# Form-Based Codes

## A Guide for Planners, Urban Designers, Municipalities, and Developers

**Daniel G. Parolek**

**Karen Parolek**

**Paul C. Crawford**

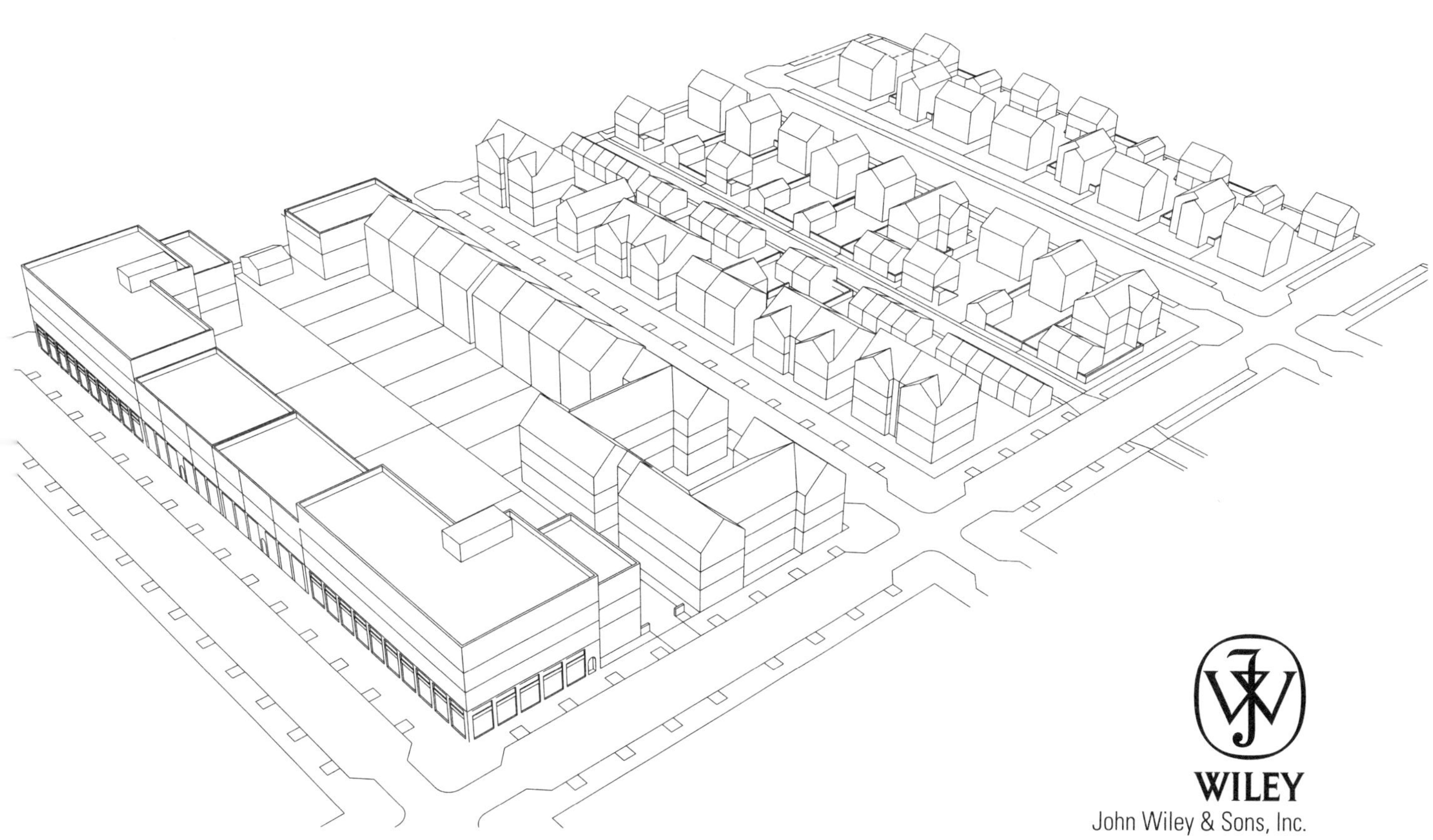

WILEY

John Wiley & Sons, Inc.

This book is printed on acid-free paper.



Published by John Wiley & Sons, Inc., Hoboken, New Jersey
Published simultaneously in Canada



Library of Congress Cataloging-in-Publication Data
Parolek, Daniel.
Form-based codes : a guide for planners, urban designers, municipalities, and developers / Daniel Parolek, Karen Parolek, and Paul Crawford.
p. cm.
Includes bibliographical references and index.
ISBN 978-0-470-04985-3 (cloth)
1. Public architecture—Planning. 2. Real estate development. 3. City planning. 4. Land use, Urban. 5. Zoning boards. 6. Municipal services. I. Parolek, Karen. II. Crawford, Paul C. III. Title.
NA9050.5.P37 2008
711'.4—dc22 2007050458

*Designed by Opticos Design*

Printed in the United States of America
10 9 8 7 6 5 4 3 2 1

To our communities
and for our communities

# Contents

# An Optimistic Moment

## A Foreword by Elizabeth Plater-Zyberk

This is a book with a point of view. Its intention is to promote the Form-Based Code, a new tool for the making and remaking of the built environment. The qualification "new" is only relative, as the goals and methods for building regulation have evolved over centuries. But the Form-Based Code's focus on the physical character and quality of public space does differ from the quantitative concerns of its predecessor, Euclidean zoning.

Zoning is a component of public policy. Policy is one of a trio of controls that shape land and building development along with design and management. Design, policy, and management vary according to type of environment, whether nature preserve, cultivated farmland, small-town main street, or urban core. Priority must be given to the management of places—their maintenance, safety, cleanliness, and other performance. In terms of variety of environment, one can easily imagine the difference in management of farmland and downtown.

Facilitating management is often a goal of design. Design provides the intended relationship among physical components of a given place: In farmland, fields are laid out to plow perpendicular to the slope in order to control erosion; in downtown, the buildings are placed to define the geometry and face of the public realm to encourage commercial activity and ensure visual monitoring of the public space. Design specifics equate to desired character of place.

Policy is the legal framework that establishes the intent for the desired relationships and performance of places. Policy can be enacted at federal, state, and local levels. For instance, federal and state environmental policies promote the preservation and continuing health of natural systems such as wetlands and drainage ways. Policy also influences the form of buildings: The Americans with Disabilities Act (ADA) is a federal policy that establishes highly specific design parameters for accessibility. There is a national fire code, too. Building codes, intended to ensure structural stability, are often enacted at the state level. The control of land use and building bulk is usually regulated at the municipal level, as the design and management goals of such policy vary by local concern. This devolution to the local level of built environment control results in a diversity of zoning regulation, and is one reason a national urban growth policy has been elusive in the United Statess.

The history of regulating the built environment is long and interesting, with recorded building restrictions dating to centuries BC. The modern American zoning code, which has determined the environment of twentieth-century cities and suburbs, however, has had a short trajectory. Its legal foundation was established by a court case of the early twentieth century, and it has evolved as the principal instrument of policy to prevent the most egregious negative impacts of siting, size, and use of buildings. Like the self-imposed rules of colonial-era settlements, early zoning consisted of simple use and dimensional restrictions. More complex documents emerged in the years after World War II, influenced by changes in urban mobility. The space reserved in the built environment for people and their work, shopping, school, and residence increasingly had to be shared with storage space for the automobile. Parking lots taking the place of buildings in downtowns changed the value of land and the size of buildings, as a larger building is required to accommodate both humans and vehicles. The convention of downtown building height regulation by mid-century was replaced by an abstraction called Floor-Area Ratio (FAR), which excluded from its calculation parking and other nonsellable areas of buildings. Zoning gradually became a numerical affair losing touch with its original qualitative intentions.

With the physical predictability of a fixed footprint and massing set aside, other relativism followed. Building height, originally correlated to the dimension of the public space in front (a 1:1 ratio of building height to street width governed some early twentieth-century downtowns) was exchanged for building area related to property size. With the introduction of a minimum setback, the location of the front wall of the building could also vary according to property size, instead of establishing the steady line of the enfronting public space. Building areas growing disproportionately with property sizes encouraged aggregation and speculation, with the result of slowing the buildout of older urban areas. Gone was the vision of a city of intention, its physical predictability inviting broad participation in its development. With the level playing field among investors lost, speculation became a better investment than construction.

Proof of the virtue of physical predictability can be seen in older residential areas, which in contrast to adjacent, often derelict commercial properties, nonetheless remain intact. Single-family neighborhoods that have maintained a consistent building envelope described by uniform setback and height requirements have maintained also their value. Those neighborhoods that were upzoned, however, took on the uncertainty of the commercial areas and experienced the slide into disrepair.

Now, at the beginning of the new century, with extreme metropolitan extension and renewed environmental concern, the Smart Growth imperative invites alternatives to suburban sprawl, including the rebuilding of the urban core and retrofitting underutilized commercial and industrial lands. The movement to restrict sprawl and densify the city has generated some policy at state levels to encourage this change. But after two decades of repeating the mantra of Smart Growth's planning goals, it must be acknowledged that the separated policies of environment, transportation, and housing have had little effect. A more detailed commitment to placemaking, initiated and controlled locally, is necessary for a culture that has forgotten how to walk, use public transit, and live in proximity to daily destinations.

Even such highly touted examples as Portland's famed urban boundary and Florida's growth-management legislation and bureaucracy, show little change to the business-as-usual of suburban sprawl. Scores of marginally effective state and county policy instruments across the country make it abundantly clear that the policy of intent is not enough. The specific details of compact transit-oriented environments must be spelled out in regulations that specify how to arrange a diversity of uses and housing in close proximity, and how to give the desired character of walkability to public space by its dimension, materials, and the qualities of the enfronting buildings. In short, Form-Based Codes tailored for local character are needed to implement the policy intent of Smart Growth.

Fortunately, new places detailed in this manner are inspiring emulation. The first of our time produced by a Form-Based Code is the Florida community, Seaside. Recognized as a radical departure from development convention in the 1980s, Seaside's town plan and design guidelines reflected the goal to build a traditional American town as not attempted since the 1920s. Seaside's plan and code produced a place of character derived from the shape of its public spaces. This emerged at a time when the decades-long architectural priority for the object building was being countered by teachers such as Colin Rowe, whose figure-ground analyses of cities provided a new awareness of the geometry and quality of public space, streets, and squares, and Leon Krier, who revived the understanding of walkable dimensions, terminated vistas, and appropriate relationships between civic and private buildings and spaces. The idea of a building as a type with multiple exemplars aggregating to form public space of specific character, represented a departure from the expectation of originality and innovation for every building. The organizing principle of urbanism as fabric and monument (of private accommodation as background to monuments of civic representation) opened the door to seeking a desired effect through instructions for design.

At the time of Seaside's inception, Walton County, Florida, had no regulations to preclude the design of the new settlement. There was nothing to prevent a graphic code in a matrix organized by building type. It was clear and easy to follow, and produced a predictable architecture. However, in ensuing years others were to discover that Walton County was a rare and lucky home for this innovation. The zoning, subdivision, and public works standards governing development across the United States literally preclude the building of traditional neighborhoods, and as well, the rebuilding of existing urbanism.

For this reason, each case study in this book represents a hard-fought victory: the result of intense commitment to principle, despite political and financial risk, by those bucking the conventions of half a century. They have changed local laws in the face of market study intransigence and the herd mentality of finance vehicles. The mere existence of these examples is a paean to the efforts of believers and activists who sought alternatives to a system of development that is now clearly identified with negative climate impact.

Guided by the principles of placemaking articulated by Smart Growth, New Urbanism, the transect, and green building, the Form-Based Code of today can take many forms, tailored to be place-specific. It may emphasize building type as did the Seaside code to ensure diversity. Or it may prioritize control of street type or building frontage type as set out by the transect-based SmartCode, an evolved instruction for community design across a range of scales. Recent codes have taken on other ambitions: the St. Lucie County Towns, Villages, and Countryside code governs a regional scale, guiding simultaneous open space preservation and compact village development; Miami 21 uses the transect and a SmartCode framework to rationalize an existing range of density and form into a set of physical parameters that ease successional growth in the booming metropolis. In all cases the Form-Based Code depends on the use of a typology, a catalogue of types, to rationalize and make predictable built form and its effect on public space.

In the legal structure of local policy, implementation can be accommodated variously. As design guidelines for a greenfield development, the Form-Based Code may provide detail under the jurisdiction of a municipal code. For a town or city, it may provide a new option within the jurisdiction's existing zoning code or it may replace the entire ordinance, incorporating those conventions that represent local culture and politics. For an historic downtown, it may be an overlay to existing zoning to ensure building forms compatible with existing character.

In their short history, Form-Based Codes have proven amenable to tailoring while maintaining a high degree of consistency and order. This capacity to rationalize the multiple elements of city-making is founded in the vision these codes share: a set of principles that lead the way to a common goal. This goal, most succinctly identified as sustainable development (Smart Growth, New Urbanism, the transect, and green building), must be maintained as the *raison d'etre* and ultimate guide for code evolution. The continuing success of Form-Based Coding depends on its adherence to the intent and principles articulated by the movements that spawned it, with attention not to abandon or misinterpret the original ideals or vision to avoid the fate of its predecessor: suburban development. To this higher standard, a holistic vision of community building, Form-Based Codes must be held. The case studies presented here might be judged for their adherence to the ideals represented by this book's point of view.

It is an optimistic moment indeed that provides enough examples of a new city-making approach to assess its effectiveness and to produce guidance for its evolution. But this is also a time of urgency for accessing and utilizing the information presented here. As global society swings into action to reduce carbon emissions, the data ever more clearly points to the need to reduce dependence on vehicular mobility, and to remake the built environment as transit- and pedestrian-friendly places of dense economic and social interaction. Only the Form-Based Code can ensure such an urbanism. And with the accelerating pressure for urban infill in the NIMBY (not in my backyard) context of a nation of homeowners, the rational structure of the Form-Based Code can engage the public in the creative process with the hope that change can be guided predictably. The authors' presentation of these examples of Form-Based Coding seeks to justify that hope.

*~Elizabeth Plater-Zyberk*

# The Time Is Now

## A Foreword by Stefanos Polyzoides

The urbanist traditions of our country are profound and have generated some of the most livable, prosperous, and equitable cities ever built in the world. This is a continent settled by immigrants of limited means. Yet its villages, towns, and cities flourished and developed well into the twentieth century, possessing a distinctive American character.

Early settlements, whether French (Biloxi and New Orleans), Spanish (Los Angeles, San Antonio, and Santa Fe), or English (Savannah, Philadelphia, and Charleston) were diverse in form but similar in principle. Unlike their European precedents, American settlements were founded under the expectation of speculative growth and profit. They were, therefore, organized under a different set of common principles than the towns of the Old World.

Hope and hype have been forms of currency and items of faith in American city-building from the beginning. Our traditional urban form was open-ended rather than predetermined. Town founders typically projected grids of streets, blocks, and lots without a fixed vision of a built outcome.

The process of completion in American towns was driven by incremental development, not holistic implementation. Individual interests were often in conflict with the common good.

Initially, the political process that regulated American urban growth was reciprocal. The property owner's right to build was absolute, but the entitlement to a particular project was relative and changeable over time. People gave their consent in promoting urban change on the assumption that their future requests for action would be similarly honored.

An American aesthetic emerged that reflected the necessity for permanence. The definition and repetition of a menu of desirable, successful building and place types were the norm. The visual prominence and imperial character of monumental composition was uncommon in North America until recently. The market drove the development process more than any overarching source of authority.

Citizen-pragmatists largely led the growth of American cities. There were few rules and fewer public meetings. There was trust in expertise and common sense. Can-do attitudes permeated every physical improvement decision. This clarity of purpose can be traced through every type of early American settlement, from the smallest to the most complex, from the most rural to the most urban.

The foundation urbanism on this continent was lightly regulated for almost 400 years, and until approximately 1920. It produced places of extraordinary character that are in many ways the basis of our American identity today: Manhattan, Kennebunkport, St. Augustine, Kansas City, Santa Barbara, and countless more.

In the aftermath of the Civil War, the country began to industrialize at a dizzying pace. The tender forms of regulation that had routinely produced harmonious settlements until this time began to falter and then fail. Inadequate parklands, poor provisions for transportation, poorly designed increased density, absence of environmental safeguards, and insensitive architectural design all produced, for the first time ever, underperforming American cities that were ugly, unhealthful, and socially and economically unredeeming.

What followed was a political crisis of unprecedented proportions. The first reaction to the faltering industrial city was an impulse to sanitize it by greening it at the center and building new suburbs at its edge. The work of Olmstead and later of the City Beautiful Movement are the best examples of this reformist urbanist agenda. With the dawn of the new century, the rate of growth, population increase, immigration, and disorderly physical change accelerated. By the 1920s, the need for new administrative instruments to control the most virulent forms of urban disarray became a pressing priority.

Zoning, as we know it today, was invented at this time. The theory behind it was sound, based on the industrialized urban conditions of the time: to separate uses, densities, and incompatibilities of all kinds in order to contain the most toxic among them. Like all good ideas, this one soon evolved by grafting itself to the dominant trends of its time, only to eventually become itself a kind of virus promoting disorderly urban growth. How did that come to pass?

From Europe came the contributions of the International Congresses for Modern Architecture (CIAM) beginning in the late 1920s. Inspired and led by Le Corbusier, the French-speaking Swiss architect and urbanist, internationalist modernists sacrificed the traditional city to the automobile by radically expanding and isolating right-of-ways, vertically separating people and vehicles, rejecting the importance of figural public space, radically expanding the size of city blocks, abandoning traditional architectural typologies, and isolating uses.

From the United States came post–World War II sprawl. Fueled by homogeneous production housing tracts, ugly commercial strips, and isolated high-rise buildings, and enabled by highway and freeway construction, American growth produced unprecedented congestion, ugliness, impermanence, and petroleum dependence.

By its immense size and modernist structure and character, the out-of-control modernist metropolis has eclipsed the settlements of all of humanity's past. There is no continent, region, or culture that has been spared cancerous, accelerating growth by abandonment, or single-use sprawl and hyper-concentration.

By default, the form of regulation that has managed and sustained this kind of untenable worldwide urban development and redevelopment is zoning. Zoning has morphed and changed over three generations, yet one thing is plainly clear. The performance of zoning over the last three quarters of a century has been a key factor in the displacement of the hallowed principles of American traditional urbanism by a tepid, project-centered, anti-urban internationalism. Harmonious urban growth cannot be properly guided by it. There is an emerging consensus that it is instead the weapon of choice by which chaotic urban form has come to prevail in the world in all of its pathological details. The sense of American pragmatism and fair dealing is offended by this gross failing.

This book is written to describe Form-Based Codes (FBCs), a method of regulating and coding, in support of another kind of urbanism—one that promotes place-based planning and development, not suburban or urban sprawl.

Since 1990, urbanists representing all key professions with a stake in the human habitat have banded together into the Congress of the New Urbanism (CNU). Their explicit purpose is to reform development and planning practice in the United States and the world. By mid-2007, this organization had been joined by an astounding 3,250 people. The imperative being sought by the CNU and its members is that cities become once again livable, prosperous, socially enabling, and beautiful. Their agenda reflects both the fundamental purposes and the emerging boldness of urbanism on the ascendant.

The Charter of the New Urbanism provides the necessary principles for visioning traditional urban form. At the core of this theory are found the directions to addressing the two fundamental challenges underlying all urbanism: How are settlements to be founded, and how are they to be managed over time in order to evolve and thrive to maximum advantage? The kind of sustainable urbanism that is practiced through the Charter of the New Urbanism aims at disciplined, varied, and permanent urban growth: forming walkable, type-diverse, and use-flexible buildings and urban places; slowing the consumption of resources; minimizing damage to the environment; and securing the agricultural countryside and nature.

Form-Based Codes have emerged as the preferred instrument for implementing new urbanist ideas of all scales and in all settings: greenfield, brownfield, infill, and both public and private projects. Many codes are already being written to secure the form and performance of municipalities and counties all over the United States.

The practice of such Form-Based Coding is centered on a theory, a process, and a format. The theory and process are common to all practitioners. The format is particular to each.

Three new urbanist tools among many others have become the necessary ingredients for the practice of Form-Based Coding: the transect; spatial organization by neighborhood, district, and corridor; and entitlement by type.

The transect describes the power of urbanism to produce immersive environments in which buildings, open space, landscape, and infrastructure are combined to produce memorable, permanent places. It describes a spectrum of choices of development intensities from urban to rural. As a means to coding, it allows the deciphering and validating of existing settings, and promotes the design of new ones as integrated physical places, not disconnected ones.

The geography of neighborhoods, districts, and corridors replaces the endlessness of sprawl with the idea of regulating within clear, identifiable spatial boundaries. This tool promotes physical variety and the presence of a rich array of uses, activities, and services within pedestrian and transit sheds. It encourages the market to accommodate many kinds of households, while minimizing dependence on the automobile as the only mobility option. As identifiable communities of common interests, people who live within neighborhoods can then be actively involved in the management of their immediate surroundings.

Organizing entitlements by building type restores Architecture to its honored place at the center of city-making. Architecture is framed in terms of generative patterns of dwelling form, not abstract metrics. Repeating these patterns as single-family houses, row houses, courts, commercial blocks, etc., generates a distinct building fabric, specific and unique to each urban setting. Some fabric can be homogeneous. Others can be diverse and highly mixed. By connecting the legal right to build with design in known and inherently compatible forms, cities can be grown that possess character specific to their culture and history.

The process common to Form-Based Coding is vision- and charrette-centered. FBCs are intentional, and they are directed to guide future growth that is particular and desirable to each community. To this end, charrettes convene professionals in many fields in one place. Urban and architectural projects of remarkable depth are then designed by them in a compressed time frame, typically a week. Charrettes engage the community, city staff, and elected officials to respond to real and diverse needs, to inspire confidence overall, and to help in project implementation. They help build consensus and political confirmation by educating participants on how to seek a balance between their best private interests and the public good. Civic engagement, fairness, and rapid resolution of private/public conflicts are often the common consequence of a well-run charrette and the foundation of a transforming Form-Based Code.

The format for FBCs may vary from jurisdiction to jurisdiction, project to project, or office to office, yet the intentions underlying the construction of these codes are remarkably similar. They are all extensively illustrated, brief, and succinct. They are typically understandable by all those with a stake in urban development: landowners, developers, councils, and commissions, and all the professionals that advise them. They are printed in large size so that their provisions can be clearly understood and assigned to particular properties.

The key difference between FBCs and conventional zoning is the relegation of regulation by use to a position ancillary and secondary to form. That is as it should be. The evidence over the centuries is overwhelming that as economies evolve, the shell of the world's most desirable cities and their buildings remains relatively stable. It is the uses they accommodate that change continually. The disposable project is a passing aberration of the twentieth century. The wealth of all nations is embodied, more than in any other way, in the constant investment, the lavishing of resources, upon their permanent buildings and cities.

Despite significant variations in the practice of Form-Based Codes, there is an emerging consensus on a common approach. The following are descriptive terms illustrating the key principles for guiding code-writing toward sustainable urban development:

**1. Vision-Centered**

Form-Based Codes are always written as part of a Master Plan. They are the outcome of a planning process that binds private and public interests onto a common vision for a desirable future. As a result, they are adopted with the complete confidence of elected and appointed officials, staffs, and the community.

**2. Purposeful**

Conventional codes are unfocused. FBCs are priority-driven and concentrate on regulating with an emphasis on those places that are prone to change. The kinds of physical adjustments that would render these places more useful and beautiful are clearly spelled out.

**3. Place-Based**

All code prescriptions are carefully calibrated to be specific to the setting to which they apply. The analysis of existing natural, physical, and social conditions within a project area is the point of departure for FBCs. Physical diversity is favored and guaranteed by providing for a wide variety of potential development and conservation intensities.

**4. Regionally Diverse**

The "one-size-fits-all" nature of zoning is replaced by a commitment to difference. FBCs reflect the environmental and cultural conditions prevailing in the different parts of our country and aim to encourage place-making that is appropriate to them. This specificity to regional context has profound environmental consequences, as the form and performance of buildings and cities are fitted to their climate, resources, and culture.

**5. Consequential**

Urbanism is not an exercise in beautification. It is an economic-development engine. Form-Based Codes typically deliver a strategy for improvement calibrated to the local economic opportunities that the market can deliver. They are operated in the interest of bolstering the fiscal health of the community.

**6. Precise**

FBCs are typological in nature. Concrete, experience-derived metrics replace abstract gauges of future development, such as Floor-Area Ratios (FARs). Ranges of preferred types for designing open space, landscape, buildings, and roads are prescribed in terms of concrete, familiar dimensional ranges. Growth by type guarantees compatibility among buildings and all other city-making ingredients as it operates within an understandable range of replicable models. Within this framework, the more one builds, the better the city gets.

**7. Integrated**

The professional autonomy that is built into so much of current planning and development practice has resulted in a process in which individuals end up working at odds with community interests. Building projects dominate, and they are often as big as possible and often deny the public realm, the multimodal use of right of ways, or the formation of an urban tree canopy. FBCs are set up to coordinate infrastructure, thoroughfares, buildings, space, and landscape design as they apply to a single project. Each project incrementally, and in accordance to its scale, completes all five dimensions of city building.

**8. Binding**

FBCs are cast in terms of standards that are obligatory, not guidelines that are optional. Standards provide development direction proactively and reward adherence to the community vision that they represent. Following the standards appropriate to a project speeds up the process of getting it entitled. As citizens begin to trust that their code routinely generates harmonious fabric, the contentious nature of the current planning process is diminished. Uncertainty about neighbors' intentions is minimized.

**9. Comprehensible**

Zoning documents have evolved into massive, complicated, mostly written tomes that are often difficult to read, internally contradictory, and impossible to understand. FBCs aim to be simply presented in a balance of words, diagrams, and tables that are clear to common folk, landowners, developers, and professionals without the need for theological interpretation from lawyers or expediters.

**10. Adjustable**

FBCs should be revisited regularly and be calibrated in the light of an evolving economy, changing community objectives, and the concrete evidence represented by work completed under their provisions. They are typically so explicit and detailed that changes small and large can be made without a fuss. A community can come to control its destiny with confidence. Currently, FBCs are being incorporated into project Master Plans and area-wide Specific Plans. Increasingly, the coding of whole cities and even counties is leading in the direction of casting General Plans (Comprehensive Plans in various states) in a new urbanist frame. Jurisdictions that have engaged in a visioning process delivering a General Plan including an FBC and appropriate environmental analysis should consider exempting individual projects from further environmental review. Such a code would also introduce a stricter and more effective level of regulation. As a matter of course, projects would be entitled more rapidly and with less scrutiny than zoning-fueled current, conventional development.

A sustainable world depends on the definitions of architectural and natural forms that in their urbanism promote rich living experiences, permanent and resource-efficient designs, limited maintenance, and reduced automobile-based mobility. This is the most conclusive response to the inconvenient truth of global warming.

This volume describes in clear argument and significant detail the issues and techniques associated with the design and management of FBCs as an antidote to zoning and sprawl. Reading it and putting it to practice is an excellent point of departure for individuals and municipalities to safeguard and to grow their communities.

*~Stefanos Polyzoides, Architect and Urbanist*

# Acknowledgments

We would like to start by thanking our generous contributing authors: Geoff Ferrell, Peter Katz, Kevin Klinkenberg, Tony Perez, Scott Polikov, Bill Spikowski, Ramon Trias, and Jeff Tumlin. We are indebted to Elizabeth Plater-Zyberk and Stefanos Polyzoides for their encouragement and forewords that set the stage for what you are about to read. A special thanks also to Emily Talen for her critical and thoughtful review of our manuscript.

We would also like to thank Peter Katz and our other co-founding board members at the Form-Based Codes Institute: Carol Wyant, Victor Dover, Andrés Duany, Geoffrey Ferrell, Joe Kohl, Mary Madden, Steve Mouzon, Stefanos Polyzoides, Sam Poole, Steve Price, Bob Sitkowski, Dan Slone, and Bill Spikowski, for their dedication and efforts in the advancement of Form-Based Coding.

Of course, Form-Based Codes (FBCs) would not have a place in this world if it were not for the pioneering and inspirational efforts of the founders of the Congress for the New Urbanism. We would like to especially thank Andrés Duany, Elizabeth Plater-Zyberk, Stefanos Polyzoides, Robert Davis, and Daryl Davis, whose personal efforts have led us to find the passion for which we lead our lives.

A special thank you to Stefan Pellegrini for his contribution to the evolution of the design and coding work at Opticos and his beautiful illustrations that are throughout this book.

Thank you to Hazel Borys, Rick Cole, Kevin Colin, Chad Emerson, Margaret Flippen, Ana Gelebert Sanchez, Luciana Gonzales, Ken Groves, Rick Hall, Joe Heckel, Susan Henderson, Nicole Horn, Marina Khoury, Jason King, Charlie Knox, Lisa Porras, Kaizer Rangwala, Sandy Sorlien, Ramon Trias, and Andrew Zitofsky for your various contributions.

Thank you to John Czarnecki, our editor at Wiley, for this incredible opportunity and his guidance throughout, as well as to Mike Olivo, Raheli Millman, and the rest of the Wiley team for helping make this book a reality.

Dan and Karen would also like to thank:

In the heartland: Our mentors Bob Amico and Dennis Doordan at the University of Notre Dame for encouraging us to write this book when we were in doubt.

In the office: Our colleagues Stefan Pellegrini, Chris Janson, John Miki, Brenda Fusté, Natasha Small, Jennifer Block, and Lisa Montana at Opticos Design, and Leo Casas, AJ Remen, Brad Devendorf, and Tara Casas at Opticos Architecture for dealing with the chaos in our offices while we disappeared for days on end to finish this book. A special thanks to Natasha for all her time and effort on the book itself.

At home: Our daughter, Abby, for putting up with our crazy schedule. When you are old enough to understand, know that you inspired us near the end of this effort with the books you began creating alongside us.

In the beginning: Our parents Kathy and Ken Hankins, and Mary and Robert Parolek, because we would not be where we are without their love, support, and sacrifices.

In the hood: Our great neighbors, friends, and family, especially Lani and Jason Gentry, who were always ready to help with meals, play dates, and moral support. Only partly because this book emphasizes the neighborhood as the building block of community do we mention that this book would not have been possible without all of them.

And finally, to Paul Crawford, for his partnership on this project and his inspirational effort to see this book completed.

Paul would also like to thank:

My wife and best friend Linda, for her constant love and support.

My generous co-authors Karen and Dan, for inviting me to join them on this important project.

Chris Clark, friend and business partner, for supporting my flitting about the country to learn and teach about FBCs.

Stefanos Polyzoides, our first and continuing FBC collaborator, and a constant source of inspiration on all things related to New Urbanism and FBCs.

Bruce Jacobson, Paul Wack, and Ron Pflugrath, for our many collaborative explorations of ways to improve the arcane zoning beast.

Friends in the charrette trenches, Tony Perez, David Sargent, Alan Loomis, Bill Dennis, Aseem Inam, Vinayak Bharne, Juan Gomez-Novy, and Orlando Gonzalez, code warriors all.

The friends I've worked with over the years at Crawford Multari & Clark who have assisted with my code work through collaboration on drafting, research, graphics, attending endless public meetings, environmental review documents, fixing my word processing disasters, and just providing general support and encouragement: Nadia Brenner, Nicole Carter, Susan DeCarli, Whitney Fisher, Ryan Gohlich, Charlie Knox, Sara Kocher, Kristen Krasnove, Jeff Legato, Jennifer Metz, Karl Mohr, Dave Moran, Mike Multari, and Lisa Wise.

And finally, our patient and enthusiastic clients, without whom there would be no FBCs.

# 1 / Introduction

# 3 Why Form-Based Codes?

When did we stop building neighborhoods where kids can ride their bikes to school? Why can't new subdivisions be more like the older neighborhoods that people love? How can I prevent suburban sprawl from destroying the character of my community and the quality of the natural environment? Why are more urban neighborhoods and small-town downtowns not being revitalized?

These and other related questions are becoming increasingly common across the country. The unfortunate reality is that the primary pattern of land development in the United States for decades has been suburban sprawl. The detrimental impacts of sprawl are becoming clearer and more critical—to our physical and mental health; to our family and community relationships; to the independence of our children, elderly, disabled, and impoverished; and to our environment.[1]

At the same time, the quality of our public realm has deteriorated. (The *public realm* is comprised of public open spaces, such as plazas, squares, and parks, and the space created and partly enclosed by the building faces on the opposite sides of a street. This space includes any front setback areas as well as the street right-of-way itself with its traffic lanes, any parking lanes, and sidewalks.) Our towns are not the great places we know are possible, and they often do not foster a sense of civic pride. They lack vibrant centers that promote healthy civic interaction,[2] and they lack a sense of place unique to themselves. In addition, the demographics of American households are changing dramatically, creating the demand for more choices in where and how we live.

Unfortunately, as developers have attempted to create projects that respond to these issues and demands, they have encountered obstacles in

**Fig. 1.1** Types of places that Form-Based Codes can protect and/or enable

existing zoning codes. And when communities have attempted to rewrite their zoning codes to accommodate these types of projects—or better yet, to require them—they have found conventional zoning techniques inadequate.

Fortunately, an alternative method of land development regulation has been created and is gaining momentum across the country as a powerful tool to effect change in the way our communities are built: The Form-Based Code.

### Form-Based Code

A method of regulating development to achieve a specific urban form. Form-Based Codes create a predictable public realm primarily by controlling physical form, with a lesser focus on land use, through city or county regulations.[3]

## A Critical Juncture

For these reasons, planning and zoning in the United States are at a critical juncture, needed to assist in the transition from the sprawling land development patterns of the last century to more compact, mixed-use, and interconnected patterns that can be applied to the creation of new communities, as well the revitalization of existing neighborhoods and town centers.

Form-Based Codes (FBCs) have been developed specifically to empower communities both to enable and to require better development patterns and individual projects. They are a cutting-edge tool for helping improve the quality of our built environment and our communities, as well as for fighting sprawl and all its detrimental effects. (See the sidebar "Linking Form-Based Codes and Sustainability").

And they have begun to show dramatic results: Communities are supporting proposed projects on parcels where there had been opposition for years.[4] Areas that had been continuously neglected are seeing renewal driven by private investment. Suburban areas are getting vibrant centers that they've never had, and the value of compact mixed-use projects, including those created under FBCs, often increases more quickly than other projects in the same area. In 2003, the sales prices per square foot for attached housing (e.g., condominiums and townhouses) was higher than that of detached housing units for the first time in American history.[5]

Interestingly, those working under implemented FBCs are their biggest proponents: city planners are excited to have a regulatory framework that has a clear intent and is easy to understand and administer; developers and builders are enthusiastic about having clear direction from the new regulations and often a streamlined approval process; and residents and elected officials are delighted to see development creating quality places that build upon the unique characteristics of their communities.

## Why This Book?

Because of these dramatic results and the quality projects they are fostering, Form-Based Codes as planning and urban design tools have quickly become accepted and encouraged by professional planning organizations,[6] builders' associations,[7] realtors' associations,[8] health experts, city staff, elected officials, community members, and developers.[9] As word has spread, the demand for information related to FBCs has grown, but there are currently few available resources and no comprehensive ones.[10]

Because of this lack of information as well as the absence of recognized standards, problems are beginning to arise from the misunderstanding of and improper implementation of Form-Based Coding concepts. Mistakes are being made that could easily be avoided. (See *Common Mistakes* in the appendix.) Unfortunately, the problems with these codes are not likely to be discovered until after the code is completed and the first few project applications are submitted that meet the code's requirements, but not the community's vision.

This book is intended to help prevent these problems by closing the information gap through a holistic look at the latest practices in Form-Based Coding. Based on their study of a wide variety of FBCs and related practices, as well as on personal experience implementing and administering them, the authors assess and describe what has happened to date while beginning to establish a common set of principles and standards for moving the practice of Form-Based Coding forward. They discuss the components of FBCs and the process by which they are created, and they present ten diverse case studies that represent the most advanced applications of this tool. The intention is for readers to use this book as a resource as they participate in the evolution of the practice and application of Form-Based Codes.

### Linking Form-Based Codes and Sustainability

The book *Growing Cooler: The Evidence on Urban Development and Climate Change*[11] presents compelling evidence that a change to more compact, blended-density, mixed-use development patterns, and a regulatory framework that promotes this type of development, plays a critical role in reducing carbon emissions in the United States.

The direct link between carbon emission and current development patterns is vehicle miles traveled (VMT). The book states that "technological improvements in vehicles and fuels are likely to be offset by continuing, robust growth in VMT," due to current segregated and sprawling development patterns.

However, the authors assert that "smart growth could, by itself reduce the total transportation related $CO_2$ emissions from current trends by 7 to 10 percent as of 2050. This reduction is feasible with land-use changes alone." They calculate that shifting 60 percent of new growth to compact patterns could save 85 million metric tons of $CO_2$ annually.

The study concludes that "the key to substantial greenhouse gas (GHG) reductions is to get all policies, funding, incentives, practices, rules, codes, and regulations... to create the right conditions for smart growth."

The authors of this book would add that because of the effectiveness Form-Based Codes have shown in facilitating smart growth, they are a powerful tool for achieving these goals of sustainable patterns of growth and development.

6

# A Brief History of Zoning

FORM-BASED CODES (FBCs) are radically revising the historical trajectory of zoning in the United States. A profound departure from the land-use zoning of the twentieth century, FBCs have significant social, cultural, economic, and environmental implications. In order to understand why FBCs are now needed, we must look briefly (very briefly) at the history of conventional zoning in the United States, the damage to American cities it has caused, and why, absent visionary and heroic zoning administration, it was incapable of producing any other outcome.

The nearly 100-year history of land-use zoning in the United States has seen a variety of evolutionary changes in the intent and scope of municipal development regulations. The initial measures of regulation in the early twentieth century were based on the authority of cities to exercise their police power (i.e., the protection of public health, safety, and welfare). Thus, the earliest regulations were intended to avoid or minimize the worst consequences of uncontrolled development and noxious land uses.

Cities began the process that has evolved into current American zoning practice by initially requiring the separation of buildings to limit the spread of fire and provide access to sunlight and air. They later limited building height to the reach of local firefighting equipment. They separated smoke-producing industry from residential uses. They isolated single-family homes from all other types of development. Eventually the practice of separating "incompatible" land uses led to a near universal segregation of each primary land-use type from others; and cities characterized by residential uses in one area, commercial in another, and industrial in still another became commonplace.

The first example of land-use zoning regulating the future use of property was in Los Angeles in 1904, while the first examples of exclusive single-family residential zones were in both Berkeley and New York City in 1916. These first instances of land-use segregation were rationalized by the concept that certain land uses function compatibly and synergistically in proximity with one another, that others do not, and that the latter must be kept physically separate from uses with which they may conflict. However, it was often the case that original efforts to segregate land uses were more the result of elitist attempts to protect property values and exclude "undesirables" from certain areas of cities. (See the sidebar "No Garment Lofts on Fifth Avenue.")

The initial creation of exclusive single-family zones was also a product of the widespread perception at the time that multifamily housing was inherently substandard and undesirable. This public bias that has lingered for decades was even reinforced by the 1926 U.S. Supreme Court case, *Village of Euclid v. Ambler Realty Company* (272 U.S. 365), which otherwise validated the constitutionality of comprehensive zoning, and eventually led to the coining of the term "Euclidean zoning."

*With particular reference to apartment houses, it is pointed out that the development of detached house sections is greatly retarded by the coming of apartment houses, which has sometimes resulted in destroying the entire section for private house purposes; that in such sections very often the apartment house is a mere parasite, constructed in order to take advantage of the open spaces and attractive surroundings created by the residential character of the district. Moreover, the coming of one apartment house is followed by others, interfering by their height and bulk with the free circulation of air and monopolizing the rays of the sun which otherwise would fall upon the smaller homes, and bringing, as their necessary accompaniments, the disturbing noises incident to increased traffic and business, and the occupation, by means of moving and parked automobiles, of larger portions of the streets, thus detracting from their safety and depriving children of the privilege of quiet and open spaces for play, enjoyed by those in more favored localities—until, finally, the residential character of the neighborhood and its desirability as a place of detached residences are utterly destroyed. Under these circumstances, apartment houses, which in a different environment would be not only entirely unobjectionable but highly desirable, come very near to being nuisances.*

### No Garment Lofts on Fifth Avenue

In *The Creative Destruction of Manhattan, 1900–1940* (University of Chicago Press, 2001), Max Page reviewed the process by which the Fifth Avenue Association pursued the process of convincing New York City to segregate certain land uses on Fifth Avenue by prohibiting garment lofts, because of their detrimental effects on the "high class stores" along the avenue.

"In a long statement to the Fifth Avenue Commission in 1913, the Fifth Avenue Association's lawyer, Bruce Falconer, argued that lofts 'have practically ruined that part of the Avenue' between 14th and 23rd Streets. They 'have utterly changed its former high-class character, and have had a derogatory effect upon the entire neighborhood': 'These buildings are crowded with hundreds and thousands of garment workers and operators who swarm down upon the Avenue for the lunch hour between 12 and 1 o'clock. They stand upon or move slowly along the sidewalks and choke them up. Pedestrians thread their way through the crowds as best they may.' The influx of immigrant workers, claims Falconer, had frightened away women shoppers, depressed property values, and encouraged an exodus of 'high-class shops and stores.'"

## Conventional Zoning Unleashed

The adverse impacts of early zoning regulations were not fully realized until the 1950s, a period of rapid economic and housing growth, which began to highlight the shortcomings of the segregation of land uses. The condition now called sprawl began when the parents of the baby boomers returned from World War II and created an unprecedented demand for housing (with the single-family home being the common dream), in the context of a zoning system that entirely separated workplaces and shopping from exclusively residential areas.

The segregation of uses inevitably required travel between them, and the dominance of single-family housing in expansive, decentralized residential areas inevitably consumed large amounts of land while increasing travel distances and making the provision of public transportation more expensive and inefficient. The cost and lack of interest in public transit in an auto-dominated society then progressively led to public streets being designed to accommodate ever-increasing traffic volumes, which made the streets less and less attractive to pedestrians for walking (as if there were anything useful within walking distance).

**Fig. 1.2** Zoned municipalities in the United States from 1904–1930

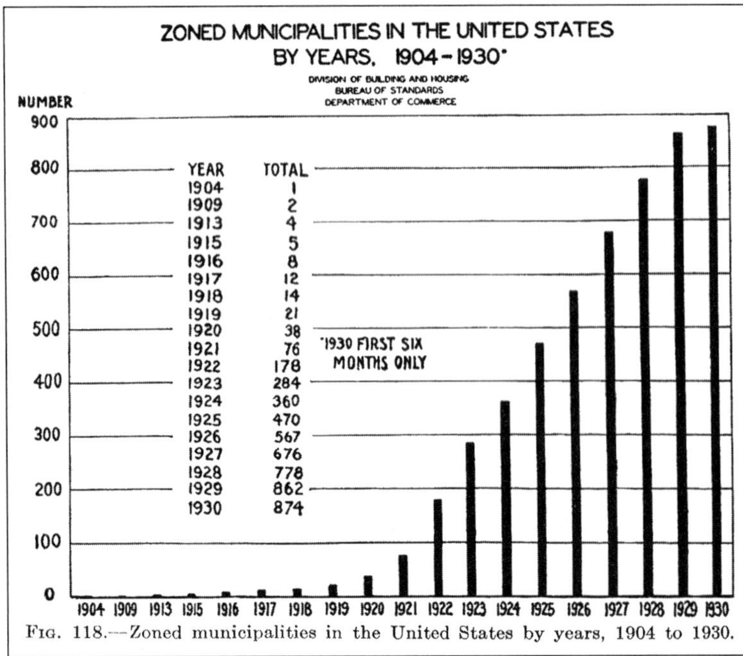

FIG. 118.—Zoned municipalities in the United States by years, 1904 to 1930.

Stating these facts is not to suggest that any were accidental. They were understood at the time, and intended, though many communities have been reevaluating their desirability since the 1980s. It is important to note that these development patterns are also a product of a planning process larger than that of drafting a zoning code, typically involving the preparation and maintenance of a "comprehensive plan," which can set the stage for a code that either facilitates sprawl or produces smart growth.

#### Attempted "Band-Aids"

As the problems of conventional zoning became more apparent over time, various modifications were implemented to try and make it work better. Ultimately the additional layers of "fixes" complicated the system even further. In the 1960s and 1970s, "Performance Zoning" was developed to provide increased flexibility in the number and types of land uses allowed in various zones by focusing on their effects on their surroundings and adjacent land uses as a basis for determining whether they could be allowed in specific zones. In the same time period, "Incentive-Based Zoning" was introduced to more gently "encourage" developers to develop specific uses in particular locations where they would be of advantage to the city, and in return developers would be provided "incentives" in the form of increases in allowed residential density, building height, Floor-Area Ratios (FAR), or lot coverage. These modifications to the regulatory system were applied in limited situations and ultimately did not make municipal development management work more efficiently for the wide range of development project types that were being proposed.

Beginning in the 1980s, many conventional code updates across the country focused on simplifying and clarifying zoning regulations, as well as reconsidering the restrictive segregation of uses that had characterized most zoning practice up to that point. So, many seemingly endless lists of permitted and conditional uses were replaced with more concise tables and matrices that instead identified fewer "generic" land-use types (for example, "general retail" often replaced a lengthy recital of specific types of retail stores and products). At the same time, the intent of specific zones with respect to the full complement of uses they allowed was often reconsidered, and a less restrictive, broader mix of uses was introduced, sometimes even allowing a mix of commercial and residential uses.

While these Band-Aids have attempted to fix the system, they have had limited success, and many communities remain dissatisfied with the character and quality of the places that conventional zoning has fostered (or as often, their *lack* of character and quality). In addition, zoning today is expected to accomplish much more. Some communities want zoning regulations that will help revitalize downtowns, create economically vital commercial areas that attract pedestrians, or otherwise facilitate development that embodies "smart growth" and "sustainability." Still others need more effective tools to help protect the existing character and quality of particular places. Many communities need to accommodate higher residential densities to increase housing supplies when land resources are limited, and must address citizen opposition to multifamily housing developments based on claims that they will cause neighborhood deterioration. But when communities have attempted to address these issues, the tools of conventional zoning have often proven inadequate.

### A New Alternative Emerges

While public agency planners were beginning to streamline conventional zoning codes in the 1980s, a group of town planners and architects dedicated to revitalizing and promoting walkable, mixed-use, sustainable communities as described in the principles of Smart Growth and the Charter of the New Urbanism worked both individually and collaboratively to formulate, test, and refine an alternative to conventional zoning. This alternative approach began to look at communities more in terms of variations in the scale and intensity of development than in differences in land uses, and its advocates proposed a complete overhaul of the existing zoning system.

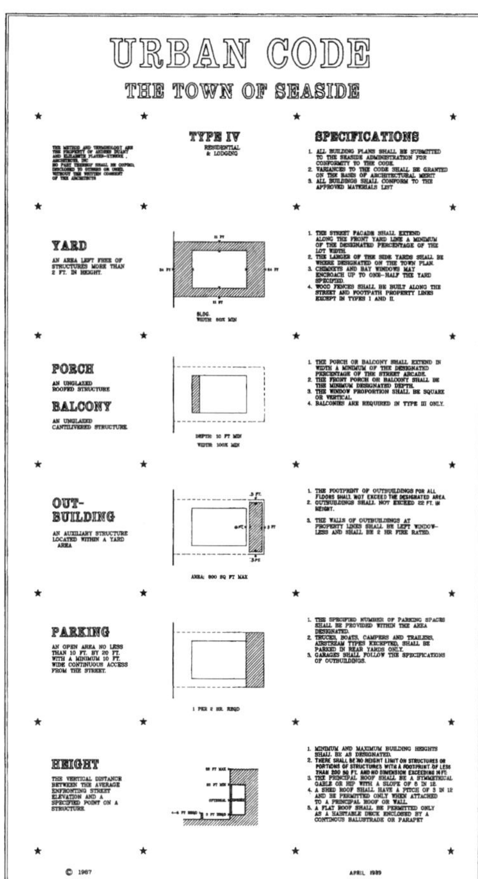


**Fig. 1.3** Building Type IV regulations from the Form-Based Code for Seaside, Florida, by Duany Plater-Zyberk (Image © Duany Plater-Zyberk & Company)

The first "on the ground" examples of the new approach were seen in the Southeast, and in the West soon after. The Development Code for Seaside, Florida, drafted by Duany Plater-Zyberk in 1981, was one of the first modern-day applications of Form-Based Coding. (See Figure 1.3.) It regulated development for Seaside with a catalog of building types that were tied to specific lots on the plan. The entire code was graphically presented on one poster. Over the course of the 1980s and into the early 1990s, several cities and counties adopted Form-Based Codes in the form of Traditional Neighborhood Development (TND) ordinances, including Key West and Dade County, Florida, and Belmont, North Carolina.

As the turn of the century arrived, the practice of Form-Based Coding continued to advance and its regulatory approach began to be extended to existing developed areas, as well as new project "greenfield" areas. Milestones included the adoption in 1998 of the City of Sonoma Development Code, prepared by Paul C. Crawford and Moule & Polyzoides, with Bruce Jacobson, Ron Pflugrath, and the City of Sonoma's Community Development Director, David Goodison; the release of the first version of the SmartCode by Duany Plater-Zyberk & Company in 2000; and the adoption of the Central Hercules Code, prepared by Dover, Kohl and Partners, by Hercules, California, in 2001.

Some of these codes regulated what types and scales of buildings were appropriate in certain areas rather than in others. They also typically coordinated standards for thoroughfares (numbers and widths of traffic lanes, width and landscaping of sidewalks, and so on) with those for building form. This alternative approach to coding was referred to by different names, including "traditional neighborhood development (TND) ordinances" and "form codes," but in 2001, Chicago consultant Carol Wyant coined the term *Form-Based Codes*, which has been the common name since.

## The Form-Based Codes Institute

The Form-Based Codes Institute (FBCI) was established in 2004 by Peter Katz, author of *The New Urbanism*, together with Carol Wyant, and 15 other New Urbanist architects, planners, and attorneys, all Form-Based Coding practitioners who collectively serve as the FBCI board of directors. The intent of the FBCI is to define Form-Based Coding, to establish best-practice standards, and to advance the practice of Form-Based Codes (FBCs) as a means of providing a regulatory framework for sustainable development. The founding board also included the authors of this book, as well as Victor Dover, Andrés Duany, Geoffrey Ferrell, Joe Kohl, Mary Madden, Stephen Mouzon, Stefanos Polyzoides, Samuel Poole, Steve Price, Robert Sitkowski, Daniel Slone, and Bill Spikowski. A nonprofit corporation, FBCI has received continuing financial support from the Richard H. Driehaus Foundation. Since its formation, FBCI has developed and taught a series of three professional development courses on the preparation, adoption, and administration of FBCs. The FBCI board members have served as volunteer faculty, and the courses have been hosted by the Virginia Institute of Technology, Rutgers University, and Arizona State University at different venues around the country. More information, including a checklist for identifying FBCs and a sample Request for Qualifications (RFQ) to find consultants to prepare an FBC, can be found on the FBCI Web site, www.formbasedcodes.org.

# A New Approach



FORM-BASED CODES are turning a page in zoning history with their new approach to development regulation. They differ from conventional zoning codes in terms of the process by which they are prepared, the substance of the standards they contain, the mechanisms by which they are implemented, and the built form they produce. (See the table on page 13.)

Form-Based Codes are vision-based and prescriptive, requiring that all development work together to create the place envisioned by the community. This requires that the community create a detailed vision at the start of the coding process and then draft and administer the FBC to enforce that vision, an inherently proactive process. While conventional zoning practices sometimes incorporate visioning processes, that visioning work is typically at a macro level scale, lacking a discussion of the details necessary to envision and implement a great place.

FBCs are holistic, addressing both private and public space design to create a whole place, including buildings, streets, sidewalks, parks, and parking. They regulate private development for the impact it has on the public realm.

FBCs are place-based, building upon and enhancing the unique characteristics of the community and region. To accomplish this, they are inherently customizable, able to regulate a specific, unique vision for each place.

Form-Based Codes are based on spatial organizing principles, such as the rural-to-urban transect, that identify and reinforce an urban hierarchy. (See more about the transect and other organizing principles in the section on Regulating Plans in Chapter 2.) Envisioning and regulating places in this way enable a sense of continuity throughout the community with smooth and often imperceptible transitions be-

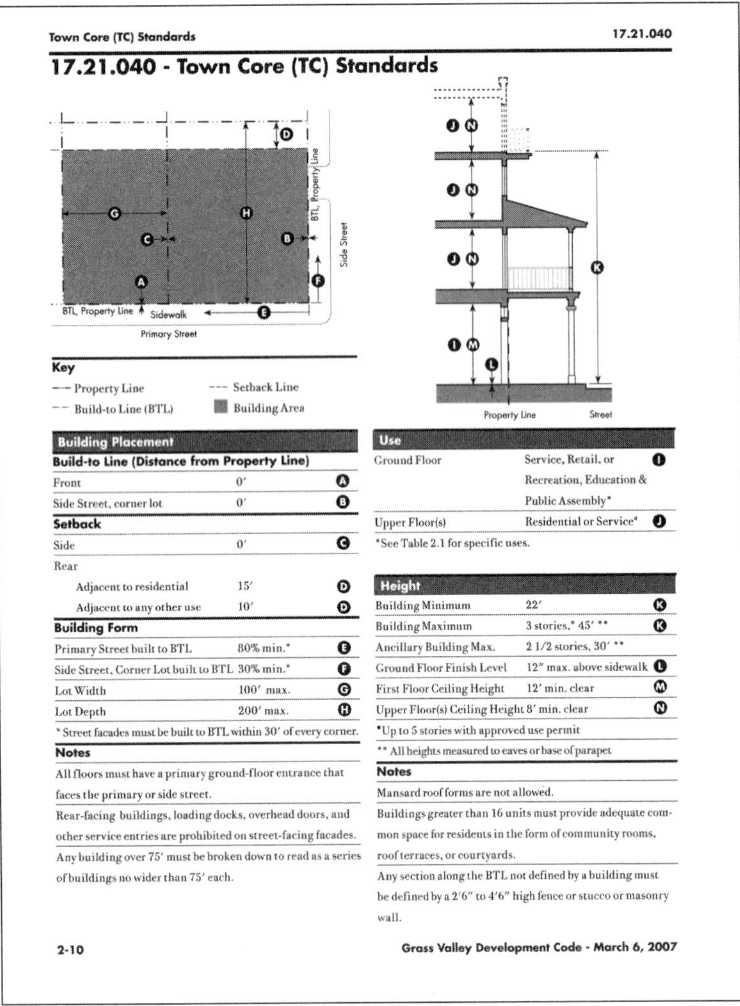
Town Core (TC) Standards 17.21.040

## 17.21.040 - Town Core (TC) Standards



**Key**

-·- Property Line — --- Setback Line — -- Build-to Line (BTL) — ■ Building Area

| Building Placement | | |
|---|---|---|
| **Build-to Line (Distance from Property Line)** | | |
| Front | 0′ | A |
| Side Street, corner lot | 0′ | B |
| **Setback** | | |
| Side | 0′ | C |
| Rear | | |
| Adjacent to residential | 15′ | D |
| Adjacent to any other use | 10′ | D |
| **Building Form** | | |
| Primary Street built to BTL | 80% min.* | E |
| Side Street, Corner Lot built to BTL | 30% min.* | F |
| Lot Width | 100′ max. | G |
| Lot Depth | 200′ max. | H |

* Street facades must be built to BTL within 30′ of every corner.

**Notes**

All floors must have a primary ground-floor entrance that faces the primary or side street.

Rear-facing buildings, loading docks, overhead doors, and other service entries are prohibited on street-facing facades.

Any building over 75′ must be broken down to read as a series of buildings no wider than 75′ each.

| Use | | |
|---|---|---|
| Ground Floor | Service, Retail, or Recreation, Education & Public Assembly* | I |
| Upper Floor(s) | Residential or Service* | J |

*See Table 2.1 for specific uses.

| Height | | |
|---|---|---|
| Building Minimum | 22′ | K |
| Building Maximum | 3 stories,* 45′ ** | K |
| Ancillary Building Max. | 2 1/2 stories, 30′ ** | |
| Ground Floor Finish Level | 12″ max. above sidewalk | L |
| First Floor Ceiling Height | 12′ min. clear | M |
| Upper Floor(s) Ceiling Height | 8′ min. clear | N |

*Up to 5 stories with approved use permit

** All heights measured to eaves or base of parapet

**Notes**

Mansard roof forms are not allowed.

Buildings greater than 16 units must provide adequate common space for residents in the form of community rooms, roof terraces, or courtyards.

Any section along the BTL not defined by a building must be defined by a 2′6″ to 4′6″ high fence or stucco or masonry wall.

2-10 Grass Valley Development Code - March 6, 2007

tween regulatory zones rather than the hard-edge separation and buffering between single-use zones that is common in places regulated by conventional zoning codes.

Form-Based Codes regulate the details that are most important for the successful implementation of walkable, human-scaled neighborhoods, focusing primarily on urban form, while also addressing use and other necessary factors. These details include certain aspects of the buildings as they form the walls of the public space, including their placement, height, width, and the particular way they interact with the public space (called the "frontage"). They also include the design and layout of streets and blocks, typically requiring narrower streets laid out in an interconnected, gridded network to accommodate pedestrians and bicyclists, as well as automobiles and transit. FBCs regulate the location of parking to create beneficial impacts, such as protecting pedestrians from moving traffic, while minimizing negative impacts, and they regulate an appropriate mix of compatible uses and building types, enabling diverse, vibrant places.

Finally, because they regulate these details to the level necessary to ensure adherence to the community's vision, FBCs can also provide a streamlined development review and approval process requiring little or no subjective review, thus encouraging appropriate development.

Yet, while FBCs differ radically from conventional zoning in many ways, they are similar in a few ways. FBCs also isolate noxious uses, such as heavy manufacturing and airports, and they generally only regulate private buildings as they affect the public good, leaving plenty of room for individual tastes and styles. As necessary, they may also contain provisions similar to conventional zoning for such issues as nonconforming uses and affordable housing.

## Potential Uses for Form-Based Codes

Form-Based Codes can be used to implement:

1. Complete Zoning and Development Code Updates
2. Downtown Master Plans
3. Corridor Revitalization Plans
4. Neighborhood Revitalization Plans
5. Specific Plan Development Standards
6. Regional Plan Implementation
7. Comprehensive Plan Implementation
8. Historic Resource Preservation Planning
9. Transit Village Implementation
10. Land Conservation through Clustered, Hamlet-Style Development
11. Greyfield Redevelopment
12. Campus Master Planning
13. University/Community Interface Plans
14. Subdivision Ordinances

With their new approach to development regulation, Form-Based Codes have the potential to change the human habitat substantially by providing communities with a tool that can help reinforce their local character and culture; revitalize and encourage reinvestment in urban, historic neighborhoods and town centers; and promote the creation of compact, walkable neighborhoods. FBCs can also play an important role in promoting sustainable planning practices by supporting and regulating development patterns that respond to global climate change and the destruction of our environment.

## Scope of This Book

This book is laid out in three primary sections: Components (Chapter 2), Process (Chapter 3), and Case Studies (Chapter 4). The components chapter introduces and defines the elements of an FBC and explains why each is important. The process chapter gives a thorough overview of the FBC process from start to post-adoption implementation, with the overall process and each of the subprocesses represented in diagrams and supporting graphics. The case studies present a diverse set of FBCs to demonstrate the wide variety of possible applications and provide examples of current best practices. At the end of the book, there are a series of appendices to provide additional information, such as a list of references, a timeline of Form-Based Coding, and a series of common mistakes to avoid.

Form-Based Coding inherently involves urban design and a public visioning process, but it is not feasible to cover all three topics in depth in one book. (See the sidebar "Form-Based Codes in Context.") The urban design details in this book focus on enabling walkable, mixed-use, sustainable communities from small, rural towns to large, urban cities—the basic te-

| Conventional Planning and Zoning Codes | Form-Based Codes |
|---|---|
| Auto-oriented, segregated land-use planning principles | Mixed use, walkable, compact development-oriented principles |
| Organized around single-use zones | Based on spatial organizing principles that identify and reinforce an urban hierarchy, such as the rural-to-urban transect |
| Use is primary | Physical form and character are primary, with secondary attention to use |
| Reactive to individual development proposals | Proactive community visioning |
| Proscriptive regulations, regulating what is not permitted, as well as unpredictable numeric parameters, like density and FAR | Prescriptive regulations, describing what is required, such as build-to lines and combined min/max building heights |
| Regulates to create buildings | Regulates to create places |

**Fig. 1.4** (Far left) Regulations for the form, placement, and use of buildings from the Grass Valley FBC by Opticos Design and Crawford, Multari & Clark Associates

**Fig. 1.5** (Above) FBCs address the public realm as a whole, regulating the design of the thoroughfares as well as the placement and form of buildings as the walls of the public space. (Image from the Sarasota County FBC by Dover, Kohl & Partners and Spikowski Planning Associates)

nets of the New Urbanism and Smart Growth movements, which the authors all strongly advocate. An effective public process is necessary to create and build support for the community's vision, as well as the FBC that will facilitate it. This book discusses some details of urban design and the public process, but only to the extent that they are necessary to understand Form-Based Coding. Suggested books and articles about New Urbanism, Smart Growth, and public visioning processes are listed among the references in the appendix.



## Form-Based Codes in Context

**by Peter Katz**
*President, Form-Based Codes Institute*

Form-Based Codes are increasingly seen as a regulatory tool that could make planners' lives easier. Indeed, they have been linked to breakthrough successes in some of the toughest planning projects in the country. And while the successes are real, the news reports haven't been telling the full story.

The most important piece of missing information is that Form-Based Codes do not work on their own. They are embedded in a suite of best practices that also includes high-quality urban design—a compelling plan, in other words—and a participatory planning methodology known as the "charrette process." Together, these linked practices form a kind of "virtuous circle" that I've come to associate with successful planning outcomes.

The process works in the following way:

During the first few days of a charrette, citizens are shown startling new visions of their community that bear little resemblance to what is there now. On first viewing, they're often taken aback. But as citizens begin to consider new possibilities, they start to wonder whether they really could have that beautiful public square or the new branch library like the one shown in the design team's renderings. And while such musings are interspersed with fears of increased density and related impacts, community members frequently come to support, and feel a sense of ownership of, ambitious growth proposals that include the features they most want in their neighborhood.

Once accepted, however, citizens again become skeptical as to whether the stunning images they're seeing could ever be realized. After all, most have seen renderings of grand plans that never got off the ground. In cases where something did get built, the final results may not have measured up to expectations generated by the initial renderings.

Form-Based Codes help to allay such concerns. The codes work best when they are developed in draft form during the multiday charrette. Presenting the proposed ordinance alongside the team's renderings brings increased confidence that what is drawn might actually be built. Furthermore, by riding the wave of enthusiasm that often accompanies the charrette process, the form-based ordinances can be written into law much more quickly, thus minimizing the inevitable watering-down process that can severely compromise a worthy development plan.

Finally, the greater precision of the Form-Based Code and the hands-on involvement of the "town architect" lead to more predictable implementation of the plan. With this step, the virtuous circle closes and gains strength as it repeats itself: a positive development experience gives citizens greater confidence in local government's ability to guide future growth and to keep private interests aligned with the goals of the community. That trust empowers local government to take on new planning challenges, knowing that there is a high probability of future success to justify their ongoing investment of time, money, and political capital.

# 2 / Components

FORM-BASED CODES (FBCs) as defined by the Form-Based Codes Institute are structured to include a set of minimum components and may also accommodate a variety of optional ones. The required components are:

*A Regulating Plan*

A plan or map assigning the code's various standards to physical locations. Extensive codes may have separate Regulating Plans for the various sections (e.g., a Building Form Standards Regulating Plan and a Public Space Regulating Plan). (See Figure 2.1.)

*Public Space Standards*

Specifications for the elements within the public realm,[1] including thoroughfares and civic spaces. For thoroughfares, these include regulations for sidewalks, travel lanes, street trees, street furniture, and the interface with the buildings. (See Figures 2.12 and 2.13.) For civic spaces, they regulate parameters, such as minimum and maximum sizes, types of spaces and their appropriate locations, their functional role within the community, and landscaping.

*Building Form Standards*

Regulations controlling the configuration, features, and functions of buildings that define and shape the public realm.[2] These typically include regulations for lot sizes, building placement and form, use, parking, encroachments, and frontage types, and may also include other regulations, such as for building types or architecture. (See Figure 2.20.)

*Administration*

Requirements for the project application and review process.[3]

*Glossary*

Definitions of uncommon technical terms and phrases used in the code, as well as definitions of the land-use types used in the code.

In addition to the required components, others may be included depending on the needs of the community and other components that may already be in place. Some of the following components have been included in adopted Form-Based Codes, while others are examples

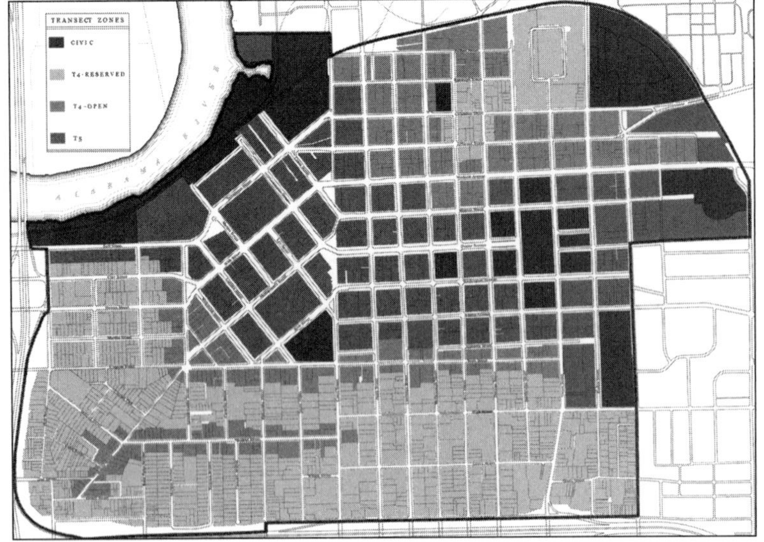

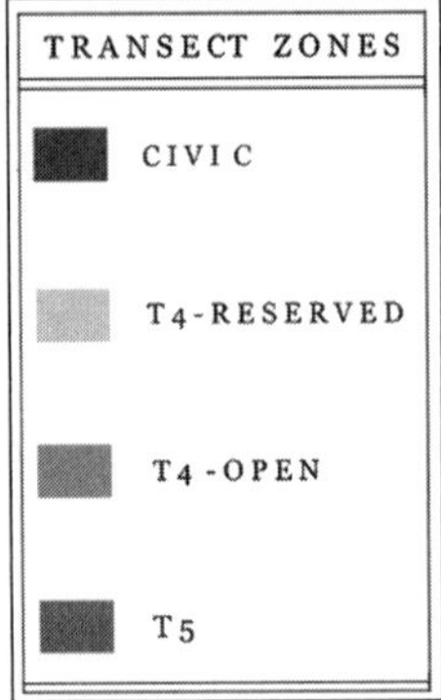


**Fig. 2.1** Regulating Plan for downtown Montgomery, Alabama, by Dover, Kohl & Partners (Also see Figure C.15 in the color section of this book.)

that could be included as the practice of Form-Based Coding continues to advance.

*Block Standards*

Regulations for dividing large sites into an interconnected and walkable network of streets and blocks. (See Figure 2.34.)

*Building Type Standards*

Specifications defining the form and function of the allowed building types. Examples of building types are townhouses, detached single-unit houses, courtyard apartments, and live/work units. (See Figures 2.37 and 2.38.)

*Architectural Standards*

Regulations to control the character and quality of buildings. (See Figures 2.45 and 2.46.)

*Green Building Standards*

Specifications for environmentally sensitive, energy efficient, and low carbon footprint buildings that assist in achieving community sustainability goals.

*Landscape Standards*

Regulations for the character and quality of the landscape within private spaces, but as it affects the public good, such as requiring native species to address water usage.

Other code components that are not exclusive to FBCs might also be included to address community-specific needs, including standards for historic preservation, storm water management, signage, and lighting, as well as nonconforming use regulations, affordable housing requirements, and lessons-learned provisions (zoning regulations developed and enacted in response to the community's past problems with particular land uses, site characteristics, and the like).

Determining which components to include is one of the first steps in calibrating the code to the local context. All the components should be coordinated to ensure that post-code development effectively works in concert to produce the intended vision for the community.

Following is a detailed description of each required FBC component, as well as a few of the most common optional ones. These descriptions include a list of regulations to consider. The list is not intended to be comprehensive, but rather to provide a solid base on which to build and customize an FBC as unique as the place being coded.

# The Regulating Plan 17

THE FIRST NECESSARY component of a Form-Based Code is a Regulating Plan. Regulating Plans have three purposes:

*Administrative*

The boundaries shown on the plan identify where different rules for development apply. That is, they provide an "index" or entry point into the code that allow a person interested in the possibilities for development or land use on a specific site to identify the applicable zone so that they can then refer to the text in the code document to determine the rules for design.

*Direct Regulation*

In some cases, a Regulating Plan will show actual development requirements (e.g., street frontages where ground-floor retail use is required; street frontages where specific frontage or building types are required; or where specific thoroughfare types are required).

*Planning*

In its most important role, the preparation of a Regulating Plan is, in itself, an act of urban design. Drawing the boundaries between zones on a Regulating Plan invokes, project-by-project and lot-by-lot, the development standards formulated in code preparation which define the critical differences in the form and character of development in each zone, and thereby also determine the configuration of the public realm.

In any development code, the various regulations are organized into sections, or zones. The Regulating Plan then designates the specific physical areas or lots to which each section of the regulations applies. Because of the specificity that is necessary for the application of the Form-Based Zones, the Regulating Plan typically applies the zones within a framework of streets and blocks, not just in large unrefined geographic areas like conventional zoning maps. This helps create a

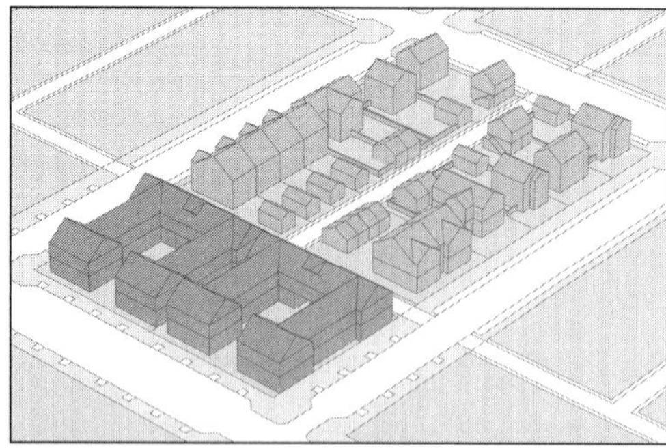

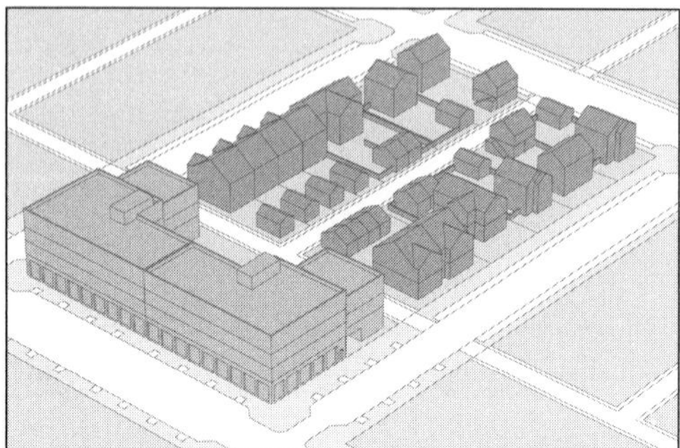

**Fig. 2.2** A typical mid-block transition between different Form-Based Zones allows for a smooth transition between different intensities and types of uses without the need for buffers. The top image shows a transition at the alley from courtyard apartment types to duplexes and then to single-unit houses. The bottom image shows a transition at the alley from a commercial block to duplexes and then to single-unit houses.

transition between zones that is seamless, not a hard edge that requires buffers or large setbacks. The boundary line between Form-Based Zones most often occurs at an alley or at the rear of lots, allowing the scale as well as the type and mix of uses to change while still being compatible. (See Figure 2.2.)

In a conventional zoning code, the primary differences between zones are the different land uses they allow. The zones may also have other standards, such as for building placement and height, but the emphasis remains on land use. Form-Based Codes, on the other hand, establish zones based on differences in building intensity and form (e.g., type, placement, height, and relationship to the public realm), as well as the features of the public realm itself, while paying less, but still careful attention to differences in allowed land uses. The primary basis for differentiating and mapping zones is the code's *organizing principle.*

## Organizing Principles

Form-Based Coding practitioners have used several organizing principles based on different approaches to regulating the type, scale, form, and intensity of allowable development. Currently, the most commonly used organizing principle is the rural-to-urban transect.

### Transect-Based Codes

The rural-to-urban transect is a means for considering and organizing the human habitat in a continuum of intensity that ranges from the most rural condition to the most urban. It provides a standardized method for differentiating between the intentions for urban form in various areas using gradual transitions rather than harsh distinctions. The zones are primarily classified by the physical intensity of the built form, the relationship between nature and the built environment, and the complexity of uses within the zone.

While the origin of the transect as a concept is in the biological and environmental analysis fields, it was first described and adapted for the purposes of Form-Based Coding by Duany Plater-Zyberk & Company (DPZ). (See Figure 2.3.) The DPZ model transect provides six zones: Natural (T1), Rural (T2), Sub-urban (T3), General Urban (T4), Urban Center (T5), and Urban Core (T6), together with a Special District (SD) designation for areas with particularly specialized purposes (e.g., heavy industrial, transportation, entertainment, or university districts, among other possibilities). Each transect zone, or T-Zone, has been designated a number. The higher numbers designate progressively more urban zones, the lower, more rural.

Among the benefits of using the transect as the organizing principle for an FBC is that it applies to most, if not all, of the elements of creating a great place, from building form and placement to parking, use, public spaces, signage, and lighting. Even green building, transit, and storm water management can be organized by transect zone. For example, it was recently used as the basis for context zone thoroughfare classification in the new "Context Sensitive Solutions in Designing Major Urban Thoroughfares for Walkable Communities" created by the ITE in partnership with the Congress for the New Urbanism (CNU).[4] (See Figures 2.4 through 2.6 for an example of transect-based standards within the SmartCode.)

### *Modifying the Transect for Application to a Community*

The six basic transect zones should be calibrated to local conditions and intentions, and sometimes may need to be expanded into subsets (e.g., T4a, T4b, and so on). Calibrating the transect zones means assigning or creating a separate zone for each unique area in the community based on urban design intention, intensity, and uses. In some instances, this also includes renaming the transect zones to make them more understandable and intuitive for local citizens, using such names as "T5-Town Center," "T4-Neighborhood General," and "T4-Neighborhood Edge." However, it is recommended that even if the transect zone name is changed, the T-Zone numeric classification (e.g., T4) should still be included at the beginning of the zone name to help enforce a common lexicon for Form-Based Coding. The details of calibrating the zones will be covered later in the Process chapter; however, following are a few examples of how transect zones have been calibrated to meet local needs. (See Figure 2.6.)

In the development code update for Grass Valley, California, a breakdown was needed for the T3 zones as they applied to the existing historic neighborhoods. The T3 zone was named Neighborhood General (NG), but the physical parameters remained similar to those typical for the Sub-urban transect zone. Because various neighborhoods had different proposed degrees of change or preservation, as well as different levels of past interventions, the NG zone

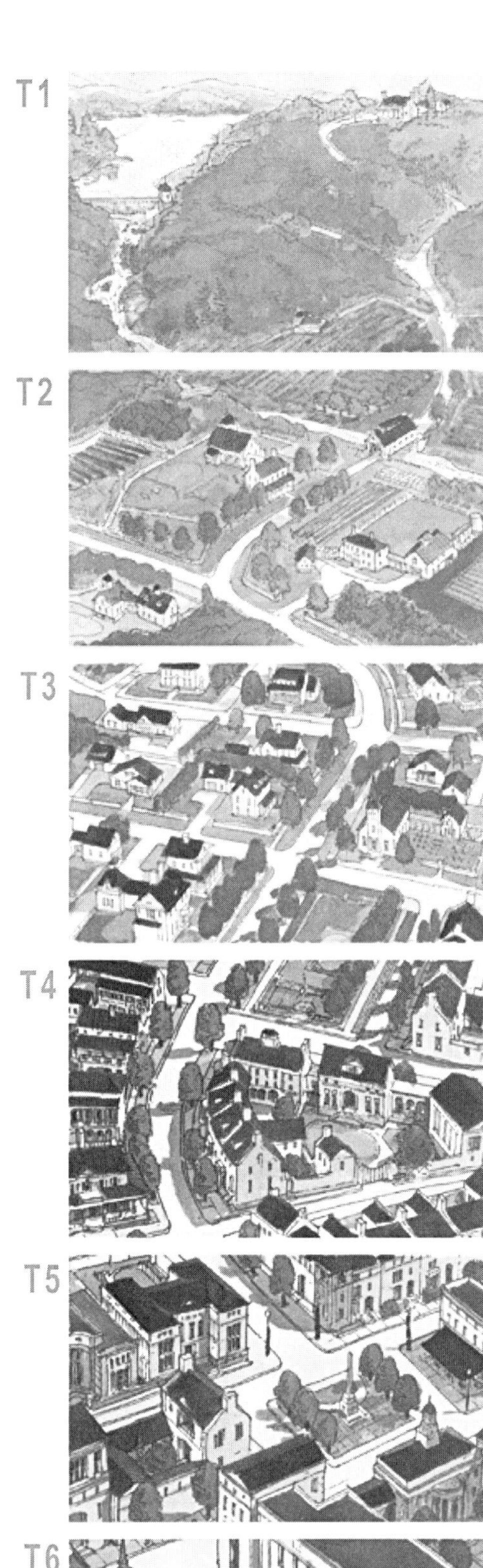


**Fig. 2.3** An illustration of the rural to urban transect (Image © Duany Plater-Zyberk & Company. Illustration by James Wassell and Eusebio Azcue.)

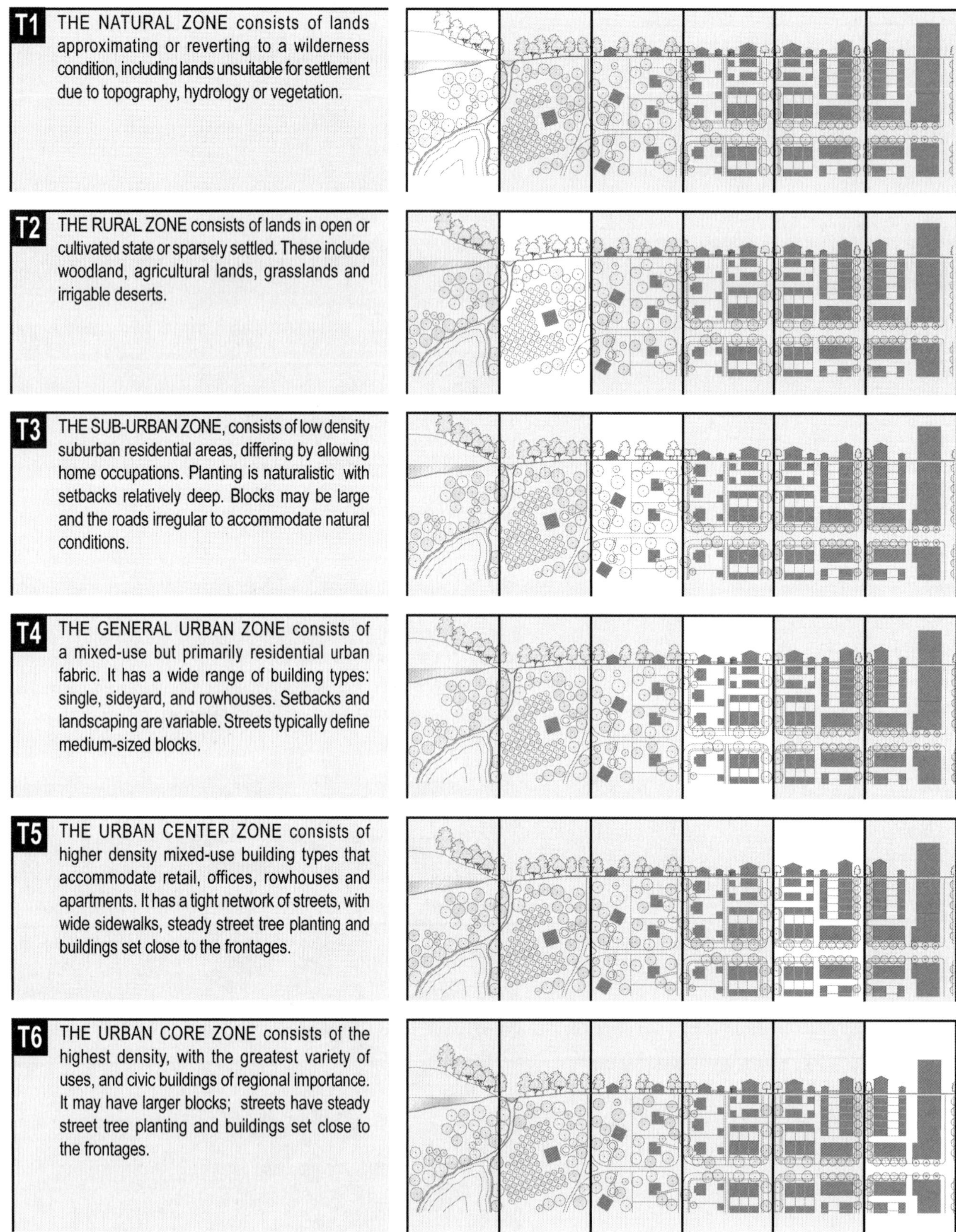

T1
THE NATURAL ZONE consists of lands approximating or reverting to a wilderness condition, including lands unsuitable for settlement due to topography, hydrology or vegetation.
T2
THE RURAL ZONE consists of lands in open or cultivated state or sparsely settled. These include woodland, agricultural lands, grasslands and irrigable deserts.
T3
THE SUB-URBAN ZONE, consists of low density suburban residential areas, differing by allowing home occupations. Planting is naturalistic with setbacks relatively deep. Blocks may be large and the roads irregular to accommodate natural conditions.
T4
THE GENERAL URBAN ZONE consists of a mixed-use but primarily residential urban fabric. It has a wide range of building types: single, sideyard, and rowhouses. Setbacks and landscaping are variable. Streets typically define medium-sized blocks.
T5
THE URBAN CENTER ZONE consists of higher density mixed-use building types that accommodate retail, offices, rowhouses and apartments. It has a tight network of streets, with wide sidewalks, steady street tree planting and buildings set close to the frontages.
T6
THE URBAN CORE ZONE consists of the highest density, with the greatest variety of uses, and civic buildings of regional importance. It may have larger blocks; streets have steady street tree planting and buildings set close to the frontages.


**Fig. 2.4** SmartCode transect zone descriptions (Credit: DPZ)

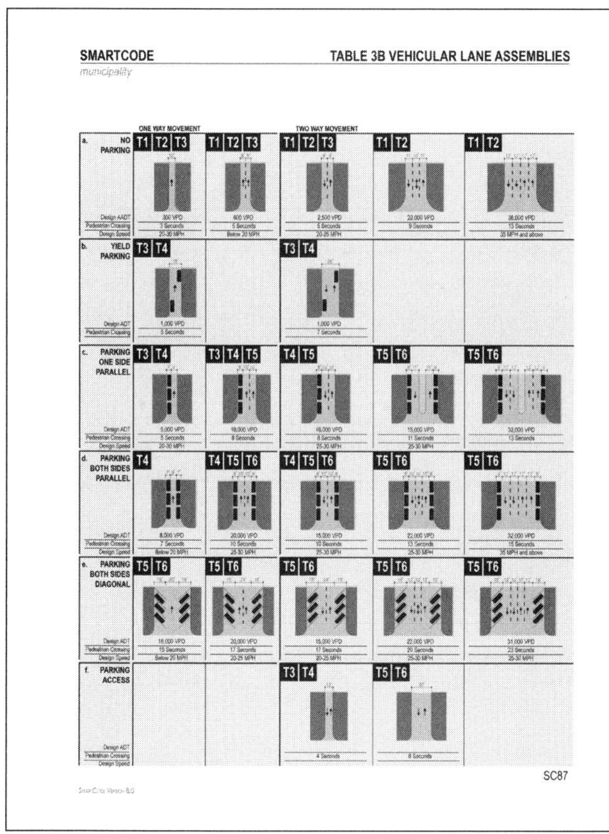

SMARTCODE
municipality

TABLE 3B VEHICULAR LANE ASSEMBLIES

ONE WAY MOVEMENT
TWO WAY MOVEMENT

a. NO PARKING — T1 T2 T3 | T1 T2 T3 | T1 T2 T3 | T1 T2 | T1 T2

b. YIELD PARKING — T3 T4 | T3 T4

c. PARKING ONE SIDE PARALLEL — T3 T4 | T3 T4 T5 | T4 T5 | T5 T6 | T5 T6

d. PARKING BOTH SIDES PARALLEL — T4 | T4 T5 T6 | T4 T5 T6 | T5 T6 | T5 T6

e. PARKING BOTH SIDES DIAGONAL — T5 T6 | T5 T6 | T5 T6 | T5 T6 | T5 T6

f. PARKING ACCESS — T3 T4 | T5 T6

SC87

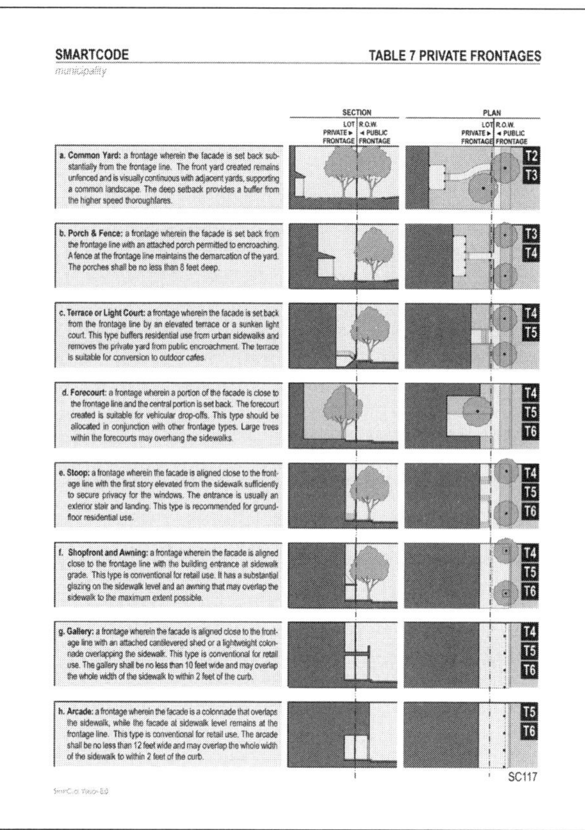

SMARTCODE
municipality

TABLE 7 PRIVATE FRONTAGES

SECTION: LOT / R.O.W.; PRIVATE FRONTAGE / PUBLIC FRONTAGE
PLAN: LOT / R.O.W.; PRIVATE FRONTAGE / PUBLIC FRONTAGE

a. **Common Yard:** a frontage wherein the facade is set back substantially from the frontage line. The front yard created remains unfenced and is visually continuous with adjacent yards, supporting a common landscape. The deep setback provides a buffer from the higher speed thoroughfares. — T2 T3

b. **Porch & Fence:** a frontage wherein the facade is set back from the frontage line with an attached porch permitted to encroaching. A fence at the frontage line maintains the demarcation of the yard. The porches shall be no less than 8 feet deep. — T3 T4

c. **Terrace or Light Court:** a frontage wherein the facade is set back from the frontage line by an elevated terrace or a sunken light court. This type buffers residential use from urban sidewalks and removes the private yard from public encroachment. The terrace is suitable for conversion to outdoor cafes. — T4 T5

d. **Forecourt:** a frontage wherein a portion of the facade is close to the frontage line and the central portion is set back. The forecourt created is suitable for vehicular drop-offs. This type should be allocated in conjunction with other frontage types. Large trees within the forecourts may overhang the sidewalks. — T4 T5 T6

e. **Stoop:** a frontage wherein the facade is aligned close to the frontage line with the first story elevated from the sidewalk sufficiently to secure privacy for the windows. The entrance is usually an exterior stair and landing. This type is recommended for ground-floor residential use. — T4 T5 T6

f. **Shopfront and Awning:** a frontage wherein the facade is aligned close to the frontage line with the building entrance at sidewalk grade. This type is conventional for retail use. It has a substantial glazing on the sidewalk level and an awning that may overlap the sidewalk to the maximum extent possible. — T4 T5 T6

g. **Gallery:** a frontage wherein the facade is aligned close to the frontage line with an attached cantilevered shed or a lightweight colonnade overlapping the sidewalk. This type is conventional for retail use. The gallery shall be no less than 10 feet wide and may overlap the whole width of the sidewalk to within 2 feet of the curb. — T4 T5 T6

h. **Arcade:** a frontage wherein the facade is a colonnade that overlaps the sidewalk, while the facade at sidewalk level remains at the frontage line. This type is conventional for retail use. The arcade shall be no less than 12 feet wide and may overlap the whole width of the sidewalk to within 2 feet of the curb. — T5 T6

SC117

**Fig. 2.5** (above) Tables from the SmartCode illustrate how the transect can be used as an organizing principle to regulate the many different elements necessary to create great places including thoroughfares (left) and frontages (right). (Credit: DPZ) **Fig. 2.6** (below) The final zones in various Form-Based Codes are displayed across the transect.

| Form-Based Code | T2 Rural | T3 Sub-Urban | T4 General Urban | T5 Urban Center | T6 Urban Core | Other |
|---|---|---|---|---|---|---|
| Whittier Uptown Specific Plan | | U-E: Uptown Edge | U-G: Uptown General | U-CT: Uptown Center | | |
| City of Grass Valley Development Code | | NG-2: Neighborhood General-2 | NG-3: Neighborhood General-3<br>NC: Neighborhood Center<br>NC-Flex: Neighborhood Center-Flex | TC: Town Core | | |
| Miami 21 | | T3: Sub-Urban, with Restricted, Limited, and Open subsets | T4: Urban General, with Restricted, Limited, and Open subsets | T5: Urban Center, with Restricted, Limited, and Open subsets | T6: Urban Core, with Restricted, Limited, and Open subsets, and T6-8, -12, -24, -36, and -48 subzones based on allowable number of floors | CI: Civic Institutional<br>DI: Work Place District<br>D2: Industrial District |
| Santa Ana Renaissance Specific Plan | | UN-1: Urban Neighborhood-1 | UN-1: Urban Neighborhood-1<br>CDR: Corridor | UC: Urban Center | RR: Rail Station Zone | R/I: Resident/Industrial |
| Benicia Downtown Form-Based Code | | NG: Neighborhood General | NG-O: Neighborhood General-Open<br>TC-O: Town Core-Open | TC: Town Core | | |
| Montgomery SmartCode | T2: Rural | T3: Sub-Urban | T4: General Urban | T5: Urban Center | T6: Urban Core | T1: Natural |
| Sarasota County | | Edge | General | Core | | Preserve |
| Peoria Development Code | | West Main-Local | Sheridan Triangle-Neighborhood Center<br>Prospect Road-Neighborhood Center<br>West Main-Neighborhood Center<br>West Main-Local Commerce | Warehouse District-General<br>Warehouse District-Local | | |
| St. Lucie County | Edge | General | Center | Core | | Countryside: Rural Fringe |
| Leander SmartCode | | T3: Sub-Urban | T4: Neighborhood General | T5: Neighborhood Center | T6: Urban Core | |
| Downtown Ventura Specific Plan | | | T4.1: Urban General<br>T4.2: Urban General 2<br>T4.3: Urban General 3<br>T4.4: Thompson Corridor | T5.1: Neighborhood Center | T6.1: Urban Core | |
| Blue Springs, MO Downtown Development Code | | T3: Sub-Urban | T4: General Urban | T5: Urban Center | | CS: Civic Space |

**Fig. 2.7** Transect photos from various cities across the country. Using photos to categorize areas of a community along the transect is a good start to calibrating the transect to the community.

was subdivided into NG-2 and NG-3 zones. In this instance, the lower the number after the transect zone name, the less intense the residential use. NG-2 applied to historic residential neighborhoods in which the primary objective of the code was to preserve and enhance the existing character. NG-3 also applied to historic residential areas, but ones that the community wanted to allow to evolve with the integration of medium-density residential building types since the areas were adjacent to mixed-use neighborhood centers.

**Tip** An effective way to introduce the transect to community residents at the onset of the visioning process is by taking the linear transect diagram and attaching several photos of each particular transect zone within the community. This immediately enables participants to understand the hierarchy of urban and rural form in their community and the role that both the urban and the rural components have in the character of the place. In no time, participants will be speaking about "T-Zones." (See Figure 2.7.)

In Miami, Florida, the Miami 21 code transect zones are broken down into subsets with Limited, Restricted, and Open categories for each that differentiate use and frontage type. This enables T4-Limited (T4-L), T4-Restricted (T4-R), and T4-Open (T4-O) zones to be located adjacent to one another, with T4-L allowing only residential uses and frontages, T4-R allowing live/work uses and shopfront frontages, and T4-O allowing residential and commercial uses, as well as residential and shopfront frontages. This code also includes various T6 zones based on the allowed height within the designated zone, such as T6-8, which allows up to 8-story buildings and T6-12, which allows up to 12-story buildings. See the Miami 21 case study later in this book for more information on this code.

### Other Organizing Principles

Depending upon the size of an area being coded and the differences in urban design outcomes desired in discrete parts of the overall area, some Form-Based Coding practitioners have also used methods other than the transect to identify areas that are subject to differing design and development standards. These organizing principle variations include differentiating standards by describing and regulating the desired form and character of individual neighborhoods, districts, and corridors; relating differences in Building Form Standards to the type of street fronting a site and showing only thoroughfare types on the regulating plan; and identifying specific named zones (e.g., "Sunset District") where special rules for development apply only in very limited areas of the city that are to be subject to Form-Based Coding. Some FBCs combine some or all of the above methods as appropriate and useful to distinguish community design intentions. Following are three of the more common methods:

### *Building Type-Based Codes*

These types of Form-Based Codes use building types as their organizing principle. Many early FBCs, especially those that were created for private projects, were based on building types. This system has since been refined to work in public regulations, and seems to work best in projects for small communities or where the project area is no more than a mile square, or two or three neighborhoods. At this scale, using Building Types as the organizing principle can produce a code that will reinforce the character of a community and encourage good development.

In this approach, specific regulations are created for a group of building types selected during the documentation and visioning processes. When the Regulating Plan is created, the applicable types are allocated to each zone. For example, in a T4 zone, townhouses, mansion apartments, courtyard housing, and small mixed-use types may be allowed. Building Form Standards sheets are then created for each type to regulate important characteristics. (See Figure 2.8.)

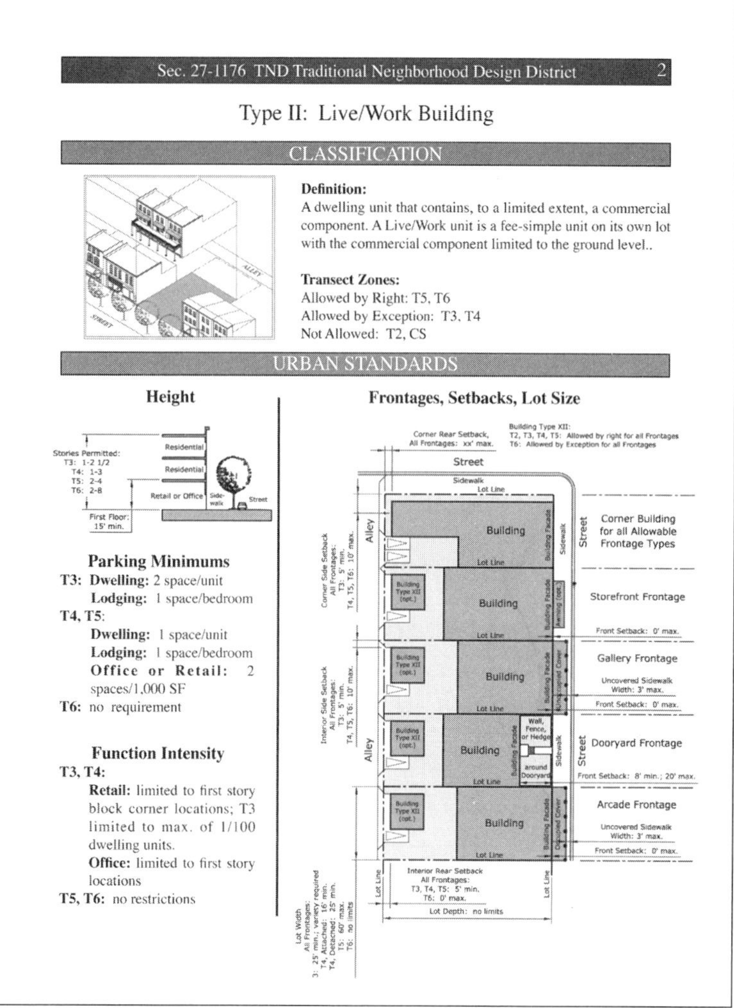

Sec. 27-1176 TND Traditional Neighborhood Design District 2

Type II: Live/Work Building

CLASSIFICATION

**Definition:**
A dwelling unit that contains, to a limited extent, a commercial component. A Live/Work unit is a fee-simple unit on its own lot with the commercial component limited to the ground level..

**Transect Zones:**
Allowed by Right: T5, T6
Allowed by Exception: T3, T4
Not Allowed: T2, CS

URBAN STANDARDS

**Height**



**Parking Minimums**
**T3: Dwelling:** 2 space/unit
**Lodging:** 1 space/bedroom
**T4, T5**:
**Dwelling:** 1 space/unit
**Lodging:** 1 space/bedroom
**Office or Retail:** 2 spaces/1,000 SF
**T6:** no requirement

**Function Intensity**
**T3, T4:**
**Retail:** limited to first story block corner locations; T3 limited to max. of 1/100 dwelling units.
**Office:** limited to first story locations
**T5, T6:** no restrictions

**Frontages, Setbacks, Lot Size**



### *Street-Based Codes*

Form-Based Codes with streets as their organizing principle focus their regulations primarily on the specific design and location of streets. The Building Form Standards typically include a section drawing that defines the dimensional requirement for the street design, such as width and number of travel lanes, allocation and width of on-street parking, planting strip widths, and sidewalk widths. In addition, the specific way that a building is required to address the street, both in height, frontage type, and build-to line, is included in the regulating street section. The allocation of the different street types and their required locations are directly applied to the Regulating Plan, designating specific street types to existing and new streets.

**Fig. 2.8** Adopted in April 2007, the Downtown Development Code for Blue Springs, Missouri, by 180° Design Studio is a good example of a Building Type-Based FBC.

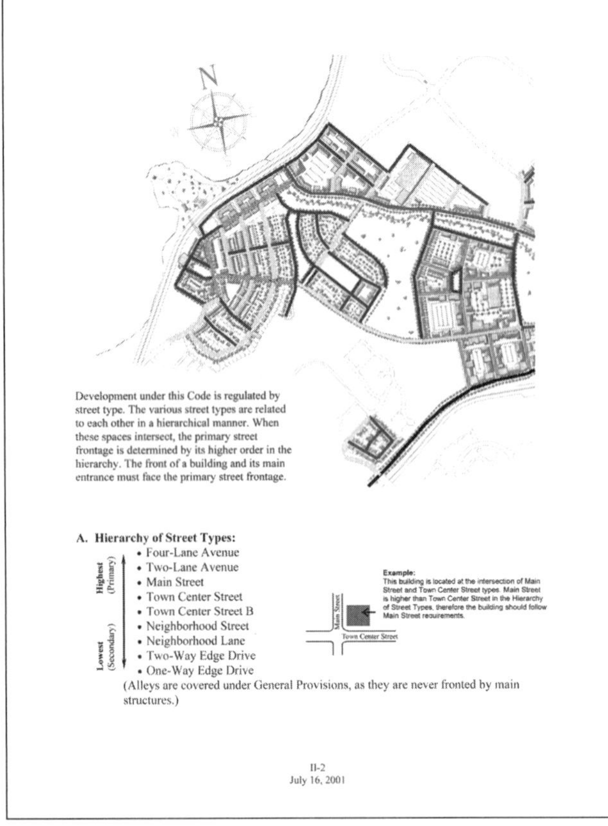


Development under this Code is regulated by street type. The various street types are related to each other in a hierarchical manner. When these spaces intersect, the primary street frontage is determined by its higher order in the hierarchy. The front of a building and its main entrance must face the primary street frontage.

A. **Hierarchy of Street Types:**

- Four-Lane Avenue
- Two-Lane Avenue
- Main Street
- Town Center Street
- Town Center Street B
- Neighborhood Street
- Neighborhood Lane
- Two-Way Edge Drive
- One-Way Edge Drive

(Alleys are covered under General Provisions, as they are never fronted by main structures.)

II-2
July 16, 2001

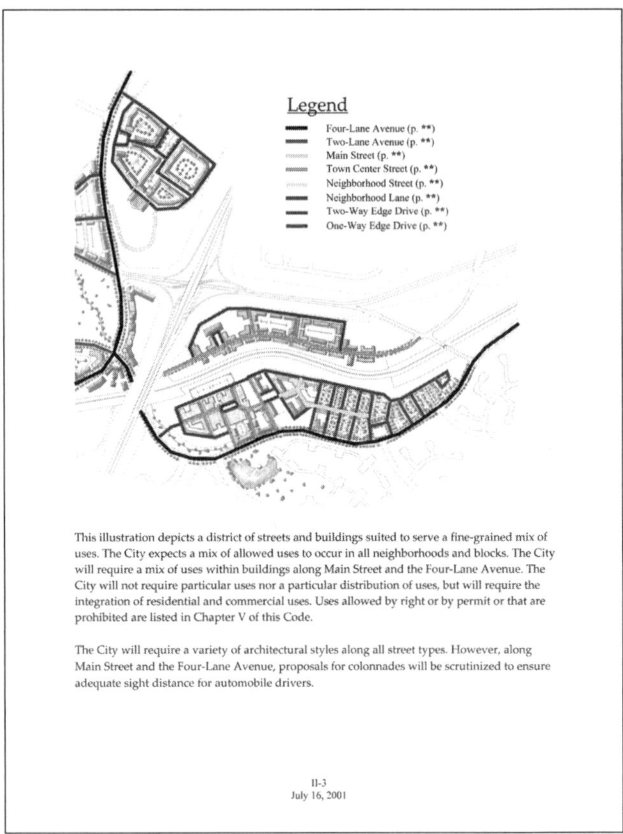


This illustration depicts a district of streets and buildings suited to serve a fine-grained mix of uses. The City expects a mix of allowed uses to occur in all neighborhoods and blocks. The City will require a mix of uses within buildings along Main Street and the Four-Lane Avenue. The City will not require particular uses nor a particular distribution of uses, but will require the integration of residential and commercial uses. Uses allowed by right or by permit or that are prohibited are listed in Chapter V of this Code.

The City will require a variety of architectural styles along all street types. However, along Main Street and the Four-Lane Avenue, proposals for colonnades will be scrutinized to ensure adequate sight distance for automobile drivers.

II-3
July 16, 2001

**Tip** During the administering of the Central Hercules Plan street-based FBC, it was helpful to meet with new developers and design consultants at the start of new projects to review the overall concept of the code, especially the dimensional requirements for each street type and the prescribed location of new streets. Without this meeting, the project designers often looked at the street allocation on the Regulating Plan without looking at the details of the sections and thought that driveways or lanes intended for access only would meet the requirements of the code. Because of the importance of the quality of the streetscape within the project area, it was important to reinforce the regulations in order to maintain a coherent street and block network throughout the new neighborhoods.

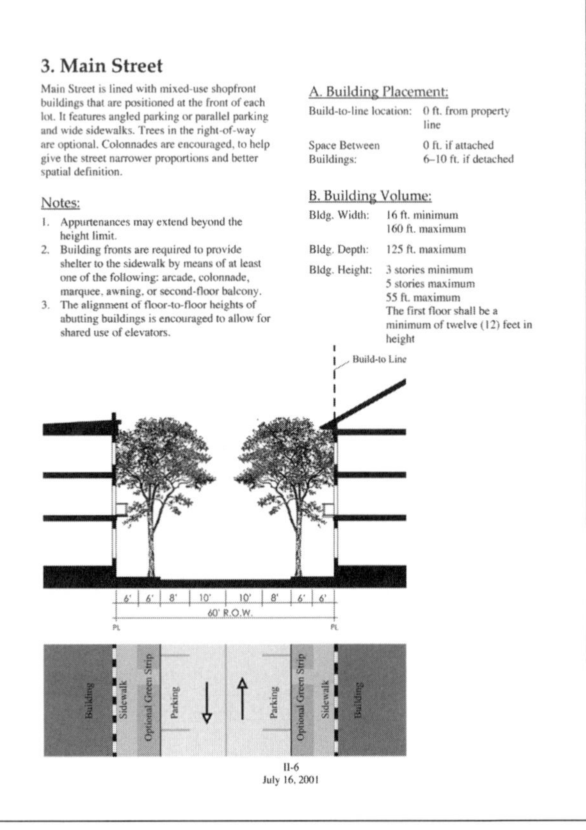

### 3. Main Street

Main Street is lined with mixed-use shopfront buildings that are positioned at the front of each lot. It features angled parking or parallel parking and wide sidewalks. Trees in the right-of-way are optional. Colonnades are encouraged, to help give the street narrower proportions and better spatial definition.

Notes:

1. Appurtenances may extend beyond the height limit.
2. Building fronts are required to provide shelter to the sidewalk by means of at least one of the following: arcade, colonnade, marquee, awning, or second-floor balcony.
3. The alignment of floor-to-floor heights of abutting buildings is encouraged to allow for shared use of elevators.

A. Building Placement:

| | |
|---|---|
| Build-to-line location: | 0 ft. from property line |
| Space Between Buildings: | 0 ft. if attached<br>6–10 ft. if detached |

B. Building Volume:

| | |
|---|---|
| Bldg. Width: | 16 ft. minimum<br>160 ft. maximum |
| Bldg. Depth: | 125 ft. maximum |
| Bldg. Height: | 3 stories minimum<br>5 stories maximum<br>55 ft. maximum<br>The first floor shall be a minimum of twelve (12) feet in height |



II-6
July 16, 2001

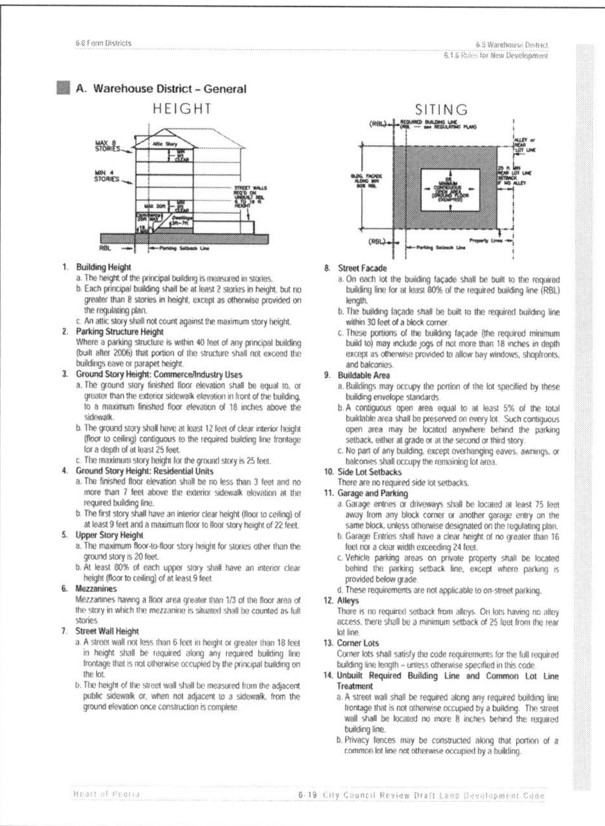

6.0 Form Districts

6.5 Warehouse District
6.1.6 Rules for New Development

### A. Warehouse District - General

HEIGHT

SITING

1. **Building Height**
   a. The height of the principal building is measured in stories.
   b. Each principal building shall be at least 2 stories in height, but no greater than 8 stories in height, except as otherwise provided on the regulating plan.
   c. An attic story shall not count against the maximum story height.
2. **Parking Structure Height**
   Where a parking structure is within 40 feet of any principal building (built after 2006) that portion of the structure shall not exceed the buildings eave or parapet height.
3. **Ground Story Height: Commerce/Industry Uses**
   a. The ground story finished floor elevation shall be equal to, or greater than the exterior sidewalk elevation in front of the building, to a maximum finished floor elevation of 18 inches above the sidewalk.
   b. The ground story shall have at least 12 feet of clear interior height (floor to ceiling) contiguous to the required building line frontage for a depth of at least 25 feet.
   c. The maximum story height for the ground story is 25 feet.
4. **Ground Story Height: Residential Units**
   a. The finished floor elevation shall be no less than 3 feet and no more than 7 feet above the exterior sidewalk elevation at the required building line.
   b. The first story shall have an interior clear height (floor to ceiling) of at least 9 feet and a maximum floor to floor story height of 22 feet.
5. **Upper Story Height**
   a. The maximum floor-to-floor story height for stories other than the ground story is 20 feet.
   b. At least 80% of each upper story shall have an interior clear height (floor to ceiling) of at least 9 feet.
6. **Mezzanines**
   Mezzanines having a floor area greater than 1/3 of the floor area of the story in which the mezzanine is situated shall be counted as full stories.
7. **Street Wall Height**
   a. A street wall not less than 6 feet in height or greater than 18 feet in height shall be required along any required building line frontage that is not otherwise occupied by the principal building on the lot.
   b. The height of the street wall shall be measured from the adjacent public sidewalk or, when not adjacent to a sidewalk, from the ground elevation once construction is complete.
8. **Street Facade**
   a. On each lot the building façade shall be built to the required building line for at least 80% of the required building line (RBL) length.
   b. The building façade shall be built to the required building line within 30 feet of a block corner.
   c. These portions of the building façade (the required minimum build to) may include jogs of not more than 18 inches in depth except as otherwise provided to allow bay windows, shopfronts, and balconies.
9. **Buildable Area**
   a. Buildings may occupy the portion of the lot specified by these building envelope standards.
   b. A contiguous open area equal to at least 5% of the total buildable area shall be preserved on every lot. Such contiguous open area may be located anywhere behind the parking setback, either at grade or at the second or third story.
   c. No part of any building, except overhanging eaves, awnings, or balconies shall occupy the remaining lot area.
10. **Side Lot Setbacks**
    There are no required side lot setbacks.
11. **Garage and Parking**
    a. Garage entries or driveways shall be located at least 75 feet away from any block corner or another garage entry on the same block, unless otherwise designated on the regulating plan.
    b. Garage Entries shall have a clear height of no greater than 16 feet nor a clear width exceeding 24 feet.
    c. Vehicle parking areas on private property shall be located behind the parking setback line, except where parking is provided below grade.
    d. These requirements are not applicable to on-street parking.
12. **Alleys**
    There is no required setback from alleys. On lots having no alley access, there shall be a minimum setback of 25 feet from the rear lot line.
13. **Corner Lots**
    Corner lots shall satisfy the code requirements for the full required building line length – unless otherwise specified in this code.
14. **Unbuilt Required Building Line and Common Lot Line Treatment**
    a. A street wall shall be required along any required building line frontage that is not otherwise occupied by a building. The street wall shall be located no more 8 inches behind the required building line.
    b. Privacy fences may be constructed along that portion of a common lot line not otherwise occupied by a building.

Heart of Peoria — 6-19 City Council Review Draft Land Development Code

<< **Fig. 2.9** (three images at left) An extremely successful example of a Street-Based FBC is the Central Hercules Plan code by Dover, Kohl & Partners, adopted in 2001. Several high-quality neighborhoods have been built by production builders under this code. (Also see Figure C.1.)

**Fig. 2.10** (above and above left) The Heart of Peoria code by Ferrell Madden Associates and Code Studio is a Frontage-Based FBC that was adopted in April 2007. (Also see Figure C.9.)

## Frontage-Based Codes

**by Geoffrey Ferrell** *Principal, Ferrell Madden Associates*

A Frontage-Based Code aspires to governmental regulation directly proportional to its necessity and appropriateness to a vital public realm (street-space) through proper building form and function.

Since the first duty is in the making of the street-space, most rules are specific to the facade and define necessary and sufficient performance—not a specific architectural solution. Government control is then in direct relation to civic responsibility, and there are likely several building types/architectural solutions (and possibly a new one) that satisfy the community need.

This approach is closely related to Street-Based Codes, its precursor. The difference is simply the separation of the 1:1 relation between the specifics of the street (lane and sidewalk widths, street tree configurations, curb radii, and so on) and the regulations governing the form and function of the private building. Coding by Frontage (versus lot) neatly avoids the problems of through-lots and consolidated properties by linking the form and performance of a property's facade to its frontage.

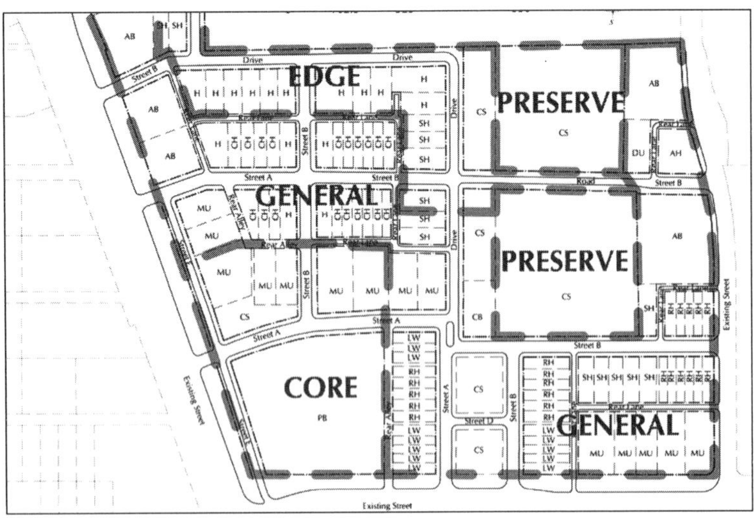


**Fig. 2.11** The transition of zones between lots and blocks in a Form-Based Code (Image from the Sarasota County FBC by Dover, Kohl & Partners and Spikowski Planning Associates)

This approach is specific about street design parameters and the way that a building should meet and define the street, but typically keeps the building type and other physical parameters out of the code. Therefore, it is best administered by a Town Architect to ensure quality implementation of projects. (See Figure 2.9.)

*Frontage-Based Codes*

FBCs with frontages as their organizing principle focus their regulations primarily on the way that buildings address the public realm, typically the street. The Regulating Plan usually designates the application of the Form-Based Zones by showing different colors on the streets instead of on the lots. This approach emphasizes the importance of the character of the public realm and often leaves what happens behind the frontage a bit more flexible. (See Figure 2.10.)

While each of these approaches is valid in appropriate places, the transect is by far the most used and most universally applicable approach. The use of the transect also helps establish a lexicon for Form-Based Coding, which is important for its advancement and use. For these reasons, the rest of this book will concentrate on transect-based Form-Based Codes.

## Implementation

### Application of Form-Based Zones

Based on the organizing principle selected, the Regulating Plan is color-coded to designate the areas where each of the transect zones applies. The purpose of defining and applying the zones is to identify specific areas within a community according to the existing character that the community wants to preserve, or the desired character into which it intends to evolve. Unlike conventional planning and zoning that may require walls, large setbacks, and landscape buffers to mitigate impacts between zones, Form-Based Coding does not require any physical delimiters and gives careful consideration to the relationship of and the transition between zones through the location of zone boundaries and the substance of the Building Form Standards. This is one of the primary urban design aspects of Form-Based Coding—transect-based zones are designed to work in a continuum, making gradual distinctions from the most urban areas of town to the most rural. (A rare exception is a case like Central Park in New York City, where abutting transect-zones jump from one end of the hierarchy to the other.) However, the application of these zones is a very precise task, often done on through lot-by-lot analysis in order to determine the appropriate location for the zone boundaries. (See Figure 2.11.)

In addition to the transect zones, the Regulating Plan often designates the required thoroughfare types and civic spaces, as well as the location of any civic buildings. Since important civic buildings are not part of the urban fabric, but instead may appropriately stand out, they are typically not required to abide by the transect zone regulations, and are designated on the Regulating Plan in a "civic building" special district.

### When Is the Regulating Plan Created?

As an essential component of a Form-Based Code, the Regulating Plan is typically created along with the rest of the code, although there are instances where the Regulating Plan is created as part of the site-specific planning of an individual development application.

The first method is the most typical. In this process, specific boundaries of the transect zones, as well as the locations of thoroughfares, lots, blocks, and civic spaces are designated on the Regulating Plan as part of drafting the FBC. For example, when an FBC is to replace an existing development code, the existing zoning map is replaced with a Regulating Plan that implements the intentions of the community's vision by including specific boundaries for the new transect zones.

The second method is used for Form-Based Codes for infill or greenfield sites that meet a certain minimum size requirement established by the code, typically 2 acres or larger, and are not planned as part of the code's visioning process. In this method, the transect zones and their regulations are defined, but their precise application through a Regulating Plan is not. Instead, a Regulating Plan is created using the percentages of T-Zones required by the FBC and submitted with each development application. In these codes, a prototypical Regulating Plan is often included to set the standard for each Regulating Plan that will be created. An example of this type of Regulating Plan implementation can be seen in the St. Lucie County and Sarasota County case studies later in this book.

In both cases, the other components, such as the Building Form Standards and the Public Space Standards, are fully defined in the code. In the latter case, they are simply applied to a Regulating Plan at a later date as part of a development application for a large parcel of land. These latter codes need to include precise regulations for the size and layout of lots, blocks, thoroughfares, and civic spaces that may be unnecessary in codes with a full Regulating Plan.

28

# Public Space Standards

The character of the parks, plazas, other open spaces, and public thoroughfares, including the features within thoroughfare right-of-ways (ROWs), profoundly affect the quality of an urban place. For this reason, Public Space Standards that address these features are an essential component of a Form-Based Code.

The Public Space Standards cover two elements: (1) thoroughfares, and (2) civic spaces. Since thoroughfares make up a large percentage of overall public space within a community, their design is one of the most critical considerations within the Form-Based Code. For example, requiring buildings to be set at the ROW in an urban environment makes sense only if the thoroughfare is designed to create a comfortable pedestrian environment. If the thoroughfare is an eight-lane, high-speed arterial that will not be redesigned, there is no reason even to consider setting buildings at the ROW because it will never be a comfortable place for pedestrians. Without the design and regulation of good thoroughfares and high-quality civic spaces in place, the positive impact of the regulations in other parts of the FBC will be marginalized.

(Terminology note: The term *thoroughfare* is the preferred technical term used to denote general transportation-oriented public spaces. The more common terms *street* or *road* are not appropriate since they are both used as specific thoroughfare types in Form-Based Codes, similar to *avenue* and *boulevard*. However, since they are generally more familiar terms, they are occasionally used in this book for general text, but not for technical descriptions.)

## Thoroughfares

Good streets form the backbone of healthy neighborhoods.[5] They perform a dual role as vehicular and pedestrian corridors, as well as the community's primary public spaces, destinations in and of themselves. The impact of their design on communities cannot be underestimated.

Unfortunately, most communities have existing thoroughfare standards that make the creation of new walkable communities impossible. In addition, in developed areas—such as downtowns and historic neighborhoods—adaptations to the historic thoroughfares, including the removal of on-street parking, the narrowing of sidewalks, the integration of higher-speed one-way thoroughfares, and the insistence of maintaining high levels of service for motor vehicles only have prevented the revitalization and improved walkability of these areas. Even in attractive and evolving cities, such as San Diego, Phoenix, and Austin, infill and redevelopment efforts could have a much stronger impact on the overall quality of the downtown and historic neighborhoods if the circulation patterns, design speeds, and overall thoroughfare design were more strongly considered.

For communities to be walkable, thoroughfares must be designed with pedestrian comfort and safety as critical goals along with the safe and efficient flow of traffic and other considerations, such as the accommodation of emergency vehicles, parking, utilities, and storm water. To elevate the importance of pedestrian safety and comfort, the focus for thoroughfare design should be on design speed rather than the volume of traffic and the level of service, especially in urban areas, which is a fundamental paradigm shift for traffic engineers and transportation planners. In addition, thoroughfares should typically be narrower than conventional thoroughfares and arranged in an interconnected, gridded network; intersections should be carefully considered, and such design details as tighter curb radii should be implemented.

Thoroughfares should be calibrated by transect level. For example, thoroughfares in T2 may be curbless and have slightly wider travel lanes as well as wider planting strips, while thoroughfares in T4 and T5 will have more curbs, narrower travel lanes, and a narrower planting strip or a tree well. Thoroughfare designs may also need to be coordinated with state and local laws. In many cases, state regulations will require augmentation.

Most FBCs regulate thoroughfares by creating a set of approved thoroughfare types in the Public Space Standards. In FBCs with a Regulating Plan, these thoroughfare types are then assigned to physical locations via the Regulating Plan. In FBCs without a Regulating Plan, they are assigned to regulating zones via the Urban Standards and then to physical locations when the Regulating Plan is submitted. As with the other components, these standards should typically be based on the documentation of existing good thoroughfares in the community.

A variety of the typical thoroughfare types can be calibrated and used in creating a walkable community, including alleys, lanes, roads, streets, commercial/main streets, avenues, and boulevards.[6] (See Figure 2.12.)

Following are the typical descriptions and regulations included for each thoroughfare type. This is not intended to be a comprehensive list, but rather a starting point for good thoroughfare design within the Form-Based Code. Include a traffic and transportation engineer on the team to help choose appropriate elements from this list and add other elements that are particular to the project area or community. Be sure they can address specific concerns from public works and emergency response of-

**Tip**

Begin conversations about thoroughfare design early in the overall FBC process because many municipal departments, such as emergency response, public works, and sanitation, often need extra time, information, and convincing to consider approving the thoroughfare regulations necessary for walkable neighborhoods.

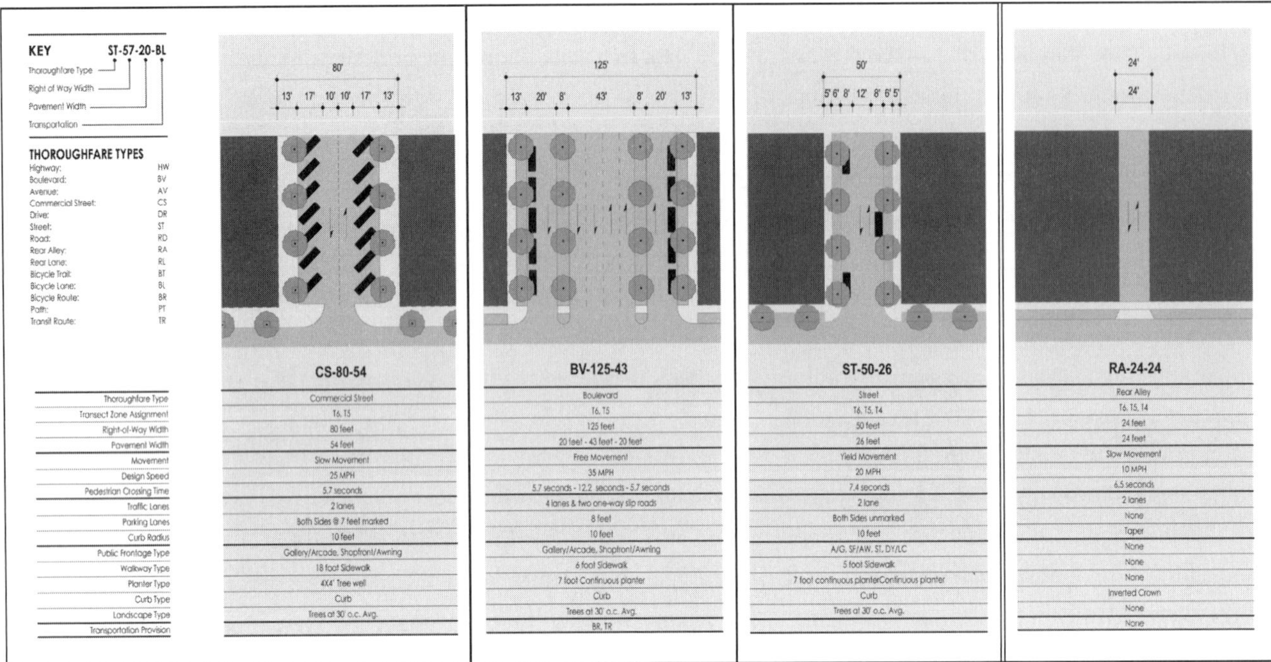


| | CS-80-54 | BV-125-43 | ST-50-26 | RA-24-24 |
|---|---|---|---|---|
| Thoroughfare Type | Commercial Street | Boulevard | Street | Rear Alley |
| Transect Zone Assignment | T6, T5 | T6, T5 | T6, T5, T4 | T6, T5, T4 |
| Right-of-Way Width | 80 feet | 125 feet | 50 feet | 24 feet |
| Pavement Width | 54 feet | 20 feet - 43 feet - 20 feet | 26 feet | 24 feet |
| Movement | Slow Movement | Free Movement | Yield Movement | Slow Movement |
| Design Speed | 25 MPH | 35 MPH | 20 MPH | 10 MPH |
| Pedestrian Crossing Time | 5.7 seconds | 5.7 seconds - 12.2 seconds - 5.7 seconds | 7.4 seconds | 6.5 seconds |
| Traffic Lanes | 2 lanes | 4 lanes & two one-way slip roads | 2 lane | 2 lanes |
| Parking Lanes | Both Sides @ 7 feet marked | 8 feet | Both Sides unmarked | None |
| Curb Radius | 10 feet | 10 feet | 10 feet | Taper |
| Public Frontage Type | Gallery/Arcade, Shopfront/Awning | Gallery/Arcade, Shopfront/Awning | A/G, SF/AW, ST, DY/LC | None |
| Walkway Type | 18 foot Sidewalk | 6 foot Sidewalk | 5 foot Sidewalk | None |
| Planter Type | 4X4' Tree well | 7 foot Continuous planter | 7 foot continuous planterContinuous planter | None |
| Curb Type | Curb | Curb | Curb | Inverted Crown |
| Landscape Type | Trees at 30' o.c. Avg. | Trees at 30' o.c. Avg. | Trees at 30' o.c. Avg. | None |
| Transportation Provision | | BR, TR | | None |

**Fig. 2.12** The typical thoroughfare types from the SmartCode are extensive and can provide a good foundation for most codes, but must be locally calibrated. (Credit: DPZ)

ficials with data and experience and a thorough knowledge of the function and flow of pedestrians, cyclists, transit, and traffic, not just design considerations.

## Movement Type

The kind of traffic flow the thoroughfare is designed to accommodate and foster.

This is not a regulation, but a general description. It helps designers and developers better understand the thoroughfare type in order to apply it appropriately to help create a good pedestrian-oriented community.

*Typical Values*

- Yield: Drivers will slow down or pull to the side to pass in opposite directions. These thoroughfares may be appropriate in all transect zones.
- Slow: Drivers will move slowly based on their perception of the environment and activity in the area, such as the presence of pedestrians. These thoroughfares are appropriate in all transect zones.
- Free: Drivers will move unimpeded at higher speeds. These thoroughfares are typically not appropriate in T3 and T4.

## Design Speed

The highest vehicle speed the thoroughfare is designed to accommodate and foster.

This is not a regulation, but a general description. It helps designers, developers, and engineers better understand the thoroughfare type in order to apply it appropriately.

The speed of cars obviously has a large impact on the safety and comfort of pedestrians. A pedestrian hit by a vehicle going 20 mph has a 95

### Perception versus Reality

Drivers may complain that narrower thoroughfares feel more dangerous. They are absolutely right about the feeling, but the reality is that they are safer. Because the thoroughfares are narrower, there are more objects within close range and less wiggle room for drivers. This perception of danger is exactly what convinces drivers to slow down, thereby actually increasing their safety, as well as the safety of the pedestrians and vehicles around them.

to 97 percent chance of survival, but only a 50 percent chance of survival if the vehicle is going 30 mph.[7] Thoroughfares intended to foster pedestrian activity need to have low design speeds. Faster speeds can be accommodated in pedestrian areas where necessary by using a boulevard, which has faster lanes in the center separated by a planting strip from slower access lanes along the edges near pedestrians.

## Pedestrian Crossing Time

The typical length of time required for a person to walk across the thoroughfare.

This is not a regulation, but a general description. It helps designers, developers, and engineers recognize the impact of thoroughfare design on pedestrians, as well as on wait times for vehicles. Crossing time is most important on thoroughfares with higher vehicle speeds.

## Transect Zones

The appropriate areas for the thoroughfare type.

This helps ensure that thoroughfare types are applied in an appropriate context.

## Right-of-Way (ROW) Width Ⓐ

The measurement across a thoroughfare of the area the municipality controls or owns. (See Figure 2.13.)

This includes the pavement area, as well as the planting strips and sidewalks, and, together with the build-to line (BTL)/Setback and the Frontage Types, effectively defines the width of the public space. Paired with the minimum and maximum height of buildings, this defines the proportion of the public space. All of these should be considered together and regulated accordingly to prescribe the desired place.

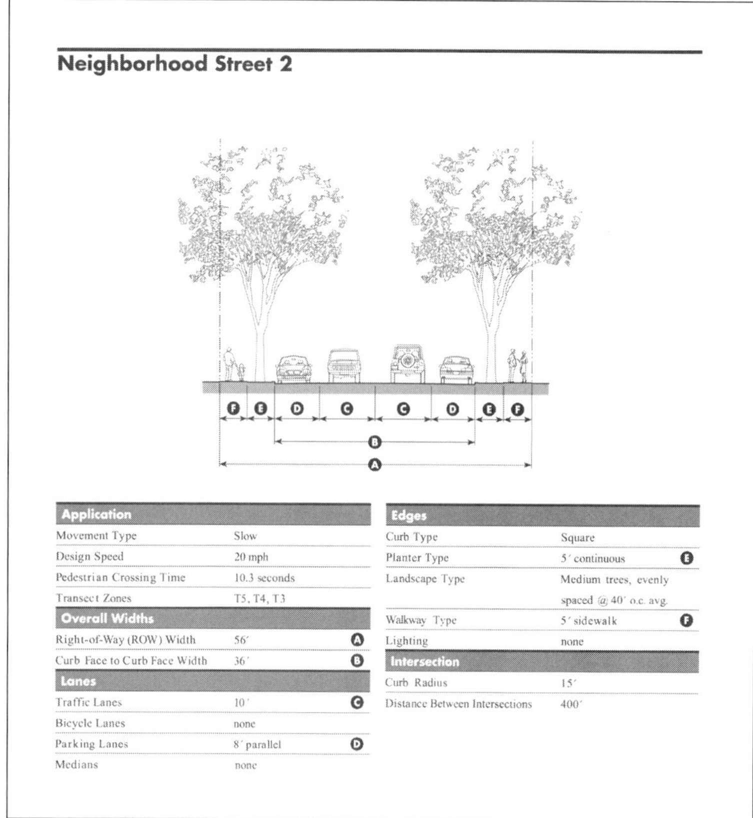


| Application | | |
|---|---|---|
| Movement Type | Slow | |
| Design Speed | 20 mph | |
| Pedestrian Crossing Time | 10.3 seconds | |
| Transect Zones | T5, T4, T3 | |
| **Overall Widths** | | |
| Right-of-Way (ROW) Width | 56′ | A |
| Curb Face to Curb Face Width | 36′ | B |
| **Lanes** | | |
| Traffic Lanes | 10′ | C |
| Bicycle Lanes | none | |
| Parking Lanes | 8′ parallel | D |
| Medians | none | |

| Edges | | |
|---|---|---|
| Curb Type | Square | |
| Planter Type | 5′ continuous | E |
| Landscape Type | Medium trees, evenly spaced @ 40′ o.c. avg. | |
| Walkway Type | 5′ sidewalk | F |
| Lighting | none | |
| **Intersection** | | |
| Curb Radius | 15′ | |
| Distance Between Intersections | 400′ | |

**Fig. 2.13** Thoroughfare Standards template by Opticos Design

## Curb Face to Curb Face Width Ⓑ

The distance across a thoroughfare between the vertical faces of the curbs, typically intended for vehicles, including any on-street parking, intermediary planting strips, and gutters. (See Figure 2.13.)

While sometimes called Pavement Width or Street Width, measurements vary from using the back of the curb to the edge of the pavement. The curb face is actually in the center of these two, and using this for the measurement most accurately represents the perceived width of the thoroughfare for drivers, and thus the likely speed of traffic. In addition, walkable thoroughfares are often parked; thus, the curb face measurement best defines the space for both movement and storage of vehicles. As the sum of its parts, this plays a major role in the function of the thoroughfare affecting the speed of vehicular travel, as well as the comfort and safety of both vehicles and pedestrians.

## Traffic Lanes C

The number and width of areas designated for vehicular travel, not including bicycle lanes. (See Figure 2.13.)

This is a primary factor in the way a thoroughfare functions. The number of lanes is a primary determinate (along with intersection control) of thoroughfare capacity. The narrower the width of each lane as well as the total width of all of the travel lanes, the slower vehicles will typically travel, thus creating a safer and more comfortable environment for pedestrians. In addition, for major thoroughfares, narrower and fewer lanes decrease the distance pedestrians must cross, again increasing their safety, decreasing the time vehicles must wait, and contributing to more compact neighborhoods. Lastly, this impacts the overall width of the public space, thus affecting the urban form.

## Bicycle Lanes

The number and width of rows designated for bicycle travel, typically demarcated by solid white stripes on the pavement.

Bicyclists should be considered when designing thoroughfares in order to ensure their safety and comfort, which also encourages more bicycle use.

*Hints for Implementation*

- Include bicycle lanes on thoroughfares with design speeds over 30 mph. Typical widths are 6 feet on thoroughfares with parallel parking and 5 feet on thoroughfares without.
- Consider not including bicycle lanes on thoroughfares with speeds under 30 mph. At these lower speeds, bicyclists and other vehicles can typically share traffic lanes. Adding bicycle lanes to these thoroughfares increases the perceived width of the thoroughfare, thus increasing the speed of the traffic, making the thoroughfare less safe for bicyclists as well as for other vehicles and pedestrians.
- Remember to carefully consider bicyclists when designing intersections.

## Parking Lanes D

The number and width of areas designated for on-street parking. (See Figure 2.13.)

The design and inclusion of on-street parking impacts a number of factors. It slows down traffic by narrowing the perceived width of the thoroughfare, provides better access to homes and businesses, and creates a physical barrier between pedestrians and moving traffic, all of which increase the comfort and safety of pedestrians. It provides more parking for residents and businesses, thus reducing the need for unattractive parking lots and garages. It distributes the parking throughout the community, providing some parking close to almost every building. Finally, it is a factor in the overall width of the thoroughfare, affecting the proportions of the public space.

Options for parking lanes include no parking, parking on one or both sides of the thoroughfare, and parallel, diagonal, or reverse diagonal parking.

*Hints for Implementation*

- Provide just enough parking to ensure that most of the parking spaces will be filled all day. If the parking spaces are not full, they cannot fulfill their role—helping slow down traffic and creating barriers between pedestrians and cars—and traffic speeds will be higher than intended.
- Consider using reverse diagonal parking in place of diagonal parking. It is can be easier to park in than parallel parking, while also being safer for both drivers and cyclists than

conventional diagonal parking. In addition, it is safer for unloading passengers since the open car door guides passengers toward the sidewalk while creating a barrier between them and the vehicular traffic.

## Curb Type

The kind of transition at the edge of the pavement.

The type of curb reinforces the desired character of place. Curbs create an edge for the vehicular area of a thoroughfare and affect the perception of the width of the thoroughfare as well as the character of an area. Square/vertical curbs are necessary in areas more urban in character to create a stronger edge between pedestrian and vehicular areas, to provide a channel for storm water runoff, and to facilitate street cleaning. In more rural areas (T2), swales can be more appropriate due to higher travel speeds, their lower cost, and their general character.

## Planter Type

The kind and width of landscaping accommodation at the edge of the thoroughfare pavement. (See Figures 2.13 and 2.14.)

The design and width of this landscaping has an integral affect on the way a thoroughfare is perceived, and thus should be considered carefully and calibrated by transect zone to achieve the desired character. Landscaping next to the pavement, particularly trees, creates a separation between vehicles and pedestrians. Swales are the most rural, planting strips work well to encourage pedestrian activity in residential areas, and tree wells are the most urban.

*Hints for Implementation*

- Coordinate the required minimum width closely with the type of trees to be planted.

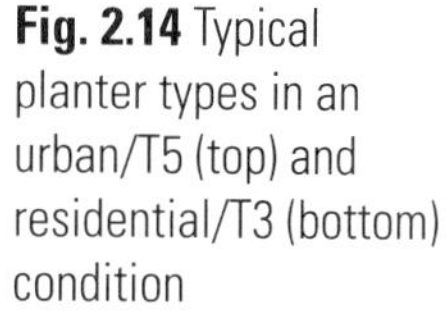

**Fig. 2.14** Typical planter types in an urban/T5 (top) and residential/T3 (bottom) condition

- In the landscape standards, designate the types of treatments and plants that are allowed in the landscaping strip to enable people to get into and out of parked cars.

## Landscape Type

The kind and spacing of trees or other landscaping to be planted. (See Figure 2.15.)

This affects the character of the streetscape, as well as the perceived proportion of the public space. It affects walkability in numerous ways. Trees create a barrier between pedestrians and vehicles, contributing to the safety and comfort of pedestrians. Trees with lower, wider canopies can reduce the perceived size of a thoroughfare, slowing down traffic. Evenly spaced, continuous rows of trees contribute to a more urban character, while clustered trees contribute to a more rural character. In warmer climates, shade trees can help keep walkways cooler, and thus more usable. In general, street trees have a major impact on the character and quality of a

**Fig. 2.15** A photo montage by Urban Advantage demonstrating the effect of trees on the streetscape (Used by permission of the National Association of Realtors®)

place, whether is it is a downtown or neighborhood, so street tree planting should be an important element in the vision and FBC.

*Hints for Implementation*

- Require regular tree spacing in all zones, except in T2 and T1.
- Place the first tree as close as possible to the corner to create the most attractive environment. While sight distance is often raised as a reason to eliminate trees from corners, it is related to vehicle speed. Sight distance is key at highway speeds above 40 mph and becomes much less significant at 15 mph.

## Walkway Type (F)

The kind and width of space allotted for pedestrians. (See Figure 2.13.)

Walkways, such as sidewalks, provide safe spaces and good surfaces for pedestrians to walk and gather, and are therefore critical in creating pedestrian-oriented places. Their design and width should be calibrated by transect zone. In more urban areas, they can also provide space for sidewalk cafés, helping enliven an area.

*Hints for Implementation*

- Avoid sidewalks that are curvilinear in plan in T6–T3, as they are too rural in character for these zones and make distances longer for pedestrians, thus decreasing the walkability of an area.
- In more urban, mixed-use areas, consider how uses are going to spill out onto the sidewalks when determining the minimum width.
- Ensure that walkways are at least 5 feet wide in T4 and T3 to provide enough space for two people to walk side by side and carry on a good conversation.

## Lighting

The type and spacing of illumination for vehicles and pedestrians.

Street lighting is critical for the comfort and safety of both pedestrians and vehicles at night and should be carefully considered. Appropriate street lighting can itself make pedestrians feel more comfortable, which in turn encourages more street life, another critical element for ensuring the comfort and safety of pedestrians in the evenings.

*Hints for Implementation*

- Ensure that lighting (both illumination level and color) is appropriate for sidewalks as well as travel lanes. In some instances, two different types of lighting fixtures may be appropriate.
- Consider additional lighting at intersections and crosswalks to ensure vehicles are able to see crossing pedestrians.

### Curb Radius

Dimension used to establish the curve of the curb at a corner. (See Figure 2.16.)

Smaller corner radii help lower the speed of vehicles turning corners, where pedestrians are mostly likely to be in the thoroughfare, and minimize crossing distances for pedestrians, thus improving the walkability of an area.

*Hints for Implementation*

- If wider radii are absolutely necessary, consider ways to mitigate their impact. (See Figure 2.17.)

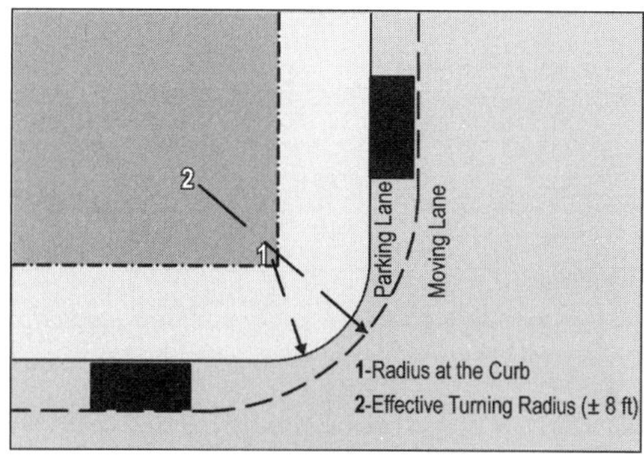


**Fig. 2.16** Illustration of a curb radius from the SmartCode (Credit: DPZ)

**Fig. 2.17** Filling the area between the desired radii and actual radii with stone pavers can help slow down traffic.

### Distance Between Intersections

The dimension between two adjacent thoroughfare crossings, typically measured from centerline to centerline.

Shorter distances between intersections help ensure the fine-grained, interconnected, gridded network of thoroughfares necessary for walkable neighborhoods.

## Civic Spaces

Well-designed and well-located civic spaces, such as parks and plazas, are critical for healthy and vibrant neighborhoods. They provide access to the outdoors, organizing elements within the structure of neighborhoods and downtowns, and public gathering places for all members of the community.

The quality of most recently built civic spaces is extremely low because current regulations primarily regulate the amount of civic space required with few standards pertaining to the quality of the space. This often leaves developers to designate leftover fragments of space as civic spaces on their plans. In addition, the regulations are typically focused on creating large, suburban-scale parks with an active recreation focus, the size of which is often prohibitive for infill and more urban conditions, and the regulations do not allow for smaller, more localized parks to meet the requirements. These regulations often prohibit high-quality infill in urban areas and foster parks that are not within walking distance of most residences. Therefore, as a means of creating walkable communities, civic space features should be specifically regulated and calibrated to the transect.

In order for civic spaces to be accessible and usable, they should be located within walking distance of residences and workplaces, typically one every 1/4 to 1/2 mile. They should be designed and sized appropriately for their transect zone. For instance, hardscaped plazas are inappropriate in T2, but work beautifully in T6. Tot lots and playgrounds should be plentiful for young families, while a range of other types of parks should be available for the rest of the population. Lushly landscaped parks may be perfect in T3 but may be inappropriate and unsafe in T6 due to the hiding places they provide for criminals.

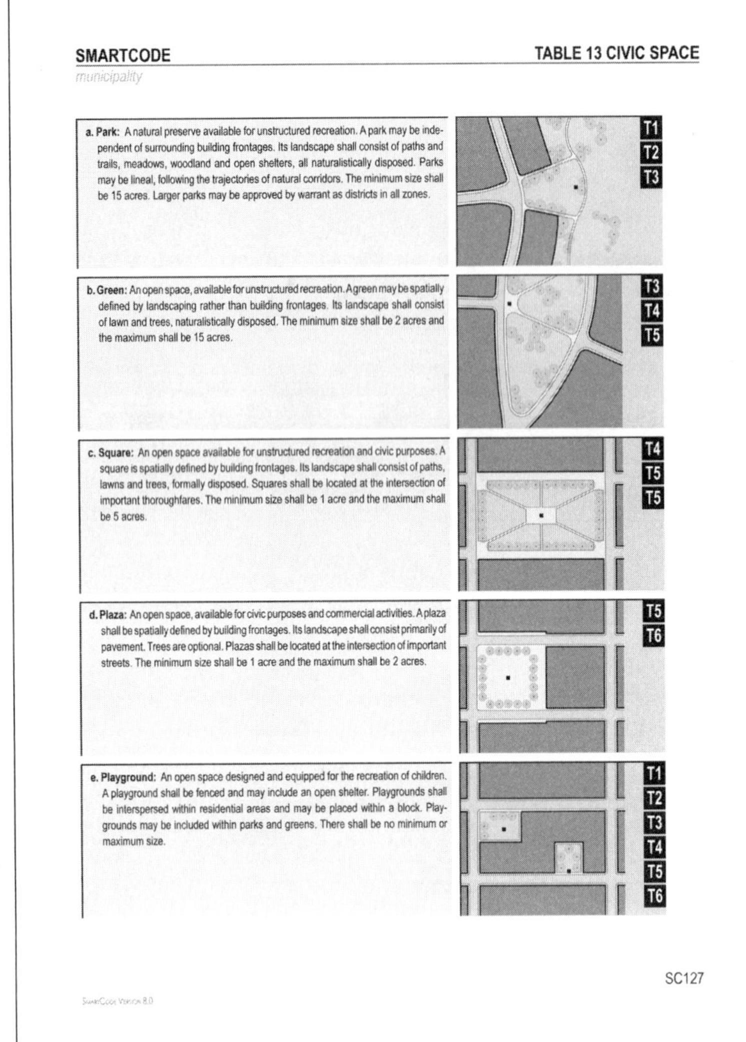

SMARTCODE — TABLE 13 CIVIC SPACE

*municipality*

**a. Park:** A natural preserve available for unstructured recreation. A park may be independent of surrounding building frontages. Its landscape shall consist of paths and trails, meadows, woodland and open shelters, all naturalistically disposed. Parks may be lineal, following the trajectories of natural corridors. The minimum size shall be 15 acres. Larger parks may be approved by warrant as districts in all zones.

T1 T2 T3

**b. Green:** An open space, available for unstructured recreation. A green may be spatially defined by landscaping rather than building frontages. Its landscape shall consist of lawn and trees, naturalistically disposed. The minimum size shall be 2 acres and the maximum shall be 15 acres.

T3 T4 T5

**c. Square:** An open space available for unstructured recreation and civic purposes. A square is spatially defined by building frontages. Its landscape shall consist of paths, lawns and trees, formally disposed. Squares shall be located at the intersection of important thoroughfares. The minimum size shall be 1 acre and the maximum shall be 5 acres.

T4 T5 T5

**d. Plaza:** An open space, available for civic purposes and commercial activities. A plaza shall be spatially defined by building frontages. Its landscape shall consist primarily of pavement. Trees are optional. Plazas shall be located at the intersection of important streets. The minimum size shall be 1 acre and the maximum shall be 2 acres.

T5 T6

**e. Playground:** An open space designed and equipped for the recreation of children. A playground shall be fenced and may include an open shelter. Playgrounds shall be interspersed within residential areas and may be placed within a block. Playgrounds may be included within parks and greens. There shall be no minimum or maximum size.

T1 T2 T3 T4 T5 T6

SmartCode Version 8.0 — SC127

**Fig. 2.18** Civic Space types from the SmartCode (Credit: DPZ)

(Central Park in New York City is now a wonderful place, but it has certainly had its rough years.) Establishing a community-wide framework of civic spaces should be part of the vision and regulated within the FBC.

Civic spaces is an area of Form-Based Coding that needs to be advanced since most FBCs to date have not addressed them to the level of detail and rigor of their other components. This being said, the SmartCode has established a good framework upon which to build.

Civic space types may include parks, greens, squares, plazas, paseos, pocket parks, playgrounds, and playing fields.[8] (See Figure 2.18.)

Overall regulations should include:

## Acreage

The minimum acreage of land required to be allocated for civic space.

This is typically a requirement for projects that are submitting their own Regulating Plan with their development application. [For citywide codes, the Regulating Plan (or the Parks Master Plan) should allocate necessary locations for parks and open space. This should not be done on a lot-by-lot basis.]

*Hints for Implementation*

- Require a minimum of 5 percent civic space for each pedestrian shed.[9]
- To provide an incentive for well-designed streets, allow them to count for up to 25 to 40 percent of the civic space requirements.
- Ensure that the overall required acreage can be implemented as a series of smaller spaces.

## Location

Requirements for the placement of civic spaces.

This helps ensure that parks are located and distributed appropriately on the Regulating Plan.

*Hints for Implementation*

- Require a playground within a six-minute walk of all residential uses.
- Require that squares and plazas be located at a prominent location in the heart of a neighborhood or downtown.
- Regulate that civic spaces shall not be made up of residual space left after buildings are placed on a site (i.e., along sound walls, tucked into corners, or the like).
- Require that civic spaces be framed by streets on at least two sides, except for play-

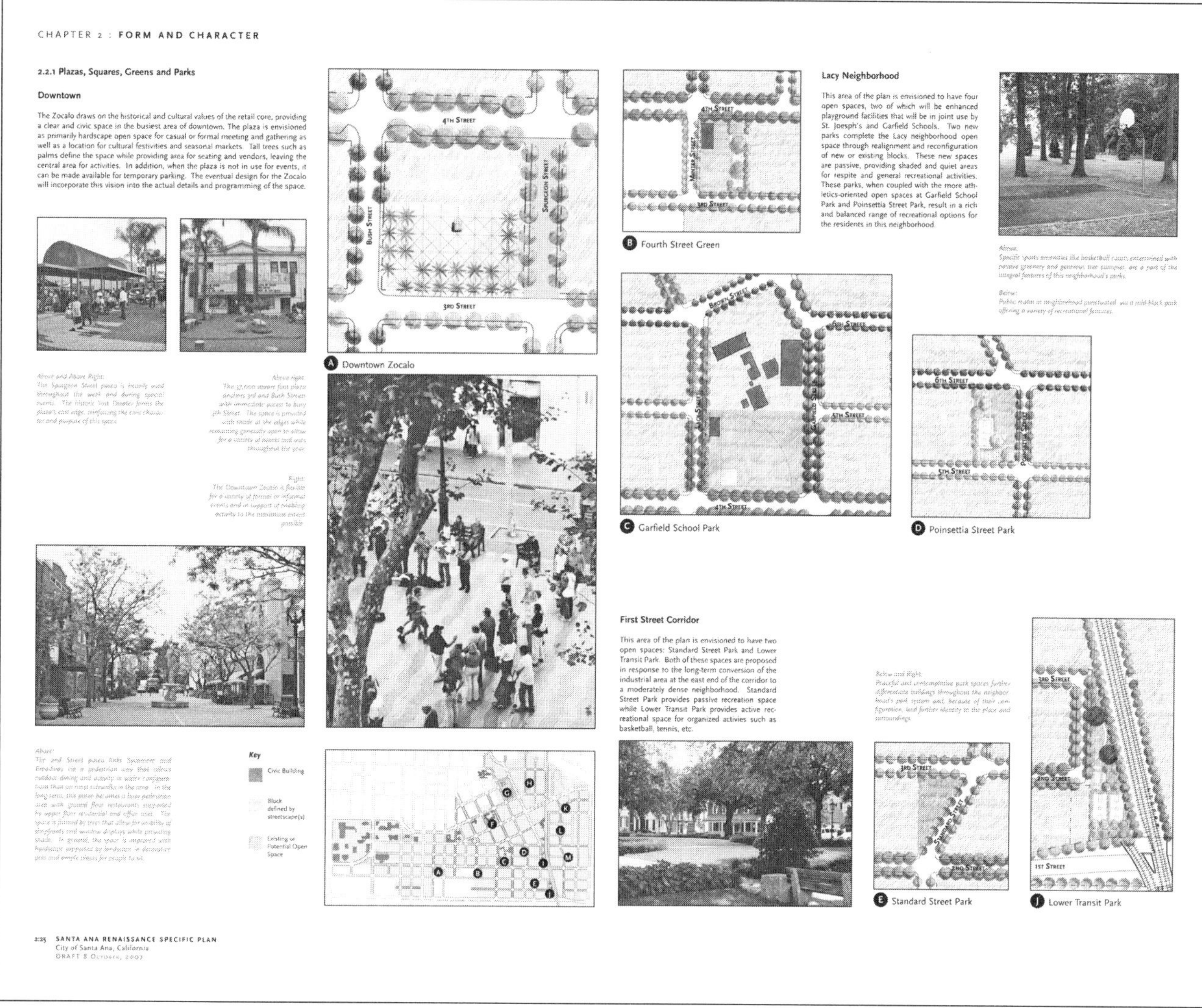

CHAPTER 2 : FORM AND CHARACTER

2.2.1 Plazas, Squares, Greens and Parks

Downtown

The Zocalo draws on the historical and cultural values of the retail core, providing a clear and civic space in the busiest area of downtown. The plaza is envisioned as primarily hardscape open space for casual or formal meeting and gathering as well as a location for cultural festivities and seasonal markets. Tall trees such as palms define the space while providing area for seating and vendors, leaving the central area for activities. In addition, when the plaza is not in use for events, it can be made available for temporary parking. The eventual design for the Zocalo will incorporate this vision into the actual details and programming of the space.

Lacy Neighborhood

This area of the plan is envisioned to have four open spaces, two of which will be enhanced playground facilities that will be in joint use by St. Joesph's and Garfield Schools. Two new parks complete the Lacy neighborhood open space through realignment and reconfiguration of new or existing blocks. These new spaces are passive, providing shaded and quiet areas for respite and general recreational activities. These parks, when coupled with the more athletics-oriented open spaces at Garfield School Park and Poinsettia Street Park, result in a rich and balanced range of recreational options for the residents in this neighborhood.

First Street Corridor

This area of the plan is envisioned to have two open spaces: Standard Street Park and Lower Transit Park. Both of these spaces are proposed in response to the long-term conversion of the industrial area at the east end of the corridor to a moderately dense neighborhood. Standard Street Park provides passive recreation space while Lower Transit Park provides active recreational space for organized activies such as basketball, tennis, etc.



2:25 SANTA ANA RENAISSANCE SPECIFIC PLAN
City of Santa Ana, California

**Fig. 2.19** Civic Space regulations from the Santa Ana Renaissance Specific Plan by Moule & Polyzoides and Crawford, Multari & Clark Associates

grounds, which may be tucked into a block, and large open parks.

Regulations for each civic space type typically include the following:

## Size

The minimum or maximum dimensions or acreage of the space.

Minimum regulations help ensure that the civic space is large enough to be usable and to achieve the desired intent. Maximum regulations help ensure that the civic space is scaled appropriately for the area and the type of space.

*Hints for Implementation*

- Do not regulate a minimum size for playgrounds, as tot lots often work well as small pocket parks.

## Allowable Transect Zones

The appropriate area for the civic space type.

This helps ensure that civic spaces are applied in an appropriate context. Although there are always exceptions, larger, more informal civic spaces tend to be more appropriate in more rural locations, while smaller, more formal civic spaces typically work better in more urban locations.

## Activity Type

The kind of recreation the civic space is intended to facilitate.

This is not a regulation, but a general description. It helps designers and developers better understand the civic space type to apply it correctly. This is typically listed as "active" or "passive" recreation.

## General Character

The intended look and feel of the space.

These may be regulations or guidelines intended to ensure that the space is appropriately designed for its context and purpose. For example, a formal civic plaza in T6 should not have a natural creek running through it, just as a large informal greenway in T2 should not be hardscaped.

*Hints for Implementation*

- Regulate the landscape treatment in civic spaces if a particular character is intended as part of the vision.
- Minimize the use of the primary civic space for storm water treatment. Instead, include secondary and tertiary civic spaces, as well as other less visible locations for this use.

# Building Form Standards



Building Form Standards are the component of an FBC that people typically visualize when they hear the term *Form-Based Code*. They have the primary role in defining the physical form of the built environment. The Building Form Standards establish specific physical and use parameters for each transect zone, such as build-to lines and heights, in addition to parameters that apply to all zones, such as frontage types and the size of parking spaces. Their preferred format is graphic, integrating simple diagrams and easy-to-read tables for ease of use and clarity of the regulations. There are typically no more than five pages of Building Form Standard regulations for each transect zone. Each of these places, or zones, is then assigned to a physical location via the Regulating Plan.

The Building Form Standards are primarily organized by zone. The typical sections in the code for each zone include the following:

- Overview of the zone
- Building placement regulations
- Building form regulations
- Parking regulations
- Allowed use types and detailed use table
- Allowed frontage types
- Allowed encroachments
- Allowed building types

It is possible that regulatory elements other than the above may be needed to address specific local conditions. These new elements will likely fit within one of the categories listed above, but the FBC team can always modify the content and format as necessary.

Although this list of elements might seem elementary, the creation of the Building Form Standards involves regulating very complex interrelationships between buildings, public spaces, and private spaces. To create the Building

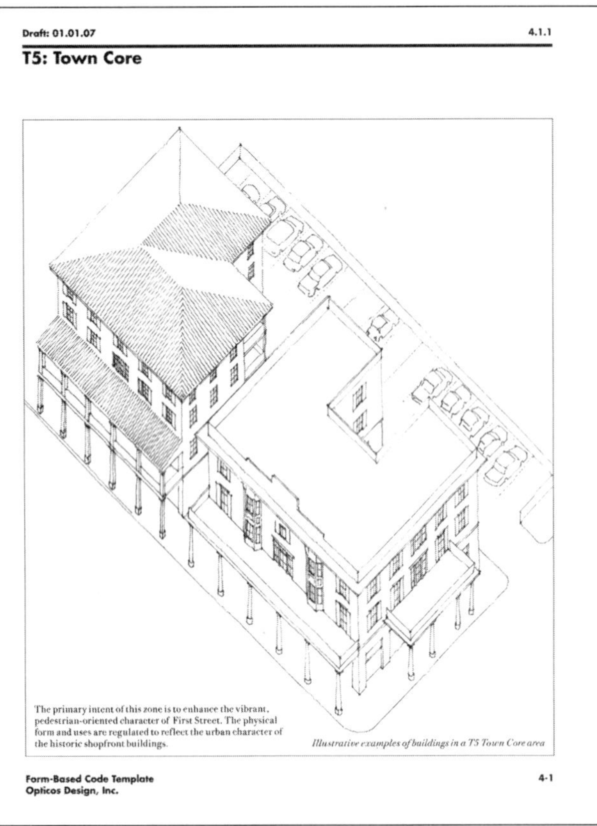

Draft: 01.01.07 4.1.1

**T5: Town Core**

The primary intent of this zone is to enhance the vibrant, pedestrian-oriented character of First Street. The physical form and uses are regulated to reflect the urban character of the historic shopfront buildings.

*Illustrative examples of buildings in a T5 Town Core area*

Form-Based Code Template
Opticos Design, Inc. 4-1

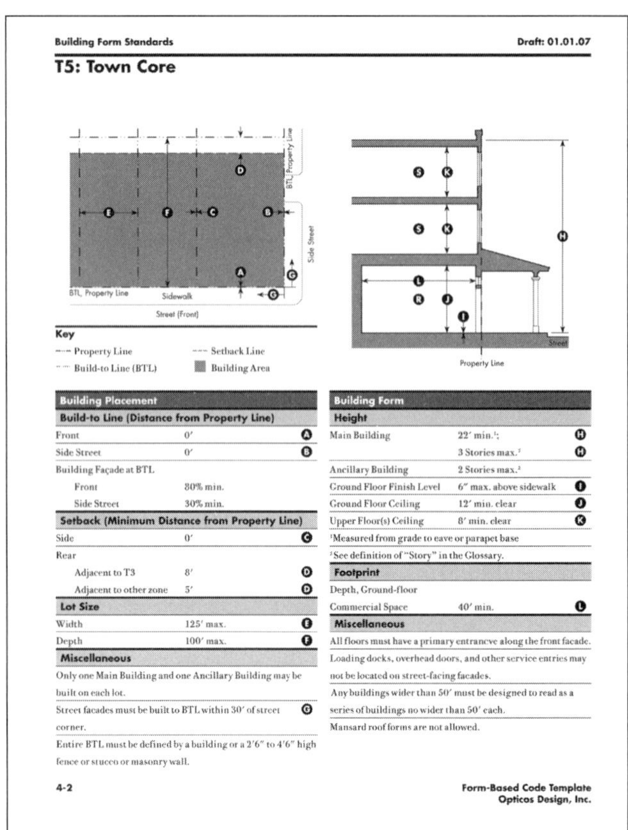

Building Form Standards Draft: 01.01.07

**T5: Town Core**



**Key**

- - - Property Line
- - - Build-to Line (BTL)
- - - Setback Line
■ Building Area

| Building Placement | | |
|---|---|---|
| **Build-to Line (Distance from Property Line)** | | |
| Front | 0′ | A |
| Side Street | 0′ | B |
| Building Façade at BTL | | |
| Front | 80% min. | |
| Side Street | 30% min. | |
| **Setback (Minimum Distance from Property Line)** | | |
| Side | 0′ | C |
| Rear | | |
| Adjacent to T3 | 8′ | D |
| Adjacent to other zone | 5′ | D |
| **Lot Size** | | |
| Width | 125′ max. | E |
| Depth | 100′ max. | F |
| **Miscellaneous** | | |
| Only one Main Building and one Ancillary Building may be built on each lot. | | |
| Street facades must be built to BTL within 30′ of street corner. | | G |
| Entire BTL must be defined by a building or a 2′6″ to 4′6″ high fence or stucco or masonry wall. | | |

| Building Form | | |
|---|---|---|
| **Height** | | |
| Main Building | 22′ min.[1]; | H |
| | 3 Stories max.[2] | H |
| Ancillary Building | 2 Stories max.[2] | |
| Ground Floor Finish Level | 6″ max. above sidewalk | I |
| Ground Floor Ceiling | 12′ min. clear | J |
| Upper Floor(s) Ceiling | 8′ min. clear | K |
| [1]Measured from grade to eave or parapet base | | |
| [2]See definition of "Story" in the Glossary. | | |
| **Footprint** | | |
| Depth, Ground-floor Commercial Space | 40′ min. | L |
| **Miscellaneous** | | |
| All floors must have a primary entrancve along the front facade. | | |
| Loading docks, overhead doors, and other service entries may not be located on street-facing facades. | | |
| Any buildings wider than 50′ must be designed to read as a series of buildings no wider than 50′ each. | | |
| Mansard roof forms are not allowed. | | |

4-2 Form-Based Code Template
Opticos Design, Inc.

**Fig. 2.20** Building Form Standards template by Opticos Design. Left to right: Page 1 includes a short descriptive overview of the zone along with an illustrative drawing of a potential desired outcome. While this page is not regulatory, it is necessary to communicate the overall intention of the zone. Page 2 includes Building Placement and Building Form.

Form Standards, the code team systematically works its way through the Illustrative Plan and other visioning documents, critically analyzing and regulating the three-dimensional characteristics of existing and proposed buildings and areas. As the Building Form Standards evolve, the team tests the regulations on existing lots.

While codes may vary, the Building Form Standards template included here covers the regulations for each zone in five pages or less to keep it concise and easy to use. (See Figure 2.20.)

## Overview of the Zone

In the Building Form Standards, the section for each transect zone begins with a narrative overview of the zone's intentions. This overview includes a short text description as well as an illustration of the vision of the intended place. The text description includes a summary of the intended physical form and complexity of uses for the zone. The text and illustration describe the basis for the very detailed regulations that follow, making the code and its intentions more understandable for developers, builders, and other users of the code. In this instance, the graphic is illustrative, not regulatory, so it should include a disclaimer to that effect. (See Figure 2.20, far left.)

## Building Placement

Because FBCs are intended primarily to regulate the character and quality of public spaces, the location and size of the building facades that front the public spaces must be regulated to define and form the edges of that space to meet the desired vision. However, these regulations should also consider the relationship between buildings, in terms of privacy and the creation of such semi-private spaces as courtyards, the required sizes of rear yards or shared open spaces, the relationship between the main and ancillary buildings, and how and where parking is integrated. (See Figure 2.21.)

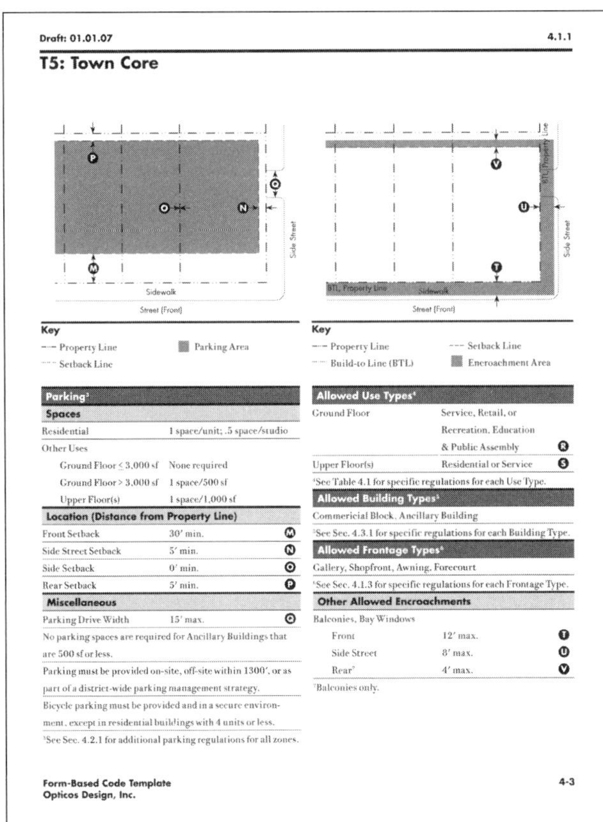

Draft: 01.01.07 4.1.1

**T5: Town Core**



**Key**

- Property Line
- Setback Line
- Parking Area

| Parking[3] | | |
|---|---|---|
| **Spaces** | | |
| Residential | 1 space/unit; .5 space/studio | |
| Other Uses | | |
| Ground Floor ≤ 3,000 sf | None required | |
| Ground Floor > 3,000 sf | 1 space/500 sf | |
| Upper Floor(s) | 1 space/1,000 sf | |
| **Location (Distance from Property Line)** | | |
| Front Setback | 30′ min. | M |
| Side Street Setback | 5′ min. | N |
| Side Setback | 0′ min. | O |
| Rear Setback | 5′ min. | P |
| **Miscellaneous** | | |
| Parking Drive Width | 15′ max. | Q |
| No parking spaces are required for Ancillary Buildings that are 500 sf or less. | | |
| Parking must be provided on-site, off-site within 1300′, or as part of a district-wide parking management strategy. | | |
| Bicycle parking must be provided and in a secure environment, except in residential buildings with 4 units or less. | | |

[3]See Sec. 4.2.1 for additional parking regulations for all zones.

**Key**

- Property Line
- Build-to Line (BTL)
- Setback Line
- Encroachment Area

| Allowed Use Types[4] | | |
|---|---|---|
| Ground Floor | Service, Retail, or Recreation, Education & Public Assembly | R |
| Upper Floor(s) | Residential or Service | S |

[4]See Table 4.1 for specific regulations for each Use Type.

| Allowed Building Types[5] |
|---|
| Commericial Block, Ancillary Building |

[5]See Sec. 4.3.1 for specific regulations for each Building Type.

| Allowed Frontage Types[6] |
|---|
| Gallery, Shopfront, Awning, Forecourt |

[6]See Sec. 4.1.3 for specific regulations for each Frontage Type.

| Other Allowed Encroachments | | |
|---|---|---|
| Balconies, Bay Windows | | |
| Front | 12′ max. | T |
| Side Street | 8′ max. | U |
| Rear[7] | 4′ max. | V |

[7]Balconies only.

Form-Based Code Template
Opticos Design, Inc.

4-3

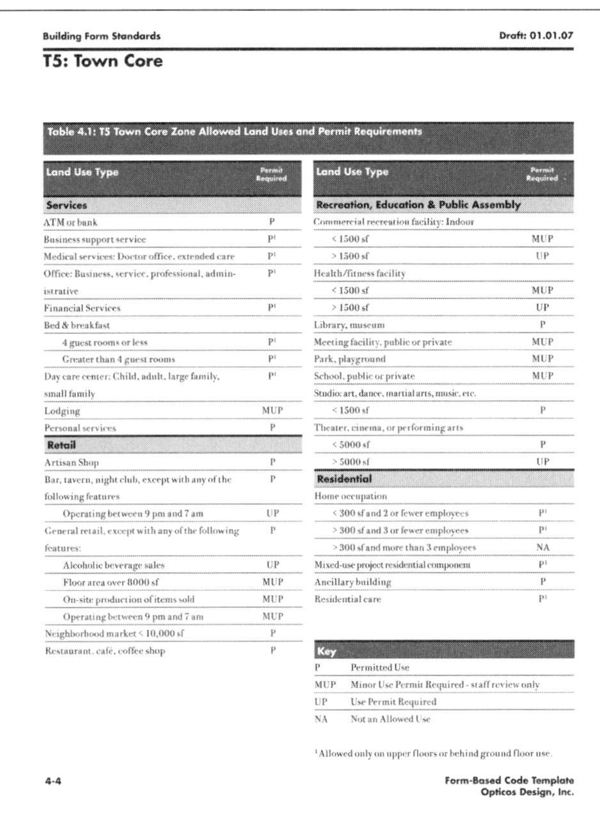

Building Form Standards Draft: 01.01.07

**T5: Town Core**

**Table 4.1: T5 Town Core Zone Allowed Land Uses and Permit Requirements**

| Land Use Type | Permit Required |
|---|---|
| **Services** | |
| ATM or bank | P |
| Business support service | P[1] |
| Medical services: Doctor office, extended care | P[1] |
| Office: Business, service, professional, administrative | P[1] |
| Financial Services | P[1] |
| Bed & breakfast | |
| 4 guest rooms or less | P[1] |
| Greater than 4 guest rooms | P[1] |
| Day care center: Child, adult, large family, small family | P[1] |
| Lodging | MUP |
| Personal services | P |
| **Retail** | |
| Artisan Shop | P |
| Bar, tavern, night club, except with any of the following features | P |
| Operating between 9 pm and 7 am | UP |
| General retail, except with any of the following features: | P |
| Alcoholic beverage sales | UP |
| Floor area over 8000 sf | MUP |
| On-site production of items sold | MUP |
| Operating between 9 pm and 7 am | MUP |
| Neighborhood market < 10,000 sf | P |
| Restaurant, café, coffee shop | P |

| Land Use Type | Permit Required |
|---|---|
| **Recreation, Education & Public Assembly** | |
| Commercial recreation facility: Indoor | |
| < 1500 sf | MUP |
| > 1500 sf | UP |
| Health/fitness facility | |
| < 1500 sf | MUP |
| > 1500 sf | UP |
| Library, museum | P |
| Meeting facility, public or private | MUP |
| Park, playground | MUP |
| School, public or private | MUP |
| Studio: art, dance, martial arts, music, etc. | |
| < 1500 sf | P |
| Theater, cinema, or performing arts | |
| < 5000 sf | P |
| > 5000 sf | UP |
| **Residential** | |
| Home occupation | |
| < 300 sf and 2 or fewer employees | P[1] |
| > 300 sf and 3 or fewer employees | P[1] |
| > 300 sf and more than 3 employees | NA |
| Mixed-use project residential component | P[1] |
| Ancillary building | P |
| Residential care | P[1] |

| Key | |
|---|---|
| P | Permitted Use |
| MUP | Minor Use Permit Required - staff review only |
| UP | Use Permit Required |
| NA | Not an Allowed Use |

[1]Allowed only on upper floors or behind ground floor use.

4-4

Form-Based Code Template
Opticos Design, Inc.

This element is typically one of the first regulated within the Building Form Standards as it provides the foundation for establishing the urban character a zone. In the most urban zones (usually T6–T4), pedestrians find comfort in the sense of enclosure provided by a continuous building wall at the edge of the sidewalk, which is typically defined using BTLs. In more rural zones where a continuous edge is not desired or necessary, setbacks are used instead.

An appropriate combination of the following regulating elements should be considered in order to produce the desired results in the built environment. The right combination and specific numbers regulated by each of these elements will be informed by the documentation of place and local calibration of the code content, as well as an architectural and urban design knowledge that will also allow the code team to understand and test the possible outcomes of these regulations. For example, the appropriate combination of building depth and distance between buildings can often create a more predictable outcome than conventional regulations for lot coverage.

## Build-to Line (BTL) 

A line parallel to the property line where the facade of the building is required to be located.

The regulated distance is from the property line or ROW to the BTL. The BTL is a regulation that was first used in Form-Based Coding practice. It prescribes a consistent plane of building facades along public frontages, including thoroughfares, parks, and sometimes alleys. This creates an edge to define a well-proportioned and comfortable, pedestrian-oriented streetscape, the location of which can be adjusted to the desired level of urbanism. It provides predictable results in the urban form by requiring a set location for the buildings as opposed to the range of possible locations that a minimum setback allows.

Page 3 includes Parking, Allowed Use Types, Allowed Frontage Types, and Allowed Encroachments, as well as Allowed Building Types if they are being regulated. Page 4 includes the Detailed Use Table. A fifth page can be added if there is any additional information that is necessary to include, such as miscellaneous notes or diagrams, or if any section needs overflow space.

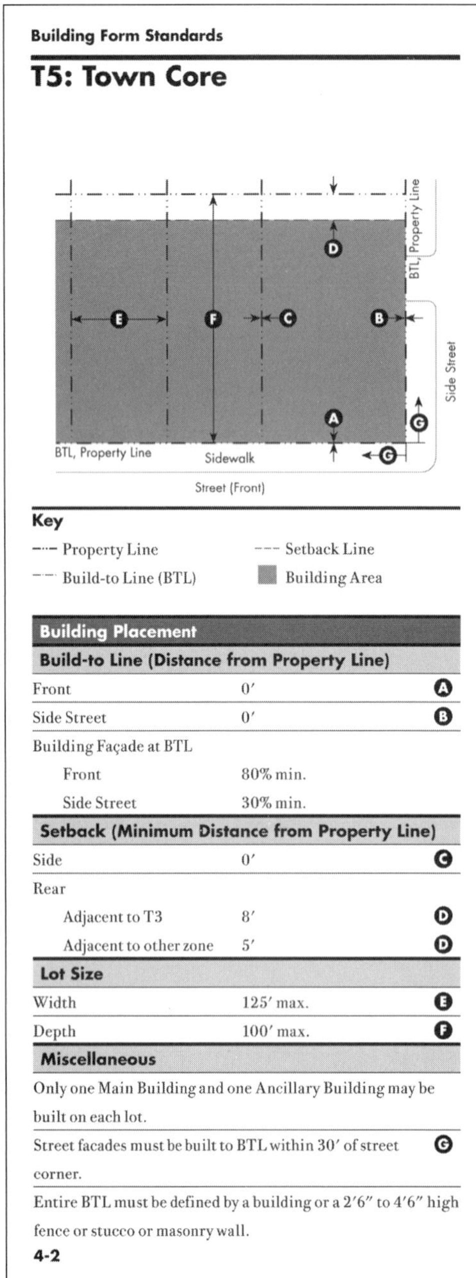

Building Form Standards

**T5: Town Core**



**Key**

–··– Property Line — — — Setback Line

– – Build-to Line (BTL) ■ Building Area

| Building Placement | | |
|---|---|---|
| **Build-to Line (Distance from Property Line)** | | |
| Front | 0′ | A |
| Side Street | 0′ | B |
| Building Façade at BTL | | |
| Front | 80% min. | |
| Side Street | 30% min. | |
| **Setback (Minimum Distance from Property Line)** | | |
| Side | 0′ | C |
| Rear | | |
| Adjacent to T3 | 8′ | D |
| Adjacent to other zone | 5′ | D |
| **Lot Size** | | |
| Width | 125′ max. | E |
| Depth | 100′ max. | F |
| **Miscellaneous** | | |
| Only one Main Building and one Ancillary Building may be built on each lot. | | |
| Street facades must be built to BTL within 30′ of street corner. | | G |
| Entire BTL must be defined by a building or a 2′6″ to 4′6″ high fence or stucco or masonry wall. | | |

4-2

**Fig. 2.21** Building placement regulations

*Typical Regulations*

- Front BTL
- Side Street BTL. This applies only to buildings on corner lots.
- Rear BTL, Ancillary Building. On blocks with alleys, use this to define the alleys with built forms.
- BTL Defined by a Building. This is typically regulated as a minimum percentage and used for more urban areas, such as T6–T5.
- Building Facade at BTL. This is typically regulated as a minimum percentage. In more residential and rural zones where a consistent, solid wall of buildings is less necessary, consider lowering this to give more flexibility while still providing enough consistency to ensure a high-quality built environment.

*Hints for Implementation*

- Use a BTL wherever a consistent building plane is desired or a defined edge is needed. This is most often in T6 and T5, and on buildings with commercial frontages in T4.
- Require a wall of fence wherever a BTL is not defined by a building in order to create a continuous built edge.
- For corner lots, consider a BTL for both the front and side street facades.
- Require a minimum distance from street corners that the BTL must be defined by a building in order to avoid corners that are not well defined. Locations of corner plazas and pocket parks should be designated in the visioning process so that the code can require that all other corners be defined by a building. G
- Do not allow landscaping between the building and the sidewalk in more urban zones (T6–T5).
- Adjust the BTL to upslope and downslope conditions if applicable to a community.

## Setback 

The distance by which a building must be separated from the property line or ROW, typically defined and regulated as a minimum.

Setbacks help regulate the placement of buildings; however, because conventional minimum setbacks define only a minimum required distance from the property line or ROW, they cannot guarantee an exact location of a building, only a range of possible locations. For this reason, they are not appropriate for the public frontages of buildings in more urban areas (T6–T4), but they may be used to regulate nonpublic spaces, such as side yards and rear yards. In more rural areas, minimum setbacks may be used for all building frontages.

*Typical Regulations*

- Front Setback
- Side Street Setback
- Side Setback, Main Building
- Side Setback, Ancillary Building
- Rear Setback, Main Building
  - Adjacent to Residential or less urban zone
  - Adjacent to Other Uses
- Rear Setback, Ancillary Building

*Hints for Implementation*

- Use both a minimum and a maximum setback wherever a relatively consistent plane of buildings is still desired, but a completely consistent plane is unnecessary.
- Consider ways setbacks may be used to transition between different intensities or uses. For example, when a higher-intensity, mixed-use zone backs onto a lower-intensity, mainly residential zone, the rear setback may need to be increased to minimize the impact and create an appropriate transition between the zones.
- When regulating small side setbacks (typically 4 feet or less), consider requiring privacy windows.

## Maximum Lot Width E

The largest allowed distance between lot corners along the front ROW.

This helps preserve the character of existing neighborhoods and downtowns, as well as create appropriately scaled development in new neighborhoods and mixed-use areas. Because a building cannot be wider than the lot, regulating the maximum lot width helps ensure that new buildings will be appropriately scaled to the desired urban form. It is in direct contrast to conventional zoning code regulations for *minimum* lot widths, which often inhibit the creation of good urbanism and new buildings in character with existing ones by preventing smaller-scaled buildings and allowing oversized ones.

*Hints for Implementation*

- Carefully calibrate this requirement to local conditions and the intended vision.
- Use this in previously developed areas where subdividable lots still exist, and preserving the existing character is the primary goal of the vision for the area.
- Use this in newly developing areas to help ensure that new buildings are in character and scale with historic areas or the desired vision.

## Minimum Lot Width

The smallest allowed distance between lot corners along the front ROW.

This helps preserve the character of more rural zones. It is most typically used in T2 zones. Paired with a maximum building width, it helps ensure the desired proportion of buildings to open space.

*Hints for Implementation*

- Try not to use this in T3 zones. If it must be used, be sure to calibrate the size based on the typical historical lot sizes within a community.
- Do not to use this in more urban zones because a side effect of its use in conventional zoning codes has been the prevention of good infill projects.

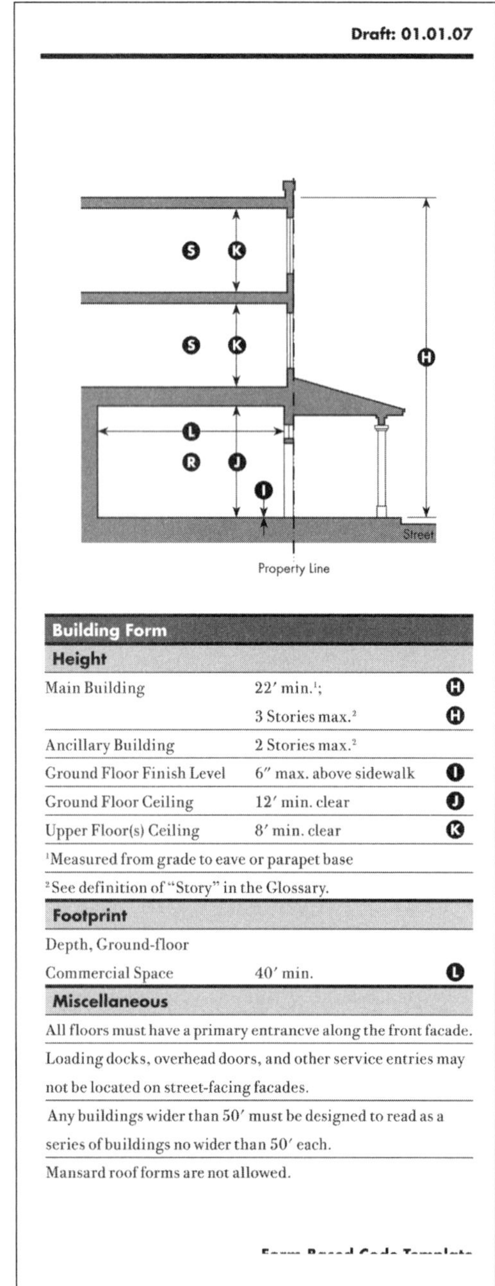


| Building Form | | |
|---|---|---|
| **Height** | | |
| Main Building | 22′ min.[1]; | H |
| | 3 Stories max.[2] | H |
| Ancillary Building | 2 Stories max.[2] | |
| Ground Floor Finish Level | 6″ max. above sidewalk | I |
| Ground Floor Ceiling | 12′ min. clear | J |
| Upper Floor(s) Ceiling | 8′ min. clear | K |
| [1]Measured from grade to eave or parapet base | | |
| [2]See definition of "Story" in the Glossary. | | |
| **Footprint** | | |
| Depth, Ground-floor Commercial Space | 40′ min. | L |
| **Miscellaneous** | | |
| All floors must have a primary entrancve along the front facade. | | |
| Loading docks, overhead doors, and other service entries may not be located on street-facing facades. | | |
| Any buildings wider than 50′ must be designed to read as a series of buildings no wider than 50′ each. | | |
| Mansard roof forms are not allowed. | | |

**Fig. 2.22** Building form regulations

## Building Form

Similarly to the Building Placement regulations, the Building Form regulations are intended to help prescribe good public spaces as well as good urban form. (See Figure 2.22.) As the "walls" of public spaces, building facades are regulated for height to ensure the correct proportion of the public spaces. The finished floor level is regulated to define the separation and transition between public, semi-public, and private spaces. The maximum size and placement of all buildings may be regulated in certain zones to help ensure that they are not intrusive on neighboring parcels. The size of all buildings, including the ancillary buildings, is regulated to ensure the buildings are an appropriate size for the intent of the area, as well as to create a hierarchy between various buildings, thereby helping to establish a rich urban form. While maximum sizes have often been regulated in conventional zoning codes, FBCs also regulate minimum sizes to prescribe an acceptable range of sizes that will help create the desired urban form.

### Minimum Building Height 

The shortest allowed vertical distance between the sidewalk and the top point of reference for a building facade along the front ROW.

This helps ensure that the building is tall enough to appropriately enclose and define a well-proportioned streetscape.

*Typical Regulations*

- Main Building Minimum Height
- Ancillary Building Minimum Height, Corner Lot: On blocks with alleys, use this to define the edge of the alley and screen views into the alley; however, make sure that this does not require the ancillary building to be larger than the primary building on the lot.

*Hints for Implementation*

- Regulate by stories rather than by feet. (See the sidebar "Regulating Height by Stories.")

### Maximum Building Height 

The largest allowed vertical distance between the sidewalk and the top point of reference for a building.

This helps ensure that new buildings will be appropriately scaled to the desired urban form.

In most FBCs, maximum building heights are regulated by stories rather than by dimensions. This enables and encourages builders and developers to use taller floor-to-ceiling heights, which leads to better buildings, and discourages them from using minimal floor heights to force as many floors into a building as possible. It also makes the form of the roof irrelevant to the regulated height of the building.

*Typical Regulations*

- Main Building Maximum Height
- Ancillary Building Maximum Height

*Hints for Implementation*

- For ancillary buildings, require privacy windows for upper-floor windows that face neighboring parcels.
- When a higher-intensity, mixed-use zone backs onto a lower-intensity, mainly residential zone, require that buildings not be more than a half-story taller than the allowed height of adjacent buildings within 30 feet of the property line to transition gradually between zones. (See the sidebar "Transitioning Between Mixed Use and Residential.")

## Ground-Floor Finished Level Height ❶

The vertical distance allowed between the sidewalk (or other common reference point) and the top of the finished floor on the ground level, regulated as a minimum or a maximum. (See Figure 2.23.)

This helps ensure an appropriate relationship between the public and private realm. Regulating a minimum height for residential uses on the ground floor is necessary to ensure a level of privacy for the residents. In addition, regulating a maximum height is necessary for retail and commercial uses to convey their semi-public status and ensure an easy transition from the sidewalk into these spaces.

*Hints for Implementation*

- Typical values are 18 inches minimum for residential units and 6 inches maximum for commercial and retail uses.
- Residential units that are closer to the sidewalk to should have higher ground-floor finished heights to provide privacy from people walking by on the sidewalk, although this must be balanced with the need to provide visitability and accessibility.

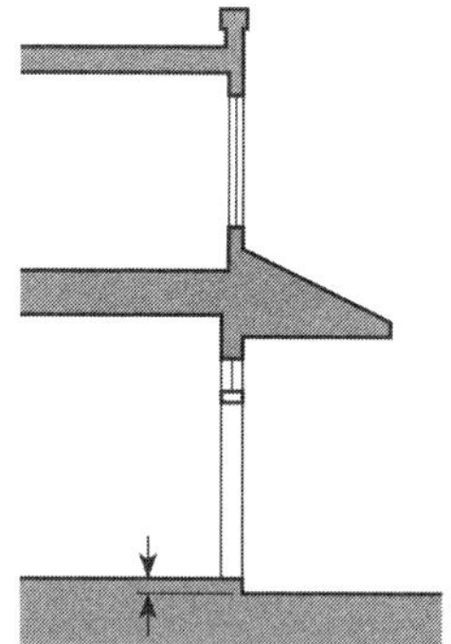

**Fig. 2.23** Ground-floor finished level height

### Regulating Height by Stories

Even after regulating maximum height by stories, many communities still ask to include a maximum height in feet or meters. This is typically unnecessary since building extremely tall stories is not cost-effective for builders and developers. It also creates an additional regulation, and one of the benefits of FBCs is their simplified content.

However, if this must be included, the height limit should be at least as tall as the maximum allowed stories with a reasonable floor-to-ceiling height. In addition, the height should be regulated to the eave or cornice line or to the base of a parapet wall in order to enable a better variety of roof forms as may be appropriate to the architectural character in the area. If height limits are regulated to the roof ridge, designers are forced to create buildings with flat roofs or with minimally sloped roofs to keep under the height limit. These roofs are often out of character with others in the area. If limits are instead created to the eave, cornice, or parapet base, designers have the flexibility to build tall sloping roof forms if they are more appropriate to the context. Examples of local vernacular styles that have been typically limited by ridge-based height limits are the Tudor style and various mountain styles that need a sloped roof to shed snow in the winter months. In general, it is best to push for story-based height limits.

### Minimum Ground-Floor Ceiling Height J

The smallest allowed vertical distance between the finished floor and ceiling on the ground floor of a building.

Typically used in more urban areas, this helps ensure that the spaces are tall enough to be viable for retail uses. In addition, this is a critical regulation for communities trying to ensure that new development is built in character with their historic architecture.

## Transitioning Between Mixed Use and Residential

The images to the right demonstrate three appropriate ways to regulate the transition from mixed-use forms along a corridor to residential forms in an adjacent neighborhood. The appropriate option for each condition will be dependent on the degree of change desired along the corridor and within the adjacent neighborhood.

The first option (top) preserves the adjacent residential intensity. The mixed use buildings step down at the rear of the lot, and the width of the buildings along the rear is minimized in order for them to be compatible and in scale with the adjacent residential buildings.

The second option (middle) assumes the evolution of the adjacent street to a larger residential scale that is more compatible with the mixed use along the corridor. The half of the block that backs onto the mixed-use lots and the facing half of the block along the adjacent street are up-zoned to allow medium density building types, such as townhouses or courtyard apartments. Projects along the mixed-use corridor are not allowed to aggregate the lot(s) behind and extend one building to the adjacent street.

The third option (bottom) maximizes the intensity of use along the mixed-use corridor, potentially to provide a transit corridor. The mixed-use buildings are allowed to extend to the adjacent street as long as they provide residential uses wrapping the parking and step down in size along the adjacent street. The facing half of the block along the adjacent street is up-zoned to allow medium density building types, such as townhouses or courtyard apartments to be compatible with this scale.

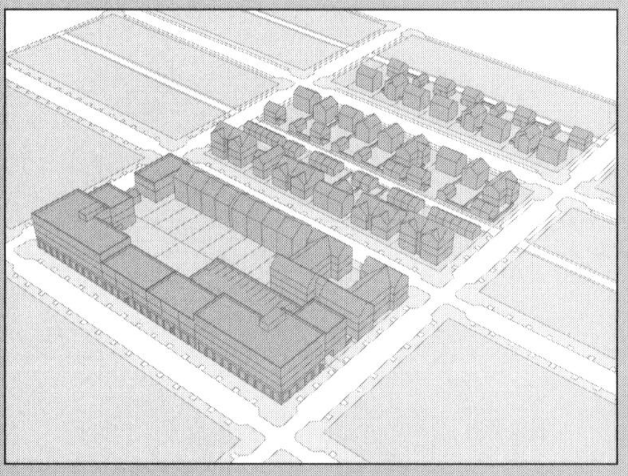

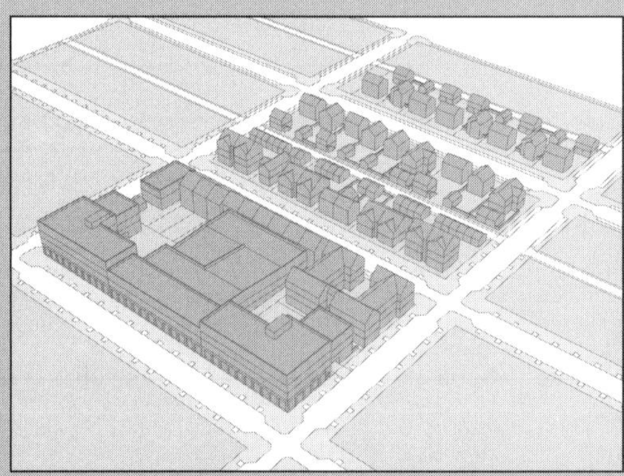

Note that retail or commercial uses are not allowed to spread to the adjacent street in any of these scenarios, as that would typically compromise the viability of retail and commercial uses along the corridor as well as the residential character of the adjacent neighborhood.

*Hints for Implementation*

- Generally, for shopfront spaces, require 12 feet minimum, although 15 feet is ideal. For residential spaces, require a 10-foot minimum.

## Minimum Upper-Floor(s) Ceiling Height K

The smallest allowed vertical distance between the finished floor and ceiling on all of the floors of a building above the ground floor.

Typically used in historic neighborhoods, this helps ensure that new buildings relate appropriately to existing buildings. It also helps allow more natural light into otherwise smaller spaces in more urban areas. These heights are most critical in communities trying to ensure that new development is built in character with their historic architecture. Otherwise, it is often seen as too restrictive to regulate.

## Maximum Building Width

The largest allowed distance between a building's two sides measured along the front right-of-way (ROW).

This helps ensure that new buildings will be appropriately scaled to the desired urban form. It is a critical regulation when maintaining the scale of an existing place is a priority. In historic neighborhoods, it helps minimize out-of-scale infill buildings, while in other infill areas it helps ensure that development on large lots is scaled to the intended vision. (See the sidebar "Maximum Building Width.")

*Hints for Implementation*

- Determine this dimension for each zone during documentation by measuring the widest existing building footprint on the base maps and verifying it in the field.
- When it is likely that new buildings will need to be wider than this dimension, consider regulating that wider buildings be designed to read as multiple separate buildings, each with this maximum width; however, consider this only in T6–T5 zones.

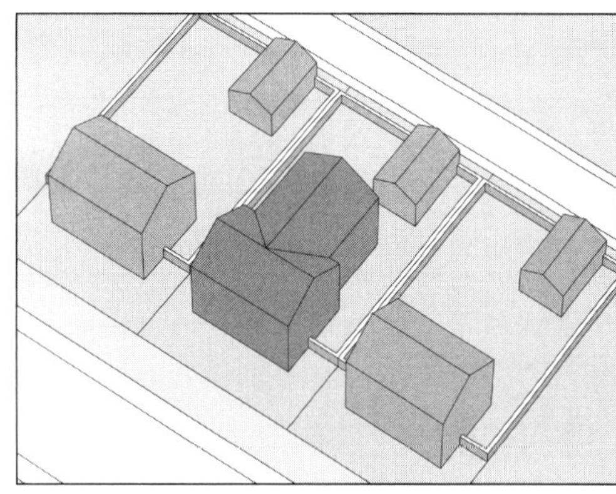

**Fig. 2.24** Regulating maximum building depth should be considered in existing neighborhoods to minimize oversized additions or new construction (as illustrated) that are incompatible with existing homes and cause privacy issues in rear yards.

## Maximum Building Depth

The largest allowed distance between a building's front facade and rear elevation.

Used in combination with maximum ancillary building sizes and minimum distance between buildings, this replaces lot coverage percentage and FAR regulations from conventional zoning codes to better regulate that new buildings are appropriately scaled to the desired urban form. It is also an important component for minimizing overscaled infill buildings in historic neighborhoods in T4 and T3, although it is less important in more urban zones, such as T6 and T5. (See Figure 2.24.)

*Hints for Implementation*

- Determine this dimension for each zone during documentation by measuring the deepest existing building footprint on the base maps and verifying it in the field.
- In existing neighborhoods, use this in combination with minimum distance between buildings and maximum depth of an ancillary building to regulate appropriate rear yard size.

## Maximum Ancillary Building Size

The largest allowed size of a secondary building, regulated as a maximum depth along with a maximum footprint square footage.

This helps ensure that ancillary buildings are hierarchically secondary to the primary buildings, which helps establish a rich urban form, and that they are not intrusive on neighboring parcels.

*Hints for Implementation*

- Ensure that ancillary buildings may not be larger than the main building, unless the area has been specifically chosen in the vision plan to evolve to a more urban form.
- Use this with a rear BTL and maximum building depth for the main building to help regulate the minimum open space on a lot.
- Use this with a minimum distance between buildings to help ensure an appropriate relationship between the main building and ancillary building.

## Maximum Building Width

These diagrams represent a hypothetical situation in which a historic neighborhood had been previously zoned for 20 units per acre without any maximum building width regulations.

The first image (top) shows the existing condition with primarily small to medium lot single-family building types on the block with ancillary units and a vacant lot that is 60 feet wide and 150 feet deep.

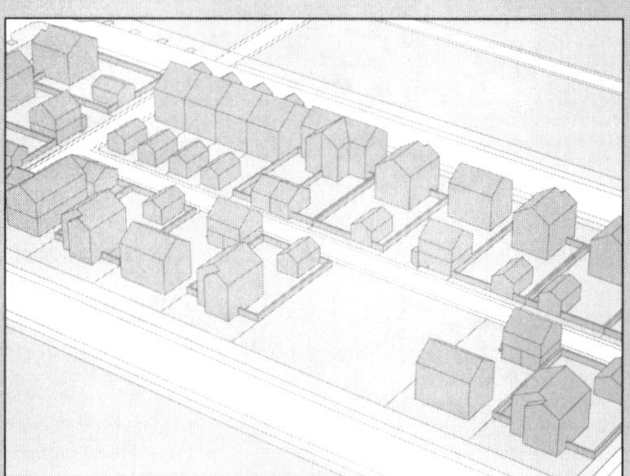

The second image (middle) shows an infill apartment building that meets the density requirements but is completely out of scale and character with the adjacent buildings. Allowing infill at this inappropriate scale will ultimately devalue the neighborhood.

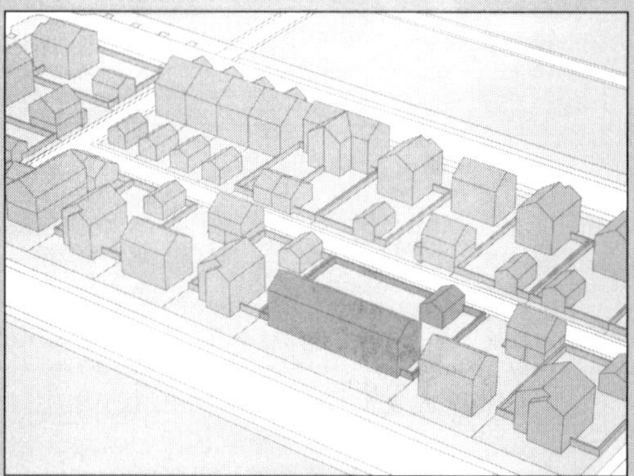

The third image (bottom) shows how by simply adding a maximum building width regulation of 25 feet along with maximum building depth, you can get appropriate infill that achieves the 20 units per acre (43,560 sf per acre ÷ 9,000 sf for the lot × 4 total units = 19.4 units/acre) through the use of single-family homes on smaller lots and ancillary or second units typical of the existing neighborhood character. Note: The same appropriate regulations of form could be achieved by regulating only single-family and ancillary unit building types in the zone as well.

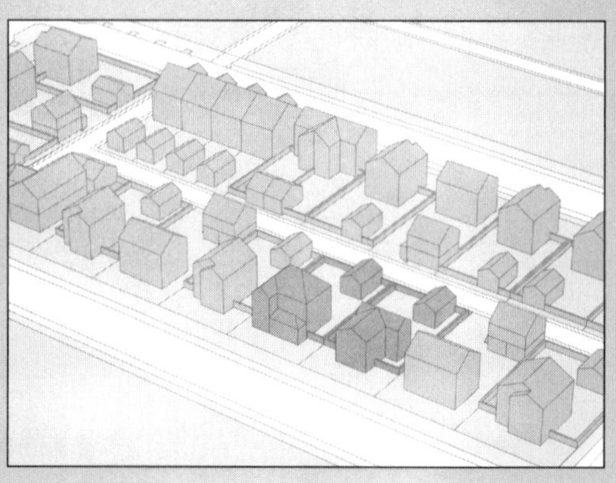

- Only allow ancillary units to be attached to the primary buildings if it is consistent with the documented local patterns.

## Notes

There are a variety of other regulations that may be included in the Building Form section dealing with such issues as the location of entrances. Following are a few to consider:

- In more urban zones, regulate that the entries to upper-floor units be provided on the front facade in order to add vibrancy to the street with the activity created by people using the entrances. Also consider requiring a minimum frequency for these entries.
- Prohibit the placement of back-of-building and service-related activities along front and side streets, except on lots that cannot accommodate these at the rear. On these lots, allow up to only 20 feet of these activities along the side street as close to the rear lot line as possible. Another way to deal with this is to create a hierarchy in the Regulating Plan with A streets and B streets. Service is then allowed only on B streets.[10]

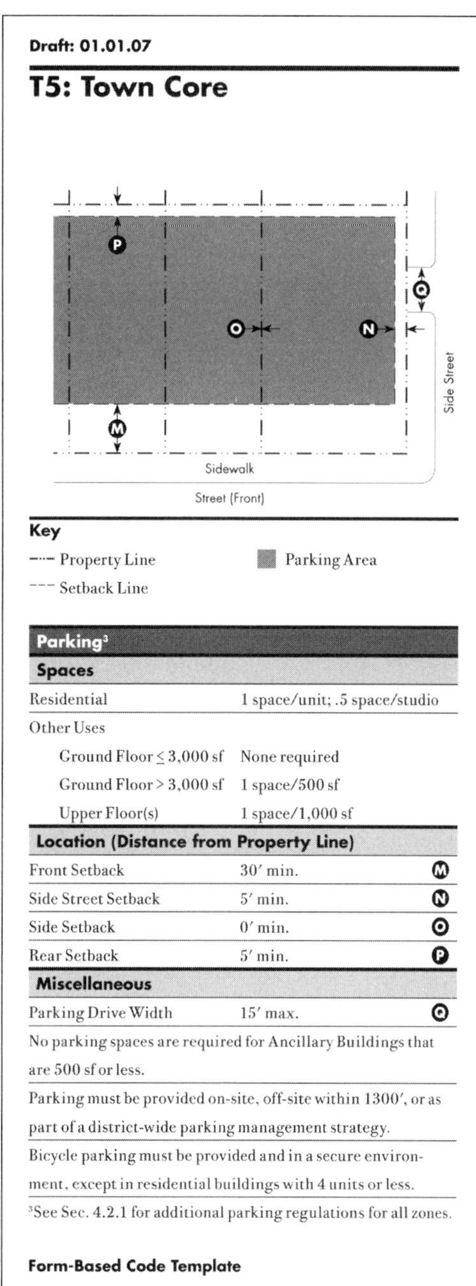

Draft: 01.01.07

**T5: Town Core**



**Key**

---- Property Line
--- Setback Line
Parking Area

| Parking[3] | | |
|---|---|---|
| **Spaces** | | |
| Residential | 1 space/unit; .5 space/studio | |
| Other Uses | | |
| Ground Floor ≤ 3,000 sf | None required | |
| Ground Floor > 3,000 sf | 1 space/500 sf | |
| Upper Floor(s) | 1 space/1,000 sf | |
| **Location (Distance from Property Line)** | | |
| Front Setback | 30′ min. | M |
| Side Street Setback | 5′ min. | N |
| Side Setback | 0′ min. | O |
| Rear Setback | 5′ min. | P |
| **Miscellaneous** | | |
| Parking Drive Width | 15′ max. | Q |
| No parking spaces are required for Ancillary Buildings that are 500 sf or less. | | |
| Parking must be provided on-site, off-site within 1300′, or as part of a district-wide parking management strategy. | | |
| Bicycle parking must be provided and in a secure environment, except in residential buildings with 4 units or less. | | |

[3]See Sec. 4.2.1 for additional parking regulations for all zones.

Form-Based Code Template

**Fig. 2.25** Parking regulations

## Parking

Parking is often one of the most contentious issues when writing an FBC and a reality that needs to be addressed appropriately. If parking is not regulated appropriately, it is often one of the most prohibitive elements to creating walkable communities. Parking lots and garages are unattractive and create gaps in the built fabric, and drives into both can be hazardous to pedestrians. Also, excessive parking takes up space that could be better used for other needed uses. Because of the destructive nature that parking has on the built environment, Andrés Duany has referred to parking as the new "noxious use."

The impacts of parking on the quality of a place can be mitigated with appropriate requirements and good design. Unlike parking requirements in conventional zoning codes that regulate suburban parking space requirements in most locations, parking requirements in a Form-Based Code should be calibrated to the transect, with fewer to no required spaces in more urban places where more alternate transportation options exist and where a percentage of the people using the commercial and retail uses will be walk-

## Parking

by Jeffrey Tumlin
*Principal, Nelson\Nygaard Consulting Associates*

Since the 1950s, minimum parking requirements have been established in planning codes in order to force private developers to supply more parking than the market would support. This market intervention is done with the following policy objectives in mind:

- By oversupplying parking for each individual land use on site, the spillover of parking demand from one land use to another is prevented.
- Different land uses need not share parking with each other.
- Existing on-street parking and other public parking need not be managed to ensure adequate availability.
- Excess supply means the market cost of parking is reduced to zero, ensuring that parking is free for end users.
- For infill sites, oversupplying parking eliminates a potential objection existing neighbors may have against new development.

Unfortunately, requirements to oversupply parking have resulted in some unintended negative consequences. These have been documented in a variety of publications, especially Donald Shoup's *The High Cost of Free Parking* (APA Planners Press, 2005). Among these consequences:

- **Housing affordability:** Each parking space associated with a residential unit typically increases the cost of that unit by up to 20 percent and decreases the number of units that can be built on a typical lot by up to 20%.[11] Each vehicle that a household can eliminate can qualify it for an additional $60,000 in mortgage.[12]
- **Walkability:** Where parking supply exceeds 3 spaces per 1,000 square feet, more area is set aside for parking than for occupiable floor space. Parking requirements are the greatest single determinant for achievable density. When density is reduced, opportunities are reduced for providing services within walking distance, and transit's potential for success is reduced.
- **Traffic congestion:** When the costs of parking are hidden in the cost of rent or goods and services, the result is a strong incentive to drive. Even in suburban locations, automobile trip generation rates can be reduced by 15 to 40 percent by eliminating parking subsidies.
- **Air and water pollution:** When parking subsidies are eliminated, the air quality, water quality, and $CO_2$ impacts of driving are also reduced.
- **Suburban bias:** While parking demand varies more by location than land-use type, parking requirements are typically set regardless of context. Parking demand data collected by the Institute of Transportation Engineers and the American Planning Association are generally from isolated, single-use locations without transit service or pedestrian accommodation. Too often, these worst-case scenario numbers are erroneously applied as minimums in mixed-use, pedestrian-friendly contexts.

To correct these problems, planners and developers have implemented a variety of tools to ensure adequate parking availability while minimizing parking's negative impacts. These tools may be more or less appropriate depending upon a project's transect zone:

- **Eliminate minimum requirements:** In most areas, government does not need to force developers to build more parking than the market would support. Minimum parking requirements are illegal as a matter of national law in the United Kingdom and have been eliminated in cities and towns of all sizes in the United States.
- **Establish maximums:** Some cities establish parking maximums as part of their overall traffic management, pollution reduction, or housing affordability strategies.

- **Require shared parking:** Arlington, Virginia's Columbia Pike FBC, for example, establishes minimum requirements for shared parking and maximum allowances for reserved parking.
- **In lieu fees:** Where minimum parking requirements are provided, permitting projects to pay a fee in lieu of building required parking can be especially helpful on awkward lots and can raise money for local improvements.
- **Unbundled parking:** Municipalities should encourage developers to unbundle the cost of parking from the cost of housing, particularly in rental and multifamily housing.
- **Market pricing:** Downtown Redwood City, California, for example, has set performance requirements for parking, adjusting public parking prices to ensure adequate availability on every block at all times of day.
- **Parking benefit districts:** Downtown Pasadena, California, for example, funnels all net parking revenue into the district in which the revenue is raised, ensuring merchant support for the parking meter program.
- **Residential parking permit programs:** Particularly where T3 neighborhoods abut denser zones, many cities allow residents to create restrictive parking districts where only residents with a special permit can park on-street. Austin, Texas, allows these districts to sell their surplus parking capacity to commuters and invest net revenue in neighborhood improvements.
- **Mechanical, tandem, and valet parking:** Rather than requiring all spaces to be independently accessible, some cities encourage more efficient parking arrangements.
- **Parking taxes:** San Francisco and Seattle have a parking sales tax used to fund local transportation improvements. Vancouver, British Columbia, has a flat, regional per-space parking tax.

**Parking along the Transect**

(See the table on the next page.)

**Calculating Parking Demand**

The Institute of Transportation Engineers' *Parking Generation* manual is the most thorough summary of parking demand data available in the United States, but it should be used with caution. Most of the data in the document is from isolated, single-use locations with no transit service or pedestrian accommodation. It is appropriate for T3 and T2 locations, but it is not useful for more urban or mixed-use areas. To estimate actual parking demand, a variety of other tools may be useful:

- The Urban Land Institute's *Shared Parking* manual is helpful for estimating peak parking accumulation and shared parking potential in mixed-use areas in suburban locations. It should be calibrated in more urban areas to reflect urban mode splits.
- By mapping household auto ownership by census block group from the U.S. Census data, planners can see how residential parking demand varies by location and adjust accordingly.
- Nothing is more useful, however, than collecting actual local parking data, or data from a comparable location. In walkable commercial areas in T5 and T4, for example, peak cumulative parking demand rarely exceeds 2.0 spaces per 1,000 square feet, even where parking is free and transit limited, simply because many motorists park once and visit a few destinations.

**Parking along the Transect** By Jeffrey Tumlin *Principal, Nelson\Nygaard Consulting Associates*

| | Commercial Supply | Residential Supply | Public Parking | Design | Management |
|---|---|---|---|---|---|
| T6 | No minimum requirement. Set maximum allowance as part of traffic management strategy. Require all parking be shared. Actual demand is typically around 1 space per 1,000 sq. ft. | No minimum requirement. Set maximum if desired to encourage housing affordability. Require cost of parking to be unbundled from cost of housing. Actual demand varies by household type; typically around 1 space per unit. Parking need not be independently accessible. | Most parking considered "public." | Encourage or require underground. Require above-ground parking to be wrapped in active uses. Restrict curb cuts on retail streets or primary pedestrian streets. | Use price to ensure adequate parking availability at all times. |
| T5 | Minimum, if any, should be aggregated for all nonresidential uses and no greater than 2 spaces per 1,000. No minimum for uses under 5,000 square feet. Shared parking should be required or encouraged. In lieu fees allowed. Consider maximum for reserved (nonshared) parking. | Minimum, if any, should be no greater than 1 space per unit. Encourage cost of parking be unbundled from cost of housing. Parking need not be independently accessible. | Same as T6. | Same as T6, but may allow exposed parking garages above ground floor facing alleys or side streets. | Same as T6. |

| | Commercial Supply | Residential Supply | Public Parking | Design | Management |
|---|---|---|---|---|---|
| **T4** | Same as T5. | Same as T5. | All on-street parking in commercial areas public. On-street parking in residential areas shared by residents and guests. | Apply T5 rules in commercial district. Greater flexibility appropriate in residential areas. | Apply T5 rules in commercial district. To achieve political support for infill projects, may be necessary to establish Residential Parking Permit Districts or Parking Benefit Districts in residential areas. |
| **T3** | Minimum parking requirements may be appropriate for ancillary commercial uses, but no greater than 4 spaces per 1,000. | Minimum parking requirements may be appropriate to achieve political support, but not necessary. On-street tandem and driveway spaces should count toward meeting minimum. | All guest parking on street. | Generally, parking at rear of lot, accessed from alley or side driveway. | Generally, no management necessary, but Residential Permit Districts or Parking Benefit Districts may be established where T3 abuts denser areas. |
| **T2** | None. | Generally not necessary. | Generally not necessary. | No requirements. | None necessary. |
| **District** | Parking demand will vary widely depending upon type of district, location, and Transportation Demand Management (TDM) programs. Require applicant to develop comprehensive TDM, and set minimum and maximum accordingly. | Similar to T3, but plan as part of overall district TDM strategy. | Varies. | Varies. | Varies. |

ing. Shared or other parking strategies may also be implemented. (See the sidebar "Parking along the Transect.")

In addition, the design should mitigate the parking's visual impact by hiding parking from view, especially from the front street. For example, in more urban areas, placing lots and garages in the center of blocks, lining them with retail and commercial spaces along the streets, and locating their entrances along side streets creates close parking locations for visitors without detracting from the pedestrian experience. In less urban places, locating the parking garages behind the houses will have a similar effect.

The impact of parking on a community must not be underestimated. It needs to be addressed in order to ensure a vibrant, walkable, mixed-use community. (See Figure 2.25.)

## Required Spaces

The mandatory number of off-street parking spaces, typically regulated by use type and size.

While including minimum parking requirements may be a political necessity in most communities, it should be seriously tempered by the impact it has on the creation of walkable neighborhoods. (See the sidebar "Parking.")

The number of required spaces should be calibrated to the transect and not simply tied to use. For example, a restaurant or café in a vibrant, mixed-use downtown should require fewer spaces and possibly no off-street spaces due to the presence of on-street parking and public parking lots.

*Hints for Implementation*

- Create parking management programs and other strategies in place of lot-by-lot requirements for mixed-use and more urban locations so that off-street parking requirements do not create obstacles for good infill development.
- Consider eliminating minimum parking requirements.
- In most cases, count on-street parking spaces in front of a building toward parking requirements.
- Require little to no parking for small uses (3,000–6,000 sf), especially in neighborhood centers to encourage small, locally owned and neighborhood-supporting businesses to move in and bring vitality to the area.
- Do not require covered spaces on residential units, as this will reduce development cost and encourage affordable housing.
- Do not require off-street parking spaces for ancillary units or granny flats as long as they are below a certain size, such as 500 square feet, in order to encourage their development. These buildings are important contributors to good communities.
- Do not require "visitor parking" in locations with on-street parking.
- Integrate maximum parking requirements to ensure that large, unattractive parking lots are not developed in new projects.
- Find ways to integrate transit alternatives in your community so that fewer people will rely on cars and need parking spaces.

## Location

The area on the lot in which parking is allowed.

This helps ensure that parking is built in appropriate locations for the desired urban form. Placing the parking out of site from the street reduces its negative visual impact. The best way to achieve this is to require underground parking, or more commonly, to use setbacks.

The sizes of parking spaces and travel lanes in lots are also regulated. (See Figure 2.26.) This table is typically located at the end of all of the various zone regulations in the Building Form Standards.

*Typical Regulations*

- Front Setback
- Side Street Setback
- Side Setback
- Rear Setback

*Hints for Implementation*

- Never allow parking in front of buildings.
- Require a minimum depth of habitable space in front of parking, typically 40 feet for commercial and retail uses and 15 feet for residential uses in more urban areas to ensure the space is deep enough to function well.
- Require any parking areas not behind or within buildings to have a 3-foot 6-inch tall hedge, wall, or fence at the front and side street ROWs.
- Regulate a maximum width of 60 feet of parking along a side street to prevent long, dead street edges.
- Allow parking that is completely underground to be built out to the lot lines.
- Encourage shared parking areas and drives.
- Consider requiring bicycle-parking locations and regulating locations in more urban areas, except for residences designed for four families or less.
- Require parking drives to be located on side streets for corner lots, and regulate their maximum width to minimize gaps in the urban fabric.

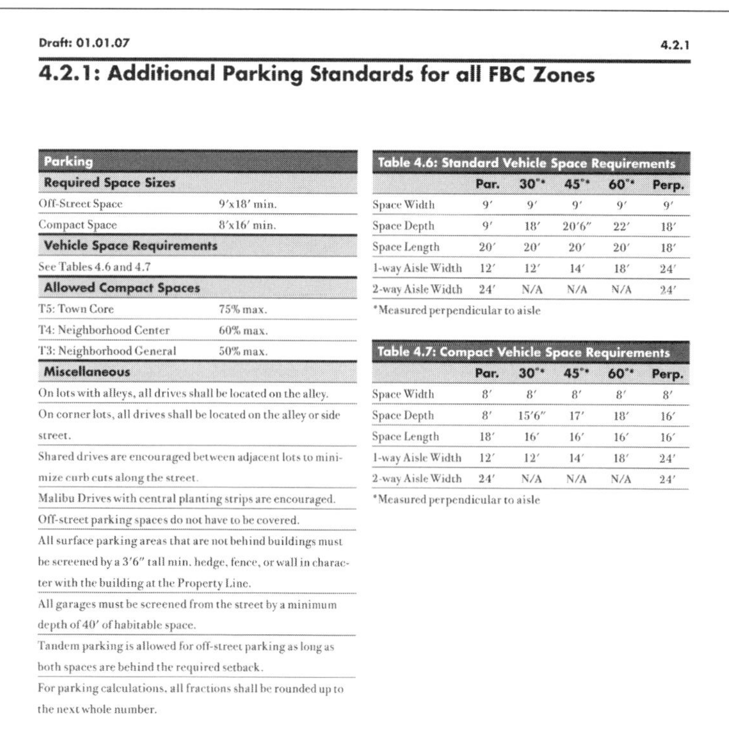

Draft: 01.01.07 4.2.1

4.2.1: Additional Parking Standards for all FBC Zones

| Parking | |
|---|---|
| **Required Space Sizes** | |
| Off-Street Space | 9′x18′ min. |
| Compact Space | 8′x16′ min. |
| **Vehicle Space Requirements** | |
| See Tables 4.6 and 4.7 | |
| **Allowed Compact Spaces** | |
| T5: Town Core | 75% max. |
| T4: Neighborhood Center | 60% max. |
| T3: Neighborhood General | 50% max. |
| **Miscellaneous** | |
| On lots with alleys, all drives shall be located on the alley. | |
| On corner lots, all drives shall be located on the alley or side street. | |
| Shared drives are encouraged between adjacent lots to minimize curb cuts along the street. | |
| Malibu Drives with central planting strips are encouraged. | |
| Off-street parking spaces do not have to be covered. | |
| All surface parking areas that are not behind buildings must be screened by a 3′6″ tall min. hedge, fence, or wall in character with the building at the Property Line. | |
| All garages must be screened from the street by a minimum depth of 40′ of habitable space. | |
| Tandem parking is allowed for off-street parking as long as both spaces are behind the required setback. | |
| For parking calculations, all fractions shall be rounded up to the next whole number. | |

Table 4.6: Standard Vehicle Space Requirements

| | Par. | 30°* | 45°* | 60°* | Perp. |
|---|---|---|---|---|---|
| Space Width | 9′ | 9′ | 9′ | 9′ | 9′ |
| Space Depth | 9′ | 18′ | 20′6″ | 22′ | 18′ |
| Space Length | 20′ | 20′ | 20′ | 20′ | 18′ |
| 1-way Aisle Width | 12′ | 12′ | 14′ | 18′ | 24′ |
| 2-way Aisle Width | 24′ | N/A | N/A | N/A | 24′ |

*Measured perpendicular to aisle

Table 4.7: Compact Vehicle Space Requirements

| | Par. | 30°* | 45°* | 60°* | Perp. |
|---|---|---|---|---|---|
| Space Width | 8′ | 8′ | 8′ | 8′ | 8′ |
| Space Depth | 8′ | 15′6″ | 17′ | 18′ | 16′ |
| Space Length | 18′ | 16′ | 16′ | 16′ | 16′ |
| 1-way Aisle Width | 12′ | 12′ | 14′ | 18′ | 24′ |
| 2-way Aisle Width | 24′ | N/A | N/A | N/A | 24′ |

*Measured perpendicular to aisle

**Fig. 2.26** Parking size regulations

## Allowed Land Uses

While not organized around land uses, FBCs still regulate them, but in a different manner and to a different degree than conventional zoning codes. The initial concept is basically the same as in conventional zoning codes, which is that land use can be regulated in three ways:

1. Through the number and types of land uses listed in all of the zones and districts provided by the code, given that if a specific use is not listed in the code and cannot reasonably be interpreted by staff to be equivalent to a listed use, it is not allowed;
2. By limiting certain land-use types to certain zones (for example by allowing heavy industrial uses only within industrial districts); and,
3. By identifying the land uses allowed within each zone or district as "permitted" or "conditional," or in the case of the SmartCode, as "open," "limited," or "restricted," and "by right" or "by warrant."

Communities choose to control the location and type of land uses in their codes for several reasons. They may have limited confidence that the local economy and real estate market will independently operate to timely locate specific, desired land uses where they will be most responsive to the needs of residents and businesses. They may be concerned about the potential for land uses with inherently incompat-

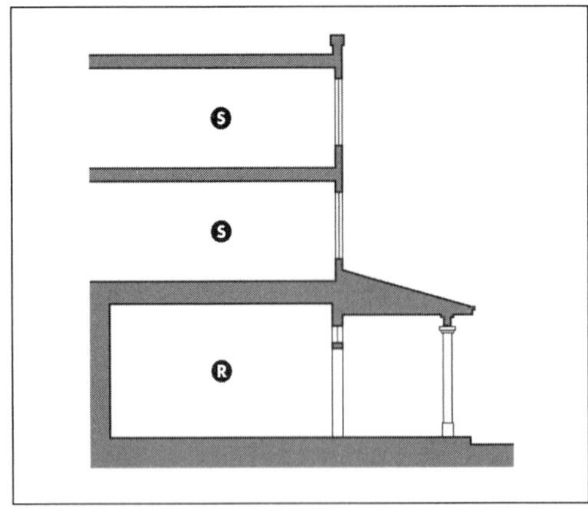


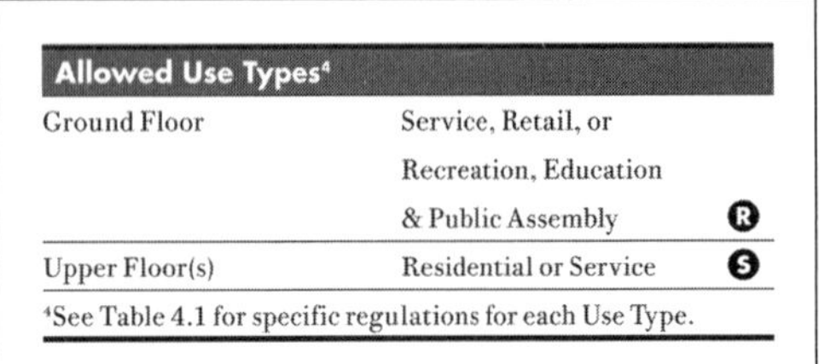

| Allowed Use Types[4] | | |
|---|---|---|
| Ground Floor | Service, Retail, or Recreation, Education & Public Assembly | R |
| Upper Floor(s) | Residential or Service | S |

[4]See Table 4.1 for specific regulations for each Use Type.

**Fig. 2.27** (top) Building section with allowed use types keyed in

**Fig. 2.28** (bottom) List of allowed use types

ible or hazardous operating characteristics to locate near more sensitive uses in the absence of land-use controls (and in the absence of common sense and/or good project design on the part of their developers). Or they may wish to pursue particular economic development goals through the distribution or clustering of certain uses in various parts of the community.

In addition to its other components, Form-Based Codes regulate the land uses allowed in each zone. Allowed uses are listed to identify and classify the activities that the community desires in each zone, and by exclusion, those that the community does not want. Individual land uses are normally identified as "permitted" if they reflect the primary purposes of the zone and if the community is confident that their most problematic effects will be avoided through compliance with the other standards in the code. Permitted uses are typically approved administratively if they clearly comply with all applicable code requirements.

Other uses that may be appropriate in a zone are typically listed as "conditional" (although the exact term used may vary depending upon specific community preferences and applicable state law requirements). Conditional uses may be compatible with, and supportive of, the permitted uses and the overall intent of the zone, but they are not "permitted" outright because the severity and/or unpredictability of their possible side effects (such as traffic, scale, hours of operation, and noise) may vary according to the design of the particular project, the location and characteristics of the site, and the nature of surrounding development.

Conditional uses are, in part, identified as such because their wide variations in potential site-specific impacts do not lend themselves to effective mitigation by the other standards in the code. A conditional use cannot be assumed to be workable on any given site without some discretionary review to verify compatibility and to enable the city to hold the project accountable for its potential adverse impacts through conditions of project approval. This review is typically part of a conditional-use permit process or other similar discretionary review process.

Choosing the type of approval required for particular land uses during the drafting of a Form-Based Code raises important policy issues that are discussed in more detail later in this book. (See "Project Review and Approval" under *Code Administration* later in this chapter.)

Unfortunately, many conventional zoning codes identify an excessive number of conditional uses because community politics and polarization over development issues have led residents to distrust staff and the existing zoning code, which has, in turn, led them to want to have a public hearing prior to most development decisions. However, it is often the case that these development controversies have little to do with actual land uses. Instead, they are the result of past failures of the ineffective physical form requirements of their zoning code and their inability to ensure that new development is consistent with the community's vision for its future or compatible with the physical design context of the site area. In some of these cases, the listings of allowed land uses are overly exhaustive (some might say obsessive), and too many uses are listed as conditional because the communities are trying to use the discretionary review required for conditional uses as a surrogate for building form standards that could otherwise reliably produce a predictable physical design outcome.

Because some of the worst consequences of conventional zoning, such as sprawl, result from how it segregates different land-use types, the obvious question is, what do Form-Based Codes do differently to avoid those consequences?

First, FBCs often provide more flexibility in the number and type of land uses allowed in mixed-use zones by listing them in a more generic form, called a use type (e.g., "General Retail" rather than "Bookstores," "Clothing Stores," "Shoe Stores," and so on). Second, and where appropriate and useful, FBCs differentiate the allowable locations and permit requirements for various land uses according to potentially bothersome operational characteristics. For example, General Retail could have subtypes that would be subject to discretionary review or prohibited in a given transect zone, while the vast majority of uses included in General Retail would be simply "permitted." (In this case, examples of subtypes might be the sale of alcohol, operation outside of normal business hours, or the sale of sexually-oriented merchandise.) Then, for administrative clarity, FBCs often illustrate the appropriate location of various use types within mixed-use buildings. (See Figures 2.27 and 2.28.) Finally, the list of allowed uses is often organized into tables with uses grouped under intuitive headings that allow a code user

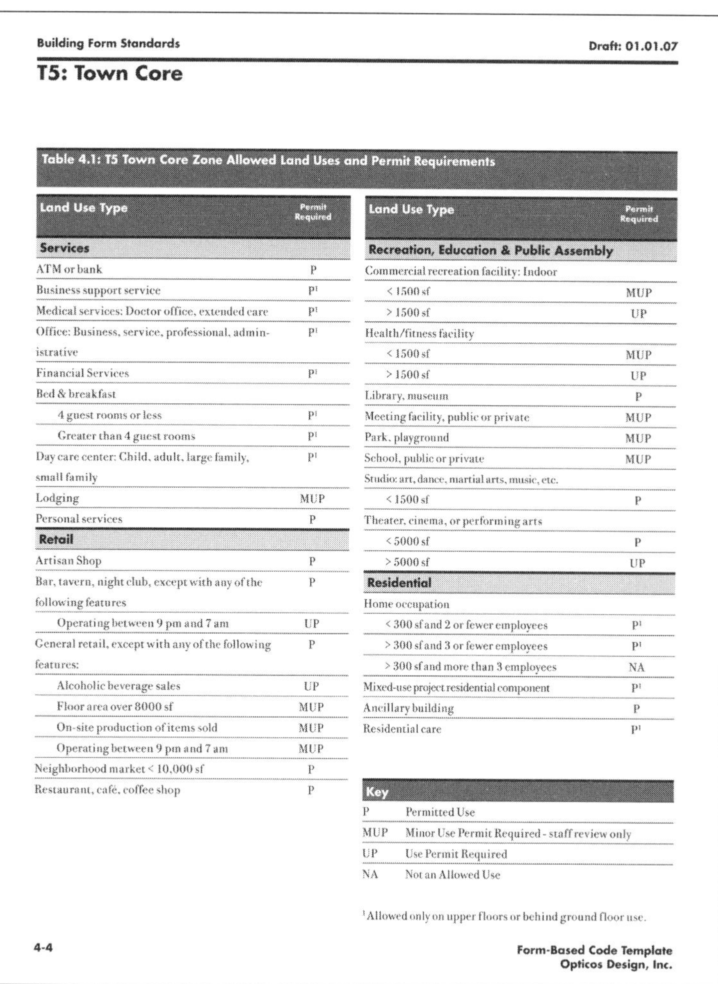
Building Form Standards — Draft: 01.01.07

**T5: Town Core**

**Table 4.1: T5 Town Core Zone Allowed Land Uses and Permit Requirements**

| Land Use Type | Permit Required |
|---|---|
| **Services** | |
| ATM or bank | P |
| Business support service | P[1] |
| Medical services: Doctor office, extended care | P[1] |
| Office: Business, service, professional, administrative | P[1] |
| Financial Services | P[1] |
| Bed & breakfast | |
| 4 guest rooms or less | P[1] |
| Greater than 4 guest rooms | P[1] |
| Day care center: Child, adult, large family, small family | P[1] |
| Lodging | MUP |
| Personal services | P |
| **Retail** | |
| Artisan Shop | P |
| Bar, tavern, night club, except with any of the following features | P |
| Operating between 9 pm and 7 am | UP |
| General retail, except with any of the following features: | P |
| Alcoholic beverage sales | UP |
| Floor area over 8000 sf | MUP |
| On-site production of items sold | MUP |
| Operating between 9 pm and 7 am | MUP |
| Neighborhood market < 10,000 sf | P |
| Restaurant, café, coffee shop | P |

| Land Use Type | Permit Required |
|---|---|
| **Recreation, Education & Public Assembly** | |
| Commercial recreation facility: Indoor | |
| < 1500 sf | MUP |
| > 1500 sf | UP |
| Health/fitness facility | |
| < 1500 sf | MUP |
| > 1500 sf | UP |
| Library, museum | P |
| Meeting facility, public or private | MUP |
| Park, playground | MUP |
| School, public or private | MUP |
| Studio: art, dance, martial arts, music, etc. | |
| < 1500 sf | P |
| Theater, cinema, or performing arts | |
| < 5000 sf | P |
| > 5000 sf | UP |
| **Residential** | |
| Home occupation | |
| < 300 sf and 2 or fewer employees | P[1] |
| > 300 sf and 3 or fewer employees | P[1] |
| > 300 sf and more than 3 employees | NA |
| Mixed-use project residential component | P[1] |
| Ancillary building | P |
| Residential care | P[1] |

| Key | |
|---|---|
| P | Permitted Use |
| MUP | Minor Use Permit Required - staff review only |
| UP | Use Permit Required |
| NA | Not an Allowed Use |

[1] Allowed only on upper floors or behind ground floor use.

4-4 — Form-Based Code Template, Opticos Design, Inc.

**Fig. 2.29** Detailed use table

to easily find uses of interest without having to read the entire table. (See Figure 2.29.) The typical use types that can be used as a basis for organizing land-use tables are listed at the right.

The distillation of a long list of land uses into a more succinct list organized under use types is one of the most challenging but critically important steps in writing an FBC. A planner who has the proven ability to distill these lists, taking into account the impact of use on the physical form desired, should be a key part of any FBC team.

*Hints for Implementation*

- In areas to be revitalized, do not restrict ground-floor uses to retail only. It is better to have a shopfront occupied by a service use than to have it sit vacant.

**Use Types**

- Assembly, Recreation, and Education
- Industry
- Residential
- Retail
- Services: Business, Financial, and Professional
- Services: General
- Transportation, Communications, and Infrastructure

- However, in successful small downtowns or other areas where there is high demand for sidewalk-fronting space, it may be necessary to restrict some service uses that can afford higher rents (such as real estate agents) to upper floors or side streets to enable access to the lower floors for local stores and restaurants.
- Allow residential, commercial, and retail uses in transitional areas adjacent to mixed-use neighborhood centers to let the market decide which use is more viable. Just be sure to regulate an appropriate form regardless of the use.
- Ensure that the detailed use table is concise, ideally not more than two pages per zone.
- Do not include prohibited uses in the table, unless it is absolutely necessary to emphasize that a certain use is not allowed.
- Avoid creating an exhaustive list of allowed uses. This will unnecessarily complicate the code, and may leave the code open to trouble if a use intended to be allowed is inadvertently not included.
- Consider using performance-based parameters, such as hours of operation, to regulate use, especially to allow uses that otherwise would need to be relegated to a special district.
- Most light industrial uses are now appropriate in mixed-use areas, while heavy industrial uses still are not. In the vision plan, clearly establish the appropriate location for heavy industrial uses in special districts; however, in the interest of creating successful, mixed-use communities, avoid unnecessarily relegating an excessive number of uses into these special districts.

## Allowed Frontage Types

The frontage is the way a building engages the public realm. The ultimate intent of regulating frontages is to ensure, after a building is located appropriately, that its interface with the public realm and the transition between the two are detailed appropriately.

In this section of the code, the allowed frontage types are listed. The detailed frontage standards are then located in a separate section of the code. For more information, see *Frontage Type Standards* later in this chapter.

## Allowed Encroachments

The allowed encroachments section regulates building elements that may extend over the BTL or into the setback, such as balconies and bay windows, typically on all sides of a building. Regulating these helps enable a rich urban form by allowing appropriate building elements to extend beyond the facade or elevation.

*Typical Regulations*

- Front Encroachment
- Side Street Encroachment
- Side Encroachment
- Rear Encroachment

## Allowed Building Types

A building type is a classification for buildings based on a combination of their form and use. Typical building types include single dwellings, duplexes, townhouses, stacked flats, commercial block buildings, parking structure liners, and others with equally intuitive names.

In this section of the code, the allowed building types are listed. The detailed building type standards are then located in a separate section of the code. For more information, see *Building Type Standards* later in this section.

# Frontage Type Standards



As stated earlier, the frontage is the way a building engages the public realm. The ultimate intent of regulating frontages is to ensure, after a building is located appropriately, that its interface with the public realm and the transition between the two are detailed appropriately. The standard eight frontage types that serve as a good starting point for most Form-Based Codes are listed in Figure 2.30. They are typically represented with a plan and section diagram and sometimes an axonometric diagram.

As with most of the regulations in the Building Form Standards, the frontage type regulations should be based on data collected during the documentation process. Typically, there are certain frontage types in a given area that should be allowed and encouraged by the code. In addition, the detailed regulations for these types should be based on measurements from good local precedents to ensure they are appropriate. For instance, setting the correct minimum depth for stoops and porches is extremely important in order to ensure that they are actually usable and that they improve the public/private interface by providing residents with a place to sit outside where they can also greet their neighbors. If a minimum for these frontages is not regulated, many unusable (too shallow) porches will be built just for stylistic or sales reasons.

In addition, care should be taken when regulating the location of the BTL or setback in combination with the depth of the encroachment to ensure the desired implementation. For example, if the BTL is 15 feet from the ROW, and a 10-foot encroachment is allowed for a front porch, the porch will be only 5 feet from the ROW or sidewalk. This may be appropriate for compact, urban neighborhoods that often have porches coming right up to the ROW, but may not be appropriate in less urban areas. The goal

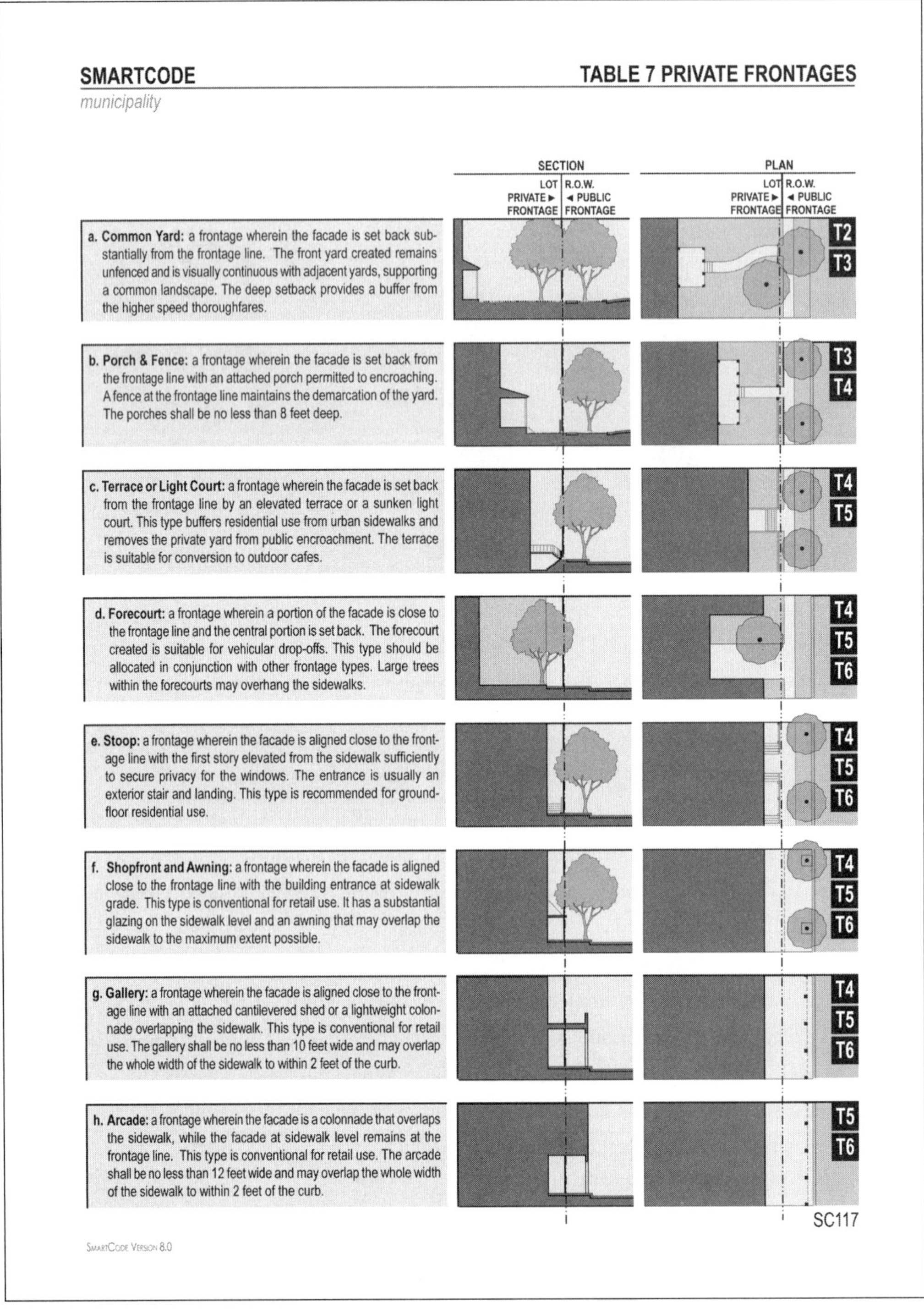

SMARTCODE — TABLE 7 PRIVATE FRONTAGES

*municipality*

| | Section / Plan (LOT: PRIVATE FRONTAGE ▸ │ ◂ R.O.W.: PUBLIC FRONTAGE) |
|---|---|
| **a. Common Yard:** a frontage wherein the facade is set back substantially from the frontage line. The front yard created remains unfenced and is visually continuous with adjacent yards, supporting a common landscape. The deep setback provides a buffer from the higher speed thoroughfares. | T2, T3 |
| **b. Porch & Fence:** a frontage wherein the facade is set back from the frontage line with an attached porch permitted to encroaching. A fence at the frontage line maintains the demarcation of the yard. The porches shall be no less than 8 feet deep. | T3, T4 |
| **c. Terrace or Light Court:** a frontage wherein the facade is set back from the frontage line by an elevated terrace or a sunken light court. This type buffers residential use from urban sidewalks and removes the private yard from public encroachment. The terrace is suitable for conversion to outdoor cafes. | T4, T5 |
| **d. Forecourt:** a frontage wherein a portion of the facade is close to the frontage line and the central portion is set back. The forecourt created is suitable for vehicular drop-offs. This type should be allocated in conjunction with other frontage types. Large trees within the forecourts may overhang the sidewalks. | T4, T5, T6 |
| **e. Stoop:** a frontage wherein the facade is aligned close to the frontage line with the first story elevated from the sidewalk sufficiently to secure privacy for the windows. The entrance is usually an exterior stair and landing. This type is recommended for ground-floor residential use. | T4, T5, T6 |
| **f. Shopfront and Awning:** a frontage wherein the facade is aligned close to the frontage line with the building entrance at sidewalk grade. This type is conventional for retail use. It has a substantial glazing on the sidewalk level and an awning that may overlap the sidewalk to the maximum extent possible. | T4, T5, T6 |
| **g. Gallery:** a frontage wherein the facade is aligned close to the frontage line with an attached cantilevered shed or a lightweight colonnade overlapping the sidewalk. This type is conventional for retail use. The gallery shall be no less than 10 feet wide and may overlap the whole width of the sidewalk to within 2 feet of the curb. | T4, T5, T6 |
| **h. Arcade:** a frontage wherein the facade is a colonnade that overlaps the sidewalk, while the facade at sidewalk level remains at the frontage line. This type is conventional for retail use. The arcade shall be no less than 12 feet wide and may overlap the whole width of the sidewalk to within 2 feet of the curb. | T5, T6 |

SmartCode Version 8.0 SC117

**Fig. 2.30** These are the eight frontage types in the SmartCode. The area within the ROW is called the "public frontage," and the area between the ROW and the front of the building is called the "private frontage." (Credit: DPZ)

is to ensure that the physical form will ultimately be consistent with the urban patterns the community wants to replicate or institute.

*Typical Regulations*

- Minimum Depth
- Height
- Width

*Hints for Implementation*

- Require an 8-foot-minimum clear depth for porches. (See Figure 2.31.) Stoops can be 6-foot-minimum clear depth, but a maximum overall percentage of stoops versus porches should be regulated so that the developers will not build only stoops because of their smaller size.

- When regulating buildings at or near the sidewalk edge, allow awnings to encroach 10 feet as long as there are no conflicts with the sidewalk depths, street trees, and lighting. For comfortable, pedestrian-oriented sidewalks, awnings are necessary to relate the larger buildings to the scale of the pedestrian and provide shade in hotter climates and protection in inclement weather for seated areas and the sidewalk. (See Figure 2.32.)
- When regulating galleries and arcades, require them to encroach into the public ROW over the sidewalk. Similarly to awnings, galleries provide shade from the sun and shelter from the rain and snow. This and any other encroachment into the public ROW will need to be approved by public works during the coding process.
- When allowing second-story galleries, prohibit the use of them as the primary means of circulation to prevent a motel-like effect.
- When regulating shopfronts, require a high percentage of glazing based on local documentation.
- Carefully regulate the depth, width, and proportions of forecourts based on local climate and typical urban conditions.
- If using axonometric drawings to illustrate the frontages, be sure either to note them as illustrative or not to include any nonregulatory information that could be interpreted as regulatory, such as style. (See Figure 2.33.)

**Fig. 2.31** The "porch" in this photo is about 3 feet deep and, therefore, neither usable nor able to successfully engage the public realm of the streetscape.

**Fig. 2.32** (left) Awnings provide weather protection for pedestrians.

**Fig. 2.33** (below) Axonometric studies completed by Opticos Design for the Grass Valley Development Code update as part of both the documentation and education process

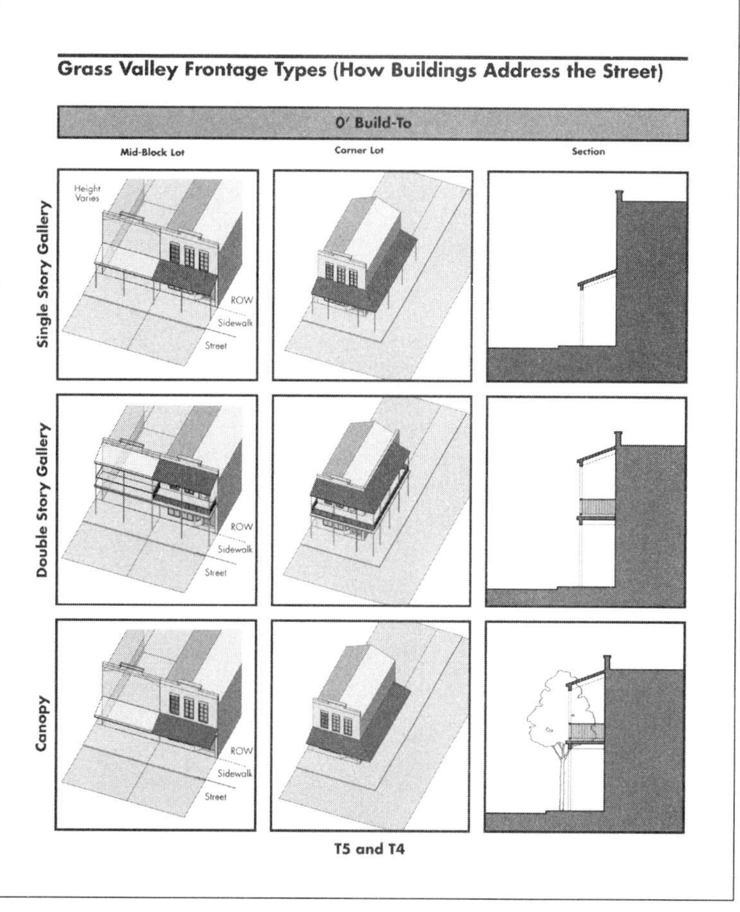

# Block Standards

An interconnected network of streets composed of small blocks is a vital component of walkable communities; therefore, regulations should be included within the FBC to ensure that this fine-grain quality of planning is implemented. These regulations typically apply to any project site that is two acres or larger.

The steps of this process should be clarified in the code as follows[13] (see Figure 2.34):

1. **Introduce Streets:** Streets taken from the Public Space Standards should be integrated into the site to break the site down into blocks that meet the established regulations for maximum block perimeter and length.
2. **Introduce Alleys:** Access to blocks should be primarily through alleys except on single-family lots wider than 50 feet, so an alley system should be integrated, using the regulated standards.
3. **Introduce Lots:** This may or may not be required or necessary, especially in T5 and T6, but in T4 and below this subdivision of blocks should establish lots that will integrate allowed building types and their standards.
4. **Introduce Building Types or Projects:** The mix of building types and program will be finalized, achieving the fine-grain urbanism that is intended by the code.

*Typical Regulations:*

- Maximum Block Length
- Maximum Block Perimeter

*Hints for Implementation:*

- Regulate maximum block length at 500 feet and maximum block perimeter at 1,600 feet unless constrained by local conditions.
- For larger sites, consider regulating a minimum mix of building types per project or per block.
- Streets and blocks do not have to be orthogonal, but require that streets be interconnected.

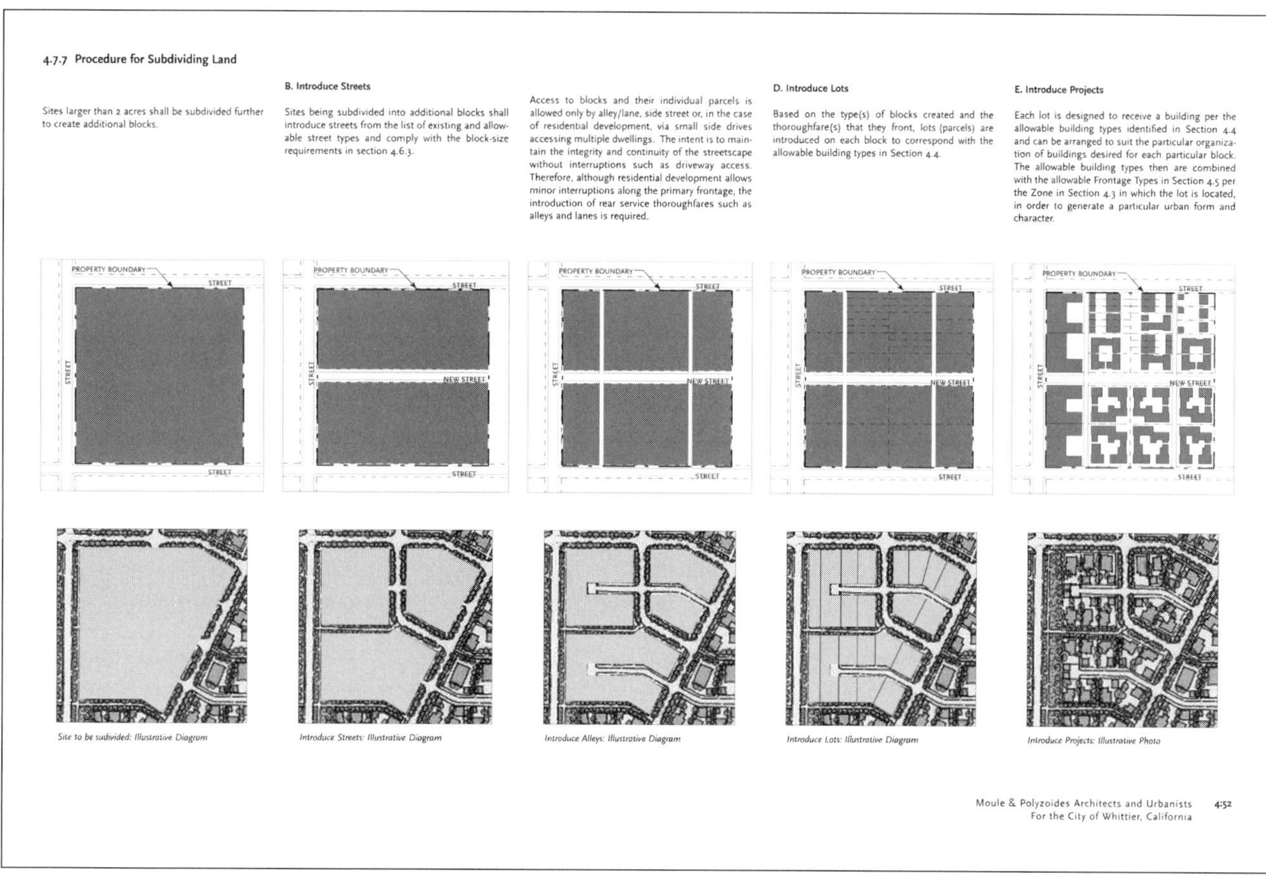

4.7.7 Procedure for Subdividing Land

Sites larger than 2 acres shall be subdivided further to create additional blocks.

B. Introduce Streets

Sites being subdivided into additional blocks shall introduce streets from the list of existing and allowable street types and comply with the block-size requirements in section 4.6.3.

Access to blocks and their individual parcels is allowed only by alley/lane, side street or, in the case of residential development, via small side drives accessing multiple dwellings. The intent is to maintain the integrity and continuity of the streetscape without interruptions such as driveway access. Therefore, although residential development allows minor interruptions along the primary frontage, the introduction of rear service thoroughfares such as alleys and lanes is required.

D. Introduce Lots

Based on the type(s) of blocks created and the thoroughfare(s) that they front, lots (parcels) are introduced on each block to correspond with the allowable building types in Section 4.4.

E. Introduce Projects

Each lot is designed to receive a building per the allowable building types identified in Section 4.4 and can be arranged to suit the particular organization of buildings desired for each particular block. The allowable building types then are combined with the allowable Frontage Types in Section 4.5 per the Zone in Section 4.3 in which the lot is located, in order to generate a particular urban form and character.



*Site to be subdivided: Illustrative Diagram* | *Introduce Streets: Illustrative Diagram* | *Introduce Alleys: Illustrative Diagram* | *Introduce Lots: Illustrative Diagram* | *Introduce Projects: Illustrative Photo*

Moule & Polyzoides Architects and Urbanists 4:52
For the City of Whittier, California

Fig. 2.34 Block and Subdivision Standards for lots two acres or larger from the Uptown Whittier Specific Plan by Moule & Polyzoides and Crawford, Multari & Clark Associates. These regulations are not necessary for areas that do not have any developable lots of this size.

- New streets must connect to existing streets, even if they are off-site.
- Street stubs must be provided when adjacent sites are vacant.
- Cul-de-sacs are not allowed, unless physical conditions provide no practical alternative.
- All buildings must face a street.
- Alleys should be required in T6, T5, and T4 zones, and in T3 zones for lots less than 50 feet in width.

# Building Type Standards

In the earliest modern Form-Based Codes, building types played a major role, so much so that the codes were often called "typological codes." These codes were typically used for project-scale regulation and were often administered privately by the developer, often through the use of a Town Architect. Examples of such codes are the Seaside, Florida, Code and the Windsor Code (Vero Beach, Florida), both created by Duany Plater-Zyberk & Company (DPZ). As the interest in FBCs grew, practitioners began exploring the various applications of FBCs at a citywide and regional scale for both greenfield and infill projects to remove regulatory obstacles for the implementation of New Urbanism and Smart Growth projects. As the scale and complexity of FBC projects grew, building types were often left out because of the already complex task of writing an FBC, as well as the challenge of finding a way to plug it into the existing regulatory system at this larger scale. However, while these codes met the minimum requirements for regulating good building form, they lacked a means for regulating a diverse stock of buildings, a critical component of vibrant urban places. As the practice of Form-Based Coding has advanced, many FBC practitioners have realized the importance of including and regulating building types and have created good systems for doing so.

The definition of building type for this urban design application is different from the typical architectural definition of building type, which is defined solely by use or function. Instead, for FBCs, the definition of building type is driven primarily by the physical form of a building and secondarily by its use or function. This prioritization of form over use mimics that of Form-Based Coding in general. (See Figure 2.35.) Two good examples of building types often included in FBCs are courtyard housing and side yard houses. Both are defined primarily by the specific placement and configuration of the building or group of buildings to create certain physical spaces between and within the buildings.

The integration of building type regulations is an important evolution within the practice of FBCs because it establishes building types as the basis for entitlements and regulation as opposed to the conventional regulations of Floor-Area Ratio (FAR) and density. Regulating by density and FAR encourages a developer to max out the buildable envelope allowed for the lot and simply to apply an architectural skin to this volume to make it fit into the area. In contrast, using building types as a primary means of regulation can instead prescribe a fine-grain mix of building types that is necessary to create a great urban form and high-quality place.

Because of their ability to help ensure diversity in building form, building types are the "building blocks" of good urbanism. Without a sensitive application and integration of building types into the regulatory framework, the quality of the built environment will suffer. Consider a high-quality historic neighborhood or town. Inevitably, it will include a fine-grained integration of a variety of building types, often within the same block, that creates the fabric of the community that is so cherished. The character and quality of this urban fabric cannot be established without the use of building types.

Many regionally adapted building types are no longer built for various reasons that include: (1) modern zoning regulations that do not allow the types and/or the fine-grain mix of types that is inherent in a highly valued historic neighborhood; (2) builders who are very set in their ways based on years of suburban development and do not believe they can mix different house sizes and types without changing their efficient system or impacting their returns; and (3) financial, insurance, and building code standards that have been established to support single-use development, and so create a dramatic increase in the complexity of financing and building alternative building types, such as the increased

**Fig. 2.35** Photos illustrating a typical palette of building types used in Form-Based Coding

**Fig. 2.36** Because of development patterns and regulations, today's choices for buyers are primarily limited to two building types: (1) isolated single-family houses (top), and (2) garden apartments that involve higher density living without the benefit of urban amenities (bottom).

insurance costs for attached units and condos. Therefore, the typical composition of development in the past 60 years has consisted primarily of two building types: (1) the single-family house, and (2) the garden apartment. With only these choices available, a person would choose to live in a garden apartment only if he or she cannot afford to buy a single-family house. This is because in most communities in the United States garden apartments are built without any surrounding urban fabric, which means there is no added value for living in smaller, attached spaces. They are, in other words, density without amenity. On the flip side, people who want to buy a new house often do not have any choice but to buy a large-lot single-family house. (See Figure 2.36.)

Compare this with historical neighborhoods that consisted of apartments over retail, small apartment buildings, townhouses, various-sized lots for single-family houses, and in-law units behind houses or above garages. In this context, the trade-off for living in a denser environment or smaller space (in an apartment or townhouse, for instance), was the proximity to stores, theaters, restaurants, and, likely, more transportation alternatives. Therefore, a person could consciously make a decision to live in a smaller place or an apartment in order to be closer to this activity. In addition, a community with a variety of building types enabled residents to stay in the neighborhood throughout their entire life, possibly living in an apartment over a local store as a young adult, moving into a townhouse with a young family, transitioning into a single-family house with older kids, and moving back into a townhouse as retirees when they no longer wanted to care for a house and yard. This helped create strong neighborhood bonds, as well as provide for a diverse age range within a community. Sadly, one of the primary reasons such a mix of building types stopped being used in development was that zoning codes outlawed them as they began to require a separation between uses and different densities of residential uses; therefore, one of the primary goals of FBCs is to reinstitute and regulate this diverse mix of building types that is vital to good urbanism.

## Integrating Building Types into the Code

There are several ways that building types have been integrated into Form-Based Codes.

*Building Types as the Organizing Principle*

In small areas, typically two or three neighborhoods at most, building types may be used as the organizing principle for the Building Form Standards and Regulating Plan. In this scenario, the regulations listed earlier for the Building Form Standards and those listed later in this section for building types are all grouped together and regulated by building type in the Building Form Standards. (See Figure 2.37.)

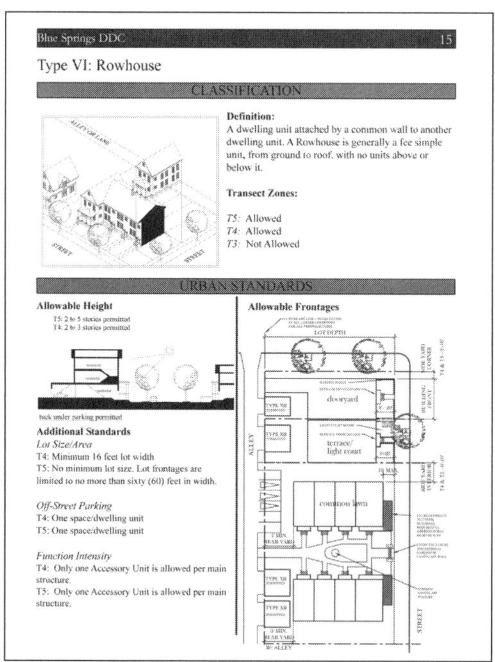

Blue Springs DDC 15

Type VI: Rowhouse

CLASSIFICATION

**Definition:**
A dwelling unit attached by a common wall to another dwelling unit. A Rowhouse is generally a fee simple unit, from ground to roof, with no units above or below it.

**Transect Zones:**

*T5:* Allowed
*T4:* Allowed
*T3:* Not Allowed

URBAN STANDARDS

**Allowable Height**

T5: 2 to 5 stories permitted
T4: 2 to 3 stories permitted

tuck under parking permitted

**Additional Standards**

*Lot Size/Area*
T4: Minimum 16 feet lot width
T5: No minimum lot size. Lot frontages are limited to no more than sixty (60) feet in width.

*Off-Street Parking*
T4: One space/dwelling unit
T5: One space/dwelling unit

*Function Intensity*
T4: Only one Accessory Unit is allowed per main structure.
T5: Only one Accessory Unit is allowed per main structure.

**Allowable Frontages**



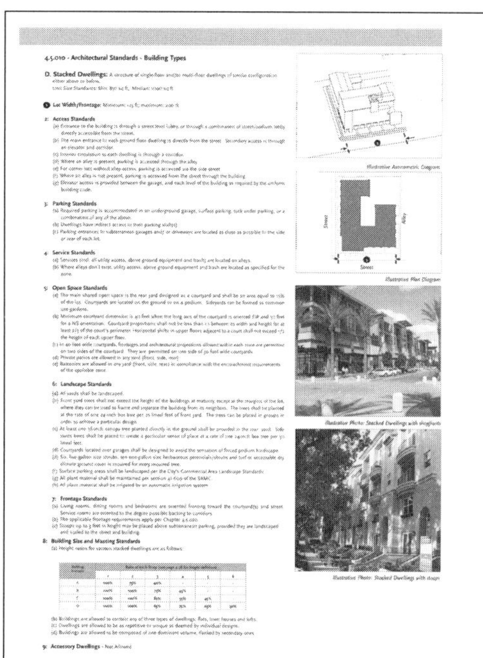

4.5.010 - Architectural Standards - Building Types

D. Stacked Dwellings:

Lot Width/Frontage:

2. Access Standards

3. Parking Standards

4. Service Standards

5. Open Space Standards

6. Landscape Standards

7. Frontage Standards

8. Building Size and Massing Standards

9. Accessory Dwellings

**Fig. 2.37** (far left) Building types are used as the organizing principle in the Downtown Development Code for Blue Springs, Missouri, by 180° Design Studio.

**Fig. 2.38** (near left) Building Type Standards from the Santa Ana Renaissance Specific Plan by Moule & Polyzoides and Crawford, Multari & Clark Associates

### *Building Types as a Land Use*

Because building types are determined by both form and use, they can be organized and assigned to regulating zones by their use in the detailed use tables. This approach then often refers to simple building type definitions in the glossary or elsewhere in the code, but could just as easily refer to detailed building type standards located later in the Building Form Standards. Two different examples of the former approach are the shown in the Miami 21 and Grass Valley case studies later in the book.

### *Building Type Standards*

The most evolved of the approaches and the most advanced for large-scale applications of Form-Based Coding is to list the allowed building types by regulating zone in the Building Form Standards, which then refer to the detailed building type standards located later in the section. This approach has the most flexibility for regulating a diverse urban form, but must be implemented carefully to consider the intersection between the general Building Form Standards and the building type standards for any given lot. (See Figure 2.38.)

## Building Type Standards

The following is a list of the most common building types used in FBCs. (See Figure 2.40.)

1. Detached single-unit house
   a. Detached garage
   b. Tuck-under garage
2. Detached, single-unit house, side yard
3. Carriage house
4. Bungalow court
5. Linear court
6. Townhouse
   a. Detached garage
   b. Tuck-under garage
7. Duplex/Triplex/Fourplex
8. Mansion apartment
9. Side yard housing
10. Courtyard apartment
11. Stacked units (low, medium, and high rise)
12. Live/work units
    a. Detached
    b. Attached
13. Commercial block (low, medium, and high rise)
14. Liner

This general list of types and the regulatory framework that goes with each of these types have been developed by Moule & Polyzoides and Paul Crawford and applied in a variety of Form-Based Codes they have created for both greenfield and infill projects, such as the Downtown Ventura Specific Plan, the Uptown Whittier Specific Plan, the Downtown Newhall Specific Plan, the Visalia Southeast Area Specific Plan, and the Placentia-Westgate Specific Plan. This list of types is primarily applicable to downtowns and neighborhoods in a typical American town. Additions and modifications to this list will likely be necessary for each individual project. When an FBC is applied to a more urban area, such as an existing or newly proposed T6 zone, it is necessary to add mid-rise buildings and possibly high-rise buildings to the palette of building types.

## The SmartCode and Building Types

The SmartCode takes a more general approach to building types than what is described in this chapter. Table 9 introduces five building types based solely on building disposition: (1) edge yard, (2) side yard, (3) rear yard, (4) courtyard, and (5) specialized, while allowing for the insertion of more specific building types onto Table 10 (Building Function) based on local calibration or market analysis for greenfield projects. (See Figure 2.39.)

Table 9 is meant to define most of the attributes of the types, with the rest of the attributes defined in the Definitions and Terms section. This approach stops short of regulating specific parameters for the building types, but it still enables a system such as the one advocated in this chapter to be plugged into the SmartCode as a module. This could be a very powerful application of building types within the SmartCode framework.

In the Miami 21 FBC by Duany Plater-Zyberk & Company, one of the most advanced and most recent applications of the SmartCode, the building types are inherent in the regulations, but they are never specifically called out or regulated. For example, in the T3-O zone, a duplex is regulated indirectly by allowing up to two attached units on a lot, whereas in the T3-L zone, two units are allowed only as a main house and a detached ancillary unit.

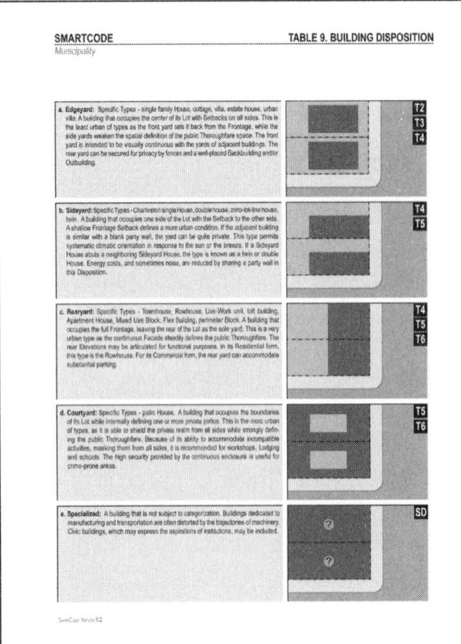

SMARTCODE — TABLE 9. BUILDING DISPOSITION

*Municipality*

a. **Edgeyard:** Specific Types - single family House, cottage, villa, estate house, urban villa. A building that occupies the center of its Lot with Setbacks on all sides. This is the least urban of types as the front yard sets it back from the Frontage, while the side yards weaken the spatial definition of the public Thoroughfare space. The front yard is intended to be visually continuous with the yards of adjacent buildings. The rear yard can be secured for privacy by fences and a well-placed Backbuilding and/or Outbuilding. (T2 T3 T4)

b. **Sideyard:** Specific Types - Charleston single House, double house, zero-lot-line house, twin. A building that occupies one side of the Lot with the Setback to the other side. A shallow Frontage Setback defines a more urban condition. If the adjacent building is similar with a blank party wall, the yard can be quite private. This type permits systematic climatic orientation in response to the sun or the breeze. If a Sideyard House abuts a neighboring Sideyard House, the type is known as a twin or double House. Energy costs, and sometimes noise, are reduced by sharing a party wall in this Disposition. (T4 T5)

c. **Rearyard:** Specific Types - Townhouse, Rowhouse, Live-Work unit, loft building, Apartment House, Mixed Use Block, Flex Building, perimeter Block. A building that occupies the full Frontage, leaving the rear of the Lot as the sole yard. This is a very urban type as the continuous Facade steadily defines the public Thoroughfare. The rear Elevations may be articulated for functional purposes. In its Residential form, this type is the Rowhouse. For its Commercial form, the rear yard can accommodate substantial parking. (T4 T5 T6)

d. **Courtyard:** Specific Types - patio House. A building that occupies the boundaries of its Lot while internally defining one or more private patios. This is the most urban of types, as it is able to shield the private realm from all sides while strongly defining the public Thoroughfare. Because of its ability to accommodate incompatible activities, masking them from all sides, it is recommended for workshops, Lodging and schools. The high security provided by the continuous enclosure is useful for crime-prone areas. (T5 T6)

e. **Specialized:** A building that is not subject to categorization. Buildings dedicated to manufacturing and transportation are often distorted by the trajectories of machinery. Civic buildings, which may express the aspirations of institutions, may be included. (SD)

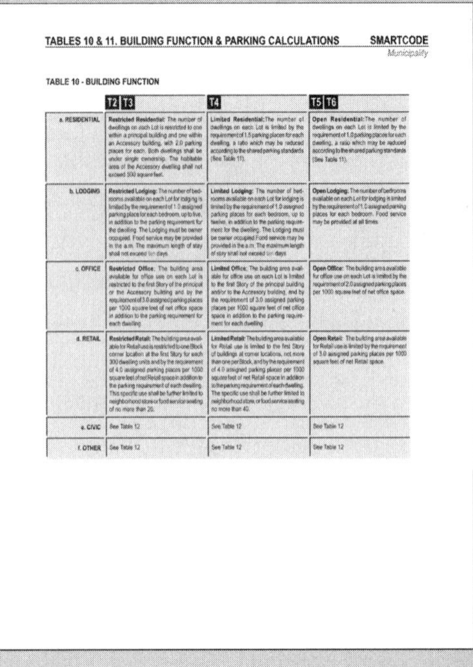

TABLES 10 & 11. BUILDING FUNCTION & PARKING CALCULATIONS — SMARTCODE

*Municipality*

TABLE 10 - BUILDING FUNCTION

| | T2 T3 | T4 | T5 T6 |
|---|---|---|---|
| a. RESIDENTIAL | **Restricted Residential:** The number of dwellings on each Lot is restricted to one within a principal building and one within an Accessory building, with 2.0 parking places for each. Both dwellings shall be under single ownership. The habitable area of the Accessory dwelling shall not exceed 500 square feet. | **Limited Residential:** The number of dwellings on each Lot is limited by the requirement of 1.5 parking places for each dwelling, a ratio which may be reduced according to the shared parking standards (See Table 11). | **Open Residential:** The number of dwellings on each Lot is limited by the requirement of 1.0 parking places for each dwelling, a ratio which may be reduced according to the shared parking standards (See Table 11). |
| b. LODGING | **Restricted Lodging:** The number of bedrooms available on each Lot for lodging is limited by the requirement of 1.0 assigned parking place for each bedroom, up to five, in addition to the parking requirement for the dwelling. The Lodging must be owner occupied. Food service may be provided in the a.m. The maximum length of stay shall not exceed ten days. | **Limited Lodging:** The number of bedrooms available on each Lot for lodging is limited by the requirement of 1.0 assigned parking places for each bedroom, up to twelve, in addition to the parking requirement for the dwelling. The Lodging must be owner occupied. Food service may be provided in the a.m. The maximum length of stay shall not exceed ten days. | **Open Lodging:** The number of bedrooms available on each Lot for lodging is limited by the requirement of 1.0 assigned parking places for each bedroom. Food service may be provided at all times. |
| c. OFFICE | **Restricted Office:** The building area available for office use on each Lot is restricted to the first Story of the principal or the Accessory building and by the requirement of 3.0 assigned parking places per 1000 square feet of net office space in addition to the parking requirement for each dwelling. | **Limited Office:** The building area available for office use on each Lot is limited to the first Story of the principal building and/or to the Accessory building, and by the requirement of 3.0 assigned parking places per 1000 square feet of net office space in addition to the parking requirement for each dwelling. | **Open Office:** The building area available for office use on each Lot is limited by the requirement of 2.0 assigned parking places per 1000 square feet of net office space. |
| d. RETAIL | **Restricted Retail:** The building area available for Retail use is restricted to one Block corner location at the first Story for each 300 dwelling units and by the requirement of 4.0 assigned parking places per 1000 square feet of net Retail space in addition to the parking requirement of each dwelling. This specific use shall be further limited to neighborhood store or food service seating of no more than 20. | **Limited Retail:** The building area available for Retail use is limited to the first Story of buildings at corner locations, not more than one per Block, and by the requirement of 4.0 assigned parking places per 1000 square feet of net Retail space in addition to the parking requirement of each dwelling. The specific use shall be further limited to neighborhood store, or food service seating no more than 40. | **Open Retail:** The building area available for Retail use is limited by the requirement of 3.0 assigned parking places per 1000 square feet of net Retail space. |
| e. CIVIC | See Table 12 | See Table 12 | See Table 12 |
| f. OTHER | See Table 12 | See Table 12 | See Table 12 |

**Fig. 2.39** SmartCode Table 9 (near right) and Table 10 (far right) (Credit: DPZ)

The typical elements for each building type include:

- General description
- Required lot size
- Pedestrian access
- Frontages
- Vehicle access and parking
- Service
- Open space
- Landscape
- Building size and massing

While it is necessary to include regulations in each section in order to effectively prescribe the appropriate building type, it is also possible to include guidelines in each section in addition to the standards as nonmandatory regulations. It can also be helpful to include an architect on the code team for this section to test the various regulations as they are being written.

## General Description

Each building type section begins with a brief explanation of the primary characteristics of the building type.

*Hints for Implementation*

- Make sure the descriptions are written in a consistent manner for all of the types.
- Ensure that local, unique aspects of type are highlighted.
- Include a three-dimensional descriptive image for each type.

## Required Lot Size

The first regulations for each building type are the minimum lot width and depth necessary for the building type. Careful consideration of lot sizes in the FBC regulations establishes the parameters for the maximum yield or density of the type while ensuring that only appropriate building types are built on a lot of an existing size and in an existing context.

*Hints for Implementation*

- Good design cannot mitigate the negative impacts of an overly sized building on a lot, so be sure to regulate minimum lot size.
- In areas with existing lots, use the typical lot sizes to help select which building types are appropriate for the area.
- For irregular sized and shaped lots, use the lot width to determine what building types are appropriate because the most important aspect to regulate is how the frontage is addressed.

## Pedestrian Access

Where and how pedestrians enter and exit the building affect the perceived level of activity at street level. Having frequent entrances into commercial, retail, and residential uses activates the street and makes it more welcoming. Also, for certain building types, the access to units is important for the function of the type. For example, on a courtyard apartment, it is desirable to have few, if any, units entered off of an interior double-loaded corridor, and to have three units or fewer entered from any stoop or stair off of a court in order to activate the main courtyard. This is in contrast to a typical stacked-flats building where a majority of units are entered off of a single corridor.

### Main Entrance Location

The primary point of access to a building.

This will have the largest percentage of activity and so should be carefully regulated. Considerations include orientation to the street, orientation to and entries from a courtyard, and access off of a corridor.

*Hints for Implementation*

- Require entries to upper-floor units from the primary street.
- Regulate the maximum distance between entries to upper-floor units on a mixed-use building.
- Regulate the typical distance between commercial or retail entries.
- Regulate the maximum distance between entries on a stacked-flats building type.

### Elevator Access

The location of vertical circulation.

In certain types, this affects the way one experiences entry to the units. In a courtyard building type, every unit should be entered from the courtyard level, so the elevator is needed only for access from the street to the courtyard level.

*Hints for Implementation*

- This regulation will be applicable only to the higher-intensity residential, mixed-use, and commercial building types.
- Ensure that the regulations are consistent with Americans with Disabilities Act (ADA) requirements and building codes.

### Interior Circulation

The path a person travels from the ground floor or parking area to the units.

This is important, especially for more urban building types, because the experience to and from a unit has a big impact on the quality of a building, and therefore should be considered more carefully than it has been in recent years.

*Hints for Implementation*

- Minimize entries off of double-loaded corridors when possible within medium- and high-density residential types to greatly increase the quality and improve the communal aspects of the building.
- Consider whether interior or exterior circulation and stairways to units are appropriate.
- Consider regulating the maximum number of units accessed by stairs off of shared public spaces to avoid a motel-like feel in the spaces.

## Frontages

The specific way that a building type addresses the street defines the transition between the public and private realms. Listing the allowable frontage types for each building type helps ensure that the public space is properly addressed and activated based on the form and use of the building.

### Rooms Facing Primary Public Spaces

The private spaces that are allowed to be located along the primary frontage of the building.

This helps ensure vibrant public spaces and streetscapes by placing the rooms that are most likely to be active along the public frontage. In addition, by placing the semi-private rooms along the public frontage and moving the private rooms to the back, it sets up an appropriate transition from public (street), to semi-private (living room), to private (bedroom) spaces.

This seems like a very basic concept, but the normal response within conventional suburban development has been to disregard this and place less active rooms along the public frontage. Therefore, in order to get the privacy needed for these rooms, the building facade had to be closed up, creating a wall between the public street and the private space, to the detriment of the public space in two ways: (1) the design of the facade suffered because it is impossible to resolve the awkwardness of the small windows, privacy windows, or a complete lack of windows; or (2) the pedestrian experience on the street side of the house was deadened due to the lack of activity from within the buildings.

*Hints for Implementation*

- Require active "living" rooms, such as the library, den, and living, dining, and family rooms, to face the street(s) and courtyards. On some of the more compact building types, this may not be completely feasible, but it is a good starting point for negotiations in the design review phase.
- Require first-floor sleeping rooms and service rooms, such as bathrooms, closets, and laundry rooms, to be located along side yards, service yards, rear yards, or corridors.
- Require the frontage to provide an appropriate transition from public to private spac-



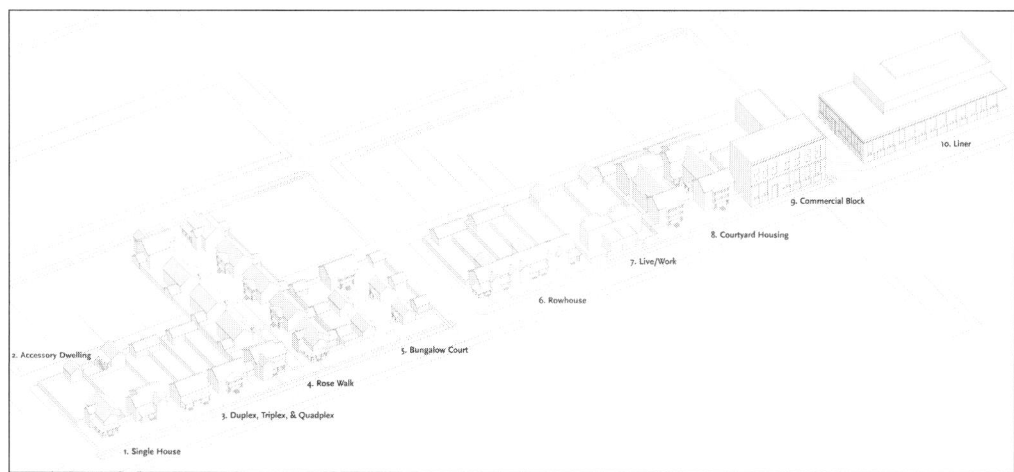


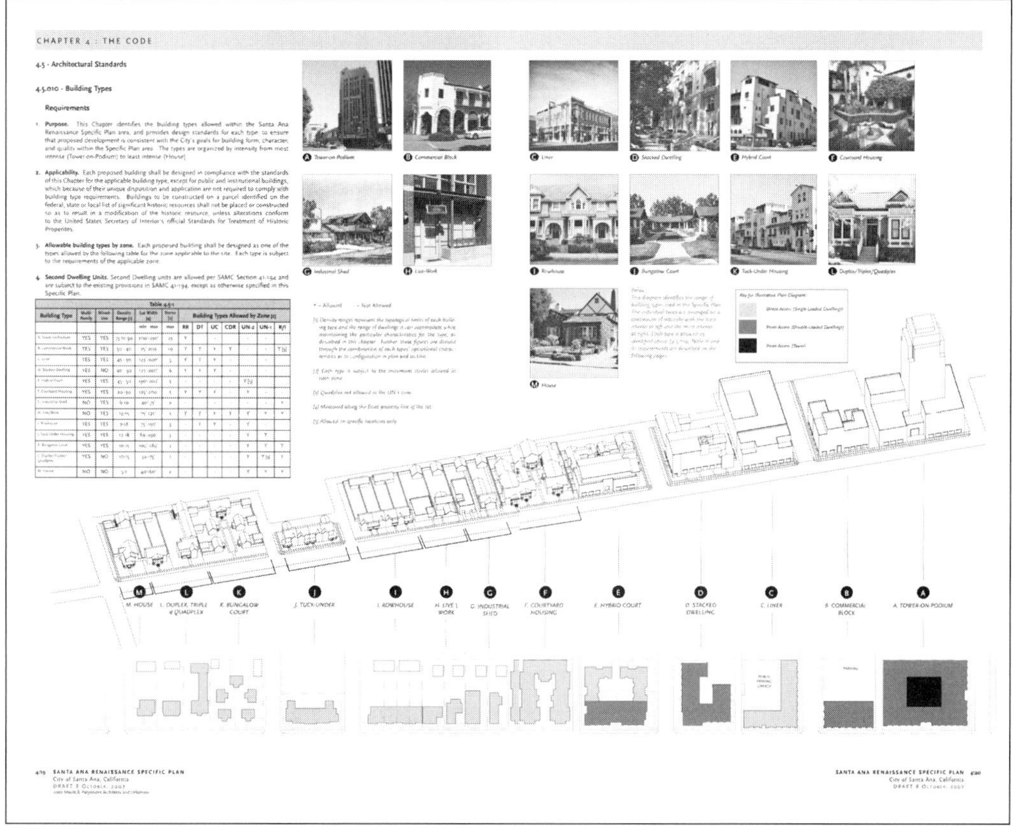


**Fig. 2.40** These two building type diagrams from Moule & Polyzoides started from the same general list and diagram of types (top). The adaptation of the diagram for Santa Ana (bottom) demonstrates the calibration of the types to the project community.

es and from indoor to outdoor spaces. This is most important, even if used only as a guideline, for smaller lots and more urban conditions. For example, a townhouse building set six feet from the sidewalk needs a raised entrance or a fence or hedge to provide a transition to the private realm.

## Allowed Frontages

The ways a building may engage the public realm.

Frontages should be regulated both by transect zone and building type to ensure their appropriate application. The list of allowed frontage types by building type should be cross-referenced with the list by transect zone to determine the permissible solutions for any given site and building.

*Hints for Implementation*

- Determine the frontage types appropriate for each building types based on information gathered during the documentation phase.
- Consider whether the list of frontage types allowed for certain building types might need to trump the list for the transect zones or vice versa. If so, be sure to clarify this in the code.

## Developing Unique Building Types

The general list of building types will not be appropriate for all Form-Based Codes. Areas with a wider diversity of uses as well as special districts may require that other building types be developed. This was true for the historic arsenal in Benicia, California. The project area was a National Register Historic District that had large heavy-industry buildings still in use adjacent to large warehouses being used for artists' work/live residences, large historic officers' mansions being used for commercial and residential uses, and other historic structures being used for large private events. A critical area within the plan where the lower-impact commercial and residential forms and uses began to transition to the larger forms and heavier uses called for the creation of a very specific light-industrial and work/live courtyard building type. (See Figure 2.41.)

This type allowed for a combination of light-industrial, commercial, and work/live uses, but it internalized the service and potential conflicting aspects of the uses, such as noise directly from the uses and truck noise. The type provided a fairly formal frontage that was appropriate to address the commercial and institutional uses across the street.

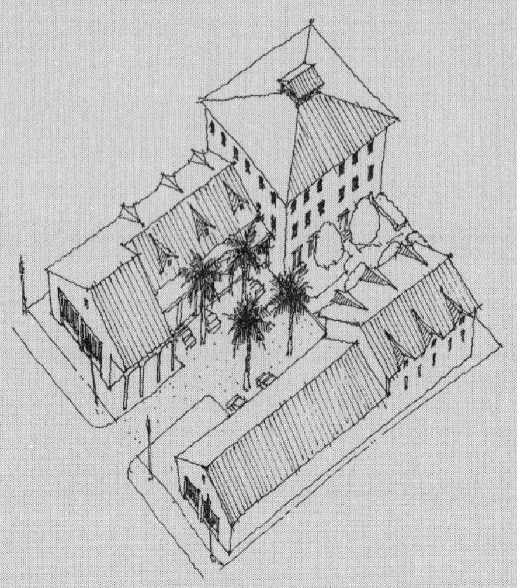

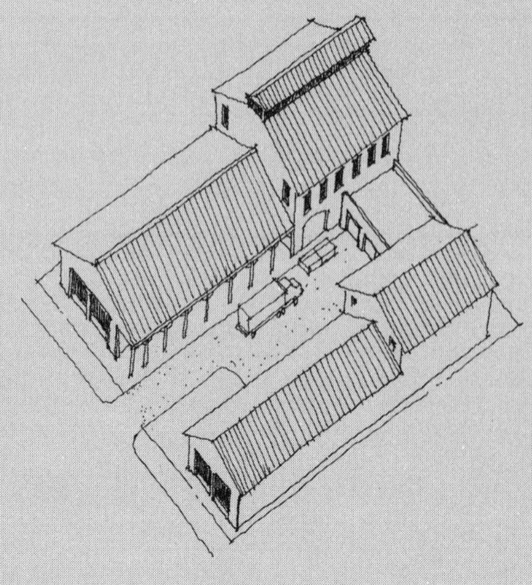

**Fig. 2.41** Adams Street light industrial and work/live building type by Opticos Design

## Vehicle Access and Parking

The type of parking and how it is accessed from programmed spaces should be addressed to ensure that they do not have a negative impact on the quality of the project as perceived from the street.

### Access to Parking

Location of the entry to parking areas.

In order for comfortable, pedestrian-oriented environments to be created, entries to parking garages need to be properly located so that they minimize the visual impact on and the sense of discomfort of pedestrians. The more garage entries that cross the paths of pedestrians, the more unsafe and uncomfortable pedestrians are. In addition, no matter how well designed they are, garage entries detract from the desired character and quality of a place.

*Hints for Implementation*

- When an alley is present, allow access only through the alley.
- When an alley is not present, allow access to corner lots only from the side street.
- When an alley is not present, allowing access to mid-block lots from the primary street may be necessary, but require the location of the entry to be as close to the side or rear of the lot as possible.
- Regulate the maximum width of parking drives either here or within the Building Form Standards.

### Access to Dwelling from Parking

The path of travel from the parking area to a residential unit.

Once a resident exits the car, he or she is a pedestrian again, and the experience from here to his or her dwelling should be considered and designed appropriately.

*Hints for Implementation*

- Be sure to address indirect or direct access, either through standards or guidelines.
- Consider the impact on the quality of the public realm and shared public spaces within a building if residents can go directly from their parking spaces into their units without passing through these public spaces.

### Allowed Parking Types

The ways that cars may be stored.

Different parking types affect a project in different ways. Based on the location and building type, certain parking types may not be acceptable for creating the urban and building form desired. Possible parking types include:

- Underground garage
- Structured parking
- Surface parking
- Tuck under parking
- Single-unit garage
- Off-site parking
- On-street parking

*Hints for Implementation*

- Consider how the allowed parking type will impact the design of buildings and their relationship with existing adjacent buildings.

## Service

The access to and location of utilities and above-ground equipment can both have a negative impact if not addressed properly.

## Location of Services

Where the utility access, above-ground equipment, and trash are placed within a building or project.

The equipment and trash are often large and unsightly, and therefore should be located at the rear of buildings so as not to negatively impact the pedestrian experience. The access to this equipment should be dealt with in a similar manner to the access to parking.



## Building Size and Massing Standards

**by José Antonio Perez**

*Senior Associate, Moule & Polyzoides*

### The Current Situation

The form of buildings is regulated by agencies in varying ways and degrees toward a common goal of mitigating a building's size to achieve physical compatibility and visual interest. Generally, two techniques are applied: Floor-Area Ratio (FAR) and building height. While FAR certainly affects the form of a building, it does so in a way that is not fully cognizant or intentional about the building's physical context or its contribution to the public realm. Building height also is very effective at controlling buildings, but it results in the unintended consequence of nearly identical building heights and massing along great distances and throughout entire neighborhoods. The first technique produces urbanism that is poorly defined, while the latter reinforces the very issues it seeks to address.

### Form-Based Code Techniques

In response to the above, form-based standards have been created to address building size and massing. These standards help buildings to incrementally contribute to the public realm while acknowledging the realities of construction and building composition. Further, because the standards are tailored by context and building type, abstract discussions about massing are avoided, enabling the designer maximum creativity and flexibility.

These standards begin with the maximum allowable building footprint and allocate percentages of that footprint to each upper story based on the scale of urbanism identified in the plan and vision being coded. For example, at the village scale, the allocations per story are far less than at the city scale in response to their respective contexts. Whether it be a neighborhood or corridor, the particular desired context informs the appropriate range of intensity, by

| Scenario (in Stories) | Ratio of each Story | | | | |
|---|---|---|---|---|---|
| | 1 | 2 | 3 | 4 | 5 |
| 2.0 | 100% | 80% | 15% | - | - |
| 3.0 | 100% | 80% | 50% | 15% | - |
| 3.5 | 100% | 90% | 65% | 25% | - |
| 4.0 | 100% | 100% | 70% | 35% | 15% |

**Fig. 2.42** Seven Fountains, a recent courtyard housing development in West Hollywood by Moule & Polyzoides, illustrates the application of form-based building size and massing standards. Note the choice to keep the street facade relatively consistent, while the interior volumes vary from two to five stories. The Seven Fountains massing requirements table is at the top right.

*Hints for Implementation*

- When an alley is present, require all services to be located along the alley.
- When an alley is not present, do not allow any services to be located along the public frontages of the site.

## Open Space

While open space may also be regulated in the Building Form Standards or Public Space Standards, certain building types require their own specific open space standards. For example, reg-



building type and by story. The overall scale is then reconciled with how each allowed building type functions typologically. It is common to find certain building types not allowed to use the maximum allowed height in a particular zone. This is the result of the type having a role within the zone but not necessarily being appropriate for use throughout the zone. For example, courtyard housing may be allowed in a zone that allows up to ten stories, but the typological realities of this type allow no more than five stories. These standards are typologically correct and, therefore, allow for appropriate selection and size of types to address particular needs throughout a zone or community.

Building size is further informed by identifying a variety of scenarios for each type that allow owners to choose whether they want the maximum size building or one somewhere in between. If the owners are not interested in a five-story building, they can, by these standards, choose a lesser scenario, such as a three-story building that clearly identifies the allowable percentages for such a building. Such scenarios are provided for each type within its typological limitations.

The examples in Figures 2.42 and 2.43 illustrate this technique in recently completed buildings by Moule & Polyzoides. Both buildings show how the allowable percentages were distributed to create more density along the front of the sites, opening up the buildings with two- and three-story volumes along the south edge and interior of the sites. These standards not only contribute to the richness of the massing, but because they are identified by "story," they directly translate into usable square footage for various dwelling types (flat, townhouse, or loft). In applying these standards, the realities of each site are recognized and the identity of the individual dwellings is maximized.

**Fig. 2.43** Granada Court's Five Stories. The upper floors are allocated a certain maximum of the allowable ground floor (footprint). It is up to the individual design of each building as to how these allocations are distributed or concentrated throughout each story.

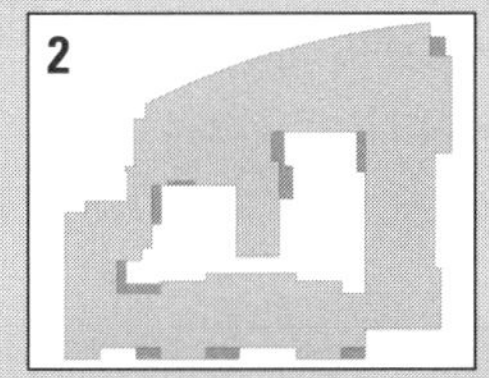


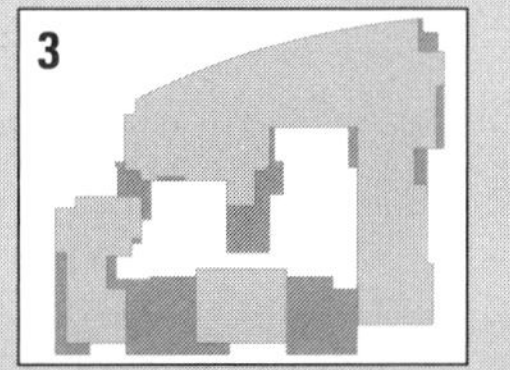


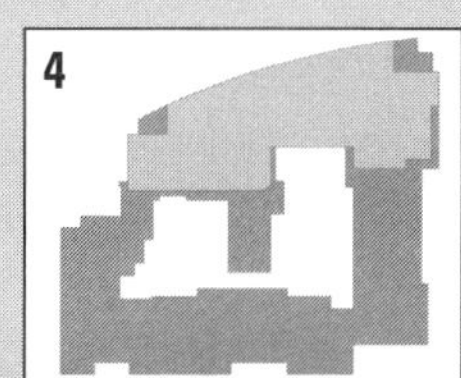


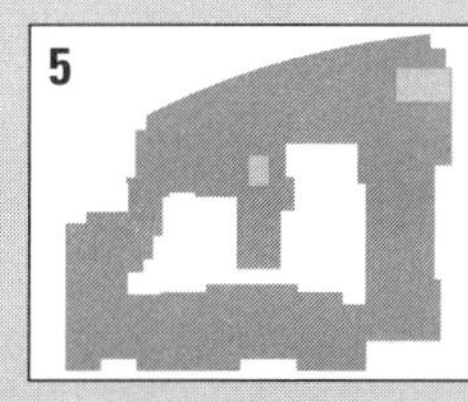

ulating the size and location of the courtyard is critical to ensuring that a courtyard building in implemented correctly. However, any element that is not specific to a building type should be regulated in the Building Form Standards.

### General Location and Size

Placement and square footage requirements for unbuilt space that is usable for its residents.

This is most critical in the more urban conditions (T6–T4), where there is less public and private open space. The appropriate location should be determined based on the physical configuration of each particular building type and the size, scale, and type of buildings that may be adjacent to them.

*Hints for Implementation*

- Regulate the size of the main (shared) open space by percentage of the lot, although dimensional parameters may be appropriate for smaller building types.
- While creating the standards, consider how open spaces within the side yard, rear yard, front yard, or courtyards are properly configured for each type.

**Courtyard**

Unlike other open spaces, courtyards are surrounded by the building on more than one side, and, therefore, the design of the courtyard affects the form of the building more than other open spaces do. The proportions, solar orientation, and size of courtyards should be carefully considered in order to create inviting, comfortable, and usable spaces.

*Hints for Implementation*

- Regulate whether a courtyard may be on a podium or on the ground.
- Regulate minimum dimensions of courtyards based on solar orientation.
- Regulate minimum proportion of the space with a width to height ratio.
- Regulate whether building projections are allowed into required open space.

## Landscape

As with open space, landscape is likely to be regulated in other sections of the code, but certain elements may be better regulated by building type.

### Minimum Required Landscape

The least amount of planting required.

For certain building types, mostly within more urban conditions, very specific landscape conditions are required to create the highest-quality environment. In addition, simple planting choices for trees and other landscaping that will provide shading can reduce passive heat gain, thus reducing the amount of energy used to cool buildings in hotter climates.

**8: Building Size and Massing Standards**

(a) Height ratios for various commercial blocks are as follows:

| Building Height (in Stories) | Ratio of each Story (see page 4:78 for definition) | | | | |
|---|---|---|---|---|---|
| | 1 | 2 | 3 | 4 | 5 |
| 2.0 | 100% | 80% | - | - | - |
| 2.5 | 100% | 75% | 40% | - | - |
| 3.0 | 100% | 75% | 55% | 10% | - |
| 4.0 | 100% | 100% | 75% | 35% | 20% |
| 4.5 | 100% | 100% | 85% | 55% | 45% |

(b) Each dwelling may have only one side exposed to the outdoors with direct access to at least a dooryard, patio, terrace or balcony.
(c) Buildings may contain any of three types of dwellings: flats, town houses and lofts.
(d) Dwellings may be as repetitive or unique as deemed by individual designs.
(e) Buildings may be composed of one dominant volume.

**Fig. 2.44** Composition regulations by target height ratios from the Santa Ana Renaissance Specific Plan by Moule & Polyzoides and Crawford, Multari & Clark Associates



*Hints for Implementation*

- Considered for front, side, and rear yards.
- Involve a landscape architect.
- Consider water use required to maintain plants.
- Include maintenance standards if the standards require planting in front yards.
- Consider regulating size of planting, such as trees if appropriate for the building type.

## Building Size and Massing

These are specific building form requirements for each building type that are in addition to the building form regulations in the Building Form Standards. These regulations will ultimately produce the diversity and complexity in the urban form that is inherent in traditional neighborhoods and downtowns.

## Composition

The way the height and massing of a building is assembled.

For most building types, the form is a critical defining factor and, therefore, should be regulated.

*Typical Regulations*

- Target height ratios regulated by percentages of each floor height allowed (See Figure 2.44.)
- Types and combination of unit types that are allowed
- Breaks in planes on the fronts and sides of buildings

# Architectural Standards

The extent to which architecture is regulated within a Form-Based Code will vary from community to community. Architectural standards are not a required component of an FBC, but it is a component that can add to the overall success of the Code, make administration more objective, and ultimately lead to higher-quality development under the Code. That being said, it is one of the most often misunderstood aspects of a Form-Based Code because it is often thought that they are primarily about regulating style. In fact, an FBC has a primary objective of prescribing a specific urban form, but the level of architectural regulation is optional. When creating the Architectural Standards, the amount of time spent regulating a specific architectural character and details should be based upon with the community's desire to regulate architectural character. If architectural character is not an important part of the community's vision, or if existing architectural guidelines have already produced successful results, then a Form-Based Code can be created without Architectural Standards.

There are generally four possible levels of architectural regulation that can be integrated into an FBC:

1. Complete regulation by style down to very specific details thoroughly drawn and dimensioned in an architectural pattern book (See Figure 2.45.)
2. Regulation by quality and general local character that is done with a combination of photos and drawings (See Figure 2.46.)
3. Very basic regulations to achieve a basic standard of quality mostly regulated through text, but sometimes with some limited supporting graphics (See Figure 2.47.)
4. No architectural standards

Following is a complete overview of elements that the team can consider regulating to ensure that new development will enhance the unique architectural character of a community. Most of the examples shown will be of traditional architecture and details since this is typically what a community asks for to preserve the unique character of its town or city. This does not mean that more modern details may not be appropriate or added to the Architectural Standards if that is what the community desires. The scope of work that the community agrees upon should decide the extent to which these elements are documented and regulated in your FBC and what the desired character is.

Comprehensive architectural standards can include all of the following elements regulated through measured drawings. If such rigorous regulation is not desired, photographs can be used instead.

1. Massing
2. Facade composition
3. Windows and doors
4. Elements and detail
5. Palette and combinations of materials

Typically, this information can be categorized or cataloged and then regulated by architectural style, but if the standards don't ultimately regulate by style, it is still a good system to use to document the architectural character of a community. This will also enable the code team to understand the diversity of architecture within a community and which details and materials work well together.

## Massing

The most important architectural element to regulate is the massing of buildings. Ultimately, creating axonometric diagrams of the massing can be very helpful in regulating architecture that is inherently "local" in character. The documentation of massing should be categorized by building type. For example, single-family homes, multiunit residential types, commercial buildings, and civic buildings will each have different massing characteristics that should be regulated individually.

*Typical Regulations*

- Primary forms: This can ensure that the overall size and shape are consistent with the community's character, which cannot be undervalued. Of all the architectural elements, this is the most critical because of its impact on the urban form. (See Figure 2.48.)
- Roof forms: Roof forms and articulation are usually very region specific based on response to local climatic conditions and therefore a large part of what establishes local character. Roof types (e.g., gables and hips) and pitch may be regulated, as well as whether and what types of dormers are allowed.
- Massing elements composition: Various secondary massing elements, such as wings and bays, may be added to the main portion of a building that enable it to accommodate a larger program. The composition of these elements along with the basic shapes and footprints create building forms that are endemic to the place or region.

### What Elements Belong in the Architectural Standards

There are different approaches among FBC practitioners as to which components should be categorized under Architectural Standards. Moule & Polyzoides have established a system in which frontage types, building types, and architectural styles are all addressed within the Architectural Standards. They established a hierarchy within the architectural standards in which style is still regulated, but it is just one of several important architectural elements to regulate, and probably the least important. Their approach to style is also different than most in that they are not simply regulating specific details, but rather the intent behind the detail within each style. See the Santa Ana case study for an example.

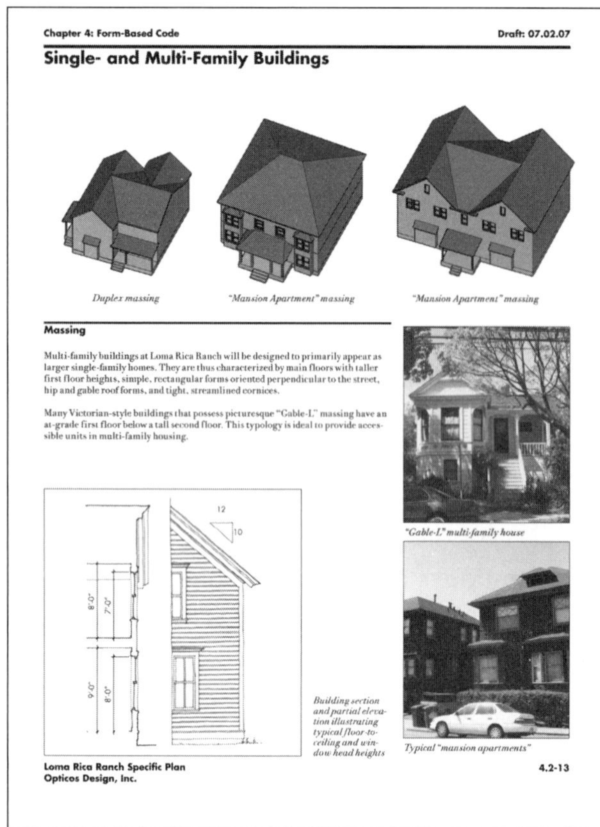
Chapter 4: Form-Based Code Draft: 07.02.07

## Single- and Multi-Family Buildings

*Duplex massing* *"Mansion Apartment" massing* *"Mansion Apartment" massing*

**Massing**

Multi-family buildings at Loma Rica Ranch will be designed to primarily appear as larger single-family homes. They are thus characterized by main floors with taller first floor heights, simple, rectangular forms oriented perpendicular to the street, hip and gable roof forms, and tight, streamlined cornices.

Many Victorian-style buildings that possess picturesque "Gable-L" massing have an at-grade first floor below a tall second floor. This typology is ideal to provide accessible units in multi-family housing.

*"Gable-L" multi-family house*

*Building section and partial elevation illustrating typical floor-to-ceiling and window-head heights*

*Typical "mansion apartments"*

Loma Rica Ranch Specific Plan
Opticos Design, Inc. 4.2-13

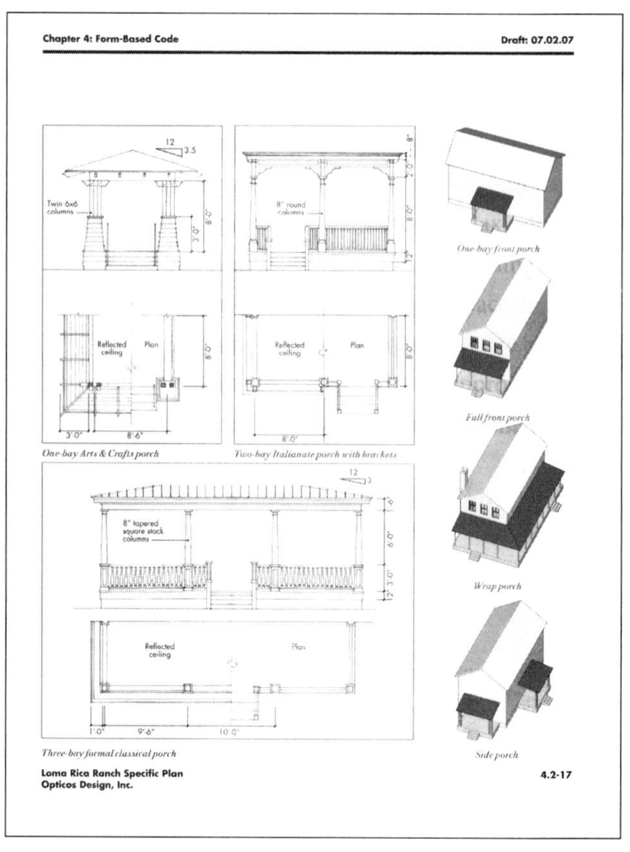
Chapter 4: Form-Based Code Draft: 07.02.07

*One-bay Arts & Crafts porch*

*Two-bay Italianate porch with brackets*

*Three-bay formal classical porch*

*One-bay front porch*

*Full front porch*

*Wrap porch*

*Side porch*

Loma Rica Ranch Specific Plan
Opticos Design, Inc. 4.2-17

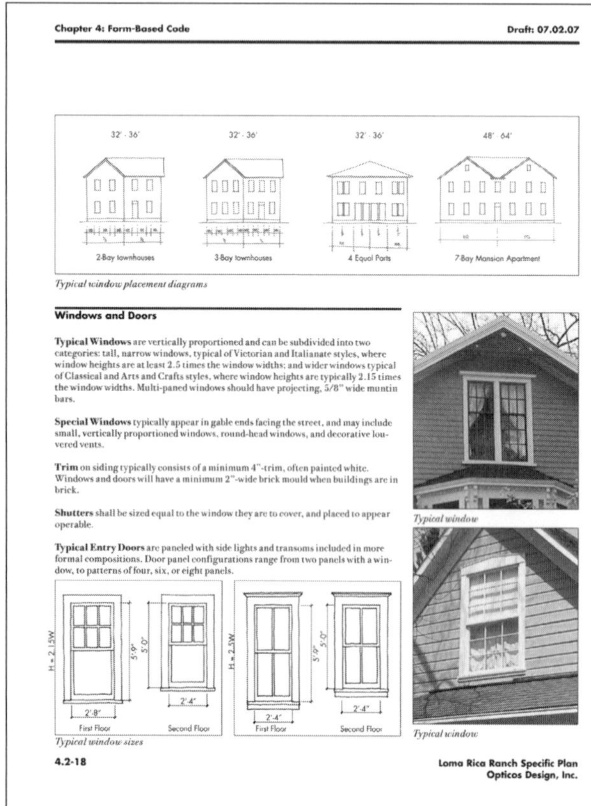
Chapter 4: Form-Based Code Draft: 07.02.07

*Typical window placement diagrams*

**Windows and Doors**

**Typical Windows** are vertically proportioned and can be subdivided into two categories: tall, narrow windows, typical of Victorian and Italianate styles, where window heights are at least 2.5 times the window widths; and wider windows typical of Classical and Arts and Crafts styles, where window heights are typically 2.15 times the window widths. Multi-paned windows should have projecting, 5/8" wide muntin bars.

**Special Windows** typically appear in gable ends facing the street, and may include small, vertically proportioned windows, round-head windows, and decorative louvered vents.

**Trim** on siding typically consists of a minimum 4"-trim, often painted white. Windows and doors will have a minimum 2"-wide brick mould when buildings are in brick.

**Shutters** shall be sized equal to the window they are to cover, and placed to appear operable.

**Typical Entry Doors** are paneled with side lights and transoms included in more formal compositions. Door panel configurations range from two panels with a window, to patterns of four, six, or eight panels.

*Typical window sizes*

*Typical window*

*Typical window*

4.2-18 Loma Rica Ranch Specific Plan
Opticos Design, Inc.

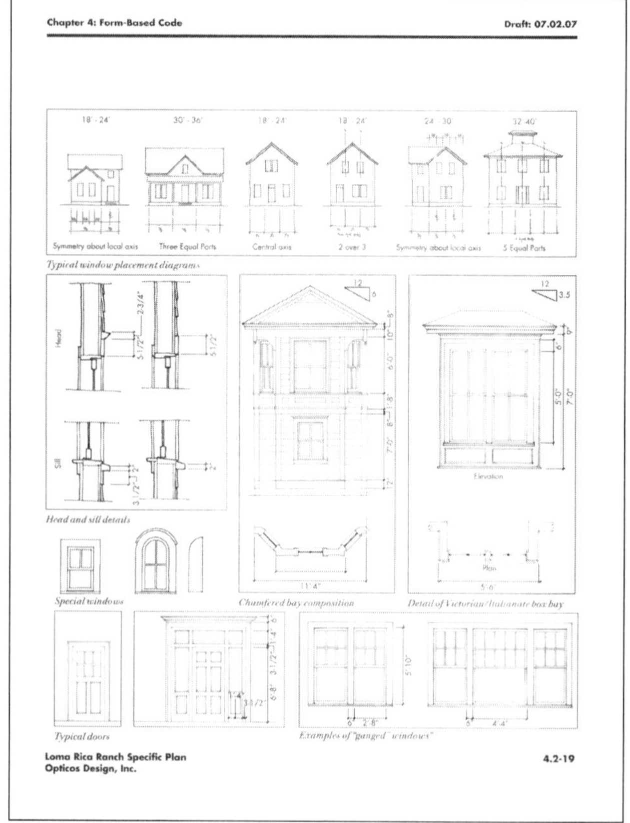
Chapter 4: Form-Based Code Draft: 07.02.07

*Typical window placement diagrams*

*Head and sill details*

*Special windows*

*Chamfered bay composition*

*Detail of Victorian/Italianate box bay*

*Typical doors*

*Examples of "ganged" windows*

Loma Rica Ranch Specific Plan
Opticos Design, Inc. 4.2-19

**Fig. 2.45** Complete regulation by architectural style in the Loma Rica Ranch Specific Plan in Grass Valley, California, by Opticos Design

CHAPTER 4: **DEVELOPMENTAL CODE**
4.6 ARCHITECTURE STYLE GUIDELINES

UPTOWN WHITTIER SPECIFIC PLAN 4:31
Whittier, California
100% PUBLIC DRAFT: December 11, 2006

**4.6.2 Craftsman**

An Arts and Crafts movement that spread throughout Europe and the United States inspired Craftsman Style architecture as a rejection to the redundancies aided by the machine-made world. In the United States, this style was initiated in the Midwest and successfully applied to the widely varying California climate and lifestyles. In California, architects Greene and Greene created modest, inexpensive, and low-profile bungalow style architecture—modest, inexpensive, and low-profile—that was easy to produce for a large demand of homes.

Buildings are composed of horizontal, single- and two-story volumes, sometimes taller. An additional floor may be concealed within the volume of the roof. In its most simple form, it is a wood box surrounded by various attached elements. Walls are typically horizontally placed wood siding, shingles or board-and-batten, with a foundation base and piers in river stone, brick or stucco. Rafter tails and porch columns are exposed, smooth, woodwork. Windows and doors are vertical in proportion, trimmed in wood. Roofs are composed of shallow sloped gabled forms, and made of wood or asphalt shingles with broad overhangs and eaves.

*Combination stone and brick base*

*Siding above painted plaster*

*Brace and exposed rafters*

*Concrete base*

*Unpainted siding above painted plaster*

*Structural elements as decoration*

*Masonry and stone base*

*Painted shingles above painted lap siding*

*Large overhangs*

**A. Base**
a. Craftsman houses invariably rest upon a base of concrete, stone, or brick.
b. Stone is largest at the bottom and smallest at the top reflecting the natural stacking of the material.
c. The lower floor may be stucco (20-30 fine sand finish) with the upper floor(s) clad in wood or shingle siding.

B. Primary Walls
a. Walls shall show no more than two materials along any vertical section of the building, with no more than 90% of the total wall surface in one material. Single family detached houses are exempt.
b. Piers are a minimum of 6"x6" if wood posts, and 18"x18" if stone or stucco.
c. Stone is largest at the bottom and smallest at the top.

**C. Roof-Wall Connections**
a. Wide eaves with exposed rafters
b. Wood braces may be used.
c. Min 3' overhang
d. Decorative, spaced boards to vent attics

*Roofs parallel to street*

*Gutter and downspout*

*Vertical openings*

*Front Porch*

*Intersecting gables with porch*

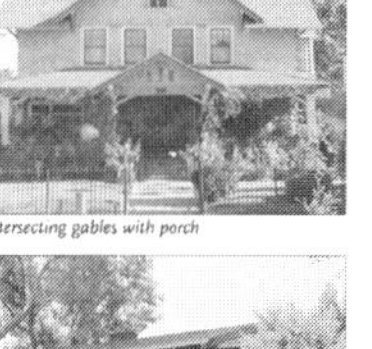

*Walls composed of natural materials to blend into landscape*

*Dormer window with pitched roof*

*Downspout*

*'Ganged' vertical openings*

*Chimney*

*Horizontal volumes, projected upper floor*

*Trellis as entry*

*Dormer with "flap-up" roof*

*Gutter and downspout*

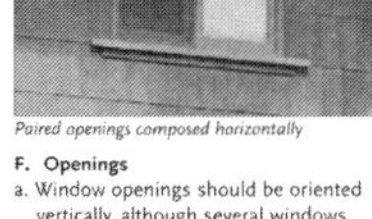

*Paired openings composed horizontally*

*Porte-cochere*

*Hip with wrap-around verandah*

*Natural materials with accented gate*

**D. Roof**
a. Principal gables are between 3:12 and 4:12, and shed slopes are less than the principal slope (between 2:12 and 6:12).
b. Dormers may be used to provide light and air to rooms in the attic space.
c. Heavy timber throughout in lookouts and brackets (6x8 min)

**E. Drainage**
a. May be conducted off pitched roofs by a traditional combination of gutters and downspouts.
b. Rainwater reaching the ground may be harvested in cisterns or temporarily collected in dry wells.
c. Downspouts are painted or copper and typically round or square.

**F. Openings**
a. Window openings should be oriented vertically, although several windows may abut to form a horizontal overall opening.
b. Window lites may be divided into equal increments or be divided on a portion of a window (such as the upper portion of a double-hung or casement window: 4 over 1, 3 over 1)

**G. Attached Elements**
a. Porches, chimneys, and trellises can encroach beyond the primary exterior surface of buildings and into their setbacks.
b. Tapered, square columns
c. Deep porches to block sun and provide shade to interiors.

**H. Massing**
a. 3rd story always concealed in roof with dormers
b. 2-story with 1-story components attached such as porches or veranda.
c. 1-story simple house forms with 1-story components attached such as porches or veranda.

**I. Site Definition and Landscape**
a. Buildings typically face a front yard.
b. Garden walls of rounded stone and/or clinker brick, brick are common.
c. Trellis and other woodwork define outdoor porches and patios.

Moule & Polyzoides Architects and Urba
For the City of Whittier, Calif
4:32

**Fig. 2.46** Regulation by general local character in the Uptown Whittier Specific Plan by Moule & Polyzoides

**Fig. 2.47** Basic standard of quality, SmartCode (Credit: DPZ)

5.3.5 **Architectural Standards (T3)**

a. Building wall materials may be combined on each Facade only horizontally, with the heavier below the lighter.

b. Streetscreens should be between 3.5 and 8 feet in height and constructed of a material matching the adjacent building Facade. The Streetscreen may be replaced by a hedge or fence by Warrant. Streetscreens shall have openings no larger than necessary to allow automobile and pedestrian access.

c. All openings, including porches, galleries, arcades and windows, with the exception of storefronts, shall be square or vertical in proportion.

d. Openings above the first Story shall not exceed 50% of the total building wall area, with each Facade being calculated independently.

e. [RESERVED].

f. Doors and windows that operate as sliders are prohibited along Frontages.

g. Pitched roofs, if provided, shall be symmetrically sloped no less than 5:12, except that porches and attached sheds may be no less than 2:12. h. The exterior finish material on all Facades shall be limited to brick, wood siding, cementitious siding and/or stucco.

h. Flat roofs shall be enclosed by parapets a minimum of 42 inches high, or as required to conceal mechanical equipment to the satisfaction of the CRC.

i. Balconies and porches shall be made of painted wood.

j. **Fences, if provided at the First Layer, shall be painted. Fences at Lot Lines may be of wood board or chain link.**

5.3.6 **Environmental Standards (T3)**

a. Transect Zones manifest a range of responses to natural and urban conditions. In case of conflict, to the extent not inconsistent with applicable state or federal law, the natural infrastructure shall have priority in the more rural zones (T1-T3) and the urban infrastructure shall have priority in the more urban zones (T4-T6) as detailed in Sections 5.2 through 5.6.

b. The landscape installed shall consist primarily of native species requiring minimal irrigation, fertilization and maintenance.

c. Impermeable surface by building shall be minimized and confined to the ratio of lot coverage by building shown in Table 14F.

SmartCode Version 8.0

## Facade Composition

Secondary to the composition of the massing elements is the composition of the facade elements. This is regulated by building widths, most importantly maximums, and an appropriate rhythm of windows, doors, and other elements that may occur, such as bay windows or balconies. (See Figure 2.49.)

*Typical Regulations*

- Primary rhythm of windows and doors: This can include the number of windows or typical bays on the main body of a building, the typical distance between the elements, whether the pattern of elements is formal or informal, and whether there is one primary rhythm or secondary and tertiary ones that are also important.
- Distances between corners and windows: Placing windows or doors too close to corners creates an awkward visual relationship between the two and often fosters a sense of instability because it visually weakens the corner of the building.
- Locations of doorways: Within the typical composition, there is usually a pattern within which the door belongs in a specific location. This will also tie into the Frontage Standards.

## Windows and Doors

The selection of appropriate and well-detailed windows and doors are important in buildings of all scales, from single-family homes to large mixed-use or commercial buildings. The depth

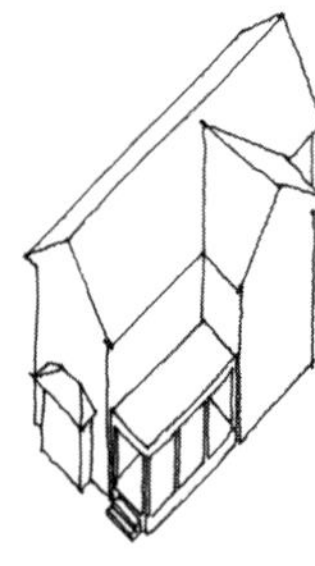
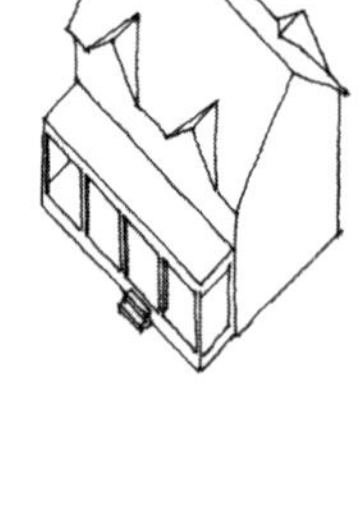
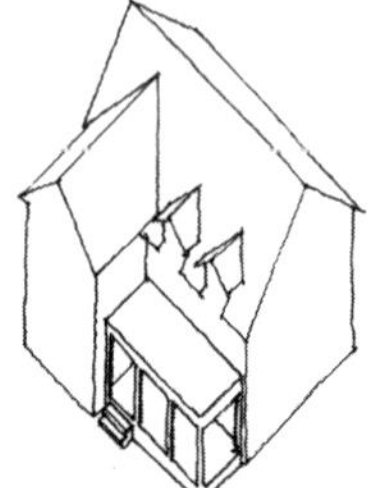
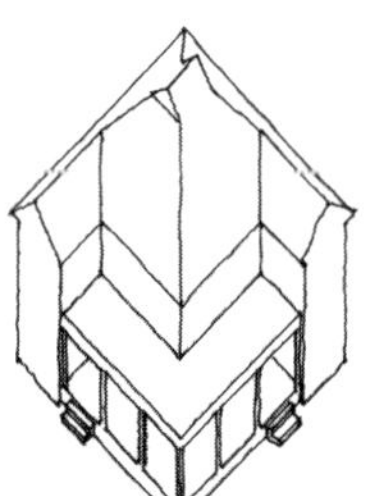
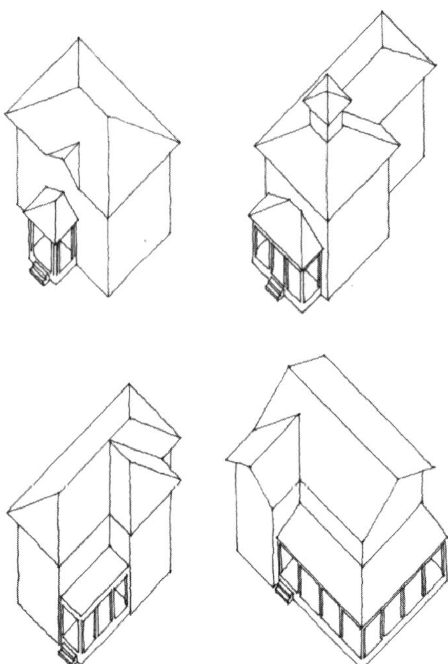

**Fig. 2.48** Documented massing elements composition for two different architectural styles: Victorian (near right) and Italianate (far right) (Credit: Opticos Design)

**Commercial Buildings**

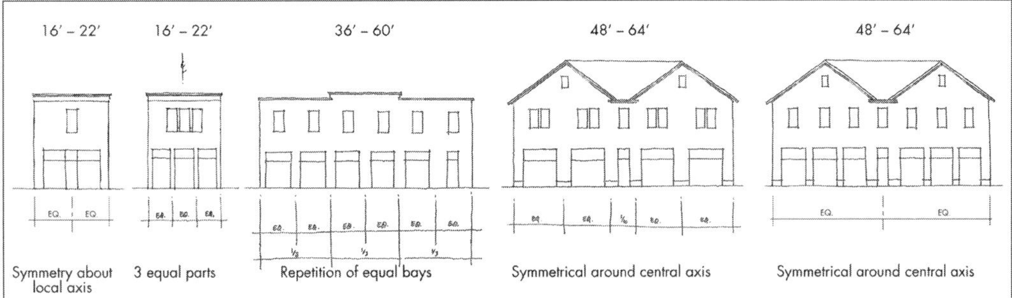


**Multi-Unit Buildings**

**Single-Unit Buildings**

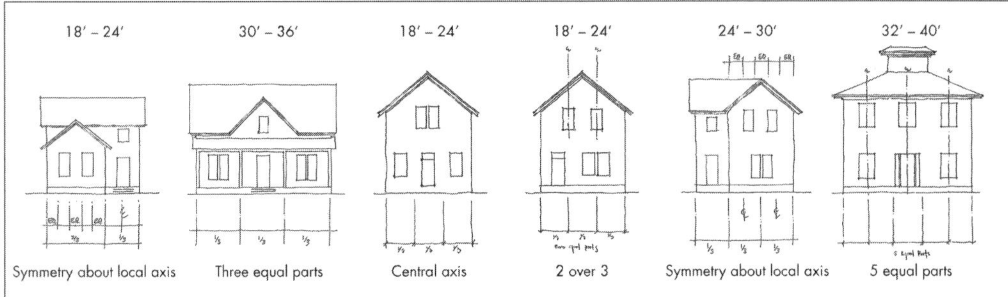


**Fig. 2.49** Facade composition diagrams by building type (Credit: Opticos Design)

of the windows provides added shadow lines and visual interest to a building's composition, the proportions and window light patterns tie the building to a particular local style, and details, such as exterior muntins, provide a sense of authenticity.

*Typical Regulations*

- Individual window types and how they are grouped: Different types of windows, such as double-hung and casement, are specific to local styles. In order to reinforce the local character of these styles, regulate that appropriate window types are used; otherwise, inappropriate windows, such as sliding windows, will be used on many new buildings.
- Proportions and typical sizes (height and width): One of the easiest ways to ruin an attractive existing building or create a new unattractive building is to use windows with poor proportions or sizes for the neighborhood. Window proportions are typically included in even basic architectural standards.
- Division patterns and profile of muntins: The pattern of lights in windows is also very specific to the time period of a building or neighborhood. In addition, the profile and placement of muntins add to the overall unifying character of a building. Do not allow internally applied muntins. It is better to not have them at all than to have bad ones. Encourage that simulated divided lights have a spacer bar between the panes of glass to imitate the pattern of the muntins.
- Minimum depth: This is probably the most important aspect of a window to regulate.

**Fig. 2.50** Minimum depth of windows (Credit: Opticos Design)

Windows on attractive local buildings typically have at least an inch in depth from the plane of the wall to the face of the windowpane. Since this depth is typically part of a window's design, window selection is an important part of quality building design. (See Figure 2.50.)

- Surround details: For stucco buildings, it is important that surrounds are detailed with a typical stucco mould or that the window has a deep reveal that is detailed in the wall to achieve some depth at the window. Do not allow foam profiles that are often used to achieve this perception of depth. For wood buildings with wood siding, the surround options should be studied as part of the documentation because it is often dealt with differently in different regions.
- Sill detail: Windowsills have historically been a tectonic part of a window, and windows look awkward without them, even to untrained eyes. Require that windows have sill, and then regulate how far the sill extends and other specific sill details as desired.
- Other specific elements, such as shutters: If shutters or other specific elements are part of the local architectural vocabulary, consider regulating how they are detailed; otherwise, inevitably, shutters will be built permanently mounted to a wall without any relationship to the size of the window. (See Figure 2.51.)

**Fig. 2.51** An example of a good unique, local shutter, found on a commercial building in the Sierra Nevada region

Ultimately these details do not typically need to be regulated to a specific measurement, but the documentation should reveal which characteristics are important to regulate in light of the goals of the community.

## Elements and Details

If architecture is going to be regulated, there are always elements that are specific to a community that should be included in addition to the primary elements above.

*Typical Regulations*

- Eave detail or cornice detail: It is important to understand how eaves are detailed because it will vary drastically from style to style and by different responses driven by climatic considerations. The depth of eaves is a detail that is extremely important to the overall character of a building, especially in styles that typically have deep overhangs, such as arts and crafts buildings. Also consider the eave treatment, such as boxed or open with exposed rafter tails or simulated rafter tails, and the typical profiles. (See Figure 2.52.)
- Rake detail: Another detail that is often overlooked is the rake's depth and detailing. This detail is best regulated with a section drawing. Often, a partial elevation detail next to this section can be helpful. Require this section early in the design review process in order to verify that the proposed rake depths are appropriate. (See Figure 2.53.)
- Porch, balcony, arcade, and gallery details: Porches seems like a simple design element, but their application is often endemic to a region. For example, while deep, wraparound porches are typical of many residen-

tial buildings in the Sierra Nevada gold-rush communities, shallow, often recessed porches are more typical in Berkeley, California, and the rest of the Bay Area, even thought the two areas are less than 100 miles apart. Consider regulating typical porch and stoop types, how they engage public ROWs in more urban conditions, and how different building types treat this element differently or similarly, down to the detail of the columns or posts as well as the railings.

The commercial equivalent of the porch is an arcade or gallery. Many communities that historically had galleries no longer have them because they were removed for fire-related issues in the late 1800s and early 1900s or they were removed as part of "modernization" efforts in the mid-1900s. When regulating these elements, include where they should be located in relationship to the public ROW. Many recent arcades and galleries have been built set back from a street, which is functionally different than those that historically extended over sidewalks to provide shade for pedestrians while helping to define the public realm. Pulling the arcade or gallery back from the sidewalk edge essentially creates two sidewalks, diluting the use and effectiveness of both.

- Bay windows: The ability to design or build a good bay window is a lost art; therefore, if these are primary elements to be reflected in a community's design standards, regulate the proportions and details in both elevation and section. Also carefully regulate profile details because the reveal and shadow created by these profiles is important for the way that a bay window reads from the street. Consider regulating the maximum heights in stories, as well as the spacing between multiple bays and commercial bay windows versus residential. (See Figure 2.54.)
- Miscellaneous elements: Consider regulating other architectural elements that help define the local character of the community. These elements may include dormer types, cupolas, or tower elements at corners or terminated vistas. (See Figure 2.56.)

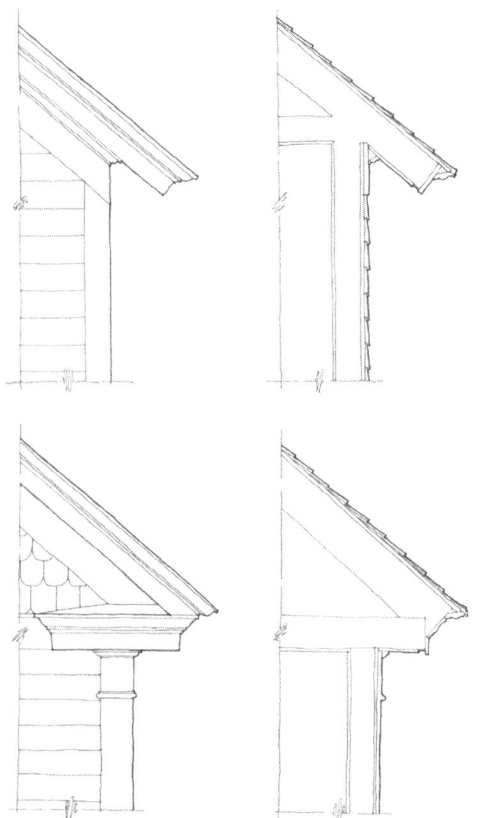

**Fig. 2.52** Eave details vary dramatically by style and context. Simple, well-designed eave details can make simple buildings feel rooted in a place. (Credit: Opticos Design)

**Fig. 2.53** Rake details are often too flat, creating a "flat" architecture that does not have any reveal or shadow, thus making it feel cartoonish. (Credit: Opticos Design)

## Materials

It is important to regulate not just a list of materials themselves, but also how the materials are typically applied and used together.

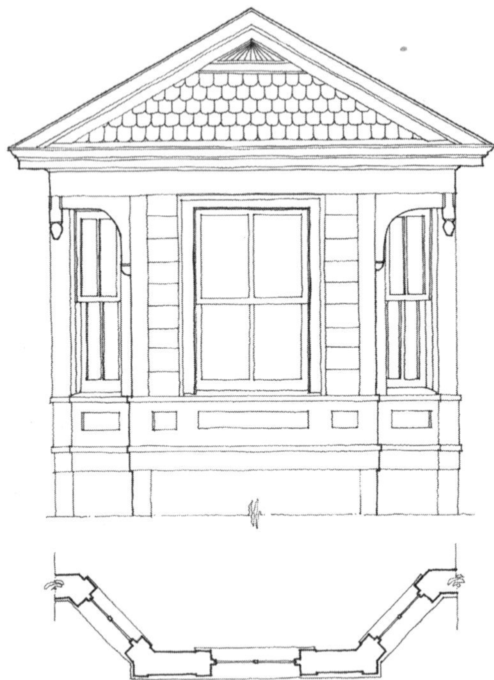

**Fig. 2.54** Be sure to include details for bay windows if they are an important aspect of the local character. (Credit: Opticos Design)

*Typical Regulations*

- Allow only horizontal changes in materials: The random application of different materials with vertical changes creates overly complex compositions and is not typical in the historic application of materials.
- Stacking of materials: Typically lighter materials should be located on top of heavier materials, not vice versa. Exceptions to this may occasionally be found in local documentation, but should not be allowed otherwise.

The level at which a community chooses to regulate architecture within their Form-Based Code should be carefully considered. The code consultant should advise the community as to which of the different approaches mentioned above are the right tools for helping to achieve the community's vision. The two biggest determinants are the abilities of the staff member(s), committee, or other group or individual who will be administering the code, and how critical and specific a certain character or style is to a community's vision.

## Window Surrounds

It is typical for architectural standards to overlook the characteristics of window surrounds; however, with the vast selection of windows available, most of which are not very well designed, it is important to understand and regulate these details. In the regulations, include typical profiles and widths of the surround and how the details differ with buildings of different materials. Common mistakes to regulate against are the use of foam profile stucco surrounds instead of typical stucco mould details or a simple deep reveal for Spanish Revival styles.

**Fig. 2.55** Locally appropriate window surrounds should be documented. (Credit: Opticos Design)

**Fig. 2.56** All the described architectural elements composed into various building types ranging from single-family to commercial blocks of varying styles (Credit: Opticos Design)

## Documentation for Regulating by Style

As mentioned above, classifying details by style is often the easiest and most coherent way to categorize all the above details. In taking this approach, the code team should be sure to document several local examples of each style and to focus on unique local applications of each style through photo documentation and details. The least time-intensive way to do this is through photographs, but drawings are much more effective in communicating intent to builders and designers. Therefore, if time does not permit much on-site sketching, a thorough analysis of the photos, including drawings, should be prepared later in the office. Also, because of local interpretations of the basic styles, it is sometimes difficult to categorize styles within a familiar style. In cases such as this, create a name for the style that ties directly to the local history of a community.

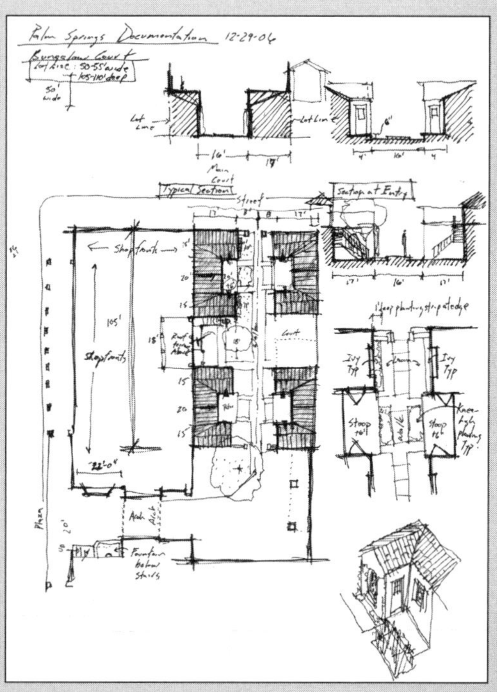


**Fig. 2.57** Documentation sketches of a Palm Springs courtyard type done on site (Credit: Opticos Design)

# Code Administration

SIMILAR TO CONVENTIONAL zoning codes, Form-Based Codes include administrative provisions that detail the procedures necessary to administer the code. The overarching procedures are obviously those for submitting, reviewing, and approving or disapproving proposed development projects. There are then numerous subprocedures that may be included for differing project circumstances, including historic resource review and the consideration of nonconformities. Finally, any rules guiding overall code administration are included, such as rules for the interpretation of code provisions, resolving any perceived conflicts between the Form-Based Code requirements and other municipal code provisions, and others.

While any zoning code should contain a variety of procedural components to support its administration, the first and the most critical in a Form-Based Code determines how individual development projects will be reviewed and approved (generically referred to as "permit requirements"), and the second consists of regulations and procedures that address nonconformities. It is also likely that a Form-Based Code will need a variance process.

## Project Review and Approval

As was the case prior to a new Form-Based Code, daily FBC administration involves both private sector and city actions. Private property owners and their agents prepare and submit development project plans for city consideration, and city staff members review the applications and proposed projects to verify their compliance with the new code. Although there may be one or more meetings with an applicant prior to application filing, staff members then either approve the applications administratively, or prepare reports and recommendations on the projects to a higher level review body (e.g., a Planning Commission or Design Review Board) to which either the Form-Based Code (or in the case of a hybrid code, the still-applicable citywide code) has assigned the authority and responsibility for the discretionary review and approval or disapproval of the particular project type.

The possibility of administrative review and approval versus discretionary review is an important distinction, and one that may be tentatively established early in code preparation, either as one of the initial overall goals for the coding process (i.e., streamline the development review and approval in the area being coded), during a charrette where the first components of the code to begin to emerge and there are opportunities for public discussion about the desirable level of public review for proposed projects, or at the conclusion of the coding process, when the various differences between the existing code and the draft new code will inevitably be highlighted and discussed during the formal public hearings where the adoption of the new code is considered.

Administrative review and approval should be technically possible for all projects that comply with applicable FBC requirements. Discretionary review is inherently subjective and can therefore undermine the intent of the community's vision and the FBC by requiring ill-advised changes to proposed projects. It should be necessary only for requests for variances from the code or where required by state law (e.g., as required by the California Coastal Act).

Allowing more administrative approvals is possible for two primary reasons: (1) the code is tied to a very specific, publicly approved vision for a city or project area; and (2) there is a much higher level of predictability in the quality and character of development when it is being regulated by a Form-Based Code. Deciding which types of development are eligible for administrative approval is an important exercise and may be critical to the political process of FBC adoption, as well as to its success thereafter. The adoption of a new code can be a challenging process due to the wide variety of constituents that may be involved and who will be affected by the code after its adoption. As discussed in Chapter 1, one benefit of an FBC to the general community is the opportunity to create an overall vision considering all aspects of the built environment and then creating a prescriptive FBC to help with the implementation of the vision. By going through this intense effort prior to code adoption, the community may confidently reduce its constant watch over individual development proposals. For developers, it can be a relief to have more detailed advance guidance about what a community is interested in seeing built, but the real value is the potential for administrative project approval. Including a process for administrative review can help convince developers to support the approval of the FBC, as well as to encourage them to develop under it. This also increases the likelihood that local owners of smaller properties will consider building or improving their existing buildings, thus providing incentives and potentially speeding up improvements to the community. (See Figures 2.58 through 2.60.)

The process for administrative review can be implemented by including a new type of project approval permit with the authority for issuance explicitly assigned to staff, provided that they first determine that the project meets the standards in the new code. The code may also retain the city's standard discretionary development permit with issuance authority assigned to an appointed body, such as the Planning Commission or a Design Review Board, after it conducts a public hearing and makes certain mandatory findings provided in the code. This may be called a "conditional use permit," a "warrant," or something similar.

A variance process may also be needed, which would allow a planning commission to relax or modify certain building design standards within the code to address design issues faced by development proposed on a site with unusual characteristics that prevent its development

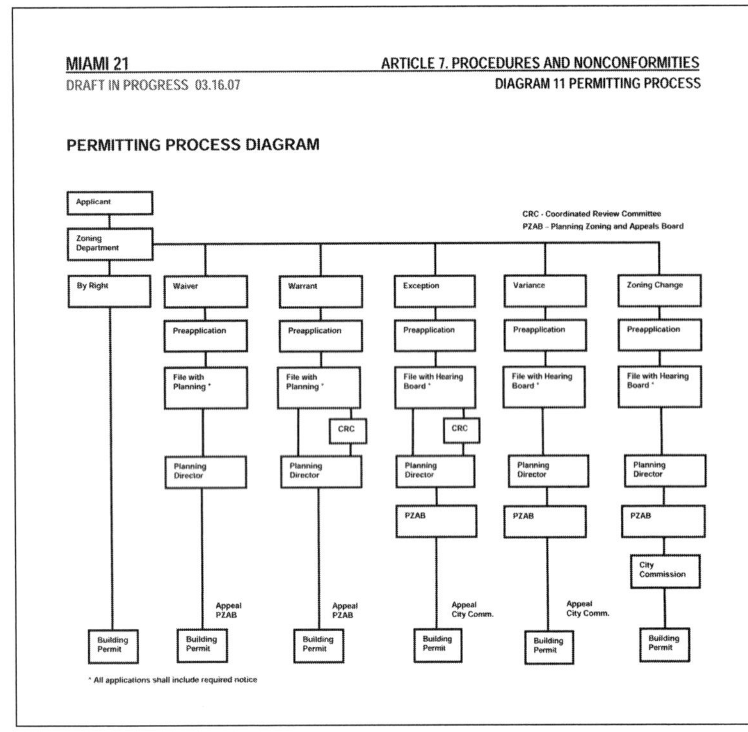


Table III-4. Summary of Approval Requirements

| Type of Decision | Development Code Reference (Municipal Code) | Role of Review Authority[1] | | | | |
|---|---|---|---|---|---|---|
| | | Director | HPC | DRC | PC | City Council |
| **Administrative and Legislative** | | | | | | |
| Interpretation | 8.10.070 | D | | | A | A |
| Development Agreement | (24.550) | R | | | R | D |
| Specific Plan Amendment | (24.555) | R | | | R | D |
| Zoning Change/Map Amendment | (24.540) | | Initiate[2] | | R | D |
| Development Code Amendment | | R | | | R | D |
| **Planning Permit/Development Approval** | | | | | | |
| Zoning Clearance | 8.10.040.F | D | | | A | A |
| Director's Permit | (24.505) | D | | | A | A |
| Planned Development Permit | (24.525) | R | | R | D | A |
| Uses Permitted by Right (P) | 8.10.040.F | D | | R[3] | A | A |
| Use Permit (U) | (24.520) | R | | | D | A |
| Administrative Coastal Development Permit[6] | (24.515) | D | | R | A | A |
| Coastal Development Permit (CDP) | (24.515) | | | R | D | A |
| Warrant | 8.10.050 | D | | | A | A |
| Exception | 8.10.050 | R | | | D | A |
| Design Review for Non-historic Resources | | | | | | |
| All new development in zones T5.1 and T6.1 | 5.10.020 | R | | D | A | A |
| All building types excluding Front Yard, Side Yard and Carriage Houses | 5.10.020 | R | | D | | |
| Additions and exterior changes to all structures providing non-residential use, except for structures with over 3 dwelling units, built prior to adoption of this Plan | 5.10.020 | R | | D | A | A |
| Design Review for Historic Resources[4] | | | | | | |
| Designation of a Historic Landmark, POI or District | (2.430) | R | R | | | D |
| Demolition of a Historic Resource | (2.430) | R | D | | A | A |
| Exterior additions or alterations to a Historic Resource | 8.10.040 | R | D | | A | A |
| New construction on property containing a Historic Resource | 8.10.040 | R | D | R | A | A |
| New construction on property contiguous to a Historic Resource | 8.10.040 | R | R | D | A | A |
| New residential construction of four units or fewer in Historic District Overlay Zones | (24.545) | R | D | | A | A |
| Flood Plain Overlay Zone Permit | (24.530) | D | | | A | A |
| Sign Permit | (24.420) | D[5] | | A | A | A |
| Access and Open Space Review | 8.10.040.L | D[5] | | A | A | A |

Notes:

1. "R" means that the Review Authority makes a Recommendation to a higher-level Review Authority, which can also be a decision-making body; "D" means that the Review Authority makes the final Decision on the matter; "A" (i.e., Appeal) means that the Review Authority may consider and decide upon the Decision of an earlier Review Authority/decision-making body, in compliance with Chapter 17.84 (Appeals) of the Municipal Code. See Review Authorities Defined, below
2. A proposed zone change may be initiated by the Planning commission or City council, or by application pursuant to section 24.500.030. A zone change to establish a Historic District Overlay Zone, or amend the boundaries thereof, may be initiated by the Historic Preservation Committee
3. Uses Permitted by Right ("P") may require Zoning Clearance if no Building Permit is required, and a Director's Permit if Design Review is required pursuant to any regulations within this Development Code.
4. Ordinary repair and replacement of Historic Resources does not require Design Review. See Definition of Historic Resource in Article IX. Glossary
5. The Director may defer action and refer the request to the Design Review Committee so that the Committee may instead make the decision.
6. In the case of a Warrant of Exception request.

**Review Authorities Defined:**

Director=Community Development Director  HPC=Historic Preservation Committee  DRC=Design Review Committee  PC=Planning Commission

City of San Buenaventura DOWNTOWN SPECIFIC PLAN
III-119

in ways similar to neighboring and other similarly situated properties. When allowed by a Form-Based Code, however, variances need additional mandatory "findings" to ensure that their approval will not circumvent the urban design intentions of the code and the community vision.

## Town Architect

Some Form-Based Codes require or recommend that the public agency hire a Town Architect (TA) to assist with the administration, more specifically the design review, of projects regulated by the Form-Based Code. In most instances, the TA is a consultant hired by the community to serve as an extension of its staff. Ideally, this should be a person or a firm who has participated in the community's visioning process, has an understanding of Form-Based Codes, understands New Urbanism and Smart Growth, and has good site-planning and architectural design sensibilities. Hiring a TA can help planning agencies with few staff to deal with the volume of review work that is likely after a Form-Based Code is adopted. The TA can also help train other city staff who will likely assist with FBC administration, as well as continue to educate elected and appointed officials. Appointing a TA may be no more expensive to the city than using a staff planner for development project review because the fees for the TA may be incorporated into the development application fees of each project.

Once appointed, the TA should work with the design team for each project early, often, and through the finest level of detail within the architecture. The idea is to be a resource for the developer/builder and team to help them get the project entitled as quickly as possible while ensuring the community's goals are met. Meeting before any time and money have been spent on design helps prevent the tension that occurs when a developer shows up to a meeting after spending tens of thousands of dollars on a design and is told that the design does not meet the FBC standards. As a project resource, TAs will often "roll up their sleeves" and have design sessions with a project's design team to ensure that the regulations within the code and the direction is clear. The TA will often work through issue areas directly with the team by drawing solutions on the spot. This review should continue through the creation of full architectural drawings, reviewing even the construction documents for design intent, and should include construction site visits to ensure the designs are being built as approved and that change orders are not being made to compromise the approved design.

The following are several points to remember in relation to a TA:

*Objective Role*

Clear standards should be in place to make TA project review as objective as possible. The true role of the TA is to enforce the standards established by the Form-Based Code; therefore, the FBC should be comprehensive in addressing the important details needed to enforce the vision. This will be primarily through the Building Form Standards, but should also include a clear intent within the Architectural Standards if a desired character is a strong component of a community's vision.

*Trusted Advisor*

The TA should have and build the trust and support of elected and appointed officials. In some instances, the TA will have the ability to approve the project administratively, but when that is not appropriate, will recommend approval or disapproval to the Planning Commission or other appointed committee. When this recommendation is made, the Planning Commission should have complete comfort in the decision made by the TA based on its support and trust that the TA is doing a good job. This support and relationship with the Planning Commission and City Council should be reinforced with frequent tours or projects being built that are pertinent to topics that are sure to arise in future review of projects, frequent presentations on similar topics, and even recent work of the TA, and occasionally workshops to address issues with current projects being reviewed.

*Clear Authority*

The TA should have clear authority to enforce the Form-Based Code. This will be tested by developers, and as soon as the authority of the TA is questioned or compromised, the review process will become ineffective.

*Single Point of Contact*

One person within a city's staff should be designated as the point of contact for the TA. The TA will be interfacing with all the different agencies within the city from public works, engineering, and planning, but should always know whom to call to discuss issues that arise.

*Meet Early and Often*

The TA should meet with a project's design team to initiate the project by reviewing the Form-Based Code and how it applied to the site. The different stages of review and what

**Authority for Proposal Review and Approval**

| | | Level of Review | | | |
|---|---|---|---|---|---|
| | | Staff & Town Architect (TA) | Planning Commission | | City Council |
| | | | Design Review Subcommittee | | |
| Type of Application | **Exception** | Approve | Information + Appeal | Information + Appeal | Information + Appeal |
| | **Design Review** | Approve | Information + Appeal | Information + Appeal | Information + Appeal |
| | **Conditional Use Permit** | Recommend | | Approve | Appeal |
| | **Variance** | Recommend | | Approve | Appeal |
| | **Parcel Maps** | Approve | | Appeal | Appeal |
| | **Subdivision Maps** | Recommend | | Approve | Appeal |
| | **Amendment** | Recommend | | Recommend | Approve |
| | **Policy Determination** | Recommend | | Recommend | Approve |

**Fig. 2.58** (far left, top) Miami 21 Permitting Process Table by DPZ

**Fig. 2.59** (far left, bottom) Table II-4: Roles of Various Review Bodies from the Downtown Ventura Specific Plan

**Fig. 2.60** (above) Authority for Proposal Review and Approval table from the Central Hercules Waterfront District by Dover, Kohl & Partners. Note the role of the Town Architect.

drawings are required for each stage should be discussed also.

*Project Guide*

The role of the TA is not to make a bad project good, but to make a bad project better or a good project great. The TA is a guide, not the project architect. The developer is responsible for hiring a team who can meet the intent of the FBC. If a developer has hired a design firm that just does not have the ability to do a good job, it is not the role of the TA to completely redesign the project. At some point, the decision makers may have to be able to tell a developer that it just does not have the right team to do the type of project that the community wants.

*Code Updates*

The TA should recommend code updates. Since the TA is using the code most often, he or she should make recommendation of changes, additions, and refinements to the code.

*Mistakes Happen*

Especially early on in the administration of an FBC, small things will slip through the cracks. This is common and should not be discouraging about the effectiveness of the process. The

## Review Process for Form-Based Codes

**by Kevin Klinkenberg**
*Principal,*
*180° Design Studio*

In communities that are striving to redevelop a neighborhood or downtown, a Form-Based Code tied to an expedited approval process can be an effective "incentive" for development, and even better, it does not require abatement of taxes or public subsidies—often thorny political issues.

Blue Springs, Missouri, is a case in point, with the Form-Based Code it adopted in April 2007. In an effort to jumpstart its languishing downtown, the city undertook a detailed master planning effort, with the new code as one important goal at the end of the process. The plan focused on the downtown core and a few surrounding residential streets, and had very specific design and policy suggestions for each block.

Key to the plan (and ultimately the code) was a thorough public involvement process. In this case, the city undertook a week-long design charrette, and multiple meetings before and after the charrette with the public and special interest groups. This type of outreach to elected officials, staff, and the public is critical to build the support necessary for doing things differently. Eliminating these steps, or doing only a few of them, runs the risk that the code never gets implemented.

The code itself then implements the plan by setting up a process that allows an appointed board (representatives of city staff, city council, planning commission, and property owners) to review and approve projects within two weeks, without a public hearing. Requested variances to the code are still reviewed by the Downtown Review Board, but they must also go through a lengthier process that requires a public hearing and the risk that entails.

In essence, this expedited process enables a property owner or developer (and the public) to have a high degree of predictability about a future investment. For example, each lot is assigned to a subzone that denotes certain building types that are preapproved, as well as rules on how the buildings meet the street. The rules are highly specific, noting the particular setback/build-to dimensions, height requirements, parking, and more, while still allowing some flexibility in design. In areas such as Blue Springs that have riskier market conditions, this element of predictability is a critical method that the jurisdiction can use to create incentive for development without dipping into its coffers.

team should continually refine the review process and communication to ensure that the same mistakes do not happen again.

## Nonconformities

Nonconformities are types and features of development that were "legal" when they were constructed—that is, they complied with all the zoning standards that applied to the site at the time of construction—but do not conform with some current standards because of more recent changes to the code itself. For example, a new Form-Based Code might allow only the "shopfront" frontage type within a particular downtown zone. The typical effect of such a change would be to prohibit the construction of a "front yard" frontage type building (including the replacement of an existing building) on the same site where one exists, the purpose being to implement the city's updated vision for the coded area as much as possible with each new development or redevelopment. A similar effect would result from a conventional zoning code update where the maximum building height limit was reduced: an existing building taller than the new height limit could not be reconstructed to its former height.

The manner in which a city treats nonconformities is an indicator of the extent and speed of the changes it hopes to achieve by updating its zoning code, which is the key public policy question raised by the issue of nonconformities. Some cities take a rigid approach toward nonconformities as described above: an existing nonconforming building cannot be replaced on its site unless the new building entirely conforms with the new zoning standards. Other cities require that nonconformities be corrected over a time period established and stated in the zoning code (a particularly problematic approach because of the institutional overhead required to track each nonconformity that must ultimately be resolved). Still others grant various case-by-case exceptions to the regulations for nonconformities to avoid imposing undue hardships on current property owners.

A new Form-Based Code brings the issue of physical nonconformities into sharper focus because its development standards and their precision are all intended to facilitate specific physical changes within the area being coded. A common question occurs where a Form-Based Code establishes a new BTL at the back of the sidewalk, but existing structures are set back farther. In this case, is it necessary for a redeveloped commercial site to have its buildings closer to the street than neighboring properties with development of the same age? The response to this question in a particular community will likely depend upon city perceptions of the demand for private redevelopment in the specific area in relation to the extent of change anticipated by the planning and coding effort in the area. All of this being said, it should be noted that nonconformities created by a Form-Based Code raise the same issues as any conventional code update that involves changes to physical development standards, so this should not be an issue that slows or hinders the implementation of a Form-Based Code. It is simply necessary for city decision makers to determine the degree of flexibility that they wish to provide physical nonconformities and for the new code to reflect their determination.

# 3 / Process

A CRITICAL ELEMENT for ensuring that a Form-Based Code (FBC) will appropriately and effectively regulate is the process by which it is created. This process distinguishes FBCs from conventional zoning codes as much as their substance.

As the process is described here, it appears neatly laid out in logical order. But any planner or other citizen who has participated in a community-planning project knows that the process itself is rarely so orderly. The technical terms that probably best describe how a typical planning process flows are iterative and recursive. That is, information gained in one step of the process may cause an earlier step to be revisited and its conclusions reexamined, and some steps may be repeated. The nontechnical term that best describes how a planning process works, particularly in a community polarized over growth and development issues, may be train wreck.

Before the official process can begin, certain decisions about the process and the project need to be made. Once these are made, the actual coding process involves three major steps: Documenting, Visioning, and Assembling the Code. (See Figure 3.1.)

**Pre–Phase 1: Scoping**

The overall process begins by making initial decisions about the size and extent of the coding project, including who will be involved, which areas of the community will be included in the code, which components of the code might be necessary, and how the code might fit in with the existing regulatory framework.

**Phase 1: Documenting**

The coding process begins by studying and documenting exemplary existing conditions in the community as well as the existing planning regulations in order to thoroughly understand the

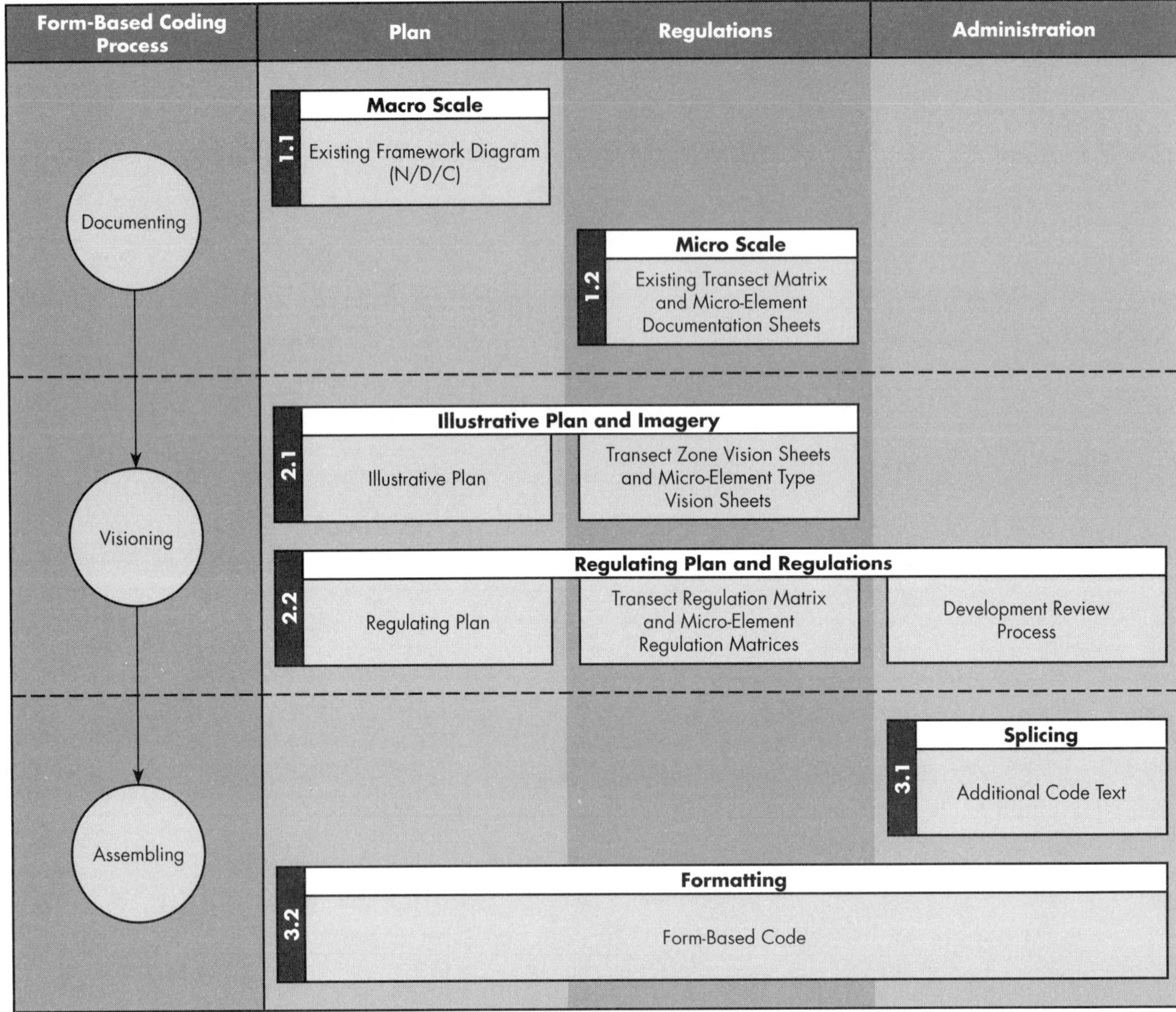


**Fig. 3.1**
Process for creating a Form-Based Code

existing place. This is critical to ensure that the vision and the code are appropriate for the community. In addition, the details of the places the community selects to emulate become the base regulatory details or DNA of the code. The Existing Framework Diagram, which documents the existing neighborhoods, districts, and corridors, is the basis for the Illustrative Plan, which ultimately is transformed into the code's Regulating Plan. The Existing Transect Matrix, which categorizes the existing areas according to the rural-to-urban transect and documents the details that make up these areas, is the basis for the regulations in the code's Building Form Standards. The other existing conditions matrices, such as the Existing Building Types Matrix and the Existing Streets Matrix, are the basis for the other regulations in the code.

### Phase 2: Visioning

Since a Form-Based Code is a prescriptive document, it needs a detailed vision to prescribe. Using the gathered information from the documentation phase as a base, the team and stakeholders work together to create a Vision Plan, a detailed vision for the future of the community. The Vision Plan includes an Illustrative Plan, a variety of three-dimensional renderings, and descriptive text to express the intentions of the vision. The Existing Framework Diagram is transformed into the Illustrative Plan by adjusting existing neighborhoods, districts, streets, blocks, and lots and adding new ones based upon the goals of the community.

In addition, in order to be detailed enough to enable the creation of a Form-Based Code, the Vision Plan should also include the preliminary versions of the Regulating Plan, Regulation Matrix, and Development Review Process. Developing these is a visioning process in and of itself, refining the vision to the level necessary for an FBC using the Illustrative Plan and micro-element documentation information as a base. Finally, the development application review process is drafted based on the desires of the community to ensure or even create incentives for development that implements the community's vision.

**Phase 3: Assembling**

Once the Form-Based Code regulations have been drafted, any additional regulations necessary to tie the code into the existing regulatory framework are drafted. Finally, the content is formatted into the final code document to ensure the code is clear, concise, and easy to use.

Following is a detailed description of each process phase.

# Pre–Phase 1: Scoping

A COMMUNITY CONSIDERING a Form-Based Code needs to make a variety of choices at the outset that will both shape the process for drafting the code and determine its content, including selecting the coding team, the process, the area to be affected, the implementation method, and the overall coding approach. These decisions will impact the success of the code before code writing has even begun, so they should be considered carefully.

## Assembling the Team

Among the powerful distinctions between the preparation of a Form-Based Code and a conventional code is that the Form-Based Coding process addresses both the short- and long-term interests of all the specialized disciplines that need to work in concert to create and maintain the framework for the evolution of a city. This occurs in two ways. First, key municipal departmental professionals (for example, public works, police, fire, parks and recreation, and the like) are included in the community visioning, charrette, and other parts of the code drafting and review process. At the same time, various consultants are typically engaged to augment the expertise of city personnel. Depending upon the overall focus and objectives of the planning and coding effort, (e.g., downtown revitalization, neighborhood preservation, or new neighborhood creation through greenfield development), the specialized professional disciplines that may be needed in Form-Based Code preparation could include several of the following: planning; architecture; urban design; landscape architecture; traffic analysis; economics, retail, and housing market analysis; fiscal analysis and municipal finance; environmental resource analysis; civil engineering; parking program design; historic resources preservation; visual simulation; legal support; graphic design; public participation; and charrette management.

It is important to note that each of these disciplines will not be essential in every Form-Based Coding project. The list is intended to comprehensively identify most, if not all, of the possibilities, so that a community embarking on a Form-Based Coding effort may have the opportunity to consider carefully which expertise is necessary to the completion of its Form-Based Code, which expertise would be helpful if time and funding permit, and which is not necessary given the scope and intent of the particular code. Often, it may be possible for current city staff to perform some of the work described above. It is also not uncommon for a team member representing one of the above specialties to be expert in one or more others as well.

## Selecting the Process

On the process side, the primary decisions regarding the scope of the coding effort relate to how the community visioning and other components of the public participation process will be configured. Because a fundamental reason for a community to prepare a Form-Based Code is to most effectively implement clear and specific community urban design intentions for the area being coded, it follows that clear and specific intentions must first be described. If the urban design intentions are indeed to reflect the aspirations of the *community*, as many segments of the community as possible should be involved in their description.

This need results in one of the most interesting differences between the preparation or update of a conventional zoning code and a Form-Based Code. That is, Form-Based Coding typically integrates a *planning* process with the drafting of specific rules for development. In contrast, preparing or updating a conventional zoning code typically focuses mostly on drafting regulations, with "planning" limited simply to the review and consideration of the most recently adopted community plan covering the same area, in terms of ensuring that regulations in the code are "consistent" with adopted plan policies. Unfortunately, the policies usually address issues unrelated to providing a clear urban design foundation for the code, such as the amount of land to be zoned for commercial development versus housing, which implies only gross differences in physical character and says nothing about the details of the public realm and how it is to be shaped by private development and public street and streetscape improvements.

This situation is a consequence of how state laws across the country structure local planning and zoning. Commonly, a two-part process is anticipated, where a municipality first prepares a "comprehensive" or "general" plan that covers all land area within the jurisdiction. Then (sometimes years) later, the community updates the zoning code to make it consistent with the plan. State planning mandates do not normally prevent a community from simultaneously updating its comprehensive plan and zoning code. But the range or nature of topics the state requires to be addressed in the plan, and/or particularly controversial local issues that need attention, can sufficiently complicate the logistics and increase the cost of a plan update, so cities most often choose to update the plan and code separately.

Depending upon the state, specific contents of the plan may be mandated or not. California, Oregon, Florida, Arizona, Texas, and a few other states specify various mandatory details for comprehensive plan content, while others simply require that a plan be prepared. Still others enable, but do not require, that plans be prepared or that zoning be used at all. As an example of state-mandated content, California requires that "general plans" explicitly address the issues of land use, housing, circulation, open space, noise, safety, and conservation. Notably lacking from state mandates, and from most comprehensive plans even where the state allows topics in addition to those mandated to be addressed at the option of a city, is any specific discussion of the community's urban design preferences or vision.

Increasingly, cities have come to realize that the lack of distinct physical identity and quality and the prevalence of monotony in the public realm are not only a consequence of ineffective conventional zoning regulations, but also a result of inadequate community attention to urban design in the overall planning process. In response, Form-Based Coding practitioners have developed and are evolving public participation and visioning techniques that can identify the community's urban design preferences in both planning and coding. While a "conventional" state-mandated planning process can, if allowed by the particular state, incorporate effective attention to urban design, (i.e., by including an urban design element or chapter in the comprehensive plan detailing desired distinctions in the character of the public realm as shaped by private development and in different parts of the city as a foundation for the code), the preparation of Form-Based Codes that are not preceded by a clear and sufficiently detailed community vision defined through other means instead accomplish the "planning" side of the exercise as an integrated component of code preparation itself.

This planning process has several purposes: to identify and document the existing physical character of the area being coded; to engage the public in the exploration and review of alternatives to the existing physical character, usually through a charrette; to describe the preferred physical character of the different places within the coded area in illustrations that clearly show how the public realm and private development will appear if the community vision is implemented; and finally, to prepare a Regulating Plan and draft the regulations. As noted in Chapter 1, the Regulating Plan identifies property boundaries between areas where differences in physical character are to occur and, therefore, where regulations for development in the Form-Based Code must differ in order to produce the intended variations in character. The details of this planning process are described later in this chapter.

Community choices between a conventional planning process with an added emphasis on urban design versus Form-Based Coding with an integrated planning and visioning process should be based upon several factors: the timing of the most recent comprehensive plan update and whether the update included sufficient community engagement and resulting urban design details in the plan; the nature of applicable state mandates and enabling legislation; and the amount of funding available for the work.

## Determining the Application Area

The options available to a community for the scope of a Form-Based Coding effort that will ultimately affect the regulatory content and effect of the code include determining the areas to be coded and the degrees of change desired. Inevitably, and properly, a number of these choices will be revisited during a community charrette and at other points during code preparation, but they should at least be considered and tentative choices made among them at the outset.

### Area to Be Coded

To date, Form-Based Coding techniques have been applied at a variety of scales: to downtowns and other specific, limited areas within cities, such as deteriorating strip commercial corridors, "dead" big-box shopping centers, one or more undeveloped "greenfield" areas adjacent to a city that are intended to accommodate growth, or existing neighborhoods or other developed areas where infill development is intended to preserve or extend existing patterns of physical character; to entire cities; and to regions that include at the time of coding both urban areas and countryside.

A city's initial choice about the area to be covered by a Form-Based Code may depend on some of the same factors described above on how to choose among public participation and visioning process alternatives, but also on whether there is a perceived need to revitalize particular areas, including reversing existing conditions of blight, or to take advantage of opportunities for the improvement of areas within the city related to changes in land ownership, parallel city plans to renovate existing street improvements or other infrastructure, and/or the availability of limited-term grants or other funding. As will be discussed regarding implementation options below, some cities have also chosen to apply Form-Based Coding to limited areas in response to political uncertainty about the desirability of Form-Based Coding in the city "by taking a small bite first," and/or to create a "pilot project" that will provide an opportunity for city staff and appointed and elected officials to gain experience in the administration of and achieving success with a Form-Based Code before applying the techniques to more extensive areas or to the entire city.

### Degrees of Change

An important part of the dialog about Form-Based Coding must necessarily be the extent of physical change that is expected and desired over time in different areas of the city. This is because physical planning, related urban design decisions, and Form-Based Coding are all fundamentally about managing change within a city. Cities will often include areas that residents love as they are in a planning and coding effort, and other areas where varying degrees of change are desired. These issues are addressed in Form-Based Coding at all stages of the preparation process, first in the documentation phase, and finally in the substance of the detailed urban and architectural standards for each area to which Form-Based Coding is applied. As communities consider physical change, the following list identifies the continuum of change that may be desired, and that a community may wish to effect through Form-Based Coding:

*Preservation*

The community is satisfied with and actively wants to retain the existing physical character of one or more neighborhoods, a downtown, or other area with distinct identity, historical or otherwise, and to ensure that infill and replacement development "fits in" with the established physical character of its context and does nothing to change that character.

*Preservation and Enhancement*

The community wants to retain the established physical character in one or more areas, but is interested in carefully conceived and targeted enhancements to them, which could be in the form of private property developments, or changes to the public realm constructed by the city.

*Evolution*

The community is interested in seeing physical change within the planning area over time, but is willing to allow change in compliance with the city's vision to occur primarily according to the timing needs and investment expectations of individual property owners within the planning area.

*Transformation*

The community wants to see desired physical change occur within the shortest possible time, so it wants Form-Based Coding to be as effective as possible in facilitating change, and is also willing to pursue other measures toward the same ends. These may include, for example, such development incentives as housing density bonuses, accelerated development application processing, street and streetscape (public realm) improvements undertaken by the municipality, and/or more rigorous code enforcement programs.

The desired extent of physical change identified through the public participation process will inform several aspects of code content, particularly Building Form Standards, frontage and building type standards, and the nature of the process for development review and approval.

## Determining the Implementation Method

Communities that find the concepts of Form-Based Coding of interest can consider several different methods of introducing these types of regulations into an established zoning and permitting system. Ultimately, the adoption of a Form-Based Code is a legislative act that requires the same type of public process as the adoption of any other plan or zoning regulation under applicable state laws, and may involve environmental review if required in the applicable state, one or more planning commission public hearings concluding with a recommendation to the local legislative body (city or town council, board of supervisors or commissioners, or the like), and one or more legislative body public hearings prior to their adoption of the regulations. Within that framework, the following alternative approaches are possible.

### Comprehensive Replacement of Existing Code (Mandatory and Freestanding)

The Form-Based Code replaces the preexisting conventional zoning code for all or part of a community, and all development within the FBCs defined application area must abide by the regulations in it.

The comprehensive replacement of an existing conventional code with a Form-Based Code creates the greatest range of opportunities for transforming targeted areas of a community while maintaining established character in others. This approach is less expensive in smaller communities than larger (as would be any conventional planning process) and also offers the advantage of any changes in regulatory vocabulary and procedures being consistent throughout the code.

### Optional/Parallel and Freestanding

The FBC is created as a standalone code but does not replace the preexisting conventional zoning code. Instead, in specific areas defined in the FBC and for project sites meeting certain specified minimum requirements (for example, 20 acres, or at least one urban block), the developer is given the choice to build under the preexisting conventional zoning code or the new Form-Based Code. The property does not have to be rezoned, but once the developer chooses a code, the entire development project must abide by it.

This method of FBC application could result in a development that is incrementally more effective at implementing the community's desired urban vision because developers will generally face a more predictable and straightforward permit process under a Form-Based Code, and the range of possible development types available to them under the FBC can be both more cost-effective to build and more marketable than those allowed by the conventional code, depending upon the particular city. However, given the complexity of planning and zoning administration generally, this approach should be considered carefully. The challenges of administering even a single zoning code are significant, and the potential for two codes to create confusion about the community's commitment to the requirements, preferences, and principles reflected in the Form-Based Code may result in development applicants attempting to pick and choose only those most beneficial to their interests, unless the terms under which each code may apply are absolutely clear.

#### Pilot Projects

A variety of cities have explored and gained experience with Form-Based Coding through a pilot project focused on a limited area. A pilot project could be executed in the form of any of the three following approaches.

#### Specific Plans and Other Limited Area Complete Codes

Certain states, such as California, Arizona, and Pennsylvania, allow this type of regulatory document (which is a subgroup of "Mandatory and Freestanding") in order to supplement broader general plans. A local government or a developer wishing to regulate a walkable, mixed-use community that is not permissible under the current zoning code prepares a Form-Based Code (including a Regulating Plan) for the area and submits it through the designated Specific Plan process to have it approved. The property does not have to be rezoned, but once approved, the Specific Plan FBC replaces the preexisting conventional zoning code regulations for the defined area.

Specific plans have been used in a number of California communities to provide a Form-Based Code for a particular area (e.g., a downtown), either as a pilot project, one of a series of plans and Form-Based Codes covering several individual places within the city, or as the only intended implementation of Form-Based Coding in the city.

#### Embedded "Form-Based Zones" (Mandatory and Integrated)

The preexisting conventional zoning code is updated by adding new Form-Based Zones with appropriate FBC regulations. The zoning map is also revised (or a new Regulating Plan is created), and certain areas are rezoned to the new Form-Based Zones. Within these areas, any and all development must abide by the new regulations for the Form-Based Zones. In addition, other regulations, such as a streamlined project approval process, may be added to the conventional zoning code, to be applicable only to areas in the new Form-Based Zones.

In this "hybrid code" example, the "conventional" zones and related standards of the existing code are retained in areas of the community that are not rezoned. This approach of introducing a few Form-Based Zones into a conventional code could be an effective pilot project in the phased replacement of an existing code, as well as an effective way of responding to near-term pressures for physical change in "sensitive" areas of the community. While this may not ultimately be as desirable as the comprehensive replacement of the existing code described above, it may be the only one feasible in a community that, for any number of reasons (including funding and time limitations), wants to move into the field gradually.

#### Floating Zone/Traditional Neighborhood Development

The preexisting conventional zoning code is updated by adding a single new zone. (It may be called a Traditional Neighborhood Development [TND] zone, or something similar.) The new zone has an FBC embedded within its regulations, including a number of Form-Based Subzones and their accompanying regulations, but typically does not include a Regulating Plan and is not yet applied to any areas on the zoning map (which is why it is a "floating" zone). A developer wishing to build under this FBC applies the Form-Based Subzones to create a Regulating Plan for the property and submits it through the designated process to have the property rezoned to the new TND zone. If approved, the property is rezoned to the TND zone with the submitted Regulating Plan attached as part of the rezoning.

An alternative but similar system requires the property owner request to have the property rezoned to the new TND zone first, to grant the initial authority to use the FBC for the project area. Regulating Plans are created later for specific parts of the project area as individual developments are proposed, reviewed, and approved.

### Floating Zone/Planned Unit Development

The preexisting conventional zoning code already has a floating zone, such as a Planned Unit Development (PUD) or Planned Development (PD) zone with virtually no requirements. A developer wishing to create a walkable, mixed-use community that is not permissible under the current zoning code prepares an FBC (including a Regulating Plan) for the property and submits it through the designated process to have the property rezoned to the new PUD zone. If approved, the property is rezoned to the PUD zone with the submitted FBC attached as part of the rezoning.

This is not actually a method for implementing FBCs, but it has been used successfully under conventional zoning codes by developers wanting to create walkable, mixed-use communities.

## Selecting an Approach to Coding

Even though Form-Based Codes have been prepared and used for a brief time in comparison with conventional zoning, there are a number of variations in practice that may be considered as workable differences in the overall approach to coding.

### Organizing Principle

The first group of choices regarding the coding approach is about the "organizing principle" used as the basis for the Regulating Plan. As described earlier, Form-Based Coding practitioners have used at least four different approaches to date to structure Regulating Plans by identifying distinct areas where different code standards will apply. Some practitioners have divided coded areas into "neighborhoods, districts, and corridors," which mirror some of the key features of urbanism identified by the Charter of the New Urbanism. Others have created Regulating Plans based on the types of thoroughfares or street frontages planned within the area being coded, where design and development standards then differ depending on the type of thoroughfare or frontage applicable to the site. Small-scale, named zones, have been used to apply Form-Based Coding standards when one or very few areas within a city are being regulated separately from the adjacent urban fabric.

Currently, the transect is the most commonly used organizing principle because it is the most effective and flexible method of addressing multiple areas within a city where development standards are to differ, and because it is highly intuitive in terms of how all components of urbanism (building and thoroughfare types, use types, landscape, and so on) should be allocated to specific transect zones based on their intensity. Choosing an organizing principle for a Regulating Plan other than the transect should be based on the size of the area to be subject to the code, whether the code is intended to cover multiple areas within city, and whether there has been earlier Form-Based Coding that is being extended into the areas currently being considered.

### Templates

The second group of choices regarding the approach to coding is interrelated and involves the type of code document itself, in terms of both the organization and the format and overall presentation of the code. Alternatives include whether the code and its standards are designed and developed locally, or are based on a predetermined "template" that has been used and proven elsewhere and that can be appropriately and effectively customized to serve local needs.

*The SmartCode*

The most notable currently available code template is the SmartCode, initially designed and written by Duany Plater-Zyberk & Company (DPZ) of Miami, and which has since undergone continual refinement, both by DPZ and its associates, and by the communities that have considered and adopted the code.

The SmartCode is a comprehensive, transect-based FBC that includes model standards and requirements for multiple scales of development by both the public and the private sectors, as well as administrative procedures for development review and approval. Many Mississippi communities are currently using it as a tool for implementing vision plans created as part of the post-Katrina "Mississippi Renewal" planning efforts, and in its largest implementation to date, it is being used as the basis for a new development code for the City of Miami, Florida.

As a template, the SmartCode is intended to be rigorously customized to the Form-Based Coding needs of each community considering its use. At minimum, after the preparation of a Regulating Plan, SmartCode customization must include the modification of administrative procedures as necessary to comply with applicable state law requirements and local regulations, and the adjustment of its model standards to ensure that proposed development is appropriate to the local area and effectively implements the community's vision as represented by the Regulating Plan.

The SmartCode can then also be customized in a variety of other ways. Some of these are anticipated by the template itself (in some cases, for example, it provides more than one version of a graphic illustrating the application of the same regulations for a city to choose from). Other aspects of SmartCode customization may include its organization and format, as well as the selection of the various components of the template that are to be used in the local code calibration (for example, whether the "Sector Plans" chapter will be included in a city's version of the code). The SmartCode template, incorporating a manual for its calibration and use, is available for download and use without charge at www.smartcodefiles.com. For examples of its implementation, see the case studies for Montgomery, Alabama; Leander, Texas; and Miami, Florida.

*Other Templates*

Depending on the preferences of the city pursuing Form-Based Coding, other Form-Based Code "templates" in addition to the SmartCode may be considered because any consultant team that has prepared more than three Form-Based Codes likely has at least one template itself. This is because a zoning code author's first code drafting experience is likely to be a bit of an experiment; his or her second code works to (among other things) correct the shortcomings of, and refine the formatting, usability, and effectiveness of, the first in the context of the second client jurisdiction; and, unless the needs of each client have been substantially different, his or her third completed code provides a model in terms of format, nomenclature, and standards that may be effectively and appropriately adapted for use in other communities, assuming adequate skill, experience, and dedication on the part of the author, as well as the necessary attention to detail.

*Selecting a Template*

A decision about whether to use a template, such as the SmartCode, may be based on several factors. As noted earlier, if Form-Based Coding is to be applied only to areas within a city so limited that more than one transect level cannot be identified within them, a transect-based solution, such as the SmartCode, may not be necessary. Beyond that issue, the remaining questions about whether to use a certain template involve the level of effort required to customize and calibrate the code template to local conditions and needs, versus that implied by other types of code documents (given that any existing code template must be calibrated and customized), and the extent to which local officials (particularly city attorneys) are confident that the template can be sufficiently calibrated and customized to comply with applicable state law requirements, including where required, consistency with the city's comprehensive plan. (Currently, this is largely not a serious issue as more Form-Based Codes, including SmartCodes, are adopted and more city attorneys become familiar with the platform.)

*Customizing and Calibrating a Template*

It is important to note here that "customization" is not the same as "calibration." Calibration is adapting and revising substantive template or other model development standards to serve local needs effectively, while customization is both modifying the format, organization, and graphic design of the template, and editing the text to improve clarity and eliminate ambiguity, to serve the information retrieval needs of code users as they are identified by local officials. Specific customization and calibration issues that should be considered by a city interested in using a template include the following, recognizing that the SmartCode and other templates can typically be calibrated and/or customized in any manner desired by a jurisdiction interested in using them:

- **Overall format, page format:** A code template should be compared to the principles for code formatting found later in this section, and the city should determine whether it wishes to implement some or all of those principles and recommendations in its new code.
- **Nomenclature:** If the template uses terminology in its standards that is different from that commonly found in other city development regulations, the city may wish to consider whether template nomenclature or citywide code nomenclature should be changed, or whether they may coexist. For example, the SmartCode refers to "building disposition," while a term such as "building placement" may be more intuitive to those who regularly work with codes, as well as to the general public.
- **Scope of development standards:** A calibration issue related to the scope of the standards in a template is that the template may not provide standards that address some development issues that the community has found to be problematic or now wishes to address. The code team will need to add regulations to address such local issues.
- **Organization:** The organization of the code should be optimized for use by project designers and municipal development project reviewers who most commonly need to access code information in a particular order: (1) what type of development and use is allowed on an individual lot (so that the owner can readily determine if the type of development project is possible at all); (2) what are the basic standards that define the limits of a building that may be located on the individual lot; (3) what other applicable devel-

opment standards will affect the project and program (for example, parking, landscaping, and sign standards, as well as any standards that may address the location, design, and operation of the specific proposed land-use type); and finally, (4) administrative and procedural provisions, which are typically the least used components in day-to-day code administration. Because the SmartCode is designed to serve as a template for the planning and regulation of development at scales ranging from the region to the individual lot, its default overall organization instead first presents its administrative provisions, then the provisions for the preparation of Sector Scale Plans, New Community Scale Plans, Existing Community Scale Plans, Building Scale Plans (which include the sections that regulate the development of individual lots), Standards and Tables, and finally, Definitions of Terms.

- **Graphics:** To help illustrate the meaning and applicability of its model standards, there should be graphics that are simple, crisp, and readable; however, they, too, need to be calibrated to illustrate the physical character objectives of the subject community. In some cases, it may be useful to augment them with photographs that show urban design conditions similar or identical to those that the community hopes to achieve. See more on formatting graphics later in this section.
- **Administration:** The SmartCode introduces a permit type called a "warrant," and also notes that "variances" are to be used in specific circumstances. The titles and use of these discretionary review procedures may need to be changed in a particular code calibration to make them consistent with applicable state law and local practice. For example, Table 10 (Building Function-Specific) allows some land-use types in some zones only with the approval of a variance. This is contrary to planning and zoning law in some states, such as California, where "land-use variances" are prohibited; so the template will simply need to be modified in these instances. (See Figure 3.2.)

SMARTCODE — TABLE 10 BUILDING FUNCTION-SPECIFIC

*municipality*

| | T1 | T2 | T3 | T4 | T5 | T6 | SD |
|---|---|---|---|---|---|---|---|
| **a. RESIDENTIAL** | | | | | | | |
| Apartment Building | | | | ■ | ■ | ■ | |
| Row House | | | | ■ | ■ | ■ | |
| Duplex House | | | | ■ | ■ | | |
| Sideyard House | | | ■ | ■ | ■ | | |
| Cottage | | | ■ | ■ | | | |
| House | | ■ | ■ | ■ | | | |
| Estate House | | ■ | | | | | |
| Accessory Unit | | ■ | ■ | ■ | ■ | | |
| Manufactured House | | | □ | | | | □ |
| Temporary Tent | □ | □ | □ | □ | □ | □ | □ |
| Live-Work Unit | | | ■ | ■ | ■ | ■ | □ |
| **b. LODGING** | | | | | | | |
| Hotel (no room limit) | | | | | ■ | ■ | □ |
| Inn (up to 12 rooms) | | □ | | ■ | ■ | ■ | |
| Inn (up to 5 rooms) | | □ | ■ | ■ | ■ | ■ | |
| S.R.O. hostel | | | □ | □ | □ | □ | □ |
| School Dormitory | | | | ■ | ■ | ■ | ■ |
| **c. OFFICE** | | | | | | | |
| Office Building | | | | ■ | ■ | ■ | □ |
| Live-Work Unit | | | ■ | ■ | ■ | ■ | □ |
| **d. RETAIL** | | | | | | | |
| Open-Market Building | | ■ | ■ | ■ | ■ | ■ | ■ |
| Retail Building | | | | ■ | ■ | ■ | □ |
| Display Gallery | | | | ■ | ■ | ■ | □ |
| Restaurant | | | | ■ | ■ | ■ | □ |
| Kiosk | | | | ■ | ■ | ■ | □ |
| Push Cart | | | | | □ | □ | □ |
| Liquor Selling Establishment | | | | | □ | □ | □ |
| Adult Entertainment | | | | | | □ | □ |
| **e. CIVIC** | | | | | | | |
| Bus Shelter | | | ■ | ■ | ■ | ■ | ■ |
| Convention Center | | | | | | □ | ■ |
| Conference Center | | | | | □ | ■ | ■ |
| Exhibition Center | | | | | | □ | ■ |
| Fountain or Public Art | | ■ | ■ | ■ | ■ | ■ | ■ |
| Library | | | | ■ | ■ | ■ | ■ |
| Live Theater | | | | | ■ | ■ | ■ |
| Movie Theater | | | | | ■ | ■ | ■ |
| Museum | | | | | □ | ■ | ■ |
| Outdoor Auditorium | | □ | ■ | | ■ | ■ | ■ |
| Parking Structure | | | | | ■ | ■ | ■ |
| Passenger Terminal | | | | | □ | □ | ■ |
| Playground | | ■ | ■ | ■ | ■ | ■ | ■ |
| Sports Stadium | | | | | | □ | ■ |
| Surface Parking Lot | | | | □ | □ | □ | ■ |
| Religious Assembly | | | | | ■ | ■ | ■ |
| **f. OTHER: AGRICULTURE** | | | | | | | |
| Grain Storage | ■ | ■ | | | | | □ |
| Livestock Pen | □ | □ | | | | | □ |
| Greenhouse | ■ | ■ | □ | | | | □ |
| Stable | ■ | ■ | □ | | | | □ |
| Kennel | ■ | ■ | □ | □ | □ | □ | □ |
| **f. OTHER: AUTOMOTIVE** | | | | | | | |
| Gasoline | | □ | | | □ | □ | ■ |
| Automobile Service | | | | | | | ■ |
| Truck Maintenance | | | | | | | ■ |
| Drive -Through Facility | | | | | □ | □ | ■ |
| Rest Stop | ■ | ■ | | | | | □ |
| Roadside Stand | ■ | ■ | | | | | □ |
| Billboard | | | | | | □ | □ |
| Shopping Center | | | | | | | □ |
| Shopping Mall | | | | | | | □ |
| **f. OTHER: CIVIL SUPPORT** | | | | | | | |
| Fire Station | | | ■ | ■ | ■ | ■ | ■ |
| Police Station | | | | ■ | ■ | ■ | ■ |
| Cemetery | | ■ | □ | □ | | | ■ |
| Funeral Home | | | | ■ | ■ | ■ | ■ |
| Hospital | | | | | □ | □ | ■ |
| Medical Clinic | | | | □ | ■ | ■ | ■ |
| **f. OTHER: EDUCATION** | | | | | | | |
| College | | | | | □ | □ | ■ |
| High School | | | | □ | □ | □ | ■ |
| Trade School | | | | | □ | □ | ■ |
| Elementary School | | | □ | ■ | ■ | ■ | ■ |
| Other- Childcare Center | | ■ | ■ | ■ | ■ | ■ | □ |
| **f. OTHER: INDUSTRIAL** | | | | | | | |
| Heavy Industrial Facility | | | | | | | ■ |
| Light Industrial Facility | | | | | | □ | ■ |
| Truck Depot | | | | | | | ■ |
| Laboratory Facility | | | | | | □ | ■ |
| Water Supply Facility | | | | | | | ■ |
| Sewer and Waste Facility | | | | | | | ■ |
| Electric Substation | □ | □ | □ | □ | □ | □ | ■ |
| Wireless Transmitter | □ | □ | | | | | ■ |
| Cremation Facility | | | | | | | ■ |
| Warehouse | | | | | | □ | ■ |
| Produce Storage | | | | | | | ■ |
| Mini-Storage | | | | | | | ■ |

■ BY RIGHT
□ BY VARIANCE

SC123

**Fig. 3.2** SmartCode building functions (Credit: DPZ)

# Phase 1: Documenting

One of the differences between Form-Based Codes and conventional development regulations is that FBCs are "place-specific" or "place-based" codes. FBCs enable and require development to build upon and strengthen the unique characteristics of a community, helping preserve the character of place and reducing or eliminating development that is devoid of character or quality. Even FBCs for greenfield sites should be based on local or regional precedent, ensuring that the new site's patterns relate to and tie into the surrounding community.

Contrary to popular belief, the unique character of most communities is not primarily established by architectural style, but rather by urban and community patterns. These patterns include lot sizes, thoroughfare design and layout, character, quality and location of public spaces, sizes and types of buildings, and relationships to such natural conditions as creek corridors and topography. By documenting the existing conditions in detail before beginning an FBC, the team gathers the information necessary to thoroughly understand the unique characteristics of the place. This enables the team to create an FBC that reinforces and builds on these unique characteristics of the place, rather than on generic or suburban characteristics that are the basis for conventional codes.

In order for the documentation to be effective in directing a Form-Based Code, it should go far beyond simply taking photographs and include a thorough analysis of a community's urban form at both a macro scale and a micro scale. This analysis includes in-the-field sketching and documentation, as well as in-office creation and analysis of drawings.

The information from the documentation process helps reintroduce an urban design component into the development regulations in two ways. First, at the macro scale, it provides a basis for understanding the framework of the existing place to inform the Vision Plan and Regulating Plan framework. Second, at the micro scale, it provides the detailed measurements for the first draft of the FBC, which will then be modified during the visioning and coding phases.

The basic elements to be considered at the macro scale are neighborhoods, districts, and corridors. These elements reinforce the overall framework of neighborhoods, towns, cities, and open spaces. The minimum elements to be considered at the micro scale are thoroughfares, buildings (form, placement, frontages, types, and use), lots and blocks, and civic spaces (parks and plazas). Additional elements, such as architecture and landscaping, may be also considered, depending on their influence on the character of the place as well as the community's interest in regulating them. These elements establish the content for the standards.

The details of the elements at both the macro and the micro scales define the character and quality of the community. They should be carefully documented because small differences in these details can have a big impact. For instance, an additional one or two feet in a thoroughfare's travel lane can increase the speed of traffic; one foot less on a finished floor height of a townhouse can reduce privacy within the home; and one foot less depth on a porch or stoop can make it unusable for anything besides getting into and out of a house.

## Process Overview

The overall process for documenting a place centers on two primary site visits. (See Figure 3.3.) The first site visit is to document the macro elements: the neighborhoods, districts, and corridors. In addition, during this site visit, the team starts creating lists of observed micro-

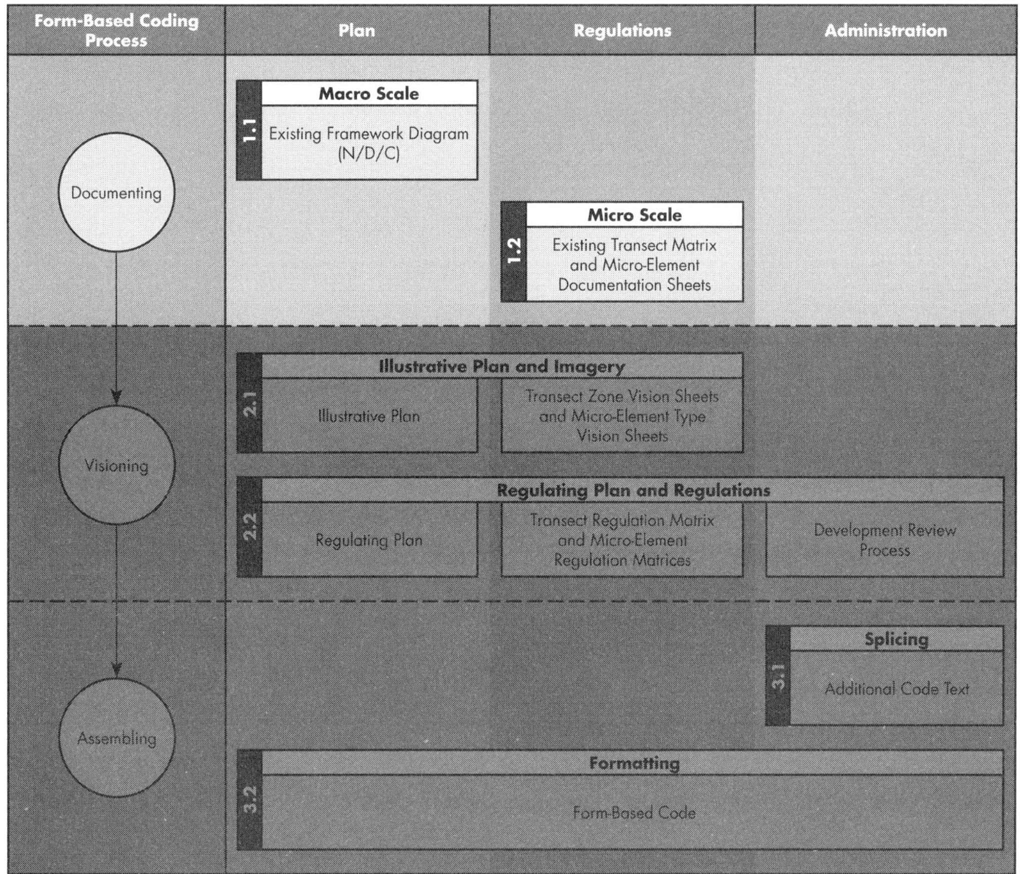


**Fig. 3.3**
Phase 1: Documenting

element types, such as thoroughfare types and building types, that will help them determine what needs to be documented during the second site visit.

The second site visit is to document the micro elements, such as building form and placement details, building types, frontage types, thoroughfare types, and park types. Once both site visits are complete, the team organizes and analyzes the gathered information to provide a basis for the visioning and coding phases.

By the end of the documentation phase, the team will have the following products:

- Existing Conditions Base Map(s)
- Existing Framework Diagram, showing neighborhoods, districts, and corridors
- Existing Transect Matrix, showing the various transect levels
- Presentation boards for each micro-element sample (thoroughfares, civic spaces, and frontage types, as well as any other components desired by the community, such as building types and architectural styles), including photos, maps, and measurement matrices

By completing this documentation, the team will gain an understanding of the existing community, which is necessary to ensure that the Form-Based Code is specific to the community and that it will regulate development to enhance the existing character. In essence, it will help ensure that a community can implement a place-specific vision.

## Budgeting and Timing of Documentation

Finding the time and budget for this extensive documentation process is not always easy. Integrating the documentation into the community's comprehensive planning efforts can alleviate part of this strain, even if the code update is not completed immediately thereafter. In fact, while this documentation process is critical to complete as the basis of the Form-Based Code, it is best completed at the beginning of the community's comprehensive planning efforts, saving the community time, money, and effort in multiple ways:

1. Gathering the information once, but using it for both processes, reduces the budget and timeline by preventing any duplication of effort.
2. It enables the community's existing framework as documented in this process to be used as the basis for both the comprehensive plan and the Form-Based Code, helping ensure that both documents are working from the same basis and toward the same goal.
3. It can help simplify the Form-Based Coding process by informing the comprehensive plan team about the level of detail that needs to be considered in their visioning process in order for a Form-Based Code to be put into place, encouraging them to consider existing elements that should not be prohibited and to include clear direction about elements that the FBC should regulate.
4. It can dramatically reduce the effort required to implement a Form-Based Code by minimizing the need to reconcile it with a contradictory comprehensive plan.

However, there is a catch: An experienced urban design and Form-Based Coding consultant should lead the documentation process, to ensure that the necessary framework for an FBC is established during the comprehensive planning process. If the budget is not available to have an experienced FBC consultant conduct the entire documentation process, it is possible to have the consultant lead the process using a team of municipal staff members or even local citizens for the groundwork. See the sidebar "Don't Try This at Home."

# 1.1 Macro Scale 

Documenting macro elements creates a basis for understanding the existing urban framework of a community. Establishing a thorough understanding of this framework helps ensure that the team creates an Illustrative Plan and a Regulating Plan that work with the existing community patterns, reinforcing them for developed areas or tying into them and replicating them for greenfield development.

The two major goals of this phase are:

1. To document the macro elements, creating the Existing Framework Diagram that will become the basis for the Illustrative Plan and the Regulating Plan
2. To list the existing micro-element types in order to prepare for the micro-scale site visit

Both of these goals are typically accomplished during a single site visit, which is at the center of the macro-scale documentation phase, but follow-up visits may be necessary based on the complexity of the community and the size of the project area.

## Process Overview

While this phase centers on a site visit, it begins with prep work to ensure the visit is productive. This prep work includes first gathering background documents and creating base drawings, and then analyzing these materials to determine which areas to explore during the site visit. (See Figure 3.4.)

At the site, the team documents and analyzes the macro elements. This includes marking a plan with the centers and boundaries of each existing neighborhood, district, and corridor, and then establishing the most likely degree of change for each. This means deciding whether the goal for each is preservation, preservation and enhancement, or evolution. It also includes noting any opportunity areas where new

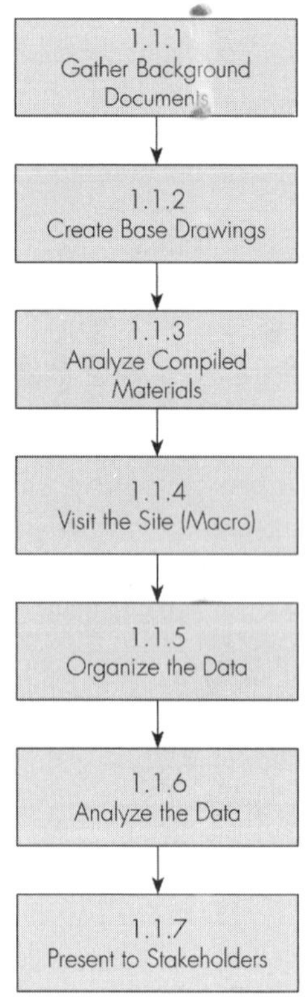


**Fig. 3.4**
1.1 Macro-Scale Documentation

neighborhoods might work well or where good infill opportunities exist. In addition, the team makes lists of observed micro-element types to help prepare for the micro-scale site visit.

After the site visit, all the gathered data is organized, analyzed, and presented to the stakeholders to review before continuing to the next phase.

## Macro Elements

Before delving into the detailed process for this phase, it is necessary to understand the basic urban design concepts behind the macro elements. The three primary macro elements are Neighborhoods, Districts, and Corridors.

In addition, in many communities, it may be necessary to document unique macro-scale conditions that have a major impact on the character of the place and the urban form, such as topography, local climate, or historic characteristics of the platting of the community.

### The Neighborhood

A primary element of town planning is the neighborhood. In Peter Katz's book *The New Urbanism*, Andrés Duany and Elizabeth Plater-Zyberk say the following about the neighborhood:

*The nomenclature may vary, but there is general agreement regarding the physical composition of the neighborhood. The "neighborhood unit" of the 1929 New York Regional Plan, the "quartier" of Leon Krier, the "traditional neighborhood development" (TND) and "transit-oriented development" (TOD) share similar attributes. They all propose a model of urbanism that is limited in area and structured around a defined center. While the population density may vary, depending on its context, each model offers a balanced mix of dwellings, workplaces, shops, civic buildings and parks.*[1]

This neighborhood structure is vital to any good urban place, and a Form-Based Code should reinforce it. In town planning terms, the neighborhood is typically defined as an area with an optimal five-minute walking radius (1/4 mile); a clearly defined center and edge; a mix of housing types, uses, and activities; a network of integrated streets; and in the more urban neighborhoods, a prominent location for civic and public buildings. A community is then a collection of individually unique neighborhoods connected by a network of streets. (See Figure 3.5.)

### The District

A district is an area of land to be used for a single purpose. Two types of districts may be

**Don't Try This at Home**

Actually, local planning staff or community members can often complete or assist with portions of the documentation process if necessary to keep the code budget lower, as long as the process is supervised by an experienced Form-Based Coding consultant to guide some of the decision-making for critical steps, such as:

1. Identifying the neighborhood framework
2. Identifying and analyzing the role of different corridors
3. Identifying the existing transect levels
4. Selecting sampling areas for the micro-scale documentation
5. Modifying the documentation sheets as necessary for local conditions
6. Identifying the typical conditions within each sampling area that will be the foundation of the Building Form Standards

On the other hand, experienced consultants will often be able to complete the documentation much more quickly, and doing it themselves will help them be better prepared for the visioning process.

healthy components of a town: certain single-use districts and incompatible-use districts.

Just about the only healthy single-use districts that still are appropriate for walkable, sustainable communities are educational campuses. Other uses that have been considered good single-use districts in the past, such as those for civic or arts uses, are in fact best integrated into mixed-use areas. If such single-use districts as educational campuses are necessary, they should be well integrated into the overall framework of a community.

Incompatible-use districts are necessary for uses that require a strong physical separation from other uses, such as airports, large-scale manufacturing, and other heavy industrial uses. This type of district is sometimes a challenge to deal with from a planning perspective but is necessary for the function of most communities. However, care should be taken when determining whether these districts are necessary. Andrés Duany and Elizabeth Plater-Zyberk state: "Thanks to industrial evolution and environmental regulation, the reason for segregating uses recede with time. The modern North American workplace is no longer a bad neighbor to dwellings and shops."[2] Most light industry can now be integrated into the mixed-use districts in town, eliminating the need for some of these incompatible-use districts.

Districts in general should be used cautiously. The overuse of districts in the past has led to many of the current planning problems. Examples of the inappropriate use of districts include business parks and monotonous single-family house neighborhoods. A core tenant of creating mixed-use neighborhoods is that businesses and residences should be integrated, not isolated.

One current trend that is completely detrimental to the creation of vibrant, healthy communities is designating an isolated area on the edge of the community as a civic center. As with any single-use district, this type of isolation forces people to drive to the location for a single purpose and then get back into their cars to drive somewhere else to complete their next task. In contrast, these civic uses could easily be placed in mixed-use environments, helping activate the area and integrating the civic functions within the heart of a community. This would also enable government workers to be able to walk to restaurants, drop off dry cleaning, or shop during lunchtime or after work without having to get in their cars. In addition, a citizen could park once to renew a driver's license, meet a friend for lunch, and walk to a gallery or do some shopping.

Another word of caution for regulating districts is to be careful of their size. Even if a district provides an essential use for a neighborhood, it still can be extremely detrimental to quality, character, and walkability if it is not scaled ap-

**Fig. 3.5** Neighborhoods with a 5-minute walking radius are the building blocks of a walkable community.

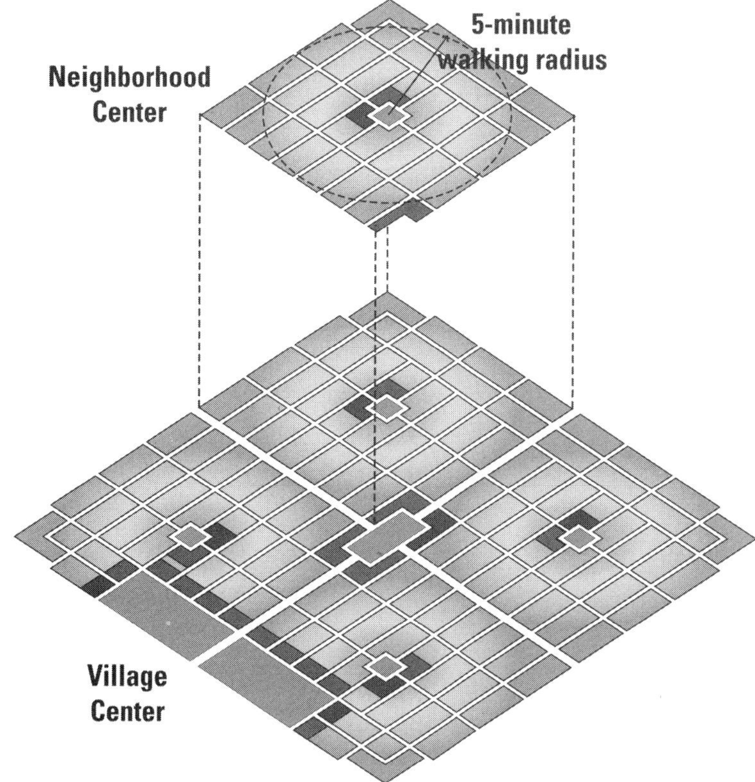

propriately for a walkable neighborhood. Many schools built today fit into this category.

**The Corridor**

The third element of the urban framework is the corridor. The definition of a corridor does not deal solely with the movement of automobiles, but more important takes into account the mobility and connectivity for pedestrians, as well as its role in physically defining neighborhoods and districts within a community.

*The corridor is at once the connector and the separator of neighborhoods and districts. Corridors include natural and man-made elements, ranging from wildlife trails to rail lines.*[3]

In addition, some corridors actually function as the center of an elliptically shaped neighborhood rather than as a neighborhood boundary or connector. The documentation of these corridors allows the code team to understand the geographic locations and function of downtowns and neighborhood centers, boundaries of neighborhoods, important entries into and connections through a community, and other elements of a community's urban framework.

| | List of Suggested Background Documents |
|---|---|
| Existing Conditions Maps: | Aerial photo<br>Topographic map<br>Street map<br>Survey<br>Layers of information in a GIS format |
| Existing Planning Documents (including plans and accompanying regulations): | Zoning map and regulations<br>Comprehensive/General plan<br>Downtown plan<br>Area plan(s)<br>District plan(s) (e.g., campus plan)<br>Streets master plan<br>Parks and open space master plan<br>Historic conservation plans<br>Historic maps |

## 1.1.1 Gather Background Documents

The first step in the documentation process is to gather the base information to help the team gain a general understanding of the area and begin to create an agenda for the first site visit. Existing conditions maps provide a graphic base for all future work, while historic maps are needed to analyze the growth patterns of the city over its history. Existing planning documents are needed for multiple reasons. First, the FBC may need to accommodate and work with any existing regulations that will remain in effect after the FBC is implemented. Second, the team will need to review any regulations that are being replaced in order to help understand the existing place and to learn from those regulations' successes and failures. Third, the team may need to incorporate any previous visioning work that was completed by the community prior to the FBC process.

**Process**

Begin by gathering as much background information as possible, including site maps, historic maps, and previous planning documents, such as the Comprehensive Plan, zoning and land-use maps, and any area-specific plans that have been completed. GIS mapping can be an excellent source, as well as the community planning department's records. See table at left for suggested of documents to gather. If the code is for a greenfield site, gather the information for the site and the neighboring communities.

**Tip:** When gathering these background documents, be sure to insist on accuracy. Inaccurate base information can cause fatal flaws in a code that can prevent it from being adopted.

**Product List**

- Existing conditions maps
- Existing planning documents

## 1.1.2 Create Base Drawings

Once all the base information is gathered, it should be organized into a few critical base drawings for use throughout the documenting and visioning phases. These will begin to help the team understand the urban framework and typical conditions, as well as to select areas to focus on during the site visit.

### Process

Begin by compiling an Existing Conditions Base Map with the following critical information:

- Public right-of-way (ROW) lines
- Lot lines
- Building footprints
- Curbs and sidewalk locations
- River and creek corridors or other natural features that will impact development

This map will be used throughout the Form-Based Coding process at many different scales, so be sure the elements are located precisely. (See Figure 3.6.) Also include any special conditions that have affected or may affect the planning of the area, such as topography. If the special conditions clutter the base map, consider creating additional base maps or analysis drawings for the special conditions, such as topography.

Next, create a Figure Ground Plan by deleting everything from the Existing Conditions Base Map (or turning off all the layers in the digital file) except for the building footprints, and then fill in the building footprints with black. (See Figure 3.7.) This is often one of the most helpful drawings for documenting and understanding existing conditions. It designates private spaces (buildings) in solid black and public spaces (streets, parks, and so on) in solid white. Nothing else is shown on the plan, although sometimes it is helpful to include the curbs in a very thin line.

**Fig. 3.6** (above) Existing Conditions Base Map for Grass Valley, California (Credit: Opticos Design)

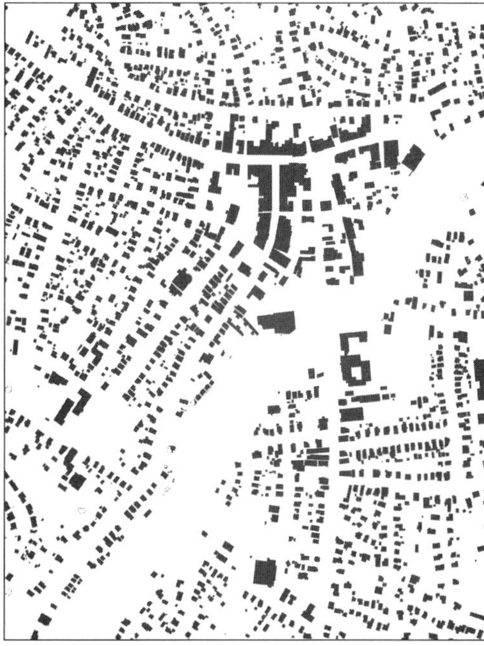

**Fig. 3.7** (left) Figure Ground Plan for Grass Valley, California. Note the large white gap where the freeway built in the 1970s cuts through the historic urban fabric. (Credit: Opticos Design)

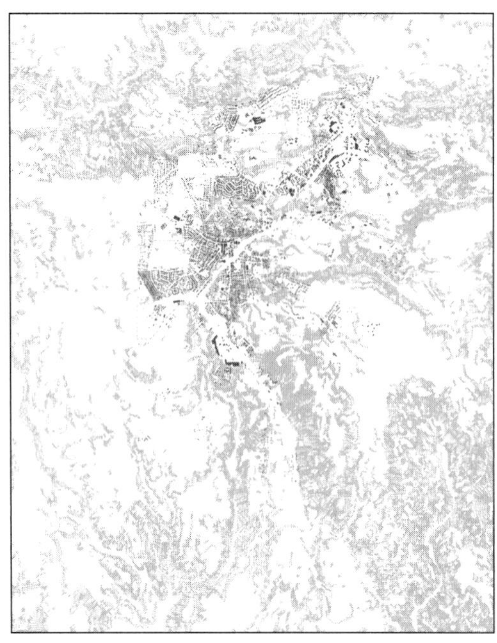

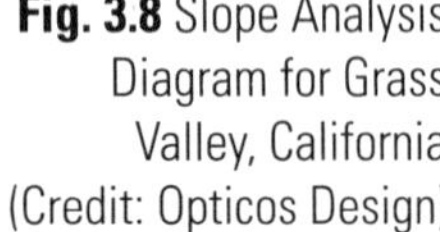

**Fig. 3.8** Slope Analysis Diagram for Grass Valley, California (Credit: Opticos Design)

This drawing is used later to help locate centers or focal points, typical development patterns from different eras, gaps within existing development, maximum building sizes, and other unique features of the urban pattern of the community. It can also potentially help the team identify building types, such as bungalow courts, and any peculiar conditions that should be verified during the site visits.

**Tip:** At this point, it can be helpful to overlay the figure ground plan on top of the existing zoning map. This helps the team locate any mixed-use commercial centers that may be the center of a neighborhood. It also begins to illustrate whether and how existing regulations are reinforcing or having a detrimental impact on an area.

Consider any other analysis diagrams that might be helpful for understanding the framework of the area. An example is a Slope Analysis Diagram for areas with variable topography that will impact development and regulations. (See Figure 3.8.)

Lastly, consider creating historic growth analysis diagrams, which can further inform the team about the typical urban patterns, while also enabling them to understand the morphology of the place. Old Sanborn fire insurance maps are very helpful for creating figure ground plans and historic versions of U.S. Geological Survey (USGS) maps are great for documenting growth patterns between different time periods at a citywide scale. (See Figure 3.9.)

#### Product List

- Existing Conditions Base Map(s)
- Figure Ground Plan
- Special Conditions Analysis Diagram(s), as necessary (e.g., Slope Analysis)
- Historic Growth Analysis Diagrams

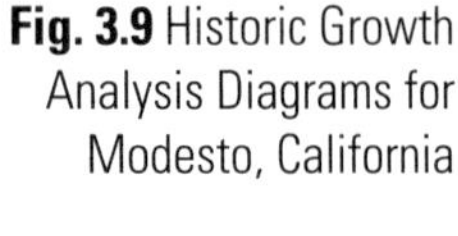

**Fig. 3.9** Historic Growth Analysis Diagrams for Modesto, California

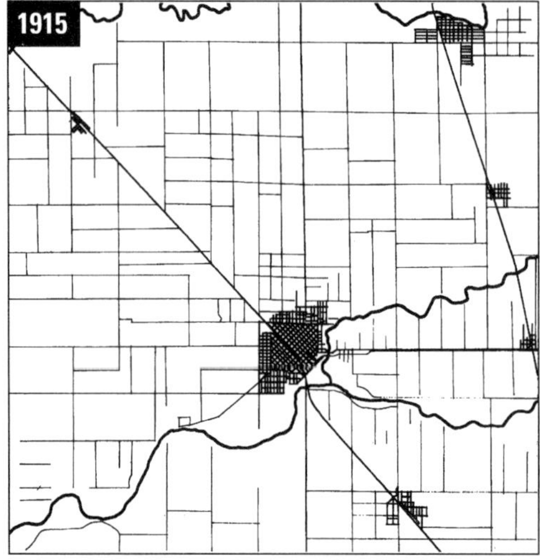


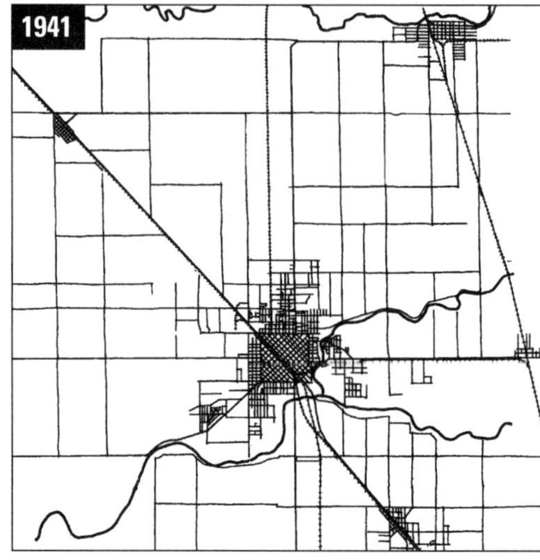

## 1.1.3 Analyze Compiled Materials

Now that the base materials and analysis drawings have been compiled, the team should review and analyze them. Extracting the important information from the analysis and base drawings is a complex task, but the following is a list of the goals for this task:

1. Begin to understand the existing neighborhood, district, and corridor framework of the community.
2. Become familiar with the land-use patterns and physical patterns of development within the community.
3. Select which areas the team needs to visit and document for the macro-scale site visit.
4. Create an initial list of transect levels that will likely be necessary for the FBC.
5. Decide if there are any gaps that require creating or locating additional maps or analysis drawings.

### Process

Print out all the base maps and analysis drawings at the same scale and pin them up side by side. Review the gathered information while beginning to mark up the drawings with answers to the following questions:

- Where are there patterns or existing zoning classifications that suggest centers or focal points?
- Where are there patterns that suggest edges?
- Which streets and roadways are regional connectors? Which are local connectors?
- What green or pedestrian corridors exist within the community?
- Which areas are currently regulated for major changes to occur in scale and possibly use?
- Which places define the identity of the community? Are historic development patterns intact in any of these places?
- Where do the building or street patterns change and what might be the reason?
- How and why has growth occurred in the past?
- Are specific areas evolving with new development?
- Which neighborhoods would benefit from the preservation of their existing character?
- Which corridors function well and do not need to be changed?
- Which corridors need to evolve in design and function?
- Are there any existing districts?
- Are there clear edges and transitions between neighborhoods?

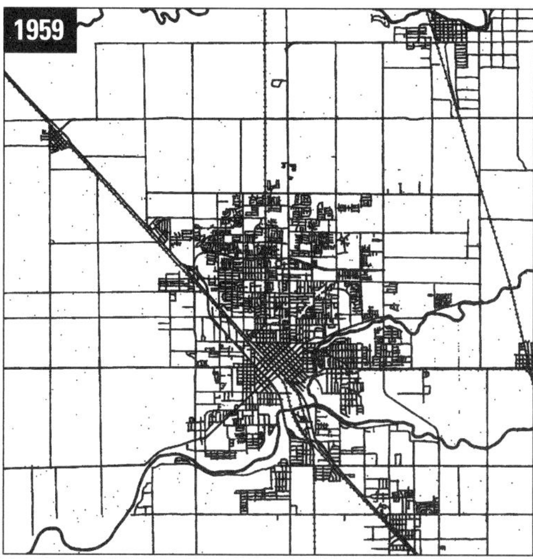


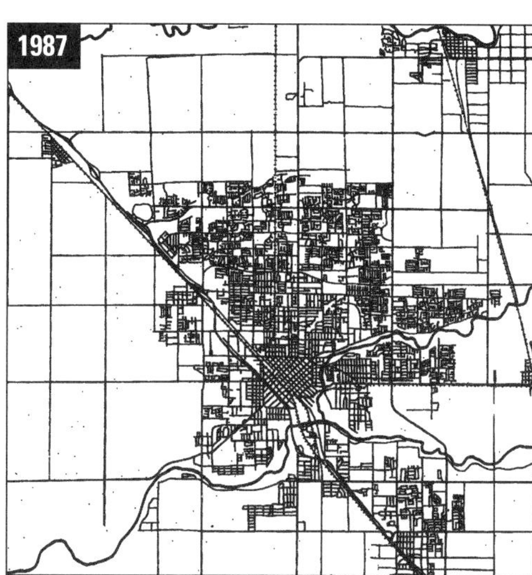

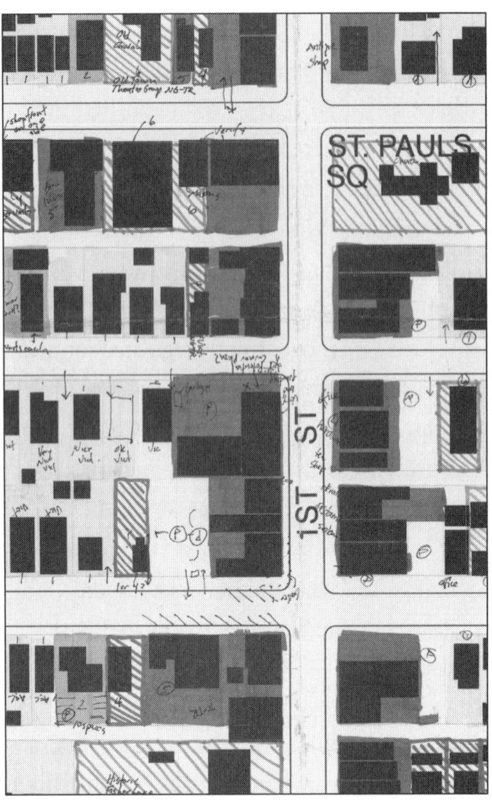


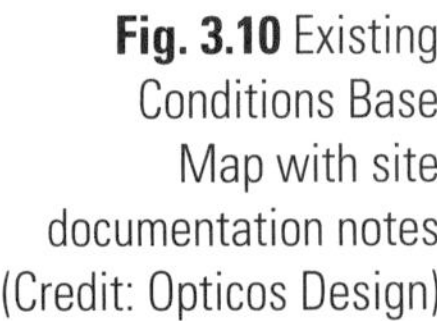
**Fig. 3.10** Existing Conditions Base Map with site documentation notes (Credit: Opticos Design)

- Which transect levels exist within the community?
- Are there other transect levels that would be appropriate that do not exist?
- Which areas do we need to visit to answer or confirm the answers to any of the questions above?

By the end of this task, the team should have a map or series of maps that are notated in reference to the questions above (in essence, a first draft of what seems to be the neighborhood framework), a draft list of the transect levels that the team feels is applicable to the community, and a list of places to visit to answer questions the team has on existing conditions of the community.

### Product List

- Notated maps
- Draft list of transect levels
- List of places to visit

## 1.1.4 Visit the Site

The next step is to visit the site. The three major purposes of this visit are:

1. To document and rate the existing macro elements, such as the location of the neighborhoods, districts, and corridors
2. To generally catalog the variety of existing micro elements, such as thoroughfare types and building types, and note locations of good examples of each
3. To refine the list of applicable transect levels

### Process

Take along the Existing Conditions Base Map to take notes, as well as a street map and an aerial photo for reference. Also, remember a camera and a sketchbook.

Walk around as much of the area as possible. Document the neighborhoods, districts, and corridors on the Existing Conditions Base Map and with photographs using the following instructions. (See Figures 3.10 and 3.11.)

*Neighborhoods*

There are two aspects of neighborhoods to document: first, the structure and location of existing neighborhoods, and second, possible locations for new neighborhoods as the community evolves.

For each existing neighborhood, note the location of both its center and outer edge on the Existing Conditions Base Map. The center is typically a crossroads, a commercial center, a school or other public use, or a park. The edge may be easy to define, such as a street, a rail line, or a creek, or it may be difficult to determine. While documenting this neighborhood framework, recognize that existing neighborhoods often do not fit the 1/4-mile radius model exactly; therefore, the actual size or shape will need to be modified as the documentation progresses. It will often be necessary to go back and forth while layering the 1/4-mile radius on the plan and trying to decide the appropriate focal point of a neighborhood as well as the edges. In addition, a downtown area may be shaped or sized differently than most neighborhoods. It will often have a 1/2-mile (10-minute) radius because it provides a wider range of uses and amenities, or it may become linear along a main street with 1/4 mile in each direction perpendicular to the street. In many instances, a neighborhood will be slightly larger or smaller, or if there is a large gap between neighborhoods, the team may determine it is appropriate to establish a new center within this gap.

Once the existing neighborhoods framework is documented, photograph and note the range of existing transect levels in each neighborhood. Then designate each neighborhood with one of three classifications for degree of change:

1. **Preserve:** A neighborhood whose size and character should be protected and maintained, such as a historic neighborhood
2. **Preserve and Enhance:** A neighborhood that needs to be strengthened
3. **Evolve and Transform:** A neighborhood that could be changed to accommodate growth in the community

Along the way, consider good potential locations for new neighborhoods and neighborhood centers and note them on the Existing Conditions Base Map.

**Tip:** The biggest opportunities for new neighborhoods and centers are typically suburban commercial corridors and suburban mall locations that are struggling to maintain their viability as retail moves farther out of town, as well as brownfield sites that have been overlooked for development due to the necessary clean up required before development can occur. These types of sites should be noted as potential future mixed-use neighborhoods to reflect a long-term vision for the area that can be reinforced by the Form-Based Code. The size, scale, and program should be determined to enable it to fit within a city's future hierarchy of centers.

**Fig. 3.11** General urban character photos

Also, begin to think about the following:

1. Will the code prevent a property owner from tearing down a building and replac-

## Documentation Site Visits

To complete the documentation, a minimum of two site visits are necessary, one for each scale. Additional visits may be added as needed to further refine the documentation. Do not shortchange these site visits or try to skip them altogether. While it may be possible to determine some of the needed information from base maps and photographs, they are no substitute for actual site visits to truly understand a place.

ing it with a new one that is not in character with the neighborhood? Should it?

2. Can the code prevent inappropriate additions or renovations?
3. How will the code provide predictability for purchasers of buildings or homes to encourage investment in the neighborhood?
4. Which neighborhoods, corridors, lots, or buildings should be encouraged or allowed to evolve? Examples of this include lots that could appropriately accommodate a higher intensity of residential uses to reinforce a neighborhood center and a prominent lot in a neighborhood center or along a corridor that has not been developed due to current development restrictions.

*Districts*

As with the neighborhoods, note each district location on the Existing Conditions Base Map and take photographs of each one. Designate each district with one of three classifications:

1. A healthy component of the community, such as an educational campus
2. An incompatible-use district, such as an airport or heavy-industrial area
3. Unnecessarily zoned as a district (These are typically districts that have been rigorously clustered into single-use zones by suburban-oriented regulations but contain uses that are more appropriately placed within a mixed-use district.)

Most communities, depending on their size, will typically have all three of these district types. It is important to understand the role of the different districts within a community and whether they need to be preserved or reconsidered based on the classifications discussed above.

For the first two types of districts, note the positive or negative impacts these districts have on adjacent areas, as well as physical or other constraints that might arise if the team decided to expand the areas. Consider the following:

- Will the district need to expand?
- Is expansion possible without impacting adjacent uses?
- Is the use no longer economically viable or is it possible it may not be within the lifespan of the code?

For the incompatible-use districts, study exactly which uses have been designated for the districts and which ones really need to be isolated. It is typically not worth spending much time documenting these districts. They usually have very little need for a pure Form-Based Code approach, except perhaps at their edges as they transition to other areas.

Finally, for the districts that have been unnecessarily zoned as such, consider the following:

- Should the code allow or require these areas to evolve into mixed-use environments? (For office parks, the answer should be yes.)
- Should the zoning allow the uses in these areas to be decided by the market within a framework of appropriate form?
- Should the use be changed to reinforce rather than degrade the character and function of an existing neighborhood? (See the sidebar "Harmful District Zoning.")

*Corridors*

Just as with the neighborhoods and districts, note each corridor location on the Existing Conditions Base Map. Take notes and photographs of each corridor about the type of corridor (such as pedestrian-oriented, auto-oriented, or a creek corridor) and whether the existing state of the corridor is helping or harming the desired nature of the community. Consider how the evolution and integration of the corridors should reinforce existing community patterns or allow for different patterns. Also, determine the appropriate balance between the efficient movement of automobile versus pedestrian traffic on these streets and how it should impact and influence the built physical form and uses. For example, for a major automobile corridor with single-family homes along its edges, there are typically two options: (1) physically redesign the thoroughfare to adjust the speed and flow of traffic to be compatible with the homes, or (2) evolve the uses along the thoroughfare, possibly from single-family residential to multifamily residential or commercial uses in order to maintain the necessary traffic flow.

*Unique Macro Elements*

The final elements that make up the urban framework are any unique characteristics. These elements will differ from city to city. The code team should study the area and consider which other elements may have had a major influence on the urban character of the place. Typical examples are topography, local climate, or historic characteristics of the platting of a community.

Similar to the elements documented and analyzed above, the analysis of these unique characteristics should inform the code team on how new development should respond to them and at the same time reinforce them. In Grass Valley, California, for instance, the team discovered that on up-sloped lots, buildings were typically set farther back from the streets, and on down-sloped lots, buildings were typically pulled closer to the sidewalk edge to improve the development potential on the lot. Patterns such as this should be reinforced by the FBC.

*Micro Elements*

While the primary purpose of this site visit is to document the macro elements, it is also necessary to use the visit to begin to catalog micro elements in preparation for the next site visit. Create a list in a sketchbook of each of the following micro elements:

- Thoroughfare types
- Civic space types
- Frontage types
- Building types
- Architectural historic periods of development
- Architectural styles

Also, take a photo and note the location of any good examples of any of the listed items for the team to consider documenting in more detail on the next visit.

**Harmful District Zoning**

In a recent citywide code update, the team documented a corridor in a historic neighborhood just outside of the downtown that had more recently been zoned into a single-use district for professional office uses. Because of this zoning, many of the preexisting homes had been converted to professional offices. While this may not be a problem in and of itself, in this case, the zoning had created three problems:

1. It did not allow these larger homes to be converted into multiple residential units that the local market needed.
2. It drew possible commercial tenants out of the downtown and neighborhood centers.
3. The commercial uses began to cause deterioration in the quality of the residential neighborhood.

Through the FBC process, the team took steps to prevent further encroachment of commercial uses into the downtown; to encourage a mix of uses, including medium-density residential, along the corridor to respond to the local residential market; and to help ensure that the sites would develop with a form that was compatible with adjacent homes.

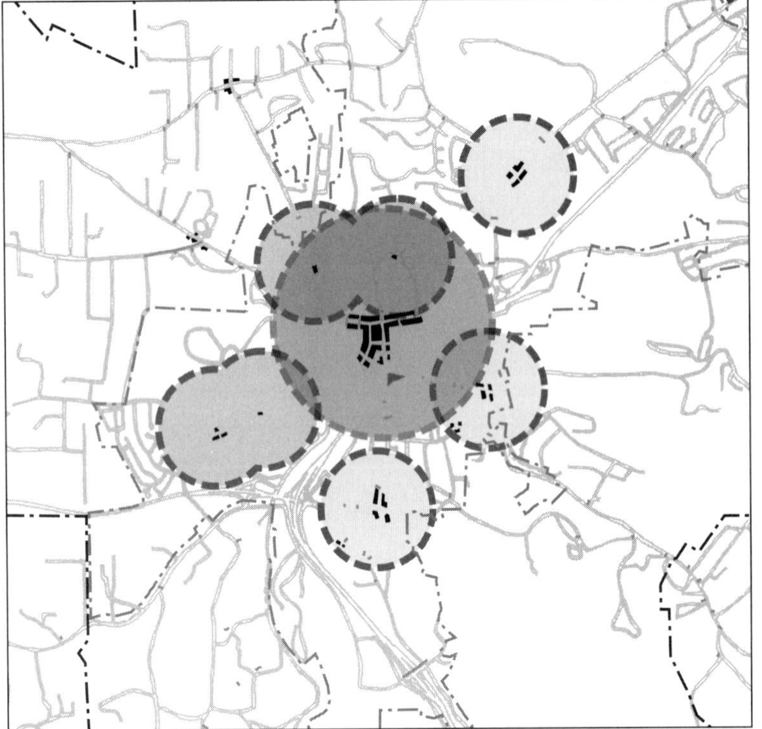

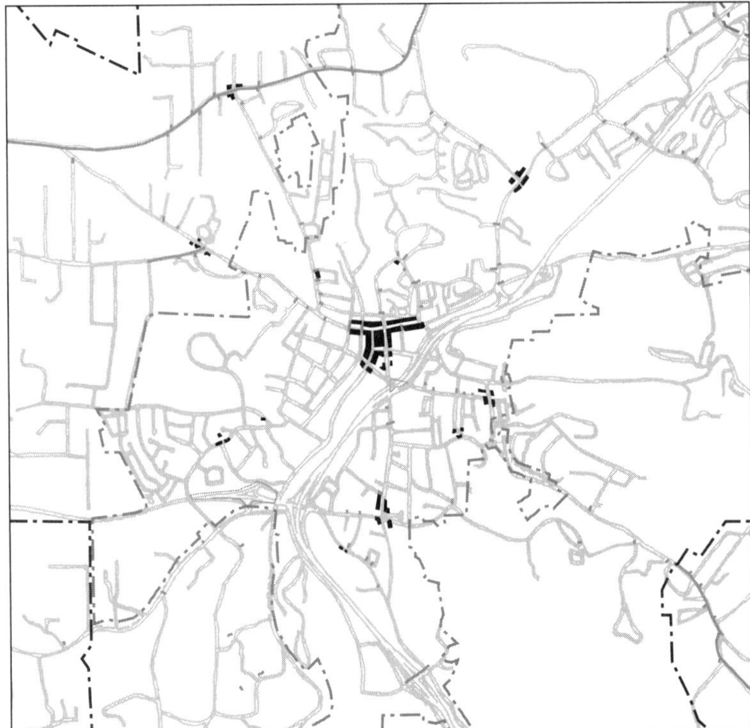

**Fig. 3.12** (top) Existing Neighborhoods Diagram for Grass Valley, California (Credit: Opticos Design)

**Fig. 3.13** (bottom) Existing Districts Diagram for Grass Valley, California (Credit: Opticos Design)

**Tip:** When listing building types, the code team may need to look very closely for types that upon first glance do not look different than a single-family house, such as duplexes, triplexes, and small apartment buildings. These are often spread intermittently throughout neighborhoods, and in some cases only a few have survived being torn down due to past zoning changes. Many times these large houses with multiple units can become a good precedent for the design, integration, and regulation for medium-density housing or small apartment buildings.

**Product List**

- Existing Conditions Base Map with notes
- Lists of observed micro elements with locations of good examples
- Photos

## 1.1.5 Organize the Data

After returning from the site, the team needs to assemble and organize the data collected to create the base drawings for the visioning and coding processes and to prepare for the next site visit. The final products will include an Existing Framework Diagram(s) and photo sheets of each transect level and each of the observed micro-element types.

**Process**

*Framework Diagrams*

Begin with the notated Existing Conditions Base Map(s) from the site visit. Transfer the information collected onto the following separate diagrams, using a clean Existing Conditions Base Map as a base:

1. Existing Neighborhoods Diagram
2. Existing Districts Diagram
3. Existing Corridors Diagram
4. Existing Special Conditions Diagram(s) (See Figures 3.12 through 3.14.)

For the neighborhoods and any corridors acting as the center of a neighborhood, note the center as well as the outer boundary of the neighborhood and list the transect levels found in each neighborhood.

Next, compile the data from all these diagrams onto a single Existing Framework Diagram, sometimes referred to as an Existing Neighborhoods, Districts, and Corridors (N/D/C) Diagram. This will become the base diagram for the Illustrative Plan, and ultimately for the Regulating Plan. (See Figure 3.15.)

*Photo Sheets*

Once the Existing Framework Diagram is complete, gather it along with all the photos taken and the micro-element lists generated during the site visit.

Review the Existing Framework Diagram for the various transect levels noted for each neighborhood. Create a separate photo sheet(s) for each existing transect level documented, and include photos from the various neighborhoods. Add a label for each photo stating the location. (See Figure 3.16.)

Next, review the lists of micro elements. Select one, such as the building types. Create a photo sheet for each building type listed and include examples from as many neighborhoods, transect levels, and historic periods as possible.

Once the building-type photo sheets are complete, repeat the process for each of the other micro-element lists, creating a photo sheet for each item on each list.

**Product List**

- Existing Neighborhoods Diagram
- Existing Districts Diagram
- Existing Corridors Diagram

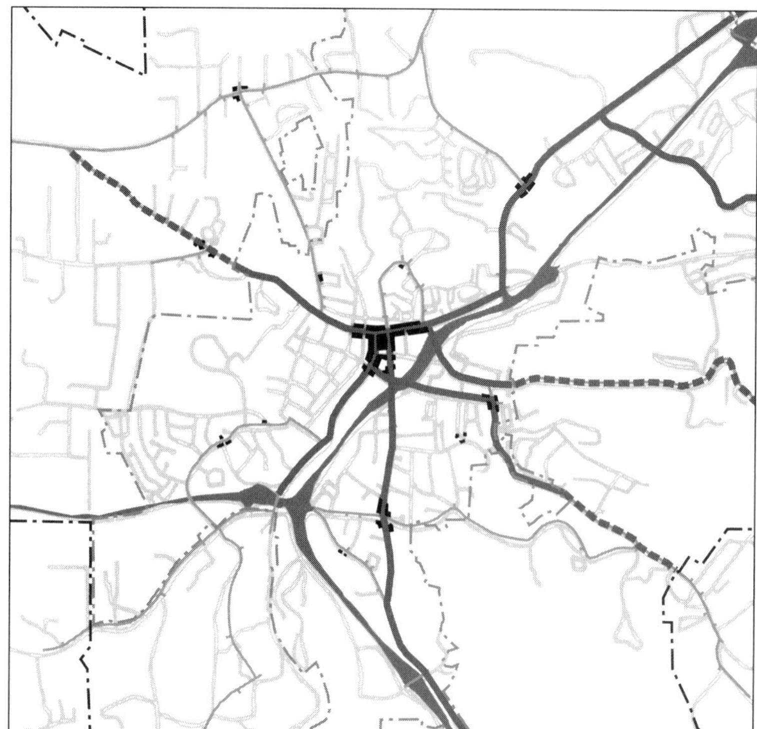

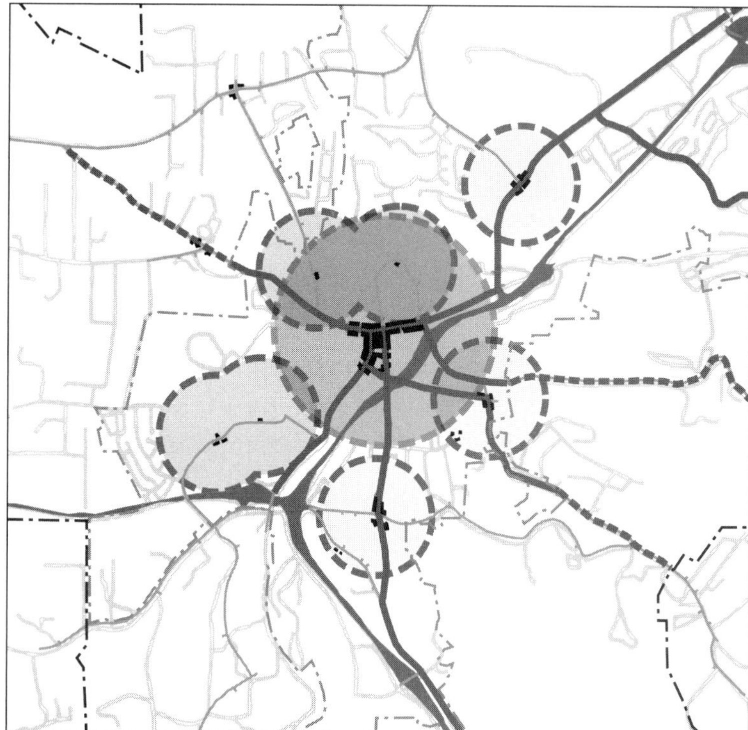

**Fig. 3.14** (top) Existing Corridors Diagram for Grass Valley, California (Credit: Opticos Design)

**Fig. 3.15** (bottom) Existing Framework (N/D/C) Diagram for Grass Valley, California (Credit: Opticos Design; Also see Figure C.6.)

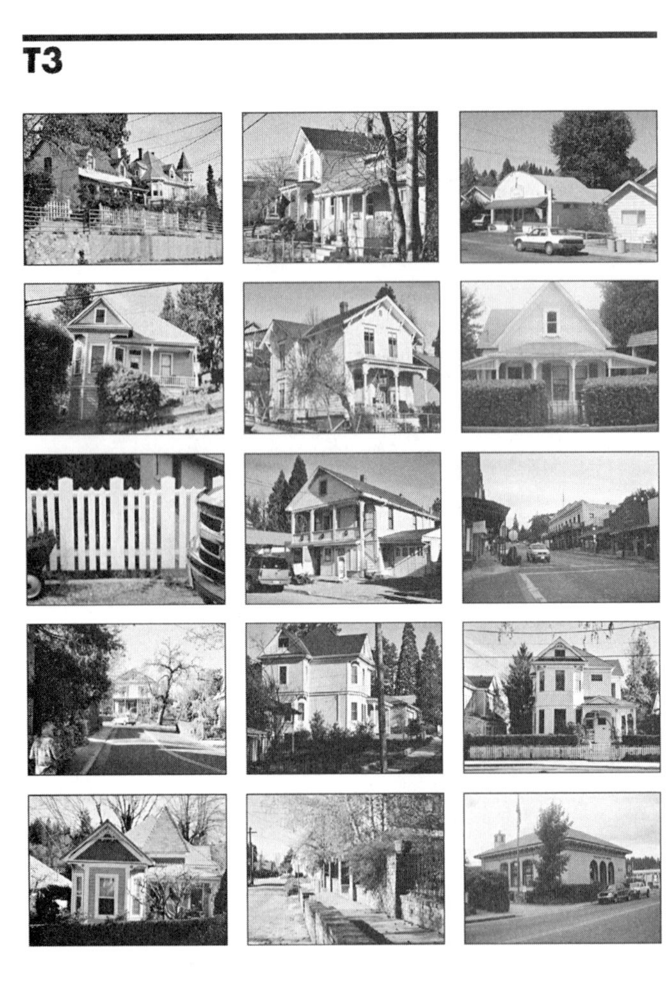


**Fig. 3.16** Photo Sheet for existing T3 transect level in Grass Valley, California

- Existing Special Conditions Diagram(s), as necessary
- Existing Framework (N/D/C) Diagram
- Photo Sheets of existing transect levels and micro element types (e.g., thoroughfare types and building types)

## 1.1.6 Analyze the Data

After having documented and organized information about the existing conditions, the team needs to determine the initial calibration of the transect to the existing community in order to be prepared for the micro-scale documentation.

### Process

Begin by gathering the transect-level photo sheets. Review them to determine whether the photographic examples on each sheet are all similar enough to belong in the same transect level. If necessary, move the photos around to different sheets or add new sheets to achieve the desired similarity. Once the team is satisfied that each photo sheet truly represents a transect level, label each photo sheet with the appropriate transect-level number (e.g., T4). If separate sheets exist that seem to be in the same transect level but have differing characteristics, create a subset, adding a different letter to the end of the transect level number for each sheet (e.g., T4a and T4b). This labeling will become the basis of the regulating zones and is an art in and of itself.

Once the sheets have been labeled, create an Existing Transect Diagram delineating the range of transect levels for each neighborhood. (See Figure 3.17.) Add each neighborhood (including corridors acting as the center of a neighborhood) as a separate row, marking where it falls along the transect range. Once all the neighborhoods have been added, add a row at the very bottom of the diagram showing the entire range existing in the area documented. This will become the base range of transect levels for the visioning process.

### Product List

- Existing Transect Diagram

## 1.1.7 Present to Stakeholders

While the consultant team can document existing conditions as external experts, they are not a substitute for community input. It is critical to involve the community early and often to ensure that the code truly represents the community's vision, not the consultants' visions. At this stage, the community can be an invaluable source to the consultant team for ensuring that all the critical areas have been documented and classified correctly. This is a good time to get

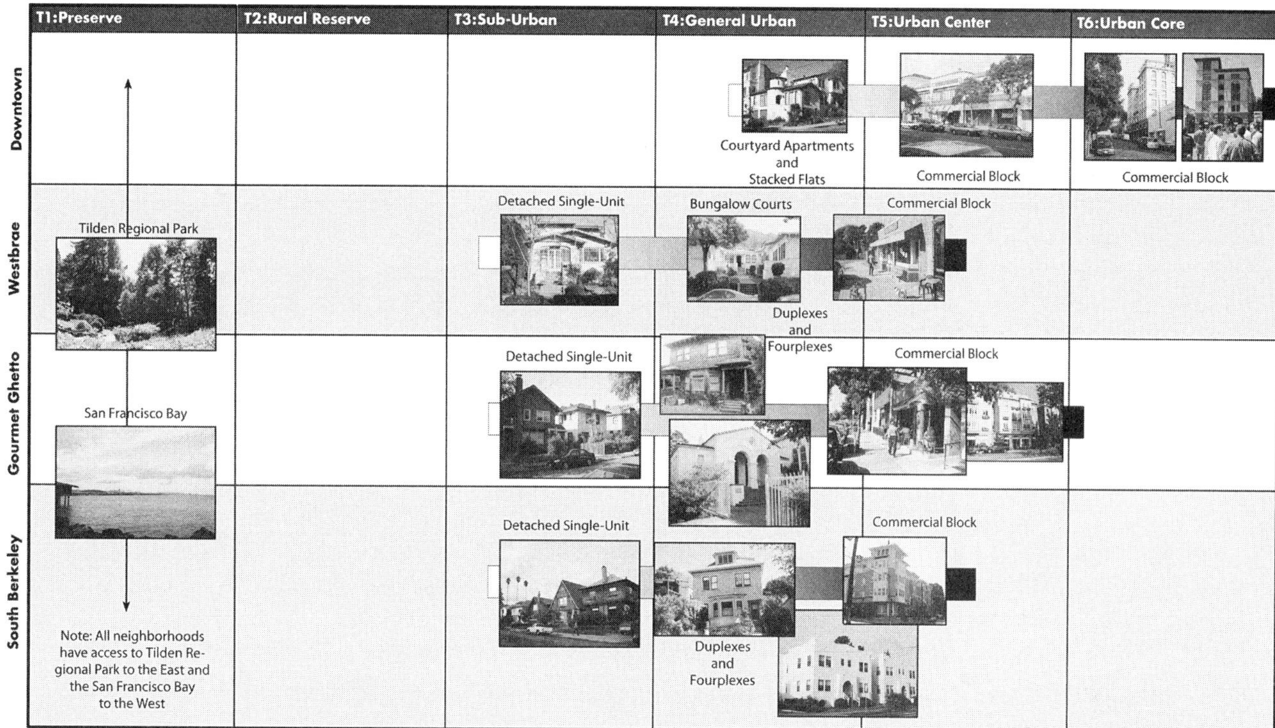




feedback on which parts of the existing community are liked and disliked by community members to consider when determining what to document during the next phase. It is also a good opportunity to have a dialog with the community about what makes a good place and how those characteristics are or are not inherent within certain parts of the community.

### Process

Hold a stakeholders' meeting, including members of the public if possible, to present the macro-scale documentation findings. If the team is using the Charrette Institute's Dynamic Planning Process, this can be part of the Outreach process. Present the existing framework diagrams, as well as the photo sheets. Determine whether any key areas were missed during the documentation. Also, gather further suggestions on which existing areas are successful, which areas need improvement, and which areas are good examples to replicate elsewhere. If the consensus is that the key areas are complete, continue to the next phase, Documenting Micro Elements. If some areas were missed, repeat steps 1.1.4 through 1.1.7 as needed.

**Fig. 3.17** Existing Transect Diagram for Berkeley, California

# 1.2 Micro Scale

In a typical comprehensive plan or code update, if documentation occurs at all, it includes only the macro elements discussed above. In creating an FBC to protect and enhance the unique character of a community, documenting the micro elements is critical. These micro-scale details are essential for a code to be successful in regulating development in character with a community. As mentioned earlier, the primary elements to document at this scale are thoroughfares, buildings (form, placement, frontages, types, and use), lots and blocks, and civic spaces (parks and plazas). Additional elements that the community is interested in regulating may also be documented, such as architectural styles or landscaping. These micro-scale details will directly inform and become the content for many of the regulations within the various components of the code, such as the Building Form Standards and Public Space Standards.

## Process Overview

Once the team has an understanding of the overall framework of the area based on the completion of the macro-scale documentation, it will visit the site to document the details of the place, the micro elements. It is not possible to document every existing micro element, so the team will first need to establish a process for sampling this information to determine typical conditions for each proposed transect level. This process is called a "synoptic survey." Once it has been determined where to take the samples, the team will visit the site to study each sample area and document its micro elements by completing documentation matrices. After the site visit(s), the team will then organize, analyze, and summarize the data to prepare for the visioning process and the initial stages of the coding. (See Figure 3.18.)

This process is used to document all the micro elements that are important content for the FBC, such as thoroughfares, buildings, and civic spaces, and typically, documenting all these elements happens in tandem during the site visit. However, since it would be too confusing to explain them all at once, the overall process is described below using buildings as the subject micro element. At the end, a brief description is provided for conducting the process for the other micro elements.

## 1.2.1 Select Sampling Areas

The details documented at the micro scale will become the base measurements, or the DNA for the Form-Based Code regulations; therefore, it is important for the documentation to be detailed and thorough. Since it is often unrealistic to assume that every micro-scale condition can be documented, nor is it really necessary, the best approach is to sample typical conditions within a community. This approach, called the "synoptic survey," is similar to the ecological sampling that is done along a transect to document and analyze environmental conditions, but in this instance, it is being used to document human habitat and the typical conditions of the built environment.[4]

### Process

To select the sampling areas, start with the Existing Transect Diagram created at the end of the macro-scale documentation. Review the range of existing transect levels in the area along with the photographs and notes that the team took on its initial documentation visits. For each transect level (including each subset level if appropriate), select four or five areas that represent the desired typical conditions. These are the "sampling areas."

In order for the data to be an accurate sampling, each of the sampling areas should be a consistent size and shape. In environmental documentation, a quadrat is used. Typically, for urban analysis and sampling, a standard block works well. However, rather than selecting a block of buildings surrounded by streets, start with a block-long street and document half a block of buildings and lots on either side to ensure that the documentation is focused on the public space (the street) and how the building forms create that public space, rather than the other way around.

In addition, be sure to spread out the sampling areas among the various neighborhoods and over the full spectrum of historical periods. Use the Figure Ground Plan to help find instances of each pattern that need to be documented.

Finally, it is important to understand the gradients that are happening within each zone, such as a transition of lot sizes; an increase or decrease in built-to locations, setbacks, or building heights; a transition of uses or building types; and the character and design of the thoroughfare and sidewalks. To help document the information about the transition between transect levels, try to select pairs of areas in abutting transect levels.

## 1.2.2 Prepare Site Visit Materials

Once the sampling blocks have been selected, the team needs to gather materials for the site visit. In addition, it is helpful to begin documenting the blocks and lots from the information on the base maps to help create a clearer understanding of historic development patterns that are unique to the community.

### Process

Print out an Existing Conditions Base Map for each sampling block. For this part of the process, the largest scale that will fit on letter or ledger size paper works best, as long as it is at

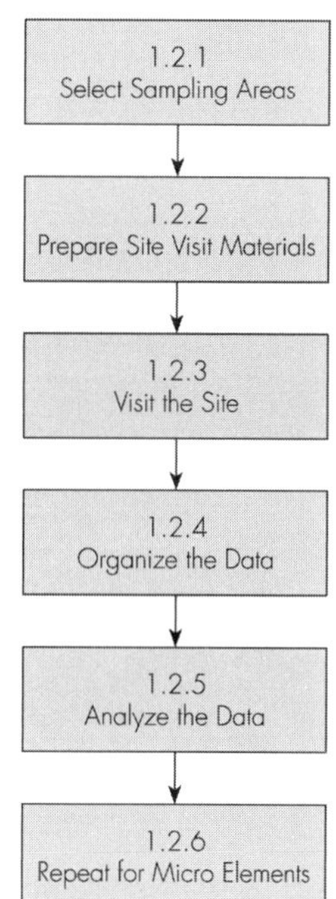


**Fig. 3.18**
1.2 Micro-Scale Documentation

least 1:100. Draw a boundary around each sampling block, and then number the lots within the boundary sequentially. (See Figure 3.19.)

Next, prepare a Block Documentation Matrix for each sampling block. Title each matrix with the location of the sampling block and the transect level, and then label the column headers with the lot numbers from the Existing Conditions Base Map for that area. (See Figure 3.20.)

Finally, before going out to the site, review the Existing Conditions Base Maps for the sampling blocks. Fill in the block perimeter, length, depth, and shape on the Block Documentation Matrix for each of the sampling blocks. Also consider the following questions:

1. How do the lot configurations typically work at the ends of the blocks (i.e., do buildings front the side street or does the end lot have a side elevation to the side street)?
2. What is the typical pattern of lot widths within a block?
3. If the shape of the block is irregular, what is causing it to be irregular?

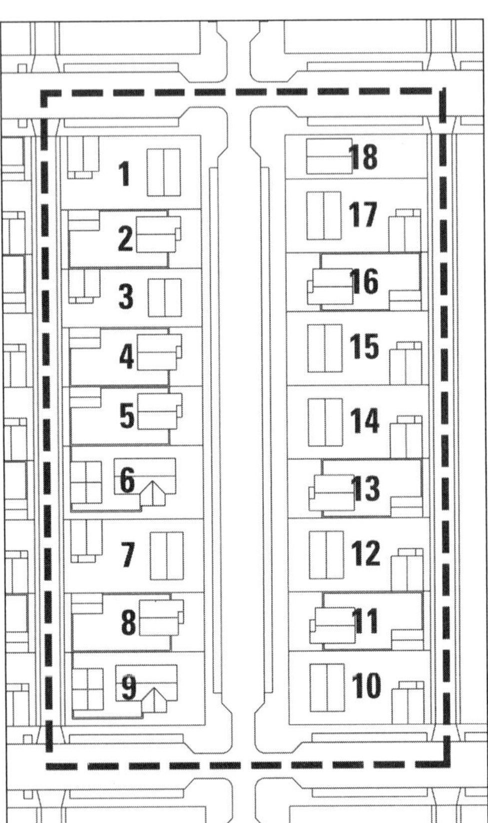


**Fig. 3.19** (near right) Enlarged Existing Conditions Base Map for a sampling block

**Product List**

- Existing Conditions Base Map for each sampling block
- Block Documentation Matrix for each sampling block

## 1.2.3 Visit the Site

The second site visit is to gather the detailed measurements that will become the base for the visioning work and the code. By knowing the existing measurements, the team can make informed decisions about the measurements to include in the final code, deciding whether to keep them as is or modify them to change the desired outcome from the existing place.

**Process**

Taking along the Existing Conditions Base Map and Block Documentation Matrix for each of the sampling blocks as well as a camera, visit each sampling block and fill in all the details for each building and lot on each Block Documentation Matrix. Include sketched diagrams if they are helpful, and take a variety of photos to include in the matrix later. At the very least, photograph building elevations to demonstrate how the buildings relate to one another, views along the sidewalk to illustrate how the buildings engage the public realm, views down the street that show how enclosed the street is by buildings and landscaping, views of the side-street conditions for corner lots, and views of how the alley is used and developed, if an alley exists. Also photograph special conditions that will be important to code, such as driveway or entry widths, distances between entries, and how edges are defined by walls, fences, buildings, or landscaping.

| <Location and Transect Level> | Format | 1 | 2 | 3 | 4 | 5 | 6 |
|---|---|---|---|---|---|---|---|
| **Instructions:** Left and right are when standing in the street facing the front of the building. Fill in before site visit | | | | | | | |
| **City** | | | | | | | |
| Width of Largest Historic Building | x′ | | | | | | |
| **Block** | | | | | | | |
| Perimeter Length | x′ | | | | | | |
| Length (Primary Street) | x′ | | | | | | |
| Depth (Secondary Street) | x′ | | | | | | |
| Shape | Rectangle (R);<br>Trapezoid (T);<br>Other (fill in description) | | | | | | |
| On-street parking spaces within 1/4-mile radius | x | | | | | | |
| Length of Building at Front BTL from Corner | | | | | | | |
| Left End of Block | x′ | | | | | | |
| Right End of Block | x′ | | | | | | |
| **Building Placement** | | | | | | | |
| **Lot Size** | | | | | | | |
| Width | x′ | | | | | | |
| Depth | x′ | | | | | | |
| Square Footage | x sf | | | | | | |
| **Distance From** | ROW (R);<br>Property Line (P);<br>Sidewalk Edge (S);<br>Curb (C) | | | | | | |
| Location of lot | Mid-block (M);<br>Corner (C) | | | | | | |
| If it is a corner lot, where does the building face? | Primary Street (P);<br>Secondary Street (S);<br>Both (B) | | | | | | |
| Front (Main Body of Building) | x′ | | | | | | |
| Side Street (Main Body of Building) | x′ | | | | | | |
| Left Side, Main Building | x′ | | | | | | |
| Right Side, Main Building | x′ | | | | | | |
| Left Side, Ancillary Building | x′ | | | | | | |
| Right Side, Ancillary Building | x′ | | | | | | |
| Rear, Main Building | x′ | | | | | | |
| Adjacent Use/Transect Level | (fill in Use or T-level) | | | | | | |
| Rear, Ancillary Building | x′ | | | | | | |
| Length of Building at Façade Line (BTL) | | | | | | | |
| Front | x% (est.) | | | | | | |
| Side Street, Main Building | x% (est.) | | | | | | |
| Side Street, Ancillary Building | x% (est.) | | | | | | |
| Width of Building/Lot Width (%) | | | | | | | |
| Front | x% (est.) | | | | | | |
| Side Street | x% (est.) | | | | | | |

**Fig. 3.20** Block Documentation Matrix template (3 pages), available for download at www.opticosdesign.com/fbcbook.html

| <Location and Transect Level> | Format | 1 | 2 | 3 | 4 | 5 | 6 |
|---|---|---|---|---|---|---|---|
| **Miscellaneous** | | | | | | | |
| Number of Buildings on Lot | x | | | | | | |
| Number of Main Buildings | x | | | | | | |
| Number of Ancillary Buildings | x | | | | | | |
| Distance between Main and Ancillary Buildings | x′ | | | | | | |
| Sidewalk Edge Treatment where There Is Not a Building | description | | | | | | |
| Treatment between Building and Sidewalk (if any) | description | | | | | | |
| **Building Form** | | | | | | | |
| **Height To:** | Eave (E);<br>Parapet Base (P).<br>Note any height variations | | | | | | |
| Main Building (stories) | x | | | | | | |
| To Eave or Parapet Base | x′ | | | | | | |
| To Ridge | x′ | | | | | | |
| Ancillary Building, Corner Lot (stories) | x | | | | | | |
| To Eave or Parapet Base | x′ | | | | | | |
| To Ridge | x′ | | | | | | |
| Ground Floor Finish Level (From Sidewalk Level) | x″ | | | | | | |
| Ground Floor Ceiling | x′ | | | | | | |
| Upper Floor(s) Ceiling | 2: x′; 3-5: x′ | | | | | | |
| **Footprint** | | | | | | | |
| Width | x′ | | | | | | |
| Depth | x′ | | | | | | |
| Depth, Ancillary Building | x′ | | | | | | |
| Footprint, Ancillary Building | x′ by x′ | | | | | | |
| Lot Coverage (All Buildings on Lot) | x% | | | | | | |
| Depth, Ground-floor Commercial Space | x′ | | | | | | |
| Depth, Ground-floor Residential Space | x′ | | | | | | |
| **Miscellaneous** | | | | | | | |
| Distance between Entries to Ground Floor | x′ | | | | | | |
| Distance between Entries to Upper Floors | x′ | | | | | | |
| Location of Entries to Upper Floors | note on plan | n.o.p | n.o.p | n.o.p | n.o.p | n.o.p | n.o.p |
| **Parking** | | | | | | | |
| **Number of spaces** | | | | | | | |
| Off-street (total) | x | | | | | | |
| Off-street covered | x | | | | | | |
| On-street along lot edges | x | | | | | | |
| Number of Residential Units | x | | | | | | |
| Number of Lodging Rooms | x | | | | | | |
| Square Footage of Non-residential Uses | | | | | | | |
| Ground Floor | x sf | | | | | | |
| Upper Floor(s) | x sf | | | | | | |
| **Distance of Off-street Parking From:** | ROW (R);<br>Property Line (P);<br>Sidewalk Edge (S);<br>Curb (C) | | | | | | |
| Front | x′ | | | | | | |
| Side Street (if any) | x′ | | | | | | |
| Right Side (not street facing) | x′ | | | | | | |
| Left Side (not street facing) | x′ | | | | | | |
| Rear | x′ | | | | | | |

| <Location and Transect Level> | Format | 1 | 2 | 3 | 4 | 5 | 6 |
|---|---|---|---|---|---|---|---|
| **Miscellaneous** | | | | | | | |
| Parking Drive Width | x′ | | | | | | |
| Parking Drive Location | note on plan | n.o.p | n.o.p | n.o.p | n.o.p | n.o.p | n.o.p |
| Shared Drive? | Yes (Y); No (N) | | | | | | |
| Character of Drive | desc. | | | | | | |
| Underground Parking? | Yes (Y); No (N) | | | | | | |
| Underground Parking Height above Sidewalk and Treatment | x′ and desc. | | | | | | |
| Number of Bicycle Parking Spaces | x | | | | | | |
| Parking Area Treatment | desc. | | | | | | |
| **Use Type(s)** | | | | | | | |
| Ground Floor | Residential (Res);<br>Retail (Ret);<br>Svcs: Bus/Fin/Pro (SB);<br>Svcs: Other (SO);<br>Rec/Educ/Assem. (E);<br>Trans/Comm/Infr.(T) | | | | | | |
| Upper Floor(s) | Residential (Res);<br>Retail (Ret);<br>Svcs: Bus/Fin/Pro (SB);<br>Svcs: Other (SO);<br>Rec/Educ/Assem. (E);<br>Trans/Comm/Infr.(T) | | | | | | |
| **Building Type** | | | | | | | |
| Building Type | Courtyard Building (C);<br>Townhouse (TH);<br>Fourplex (4);<br>Triplex (3);<br>Duplex (2);<br>Single Unit House (1) | | | | | | |
| **Frontage Type** | | | | | | | |
| Frontage Type | Gallery (G);<br>Arcade (Arc);<br>Shopfront (Sh);<br>Awning (Awn);<br>Stoop (St);<br>Forecourt (F);<br>Terrace or Light Court (T);<br>Porch and Yard | | | | | | |
| Frontage Depth | x′ | | | | | | |
| Frontage Height | x′ | | | | | | |
| Frontage Width | x′ | | | | | | |
| **Other Allowed Encroachments** | | | | | | | |
| Other Encroachment Types | Balconies (BAL);<br>Bay Windows (BW) | | | | | | |
| Typical Front Encroachment | x′ | | | | | | |
| Typical Side Street Encroachment | x′ | | | | | | |
| Typical Side Encroachment | x′ | | | | | | |
| Typical Rear Encroachment | x′ | | | | | | |

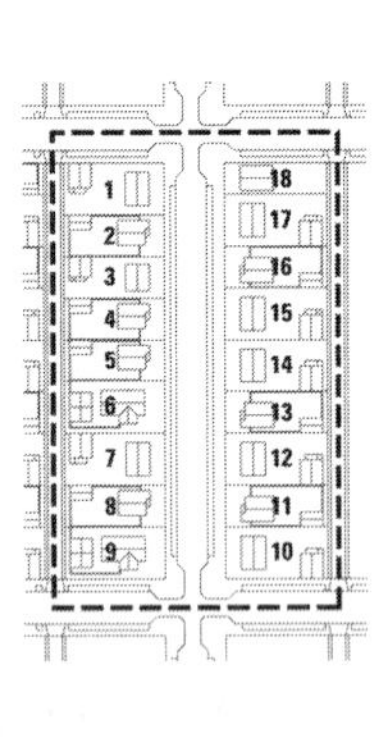

| Sample Block #1: Oak bet. Elm and Maple: T3 | 1 | 2 | 3 | 4 | 5 | 6 | Typical Mid-block | Typical Corner |
|---|---|---|---|---|---|---|---|---|
| **Building Placement** | | | | | | | | |
| **Lot Size** | | | | | | | | |
| Width | 50' | 45' | 45' | 35' | 45' | 50' | 45' | 50' |
| Depth | 110' | 110' | 110' | 110' | 110' | 110' | 110' | 110' |
| Square Footage | 5,500 | 4,950 | 4,950 | 3,850 | 4,950 | 5,500 | 4,950 | 5,500 |
| **Distance From** | P | P | P | P | P | P | P | P |
| Location of lot | C | M | M | M | M | C | M | C |
| If it is a corner lot, where does the building face? | P | — | — | — | — | P | — | P |
| Front (Main Body of Building) | 15' | 15' | 20' | 15' | 18' | 15' | 15'-20' | 15' |
| Side Street (Main Body of Building) | 15' | — | — | — | — | 15' | — | 15' |
| Left Side, Main Building | N/A | 8' | 8' | 8' | 8' | 8' | 8' | 8'-10' |
| Right Side, Main Building | 10' | 12' | 10' | 6' | 12' | N/A | | |
| Left Side, Ancillary Building | 0' | 5' | — | 5' | — | — | 5' | 8'-25' |
| Right Side, Ancillary Building | 25' | 10' | — | 8' | — | — | | |
| Rear, Main Building **(From ROW)** | 50' | 45' | 50' | 50' | 40' | 50' | 50' | 50' |
| Adjacent Use/Transect Level | T3 | T3 | T3 | T3 | T3 | T3 | T3 | T3 |
| Rear, Ancillary Building | 8' | 8' | — | 8' | — | — | 8' | 8' |
| Length of Building at Façade Line (BTL) | | | | | | | | |
| Front | 80% | 60% | 60% | 100% | 60% | 80% | 60%-100% | 80% |
| Side Street, Main Building | 30% | — | — | — | — | 30% | — | 30% |
| Side Street, Ancillary Building | 100% | — | — | — | — | 100% | — | 100% |
| Width of Building/Lot Width (%) | | | | | | | | |
| Front | 50% | 55% | 60% | 60% | 55% | 55% | 55% | 50% |
| Side Street | 55% | N/A | N/A | N/A | N/A | 55% | — | 55% |
| **Miscellaneous** | | | | | | | | |

**Fig. 3.21** Presentation board for a sampling block with typical condition columns added to the Block Documentation Matrix. Note that the boards should include the columns for all the lots on the block, as well as all the rows of the matrix, not just the subset shown here.

If there is time, also include a complete panoramic view of the street elevation.

### Product List

- Completed Block Documentation Matrix for each sampling block

## 1.2.4 Organize the Data

Once the data is collected, it needs to be organized to prepare for the visioning process.

### Process

Begin by cleaning up the Block Documentation Matrices as necessary in order to make them readable and presentable. Next, add two columns to the far right of each matrix, one titled "Typical Mid-block" and one titled "Typical Corner." Analyze the sample data for the block, and fill in the two columns with the values best exemplifying the typical conditions from the samples on the matrix. The final numbers should not be averages, but rather the most typical condition.

Once the matrices are complete, create a presentation board for each sampling block. Include the Existing Conditions Base Map, the Block Documentation Matrix, and some of the photos taken during the site visit. (See Figure 3.21.)

### Product List

- Presentation board for each sampling block

## 1.2.5 Analyze the Data

Before the data can be used for the visioning phase, it needs to be analyzed and summarized. This summary data will become the predraft of the content of the code regulations.

### Process

Group all the Block Documentation Matrices by transect level (or subset level). For each group (transect level), create a new matrix and copy both typical condition columns from each Block Documentation Matrix in the group to the new matrix, called an "Existing Transect Level Matrix." (See Figure 3.22.)

Once all the Existing Transect Level Matrices are complete, repeat the process once more. Begin by adding two columns to the far right of each Existing Transect Level Matrix, one titled "Typical Mid-block Condition" and one titled "Typical Corner Condition." Analyze the sample data across all the transect level sampling areas, and fill in the two columns with the regulations best exemplifying the typical conditions. (See Figure 3.23.) Complete these additional columns on each of the Existing Transect Level Matrices.

Finally, copy both typical conditions columns from each Existing Transect Level Matrix to a

| T3 | Block 1 | | Block 2 | | Block 3 | |
|---|---|---|---|---|---|---|
| | Typical Mid-block | Typical Corner | Typical Mid-block | Typical Corner | Typical Mid-block | Typical Corner |
| **City** | | | | | | |
| Width of Largest Historic Building **(Historic Hotel)** | 115' | | — | | — | |
| **Block** | | | | | | |
| Perimeter Length | 1530' | | 1530' | | 1280' | |
| Length (Primary Street) | 525' | | 525' | | 400' | |
| Depth (Secondary Street) | 240' | | 240' | | 240' | |
| Shape | R | | R | | R | |
| On-street parking spaces within 1/4-mile radius | 250 | | 250 | | 200 | |
| Length of Building at Front BTL from Corner | | | | | | |
| Left End of Block | 150' | | 80' | | 0' corner chamfer | |
| Right End of Block | 80' | | 80' | | 80' | |
| **Building Placement** | | | | | | |
| **Lot Size** | | | | | | |
| Width | 45' | 50' | 50' | 60' | 45' | 50' |
| Depth | 110' | 110' | 110' | 110' | 110' | 110' |
| Square Footage | 4,950 | 5,500 | 5,500 | 6,600 | 4,950 | 5,500 |
| **Distance From** | P | P | P | P | P | P |
| Location of lot | M | C | M | C | M | C |
| If it is a corner lot, where does the building face? | — | P | — | P | — | P |
| Front (Main Body of Building) | 15'-20' | 15' | 20' | 20' | 15' - 20' | 15' |
| Side Street (Main Body of Building) | — | 15' | — | 15' - 20' | — | 15' |
| Left Side, Main Building | 8' | 8'-10' | 8' | 8' - 10' | 8' | 8' - 10' |
| Right Side, Main Building | | | | | | |
| Left Side, Ancillary Building | 5' | 8'-25' | 0' - 60' | 0' | 0' - 60' | 0' |
| Right Side, Ancillary Building | | | | | | |
| Rear, Main Building | 50' | 50' | 40' | 40' | 40' | 40' |
| Adjacent Use/Transect Level | T3 | T3 | T4 | T4 | T4 | T4 |
| Rear, Ancillary Building | 8' | 8' | 8' | 8' | 6' | 6' |
| Length of Building at Façade Line (BTL) | | | | | | |
| Front | 60% - 100% | 80% | 50% - 90% | 45% - 85% | 60% - 100% | 80% |
| Side Street, Main Building | — | 30% | — | 35% | — | 30% |
| Side Street, Ancillary Building | — | 100% | — | 100% | — | 100% |
| Width of Building/Lot Width (%) | | | | | | |
| Front | 55% | 50% | 35% | 35% | 40% | 40% |
| Side Street | — | 55% | 55% | 60% | 60% | 65% |
| **Miscellaneous** | | | | | | |
| Number of Buildings on Lot | 2 | 2 | 2 | 2 | 2 | 2 |
| Number of Main Buildings | 1 | 1 | 1 | 1 | 1 | 1 |
| Number of Ancillary Buildings | 1 | 1 | 1 | 1 | 1 | 1 |
| Distance between Main and Ancillary Buildings | 30' | 27' | 25' - 30' | 25' - 30' | 27' - 32' | 27' |
| Sidewalk Edge Treatment where There Is Not a Building | 3' fence | 3' fence | 3' fence | — | 3' hedge | — |
| Treatment between Building and Sidewalk (if any) | lawn | lawn | lawn | lawn | lawn | lawn |

**Fig. 3.22** Existing Transect Level Matrix for the T3 level with the typical conditions from each of the documented blocks in T3

| T3 | Block 1 | | Block 2 | | Block 3 | | Typical | |
|---|---|---|---|---|---|---|---|---|
| | Typical Mid-block | Typical Corner | Typical Mid-block | Typical Corner | Typical Mid-block | Typical Corner | Mid-block | Corner |
| **City** | | | | | | | | |
| Width of Largest Historic Building **(Historic Hotel)** | 115' | | — | | — | | 115' | |
| **Block** | | | | | | | | |
| Perimeter Length | 1530' | | 1530' | | 1280' | | 1530' | |
| Length (Primary Street) | 525' | | 525' | | 400' | | 525' | |
| Depth (Secondary Street) | 240' | | 240' | | 240' | | 240' | |
| Shape | R | | R | | R | | R | |
| On-street parking spaces within 1/4-mile radius | 250 | | 250 | | 200 | | 250 | |
| Length of Building at Front BTL from Corner | | | | | | | | |
| Left End of Block | 150' | | 80' | | 0' corner chamfer | | | |
| Right End of Block | 80' | | 80' | | 80' | | | |
| **Building Placement** | | | | | | | | |
| **Lot Size** | | | | | | | | |
| Width | 45' | 50' | 50' | 60' | 45' | 50' | 45' - 50' | 50' - 60' |
| Depth | 110' | 110' | 110' | 110' | 110' | 110' | 110' | 110' |
| Square Footage | 4,950 | 5,500 | 5,500 | 6,600 | 4,950 | 5,500 | 5,500 | 6,600 |
| **Distance From** | P | P | P | P | P | P | P | P |
| Location of lot | M | C | M | C | M | C | M | C |
| If it is a corner lot, where does the building face? | — | P | — | P | — | P | — | P |
| Front (Main Body of Building) | 15'-20' | 15' | 20' | 20' | 15' - 20' | 15' | 15' - 20' | 15' - 20' |
| Side Street (Main Body of Building) | — | 15' | — | 15' - 20' | — | 15' | — | 15' - 20' |
| Left Side, Main Building | 8' | 8'-10' | 8' | 8' - 10' | 8' | 8' - 10' | 8' | 8' - 10' |
| Right Side, Main Building | | | | | | | | |
| Left Side, Ancillary Building | 5' | 8'-25' | 0' - 60' | 0' | 0' - 60' | 0' | 0' - 60' | 0' |
| Right Side, Ancillary Building | | | | | | | | |
| Rear, Main Building | 50' | 50' | 40' | 40' | 40' | 40' | 40' | 40' |
| Adjacent Use/Transect Level | T3 | T3 | T4 | T4 | T4 | T4 | T4 | T4 |
| Rear, Ancillary Building | 8' | 8' | 8' | 8' | 6' | 6' | 6' - 8' | 6' - 8' |
| Length of Building at Façade Line (BTL) | | | | | | | | |
| Front | 60% - 100% | 80% | 50% - 90% | 45% - 85% | 60% - 100% | 80% | 60% - 100% | 50% - 80% |
| Side Street, Main Building | — | 30% | — | 35% | — | 30% | — | 30% - 35% |
| Side Street, Ancillary Building | — | 100% | — | 100% | — | 100% | — | 100% |
| Width of Building/Lot Width (%) | | | | | | | | |
| Front | 55% | 50% | 35% | 35% | 40% | 40% | 35% - 55% | 35% - 50% |
| Side Street | — | 55% | 55% | 60% | 60% | 65% | 60% | 60% |
| **Miscellaneous** | | | | | | | | |
| Number of Buildings on Lot | 2 | 2 | 2 | 2 | 2 | 2 | 2 | 2 |
| Number of Main Buildings | 1 | 1 | 1 | 1 | 1 | 1 | 1 | 1 |
| Number of Ancillary Buildings | 1 | 1 | 1 | 1 | 1 | 1 | 1 | 1 |
| Distance between Main and Ancillary Buildings | 30' | 27' | 25' - 30' | 25' - 30' | 27' - 32' | 27' | 25' - 30' | 25' - 30' |
| Sidewalk Edge Treatment where There Is Not a Building | 3' fence | 3' fence | 3' fence | — | 3' hedge | — | 3' fence | — |
| Treatment between Building and Sidewalk (if any) | lawn | lawn | lawn | lawn | lawn | lawn | lawn | lawn |

**Fig. 3.23** Existing Transect Level Matrix for the T3 level with the typical conditions determined for the entire transect level

| | T3 | | T4 | | T5 | |
|---|---|---|---|---|---|---|
| | Typical Mid-block | Typical Corner | Typical Mid-block | Typical Corner | Typical Mid-block | Typical Corner |
| **City** | | | | | | |
| Width of Largest Historic Building | | | 120' Apartment Bldg | | | |
| **Block** | | | | | | |
| Perimeter Length | 1530' | | 1600' | | 1600' | |
| Length (Primary Street) | 525' | | 400' | | 400' | |
| Depth (Secondary Street) | 240' | | 400' | | 400' | |
| Shape | R | | R | | R | |
| On-street parking spaces within 1/4-mile radius | 250 | | 200 | | 200 | |
| Length of Building at Front BTL from Corner | | | | | | |
| Left End of Block | | | 80' | | 100' | |
| Right End of Block | | | 100' | | 100' | |
| **Building Placement** | | | | | | |
| **Lot Size** | | | | | | |
| Width | 45' - 50' | 50' - 60' | 25' | 30' | 75' - 125' | 75' - 125' |
| Depth | 110' | 110' | 100' | 100' | 100' - 150' | 100' - 150' |
| Square Footage | 5,500 | 6,600 | 2,500 | 3,000 | 12,500 | 12,500 sf |
| **Distance From** | P | P | P | P | P | P |
| Location of lot | M | C | M | C | M | C |
| If it is a corner lot, where does the building face? | — | P | — | P | — | P |
| Front (Main Body of Building) | 15' - 20' | 15' - 20' | 5' | 5' | 0' | 0' |
| Side Street (Main Body of Building) | — | 15' - 20' | — | 5' | — | 0' |
| Left Side, Main Building | 8' | 8' - 10' | 0' | 0' | 0' | 0' |
| Right Side, Main Building | | | | | | |
| Left Side, Ancillary Building | 0' - 60' | 0' | 0' | 0' | — | — |
| Right Side, Ancillary Building | | | | | | |
| Rear, Main Building | 40' | 40' | 40' | 40' | — | — |
| Adjacent Use/Transect Level | T4 | T4 | t4 & T5 | T4 & T5 | — | — |
| Rear, Ancillary Building | 6' - 8' | 6' - 8' | 6' | 6' | — | — |
| Length of Building at Façade Line (BTL) | | | | | | |
| Front | 60% - 100% | 50% - 80% | 100% | 100% | 90% - 100% | 90% - 100% |
| Side Street, Main Building | — | 30% - 35% | — | 70% | — | 90% - 100% |
| Side Street, Ancillary Building | — | 100% | — | 70% | — | — |
| Width of Building/Lot Width (%) | | | | | | |
| Front | 35% - 55% | 35% - 50% | 100% | 80% - 100% | 80% - 100% | 80% - 100% |
| Side Street | 60% | 60% | — | 70% | — | 80% - 100% |

**Fig. 3.24** Existing Transect Matrix

new matrix called the "Existing Transect Matrix," and add a good example photo of each transect level to the matrix. (See Figure 3.24.) This is now the base matrix to be used to inform the visioning process and ultimately to be used for the Form-Based Code regulations.

**Product List**

- Existing Transect Level Matrices
- Existing Transect Matrix

## 1.2.6 Repeat for Other Micro Elements

For each of the micro elements, repeat steps 1.2.1 through 1.2.4. (Step 1.2.5 is necessary only for documenting the transect levels.) See the sidebar "Repeating Process for Building Types." (See Figures 3.25 through 3.27 for documentation sheet templates for some of the most common micro elements.) Following are some additional considerations and tips.

**Product List**

- Completed Micro-Element Documentation Sheets
- Presentation board for each micro-element sample

**Thoroughfare Types**

The vast majority of the micro-scale documentation is to document precedents to use to either preserve current places or replicate them elsewhere. However, documenting thoroughfares is necessary for a couple of other reasons. Documenting historic thoroughfares can help stakeholders and decision makers recognize the feasibility of narrower thoroughfare designs, as well as provide base measurements for the code's thoroughfare standards. Documenting selected hierarchical thoroughfares can help the team understand the existing thoroughfare hierarchy to better build upon it, connect into it, adjust it, or replicate it. Documenting dysfunctional thoroughfares provides the base measurement

### Repeating Process for Building Types

1.2.1 Begin by reviewing the list of building types recorded during the macro-scale documentation as well as the standard list provided in Section 2: Building Type Standards. Select several samples for each building type to document, making sure to vary the selections across all transect levels, neighborhoods, and historic eras where possible. Note each selected sample location on the Existing Conditions Base Map and number the samples.

1.2.2 Create a Building Type Documentation Sheet for each building type sample. Label each sheet with the building type and the sample number from the Existing Conditions Base Map. (See Figure 3.27.)

1.2.3 Fill out each sheet during the site visit, creating a sketch of the building and taking a variety of photos.

**Tip:** For buildings that were originally constructed as a single-family house but were subsequently converted into multiple units, also document how they have been converted, what densities they achieve, and how they function within their neighborhood. These buildings can likely be the basis for the regulations for a mansion apartment type.

1.2.4 Clean up the Building Type Documentation Sheets to make them presentable, and add a photo of the sample building to each sheet. Group the sheets by building type, and create a presentation board for each group.

**Product List**

- Completed Building Type Documentation Sheets
- Presentation boards for each micro element sample

## Location:
## Thoroughfare Type:



| Application | | |
|---|---|---|
| Movement Type | Yield \| Slow \| Free | |
| Speed Limit | mph | |
| Pedestrian Crossing Time | seconds | |
| Transect Level | | |
| **Overall Widths** | | |
| Right-of-Way (ROW) Width | *(note on section)* | A |
| Curb Face to Curb Face Width | *(note on section)* | B |
| **Lanes** | | |
| Traffic Lanes | Single \| Yield | C |
| Bicycle Lanes | *(note on section)* | D |
| Parking Lanes | Parallel \| Diagonal<br>Reverse Diagonal | E |
| Medians | *(note on section)* | F |

| Edges | | |
|---|---|---|
| Curbs | Square \| Rolled \| Swale | |
| Planters | Continuous Planter<br>Continuous Swale<br>Tree Well | G |
| Landscaping | | |
| Type | | |
| Spacing Type | Evenly-spaced \| Clustered | |
| Spacing | o.c. avg. | |
| Walkways | Sidewalk \| Path | H |
| Lighting | | I |
| Type | | |
| Spacing | o.c. avg. | |
| **Intersection** | | |
| Curb Radius | | |
| Distance between Intersections | | |

**Fig. 3.25** Thoroughfare Documentation Sheet template

Location: #4: Oak St. bet. Elm and Maple
Thoroughfare Type: Street


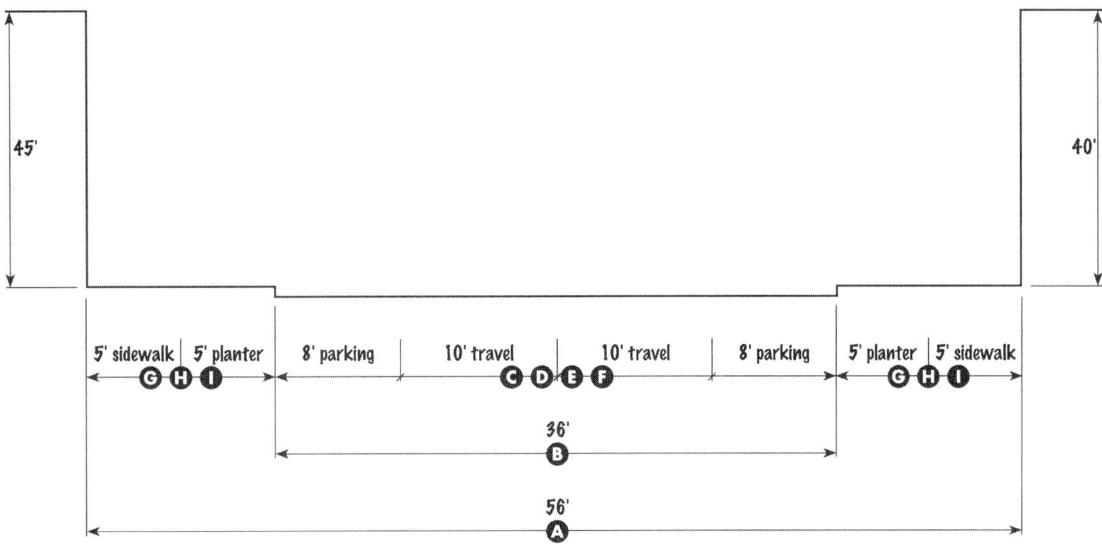


| Application | | |
|---|---|---|
| Movement Type | Yield \| Slow \| Free | |
| Speed Limit | 20 mph | |
| Pedestrian Crossing Time | 10.3 seconds | |
| Transect Level | T4 | |
| **Overall Widths** | | |
| Right-of-Way (ROW) Width | *(note on section)* | A |
| Curb Face to Curb Face Width | *(note on section)* | B |
| **Lanes** | | |
| Traffic Lanes | Single \| Yield | C |
| Bicycle Lanes | *(note on section)* | D |
| Parking Lanes | Parallel \| Diagonal<br>Reverse Diagonal | E |
| Medians | *(note on section)* | F |

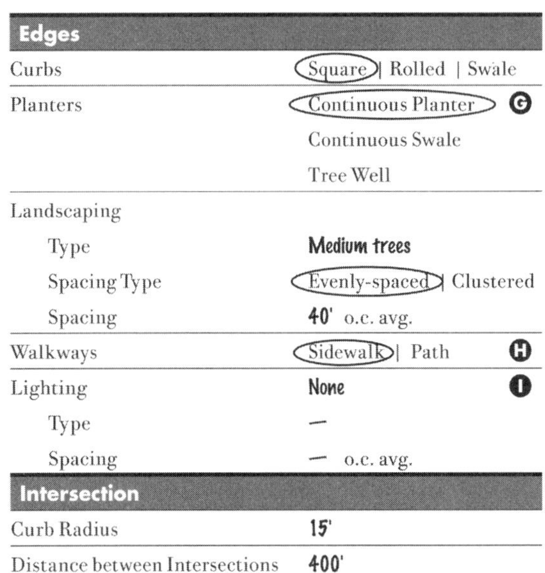

| Edges | | |
|---|---|---|
| Curbs | Square \| Rolled \| Swale | |
| Planters | Continuous Planter<br>Continuous Swale<br>Tree Well | G |
| Landscaping | | |
| Type | Medium trees | |
| Spacing Type | Evenly-spaced \| Clustered | |
| Spacing | 40' o.c. avg. | |
| Walkways | Sidewalk \| Path | H |
| Lighting | None | I |
| Type | — | |
| Spacing | — o.c. avg. | |
| **Intersection** | | |
| Curb Radius | 15' | |
| Distance between Intersections | 400' | |

Template available for download at www.opticosdesign.com/fbcbook.html

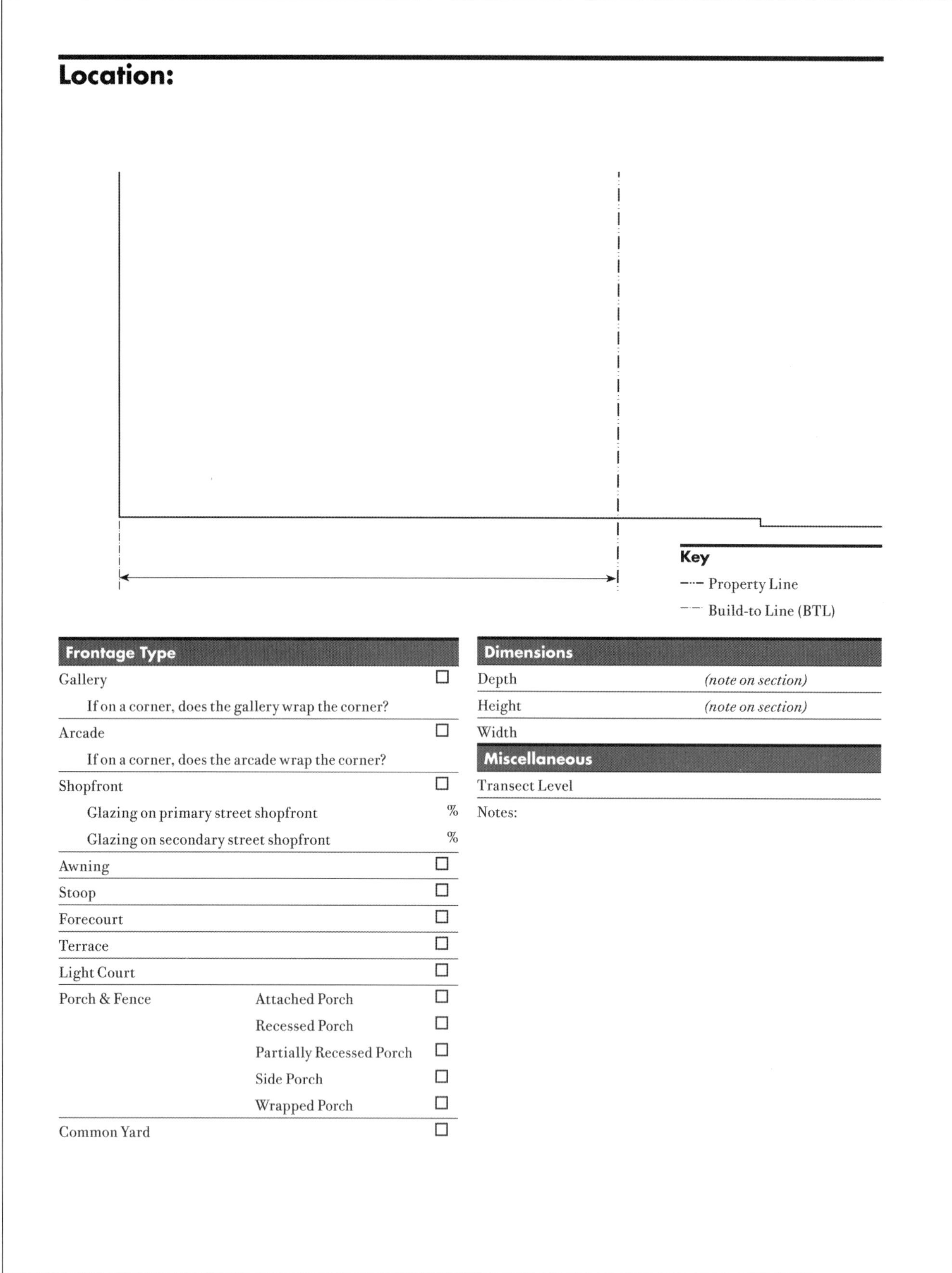

## Location:

**Key**

Property Line

Build-to Line (BTL)

| Frontage Type | | |
|---|---|---|
| Gallery | | ☐ |
| If on a corner, does the gallery wrap the corner? | | |
| Arcade | | ☐ |
| If on a corner, does the arcade wrap the corner? | | |
| Shopfront | | ☐ |
| Glazing on primary street shopfront | | % |
| Glazing on secondary street shopfront | | % |
| Awning | | ☐ |
| Stoop | | ☐ |
| Forecourt | | ☐ |
| Terrace | | ☐ |
| Light Court | | ☐ |
| Porch & Fence | Attached Porch | ☐ |
| | Recessed Porch | ☐ |
| | Partially Recessed Porch | ☐ |
| | Side Porch | ☐ |
| | Wrapped Porch | ☐ |
| Common Yard | | ☐ |

| Dimensions | |
|---|---|
| Depth | *(note on section)* |
| Height | *(note on section)* |
| Width | |

| Miscellaneous | |
|---|---|
| Transect Level | |
| Notes: | |

**Fig. 3.26** Frontage Type Documentation Sheet template

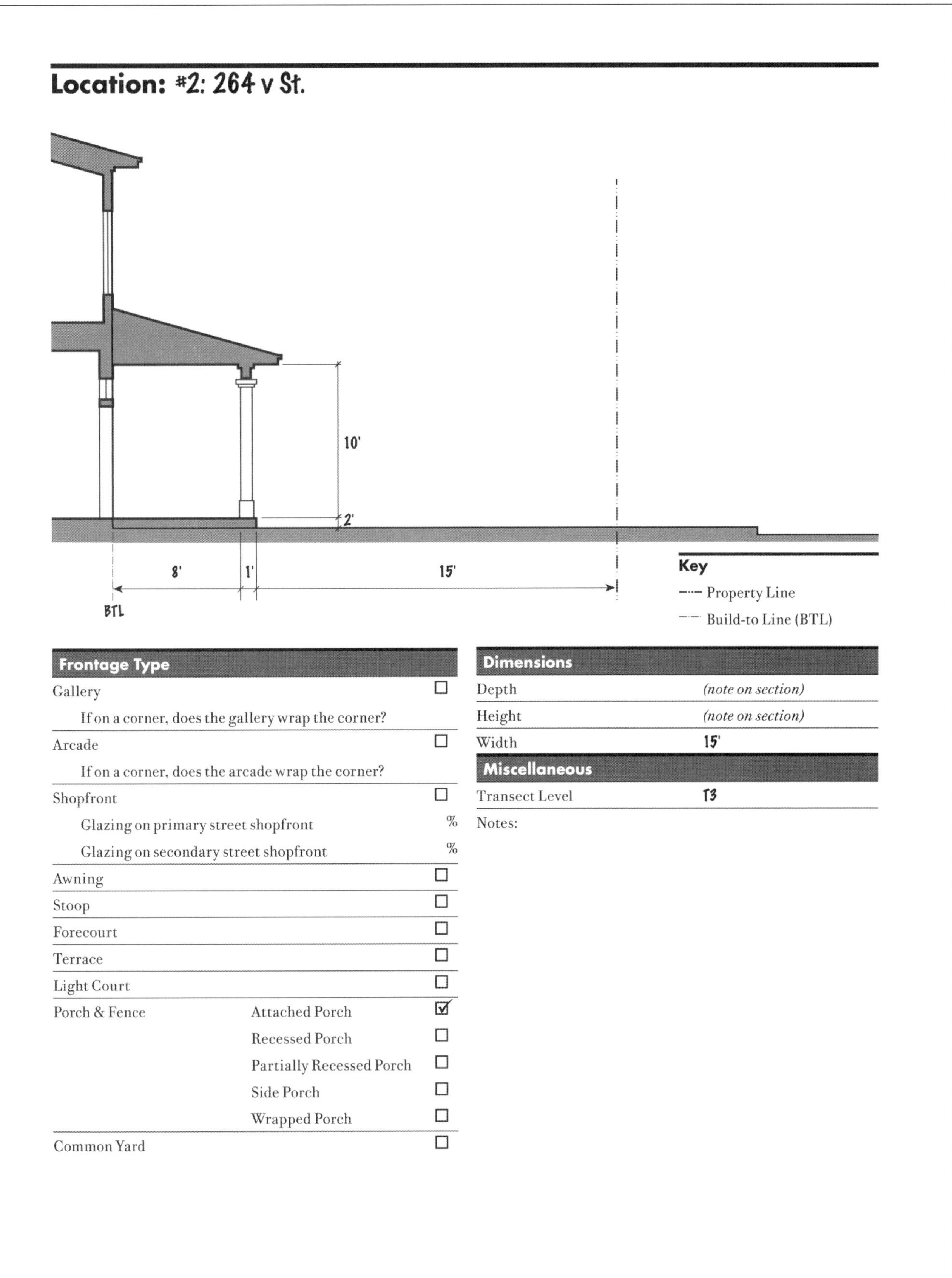

## Location: #2: 264 v St.



| Frontage Type | | |
|---|---|---|
| Gallery | | [ ] |
| If on a corner, does the gallery wrap the corner? | | |
| Arcade | | [ ] |
| If on a corner, does the arcade wrap the corner? | | |
| Shopfront | | [ ] |
| Glazing on primary street shopfront | | % |
| Glazing on secondary street shopfront | | % |
| Awning | | [ ] |
| Stoop | | [ ] |
| Forecourt | | [ ] |
| Terrace | | [ ] |
| Light Court | | [ ] |
| Porch & Fence | Attached Porch | [x] |
| | Recessed Porch | [ ] |
| | Partially Recessed Porch | [ ] |
| | Side Porch | [ ] |
| | Wrapped Porch | [ ] |
| Common Yard | | [ ] |

| Dimensions | |
|---|---|
| Depth | *(note on section)* |
| Height | *(note on section)* |
| Width | 15' |

| Miscellaneous | |
|---|---|
| Transect Level | T3 |

Notes:

## Location:
## Building Type:

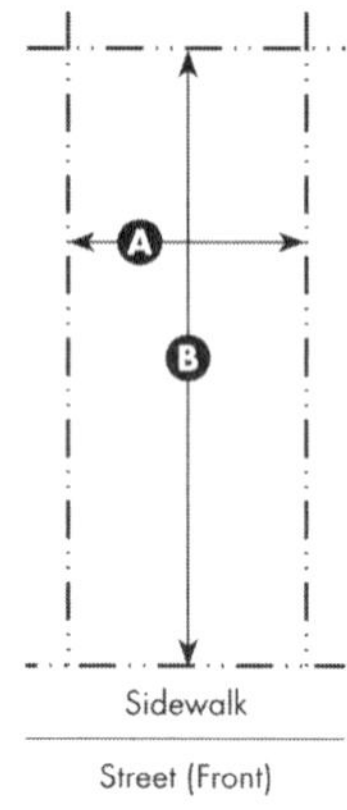


**Key**

| | |
|---|---|
| Property Line | Setback Line |
| Build-to Line (BTL) | Building Area |

| Lot Size | |
|---|---|
| Lot Width | ft. |
| Lot Depth | ft. |

| Pedestrian Access | |
|---|---|
| Entry to units is oriented toward a street or courtyard. | ☐ |
| Upper floor units have an entrance from the street. | ☐ |
| Elevator goes from ________________ to ________________ | |
| Distance between entries to upper floors | ft. |
| Distance bet. doors at street | ft. |
| Notes: | |

| Landscape |
|---|
| Are there landscape characteristics specific to this type that are important to the way the type functions? |
| Notes: |

| Vehicular Access and Parking | |
|---|---|
| **Type of Parking** | |
| Single-unit garage (detached) | ☐ |
| Single-unit garage (tuck-under) | ☐ |
| Off-street parking | ☐ |
| On-street parking | ☐ |
| Underground parking garage | ☐ |
| Parking | ☐ |
| **Parking Access** | |
| Direct | ☐ |
| Indirect | ☐ |
| **Other** | |
| How is trash serviced? | |
| Where are utilities and above-ground equipment located? | |
| Notes: | |

**Fig. 3.27** Building Type Documentation Sheet template

**Building Size and Massing**

Breaks in planes on front elevation? ☐

If yes, how many or how often?

Breaks in planes on side elevation? ☐

If yes, how many or how often?

Heights

**Unit Types**

Flats ☐

Townhouses ☐

Lofts ☐

Live/Work ☐

Combination of Units:

In relation to open space and orientation?

Notes:

**Open Space**

Provided? Yes | No

**Location**

Rear Yard ☐

Side Yard ☐

Courtyard ☐

Other ☐

**Miscellaneous**

Size ft. x ft.

Projections into the space?

Direct Yes | No

Indirect Yes | No

Intended Use

General Character

Notes:

**Miscellaneous**

Transect Level

Corner lot?

Number of Units (if Applicable)

Percentage Build-to %

**Frontages**

Which types of rooms face the street?

Which types of rooms face the rear?

What type of transition exists from public to private street?

Notes:

information for them to be transformed. The selection of which thoroughfares to document will be based on which of these reasons exist within the scope of the project.

When selecting thoroughfares to document, consider the reasons the information is needed as discussed above. For historic thoroughfares, select as many good ones as possible to cover the existing range of thoroughfare types and transect levels. To understand the existing framework, study the Existing Framework Diagram and select a sampling of thoroughfares for each level in the thoroughfare hierarchy. Finally, select all thoroughfares that may need to be transformed as part of the project.

### Civic Spaces

Documenting civic spaces is necessary to demonstrate to the team members and other vision-

## When Good Local Precedent Doesn't Exist

In some instances, a good local precedent of an appropriate urban form may not exist to use as a basis for a Form-Based Code. Three such instances are:

1. A community that has been completely developed in a post–World War II suburban pattern and has decided that it wants to require new development to be more walkable and sustainable, possibly including adding a new town center
2. A community that is calling for major transformation and evolution that will incorporate development beyond the scale of what currently exists in the community
3. A community that wants future development within the entire community or a specific planning area to respond environmentally to its location in a way that past development did not

In these situations, the Form-Based Code team should expand the documentation area, first looking regionally for precedent, and if appropriate examples are not found regionally, then looking beyond to other areas with similar climates for examples of built environments that can serve as precedents for character, form, and function. For example, consider a community in the Southwest that has a desert climate and desires a more environmentally sensitive approach to its development. The code team could first look regionally throughout the Southwest for other towns that have more successfully integrated climatic concerns into their planning. If none are found, they could then look at examples in Central or South America, where the urban form responds directly to the climate with the integration of courtyard homes to provide usable private spaces for the residents, shaded walkways with the use of arcades or more vertically proportioned streets to encourage walkability, minimal landscaping to reduce the use of water, and the integration of passive solar heating and cooling into the building forms. (See Figure 3.28.)

Selecting a precedent for a Form-Based Code outside the region can be challenging and should be considered carefully. First, consider the quality and intensity of the urbanism and character of the place trying to be achieved. As discussed above, often these outside examples can enable a community to respond to such specific local conditions as climate, but they can also enable a community to consider typical physical conditions, such as topography in its ultimate physical form. In taking this approach, public planning agencies in particular need to be careful to understand the feasibility within the local development market, construction costs and constraints,

ing participants how the size, function, and role of civic spaces vary across transect levels. Make sure to select a variety of civic space types across the full range of transect levels to document.

## Conclusion

By the end of the documentation phase, the team will have a thorough understanding of the physical parameters of the community represented in the Existing Transect Matrix and the documentation sheets for thoroughfares, civic spaces, and any other micro elements documented. This will represent a wealth of information that is representative of the DNA of a community. These, in combination with the Existing Framework Diagram, will become the foundation for the vision plan and will evolve into the content of the FBC.



and development potential. This being said, communities should not be afraid to push these parameters within reason. The Central Hercules Planning District in Hercules, California, is a good example of this approach by a city. Hercules, which historically had been a bedroom community for the San Francisco Bay Area developed in suburban pattern, hired Dover, Kohl & Partners to establish a vision for a new town center and a series of traditional neighborhoods. After establishing this vision, Dover Kohl wrote an FBC to implement the vision. Many of the builders complained about the code, saying that the local market was not in place for such a project, nor was it economically viable. With strong opposition from builders, the city held its ground and made the early builders adhere to the code. In the end, the market responded to the first phase, and the value of the homes have since been higher per square foot than others in the area.

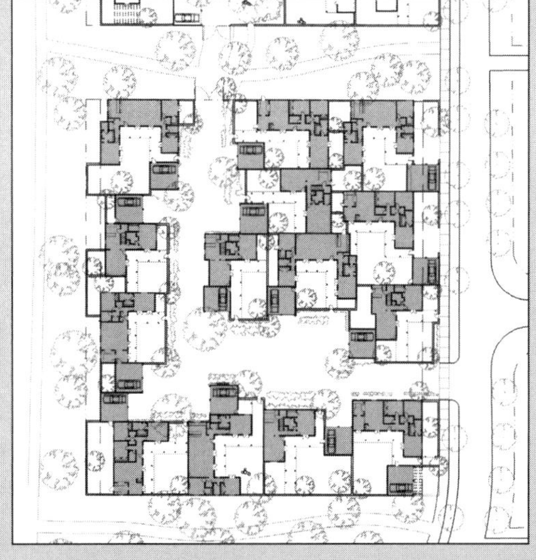

**Fig. 3.28** Plan and illustration of urban form, building form, and landscape responding appropriately to a desert climate based on appropriate precedent studies (Civano Housing images © 2007 Moule & Polyzoides, Architects and Urbanists)

# Phase 2: Visioning

A CRITICAL COMPONENT of creating a Form-Based Code is the visioning process. As discussed earlier, one of the primary reasons to use a Form-Based Code is because it helps ensure a predictable outcome for the built environment. However, there must be a desired outcome (a vision) in order to create a code that prescribes it.

In addition, it is critical that it be a *good* vision that is detailed enough to put a Form-Based Code in place. Technically, a good Form-Based Code is one that successfully prescribes the vision defined by the community. A Form-Based Code can enable the creation of a good place only if both the code *and* the vision are good.

A good vision has three characteristics: (1) It is a vision of a place the community really wants, after having a thorough understanding all the implications of the design. (2) It is detailed to a very refined level—much more refined than the visioning processes most communities and planners are familiar with from comprehensive or general plans. A "bubble diagram" will not work. (3) It is implementable. A multidisciplinary team should be involved to test the vision for feasibility as it evolves to ensure that it is practical and implementable.

The first requirement is beyond the scope of this book, although the process and products from the documentation phase as well as the information in the components section are certainly intended to help facilitate good communication and decision making toward this goal. The second requirement is the focus of the following instructions for this phase.

Also, the following process is intended for codes that will include a Regulating Plan as part of the approved code. For codes that will not have a Regulating Plan until it is submitted as part of each project's development application, the details of this process will need to be modified to include the creation of the additional necessary components, such as the Block Standards, as well as to assign such elements as thoroughfare types and civic space types to the transect zones rather than to a Regulating Plan.

## Process Overview

The products from the documentation phase are the foundation for the visioning phase, and so are presented to all participants to begin the visioning dialogue. (See Figure 3.29.) The visioning work is then begun by laying out the framework of the intended place on an Illustrative Plan and illustrating each of the transect zones and micro elements necessary to implement the vision. For coding projects that include areas with an existing built environment, the visioning team and participants make decisions about what degree of change is appropriate for the existing places. For greenfield and large infill projects, they design the new places.

To further detail the intended vision, the preliminary regulations are drafted, including the Regulating Plan, Regulations Matrix, and Development Review Process. The Illustrative Plan and related imagery are used to establish the physical locations and boundaries of the regulating zones on the Preliminary Regulating Plan. The Existing Transect Matrix is then used to fill out the Preliminary Transect Matrix, adjusting the regulations and values to reflect the desired vision of the community rather than the existing place. The micro-element documentation sheets are used in a similar fashion to develop the Preliminary Element Matrices. Finally, the development review process is drafted based on input from the stakeholders about the amount of discretionary review desired.

By the end of the visioning process, there should be a clear view of the intentions for the future of the community documented in enough detail to be able to begin the final coding process. All the products are then assembled into a Vision Plan, a document describing the desired intentions for the built environment.

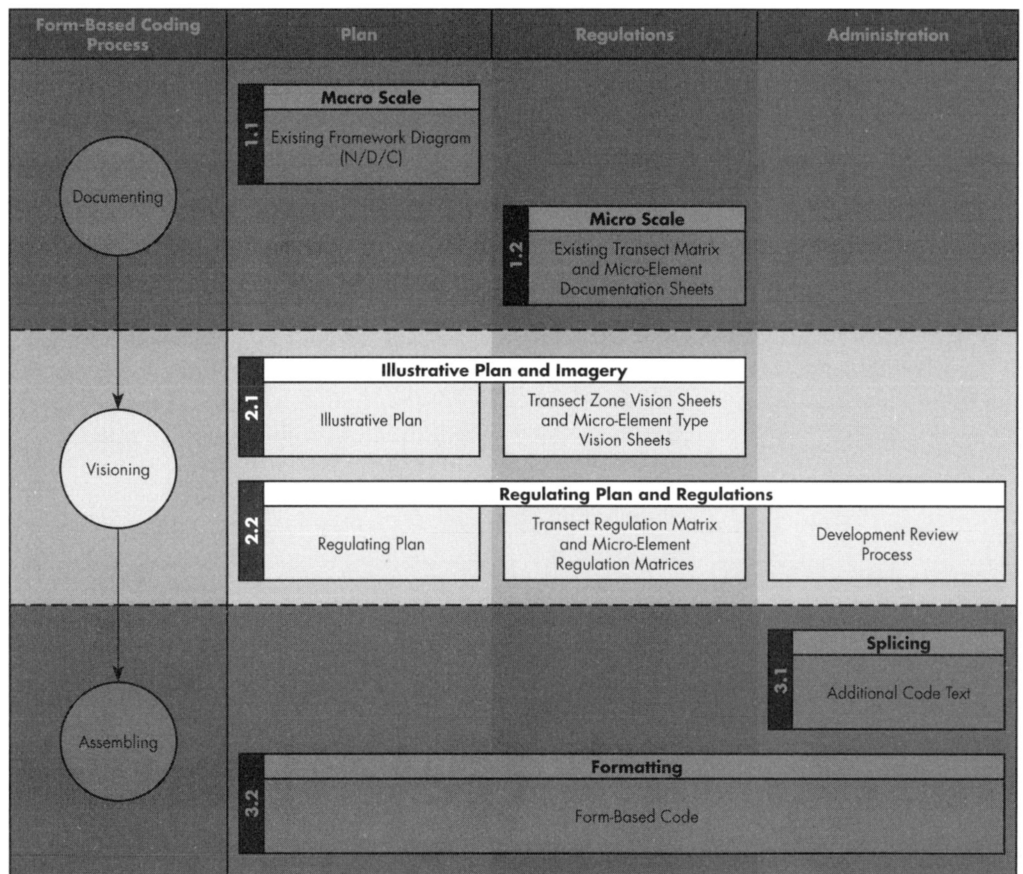


**Fig. 3.29**
Phase 2: Visioning

## Public Visioning Process

The creation of a vision is a collaborative effort that requires the input of a variety of professionals as well as other stakeholders, such as the developer, the municipality, and the neighbors. In addition, a Form-Based Code is a legal public document that inherently affects its community. For that reason, it is only right that the public has a critical part in defining the vision that the FBC helps implement. Finally, because an FBC will ultimately need to be approved by local public agencies to be made legal, its creation is inherently a political process.

For these reasons and more, the authors strongly recommend the National Charrette Institute's Dynamic Planning Process for the visioning work required as part of creating a Form-Based Code. The highlight of this Dynamic Planning Process is a four- to seven-day charrette involving all the stakeholders on the project, including the public.

This process has multiple benefits, all of which assist in the success of creating a Form-Based Code. The two most important benefits are:

1. A shortened visioning (and coding) process, which can speed up both the visioning process and the public approval process.
2. A collaborative public process that creates public momentum behind a shared vision. This wave of momentum is often critical in getting a Form-Based Code through the difficult waters of the public approval process.

More resources about the public visioning process can be found in the Resources section at the end of this book.

# 2.1 Illustrative Plan and Imagery



THE VISIONING PROCESS begins with the creation of the Illustrative Plan and Vision Sheets. The Illustrative Plan is the defining drawing of the vision, showing the envisioned layout of the community. It includes the locations of neighborhoods, districts, corridors, and, depending on the scope and scale of the project, other elements, such as thoroughfares, civic spaces, buildings, and transit lines.

As the Illustrative Plan is developed, decisions are made about which transect zones and micro-element types are necessary to fulfill the vision. The Vision Sheets include illustrations and written descriptions of each of these to help communicate their intention.

## Process Overview

The creation of the Illustrative Plan includes three steps. (See Figure 3.30.) First, a meeting is held with all the team members, stakeholders, and other visioning participants to present the documentation information and begin the visioning dialog. This ensures that everyone understands the scope of the project and the existing conditions before beginning the visioning. Second, the Illustrative Plan is begun by locating the macro elements: neighborhoods, districts, and corridors. Third, if appropriate to the scope of the project, certain micro elements are added, typically thoroughfares, civic spaces, and buildings.

Based on the lists of transect zones on the Illustrative Plan, a Transect Zone Vision Sheet is then created for each zone with an illustration and descriptive text, as well as a list of micro elements needed for the zone. Finally, an Element Type Vision Sheet is created for each necessary micro element based on these lists as well as the lists of thoroughfare types and civic space types on the Illustrative Plan.

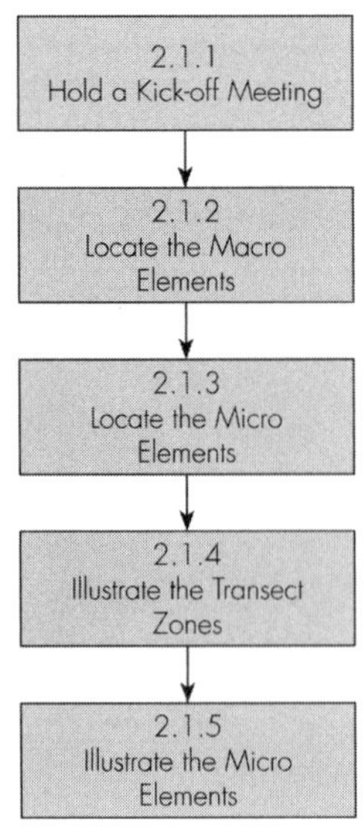


**Fig. 3.30**
2.1 Illustrative Plan and Imagery

## 2.1.1 Hold a Kickoff Meeting

Gather all the materials from the documentation process, especially the Existing Framework Diagram, the Existing Transect Matrix, and the micro-element documentation sheets. Present them at a meeting with all the team members, stakeholders, and other visioning participants. (See Figure 3.31.)

After the presentation, begin the discussion about the vision, asking the participants which aspects of the community should remain, what should change, what should be replicated, and what is desired overall. The answers to these questions will lead to the initial formation of the vision.

## 2.1.2 Locate the Macro Elements

Based on this input from the visioning team, create the Illustrative Plan, beginning with the macro-level elements. Use the Existing Framework Diagram as a base, unless the code is for a greenfield site, in which case use it for context and for tying the new framework into the existing one. Start with the neighborhoods, marking the intended center and boundary (walking radius) of new neighborhoods and adjusting existing ones. Note the intended transect zones (including subset zones) for each neighborhood, both existing and new, from the list on the Existing Transect Matrix. Also note any new transect zones that are needed, as well as any characteristics or intentions that are

**Fig. 3.31** (above)
Visioning process kickoff meeting

**Fig. 3.32** (near right)
Illustrative Plan with macro elements from Miami 21 by DPZ
(Also see Figure C.4.)

**Fig. 3.33** (far right)
Illustrative Plan with micro elements from the Santa Ana Renaissance Specific Plan by Moule & Polyzoides

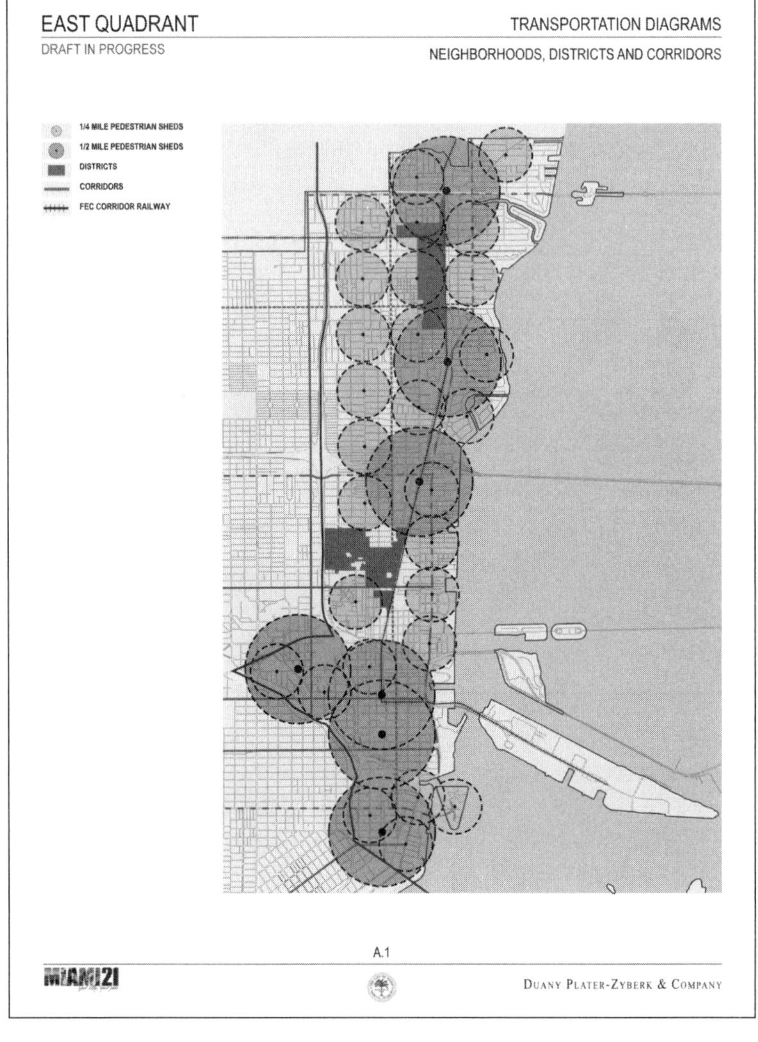

unique to the neighborhood and may need to be included in the code, such as unusual uses or unique lot conditions. In addition, for existing neighborhoods, determine and note the degree of change desired (preserve, preserve and enhance, evolve, or transform). If necessary, also designate or adjust any districts and corridors and their boundaries, making similar notes for each. (See Figure 3.32.)

## 2.1.3 Locate the Micro Elements

Next, if appropriate to the scope of the code project, continue to the micro elements. As applicable, adjust existing thoroughfares, blocks, civic spaces, and buildings, and lay out new ones, referring to the micro-scale documentation materials to replicate existing patterns where appropriate. For each thoroughfare and civic space, note whether it will be designed based on an existing precedent from the documentation process or whether a new type will need to be created. (See Figure 3.33.)

**Product List**

- Illustrative Plan

## 2.1.4 Illustrate the Transect Zones

As the Illustrative Plan is being created, begin a list of all the necessary transect zones from the notes for each of the neighborhoods. For each transect zone listed, create a three-dimensional

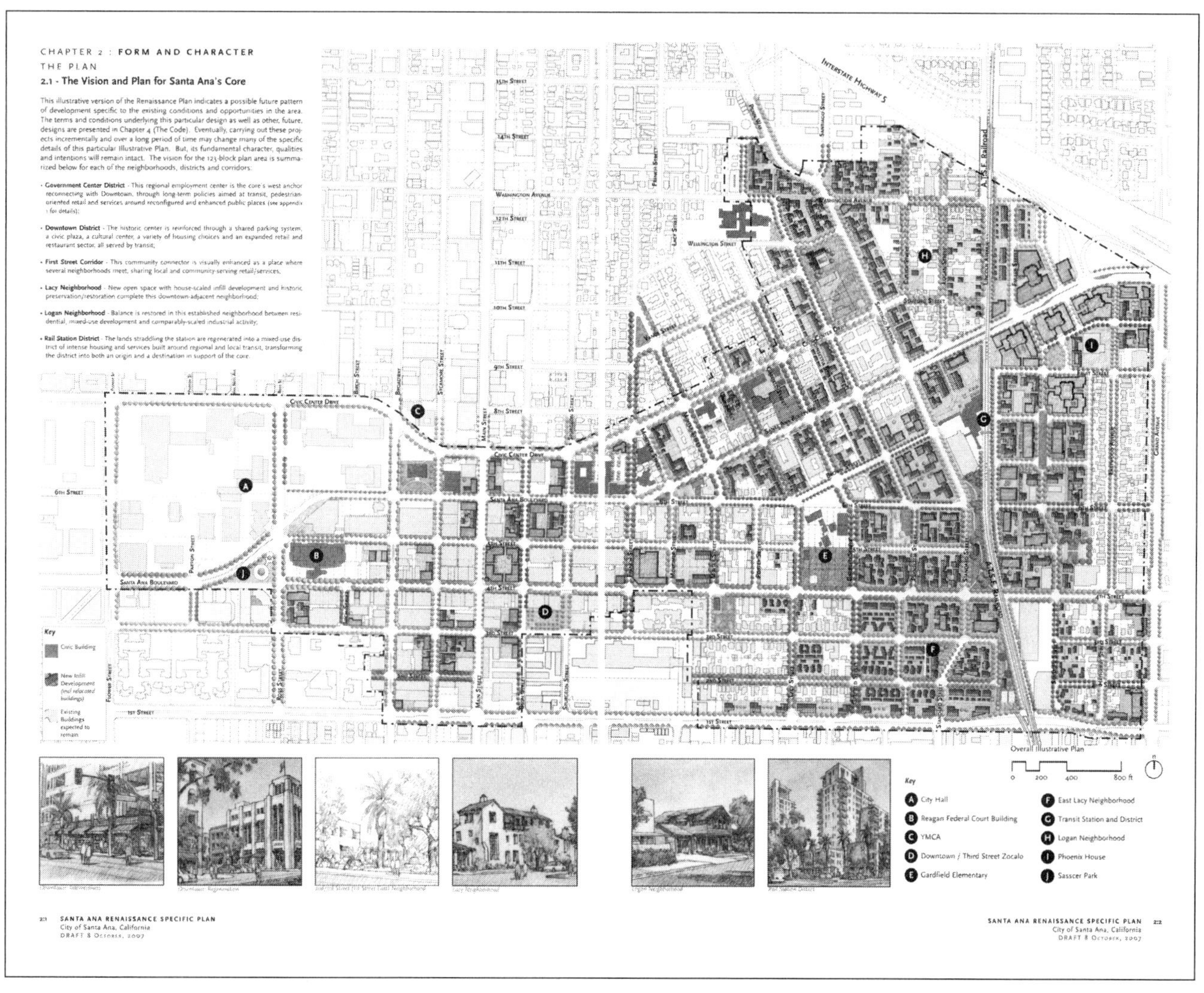
CHAPTER 2 : FORM AND CHARACTER

THE PLAN

2.1 - The Vision and Plan for Santa Ana's Core

This illustrative version of the Renaissance Plan indicates a possible future pattern of development specific to the existing conditions and opportunities in the area. The terms and conditions underlying this particular design as well as other, future, designs are presented in Chapter 4 (The Code). Eventually, carrying out these projects incrementally and over a long period of time may change many of the specific details of this particular Illustrative Plan. But, its fundamental character, qualities and intentions will remain intact. The vision for the 123-block plan area is summarized below for each of the neighborhoods, districts and corridors:

- **Government Center District** - This regional employment center is the core's west anchor reconnecting with Downtown, through long-term policies aimed at transit, pedestrian-oriented retail and services around reconfigured and enhanced public places (see appendix 1 for details);
- **Downtown District** - The historic center is reinforced through a shared parking system, a civic plaza, a cultural center, a variety of housing choices and an expanded retail and restaurant sector, all served by transit;
- **First Street Corridor** - This community connector is visually enhanced as a place where several neighborhoods meet, sharing local and community-serving retail/services;
- **Lacy Neighborhood** - New open space with house-scaled infill development and historic preservation/restoration complete this downtown-adjacent neighborhood;
- **Logan Neighborhood** - Balance is restored in this established neighborhood between residential, mixed-use development and comparably-scaled industrial activity;
- **Rail Station District** - The lands straddling the station are regenerated into a mixed-use district of intense housing and services built around regional and local transit, transforming the district into both an origin and a destination in support of the core.



2:1 SANTA ANA RENAISSANCE SPECIFIC PLAN
City of Santa Ana, California
DRAFT 8 October, 2007

SANTA ANA RENAISSANCE SPECIFIC PLAN 2:2
City of Santa Ana, California
DRAFT 8 October, 2007

## T5: Town Core

**Description**

The primary intent of this zone is to enhance the vibrant, pedestrian-oriented character of First Street. The physical form and uses are regulated to reflect the urban character of the historic shopfront buildings.

**Use Types**

| | |
|---|---|
| Ground Floor | Service, Retail, Recreation, Education & Public Assembly |
| Upper Floors | Residential or Service |

**Building Types**

Commercial Block, Ancillary Building

**Frontage Types**

Gallery, Shopfront, Awning, Forecourt

Opticos Design, Inc.

**Fig. 3.34** Transect Zone Vision Sheet

rendering(s) and a short written description of the intended vision.

Next, begin to assemble the details and elements necessary to implement the vision of each transect zone. First, consider and list the Use Types appropriate for each. (See Section 2: Building Form Standards for a list of Use Types.) Next, review the Building Type Documentation Sheets and Frontage Type Documentation Sheets and list the building and frontage types necessary for each transect zone, adding new types as necessary. Compile this information onto a sheet for each transect zone, called the "Transect Zone Vision Sheet." (See Figure 3.34.)

**Product List:**

- Transect Zone Vision Sheets

## 2.1.5 Illustrate the Micro Elements

Review the notes from the Illustrative Plan as well as the Transect Zone Vision Sheets for the various micro elements and element types that will be regulated, such as the thoroughfares, civic spaces, building types, and frontage types. For each element, create a list of all the necessary element types. Create an Element Type Vision Sheet for each element type that includes appropriate descriptive imagery, text, and whatever else is necessary to communicate the vision. For example, if thoroughfares will be regulated, create a list of all the thoroughfare types needed, and then create a Thoroughfare Type Vision Sheet for each thoroughfare type that includes a section drawing of the intended thoroughfare design. (See Figure 3.35.)

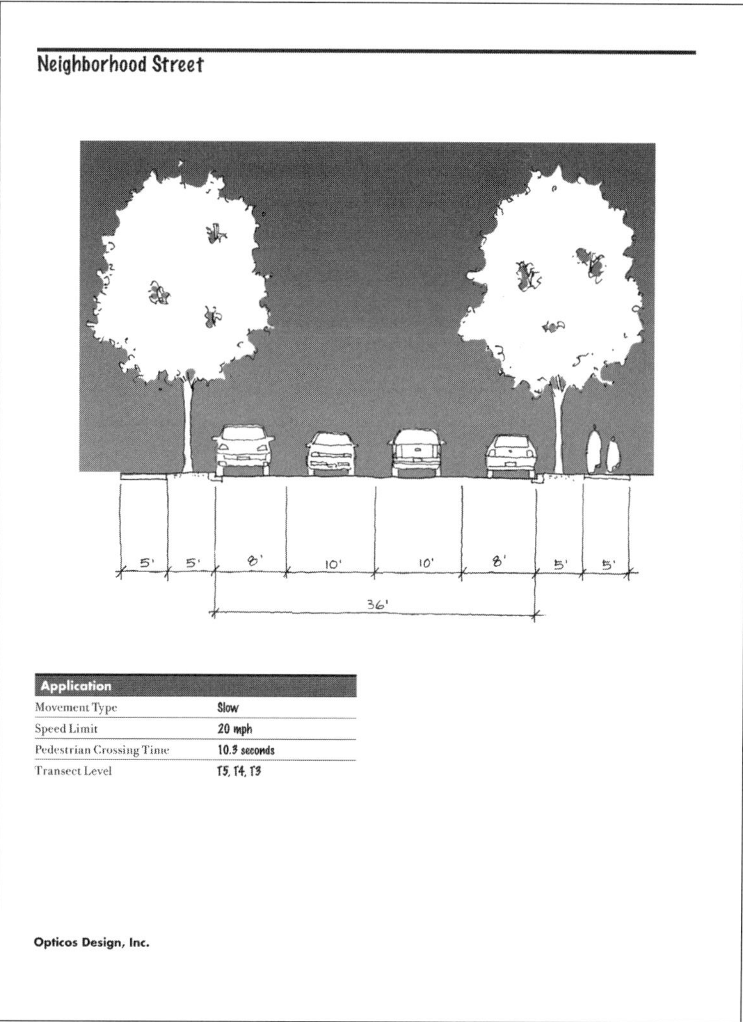

Neighborhood Street

5' 5' 8' 10' 10' 8' 5' 5'

36'

| Application | |
|---|---|
| Movement Type | Slow |
| Speed Limit | 20 mph |
| Pedestrian Crossing Time | 10.3 seconds |
| Transect Level | T5, T4, T3 |

Opticos Design, Inc.

**Fig. 3.35** Micro-Element Type Vision Sheet for a thoroughfare

Finally, determine whether there are any other optional elements the community wants to regulate, such as architectural style. For each of these elements, determine the types or styles to be included in the vision and the code and create appropriate descriptive imagery and text for each.

Once these visioning materials are completed, consider presenting them to the stakeholders and other participants for confirmation before continuing on to the next step.

**Product List:**

- Micro-Element Type Vision Sheets (e.g., Thoroughfare Type Vision Sheets, Civic Space Type Vision Sheets, and Building Type Vision Sheets)

# 2.2 Regulating Plan and Regulations

ONCE THE ILLUSTRATIVE Plan and Vision Sheets are complete, the visioning process continues with the creation of the code regulations, including the Regulating Plan, the transect zone regulations, the micro-element regulations, and the Development Review Process.

The Regulating Plan is one of the core components of a Form-Based Code. (See Figure 3.36.) Its creation is inherently part of the visioning process since it involves making decisions about the precise application of the transect zones to physical locations; however, in order to make these decisions, the transect zones initially described on the Transect Zone Vision Sheets need to be further defined with detailed regulations. These regulations are filled in on a Transect Regulation Matrix, which lists each regulation for each transect zone. (See Figure 3.37.) The Micro-Element Regulation Matrices provide the same level of detailed visioning for the micro elements. (See Figure 3.38.)

The Development Review Process is the last visioning product necessary to enable the creation of a Form-Based Code. This defines the process necessary for the submission and approval of development proposals once the FBC is in place. A good Development Review Process can be critical to the success of the code and, more important, to the implementation of the vision. Since this is often a political topic, it is important to address it during the public visioning process.

The final visioning product is the Vision Plan itself, which is a compilation of all the other visioning products assembled to fully communicate and establish a written record of the vision. (See Figure 3.39.)

**Tip:** It is important to set public expectations that while the core components of the code will be drafted during the visioning process, the code will not be complete until it is refined and formatted during the Assembling process.

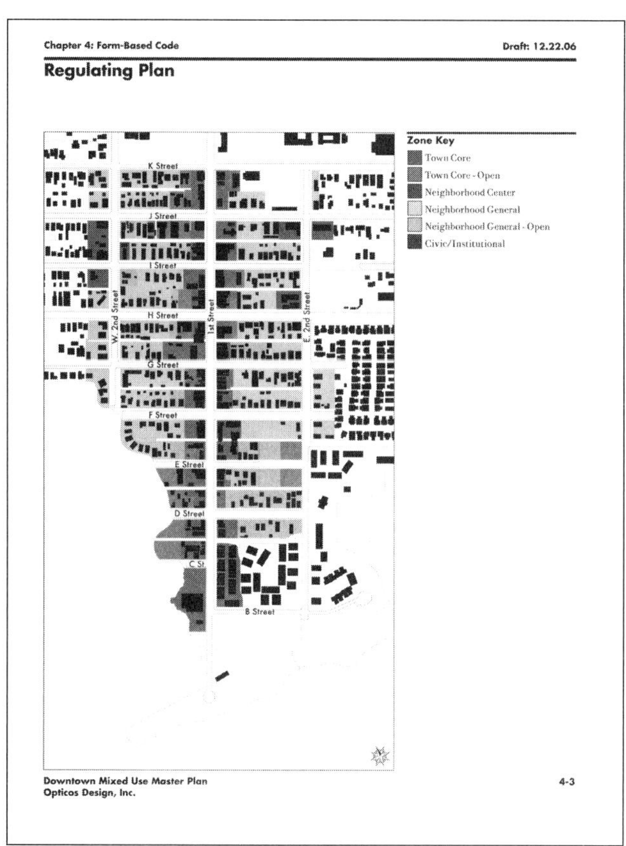

Chapter 4: Form-Based Code | Draft: 12.22.06

**Regulating Plan**



Downtown Mixed Use Master Plan
Opticos Design, Inc. | 4-3

Fig. 3.36 Regulating Plan (Also see others in the color section.)

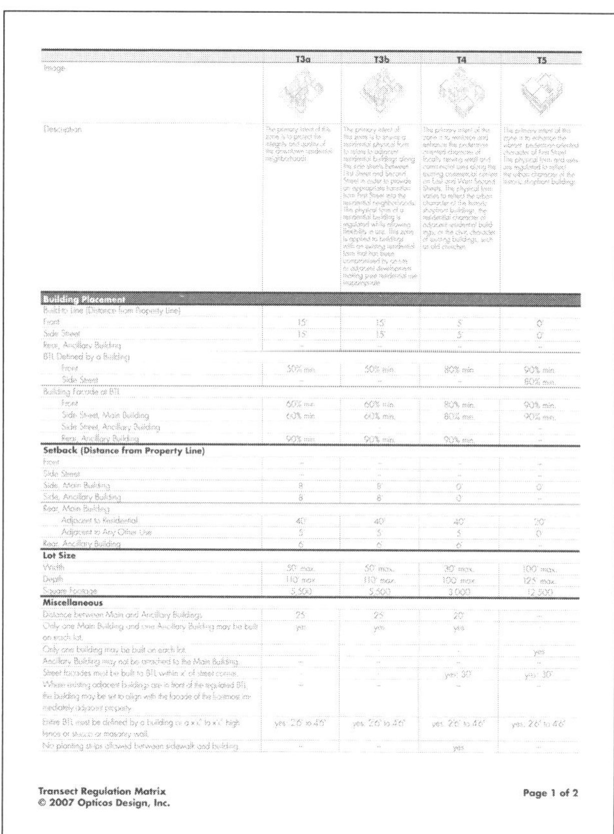

| | T3a | T3b | T4 | T5 |
|---|---|---|---|---|
| Image | | | | |
| Description | The primary intent of this zone is to protect the integrity and quality of the downtown residential neighborhood. | The primary intent of this zone is to ensure a residential physical form to relate to adjacent residential buildings along the side streets between First Street and Second Street in order to provide an appropriate transition from First Street into the residential neighborhoods. The physical form of a residential building is regulated while allowing flexibility in use. This zone is applied to buildings with an existing residential form that has been compromised by use or adjacent development making pure residential use inappropriate. | The primary intent of this zone is to reinforce and enhance the pedestrian oriented character of locally serving retail and commercial uses along the existing commercial spines on East and West Second Streets. The physical form varies to reflect the urban character of the historic shopfront buildings, the residential character of adjacent residential buildings, or the civic character of existing buildings, such as old churches. | The primary intent of this zone is to enhance the vibrant, pedestrian-oriented character of First Street. The physical form and uses are regulated to reflect the urban character of the historic shopfront buildings. |
| **Building Placement** | | | | |
| Build-to Line (Distance from Property Line) | | | | |
| Front | 15' | 15' | 5' | 0' |
| Side Street | 15' | 15' | 5' | 0' |
| Rear, Ancillary Building | -- | -- | -- | -- |
| BTL Defined by a Building | | | | |
| Front | 50% min. | 50% min. | 80% min | 90% min. |
| Side Street | -- | -- | -- | 80% min. |
| Building Facade at BTL | | | | |
| Front | 60% min. | 60% min. | 80% min. | 90% min. |
| Side Street, Main Building | 60% min. | 60% min. | 80% min. | 90% min. |
| Side Street, Ancillary Building | - | - | - | -- |
| Rear, Ancillary Building | 90% min. | 90% min. | 90% min. | -- |
| **Setback (Distance from Property Line)** | | | | |
| Front | -- | -- | - | -- |
| Side Street | -- | -- | -- | -- |
| Side, Main Building | 8' | 8' | 0' | 0' |
| Side, Ancillary Building | 8' | 8' | 0' | -- |
| Rear, Main Building | | | | |
| Adjacent to Residential | 40' | 40' | 40' | 20' |
| Adjacent to Any Other Use | 5' | 5' | 5' | 0' |
| Rear, Ancillary Building | 6' | 6' | 6' | -- |
| **Lot Size** | | | | |
| Width | 50' max. | 50' max. | 30' max. | 100' max. |
| Depth | 110' max. | 110' max. | 100' max. | 125' max. |
| Square Footage | 5,500 | 5,500 | 3,000 | 12,500 |
| **Miscellaneous** | | | | |
| Distance between Main and Ancillary Buildings | 25' | 25' | 20' | -- |
| Only one Main Building and one Ancillary Building may be built on each lot. | yes | yes | yes | - |
| Only one building may be built on each lot. | - | - | - | yes |
| Ancillary Building may not be attached to the Main Building. | -- | -- | -- | -- |
| Street facades must be built to BTL within x' of street corner. | - | - | yes; 30' | yes; 30' |
| Where existing adjacent buildings are in front of the regulated BTL, the building may be set to align with the facade of the frontmost immediately adjacent property. | -- | -- | -- | -- |
| Entire BTL must be defined by a building or a x'x" to x'x" high fence or stucco or masonry wall. | yes; 2'6" to 4'6" | yes; 2'6" to 4'6" | yes; 2'6" to 4'6" | yes; 2'6" to 4'6" |
| No planting strips allowed between sidewalk and building. | -- | -- | yes | -- |

Transect Regulation Matrix
© 2007 Opticos Design, Inc. | Page 1 of 2

Fig. 3.37 Transect Regulation Matrix

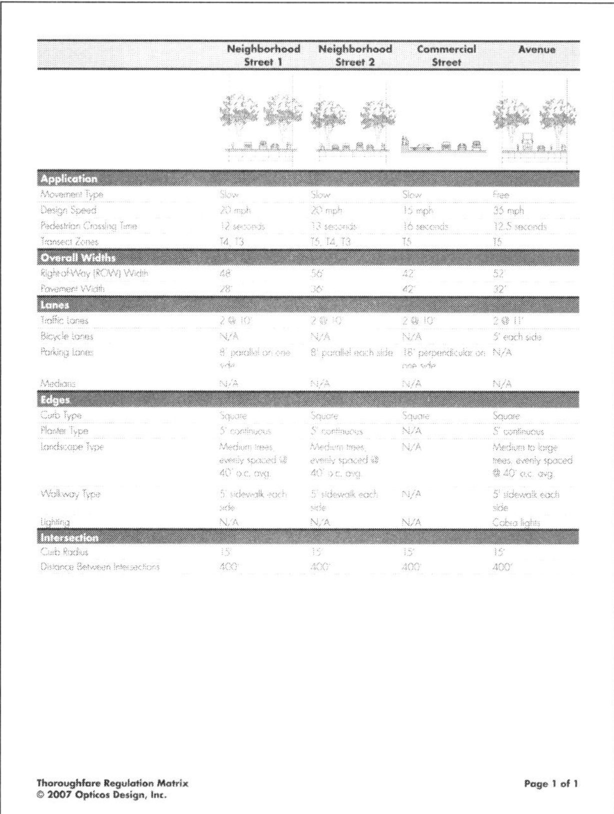

| | Neighborhood Street 1 | Neighborhood Street 2 | Commercial Street | Avenue |
|---|---|---|---|---|
| **Application** | | | | |
| Movement Type | Slow | Slow | Slow | Free |
| Design Speed | 20 mph | 20 mph | 15 mph | 35 mph |
| Pedestrian Crossing Time | 12 seconds | 13 seconds | 16 seconds | 12.5 seconds |
| Transect Zones | T4, T3 | T5, T4, T3 | T5 | T5 |
| **Overall Widths** | | | | |
| Right-of-Way (ROW) Width | 48' | 56' | 42' | 52' |
| Pavement Width | 28' | 36' | 42' | 32' |
| **Lanes** | | | | |
| Traffic Lanes | 2 @ 10' | 2 @ 10' | 2 @ 10' | 2 @ 11' |
| Bicycle Lanes | N/A | N/A | N/A | 5' each side |
| Parking Lanes | 8' parallel on one side | 8' parallel each side | 18' perpendicular on one side | N/A |
| Medians | N/A | N/A | N/A | N/A |
| **Edges** | | | | |
| Curb Type | Square | Square | Square | Square |
| Planter Type | 5' continuous | 5' continuous | N/A | 5' continuous |
| Landscape Type | Medium trees, evenly spaced @ 40' o.c. avg. | Medium trees, evenly spaced @ 40' o.c. avg. | N/A | Medium to large trees, evenly spaced @ 40' o.c. avg. |
| Walkway Type | 5' sidewalk each side | 5' sidewalk each side | N/A | 5' sidewalk each side |
| Lighting | N/A | N/A | N/A | Cobra lights |
| **Intersection** | | | | |
| Curb Radius | 15' | 15' | 15' | 15' |
| Distance Between Intersections | 400' | 400' | 400' | 400' |

Thoroughfare Regulation Matrix
© 2007 Opticos Design, Inc. | Page 1 of 1

Fig. 3.38 Micro-Element Regulation Matrix for thoroughfares

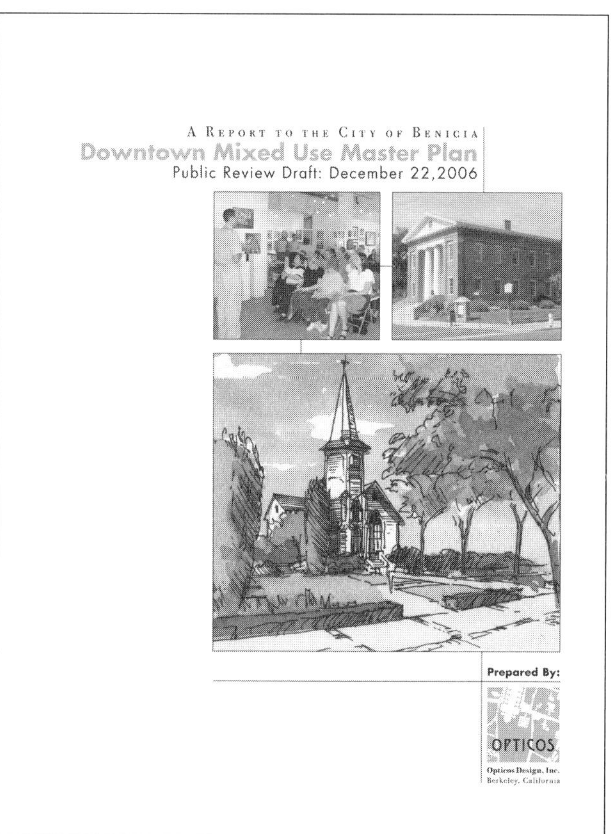

A Report to the City of Benicia
**Downtown Mixed Use Master Plan**
Public Review Draft: December 22,2006

Prepared By:



Opticos Design, Inc.
Berkeley, California

Fig. 3.39 Vision Plan

## Process Overview

The creation of the Regulating Plan and the accompanying Transect Regulation Matrix is an iterative process, going back and forth between the two documents. Based on the information on the Illustrative Plan and the Transect Zone Vision Sheets, the boundaries for a regulating zone are determined and drawn on the Regulating Plan. A column is then added to the Transect Regulation Matrix for the appropriate transect zone, and the values are filled in to regulate the intentions for the newly established regulating zone. These values are mainly based on the documentation information from the Existing Transect Matrix.

Once the first regulating zone and accompanying regulations are complete, the process is repeated. First, the boundaries of a regulating zone are drawn on the Regulating Plan, then the regulations and values for the regulating zone are determined and filled in on the Transect Regulation Matrix.

At some point, an earlier regulating zone will already have established the transect zone needed for the newly drawn regulating zone. In this case, the regulations on the Transect Regulation Matrix for the transect zone are reviewed to make sure they are all applicable. If not, they are either revised for all of the corresponding regulating zones, or a new transect zone will be created, typically as part of a subset.

This process is repeated until all the areas have been placed into regulating zones and the Regulating Plan and Transect Regulation Matrix are complete.

Next, the process is repeated again for each of the micro elements, assigning each micro-element type to the Regulating Plan or to transect zones and then creating Micro-Element Regulation Matrices for each.

Finally, the first draft of the Development Review Process is written and all the products from the visioning process are assembled into the Vision Plan document.

## Using This Section

The process for developing the regulations is iterative, and the process for each repetition varies. In order to follow the process, use the flow chart in Figure 3.40 while following the instructions given at the end of the various steps. Do not attempt to read this section from start to finish.

## 2.2.1 Create the Transect Regulation Matrix

Gather the Existing Transect Matrix from the documentation along with the Transect Zone Vision Sheets created in the first part of the visioning process. Create a new matrix, called the "Transect Regulation Matrix," using a sample template or one provided by the coding consultant. (See Figures 3.41 through 3.43.)

The template provides the list of potential regulations organized into sections. The various Building Form Standards templates shown in Figures 3.41 through 3.43 all enable the regulation of vibrant, walkable mixed-use places using the basic components and regulations listed earlier while varying the particular organization and specific regulations. Selecting a template that has been rigorously vetted will help ensure that the necessary regulations and components are included.

*Next Step*
Continue to Step 2.2.2.

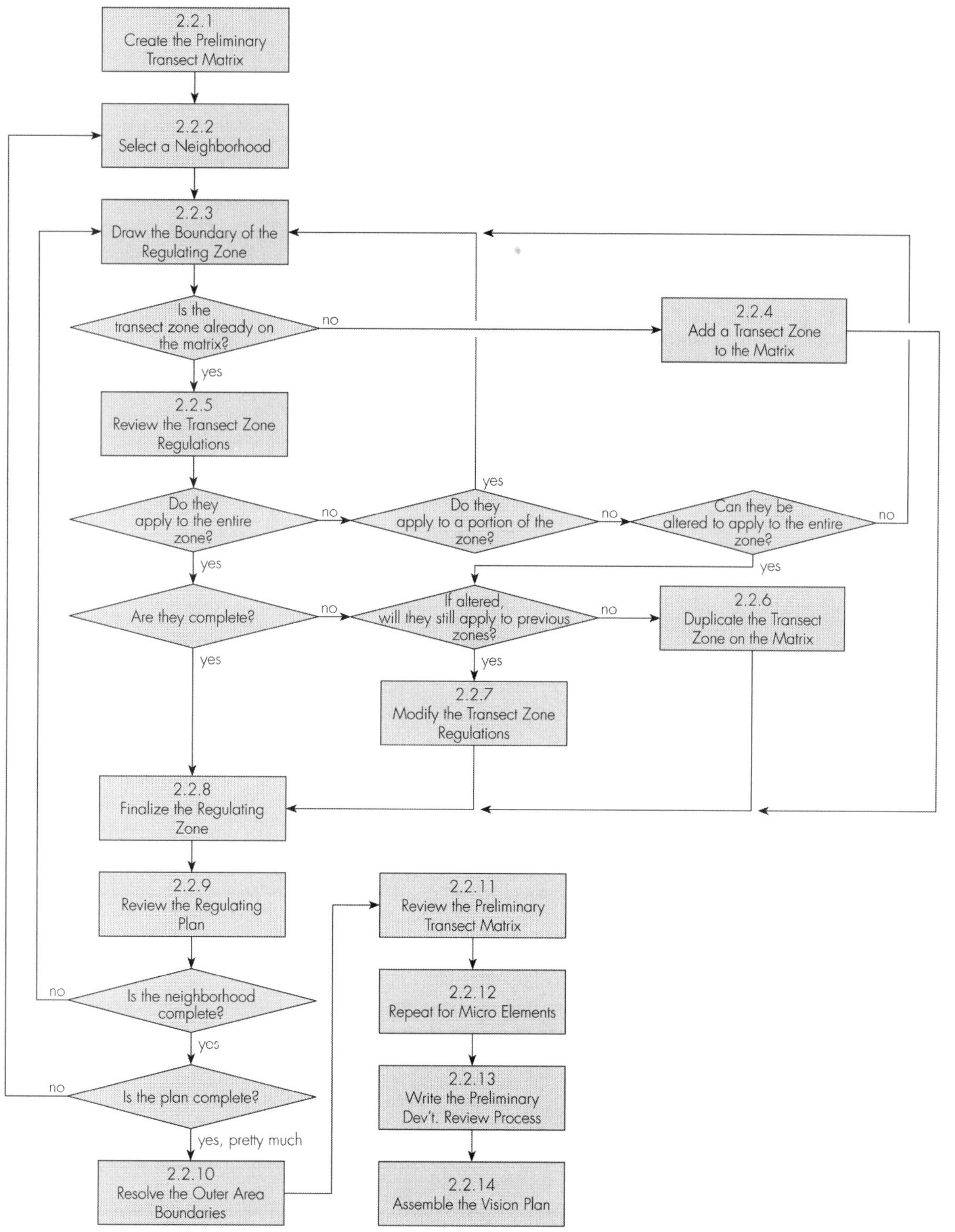


**Fig. 3.40**
2.2 Regulating Plan and Regulations
Do not attempt to read this section from start to finish. Follow the instructions under "Next Steps" for guidance through this process.

| | | | |
|---|---|---|---|
| Image | | | |
| Description | | | |
| **Building Placement** | | | |
| Build-to Line (Distance from Property Line) | | | |
| Front | | | |
| Side Street | | | |
| Rear, Ancillary Building | | | |
| BTL Defined by a Building | | | |
| Front | | | |
| Side Street | | | |
| Building Facade at BTL | | | |
| Front | | | |
| Side Street, Main Building | | | |
| Side Street, Ancillary Building | | | |
| Rear, Ancillary Building | | | |
| **Setback (Distance from Property Line)** | | | |
| Front | | | |
| Side Street | | | |
| Side, Main Building | | | |
| Side, Ancillary Building | | | |
| Rear, Main Building | | | |
| Adjacent to Residential | | | |
| Adjacent to Any Other Use | | | |
| Rear, Ancillary Building | | | |
| **Lot Size** | | | |
| Width | | | |
| Depth | | | |
| Square Footage | | | |
| **Miscellaneous** | | | |
| Distance between Main and Ancillary Buildings | | | |
| Only one Main Building and one Ancillary Building may be built on each lot. | | | |
| Ancillary Building may not be attached to the Main Building. | | | |
| Street facades must be built to BTL within x' of street corner. | | | |
| Where existing adjacent buildings are in front of the regulated BTL, the building may be set to align with the facade of the frontmost immediately adjacent property. | | | |
| Entire BTL must be defined by a building or a x'x" to x'x" high fence or stucco or masonry wall. | | | |
| No planting strips allowed between sidewalk and building. | | | |
| **Building Form** | | | |
| **Height** | | | |
| Main Building | | | |
| Ancillary Building, Corner Lot | | | |
| Ground Floor Finish Level | | | |
| Ground Floor Ceiling | | | |
| Upper Floor(s) Ceiling | | | |
| **Footprint** | | | |
| Width | | | |
| Depth | | | |
| Depth, Ancillary Building | | | |
| Footprint, Ancillary Building | | | |
| Lot Coverage | | | |
| Depth, Ground-Floor Commercial Space | | | |
| Depth, Ground-Floor Residential Space | | | |
| **Miscellaneous** | | | |
| Distance Between Entries to Ground Floor | | | |
| Distance Between Entries to Upper Floor(s) | | | |
| All floors must have a primary entrance along the front facade. | | | |
| Loading docks, overhead doors, and other service entries may not be located on street-facing facades. | | | |
| Any buildings wider than x' must be designed to read as a series of buildings no wider than x' each. | | | |
| Privacy windows are required on all side and rear elevations. | | | |
| Within x' of the rear property line, buildings may not be more than a half-story taller than the allowed height of adjacent buildings. | | | |
| Mansard roof forms are not allowed. | | | |

**Fig. 3.41** Transect Regulation Matrix template by Opticos Design

| **Parking** | | | |
|---|---|---|---|
| **Spaces** | | | |
| Residential Uses | | | |
| Studio Unit | | | |
| 1-2 Bedroom Unit | | | |
| 3+ Bedroom Unit | | | |
| Lodging Uses | | | |
| Other Uses | | | |
| Ground Floor < x sf | | | |
| Ground Floor > x sf | | | |
| Upper Floor(s) | | | |
| **Location (Distance from Property Line)** | | | |
| Front Setback | | | |
| Side Street Setback | | | |
| Side Setback | | | |
| Rear Setback | | | |
| **Miscellaneous** | | | |
| Parking Drive Width | | | |
| On lots with alleys, all drives shall be located on the alley. | | | |
| On corner lots, all drives shall be located on the alley or side street. | | | |
| Shared drives are encouraged between adjacent lots to minimize curb cuts along the street. | | | |
| Malibu Drives with central planting strips are encouraged. | | | |
| x% of the on-street parking spaces located adjacent to the lot count toward required parking. | | | |
| No parking spaces are required for Ancillary Buildings that are 500 sf or less. | | | |
| Parking must be provided on-site, off-site within x', or as shared parking. | | | |
| Off-street parking spaces do not have to be covered. | | | |
| Underground parking may be placed up to the property line. | | | |
| Underground parking must not project more than 2' above the level of the sidewalk and must not be visible to pedestrians. | | | |
| Bicycle parking must be provided and in a secure environment, except in residential buildings with 4 units or less. | | | |
| If park-lifts or mechanically-ventilated garages are used next to residential uses, the noise and vibration of the mechanical systems must be mitigated. | | | |
| On corner lots less than 100' wide, a maximum length of 60' of parking podium or garage is allowed along a side street. | | | |
| All surface parking areas that are not behind buildings must be screened by a x'x" tall min. hedge, fence, or wall in character with the building at the ROW. | | | |
| All garages must be screened from the street by a minimum depth of x' of habitable space. | | | |
| Tandem parking is allowed for off-street parking as long as both spaces are behind the required setback. | | | |
| **Allowed Use Types** | | | |
| Ground Floor | | | |
| Upper Floor(s) | | | |
| **Allowed Building Types** | | | |
| List Types | | | |
| **Allowed Frontage Types** | | | |
| List Types | | | |
| **Other Allowed Encroachments** | | | |
| List Types | | | |
| Front | | | |
| Side Street | | | |
| Side | | | |
| Rear | | | |

## Code Framework and Regulations

**Template for Adjustment to Plan**

The individual regulations for each of the zones in the plan area are expressed for each zone to carry out the intentions and vision of the plan. These regulations work in combination with the regulating plan.

NA = not applicable
- = not allowed

| | Town Center Zone | | Special District Zone |
|---|---|---|---|
| | The TC Zone is applied to the area planned to serve regional and community-level needs. Streetscapes are pedestrian-oriented, regular in planting and detail to support an inviting and effective commercial environment. Buildings are close to or at the sidewalk with outdoor extensions and activities. Parking is shared in a 'park-once' system of on-street and off-street spaces. | The COR Zone is applied to areas along major thoroughfares to serve community-level needs. Buildings front streets and cover most of the frontage with parking on-street and off-street along and behind buildings. Streetscapes are pedestrian-oriented, regular in planting and detail to provide spatial definition along these community-connecting streets. | The SD Zone is applied to areas that are single-purpose in nature and, due to their configuration and use, are not intended as mixed-use neighborhoods or districts (e.g., Sports Complex, Racetrack, Power Generator, industrial areas). Parking is on-street and off-street. |
| **Character** | | | |
| **Development Potential** | Commercial: 000,000<br>Industrial: 000,000<br>Residential: 12345 | Commercial: 000,000<br>Industrial: 000,000<br>Residential: 12345 | Commercial: 000,000<br>Industrial: 000,000<br>Residential: 12345 |
| **Permitted Uses** | Regional / Community-retail, office, medical, lodging, residential, civic | Retail, office, light industrial, residential, civic | Racetrack, Power Generator, Stadium |
| **Blocks / Subdivision of Land**<br>O = Orthogonal<br>T = Trapezoidal | O - Depth: min 200, max 500<br>Length: min 200, max 500<br>T - Depth/Length: 500 avg longest 2 sides | O - Depth: min 200, max 500<br>Length: min 200, max 500<br>T - Depth/Length: 500 avg longest 2 sides | O - Depth: min 500, max 700<br>Length: min 300, max 700<br>T - Depth/Length: 500 avg longest 2 sides |

### Building Type Standards

| | Type | Lot Width | Units per Acre | Max Stories | Open Space | Town Center Zone | COR Zone | Special District Zone |
|---|---|---|---|---|---|---|---|---|
| More Urban | Tower-on-Podium | 200-400 | 90-110 | 25 | 10% | Tower-on-Podium | - | per Design Review |
| | Podium | 200-400 | 50-70 | 7 | 15% | Podium | - | |
| | Hybrid Court [*] | 150-250 | 45-60 | 5.5 | 15% | Hybrid Court | Hybrid Court | |
| | Commercial Block | 125-200 | 35-50 | 5 | 15% | Commercial Block | Commercial Block | |
| | Liner | 125-250 | 35-50 | 4 | 5% | Liner | Liner | |
| | Stacked Dwellings | 125-200 | 40-50 | 4 | 15% | Stacked Dwellings | Stacked Dwellings | |
| | Industrial Block | 125-200 | - | 2 | NA | Live-Work | Live-Work | |
| | Industrial Shed | 40-75 | - | 1.5 | NA | - | Industrial Block | |
| Less Urban (Walk-up Access) | Live-Work | 25-125 | 15-20 | 2.5 | 15% | - | - | |
| | Courtyard Housing | 125-250 | 25-35 | 3.5 | 15% | Courtyard Housing | Courtyard Housing | |
| | Rowhouse | 25-150 | 18-20 | 2 | 20% | Rowhouse | Rowhouse | |
| | Bungalow Court | 125-200 | 15-20 | 2.5 | 35% | - | - | |
| | Rosewalk | 125-200 | 10-18 | 2.5 | 35% | - | - | |
| | Duplex to Quadplex | 50-75 | 10-15 | 2.5 | 25% | - | - | |
| | Single Dwelling | 40-75 | 6-10 | 2 | 25% | - | - | |
| | Accessory Dwelling | 40-75 | 6-10 | 1 | NA | - | - | |

[*] Hybrid Court combines walk-up access with lobby access

### Building Placement Standards

| Setbacks | TC min | TC max | TC other | COR min | COR max | COR other | Special District Zone |
|---|---|---|---|---|---|---|---|
| Front (F:) | 0 | 5 | NA | 0 | 10 | 50% of lot | by conditional use permit |
| Rear (R:) | 0 | 10 | NA | 0 | 5 | 50% of lot | |
| Side (S:) | 0* | na | * (3 if provided) | 0* | NA | *(3 if provided) | |
| Street Side (St S:) | 5 | na | NA | 10 | NA | NA | |

### Building Profile Standards

| | Town Center Zone | COR Zone | Special District Zone |
|---|---|---|---|
| Min and Max Building Height (to eave) | 3 25 | 2 4 | NA NA |
| Types of Encroachments into Setbacks | Arcade, Gallery, Balcony, Bay, Sign, Awning | Arcade, Gallery, Balcony, Bay, Sign, Awning | Arcade, Gallery, Balcony, Bay, Sign, Awning |
| Max Front | F: 10 | F: 10 | F: NA |
| Max Rear | R: 10 | R: 10 | R: NA |
| Max Side | S: 3 | S: 3 | S: NA |
| Max Street Side | St S: 6 | St S: 6 | St S: NA |

### Frontage Type Standards

| | Type | Width | Depth | Height | Other | Town Center Zone | COR Zone | Special District Zone |
|---|---|---|---|---|---|---|---|---|
| More Urban | Arcade | 50% min | 10 min | 10 min | - | Arcade | Arcade | Arcade |
| | Gallery | 50% min | 10 | 10 min | - | Gallery | Gallery | Gallery |
| | Shopfront | 75% min | - | 12 min | - | Shopfront | Shopfront | Shopfront |
| | Stoop | at entries | 4 | - | - | Stoop | Stoop | Stoop |
| | Forecourt | 20 min | 40 max | - | - | Forecourt | Forecourt | Forecourt |
| Less Urban | Walled Front Yard | 65% min | - | 10 max | - | - | - | Walled Front Yard |
| | Porch & Garden Wall | 65% min | 6 | 10 max | - | - | - | Porch & Garden Wall |
| | Fence | 65% min | - | 4 max | - | - | - | Fence |
| | Common Lawn | 65% min | per zone | - | - | - | - | Common Lawn |
| | other | - | - | - | - | - | - | other |
| | other | - | - | - | - | - | - | other |

### Parking & Parking Placement Standards

| | TC min | TC max | COR min | COR max | SD min | SD max |
|---|---|---|---|---|---|---|
| Location | **Location:** behind buildings | | **Location:** along or behind buildings | | **Location:** anywhere on lot | |
| (spaces per bedroom) Residential | 1 | 2 (except single dwelling) | 1 | 2 | NA | NA |
| (spaces per unit) Live/Work | 1.5 | 3 | 1.5 | 3 | NA | NA |
| (spaces per sq. ft.) Commercial/Office | 3/1000 (park-once) | NA | 2/1000 | 3/1000 | 3/1000 | 4/1000 |
| (spaces per sq. ft.) Industrial | 0 | NA | 3/1000 | NA | 2/1000 | 4/1000 |

More Urban

Title -------------- Plan
Client Name

**Fig. 3.42** Transect Regulation Matrix template by Moule & Polyzoides. The original is poster size and intended to be mounted on the wall during the public visioning process. (© 2007 Moule & Polyzoides, Architects and Urbanists)

| | | Neighborhood General 1 Zone | | Open Space Zone |
|---|---|---|---|---|
| The NC Zone is applied to areas to serve local, neighborhood needs through mixed use development of retail, office and residential uses. Buildings are close to or at the sidewalk. Streetscapes are pedestrian-oriented, regular in planting and detail to reinforce the neighborhood focus of the area. Parking is shared in a 'park-once' system of on- and off-street spaces. | The NG 2 Zone is applied to areas intended to accommodate the widest variety of attached and detached building types and uses at the local, neighborhood level. Streetscapes are pedestrian-oriented, regular and irregular in planting and detail to provide spatial definition to the wide range of street types. Parking is provided on each lot. | The NG 1 Zone is applied to areas intended to accommodate the widest variety of attached and detached building types and uses at the local, neighborhood level. Streetscapes are pedestrian-oriented, regular and irregular in planting and detail to provide spatial definition to the wide range of street types. Parking is provided on each lot. | The NE Zone is applied to areas intended for the least intense of development in the plan area through detached building types. Streetscapes are pedestrian-oriented and irregular to provide the physical contrast with the rest of the plan area. Parking is provided on each lot. | The OS Zone is applied to areas intended for no development while allowing for appropriate passive and active recreation. Streetscapes are pedestrian-oriented and irregular to provide the physical contrast with the rest of the plan area. Parking is provided along street frontages or, in the case of parks and greenways, in lots. |
|  |  |  | | |
| Commercial: 000,000<br>Industrial: 000,000<br>Residential: 12345 | Commercial: 000,000<br>Industrial: 000,000<br>Residential: 12345 | Commercial: 000,000<br>Industrial: 000,000<br>Residential: 12345 | Commercial: 000,000<br>Industrial: 000,000<br>Residential: 12345 | Commercial: 000,000<br>Industrial: 000,000<br>Residential: 12345 |
| Local retail, office, live-work, residential, light-industrial | Residential, live-work [1] | Residential, live-work [1] | Residential, home-occupation | Residential, home-occupation |
| O - Depth: min 200, max 400<br>Length: min 200, max 400<br>T - Depth/Length: 500 avg longest 2 sides | O - Depth: min 220, max 400<br>Length: min 200, max 500<br>T - Depth/Length: 500 avg longest 2 sides | O - Depth: min 220, max 400<br>Length: min 200, max 500<br>T - Depth/Length: 500 avg longest 2 sides | O - Depth: min 220, max 400<br>Length: min 200, max 600<br>T - Depth/Length: 500 avg longest 2 sides | More Urban / Less Urban<br>Type / Acreage / Min Street Frontage<br>Plaza / 0.1 - 1.0 / 3<br>Square / 0.1 - 1.0 / 2<br>Green / 0.1 - 4.0 / 2<br>Park / 1.0 - 15.0 / 1<br>Greenway / 1.0 - na / 1 |
| -<br>-<br>-<br>Commercial Block<br>Liner<br>-<br>Live-Work<br>- | -<br>-<br>-<br>Commercial Block<br><br><br>Live-Work | -<br>-<br>-<br>Commercial Block<br><br>Live-Work | -<br>-<br>-<br>-<br>-<br>-<br>-<br>- | Civic Building(s)<br>per Design Review |
| -<br>Courtyard Housing<br>Rowhouse<br>-<br>-<br>-<br>-<br>- | Industrial Shed<br>Courtyard Housing<br>Rowhouse<br>Bungalow Court<br>Rosewalk<br>Duplex to Quadplex<br>Single Dwelling<br>Accessory Dwelling | Industrial Shed<br>Courtyard Housing<br>Rowhouse<br>Bungalow Court<br>Rosewalk<br>Duplex to Quadplex<br>Single Dwelling<br>Accessory Dwelling | -<br>-<br>-<br>-<br>Rosewalk<br>Duplex to Quadplex<br>Single Dwelling<br>Accessory Dwelling | |
| min / max / other<br>F: 0 / 5 / NA<br>R: 0 / 10 / NA<br>S: 5 / NA / NA<br>St S: 5 / NA / NA | min / max / other<br>F: 5 / 10 / NA<br>R: 0 / 5 / NA<br>S: 7 / NA / NA<br>St S: 10 / NA / NA | min / max / other<br>F: 5 / 10 / NA<br>R: 0 / 5 / NA<br>S: 7 / NA / NA<br>St S: 10 / NA / NA | min / max / other<br>F: 10 / NA / NA<br>R: 0 / 10 / NA<br>S: 10 / NA / NA<br>St S: 20 / NA / NA | min / max / other<br>F: 10 / NA / NA<br>R: 0 / 10 / NA<br>S: 10 / NA / NA<br>St S: 20 / NA / NA |
| 2 4<br>Arcade, Gallery, Balcony, Bay, Sign, Awning<br>F: 10<br>R: 10<br>S: 3<br>St S: 6 | 1 3.5<br>Balcony, Bay, Sign, Awning<br>F: 10<br>R: 10<br>S: 3<br>St S: 6 | 1 3.5<br>Balcony, Bay, Sign, Awning<br>F: 10<br>R: 10<br>S: 3<br>St S: 6 | 1 2<br>Balcony, Bay, Sign, Awning<br>F: 10<br>R: 10<br>S: 3<br>St S: 6 | Civic Building(s)<br>per Design Review |
| Arcade<br>Gallery<br>Shopfront<br>Stoop<br>Forecourt | -<br>-<br>-<br>Stoop<br>Forecourt | -<br>-<br>-<br>Stoop<br>Forecourt | -<br>-<br>-<br>-<br>- | |
| -<br>-<br>-<br>-<br>-<br>- | Walled Front Yard<br>Porch & Garden Wall<br>Fence<br>Common Lawn<br>other<br>other | Walled Front Yard<br>Porch & Garden Wall<br>Fence<br>Common Lawn<br>other<br>other | Walled Front Yard<br>Porch & Garden Wall<br>Fence<br>Common Lawn<br>other<br>other | |
| **Location:** behind buildings | **Location:** behind buildings | **Location:** behind buildings | **Location:** in front or behind buildings | **Location:** along street frontage[2] |
| min / max<br>1 / 2 (except single dwelling)<br>1.5 / 3<br>2/1000 (park-once) / 3/1000<br>NA / NA | min / max<br>1 / 2 (except single dwelling)<br>1.5 / 3<br>2/1000 / 2/1000<br>2/1000 / 2/1000 | min / max<br>1 / 2 (except single dwelling)<br>1.5 / 3<br>2/1000 / 2/1000<br>2/1000 / 2/1000 | min / max<br>1 / 2 (except single dwelling)<br>NA / NA<br>NA / NA<br>0 | [2] Parks and Greenways are allowed to have individual parking lots of no more than ___ spaces. |

Less Urban

## SMARTCODE

*Municipality*

## TABLE 14. SMARTCODE SUMMARY

Note: All requirements in this Table are subject to calibration for local context.

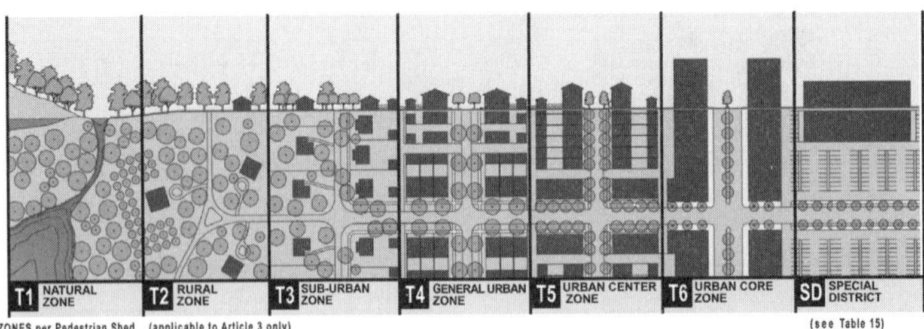

| | T1 NATURAL ZONE | T2 RURAL ZONE | T3 SUB-URBAN ZONE | T4 GENERAL URBAN ZONE | T5 URBAN CENTER ZONE | T6 URBAN CORE ZONE | SD SPECIAL DISTRICT |
|---|---|---|---|---|---|---|---|
| **a. ALLOCATION OF ZONES per Pedestrian Shed (applicable to Article 3 only)** | | | | | | | (see Table 15) |
| CLD requires | no minimum | 50% min | 10 - 30% | 20 - 40% | not permitted | not permitted | |
| TND requires | no minimum | no minimum | 10 - 30% | 30 - 60 % | 10 - 30% | not permitted | |
| RCD requires | no minimum | no minimum | not permitted | 10 - 30% | 10 - 30% | 40 - 80% | |
| **b. BASE RESIDENTIAL DENSITY (see Section 3.4)** | | | | | | | |
| By Right | not applicable | 1 unit / 20 ac avg. | 2 units / ac. gross | 4 units / ac. gross | 6 units / ac. gross | 12 units / ac. gross | |
| By TDR | by Variance | by Variance | 6 units / ac. gross | 12 units / ac. gross | 24 units / ac. gross | 96 units / ac. gross | |
| Other Functions | by Variance | by Variance | 10 - 20% min | 20 - 30% min | 30 - 50% min | 50 - 70% min | |
| **c. BLOCK SIZE** | | | | | | | |
| Block Perimeter | no maximum | no maximum | 3000 ft. max | 2400 ft. max | 2000 ft. max | 2000 ft. max * | |
| | | | | | | * 3000 ft. max with parking structures | |
| **d. THOROUGHFARES (see Table 3 and Table 4)** | | | | | | | |
| HW & RR | permitted | permitted | permitted | not permitted | not permitted | not permitted | |
| BV | not permitted | not permitted | permitted | permitted | permitted | permitted | |
| SR | not permitted | not permitted | permitted | permitted | not permitted | not permitted | |
| RS | not permitted | not permitted | permitted | permitted | not permitted | not permitted | |
| SS & AV | not permitted | not permitted | not permitted | not permitted | permitted | permitted | |
| CS & AV | not permitted | not permitted | not permitted | not permitted | permitted | permitted | |
| Rear Lane | permitted | permitted | permitted | permitted | not permitted | not permitted | |
| Rear Alley | not permitted | not permitted | permitted | required | required | required | |
| Path | permitted | permitted | permitted | permitted | not permitted | not permitted | |
| Passage | not permitted | not permitted | permitted | permitted | permitted | permitted | |
| Bicycle Trail | permitted | permitted | permitted | not permitted * | not permitted | not permitted | |
| Bicycle Lane | permitted | permitted | permitted | permitted | not permitted | not permitted | |
| Bicycle Route | permitted | permitted | permitted | permitted | permitted | permitted | |
| | | | | | | * permitted within Open Spaces | |
| **e. CIVIC SPACES (see Table 13)** | | | | | | | |
| Park | permitted | permitted | permitted | by Warrant | by Warrant | by Warrant | |
| Green | not permitted | not permitted | permitted | permitted | permitted | not permitted | |
| Square | not permitted | not permitted | not permitted | permitted | permitted | permitted | |
| Plaza | not permitted | not permitted | not permitted | not permitted | permitted | permitted | |
| Playground | permitted | permitted | permitted | permitted | permitted | permitted | |
| **f. LOT OCCUPATION** | | | | | | | DISPOSITION |
| Lot Width | not applicable | by Warrant | 72 ft. min 120 ft. max | 18 ft. min 96 ft. max | 18 ft. min 180 ft. max | 18 ft. min 700 ft. max | |
| Lot Coverage | not applicable | by Warrant | 60% max | 70% max | 80% max | 90% max | |
| **g. SETBACKS - PRINCIPAL BUILDING** | | | | | | | |
| Front Setback (Principal) | not applicable | 48 ft. min | 24 ft. min | 6 ft. min 18 ft. max | 0 ft. min 12 ft. max | 0 ft. min 12 ft. max | |
| Front Setback (Secondary) | not applicable | 48 ft. min | 12 ft. min | 6 ft. min 18 ft. max | 0 ft. min 12 ft. max | 0 ft. min 12 ft. max | |
| Side Setback | not applicable | 96 ft. min | 12 ft. min | 0 ft. total min | 0 ft. min 24 ft. max | 0 ft. min 24 ft. max | |
| Rear Setback | not applicable | 96 ft. min | 12 ft. min | 3 ft. min * | 3 ft. min * | 0 ft. min | |
| Frontage Buildout | not applicable | not applicable | 60% min | 70% min | 80% min | 90% min | |
| **h. SETBACKS - OUTBUILDING** | | | | | | | |
| Front Setback | not applicable | 20 ft. min +bldg setback | 20 ft. min +bldg setback | 24 ft. min +bldg setback | 40 ft. max from rear prop | not applicable | |
| Side Setback | not applicable | 3 ft. or 6 ft. | 3 ft. or 6 ft. | 0 ft. min or 3 ft. | 0 ft min | not applicable | |
| Rear Setback | not applicable | 3 ft. min | 3 ft. min | 3 ft. | 3 ft. max | not applicable | |
| **i. BUILDING DISPOSITION (see Table 9)** | | | | | | | |
| Edgeyard | permitted | permitted | permitted | permitted | not permitted | not permitted | |
| Sideyard | not permitted | not permitted | not permitted | permitted | permitted | not permitted | |
| Rearyard | not permitted | not permitted | not permitted | permitted | permitted | permitted | |
| Courtyard | not permitted | not permitted | not permitted | not permitted | permitted | permitted | |
| **j. PRIVATE FRONTAGES (see Table 7)** | | | | | | | CONFIGURATION |
| Common Yard | not applicable | permitted | permitted | not permitted | not permitted | not permitted | |
| Porch & Fence | not applicable | not permitted | permitted | permitted | not permitted | not permitted | |
| Terrance or L.C. | not applicable | not permitted | not permitted | permitted | permitted | not permitted | |
| Forecourt | not applicable | not permitted | not permitted | permitted | permitted | permitted | |
| Stoop | not applicable | not permitted | not permitted | permitted | permitted | permitted | |
| Shopfront & Awning | not applicable | not permitted | not permitted | permitted | permitted | permitted | |
| Gallery | not applicable | not permitted | not permitted | permitted | permitted | permitted | |
| Arcade | not applicable | not permitted | not permitted | not permitted | permitted | permitted | |
| **k. BUILDING CONFIGURATION (see Table 8)** | | | | | | | |
| Principal Building | not applicable | 2 Stories max | 2 Stories max | 3 Stories max, 2 min | 5 Stories max, 2 min | 8 Stories max, 2 min | |
| Outbuilding | not applicable | 2 Stories max | 2 Stories max | 2 Stories max | 2 Stories max | not applicable | |
| **l. BUILDING FUNCTION (see Table 10 &Table 12)** | | | | | | | FUNCTION |
| Residential | not applicable | restricted use | restricted use | limited use | open use | open use | |
| Lodging | not applicable | restricted use | restricted use | limited use | open use | open use | |
| Office | not applicable | restricted use | restricted use | limited use | open use | open use | |
| Retail | not applicable | restricted use | restricted use | limited use | open use | open use | |

SECTION 5

SECTION 2, 3, 4

SmartCode Version 9.0

**Fig. 3.43** Transect Regulation Matrix template from the SmartCode (Credit: DPZ)

## 2.2.2 Select a Neighborhood

Lay a sheet of tracing paper over the Illustrative Plan to begin the Regulating Plan. Study the Illustrative Plan, and review the various macro elements (neighborhoods, districts, and corridors) established during the visioning process. Select one to start with. It is often easier to begin with a small, minimally complicated area like a small neighborhood and return to the more complicated areas later.

*Next Step*

Continue to Step 2.2.3.

## 2.2.3 Draw the Boundary of the Regulating Zone

Find or establish the focal point of the selected neighborhood. This will typically be the most urban portion. Reviewing the Illustrative Plan of the area, the Transect Zone Vision Sheets, and any applicable background documents, such as the existing zoning map or comprehensive plan land-use map, select an applicable transect zone. Using the parameters from the selected Transect Zone Vision Sheet and the existing lot lines, draw a boundary around a contiguous portion of the area surrounding the focal point that matches the form and use parameters of the selected transect zone. (They may not match perfectly, but should be close.) This boundary line now defines a regulating zone. (See Figure 3.44.)

*Instructions for Later Repetitions*

When returning to this step for later portions of the same neighborhood, work on defining the next outer concentric area from the previously defined regulating zone. (See Figure 3.45.) If this is the last portion of the neighborhood, drawing the boundary line may take some finessing in order to determine where the neighborhood ends and another one begins. Often, a corridor will help define this edge.

When returning to this step for later neighborhoods, the Transect Regulation Matrix will already have some zones completed. Make sure to review these established zones along with the Transect Zone Vision Sheets when selecting an applicable transect zone.

*Next Step*

Does the appropriate transect zone for the newly defined regulating zone already exist on the Transect Regulation Matrix? If yes, skip to Step 2.2.5. If no, continue to Step 2.2.4.

## 2.2.4 Add a Transect Zone to the Matrix

Find the Transect Zone Vision Sheet for the applicable transect zone. Create a new column on the matrix for the transect zone, and add the name, image and description from the Transect Zone Vision Sheet to the top of the column.

Next, begin filling in the regulation values. For transect zones based on an existing transect level in the community, find that transect level on the Existing Transect Matrix from the documentation process for reference. Starting at the top of the Transect Regulation Matrix, review each regulation one by one. If the regulation is necessary to implement the vision, transfer the appropriate value for that regulation from the Existing Transect Matrix to the Transect Regulation Matrix. If it is not necessary, simply fill in "Not Applicable." (See Figure 3.46.)

For transect zones that are new to the community, use documentation information from other appropriate precedents to fill in the values. Typically, the consultant team will bring the knowledge and expertise on a variety of other

**Fig. 3.44** Beginning of the Regulating Plan

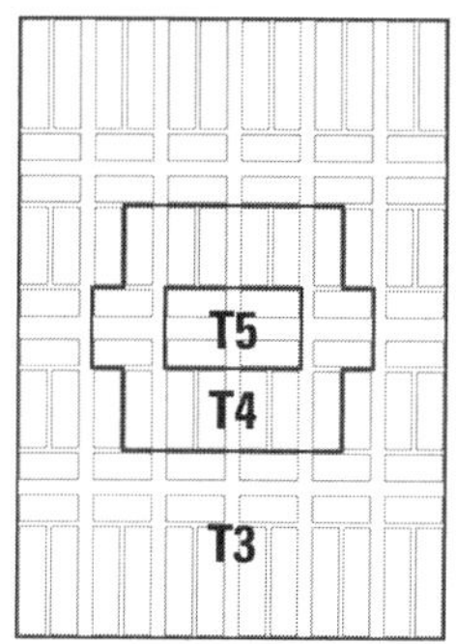


**Fig. 3.45** Continuation of the Regulating Plan

precedents necessary to be able to fill in these regulations, but if necessary someone can always be sent out to find and document appropriate precedents. (See the sidebar on page 142, "When Good Local Precedent Doesn't Exist.")

Finally, review each of the regulations and values to determine if any of them need to be adjusted. For existing places, if the intention is to preserve the area, the values will be only minimally adjusted, if at all. If the intention is to preserve and enhance the area, the values may be adjusted a little more to "enhance" the area. Typically, this means adjusting the value in the direction of the one for the next transect zone. If the transect zone is new to the community and based on an appropriate but not a local precedent, the values may need to be adjusted a little more to calibrate them to the local community.

The values may also need to be adjusted based on local realities. First, take into consideration local building codes. For example, some aspects of historic building practices are no longer legal under current building codes, so the regulation values based on historic models may need to be adjusted; however, do this cautiously and thoughtfully so as not to inadvertently negate an important observed historic condition. Second, consider the need to compensate for current development practices and economic realities. For example, when dealing with production builders, it may be impossible to get them to build houses with crawl spaces similar to the historic homes, but it is possible to require them to elevate the foundation slabs with stem walls at the front of the houses to get the required minimum height of a finished first floor in residential units.

| | T3a |
|---|---|
| Image | |
| Description | The primary intent of this zone is to protect the integrity and quality of the downtown residential neighborhoods. |
| **Building Placement** | |
| Build-to Line (Distance from Property Line) | |
| Front | 15' |
| Side Street | 15' |
| Rear, Ancillary Building | – |
| BTL Defined by a Building | |
| Front | 50% min |
| Side Street | – |
| Building Facade at BTL | |
| Front | 60% min. |
| Side Street, Main Building | 60% min. |
| Side Street, Ancillary Building | - |
| Rear, Ancillary Building | 90% min. |
| **Setback (Distance from Property Line)** | |
| Front | – |
| Side Street | – |
| Side, Main Building | 8' |
| Side, Ancillary Building | 8' |
| Rear, Main Building | |
| Adjacent to Residential | 40' |
| Adjacent to Any Other Use | 5' |
| Rear, Ancillary Building | 6' |
| **Lot Size** | |
| Width | 50' max. |
| Depth | 110' max. |
| Square Footage | 5,500 |
| **Miscellaneous** | |
| Distance between Main and Ancillary Buildings | 25' |
| Only one Main Building and one Ancillary Building may be built on each lot. | yes |
| Only one building may be built on each lot. | - |
| Ancillary Building may not be attached to the Main Building. | – |
| Street facades must be built to BTL within x' of street corner. | - |
| Where existing adjacent buildings are in front of the regulated BTL, the building may be set to align with the facade of the frontmost immediately adjacent property. | – |

**Fig. 3.46** Beginning of the Transect Regulation Matrix. Start with the values from the documentation process to fill this in.

While completing this task, remember that the values being assigned are defining the intended place. Make sure to consider each one carefully for its impact on the character and quality of the intended place, as well as on the potential for development in the community. Review the Building Form Standards section in the Components chapter of this book for tips on determining the appropriate regulations.

*Next Step*

Skip to Step 2.2.8 to finalize the regulating zone.

## 2.2.5 Review the Transect Zone Regulations

Find the column for the applicable transect zone on the Transect Regulation Matrix. Review the regulations and values to determine if they are appropriate to the newly defined regulating zone. Answer the following questions and continue according to the accompanying directions.

*Next Step*

1. Do all the regulations and values for the selected transect zone apply to the entire

regulating zone? If yes, skip to question 4. If no, continue to the next question.

2. Do all the regulations and values for the selected transect zone apply to any portion of the regulating zone? If yes, return to Step 2.2.3, and redraw the boundary of the regulating zone around only the portion of the area to which all the regulations apply. If no, continue to the next question.
3. Can the regulations and values for the selected transect zone be modified to be correct and complete for the entire newly defined regulating zone? If yes, skip to question 5. If no, the newly defined regulating zone is too large. Return to Step 2.2.3, and redraw the boundary of the regulating zone around a smaller area to which a single set of regulations will apply.
4. Are the regulations for the selected transect zone complete for the newly defined regulating zone? If yes, skip to Step 2.2.8 to finalize the regulating zone. If no, continue to the next question.
5. If the regulations for the selected transect zone are modified to be correct and complete for the newly defined regulating zone, will they still work for all the previously defined regulating zones corresponding to this transect zone? If yes, skip to Step 2.2.7 to modify the transect zone regulations. If no, continue to Step 2.2.6 to create a duplicate transect zone on the Transect Regulation Matrix that can then be modified.

## 2.2.6 Duplicate the Transect Zone on the Matrix

Since the modifications necessary for the newly defined regulating zone are not appropriate to the previously defined regulating zones, the modifications cannot be made to the existing transect zone column on the Transect Regulation Matrix. Instead, make a duplicate of the transect zone column on the matrix. This duplication automatically creates a subset within the transect zone, assuming one did not already exist. As discussed earlier, subsets include zones that have a similar level of urbanism, but different distinguishing characteristics.

Rename the two transect zones with sequential letters (e.g., T3a and T3b), making sure to take into account the names of any other zones in the subset, if any. Determine which column on the matrix will be *not* be modified, based on whether the new transect zone will be modified to be more or less urban than the existing transect zone and remembering to keep the Transect Matrix organized from most rural to most urban. (See Figure 3.47.) Using the revised name of the unmodified transect zone column, find any previously defined regulating zones corresponding to that transect zone and rename them on the Regulating Plan.

**Fig. 3.47** Transect Regulation Matrix with a transect zone subset

| | T3a | T3b |
|---|---|---|
| Image | | |
| Description | The primary intent of this zone is to protect the integrity and quality of the downtown residential neighborhoods. | The primary intent of this zone is to protect the integrity and quality of the downtown residential neighborhoods. |
| **Building Placement** | | |
| Build-to Line (Distance from Property Line) | | |
| Front | 15' | 15' |
| Side Street | 15' | 15' |
| Rear, Ancillary Building | – | – |
| BTL Defined by a Building | | |
| Front | 50% min. | 50% min. |
| Side Street | – | – |
| Building Facade at BTL | | |
| Front | 60% min. | 60% min. |
| Side Street, Main Building | 60% min. | 60% min. |
| Side Street, Ancillary Building | - | - |
| Rear, Ancillary Building | 90% min. | 90% min. |
| **Setback (Distance from Property Line)** | | |
| Front | – | – |
| Side Street | – | – |
| Side, Main Building | 8' | 8' |
| Side, Ancillary Building | 8' | 8' |
| Rear, Main Building | | |
| Adjacent to Residential | 40' | 40' |
| Adjacent to Any Other Use | 5' | 5' |
| Rear, Ancillary Building | 6' | 6' |
| **Lot Size** | | |
| Width | 50' max. | 50' max. |
| Depth | 110' max. | 110' max. |
| Square Footage | 5,500 | 5,500 |
| **Miscellaneous** | | |
| Distance between Main and Ancillary Buildings | 25' | 25' |
| Only one Main Building and one Ancillary Building may be built on each lot. | yes | yes |
| Only one building may be built on each lot. | - | - |
| Ancillary Building may not be attached to the Main Building. | – | – |
| Street facades must be built to BTL within x' of street corner. | - | - |
| Where existing adjacent buildings are in front of the regulated BTL, the building may be set to align with the facade of the frontmost immediately adjacent property. | – | – |

Now that the original transect zone has been safely preserved on the Transect Regulation Matrix, edit the regulations and values for the new duplicate transect zone as needed for the newly defined regulating zone. This may entail deleting existing regulations, modifying their values, and/or adding new regulations.

*Next Step*
Skip to Step 2.2.8.

## 2.2.7 Modify the Transect Zone Regulations

On the Transect Regulation Matrix, edit the regulations and values for the transect zone as needed for the newly defined regulating zone, making sure that the changes also apply to all the previously defined regulating zones corresponding to this transect zone. This may entail deleting existing regulations, modifying their values, and/or adding new regulations.

*Next Step*
Continue to Step 2.2.8.

## 2.2.8 Finalize the Regulating Zone

Now that the transect zone regulations are all appropriate and complete for the newly defined regulating zone, the regulating zone is complete. Label the regulating zone on the Regulating Plan with the name of the transect zone from the Transect Regulation Matrix.

*Next Step*
Continue to Step 2.2.9.

## 2.2.9 Review the Regulating Plan

Next, review the Regulating Plan along with the Illustrative Plan to determine whether all the areas are now in regulating zones. Answer the following questions, and continue according to the accompanying directions.

*Next Step*
1. Are all portions of the neighborhood (or other macro element) selected in Step 2.2.2 now in defined regulating zones? If yes, continue to the next question. If no, return to Step 2.2.3 to define the boundary for the next outer concentric zone in the neighborhood.
2. Are all the neighborhoods, districts, and corridor areas on the Illustrative Plan now in defined regulating zones, except for possibly remnant outer edges? If yes, continue to Step 2.2.10 to resolve the outer area boundaries. If no, return to Step 2.2.2 and start defining regulating zones for the next neighborhood or other macro element.

## 2.2.10 Resolve the Outer Area Boundaries

Review the boundary lines for all of the defined regulating zones. If there are any portions of the plan that are not in a regulating zone, consider whether to expand some existing regulating zones to encompass those areas or to create new zones for them. Complete Steps 2.2.3 to 2.2.8 for each new regulating zone created. Once all the outer edges have been assigned to a regulating zone, the first drafts of the Transect Regulation Matrix and the Regulating Plan are complete.

### Transect Subzones

In some cases, the two zones will be almost identical except for one or two differentiating regulations that are critical to keep. In this case, one option is to create a transect subzone. This can be implemented by coloring the entire transect zone a single color on the Regulating Plan and then adding a hatch (or some other visual variation) over the color for the subzone. On the Transect Regulation Matrix, the variable regulations can then be identified with footnotes However, this method also makes the code more complicated; use it only if absolutely necessary.

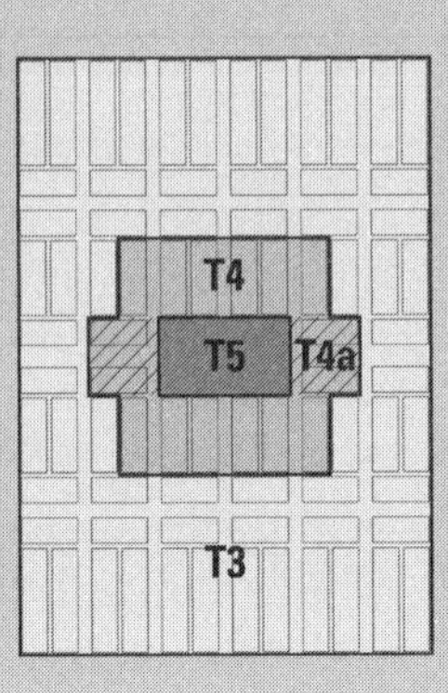

*Next Step*

Continue to Step 2.2.11.

## 2.2.11 Review the Transect Regulation Matrix

Once the Regulating Plan is complete, review the Transect Regulation Matrix to ensure that all the transect zones listed are actually necessary. Including unnecessary zones complicates the code for both developers and the staff responsible for maintaining the code.

Starting at one end of the matrix, review each pair of codes to determine whether the differences are great enough to warrant separate zones. If they are, continue to the next pair of zones. If they are not, combine the two, selecting the regulations that apply to all the regulating zones corresponding to both transect zones. Select a name for the transect zone and rename the corresponding regulating zones on the Regulating Plan. Repeat this process until the team is convinced that each transect zone is necessary. (See the sidebar "Transect Subzones.")

Finally, finalize the Transect Regulation Matrix by renaming the remaining transect zones as necessary to ensure an even continuum and consistent naming.

*Next Step*

Continue to Step 2.2.12.

## 2.2.12 Repeat for Micro Elements

Select a micro element that needs to be regulated to implement the vision. Repeat Steps 2.2.1 to 2.2.9 for the micro element using the following adjustments. (See the sidebar "Repeating the Process for Building Types.")

When creating the Micro-Element Regulation Matrix (e.g., Thoroughfare Regulation Matrix), create a column for each micro-element type (e.g., a column for each thoroughfare type).

When working on the thoroughfares and civic spaces, assign an appropriate thoroughfare or civic space type on the Regulating Plan, similarly to the regulating zones. However, for the other micro elements, assign the types to the transect zones on the Transect Regulation Matrix instead of to the Regulating Plan.

As with the transect zones, refer to the Components section of this book for tips on determining the appropriate regulations.

*Next Step*

Are all the necessary Micro-Element Regulation Matrices complete? If yes, continue to Step 2.2.13. If not, repeat this step for the next micro element.

**Product List**

- Regulating Plan
- Transect Regulation Matrix
- Micro-Element Regulation Matrices (e.g., Thoroughfare Regulation Matrix and Civic Space Regulation Matrix)

### Multiple Regulating Plans

In the interest of keeping the code simple and easy to use, it is typically best to keep all the necessary information on a single Regulating Plan. If the plan starts to become overwhelming with too much information, it may be appropriate to separate it into multiple Regulating Plans, typically creating one for each code component (e.g., a Building Form Standards Regulating Plan and a Public Space Regulating Plan). However, this requires code users to refer to multiple plans when determining which regulations apply to their property, so it should be considered only if this would be easier than trying to decipher the information on a single, overburdened Regulating Plan.

## 2.2.13 Write the Development Review Process

Gather the visioning participants together to discuss the possible development review processes and the pros and cons of each. Refer to the Administration section in the Components chapter of this book for tips on determining the appropriate process. Based on the input from the participants, write the development review process to include in the Vision Plan.

*Next Step*
Continue to Step 2.2.14.

**Product List**

- Development Review Process

## 2.2.14 Assemble the Vision Plan

Gather all the products from the visioning process, and assemble them into a single document called the Vision Plan. The Vision Plan can take many forms and include a variety of information, depending on the intention and scope of the overall project, of which a Form-Based Code may be only one piece; however, in order to be a suitable base for an FBC, the Vision Plan should include all the products listed below.

**Product List**

- Vision Plan, including at minimum:
  - Illustrative Plan
  - Transect Zone Vision Sheets
  - Element Vision Sheets (e.g., Thoroughfare Type Vision Sheets, Civic Space Vi-

### Repeating the Process for Building Types

2.2.1: Gather the Building Type Documentation Sheets from the documentation process along with the Building Type Vision Sheets created in the first part of the visioning process. Create a new matrix, called the "Building Type Regulation Matrix," using a template such as the one shown at the right.

2.2.2: Select a transect zone from the Transect Regulation Matrix.

2.2.3: Select a building type from the list for the transect zone.

2.2.4: Find the Building Type Vision Sheet for the applicable building type. Create a new column on the Building Type Regulation Matrix for the building type, and add the name and image from the Building Type Vision Sheet to the top of the column.

Next, begin filling in the regulations. If the building type is based on an existing building type in the community, find the Building Type Documentation Sheets for that building type for reference. Starting at the top of the Building Type Regulation Matrix, review each section one by one. Determine which regulations are necessary, and fill them in based on the information on the Building Type Documentation Sheets.

For building types that are new to the community, use documentation information from other appropriate precedents to fill in the regulations. Finally, review each of the regulations and values to determine if any of them need to be adjusted. As with the transect zones, the building type regulations may also need to be adjusted based on local realities. Review the Building Type Standards section in the Components chapter of this book for tips on determining the appropriate regulations.

2.2.8: The building type is complete.

2.2.9: Review the Transect Regulation Matrix.

*Next Step*

1. Are all building types in the transect zone selected in Step 2.2.2 now defined on the Building Type Regulation Matrix? If yes, continue to the next question. If no, return to Step 2.2.3 to define the next building type.
2. Are all the building types in all the transect zones now defined on the Building Type Regu-

sion Sheets, and Building Type Vision Sheets)

- Regulating Plan
- Transect Regulation Matrix
- Micro-Element Regulation Matrices (e.g. Thoroughfare Regulation Matrix, Civic Space Regulation Matrix, and Building Type Regulation Matrix)
- Development Review Process

lation Matrix? If yes, continue to Step 2.2.12 for the next micro element. If no, return to Step 2.2.2 and start defining building types for the next transect zone.

As additional transect zones are reviewed, building types may be reused, just as the transect zones were reused for additional regulating zones. Follow the instructions in Steps 2.2.5 through 2.2.7 for modifying building types already on the Building Type Regulation Matrix.

**Product List**

- Building Type Regulation Matrix
- Updated Transect Regulation Matrix

| | Commercial Block | Duplex | Fourplex | Detached Single Unit House A | Detached Single Unit House B |
|---|---|---|---|---|---|
| Sketch or Photo | | | | | |
| Description | | | | | |
| **Required Lot Size** | | | | | |
| Min. lot width | | | | | |
| Min. lot depth | | | | | |
| **Pedestrian Access** | | | | | |
| Main Entrance Location | | | | | |
| Elevator Access | | | | | |
| Interior Circulation | | | | | |
| **Frontages** | | | | | |
| Rooms Facing Primary Public Spaces | | | | | |
| Frontages Allowed | | | | | |
| **Vehicle Access and Parking** | | | | | |
| Access to Parking | | | | | |
| Access to Dwelling from Parking | | | | | |
| Allowed Parking Types | | | | | |
| **Service** | | | | | |
| Location of Services | | | | | |
| **Open Space** | | | | | |
| General Location and Size of Open Space | | | | | |
| **Landscape** | | | | | |
| Minimum Required Landscape | | | | | |
| **Building Size and Massing** | | | | | |
| Composition | | | | | |

**Building Type Regulation Matrix**

**Page 1 of 1**

# Phase 3: Assembling

ONCE THE VISIONING is complete, the code content can be supplemented if necessary to fit the code into the existing regulatory framework, and then formatted to create the final code document. While some of the precursors to regulatory Form-Based Codes were presented as a poster or other succinct document, today's FBCs tend to be a bit longer to accommodate their regulatory nature and address concerns that have arisen from some of the earlier codes; however, keeping the FBC concise is still a priority. In fact, one of the numerous reasons for the popularity of Form-Based Codes is their ease of use. Just as the regulatory basis of conventional zoning codes have been rethought, so have their organization and formatting. Form-Based Codes are shorter, less complicated, more graphically oriented, and generally more user-friendly than conventional zoning codes.

## Process Overview

Once the vision is complete, including all the necessary regulations, only two steps remain. First, if the FBC is being implemented alongside or within the existing zoning code rather than replacing it completely, any additional parts that are necessary to plug it into the existing regulatory framework must be written. Finally, all the code content must be organized and formatted into the code document. (See Figure 3.48.)

Also, as mentioned earlier, the code content that was created during the visioning process might also be refined throughout this phase.

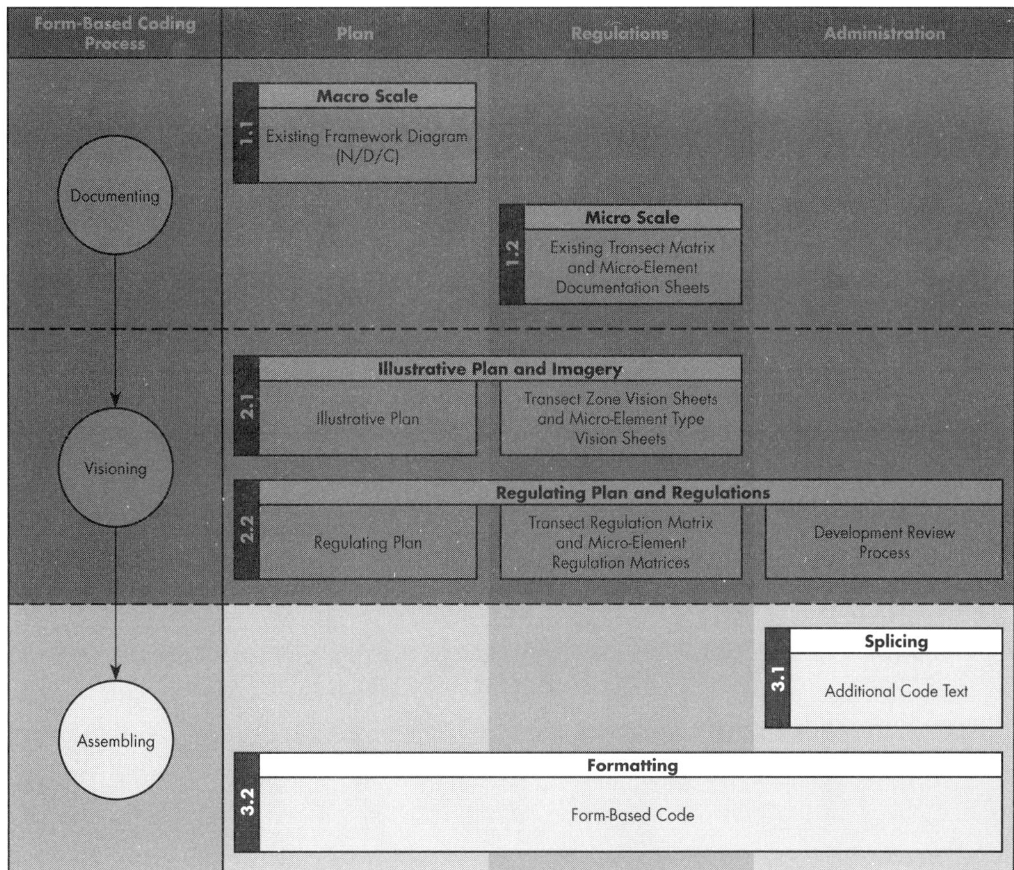
Form-Based Coding Process
Plan
Regulations
Administration
Documenting
Visioning
Assembling
1.1
Macro Scale
Existing Framework Diagram (N/D/C)
1.2
Micro Scale
Existing Transect Matrix and Micro-Element Documentation Sheets
2.1
Illustrative Plan and Imagery
Illustrative Plan
Transect Zone Vision Sheets and Micro-Element Type Vision Sheets
2.2
Regulating Plan and Regulations
Regulating Plan
Transect Regulation Matrix and Micro-Element Regulation Matrices
Development Review Process
3.1
Splicing
Additional Code Text
3.2
Formatting
Form-Based Code

**Fig. 3.48**
Phase 3: Assembling

# 3.1 Splicing

UNLESS THE FBC is replacing the preexisting development code for the entire community or it is being implemented under a PUD zone, the integration of Form-Based Code standards into a more extensive conventional code requires careful attention to the relationships between the standards and procedures in each code in the event that conflicts between them are perceived. The FBC will need to include one or more definitive statements to "splice" the new FBC standards to those remaining in the preexisting development code, as well as to identify the circumstances under which either the preexisting code standards or the Form-Based Code standards control for the purposes of project design, and/or review and approval. Depending on the community's objectives, still-operative citywide code standards may include such standards as requirements for the operation of home occupations, sign regulations, and other similar regulations.

Because of the infinite variations in local and state regulatory frameworks as well as the legal aspects involved, it is beyond the scope of this book to cover this topic beyond this mention. The team's planning expert will need to address this concern.

# 3.2 Formatting 

Carol Wyant, a consultant at Pathfinder Consulting, coined the term *Form-Based Codes* in 2001. Prior to that time, Form-Based Codes were known by a variety of names as people tried to determine exactly what they were and what they should be called. One of the more popular names was "Graphic Codes" because the codes were easily recognizable by their graphic nature. This was a significant difference from conventional zoning regulations, which were almost solely text. Many people latched onto this difference not only because the graphics made these codes so quickly identifiable, but also because they made them much easier to use. The codes were becoming popular not only for the changes they were enabling in the development of great places, but also because they were so much easier to use than conventional zoning documents.

Coincidentally, a similar movement was happening at the same time on the Internet. As more people began using the Internet, especially for shopping, Web site owners began recognizing that a bad Web site design could lose them business. If their site's visitors (or "users") could not find the items they were looking for or could not figure out how to actually purchase the item, not only did the business lose that sale, but more than likely, the user would never come back to the site and all future sales were also lost. It became critical to make sure the Web site was easy to use, or "usable." A relatively small design practice known as "usability design" became the mainstream.

The focus of this type of design is the "user." As a Web site (or code) is being designed, the user's viewpoint is constantly considered. The key is always to remember that the site is not being designed for the site's owners, designers, and developers, who are all too familiar with the site and its content and often much more comfortable using a computer and the Internet than most users. The designers need to constantly consider what it is like for their users to use the site.

This "usability design" practice is a key component to the success of Form-Based Codes. As with Web sites, there are critical problems that occur when a Form-Based Code is not designed well, and users get confused and misinterpret the intent of the code. This is often the case with conventional zoning codes. For example, a property owner might interpret a specific item one way, but the staff planner reviewing his or her proposed project interprets it a different way. This obviously leads to disagreement, and the process gets delayed trying to determine which interpretation is correct. At best, negotiation leads to an outcome that both parties are happy with; at worst, attorneys are brought in and litigation ensues. Either way, there is a good likelihood that the original intent of the code will be lost. In the end, the poor design of the code led to the loss of time, money, and quality of the development. This process can repeat itself from project to project until the entire intent of the code has been lost and the quality of development begins to negatively impact the quality of life of the residents. Therefore, taking the time to design the code correctly is a necessity to ensure that the intent is clear and the document is user-friendly.

## Know Your Users

In order to design a good FBC, it is essential to know and understand the code's users. Critical to this understanding is recognizing the wide variety of people who will be using the code. These include staff planners, property owners, developers, architects, planners, business owners, local politicians, potential property owners and residents, general citizens, and, last but not least, attorneys and judges. Each of these people will be looking at the code for answers to a multitude of different questions, all of which should be easy to find and understand from each person's point of view.

For this reason, the code should be written and designed considering the lowest common denominators of user traits. For example, even though many users will be familiar with the local geographic area, some will not. In order for those unfamiliar with the area to be able to understand the code, it should be written assuming that all users are not familiar with the area.

The key is to remember that the primary intention of the code is to ensure the implementation of the vision. This begins with the designing and writing of the code to enforce the vision. Once they are complete, and the code has been approved and become law, it continues with the development review process, which the code should be written and designed to support.

The various players in the development review process are the code's primary users. These are the staff planners as well as the design consultants, property owners, and developers. Secondary users are those will also use the document, but are not generally part of the design review process. These are typically general citizens, politicians, and judges.

First on the list of primary users are staff planners. This may include the Town Architect. They will be responsible for ensuring that the projects that come in for review meet the regulations in the code; therefore, they should be able to both understand and enforce the code. Second are design professionals, such as planners, architects, and designers. They are in a good position to help ensure a smooth process by creating designs that meet the community's needs and wishes; however, to do this, they should be able to understand the code.

Third are property owners and developers. This user group can encompass a wide variety of people and intentions. It could include someone who owns a small piece of property with a single-family house on it, a business owner who wants to build a new office in town, or a large developer who wants to build a mixed-use neighborhood on a large piece of land. Understanding that there are a large variety of property owners and developers with an equally large variety of intentions is important. For example, one developer might be interested in building a restaurant in town and is looking to the code to determine where that is allowable. Another developer might already own a piece of property and be trying to determine what can be built on the site. The way the document is organized should meet both of these needs.

Outside of the development review process, general citizens should also be considered when designing the code. For those who participate in the community visioning process, the code should be designed so that they can see that their vision is what was actually codified. Those who did not participate or who are considering moving to town should be able to understand what future development might happen in the community.

In addition, the local politicians and/or board members who must approve the code should be considered. They should be able to easily see and understand the intention of the code and what it will and will not do. The easier the code is to understand, the more likely its approval process will be straightforward as there won't be a debate about what the code is actually implementing.

Finally, lawyers and judges should be considered as users. At the end of the day, this is a legal document, and if there is any disagreement, it may end up on a judge's desk. Ensuring that the final judgment is made to uphold the community's vision is critical. The code should be written and designed to be legally understandable and enforceable.

Based on this consideration of the variety of potential users, the design will be impacted most by a few specific traits. First, as mentioned above, while most users will likely be familiar with the local geographic area, a substantial number will not, such as a new staff planner, a new property owner, or a judge—all critical users. The code should be designed assuming that the reader is not familiar with the area.

Second, over the life of a Form-Based Code, most users will not have been part of the community visioning process that led to the writing of the code. During the writing of a code, it is easy to assume that everyone understands the intention of the code because everyone involved at the time does understand it. However, the code, once approved, is likely to remain in force for many years, during which townspeople move away, staff planners find other opportunities, and new politicians are elected. Before you know it, there are a new city council, an entire new team of staff planners, and a new generation of citizens, none of whom were around when the code was written. This cannot be over emphasized. The code should be written assuming that the user is not familiar with the community vision or the process that took place to create that vision, and that no one else is either. The code should be able to stand alone.

Third, with a variety of users comes a variety of abilities with regard to graphics and drawings. Some users, such as the design professionals, will be trained in architecture or planning and will be able to easily understand line drawings and computer-assisted design (CAD) plans; however, many of the code's users will not have any such training and will have no ability to

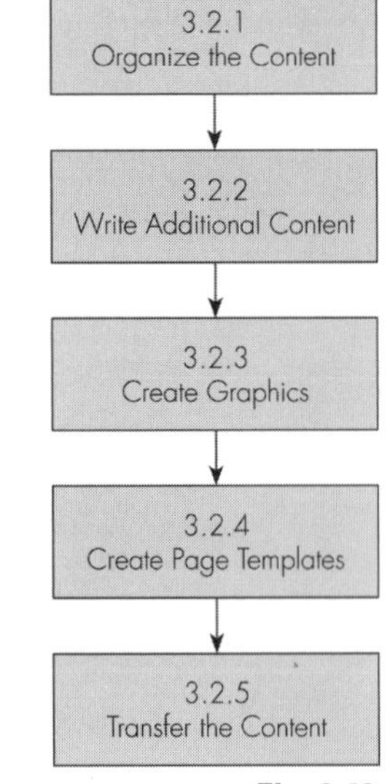


**Fig. 3.49**
3.2 Formatting

read complicated drawings. The code should be equally understandable to both types of users. For this reason, special consideration should be taken with all graphics to ensure that they are simple and easy to understand.

There are, no doubt, other considerations for specific users. The key is to critically examine the design of the document and consider the widest variety of users and their concerns when trying to make a design decision. When in doubt, use the lowest common denominator and remember that the users are the ones who have to understand the code, not the code team.

## Graphic Design

The layout and formatting of the code are also critically important to a code's usability. FBCs are filled to the brim with information, and a good graphic design can help the users wade through this information. Throughout this section, there are a variety of graphic design guidelines that can help create a usable code. They have been written specifically for designing code documents, although they can certainly be applied to many other types of documents.

When formatting a code document, remember these two overarching guidelines:

**1. Keep It Simple**

The intention of the graphic design elements and techniques in the following sections is to help code users better find and understand the information they are looking for. The intention is not to draw attention to the graphic design; it is to enhance the information, not overtake it. Therefore, the design tactics advocated here are purposefully simple and straightforward. Using these guidelines may not help create an award-winning graphic design, but they will help ensure that the code is easy to understand and use, while being graphically sound.

**2. Use Plenty of White Space**

White space is exactly what it sounds like: any space on a page that is left blank. As users read through a code, their eyes (and minds) are likely to get tired. White space provides places for their eyes to rest. In addition, white space provides cues for the eye to recognize divisions of information. For example, a tab at the beginning of a paragraph is a bit of white space that tells the reader that a new paragraph has begun. While increasing white space may make the code a bit longer, the usability of the code will be increased tenfold. It is worth the trade-off, especially for such a dense and dry document.

## Process Overview

To begin, all of the code's content is organized into sections to create a final code document order that will best facilitate the needs of all the users. Next, any remaining necessary content, such as the glossary, is written and graphics are created. Once the content is complete, the graphic design of the document and its impact on the usability of the code are considered while page templates are created. Once the templates are ready, the content is transferred in to complete the final Form-Based Code document. (See Figure 3.49.)

## 3.2.1 Organize the Content

There are many factors that influence a code's usability, including graphic design, the ordering of the content, the inclusion of certain sections (such as a table of contents and a glossary), and the design of the graphic images themselves. Beginning with the overall organization, consider the primary users and their intentions. For developers and their project designers, the primary questions are: What can I build on my lot or site, and what do I have to include? For staff planners, the questions are essentially the same. While there may be other viewpoints, organize the code's content to answer these primary questions.

In order to best determine this organization system, create a flowchart for how each of the primary users will use the code.

Depending on the size and reach of the code, this typically includes:

1. A developer of a small lot
2. A developer of a large site (one that will need to consider street, lot, and block design)
3. A staff planner who will review a submitted design for compliance with the code

Next, begin to create the table of contents to comply with these flowcharts, working back and forth between all of them. Before they are complete, consider any secondary users and usage scenarios that might be likely; however, be sure to weigh them against the primary scenarios before determining the best content organization. The secondary scenarios typically include:

1. A developer trying to determine where it is possible to build a certain type of project. For this, a single use table showing all the regulating zones is helpful; however, for users in the usage scenarios listed above, it is more helpful to have individual use tables in each of the regulating zone sections. Weigh the likelihood of each scenario and the next scenario to determine the best solution.
2. A staff planner making edits to the code. This typically means including each regulation only once in the code so that if that regulation must be edited, it needs to be edited in only one place. Every time a regulation is included more than once, there is a possibility that only one of the instances may get edited, creating inconsistency and confusion. In some instances, this may mean pulling regulations that apply to all the regulating zones out into a single section, such as the standards for parking space sizes; however, this should always be weighed against the usability aspects of the primary usage scenarios, and the final answer will depend on the overall size, scope, and complexity of the code document. In other instances, like the above for the use tables, it may be worth the potential for inconsistencies to include two different use tables, one at the beginning of the Building Form Standards, and one within each regulating zone section of the Building Form Standards.
3. A developer wondering, "Why do I have to do this?" Besides the obvious answer of "Because the code says so," it is often beneficial to know about the community's vision and the visioning process. This helps developers recognize that the regulations were created for a good reason, and that the community stands behind the regulations. The best solution for this is to include a section at the beginning of the code with images and a narrative about the vision and the visioning process.
4. A developer trying to determine what a term means. It is critical to include a glossary in the FBC. As mentioned earlier, many users of Form-Based Codes are not trained architects or planners. Even those who have formal training may not know anything about Form-Based Codes or the specific terms used in them. The glossary should contain any term that someone without a planning or architecture degree or someone unfamiliar with Form-Based Codes would not know (e.g., Build-to Line [BTL], Frontage). It should also contain any term that has specific regulations around it (e.g., Balcony), including all the uses from the use tables. Finally, it should contain any term that has an unconventional meaning (e.g., Building Type or District). A great way to

determine the list of terms to be defined in the glossary is to have a few general citizens read the code and highlight any terms they do not understand.

Based on the above considerations, the following is the recommended organization for a Form-Based Code to create an efficient flow through the code:

1. Table of Contents
2. Introduction
3. Regulating Plan
4. Building Form Standards
5. Block Standards
6. Public Space Standards
7. Administration
8. Glossary

The table of contents is often the first stop for readers. It gives them an overview of the document and helps them find specific items of interest. The introduction provides background information on the code and the community visioning process and acts as a transition into the core of the document. It also includes instructions on how to use the rest of the code.

The core of the document is the Regulating Plan and the Building Form, Block, and Public Space Standards. The Regulating Plan should be presented first, since the standards tie into it. Also, most users are likely to start by locating their property on the Regulating Plan. From there, most development applicants will be working with single lots, involving no land subdivision or changes to abutting streets, so the Building Form Standards should follow. Finally, for larger sites and as necessary, a code user will refer to the Block Standards and/or Public Space Standards.

The Administration section includes instructions for submitting, reviewing, and approving the project. Since it is not a part of the core standards, nor is it particularly juicy material, it generally works best toward the end of the document. The last section of the document should be a glossary, which users can easily refer to as necessary.

The following components are included specifically to aid in the usability of the code.

#### Table of Contents

It is highly unlikely that anyone will ever read an FBC from start to finish, except maybe for the staff planners who are responsible for enforcing it, and even they will probably never get through the whole code. Besides the fact that codes are inherently dry documents, there will never be a single project that involves the entire code. For instance, the designers of a new building in a T5 zone can completely ignore the Building Form Standards for the other transect zones. There is simply no need for anyone to read the code cover to cover; therefore, just about every person who picks up the code will refer to the table of contents to determine which sections they need to read. It also provides a quick overview of the entire document for those unfamiliar with it, as it is the first glimpse of the code for most users. Finally, it is important to include enough detail in the table of contents to enable users to find the specific items they need. Typically, one or two levels below the chapter listing is appropriate.

#### Introduction

A Form-Based Code is only as good as the political will to enforce it. The best-designed code for the best-designed place is useless if it is ignored or continuously overridden with variances. The public process that takes place to create a community vision is often what generates the enthusiasm and political will to turn that vision into an FBC and to get the code approved. It is critical to ensure that both the enthusiasm and the political will thrive once it is time to enforce the code, but this can be challenging as time goes on, newcomers enter the picture, and planning staff and community members who participated in the visioning process and code approval move away. A good introduction can help sustain and even propagate this enthusiasm by educating newcomers about the history of the community's vision, the process, and the code. This will meet the need of many of the users discussed earlier who are not familiar with this history.

In addition, a well-written introduction can help prevent unacceptable submissions and applications for variances by uninformed developers, which can save the developers' and the planning staffs' time and energy, as well as prevent unacceptable development. For these developers, it is critical that the introduction explain the background of the code, especially the community visioning process and documentation of place information. These will help the developer understand that the code was not pulled out of thin air, and that it has the support of the entire community. This can go a long way toward preventing these developers from attempting to thwart the code and the community's intention.

The following are recommended components of the introduction:

1. Intent of the Code
    a. History of the Code and the Community Vision
    b. Documentation of Place
2. How to Use the Code (typically, flow charts for the most likely usage scenarios)

#### Glossary

As mentioned earlier, many users of FBCs are not trained architects or planners. Even those who have formal training may not know much about Form-Based Codes or the specific terms used; therefore, it is critical to include a glossary. The glossary should contain all terms that someone without a planning or architecture degree or someone unfamiliar with FBCs might not know (e.g., Build-to Line [BTL], Frontage). It should also contain all terms that have specific regulations around them (e.g., Balcony), including the uses from the use tables, and all terms that have an unconventional meaning (e.g., Building Type). Finally, it should contain all acronyms used in the code.

However, the glossary should contain only definitions, *not* regulations. Most users will not find regulations listed in a glossary definition and will be surprised and dismayed when these regulations are brought up during the project application review.

### 3.2.2 Write Additional Content

Based on the decisions about the necessary components, write any additional sections that are necessary for the usability of the document, such as the introduction and the glossary.

### 3.2.3 Create Graphics

Next, consider any additional graphics that may be helpful to illustrate the regulations. As mentioned earlier, many Form-Based Code users are not able to read architectural or planning drawings. The key to creating graphics that most users can understand is, once again, to *simplify*.

Include only the information that is necessary to help users understand the code. Avoid graphics that look like typical architectural drawings, which have too many details for an FBC. The simpler the drawings, the more likely users will be able to understand them.

To better understand creating simple graphics, consider a plan within the Building Form Standards. (See Figure 3.50.)

Typically, the lines listed in the table below are all that are necessary for the base drawing. To differentiate these lines, use different line weights and dash patterns, but remember that only one attribute of a line needs to be different (e.g., line weight or dash, but not necessarily both). For solid objects that exist in real life, such as the building and curbs, use solid lines. For nonsolid objects, such as the property line, use dashed lines. To differentiate between the solid lines, use different line weights: for items of central focus, such as the ROW, use a heavyweight line; for items of lesser focus, such as the curb lines, use a lightweight line.

Also, consider using a gray fill to highlight an item of focus, such as the building or parking area, depending on what the related code guidelines are focusing on; however, remember not to highlight more than one or two items in order to keep the focus where it is intended.

Once this simple base drawing is in place, begin to add the notes, typically labels, dimensions, and callouts. The key is to include all critical information without including any unnecessary information. Following are a few guidelines:

- Align text labels along a shared guideline whenever possible.
- Use the same typeface and type size for all the notes.
- Keep leader lines vertical or horizontal whenever possible to avoid a mass of diagonal lines streaking across the drawing.
- Keep arrows small and out of the way.
- Set a standard outline size for all graphics. A 0.5 point line weight works well.

**T4: Neighborhood Center**

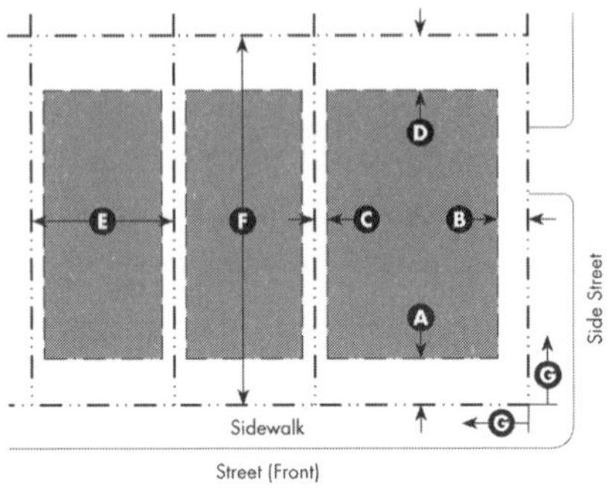

Sidewalk

Street (Front)

Side Street

**Key**

Property Line — Setback Line — Build-to Line (BTL) — Building Area

| Building Placement | | |
|---|---|---|
| **Build-to Line (Distance from Property Line)** | | |
| Front | 12′ | A |
| Side Street | 8′ | B |
| Building Façade at BTL | | |
| Front | 80% min. | |
| Side Street | 30% min. | |
| **Setback (Minimum Distance from Property Line)** | | |
| Side | 3′ min., 10′ max. | C |
| Rear | | |
| Adjacent to T3 | 10′ | D |
| Adjacent to other zone | 5′ | D |
| **Lot Size** | | |
| Width | 75′ max. | E |
| Depth | 150′ max. | F |
| **Miscellaneous** | | |
| Only one Main Building and one Ancillary Building may be built on each lot. | | |
| Street facades must be built to BTL within 30′ of street corner. | | G |
| Entire BTL must be defined by a building or a 2′6″ to 4′6″ high fence or stucco or masonry wall. | | |

**Fig. 3.50** Building placement plan

| Line | Type | Weight | Graphic |
|---|---|---|---|
| Right-of-Way (ROW) | Dashed 1 | 1 pt | — · · — · · — |
| Build-to Line (BTL) | Dashed 2 | 0.5 pt | — — — — |
| Setback Line | Dashed 3 | 0.5 pt | — · — · — · · |
| Curbs | Solid | 0.25 pt | ——— |
| Building outline (kept simple by not including doors and windows) | Fill with no line | 45% gray | ■ |

### Dimensions

The Building Form Standards and the Thoroughfare Standards pages often have tables as well as graphics with the pertinent regulatory dimensions listed. Listing these dimensions in tables makes them easy to locate, as well as to compare them with other regulatory dimensions; however, including graphic plans and sections with the same regulatory dimensions on the same pages is a part of what makes Form-Based Codes so usable. In this case, it could be argued that it is important to duplicate the dimensions in both cases. At least they are both on the same page, so it is more likely that the editor will catch both instances.

However, there is another option that uses notation graphics to tie the two regulation instances together. (See Figure 3.51.) For this option, the regulatory dimension is listed in the table, along with a bold graphic notation. Then the notation, rather than the dimension, is listed on the plan or section graphic. This system may not be quite as perfectly usable as including the actual dimension in both places, but it nicely balances the need for usability with the need for consistency. There are a couple of added benefits to this system. First, the plan and section graphics are actually cleaner because the notation graphics are more uniform than dimension numbers. This helps make the graphics easier to read. In addition, editing the dimensions is easier when the graphics have been created in a separate program and placed into the code document because it is not necessary to go into the graphic file to change the dimension; it can be done in the text document.

### The Regulating Plan

The most important graphic in the FBC is the Regulating Plan. Every user will need to read and understand it, so special care should be taken when designing it.

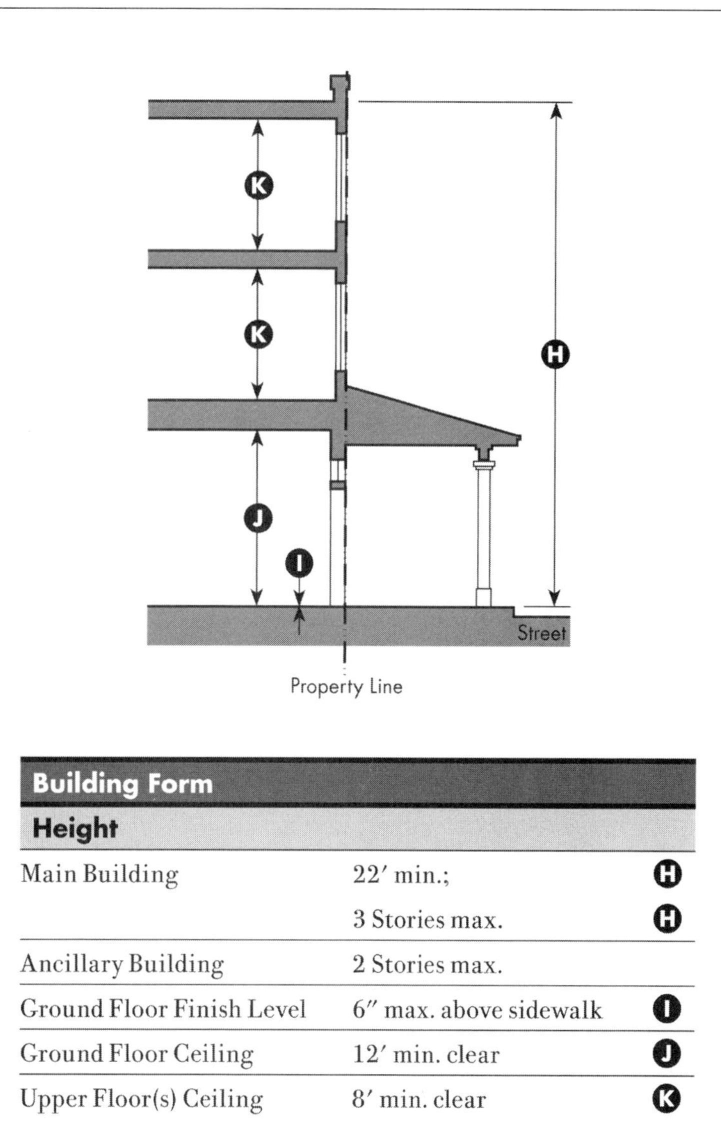


| Building Form | | |
|---|---|---|
| **Height** | | |
| Main Building | 22′ min.; | H |
| | 3 Stories max. | H |
| Ancillary Building | 2 Stories max. | |
| Ground Floor Finish Level | 6″ max. above sidewalk | I |
| Ground Floor Ceiling | 12′ min. clear | J |
| Upper Floor(s) Ceiling | 8′ min. clear | K |

**Fig. 3.51** The regulations are tied to the diagrams with notations so that there is only one place where each regulation must be edited.

The Regulating Plan is a graphic, just like all the others mentioned above, so it follows the same basic guidelines:

- Keep it simple.
- Use line weight and dashed-line patterns to differentiate between different lines while keeping variation to a minimum.
- Include only the necessary information. Edit out everything else.

Also, since the Regulating Plan reads best as a large graphic, consider using an 11 × 17-inch horizontal page folded into an 8-1/2 × 11-inch vertical document.

The Regulating Plan has some other specific considerations. The intention of the plan is to designate physical areas (or zones) to which certain aspects of the code apply. There are a number of ways to graphically identify these areas: color, hatch patterns, grays, and outlines along with text labels. Color is by far the best option. Although there are certain cost considerations with printing in color, it is possible to alleviate some of the concerns by printing only the Regulating Plan in color rather than the entire document. The alternatives significantly reduce the readability of the Regulating Plan.

For example, hatch patterns are one alternative that are incredibly difficult to read. While architects using CAD software may have become immune to their effect, most people are not used to reading hatch patterns. These patterns are very distracting visually and create a lot of noise on the page. They make a conceivably simple drawing look very messy and hard to read. Try to avoid hatch patterns.

Another option is to use a different gray for each of the areas. In order to differentiate between two different grays, the grays need to be at least 15 percent different (e.g., 10 percent gray and 25 percent gray). This means that there can be only six different grays, and most Regulating Plans have more than six areas to designate. If there are six areas or less, it may be acceptable to use gray rather than color. However, even with a 15 percent difference, grays are harder to differentiate than color, so color is still recommended.

A third option is to put a heavy outline around each area and include a text label; however, Regulating Plans already have many lines on them, so adding more lines, even heavyweight ones, generally adds more confusion and clutter.

If color is simply not feasible, the second best option is to use a combination of grays with outlines and labels. The gray areas with outlines create solid objects to identify, while the labels help differentiate between areas. In the end, though, do everything possible to use color since this is the most critical drawing in the entire code.

Finally, once the different areas are defined on the plan, add labels and/or a key.

## Software Programs

As the templates are being created, the team needs to determine which software program to use. The answer is not as simple as it seems, partially because it can vary depending on the project circumstances.

For the code team, the preferred method is typically to use a page-layout program, such as QuarkXPress or Adobe InDesign, along with an illustration program, such as Adobe Illustrator, and usually a photo program, such as Adobe Photoshop. These enable the best control of page layout and graphics, as well as easy setup templates.

Many municipal clients, however, prefer programs that they already have and know how to use. This is based on the expectation that, at some point, the code document will be turned over to them to manage and edit. While this is a completely reasonable request for municipal clients, the effort (and cost) to do it this way is considerably greater. Typically, this limits software choices to a word-processing program and maybe a CAD program. Neither of these program types is designed to create book graphics, although they can sometimes be made to do so with extra time, effort, patience, and a considerable amount of program expertise. Clients who insist on this option need to have the extra budget to pay for the additional time and expertise it takes to make them work.

A third option is to combine the two methods, using a word-processing program for the text-heavy sec-

## 3.2.4 Create Page Templates

Once the content has been created, begin to design the final document. When designing a Form-Based Code, many design elements must be considered, including the page format, page orientation, and typography. It is best to consider all these elements before beginning to format the content and while creating templates. This ensures a cohesive design that can accommodate all the content. It also helps avoid having to reformat the entire document at the end of the process when a situation arises that was not considered at the beginning.

### Page Size and Orientation

First, decide which size paper and orientation to use. In the United States, there are two size choices: letter (8-1/2 × 11 inches) or ledger (11 × 17 inches, also known as tabloid). (The considerations for metric-sized paper, A4 and A3, respectively, are similar.) Letter size is easier to read, easier to handle, and cheaper to reproduce, and it fits better on most bookshelves. On the other hand, ledger size provides more space for drawings on a single page and will generate a thinner document. If the code has any long text sections, such as the introduction or administration section, using letter-size paper will make them easier to read. When deciding, consider the orientation. A letter-size page, vertically oriented, is the easiest to read and handle, while either size page horizontally oriented can provide the extra space needed for certain drawings. (See Figure 3.52.)

In general, the best option is to use vertically oriented letter-size paper because it is more economic, easier to read, and easier to handle. Also, most people have a printer for letter-size paper, not ledger-size, which makes it more feasible to place the code online for people to access and print themselves. This option also works very nicely with an occasional horizontally oriented ledger-size page inserted for critical pages, such as the Regulating Plan. (See Figure 3.53.)

8-1/2" x 11"
vertical

8-1/2" x 11"
horizontal

11" x 17"
horizontal

**Fig. 3.52** Various page-size options

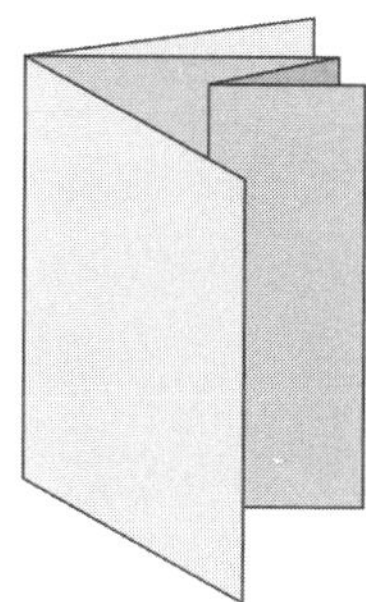

**Fig. 3.53** Horizontally oriented ledger-size page inserted into a vertically oriented letter-size document

tions of the document, such as the Administration section, and a graphic program for the more graphically intense sections, such as the Building Form Standards. In this case, once the code is turned over, the client can still do most of the editing, but would call the code designer to make any changes to the graphic sections. Since the changes to the graphic sections are less likely, this solution often works.

A fourth option is to use an illustration program for all of the graphics and a word-processing program for the entire layout. When this option is used, special care should be take when creating the graphics to minimize the amount of editable information in them. For example, it would be best in this instance to use letter-coded symbols for each of the dimension strings and notes on a graphic, and then put the actual dimensions and notes in an editable table in the word-processing program. (See Figure 3.51.)

In the end, it actually takes more expertise and design capabilities to design a good, usable document using a word-processing program. For those who are just learning how to create a good graphic code from this chapter, it will be nearly impossible. It is often better to spend a little extra money to buy one copy of a good graphic software package and train a staff member or two on how to use it for simple edits than to spend the extra time it takes to coax a good document out of a word-processing program.

### Single-Sided or Double-Sided Pages

Next, determine whether the document will be single- or double-sided. Whenever possible, design a double-sided document, which will be half as thick and will reduce paper consumption. In addition, if the code is on vertically oriented letter-size paper, two pages shown side by side, called a "spread," will provide an overall horizontal orientation to lay out drawings and plans, which is typically preferable. (See Figure 3.54.) However, make sure the client has the resources necessary to print double-sided pages (a local copy shop or a duplexer for the printer). Once the code has been designed to be double-sided, it will be less usable if printed single-sided, because it will have been designed to read in spreads.

### Color

Next, determine whether the document will include color. Once a graphic is designed in color, it will not read as well if it is then printed in black and white. Since the code designer will be spending valuable time designing quality, easy-to-read graphics, it is critical to know ahead of time whether color will be available to enhance their usability. Because of the added expense of printing in color and the tight budgets of most municipalities, codes are typically black and white; however, there are certain key elements in the code for which color needs to be considered, the most prominent of which is the Regulating Plan, discussed later in this chapter. As you'll see, it is very difficult to create a usable Regulating Plan without color, except in the simplest of localities. For this reason, plan to have a few pages printed in color and inserted into the document. These are often the same pages that need to be printed on ledger-size paper and inserted, so they can be easily coordinated.

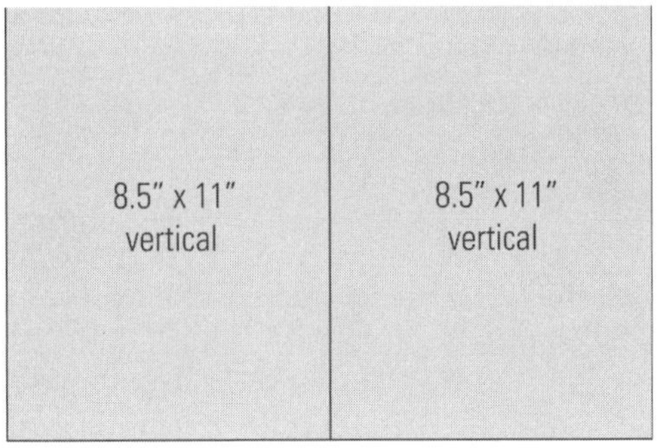

| 8.5" x 11" vertical | 8.5" x 11" vertical |
|---|---|

**Fig. 3.54**
A "spread" of two vertically oriented letter-size pages gives an overall horizontal orientation to the document.

### Margins

Once the page size and orientation have been determined, begin to lay out the page templates. First, determine the margins. Typically, the top margin should be the smallest and the bottom margin should be the largest. For a single-sided document, the two side margins may be equal, but for a double-sided document, the inside margins are next to one another, effectively reading as one margin. To account for this additive effect, the inside margins should be smaller than the outside margins. (See Figure 3.55.)

Also remember to account for the binding itself. Depending on the type of binding, it may be necessary to increase the size of the inside margin. For most FBCs, spiral binding works best since it can easily be done at a local copy shop, and it permits a reader to open the document and lay it out flat on a desk as a reference. If the document is spiral bound, there is no need to leave extra space in the margin.

### Header and Footer Elements

Next, determine the headers and footers, including any information that needs to be on every page of the document. First, consider a user who may be seeing a page of the code copied out of context and include any information that person needs to provide context and to help find the entire code if needed. This might include the document title, the project location, the draft date, and the page number. Second, consider a user looking at a page within the code and include any items that would be useful to provide context within the document. These might include the chapter name and the page number.

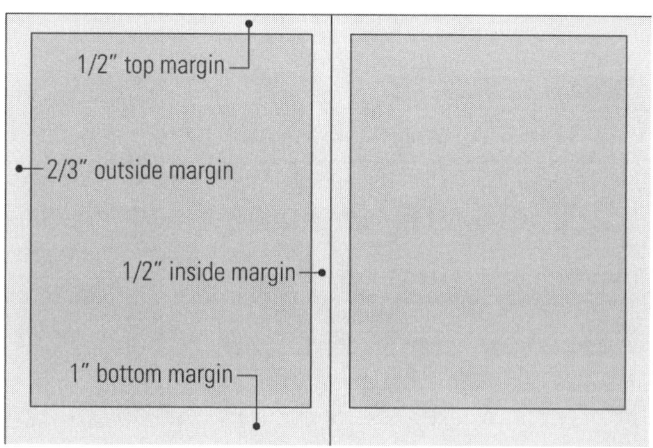


**Fig. 3.55** Sample margins for a single-sided document (far left). For double-sided pages (near left), the side margins will be unequal. The "inside" margin is the margin where the binding is. The "outside" margin is the outer edge of the book.



Elements to consider for each page include:

- **Document Title** and **Project Location**
- **Page Number** and **Chapter**: Consider numbering the pages by chapter, such as 1-18 (Chapter 1, page 18) and 4-12 (Chapter 4, page 12). Form-Based Codes are edited many times both before and after final approval. When a page is added or deleted, it is much easier to renumber a single chapter than the entire document.
- **Draft Date**: If nothing else is included besides a page number, be sure to include a draft date on every page. As mentioned earlier, Form-Based Codes go through multiple drafts throughout their life, and pages are copied out and distributed at random throughout the process. The draft date is the only way users can know which version of the document they are looking at. The draft date should be removed only after final approval of the code. Even then, consider changing it to **Record Date** and keeping the date on every page since even "final" codes can be revised.

### Typography

Finally, determine how the text will be handled. As with all the other graphic design elements, it is important to keep the typography simple. Its job is to help make the information clearer, not to draw attention to itself. Begin by selecting the typefaces, choosing no more than two or maybe three. Using a sans-serif typeface for the page titles and headers along with a serif typeface for the general text often works nicely.

Next, determine the type sizes, again limiting the number of sizes to be used. Typically, one size for the page titles, one for the page text, including headings, and one for the captions and callouts on images are all that are needed.

AVOID USING ALL CAPITAL LETTERS (KNOWN AS ALL CAPS). ALL CAPS ARE VERY DIFFICULT TO READ WHEN THERE ARE MORE THAN A FEW WORDS BECAUSE THERE IS NO VARIATION IN THE HEIGHT OF THE LETTERS TO HELP YOUR EYE DISTINGUISH ONE LETTER FROM THE NEXT. THIS MAKES MORE WORK FOR YOUR EYES, REDUCING LEGIBILITY.

The same is true for condensed (narrow) type, except in this case, there is less horizontal variation in the letters. Again, this lack of variation makes the type harder on the eyes. Condensed type may be used for short sections of text (such as the sidebars in this book), but should not be used as the primary typeface in a long document.

Finally, use only bold and italics as highlighting methods. All other methods available in most software is inappropriate for a document such

Serif Typeface

Sans-serif Typeface

**Left Justified**
For lots 70 feet wide or wider, the courtyard must be enclosed by the building on at least three sides.

**Center Justified**
For lots 70′ wide or wider, the courtyard must be enclosed by the building on at least three sides.

**Fully Justified**
For lots 70 feet wide or wider, the courtyard must be enclosed by the building on at least three sides.

**Fig. 3.56** Justification styles

as a Form-Based Code. (See the sidebar "Highlighting Techniques.")

While it may seem like all the options have been taken away, the reality is that with two fonts, three type sizes, and two highlighting methods (bold and italic), there are 12 different typographic variations to use throughout the document ($2 \times 3 \times 2 = 12$). This is more than enough to create an effective and usable code. Most of the other variations described above (such as all caps and shadow letters) were originally created for graphic artwork, such as book covers and posters. With the increase in the use of personal computers, they are used much more routinely than was ever intended.

Paul Rand, one of the twentieth century's most acclaimed graphic designers, said, "If you can't make it good, make it big. If you can't make it big, make it red." We've all seen too many big, red words in our lifetime. With a little thought and frugality, it can be good instead.

*Justification*

Justification is the way text is aligned on a page. (See Figure 3.56.) Once the typefaces have been selected, determine how the text will be justified. For general text, use left justification, which is the easiest to read for long passages and normal column widths. Do not use center, right, or full justification for general text. Center justification may be used for titles or in tables, as long as it is used for no more than two lines at a time. Full justification is for very narrow columns, such as those in a newspaper, and must be implemented with a good software program to ensure that the word spacing is not distracting. For most FBCs, left justification is the best option.

*Text Column Widths*

In addition to considering justification, determine how wide the text columns will be. While the guidelines vary a bit, typically keep the line lengths to about 8–12 words. If the lines are much longer, a reader's eyes will get lost as they travel from the end of one line back to the beginning of the next line. If the lines are much shorter, their eyes bounce back and forth down the page without time to rest.

## 3.2.5 Transfer the Content

Once the page templates have been determined, transfer the code content into the templates using the organization determined earlier.

### Highlighting Techniques

Be very cautious with the use of typographic highlighting techniques, such as bold and italics. These techniques can be very effective when used judiciously, but they become useless and distracting when used in abundance. Their design intent is to call attention to certain items on a page. In order to be effective, they should contrast with the majority of the other items. If everything on a page is bold, nothing stands out because there is no contrast. The best way to ensure that these items are used successfully is to write the entire code without them. After the code is written, read through it, looking for the most important items to highlight, ensuring that you are being very critical in your selections.

Of the highlighting methods available, bold and italics are the most useful. Underlining, which used to be acceptable as a highlighting method, should no longer be used. With the rise in popularity of the Internet, underlining now reads as a hyperlink, even when seen in print. It makes users think they are missing information by not being able to click on the link. Also, avoid all other highlighting methods, such as strikethrough, shadow, and outline, as they are more distracting than helpful. In essence, ignore most of the options in your font menu, except bold and italics.

### Text versus Tables

One key is to remember that users want to get the information as quickly and easily as possible. Tables rather than narrative text work best for readers to be able to scan quickly. Table-formatted text minimizes the use of words, so there is less to read. In addition, tables facilitate comparison. This keeps readers focused on critically examining the information rather than parsing through narrative text for the important pieces of information.

Certain sections of a Form-Based Code lend themselves well to narrative text, while tables work best in others. The introduction is a section that is typically best in narrative format because it is essentially telling the story of how and why the code came about. The Building Form Standards are almost always a combination of tables and graphics, with little or no narrative text. Because this section is at the core of the document, it should be formatted so that readers do not miss any critical data. In sections such as this, tables will work for most of the information, but maybe not all of it. In this situation, first try to put as much as possible into tables, without missing any critical information. Once this is completed, try to put the rest of the information at the bottom of the table as bullet points (typically 7–10 words and with or without and actual "bullet point"). Only when absolutely necessary, include the final bits as narrative text.

### Table Design

In order for the tables to be effective, they should be designed well. The key to good table design is to pay special attention to the table dividers or section headers. These enable users to scan through the headers looking for the section they need. Typically, there will be multiple levels of headers. For instance, the primary header is the table title and the secondary headers are the table sections. Each header type should have a different design. As with the general text pages, start by creating the entire table in the standard typeface. Next, highlight the secondary headers by changing one graphic aspect. For instance, use a different, heavier typeface, or simply bold them. The key is to make them stronger than the typical text. Last, format the primary header or table title by changing a second graphic aspect. For example, make the row background dark gray and the text white.

| **Parking** | |
|---|---|
| **Required Space Sizes** | |
| Off-Street Space | 9′x18′ min. |
| Compact Space | 8′x16′ min. |
| **Vehicle Space Requirements** | |
| See Tables 4.6 and 4.7 | |
| **Allowed Compact Spaces** | |
| T5: Town Core | 75% max. |
| T4: Neighborhood Center | 60% max. |
| T3: Neighborhood General | 50% max. |
| **Miscellaneous** | |
| On lots with alleys, all drives shall be located on the alley. | |
| On corner lots, all drives shall be located on the alley or side street. | |
| Shared drives are encouraged between adjacent lots to minimize curb cuts along the street. | |
| Malibu Drives with central planting strips are encouraged. | |

**Fig. 3.56** Sample table design

Once the headers are called out, consider whether to add borders to the table. Generally, using full borders adds too many extra lines to the page without enhancing usability. Vertical borders are typically unnecessary because the left justification of the text in each column reads as a vertical line along the left.

However, it is much more difficult to differentiate between the horizontal rows of information, especially when the rows have different numbers of text lines. In this case, horizontal borders add necessary visual information that aids in the usability of the table. (See Figure 3.51.)

### Product List

- Form-Based Code (See the case studies in the next chapter.)

## Future Considerations

The design of Form-Based Codes continues to develop at a rapid pace. Following are some cutting-edge ideas to consider when developing your code.

### Web-Based Code

As mentioned earlier, Form-Based Codes are not read cover to cover. Users skip through to the sections that are relevant to their particular project or interests. This type of use would be much better served by a Web-based code, which is based on a hyperlink structure, rather than a book-based code, which is organized in a linear fashion. In fact, one of the great things about a hyperlink-based structure is that it allows access to information in multiple ways. A Web-based code could be designed to include various access routes to pertinent information, including a linear route to mimic a book design, if so desired. The most enticing aspect would be a Web-based code in which a developer could enter the project information on the first page and the site would filter the code to display only the portions of the code relevant to the project site. For instance, property owners could enter their property address and the site would show only information relevant to that particular site, such as the uses and building types allowed. Another example: business owners could enter their type of business and the site would show where that use is allowed.

Other benefits of a Web-based code include better accessibility, less expense, and less harm to the environment. Printed codes are inherently more difficult for most people to access than Web-based codes because people must physically go to the municipality to get a copy, then check in occasionally for updates. In addition, this requires staff time to make sure copies are kept available. With a Web-based code, citizens can see the code from their computer. In addition, there are services available that will send them an email whenever the site is updated. Printed codes are also more expensive due to the printing costs, and they waste trees. Of course, a few printed copies would need to be kept on hand for those without computer access.

There is a caveat: as you have read throughout this chapter, a dedicated effort is required to design a usable printed Form-Based Code. A similar effort is required to create an effective and usable Web-based code; however, while the concerns are similar, the design will be very different. It is highly recommended that a professional Web usability designer be engaged to ensure the code is designed well.

### Guide Sheets

Short of creating a Web-based code, guide sheets are another possibility to improve usability of printed Form-Based Codes. A guide sheet is a one-page list of items relevant to a particular interest. For instance, a guide sheet could be created for each area in the regulatory plan. Each area guide sheet would list the sections in the code that are relevant to that particular area, such as the permissible building types, enabling users to easily skip sections of the code not pertinent to their property.

# 4 / Case Studies

THE CASE STUDIES in this section represent the advanced practice of Form-Based Coding. They were selected to explore a variety of project types, scales, locations, and organizing principles. Some have not yet been adopted, but they are used here to demonstrate advanced applications of Form-Based Coding.

The case studies are mostly for single Form-Based Codes (FBCs), except for Montgomery, Alabama, and Ventura, California, which have adopted multiple Form-Based Codes. The codes in all the case studies use the transect as the organizing principle, except for the Heart of Peoria code, which uses frontages.

Each case study is presented primarily graphically with a short written description about the most important aspects of the code and coding process. The case study images illustrate various aspects of the documenting and visioning, as well as the final codes to highlight the importance of the process in creating a good Form-Based Code.

The chapter begins with a set of Regulating Plans and other color images, which are provided as a reference while reading each of the case studies. In addition, links to full versions of these codes will be listed as they are available at www.opticosdesign.com/fbcbook.html.

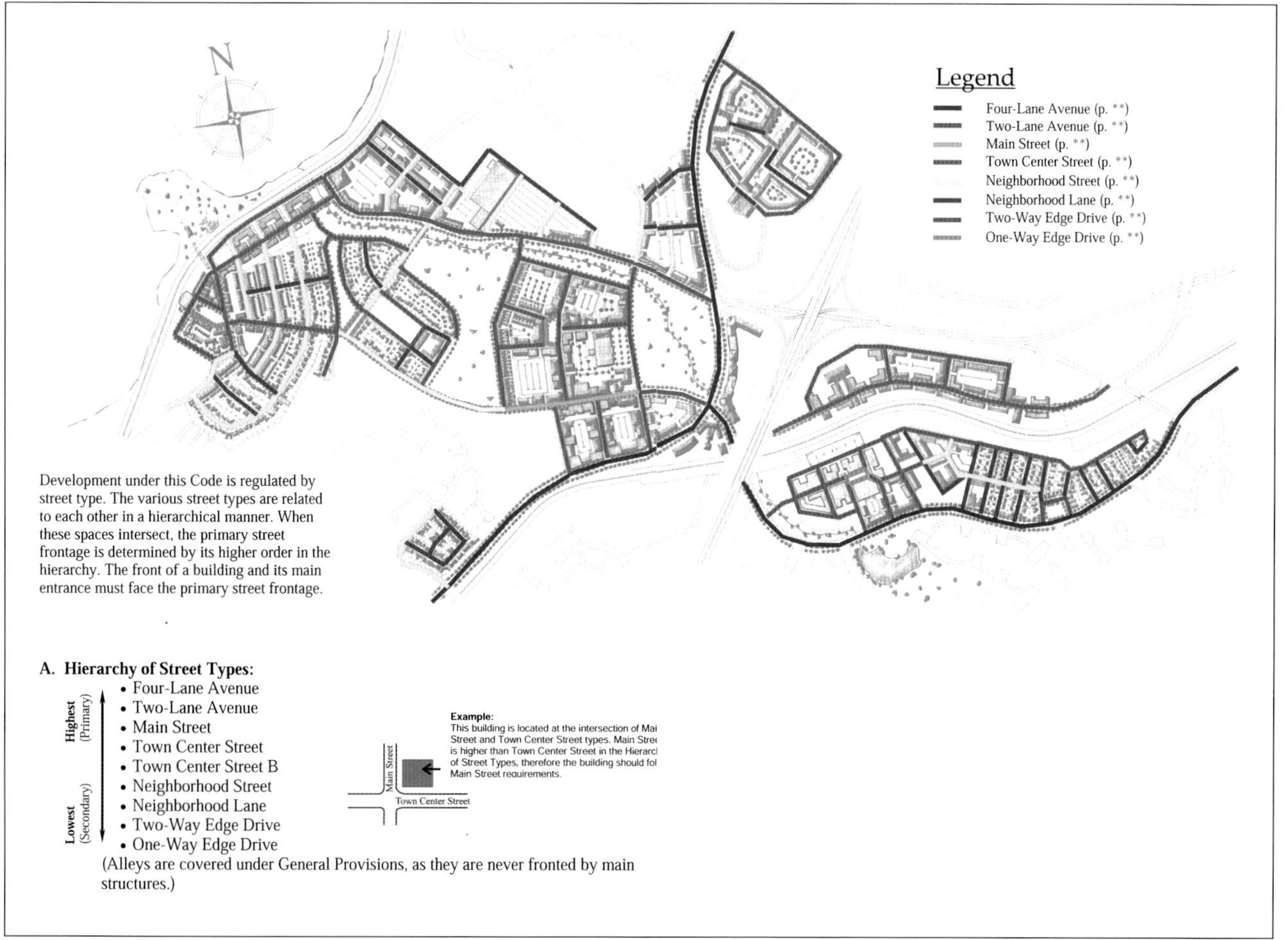


**Fig. C.1** Central Hercules Plan FBC Regulating Plan (from Chapter 2)

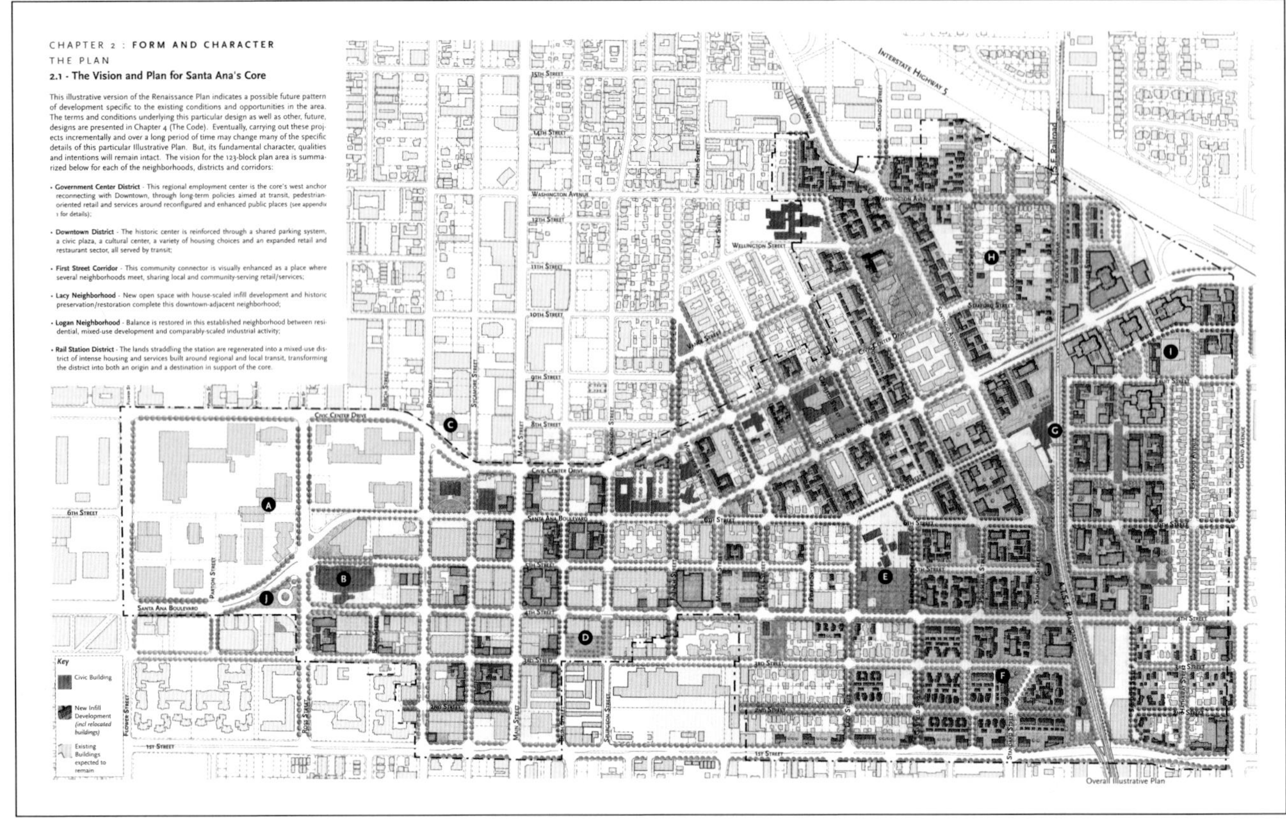


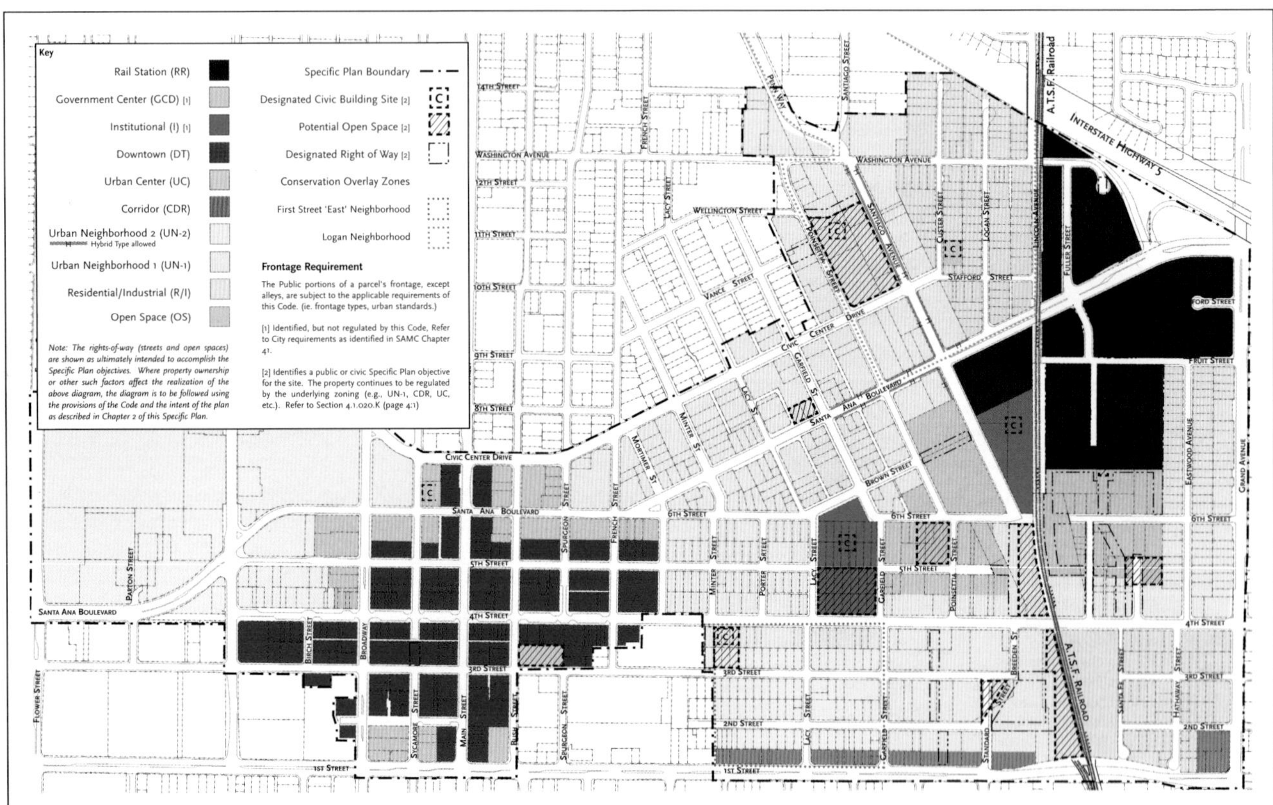


**Fig. C.2** Santa Ana Downtown Renaissance Specific Plan Illustrative Plan (top ) and Regulating Plan (bottom)

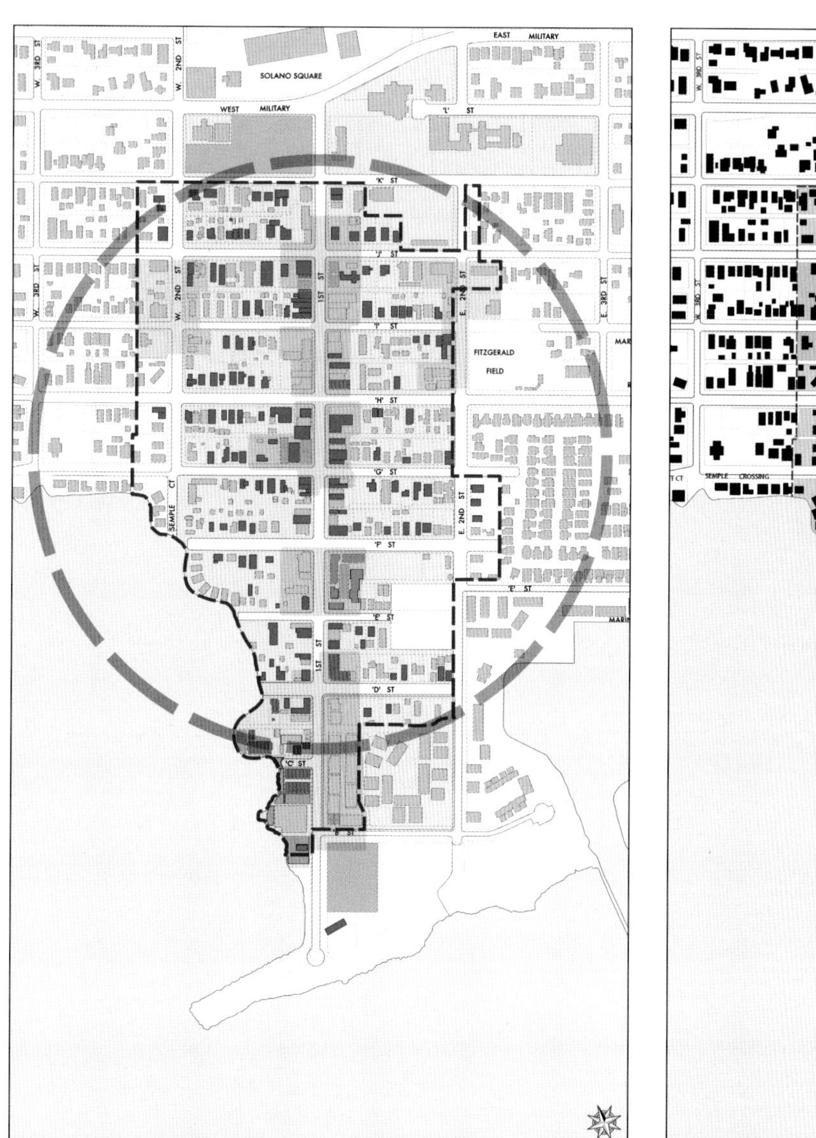

**Fig. C.3** Downtown Benicia Illustrative Framework Plan (left) and Regulating Plan (right)

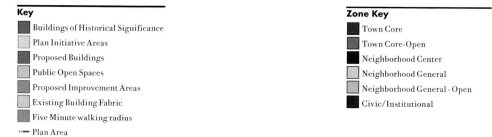

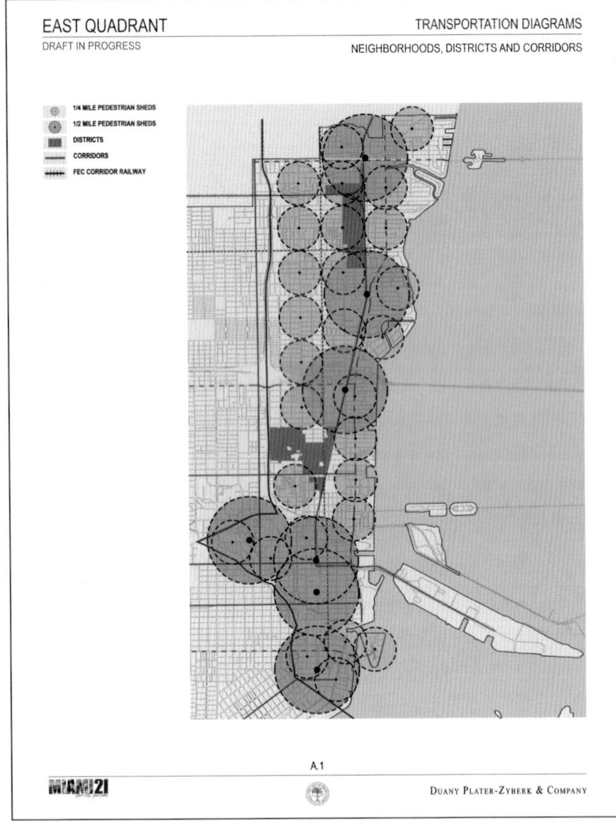

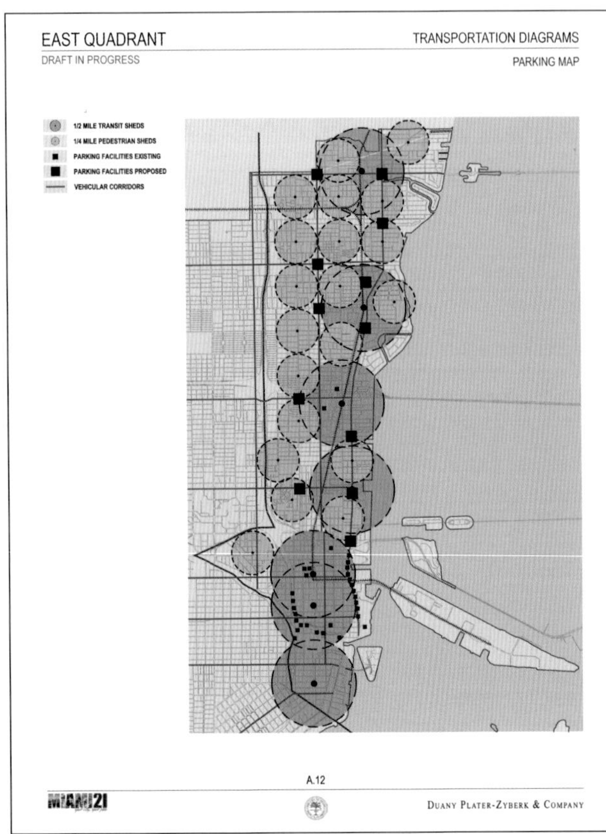


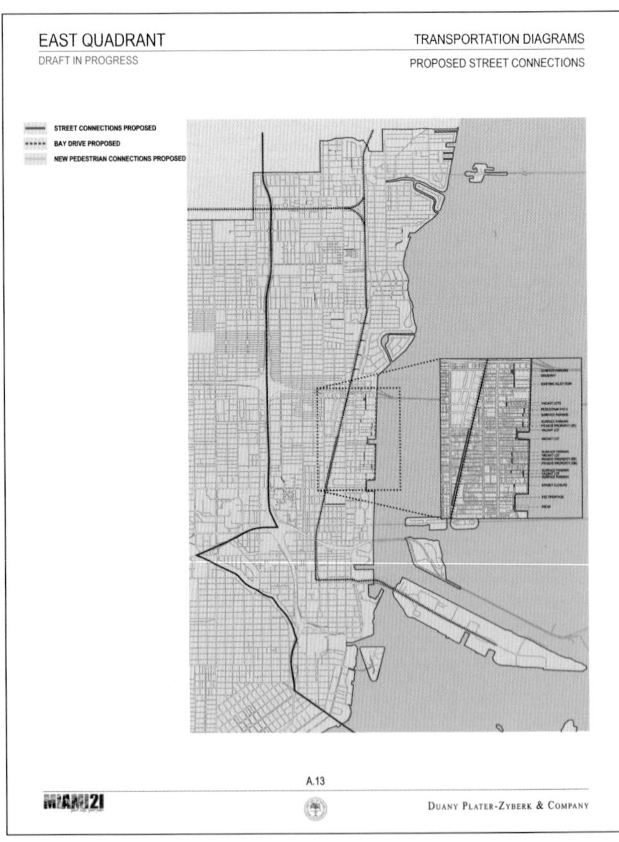


**Fig. C.4** Miami 21 SmartCode Illustrative Plans: Neighborhoods, districts, and corridors (top left); transit oriented development (top center); recreational greenways (top right); parking (bottom left); proposed street connections (bottom center); bus transit (bottom right)

EAST QUADRANT
TRANSPORTATION DIAGRAMS
DRAFT IN PROGRESS
RECREATIONAL GREENWAYS
GREENWAYS EXISTING & PROPOSED
UNITY TRAIL
FLAGLER TRAIL
VENETIAN LINK
MIAMI RIVER WALK
M-PATH TRAIL
EXISTING BAYWALK
BAYWALK PROPOSED
BIKE ROUTES (TBD) PROPOSED
UNITY TRAIL
FLAGLER
BAYWALK
VENETIAN LINK
MIAMI RIVER TRAIL
M-PATH TRAIL
BAYWALK
A.14
MIAMI21
DUANY PLATER-ZYBERK & COMPANY

EAST QUADRANT
TRANSPORTATION DIAGRAMS
DRAFT IN PROGRESS
BUS TRANSIT
BUS ROUTES EXISTING
BUS ROUTES PROPOSED
FEC CORRIDOR RAILWAY
FEC RAILWAY CROSSINGS
A.6
MIAMI21
DUANY PLATER-ZYBERK & COMPANY

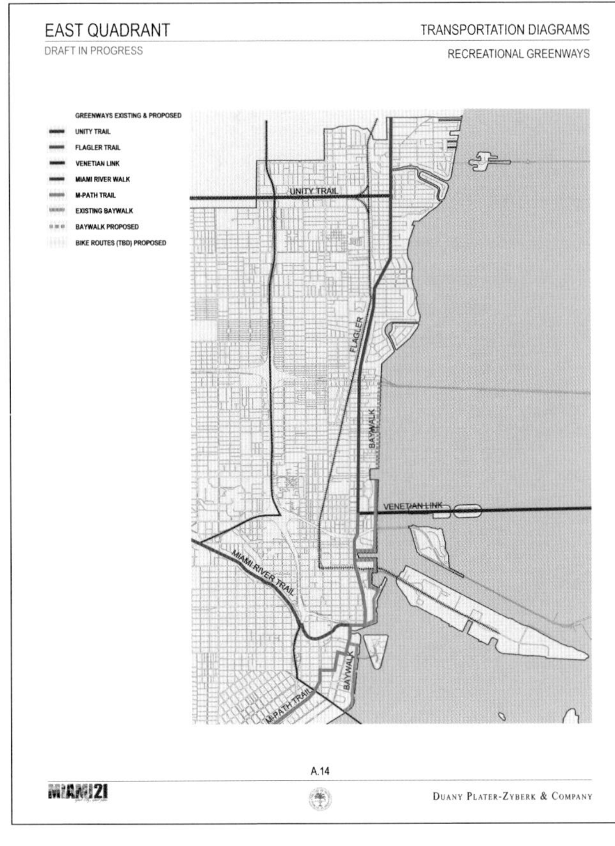

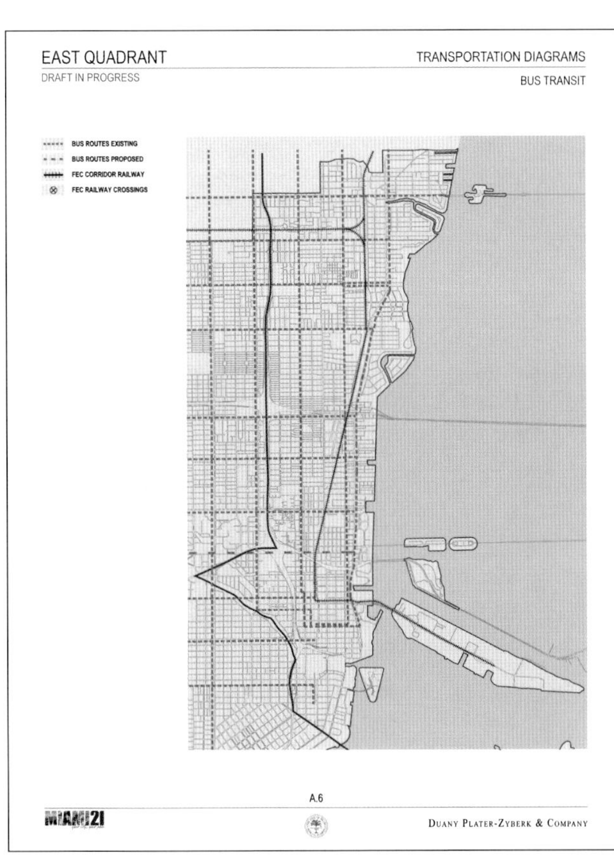

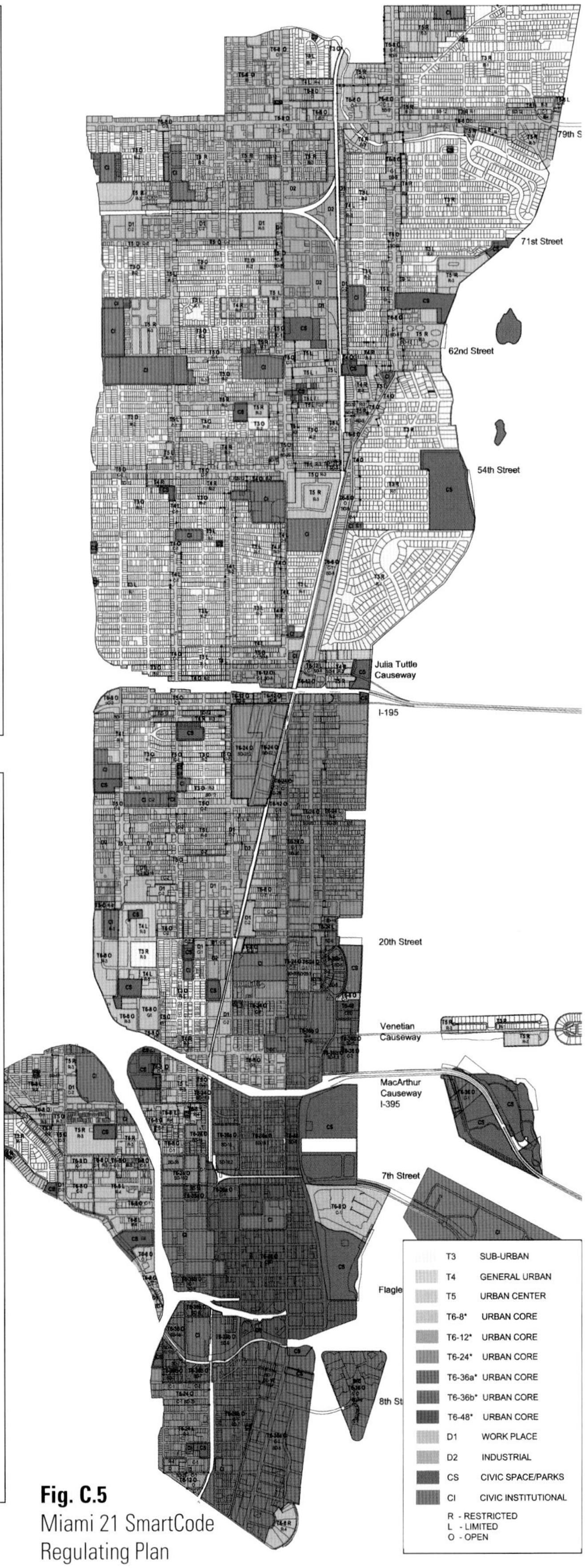

79th St
71st Street
62nd Street
54th Street
Julia Tuttle Causeway
I-195
20th Street
Venetian Causeway
MacArthur Causeway I-395
7th Street
Flagle
8th St
T3 SUB-URBAN
T4 GENERAL URBAN
T5 URBAN CENTER
T6-8* URBAN CORE
T6-12* URBAN CORE
T6-24* URBAN CORE
T6-36a* URBAN CORE
T6-36b* URBAN CORE
T6-48* URBAN CORE
D1 WORK PLACE
D2 INDUSTRIAL
CS CIVIC SPACE/PARKS
CI CIVIC INSTITUTIONAL
R - RESTRICTED
L - LIMITED
O - OPEN

**Fig. C.5**
Miami 21 SmartCode Regulating Plan

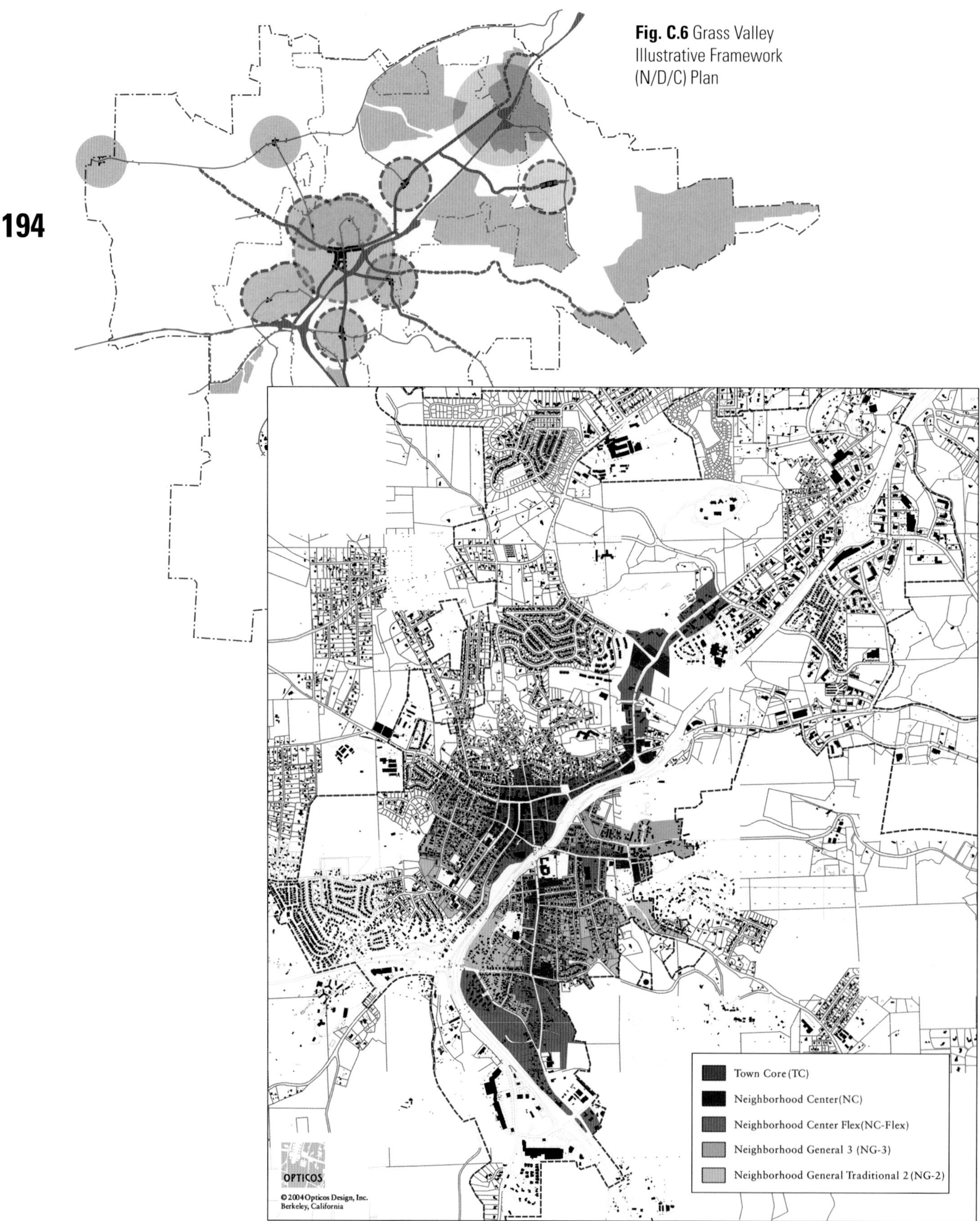


**Fig. C.6** Grass Valley Illustrative Framework (N/D/C) Plan

**Fig. C.7** Grass Valley Form-Based Code Regulating Plan

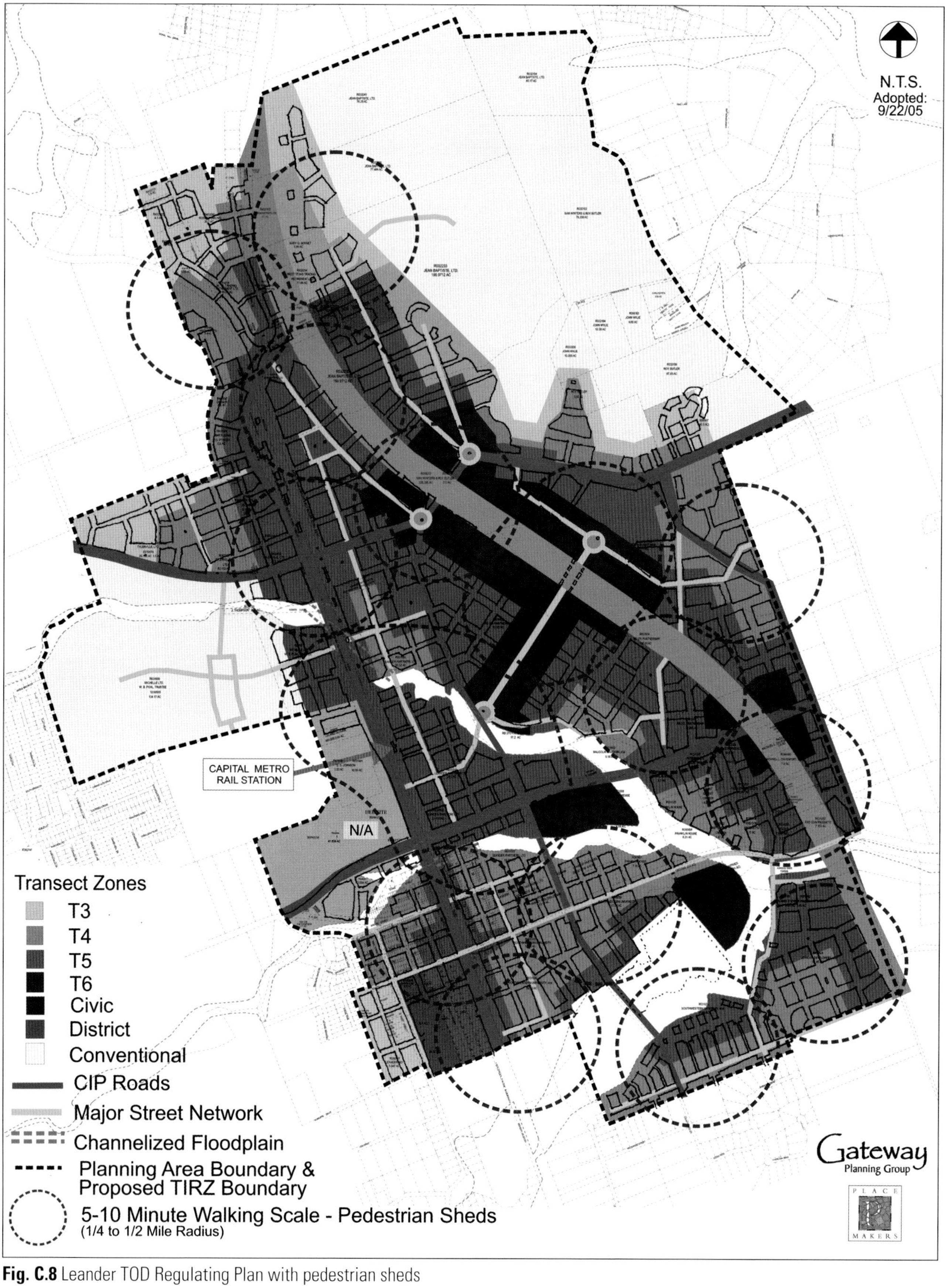

N.T.S.
Adopted:
9/22/05

CAPITAL METRO
RAIL STATION

N/A

Transect Zones
T3
T4
T5
T6
Civic
District
Conventional
CIP Roads
Major Street Network
Channelized Floodplain
Planning Area Boundary &
Proposed TIRZ Boundary
5-10 Minute Walking Scale - Pedestrian Sheds
(1/4 to 1/2 Mile Radius)

Gateway
Planning Group

PLACE
MAKERS

**Fig. C.8** Leander TOD Regulating Plan with pedestrian sheds

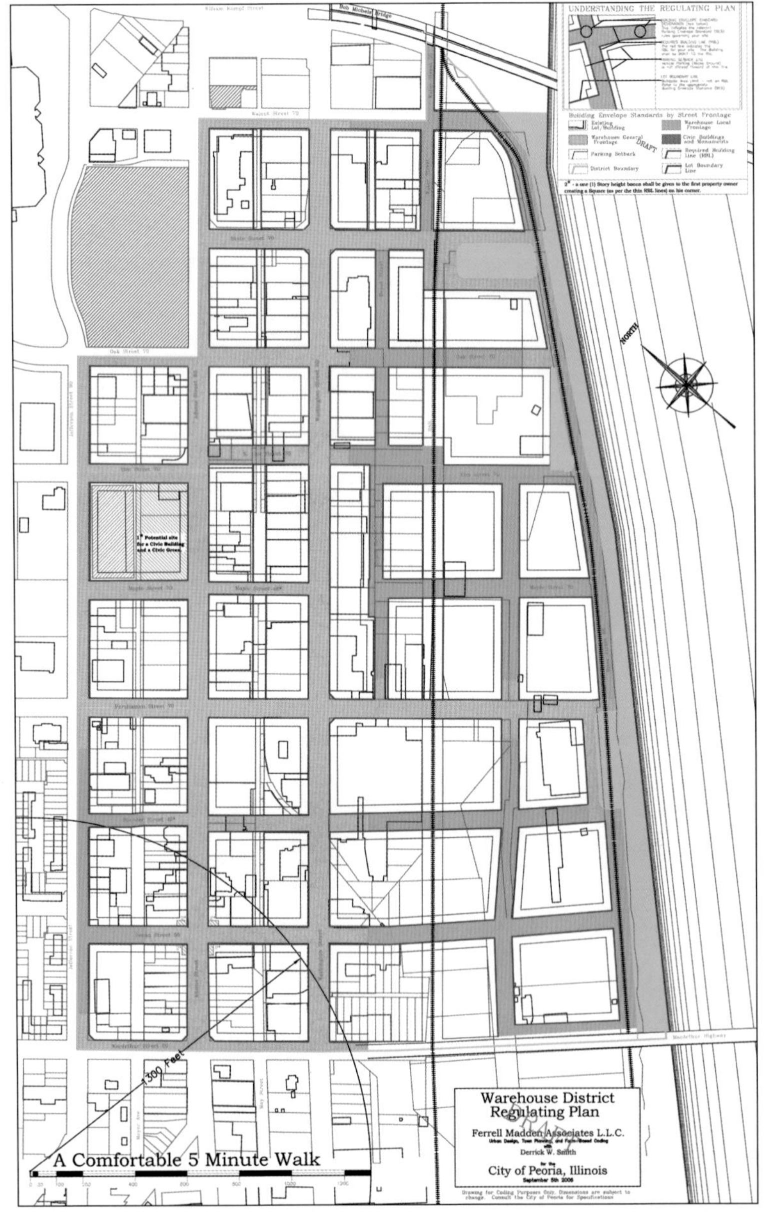

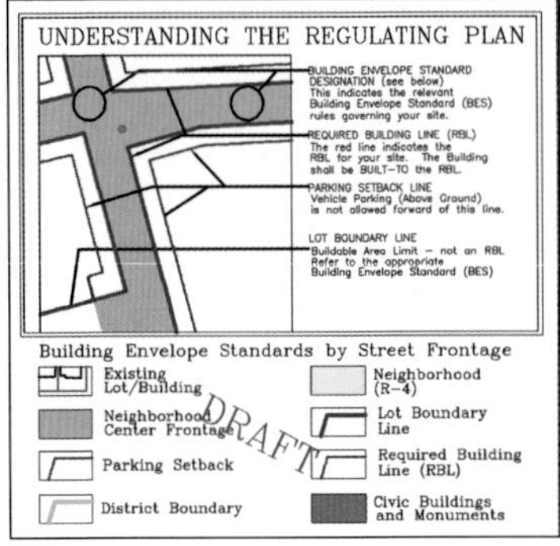


**Fig. C.9** Heart of Peoria Regulating Plans: Warehouse District (above left), Prospect Avenue (above right), and Sheridan Triangle (right)

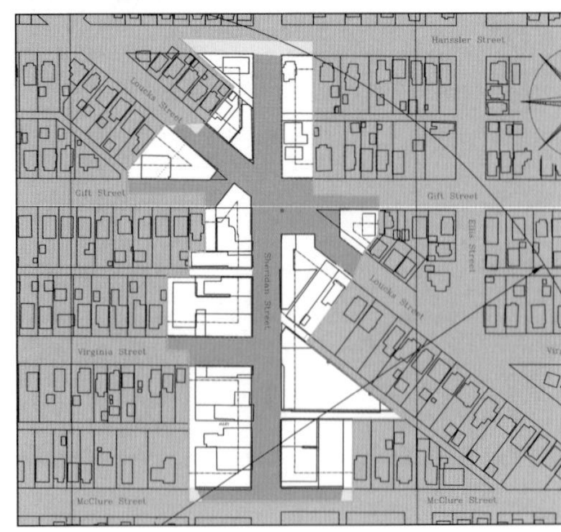

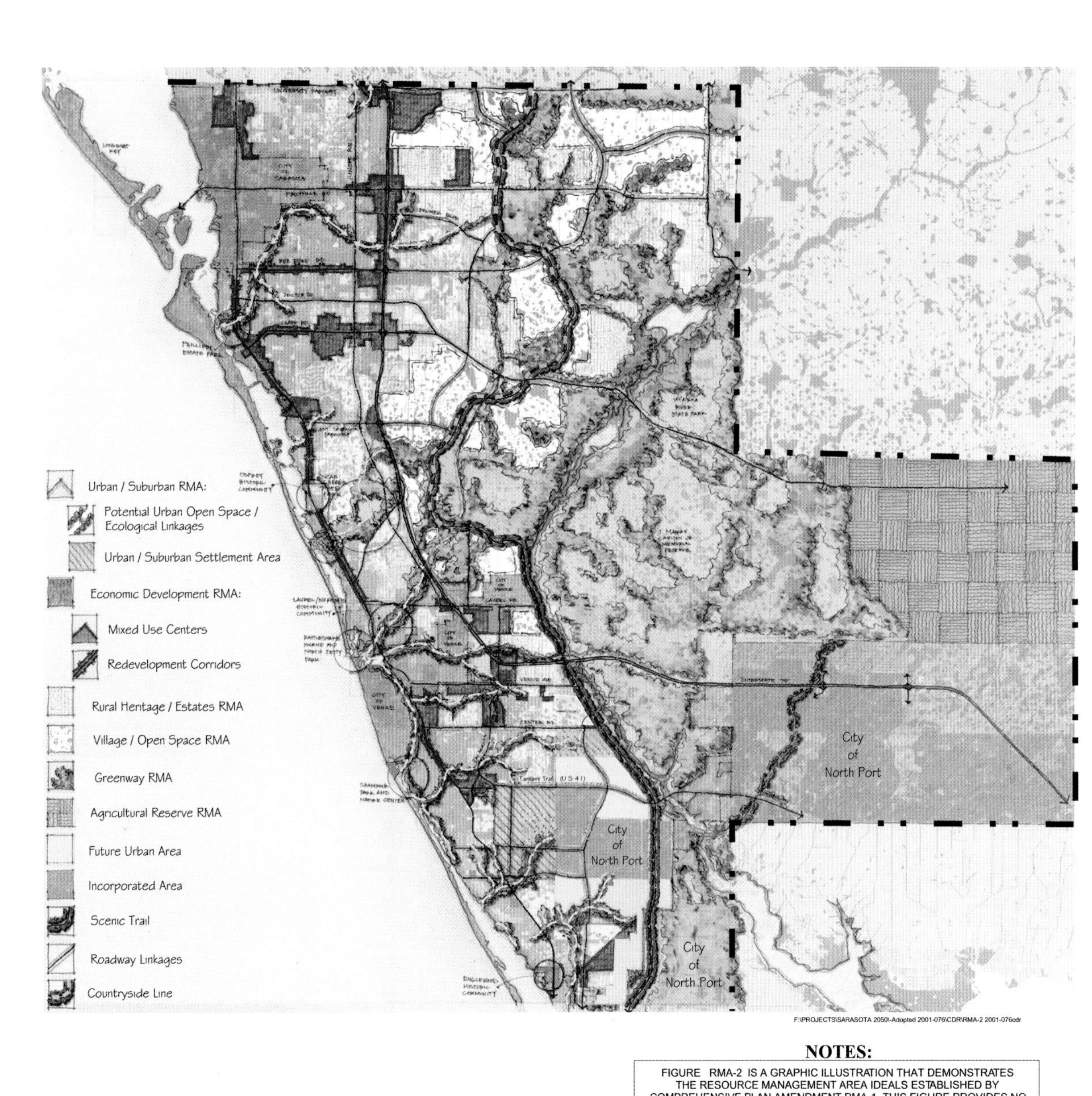


**NOTES:**

FIGURE RMA-2 IS A GRAPHIC ILLUSTRATION THAT DEMONSTRATES THE RESOURCE MANAGEMENT AREA IDEALS ESTABLISHED BY COMPREHENSIVE PLAN AMENDMENT RMA-1. THIS FIGURE PROVIDES NO REGULATORY FUNCTION WITHIN THE COMPREHENSIVE PLAN. THIS FIGURE CANNOT BE CORRECTLY INTERPRETED INDEPENDENT OF THE SARASOTA COUNTY COMPREHENSIVE PLAN AS ADOPTED BY SARASOTA COUNTY ORDINANCE NO. 89-18, AS THE SAME MAY BE AMENDED FROM TIME TO TIME. THE BOUNDARIES OF LAND USE DESIGNATIONS, WHERE THEY HAVE BEEN ESTABLISHED, MAY BE REVIEWED AT SARASOTA COUNTY GROWTH MANAGEMENT, 1660 RINGLING BOULEVARD, SARASOTA, FLORIDA.

**FIGURE RMA-2**
**SARASOTA 2050 STRUCTURE GRAPHIC**

***Future Land Use***
***Sarasota County Comprehensive Plan***

7/05/02

*Page 9-RMA-71*

ORD. NO 2001-076

**Fig. C.10** Sarasota 2050 Framework Plan

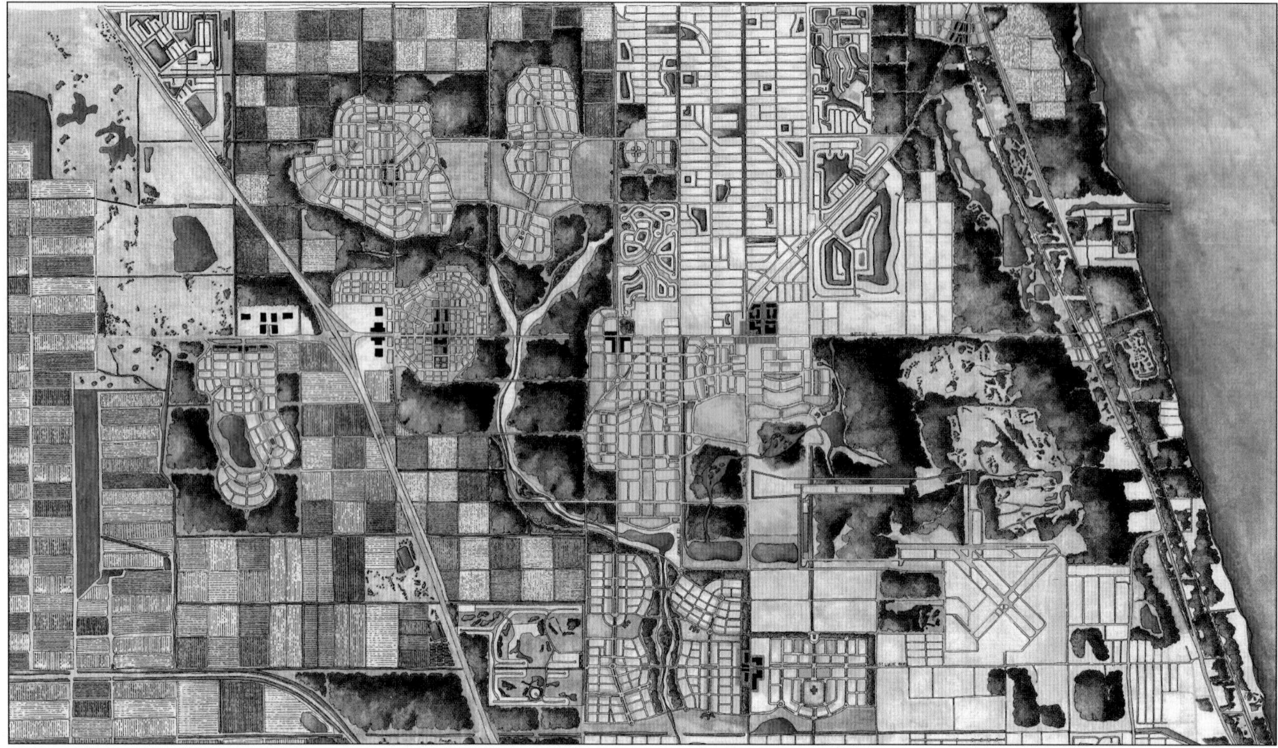

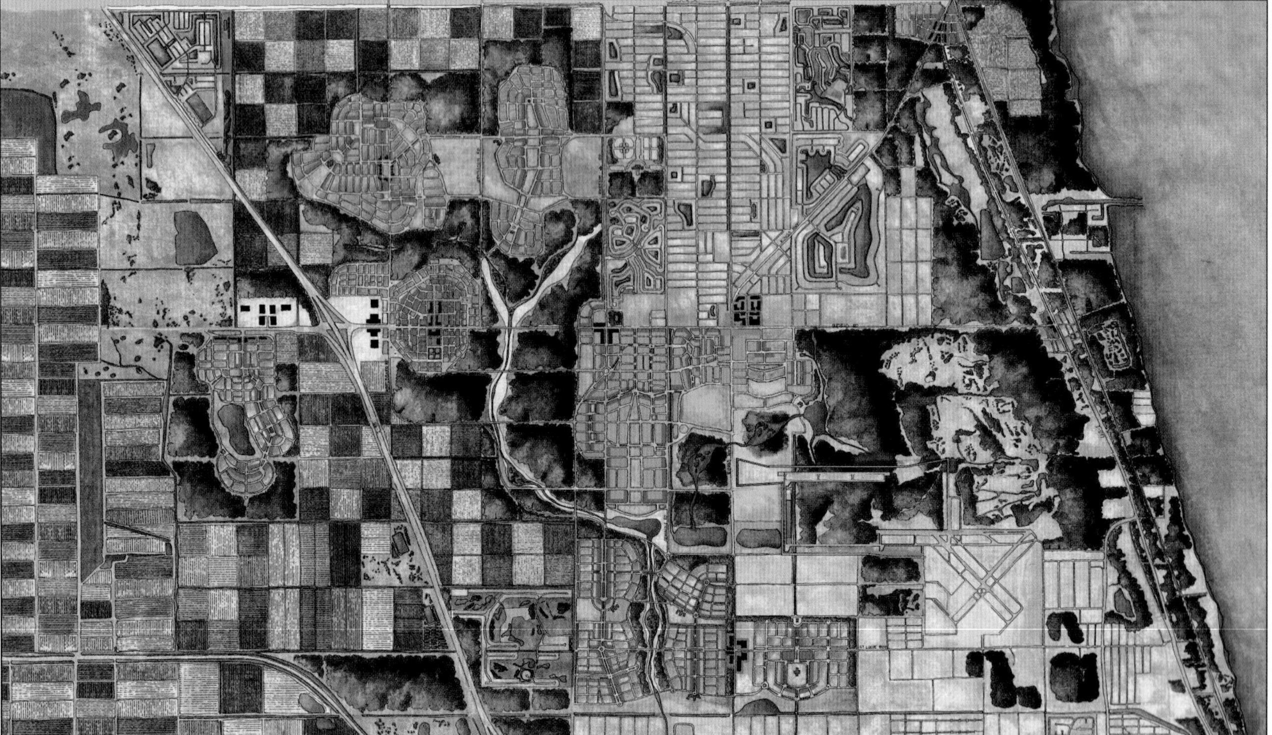

**Fig. C.11** St. Lucie County Illustrative Plan (top left), Greenways, Parks, and Open Space Plan (bottom left), Retail Forecast Locator Map (top right), and Water Management Plan (bottom right)

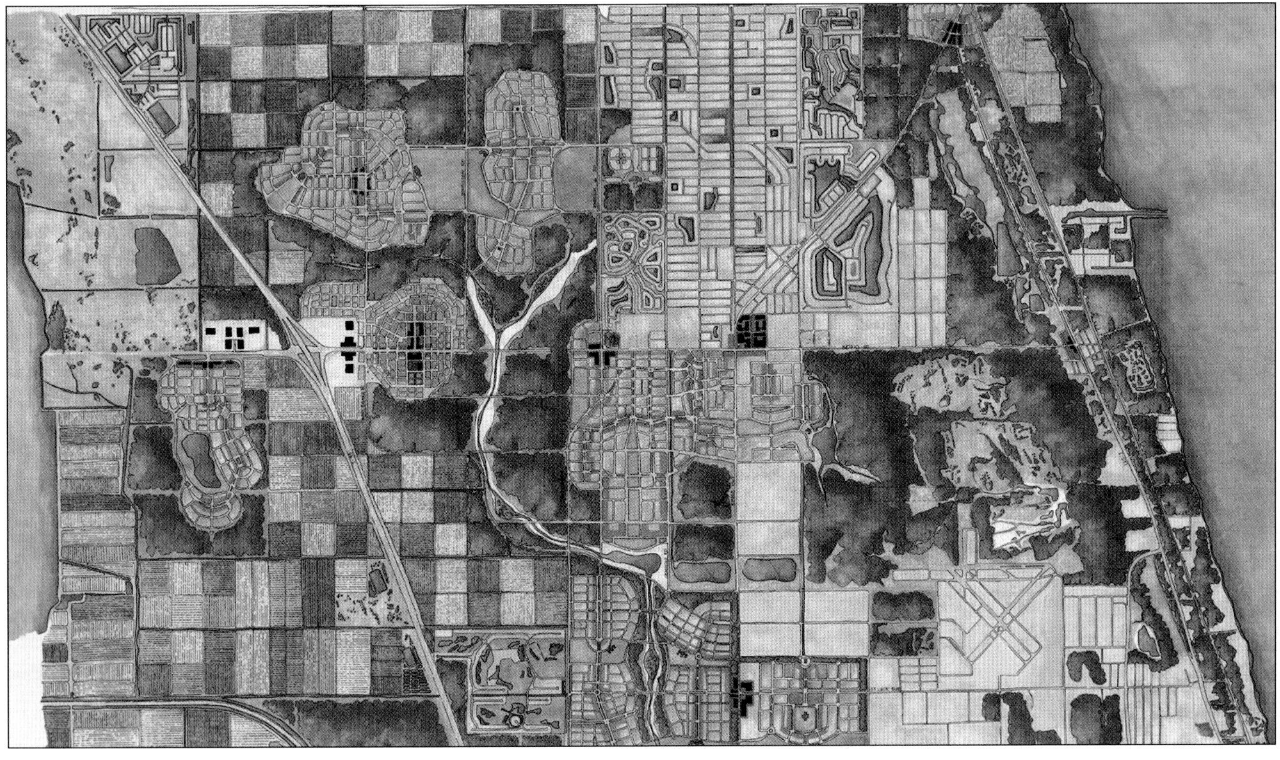

**Fig. C.12** Ventura General Plan: Overall General Plan diagram (top left); infill areas (top right); bus and rail routes (bottom left)



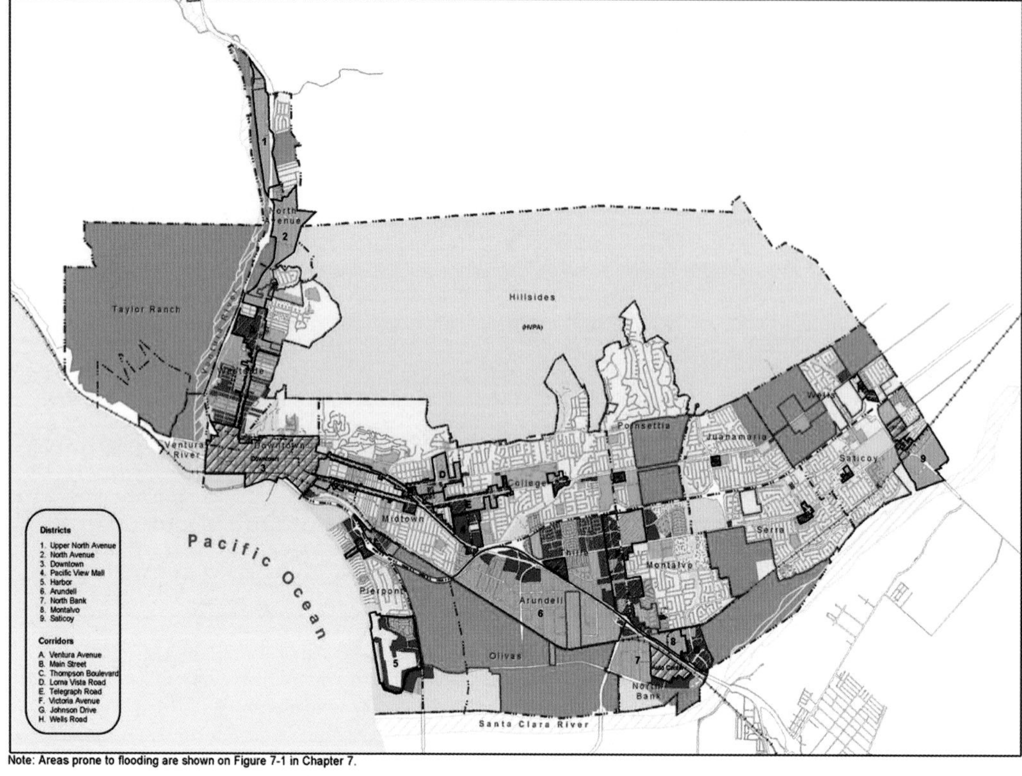


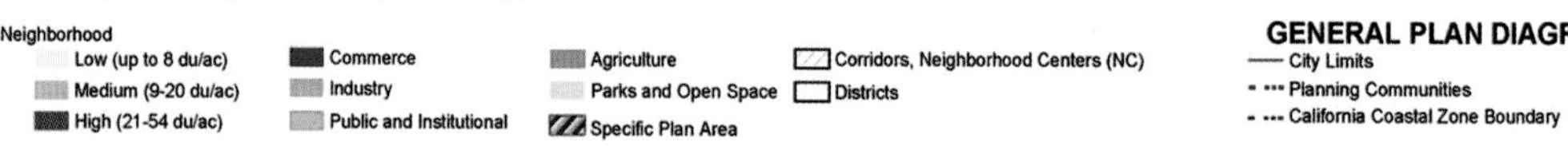

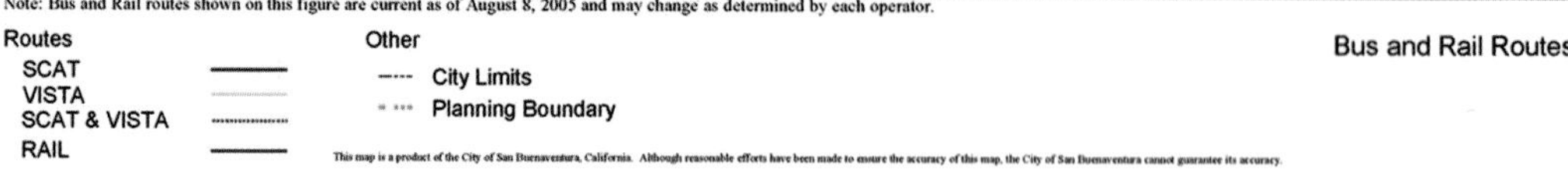

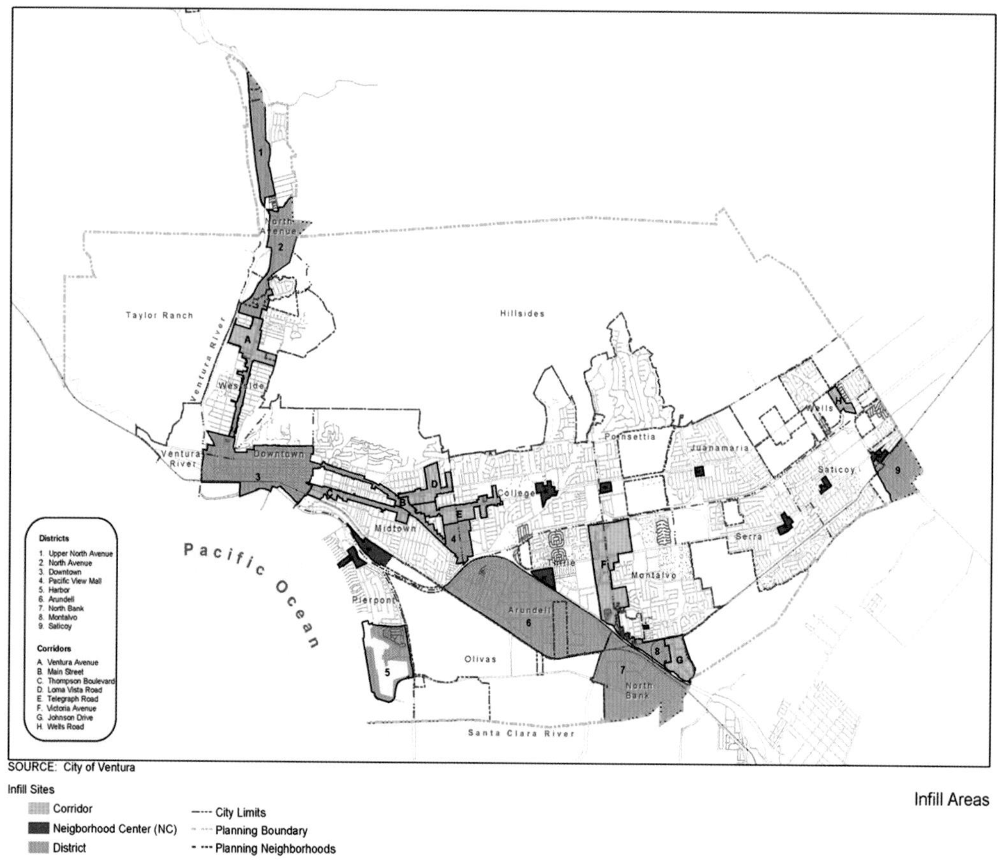


SOURCE: City of Ventura



Infill Areas

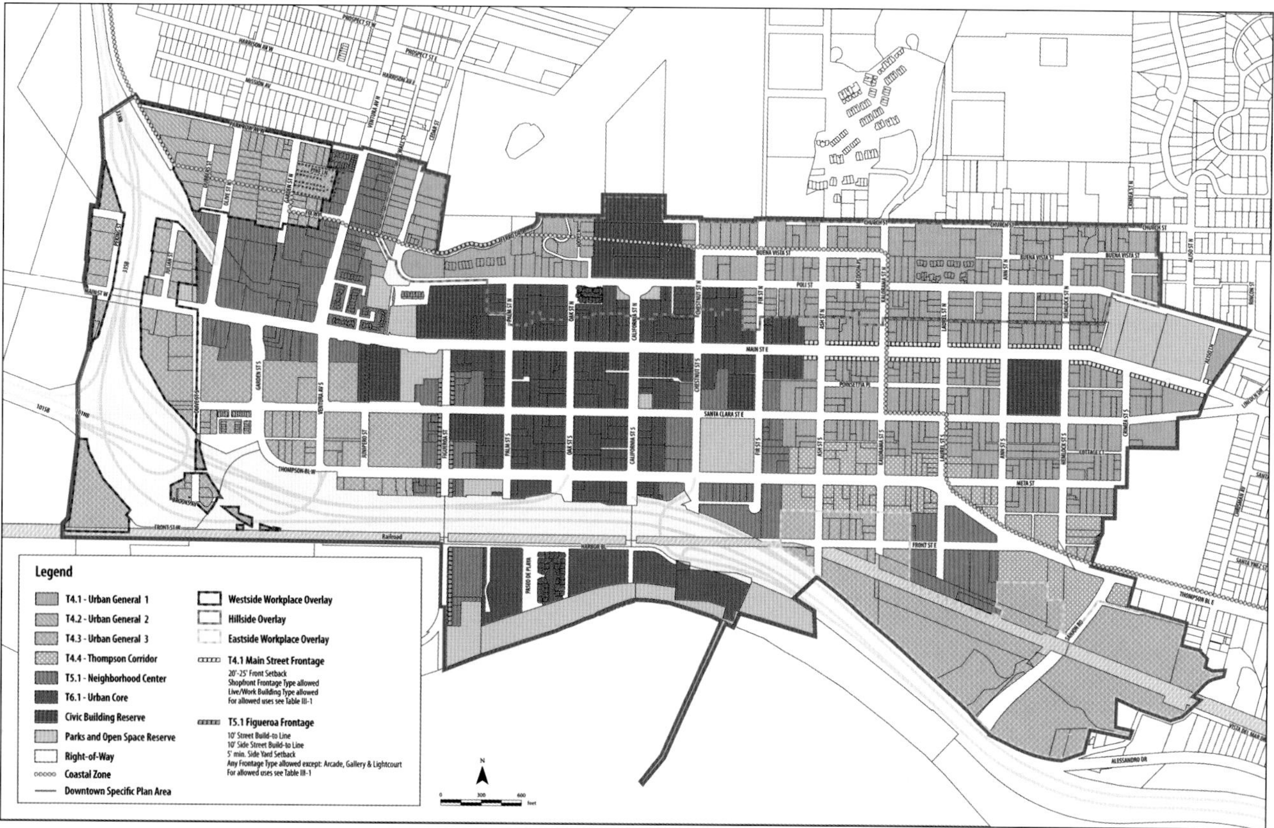


**Fig. C.13** Ventura Downtown Specific Plan Regulating Plan

**Fig. C.14** Probable build-out scenarios for Montgomery under the preexisting conventional zoning code (left page) and under the new SmartCode (right page)

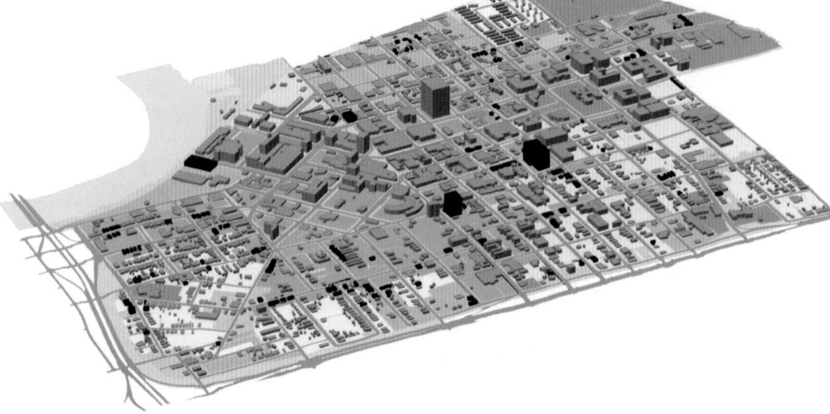

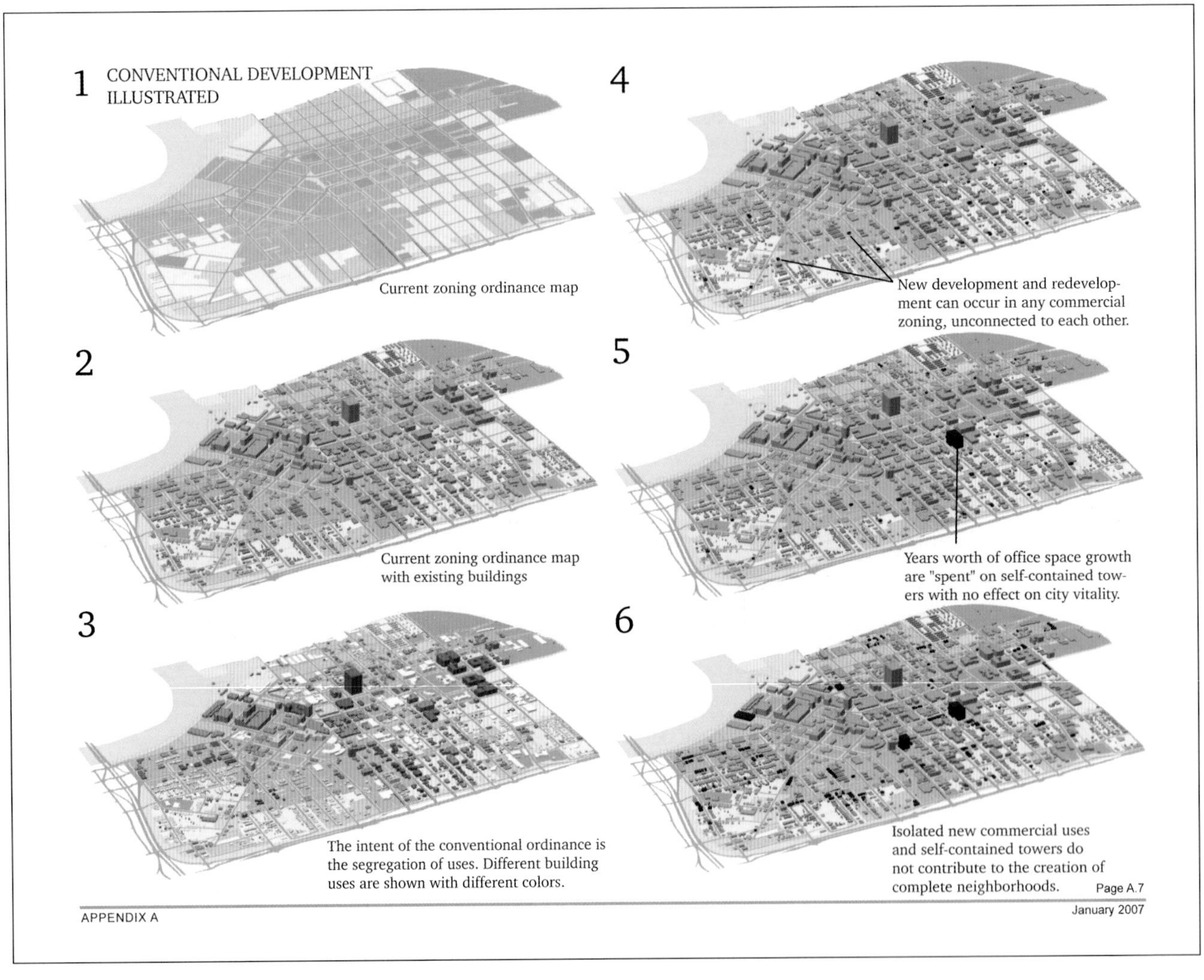

1 CONVENTIONAL DEVELOPMENT ILLUSTRATED

Current zoning ordinance map

2

Current zoning ordinance map with existing buildings

3

The intent of the conventional ordinance is the segregation of uses. Different building uses are shown with different colors.

4

New development and redevelopment can occur in any commercial zoning, unconnected to each other.

5

Years worth of office space growth are "spent" on self-contained towers with no effect on city vitality.

6

Isolated new commercial uses and self-contained towers do not contribute to the creation of complete neighborhoods.

Page A.7

APPENDIX A

January 2007

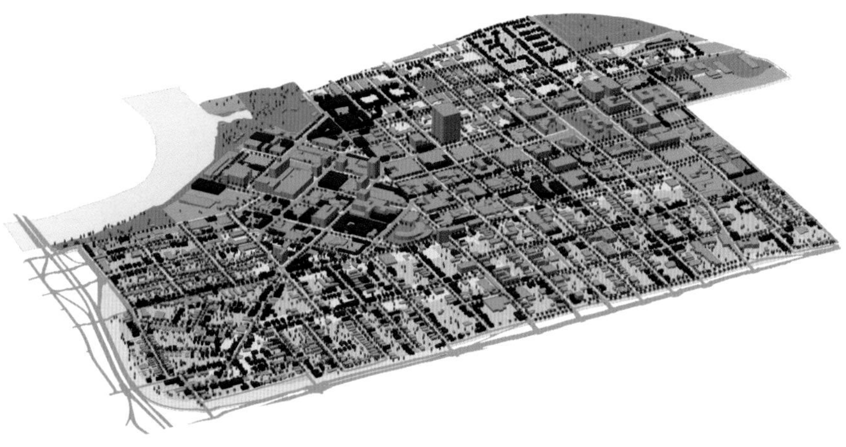

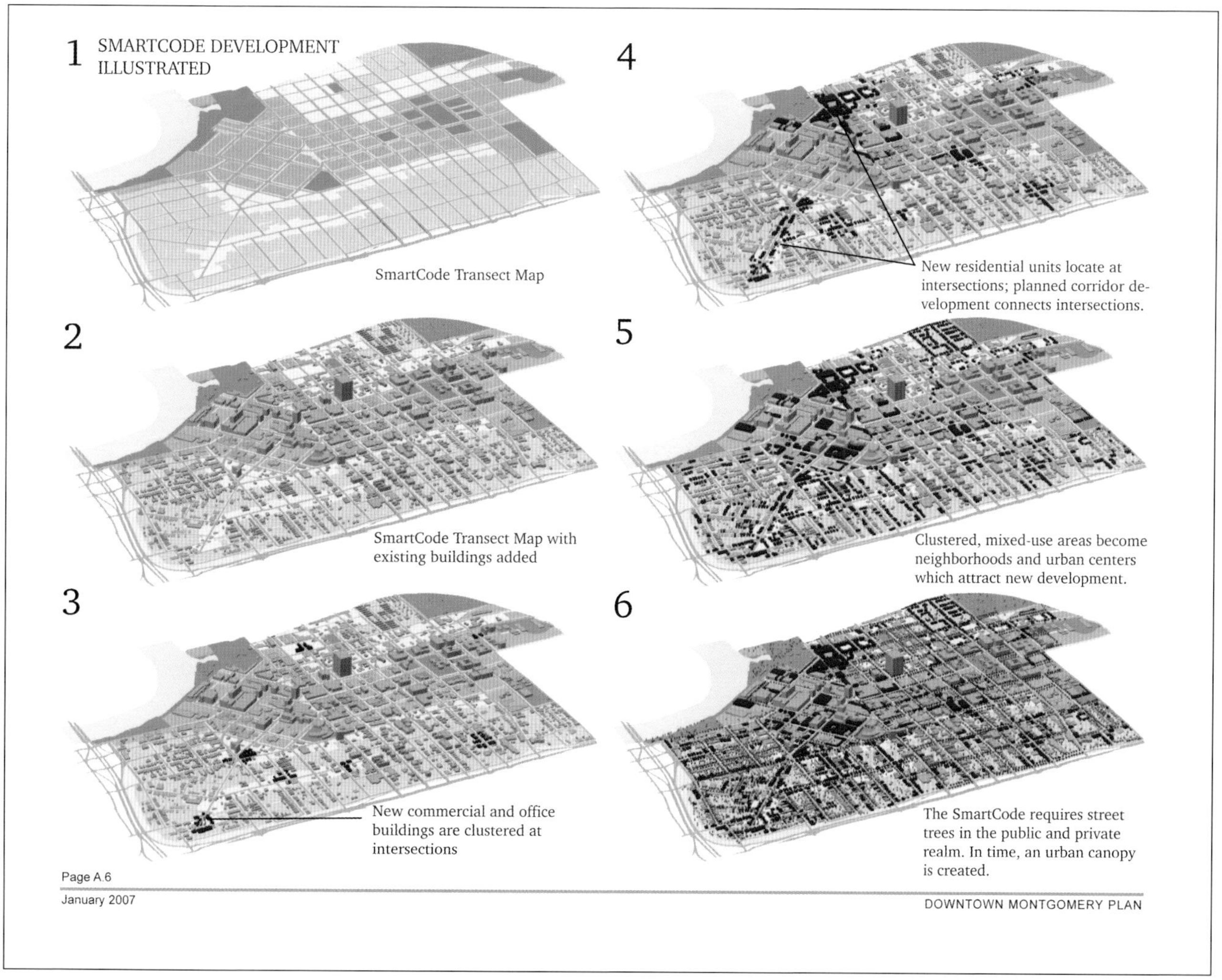

1 SMARTCODE DEVELOPMENT ILLUSTRATED

SmartCode Transect Map

2

SmartCode Transect Map with existing buildings added

3

New commercial and office buildings are clustered at intersections

4

New residential units locate at intersections; planned corridor development connects intersections.

5

Clustered, mixed-use areas become neighborhoods and urban centers which attract new development.

6

The SmartCode requires street trees in the public and private realm. In time, an urban canopy is created.

Page A.6

January 2007

DOWNTOWN MONTGOMERY PLAN

**Fig. C.15** Downtown Montgomery Master Plan Regulating Plan

# Santa Ana Downtown Renaissance Specific Plan

## Santa Ana, California

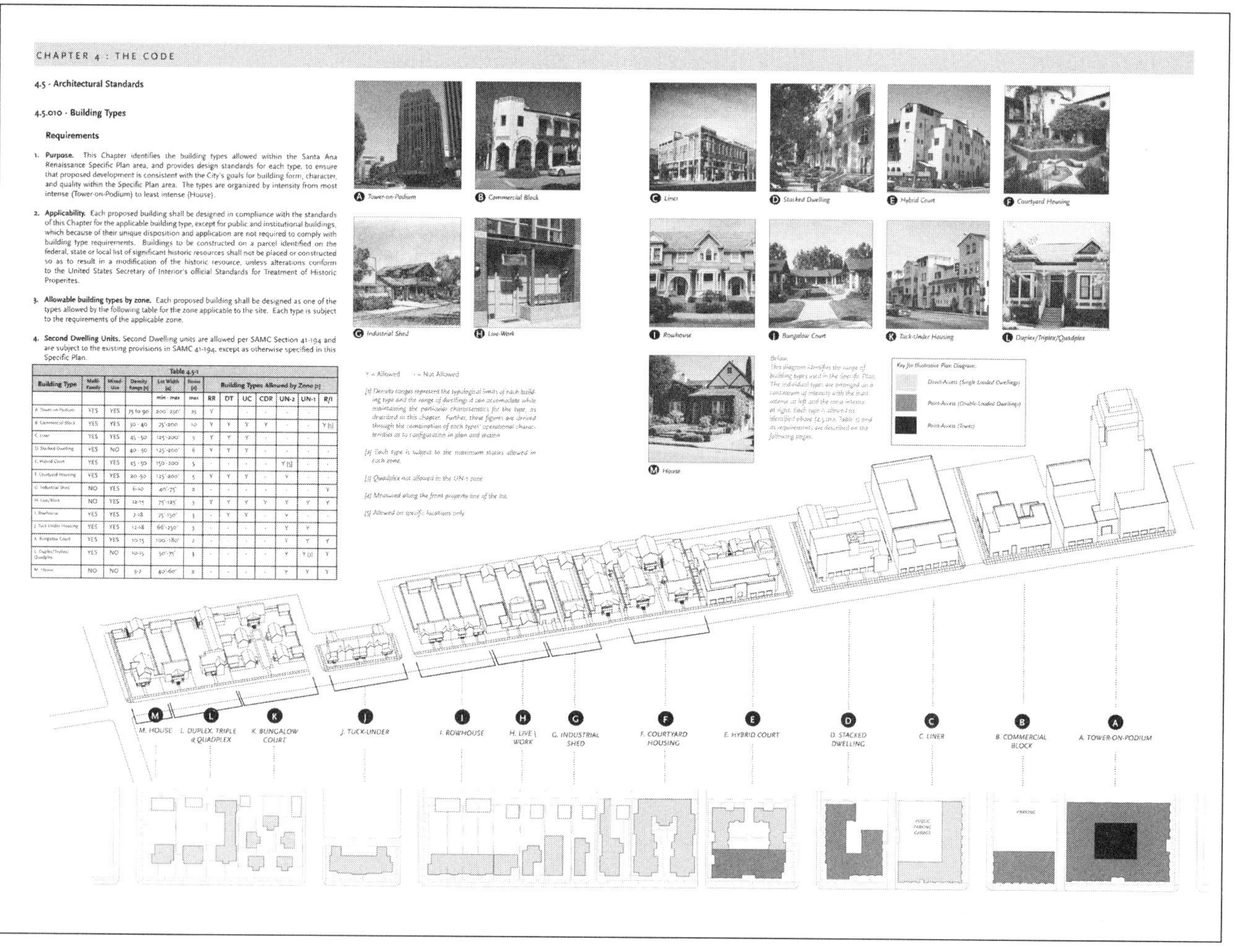

CHAPTER 4 : THE CODE

4.5 · Architectural Standards

4.5.010 · Building Types

Requirements

1. **Purpose.** This Chapter identifies the building types allowed within the Santa Ana Renaissance Specific Plan area, and provides design standards for each type, to ensure that proposed development is consistent with the City's goals for building form, character, and quality within the Specific Plan area. The types are organized by intensity from most intense (Tower-on-Podium) to least intense (House).
2. **Applicability.** Each proposed building shall be designed in compliance with the standards of this Chapter for the applicable building type, except for public and institutional buildings, which because of their unique disposition and application are not required to comply with building type requirements. Buildings to be constructed on a parcel identified on the federal, state or local list of significant historic resources shall not be placed or constructed so as to result in a modification of the historic resource, unless alterations conform to the United States Secretary of Interior's official Standards for Treatment of Historic Properites.
3. **Allowable building types by zone.** Each proposed building shall be designed as one of the types allowed by the following table for the zone applicable to the site. Each type is subject to the requirements of the applicable zone.
4. **Second Dwelling Units.** Second Dwelling units are allowed per SAMC Section 41-194 and are subject to the existing provisions in SAMC 41-194, except as otherwise specified in this Specific Plan.

Table 4.5-1

| Building Type | Multi-Family | Mixed-Use | Density Range [1] | Lot Width [4] | Stories [2] | Building Types Allowed by Zone [1] | | | | | | |
|---|---|---|---|---|---|---|---|---|---|---|---|---|
| | | | | min - max | max | RR | DT | UC | CDR | UN-2 | UN-1 | R/I |
| A. Tower-on-Podium | YES | YES | 75 to 90 | 200'-250' | 25 | Y | - | - | - | - | - | |
| B. Commercial Block | YES | YES | 30 - 40 | 75'-200 | 10 | Y | Y | Y | Y | - | - | Y [5] |
| C. Liner | YES | YES | 45 - 50 | 125'-200' | 5 | Y | Y | Y | - | - | - | |
| D. Stacked Dwelling | YES | NO | 40 - 50 | 125'-200' | 8 | Y | Y | Y | - | - | - | - |
| E. Hybrid Court | YES | YES | 45 - 50 | 150'-200' | 5 | - | - | - | - | Y [5] | - | - |
| F. Courtyard Housing | YES | YES | 20 -50 | 125'-200' | 5 | Y | Y | Y | - | Y | - | - |
| G. Industrial Shed | NO | YES | 6-10 | 40'-75' | 2 | - | - | - | - | - | - | Y |
| H. Live/Work | NO | YES | 12-15 | 75'-125' | 3 | Y | Y | Y | Y | Y | Y | Y |
| I. Rowhouse | YES | YES | 7-18 | 75'-150' | 3 | - | Y | Y | - | Y | - | - |
| J. Tuck-Under Housing | YES | YES | 12-18 | 66'-250' | 3 | - | - | - | - | Y | Y | |
| K. Bungalow Court | YES | YES | 10-15 | 100'-180' | 2 | - | - | - | - | Y | Y | Y |
| L. Duplex/Triplex/Quadplex | YES | NO | 10-15 | 50'-75' | 3 | - | - | - | - | Y | Y [3] | Y |
| M. House | NO | NO | 5-7 | 40'-60' | 2 | - | - | - | - | Y | Y | Y |

Y = Allowed - = Not Allowed

[1] Density ranges represent the typological limits of each building type and the range of dwellings it can accomodate while maintaining the particular characteristics for the type, as described in this chapter. Further, these figures are derived through the combination of each types' operational characteristics as to configuration in plan and section.

[2] Each type is subject to the maximum stories allowed in each zone.

[3] Quadplex not allowed in the UN-1 zone.

[4] Measured along the front property line of the lot.

[5] Allowed on specific locations only.

A Tower-on-Podium

B Commercial Block

C Liner

D Stacked Dwelling

E Hybrid Court

F Courtyard Housing

G Industrial Shed

H Live-Work

I Rowhouse

J Bungalow Court

K Tuck-Under Housing

L Duplex/Triplex/Quadplex

M House

Below.
This diagram identifies the range of building types used in the Specific Plan. The individual types are arranged on a continuum of intensity with the least intense at left and the most intense at right. Each type is allowed as identified above (4.5.010, Table 1) and its requirements are described on the following pages.

Key for Illustrative Plan Diagram:

Direct-Access (Single Loaded Dwellings)

Point-Access (Double-Loaded Dwellings)

Point-Access (Tower)

*Written by José Antonio Perez, Senior Associate, Moule & Polyzoides*

SANTA ANA IS the most highly populated city in Orange County, with a population of approximately 340,000 people.[1] For this project, the consultant was hired to prepare a Specific Plan for the regeneration of a 447-acre area of the city's core, representing three districts and three neighborhoods that have been devastated by urban renewal and traffic-engineering solutions aimed at facilitating access to and from the county seat. Despite enormous pressure to approve development today, the city asked that we reevaluate the entire area for appropriate regeneration and then produce a plan and code that would address the development pressure.

### Client's Background in Form-Based Coding

The planning and building agency had attended various sessions on Form-Based Coding and was familiar with a nearby community developing such a code to deal with regeneration issues.

## Code Components

All the Form-Based Code components were created for this plan. Soon before hiring the consultant team, the city completed a three-year effort for citywide design guidelines that applied to the plan area. The city will be removing the guidelines' applicability to the specific plan area.

### Organizing Principle

The transect was selected as the organizing principle because of the easily understood and applied concept of intensity across a wide variety of subjects and issues.

## Code Process

This coding process was oriented around a public outreach process within which the community established issues and expectations for the project area revitalization framework. The FBC was created to implement the neighborhood, district, and corridor vision for the project area that was a product of this process. The outreach was supported by extensive analysis of the existing conditions by the consultant team, consisting of physical and fiscal information in diagnostic fashion easily digested by participants.

### Public Participation

The public process involved a three-pronged approach:

1. **Precharrette:** Using the existing conditions analysis and interviews of each city department, the team facilitated four geographically based discovery workshops with the community to establish the issues to be addressed and the credibility with which to help solve those issues. The team then re-

| | Santa Ana Downtown Renaissance Specific Plan |
|---|---|
| Status: | Submitted (Anticipated adoption date: April 2008) |
| Scale: | Part of a City/Town (447 acres/135 blocks) |
| Implementation Method: | Specific Plan |
| Site Context: | Redevelopment/Infill |
| Site Size: | 447 acres/135 blocks |
| Administration: | City/County staff |
| Organizing Principle: | Transect |
| Code Consultants(s): | Moule & Polyzoides; Crawford, Multari & Clark Associates |
| Agency: | City of Santa Ana Planning and Building Agency |

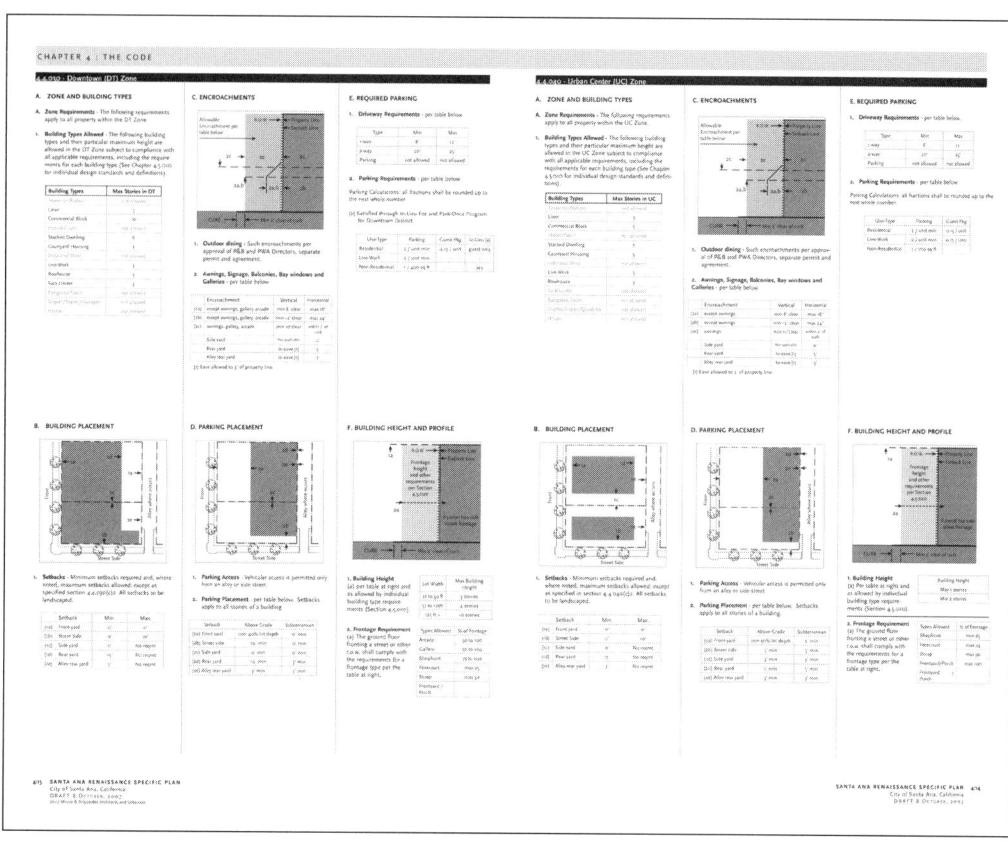

**Fig. 4.1** (previous page)
Building types overview

**Fig. 4.2** (left)
Building Form Standards



ported this feedback to each of the city departments for reaction and feedback. This subsequent feedback was discussed with the community to appropriately define the issues and challenges.

2. **Charrette phase:** The entire team was brought in for seven days and essentially prepared all the project diagrams, projections, and details as the "structural content" for the administrative draft of the Specific Plan, including a full FBC.
3. **Postcharrette phase:** The charrette results and certain adjustments and refinements that became necessary were communicated to participants in reverse order of the discovery workshops mentioned above. This enabled the preparation of the Specific Plan.

## Advanced Application of FBCs

The Building Type standards, Regulating Plan, Frontage Types, and Open Space Types are advanced applications of Form-Based Coding.

### Building Types

The building type regulations in this code are some of the most developed and comprehensive standards for building types of any Form-Based Code in the country. The complete matrix of 12 building types, established through the documentation process, features tower-on-podium, liner, hybrid courtyard, commercial block, stacked dwelling, courtyard housing, industrial shed, live/work, row house, duplex/triplex/quadplex, and single dwelling building types. At the beginning of the Building Types Standards, a table regulates the building types allowed for each of the zones. Each of the building types then has a page of extensive standards that pertain specifically to the type. These standards include minimum lot width, access, parking, service, open space, landscape, frontage, and building size and massing. These standards are intended to make building types the primary aspect of regulation and entitlement, as compared to density and Floor-Area Ratio (FAR), which are the primary aspects of regulation and entitlement in conventional codes. Figures 4.5 and 4.6 show examples of the standards for two of the types. Each of the building types has a similar page of standards.

#### Regulating Plans

This Regulating Plan is expressed through two diagrams: existing right-of-way (ROW) and future ROW. This is the direct result of the complexity of the individual proposed changes due to a very mature ownership and parcel pattern and the objectives to regenerate community fabric at the historic scale and pattern of the community. In addition, historic preservation is coded through the establishment of two conservation overlays, which have specific requirements for historic structures in or relocated to the area.

#### Frontage Types

Beyond identifying the appropriate frontage types, the individual components of each type are described along with appropriate numerical and proportional standards.

#### Open Space Types

Each type is identified on the Regulating Plan and supported through measurable standards that assist in the space's response to the intended context along with siting requirements (e.g., minimum number of streets fronting each particular type).

#### Reinforcing the Unique Local Character

The following are ways that the code protects and enhances the unique aspects of the community.

*Precise Allocation of Zones to Existing Conditions*

This provision ensures that each zone truly serves a purpose in the overall mosaic by testing whether other closely related zones could accomplish the purpose. One example is the allocation of the Hybrid Court building type along two segments of streets in the UN-2 zone

**Fig. 4.3** Illustrative Plan

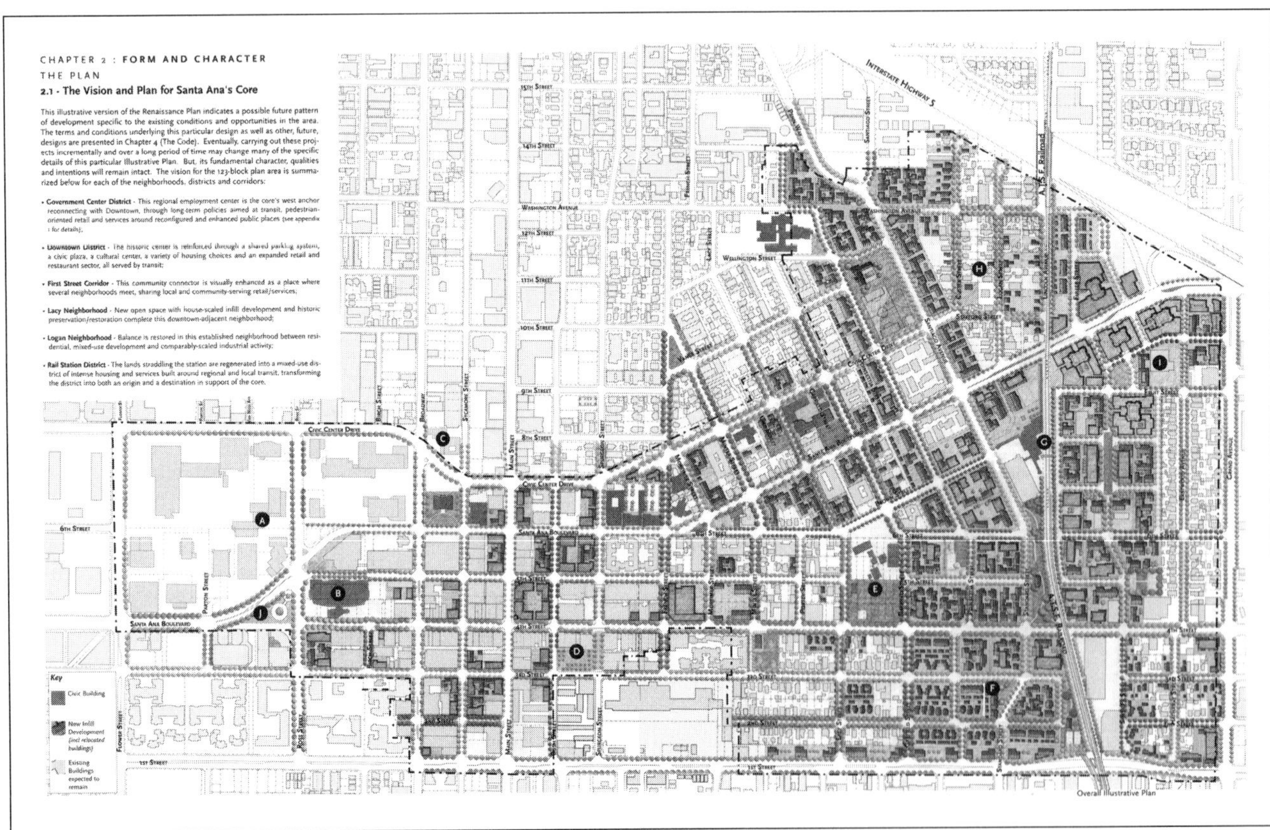

that truly warrant more intensity than the UN-2 zone allows but have immediate neighbors that are far less intense. Initially, the city wanted to apply the UC zone to allow commercial types that would accommodate this need. However, the team identified the unintended consequences of such an action and surgically allocated the Hybrid type for only these two areas.

*Regulating Building Size and Massing*

Allocating percentages of the building's allowed footprint for any upper stories (item 8 in the individual Building Type standards) eliminates the risk of cookie-cutter, single-height buildings. Instead, each building's designer chooses how to distribute the allowed percentage, by story, to address site conditions, solar orientation, or simply visual preferences. The result is twofold:

1. More flexibility for the owner/designer as compared to abstract FAR requirements, which don't always enable good design
2. A higher likelihood of variety among buildings due to their individual owner's choices

## Implementation

### Code Administration

The Planning and Building Agency will primarily administer the Form-Based Code, with the Public Works Agency administering the street standards in the code.

Because of the enormous development pressure in the community, early proposals based on the draft specific plan and code are being submitted to the planners for early reaction. The few we have seen show a dramatically positive change in the urban quality of proposals from those we were shown early in the process.

*Rail Station District*

*Downtown: Regeneration*

*Downtown: Interventions*

*Lacy Neighborhood*

**Fig. 4.4** Images from the visioning process

### Lessons Learned

We would work more extensively with Public Works and Traffic staff on the changing practice of traffic engineering. Particular effort would be directed toward the issue of large curb radii (minimum 25 feet throughout) and restoring on-street parking and two-way circulation.

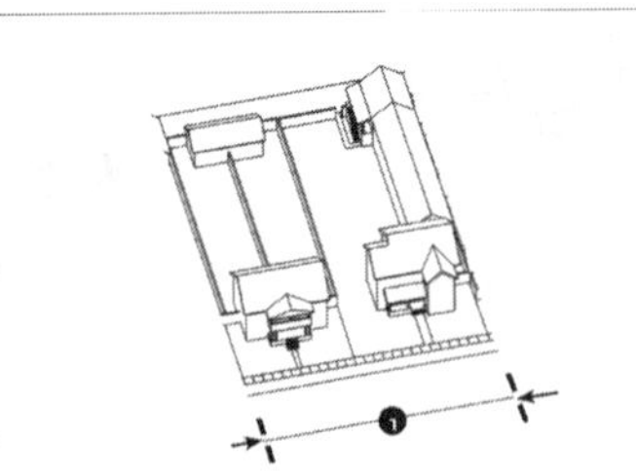

*Illustrative Axonometric Diagram*

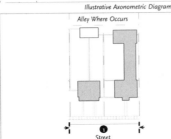

Alley Where Occurs

1

Street

*Illustrative Plan Diagram*

*Illustrative Photo: Quadplex with stoop frontage*

*Illustrative Photo: Triplex with frontyard frontage*

*Illustrative Photo: Duplex with frontyard and porch frontage*

### 4.5.010 - Architectural Standards - Building Types

**L. Duplex, Triplex, and Quadplex:** Duplexes, triplexes, and quadplexes are multiple dwelling types that are architecturally presented as large single-family houses in their typical neighborhood setting.
Unit Size Standards: Min: 850 sq ft

**1 Lot Width/Frontage:** Minimum: 50 ft; maximum: 75 ft.

**2: Access Standards**
(a) The main entrance to each dwelling shall be accessed directly from and face the street. Access to second floor dwellings shall be by a stair, which may be open or enclosed.
(b) Where an alley is present, parking and services shall be accessed through the alley.
(c) Where an alley is not present, parking and services shall be accessed by of a driveway 8 to 10 feet wide, and with 2-foot planters on each side.
(d) On a corner lot without access to an alley, parking and services shall be accessed by driveways up to 8 feet wide, and 2-foot planters on each side.

**3: Parking Standards**
(a) Required parking shall be within individual garages, which shall contain up to four cars.
(b) Garages on corner lots without alleys can front onto the side street only if provided with 1-car garage doors, and with driveways up to 8 feet wide that are separated by planters at least 2 feet wide.

**4: Service Standards**
(a) Where an alley is present, services, including all utility access and above ground equipment and trash container areas shall be located on the alley.
(b) Where an alley is not present, utility access, above ground equipment and trash container areas shall be located at least 10 feet behind the front of the house, and be screened from view from the street with a hedge or fence, as specified for the zone.

**5: Open Space Standards**
(a) Each ground floor dwelling shall have a private or semi-private yard of at least 150 square feet
(b) Required yards shall be at least 8 feet wide, and enclosed by a fence, wall or hedge.
(c) Front yards are defined by the applicable setback and frontage type requirements.
(d) Porches, stoops and dooryards may encroach into a required yard, as specified for the zone.

**6: Landscape Standards**
(a) All yards shall be landscaped.
(b) Landscape shall not obscure front yards on adjacent lots. Front yards trees shall not exceed 1.5 times the height of the porch at maturity, except at the margins of the lot, where they may be no more than 1.5 times the height of building at maturity. The trees shall be planted at the rate of one 36-inch box tree per 25 lineal feet of front yard. The trees can be placed in groups in order to achieve a particular design.
(c) At least one 24-inch canopy tree shall be provided in the rear yard for shade and privacy.
(d) Side yards trees shall be placed a rate of one 24-inch box tree per 30 lineal feet to protect the privacy of neighbors.
(e) Six, five-gallon size shrubs, ten one-gallon size herbaceous perennials/shrubs and turf or acceptable dry climate ground cover is required for every required tree.
(f) All plant material shall be maintained per section 41-609 of the SAMC. All plant material shall be irrigated by an automatic irrigation system.

**7: Frontage Standards**
(a) Dwellings abutting front yards shall be designed so that living areas (e.g., living room, family room, dining room, etc.), rather than bedrooms and service rooms, are oriented toward the fronting street to the extent possible.
(b) The applicable frontage requirements apply per Chapter 4.5.020.
(c) On corner lots, entrances to triplex and quadplex dwellings on both frontages is required.
(d) See requirements of applicable zone for allowed encroachments into required setbacks.

**8: Building Size and Massing Standards**
(a) Building elevations abutting side yards shall be designed to provide at least one horizontal plane break of at least three feet, and one vertical break of at least two feet.
(b) Buildings on corner lots shall be designed with two front facades.
(c) Buildings shall be massed as large houses, composed principally of two story volumes, each designed to house scale.
(d) Dwellings within buildings may be flats and/or townhouses.

| Scenarios (in Stories) | Ratio of each Story (see page 4:17 for height definition) | | |
|---|---|---|---|
| | 1 | 2 | 3 |
| A | 100% | 80% | - |
| B | 100% | 75% | 40% |

**9: Accessory Dwellings**
Allowed. See SAMC section 41-194.




**Fig. 4.5** Building Type Standards for Duplex, Triplex, and Quadplex

## 4.5.010 - Architectural Standards - Building Types

**F. Courtyard Housing:** A structure type consisting of residences that can be arranged in four possible configurations: townhouses, townhouses over flats, flats, and flats over flats. These are arrayed next to each other, on one or more courts, to form a shared type that is partly or wholly open to the street.
Unit Size Standards: Min: 850 sq ft, Median: 1000 sq ft

❶ **Lot Width/Frontage**: Minimum: 125 ft; maximum: 200 ft.

**2: Access Standards**
(a) The main entry to each ground floor dwelling is directly off a common courtyard or from the street
(b) Access to second story dwellings shall be through an open or roofed stair, serving up to 2 dwellings
(c) Elevator access, if any, is provided between the garage and courtyard/podium only.
(d) Where an alley is present, parking and service shall be accessed through the alley.

**3: Parking Standards**
(a) Required parking shall be in an underground garage, or can be surface parking, tuck under parking, an aboveground garage, or a combination of any of the above.
(b) Dwellings can have direct on indirect access to their parking stall(s), or direct access to stalls enclosed within the garage.
(c) Entrances to subterranean garages and/or driveways shall be located as close as possible to the side or rear of each lot.
(d) Where an alley is not present, parking shall be accessed from the street by side yard driveways flanked by planters, at least 1-foot wide.
(e) On a corner lot without alley-access, parking shall be accessed from the side street and services shall be underground and/ or in the side and rear yards.

**4: Service Standards**
(a) Where an alley is present, services, including all utility access and above ground equipment and trash container areas shall be located on the alley.
(b) Where an alley is not present, services shall be located in compliance with the setback requirements.
(c) Where an alley is not present, parking and services shall be accessed from the street by side yard driveways flanked by planters, at least 1-foot wide.
(d) On a corner lot without alley-access, parking and services shall be accessed from the side street and services shall be underground and/ or in the side and rear yards as specified for the zone.

**5: Open Space Standards**
(a) Courtyard housing shall be designed to provide a central courtyard and/or partial, multiple, separated or interconnected courtyards of a size of at least 15% of the lot.
(b) In a project with multiple courtyards, at least two of the courtyards shall conform to the patterns below. Courtyard proportions shall not be less than 1:1 between the width and height for at least 2/3 of the court's perimeter. Horizontal shifts in upper floors adjacent to a court shall not exceed 1/2 the height of each upper floor.
(c) Minimum courtyard dimensions are 40 feet when the long axis of the courtyard is oriented East/West and 30 feet when the courtyard is oriented North/South.
(d) In 40-foot wide courtyards, the frontages and architectural projections allowed are permitted on two sides of the courtyard and on one side of 30-foot wide courtyards.
(e) Private patios are allowed in any yard (front, side, rear)
(f) Balconies are allowed in any yard (front, side, rear) in compliance with the encroachment requirements of the applicble zone.
(g) Courtyards shall be connected to each other and to the public way by zaguans or paseos.
(h) Surface parking (five cars max) allowed in a front garden, screened from street by a decorative wall.

**6: Landscape Standards**
(a) All yards shall be landscaped.
(b) Landscape shall not obscure front yards on adjacent lots or the shopfront of ground floor flex space. Front yard trees shall not exceed 1.5 times the height of the porch at maturity, except at the margins of the lot, where they may be no more than 1.5 times the height of building at maturity. Trees shall be planted at the rate of one, 36-inch box tree per 25 lineal feet of front yard. Trees can be placed in groups in order to achieve a particular design.
(c) At least one, 24-inch canopy tree planted directly in the ground shall be provided in the rear yard.
(d) At least one, 36-inch box canopy tree shall be planted directly in the ground in one courtyard for shade, privacy and scale.
(e) One, 15 gallon/24" box size tree of small scale (12-15' height at maturity) or similar tall shrubs shall be used for planters in courtyards over garages. Layering of all plant materials is recommended.
(f) Side yard trees shall be placed at a rate of one 24-inch box tree per 30 lineal feet for privacy of neighbors.
(g) Six, five-gallon size shrubs, ten, one-gallon size herbaceous perennials/shrubs and turf or acceptable dry climate ground cover is required for every required tree.
(h) Surface parking areas shall be landscaped per the City's Commercial Area Landscape Standards.
(i) All plant material shall be maintained per section 41-609 of the SAMC.
(j) All plant material shall be irrigated by an automatic irrigation system.

**7: Frontage Standards**
(a) Entrance doors, living space (e.g., living rooms and dining rooms) shall be oriented toward the courtyard(s) and the fronting street to the degree possible. Service rooms shall be oriented backing to sideyards, service yards and rear yards to the degree possible.
(b) Features such as arcades, galleries, porches, towers, loggias, entry stairs and stoops are allowed but shall not encroach into the required minimum width of a courtyard.
(c) Stoops up to 3 feet in height may be placed above subterranean parking, provided they are landscaped and scaled to the street and building.
(d) The applicable frontage and encroachment requirements apply per Chapter 4.5.020.

**8: Building Size and Massing Standards**
(a) Buildings shall be composed of one, two and three story masses, each designed to house scale, and not necessarily representing a single dwelling.
(b) The intent of these regulations is to provide for courtyard housing projects with varying building heights.
Height ratios for courts are as follows:

| Building Scenario | Ratio of each Story (see page 4:78 for height definition) | | | | |
|---|---|---|---|---|---|
| | 1 | 2 | 3 | 4 | 5 |
| A | 100% | 80% | - | - | - |
| B | 100% | 75% | 40% | - | - |
| C | 100% | 75% | 55% | 20% | - |
| D | 100% | 100% | 75% | 40% | 25% |

(c) 3-story buildings shall be composed of single loaded and stacked dwellings. In this case, the visibility of elevators and of exterior corridors at the third story shall be minimized by incorporation into the mass of the building.
(d) Buildings are allowed to contain any of 4 combinations: flats, flats over flats, townhouses, and townhouses over flats.
(e) Dwellings are allowed to be as repetitive or unique as deemed by individual designs.
(f) 4 and 5-story masses shall be minimized inside courtyards and apparent on street frontages.

**9: Accessory Dwellings** - Not allowed

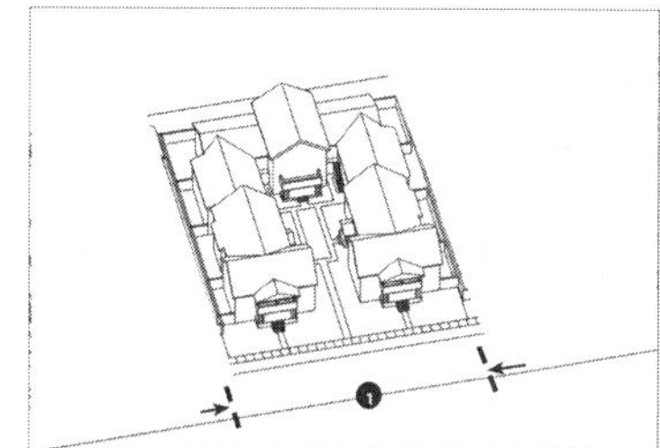


*Illustrative Axonometric Diagram*

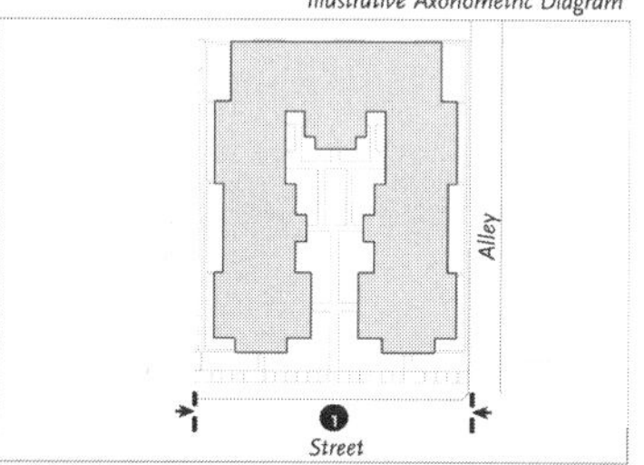


*Illustrative Plan Diagram*

*Illustrative Photo: Courtyard with frontyard frontage and zaguan*

*Illustrative Photo: Courtyard with zaguan linking two courtyards*

SANTA ANA RENAISSANCE SPECIFIC PLAN 4:26
City of Santa Ana, California
DRAFT 8 October, 2007

**Fig. 4.6** Building Type Standards for Courtyard Housing

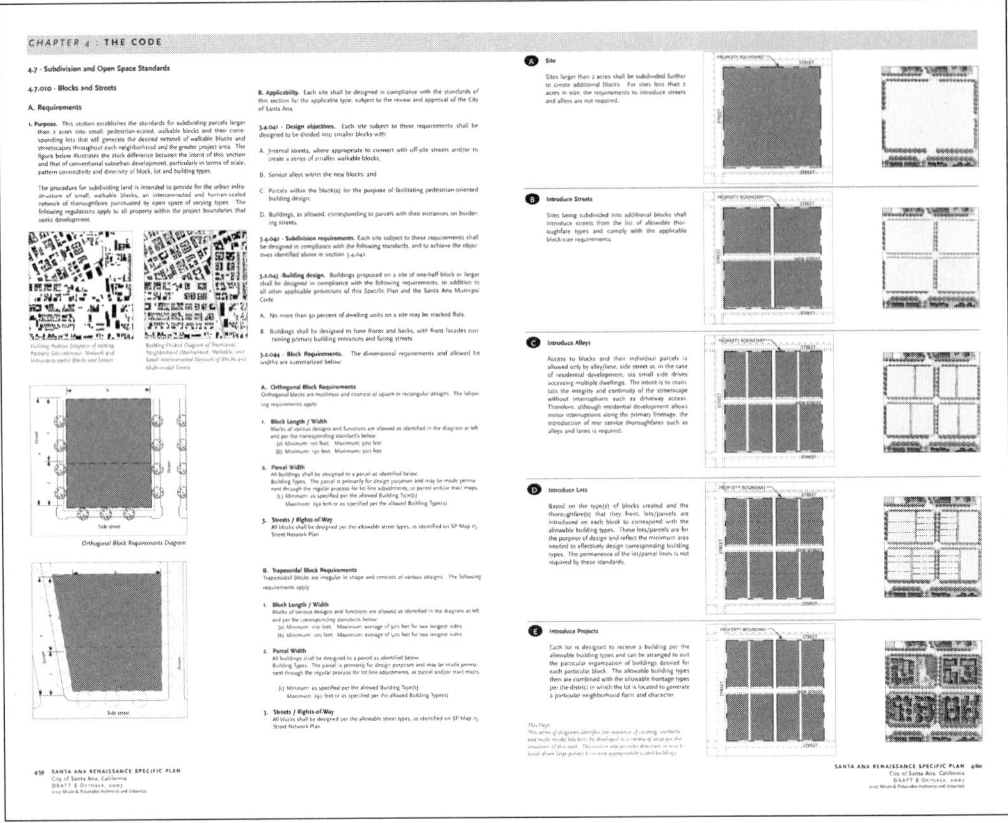
Fig. 4.7 Subdivision Standards

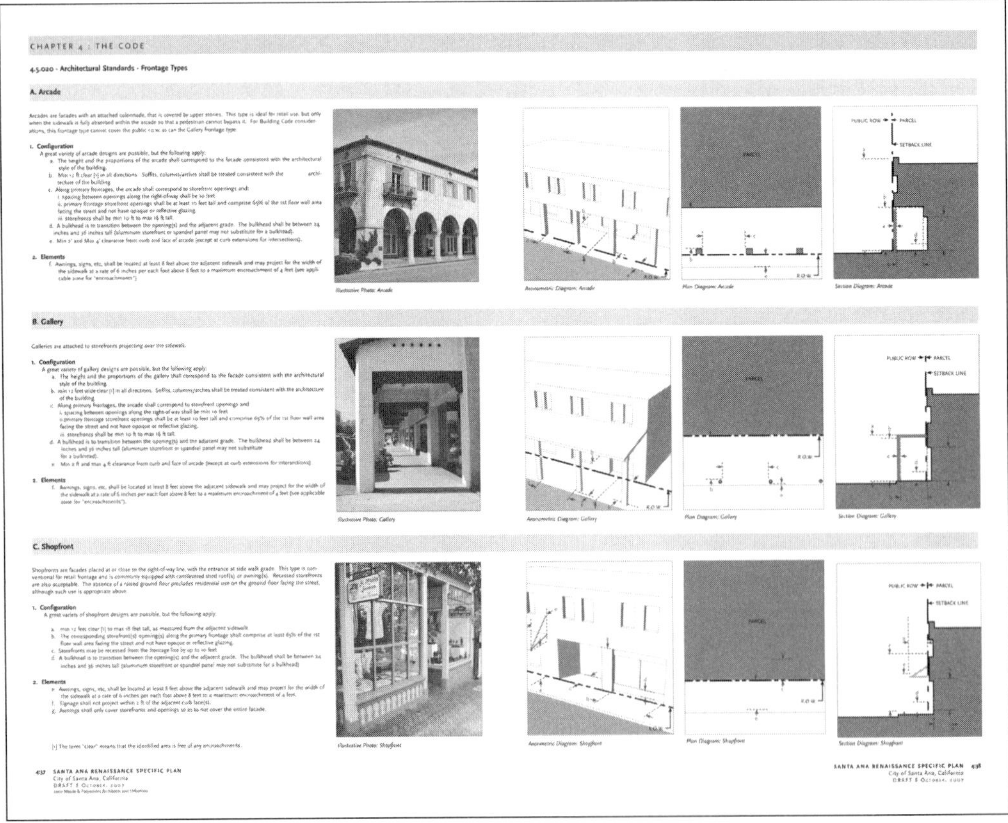
Fig. 4.8 Frontage Standards

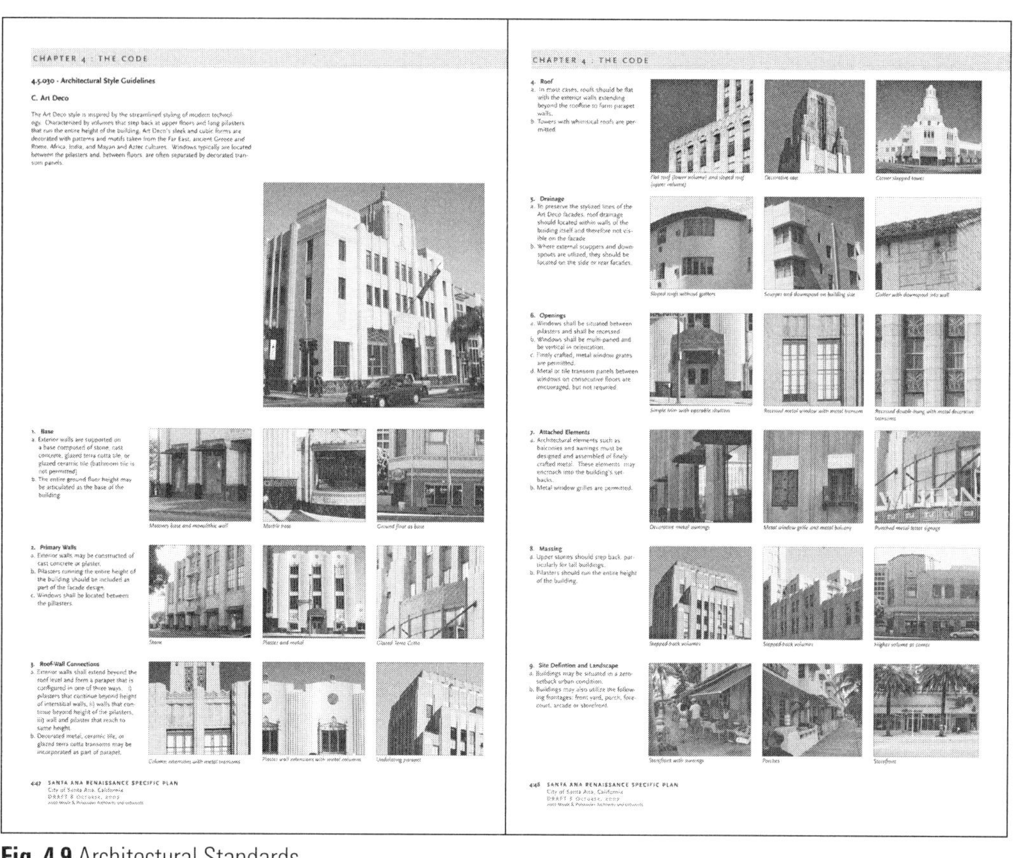
CHAPTER 4 : THE CODE

4.5.030 - Architectural Style Guidelines

C. Art Deco

**Fig. 4.9** Architectural Standards

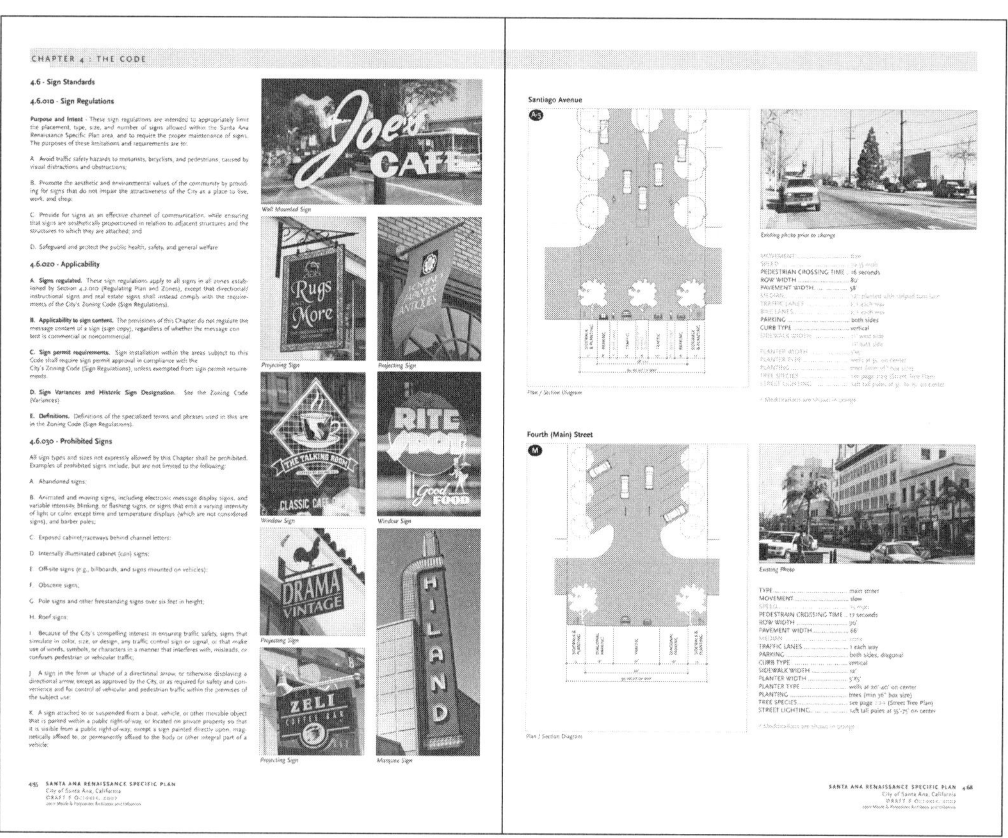
CHAPTER 4 : THE CODE

4.6 - Sign Standards

4.6.010 - Sign Regulations

4.6.020 - Applicability

4.6.030 - Prohibited Signs

Santiago Avenue

Fourth (Main) Street



**Fig. 4.10** Signage Standards (left page) and Street Standards (right page)

CHAPTER 4 : THE CODE

### 4.3 - Use Standards

#### 4.3.010 Allowable Land Uses and Permit Requirements

**A. Allowable Land Uses.** A parcel or building within the specific plan area shall be occupied by only the land uses allowed by Table 4-3-1 within the zone applied to the site by the Regulating Plan. Each land use listed in the table is defined in the glossary of this Specific Plan (chapter 4.8) or in SAMC( Definitions, Ch 41).

**B. Multiple Uses.** Any one or more land uses identified by Table 4-3-1 as being allowable within a specific zone may be established on any parcel within that zone, subject to the planning permit requirement listed in the table, and in compliance with all applicable requirements of this Code.

**C. Use Not Listed.** A land use that is not listed in Table 4-3-1 is not allowed within the specific plan area. A land use that is listed in the table, but not within a particular zone, is not allowed within that zone.

**D. Similar and compatible use may be allowed.** The PBA Director may determine that a proposed use not listed in Table 4-3-1 is similar to a use described in SAMC Chapter 41.

**E. Temporary and Ancillary uses.** Temporary and Ancillary uses are allowed within the specific plan area in compliance with the operational and development standards of the SAMC Chapter 41. Ancillary uses including, but limited to garage sales; temporary outdoor activities, such as selling alcohol, at an event wireless communication facilities exterior pay phones, outdoor vending machines, keep, laundromats.

**F. Drive-through facilities.** Such facilities shall not be permitted in the Specific Plan area.

**G. New section:** Operational Standards General. Please refer to section 4.1.020 (4.b.ii)
All property shall be maintained in a safe, sanitary and attractive condition, including but not limited to structures, landscaping, parking area, walkways, and trash enclosures.

**H. Operational standards for auto or motor vehicle service or repair**

(a) No automobile servicing or repair within three hundred (300) feet of property used or zoned for residential purposes shall be conducted before 6:00 a.m. or after 10:00 p.m. on any day of the week.

(b) Outdoor/overnight vehicle storage is not permitted.

**I. Operational standards for nonresidential uses**

**Commercial**
(a) All business activities shall be conducted and located within an enclosed building, except that the following business activities, to the extent permitted under section 4-3-1, may be conducted outside of an enclosed building:

(1) Plant nurseries.
(2) Newsstands
(3) Flower Stands
(4) Recreational or entertainment uses.

(b) There shall be no manufacturing, processing, compounding, assembling or treatment of any material or product other than that which is clearly incidental to a particular retail enterprise, and where such goods are sold on the premises.

(c) Storage of goods and supplies shall be limited to those sold at retail on the premises or utilized in the course of business.

(d) Public utility electric distribution and transmission substations shall be screened by a fence at least eight (8) feet high, except as restricted by sections 36-45, 36-46, and 36-47 of the SAMC.

TABLE 4-3-1

Allowed Land Uses and Permit Requirements for Zones

P = Permitted Use, Use-Clearance required
LUC = Land Use Certificate required
CUP = Conditional Use Permit required
- = Use not allowed

| Land Use Type | Permit Required by Zone | | | | | | |
|---|---|---|---|---|---|---|---|
| | RR | DT | UC | CDR | UN-2 | UN-1 | R/I |
| **INDUSTRY, MANUFACTURING AND PROCESSING, WAREHOUSING AND DISTRIBUTION** | | | | | | | |
| Artisan/craft product manufacturing | - | CUP | CUP- | - | CUP | - | P |
| Businesses operating between 12 and 5am | CUP | CUP | CUP | - | CUP | CUP | CUP |
| Furniture and fixture manufacturing, cabinet shop | - | - | - | - | - | - | P |
| Laboratory - medical - analytical | - | - | P(1) | - | - | - | P |
| Manufacturing - light | - | - | - | - | - | - | P |
| Manufacturing - medium intensity | - | - | - | - | - | - | CUP |
| Media production - office or storefront type (no sound stage) | P | P | P(1) | - | - | - | P |
| Printing and publishing | - | P(1) | P | - | - | - | P |
| Research and development | - | - | - | - | - | - | P |
| Outdoor storage - max stacking height 10ft | - | - | - | - | - | - | P |
| **RESIDENTIAL USES** | | | | | | | |
| Home Occupation, excluding alcohol sales | P(1) | P(1) | P(1) | - | P | P | P |
| Live-Work Use / Joint living-working quarters | LUC | LUC | LUC | LUC | CUP | CUP | CUP |
| Residential Component of Mixed-Use Building | P(1) | P(1) | P(1) | P(1) | P | P | P |
| Ground Floor Residential | - | - | - | - | P | P | P |
| Care Homes | CUP | CUP | CUP | CUP | CUP | CUP | CUP |
| Caretaker Residential Use | - | P(1) | P(1) | P(1) | P | P | P |
| Carriage House/Second Dwelling, Single Dwelling | - | - | - | - | P | P | P |
| Multi-Family Building (as allowed on page 4:17) | CUP | CUP | CUP | CUP | CUP | CUP | CUP |
| Mixed-Use Building (as allowed on page 4:17) | CUP | CUP | CUP | CUP | CUP | - | CUP |
| **RECREATION, EDUCATION AND ASSEMBLY** | | | | | | | |
| Businesses operating between 12 and 7am | CUP | CUP | CUP | CUP | CUP | CUP | CUP |
| Community assembly | P(1) | CUP | CUP | P | CUP | CUP | CUP |
| Health/fitness facility | - | - | P | P | CUP | - | - |
| Indoor recreation facility - commercial/billiards | CUP | CUP | CUP | CUP | - | - | - |
| Library, museum | - | P | P | P | P | - | - |
| School - public or private | - | CUP(1) | CUP | P | CUP | CUP | - |
| Studio - art, dance, martial arts, etc | P | P | P | P | CUP | CUP | - |
| Theater, cinema or performing arts | P | P | P | - | - | - | - |
| Cyber cafe- subject to 41.198.200 | LUC | LUC | LUC | LUC | LUC | - | LUC |
| **RETAIL** | | | | | | | |
| Antique or collectible store | P | P | CUP | - | - | - | - |
| Bar, tavern, night club, live entertainment (fee or no fee) | CUP | CUP | CUP | CUP | - | - | - |
| Building and landscape material sales | - | - | - | - | - | - | CUP |
| General retail, except with any of the following features | P | P | P | P | P(2) | - | - |
| • Alcoholic beverage sales | CUP | CUP | CUP | CUP | - | - | CUP |
| • Auto or motor vehicle service | - | - | - | CUP | - | - | - |
| • Auto or motor vehicle repair | - | - | - | - | - | - | CUP |
| • Floor area over 20,000 per tenant | CUP | CUP | CUP | - | CUP | - | - |
| • Operating between 12 and 7am | CUP | CUP | CUP | CUP | CUP | - | CUP |
| Eating establishments | P | P | P | P | P(2) | - | P |
| Operations between 12 and 5 am | CUP | CUP | CUP | CUP | CUP | - | CUP |

4:7 SANTA ANA RENAISSANCE SPECIFIC PLAN
City of Santa Ana, California
DRAFT 8 OCTOBER, 2007
2007 Moule & Polyzoides Architects and Urbanists

**Fig. 4.11** (left and right) Land-use tables

| TABLE 4.3-1, continued<br>Allowed Land Uses and Permit Requirements for Zones | P = Permitted Use, Use-Clearance required<br>LUC = Land Use Certificate required<br>CUP = Conditional Use Permit required<br>- = Use not allowed | | | | | |
|---|---|---|---|---|---|---|---|
| Land Use Type | Permit Required by Zone | | | | | | |
| | RR | DT | UC | CDR | UN-2 | UN-1 | R/I |
| **SERVICE GENERAL** | | | | | | | |
| Banquet facility - catering - subject to 41.199.1 | CUP | CUP | CUP | CUP | - | - | - |
| Businesses operating between 12 and 5am | CUP | CUP | CUP | CUP | CUP | CUP | CUP |
| Child day care - more than 8 and up to 14 children | LUC | - | - | P | LUC(2) | LUC | LUC |
| Day care center - child or adult subject to 41.199.2 | CUP | CUP | CUP | P | CUP | CUP | - |
| Equipment rental, indoor type only | - | - | - | P | - | - | P |
| Lodging - bed and breakfast inn | - | CUP | CUP | - | CUP | - | - |
| Lodging - hotel / motel, excl. transcent residential hotel | CUP | CUP | CUP | - | - | - | - |
| Mortuaries, funeral homes | - | - | CUP | P | - | - | - |
| Personal services | P | P | P | P | P(2) | - | P |
| Personal services - restricted | - | - | CUP | CUP | - | - | - |
| **SERVICES-BUSINESS-FINANCIAL-PROFESSIONAL** | | | | | | | |
| Bank, financial services | P | P | P | P | - | - | - |
| Business support service | P | P | P | P | P(2) | - | - |
| Businesses operating between 12 and 5am | CUP | CUP | CUP | CUP | CUP | - | CUP |
| Medical services - clinic, urgent care | - | - | CUP | CUP | - | - | - |
| Medical services - doctor, dentist, chiropractor, etc, office | P(1) | P(1) | P(1) | P | - | - | - |
| Medical services - extended care | - | - | - | - | CUP | - | - |
| Office - service | P | P | P | P | P(2) | - | P |
| Professional / administrative | P(1) | P(1) | P(1) | P | P(2) | - | |
| **TRANSPORTATION, COMMUNICATION, INFRASTRUCTURE** | | | | | | | |
| Helistops | CUP | CUP | CUP | - | - | - | - |
| Parking facility - public or commercial | P | P | P | P | - | - | - |
| Transit station or terminal | CUP | - | - | CUP | - | - | - |
| Public utility structure, excluding cell sites | - | - | - | - | CUP | - | CUP |

**Key to Zone Symbols**

| | | | |
|---|---|---|---|
| RR | Rail Station Zone | UN-2 | Urban Neighborhood 2 |
| DT | Downtown | UN-1 | Urban Neighborhood 1 |
| UC | Urban Center | R/I | Residential/Industry |
| CDR | Corridor | | |

**Key to Permit Types**

P Permitted Use
LUC Land Use Certificate Required
CUP Use-Permit Required
- Use not allowed

**Notes:**

(1) Use allowed only on second or upper floors, or behind ground floor street frontage use.
(2) Allowed only as part of a vertical mixed use project, with upper floor residential

Note: A definition of each listed use type is in section 4.9

(e) No sales shall be made directly from a building to persons on a public sidewalk, either trough

a window or similar opening or by means of any coin-operated device (excluding ground floor garage-liners)

(f) Youth amusement rides shall comply with Sec. 41-366 of the SAMC.

**Industrial**

(a) Any activity permitted in this district shall be conducted in such a manner as not to have a detrimental effect on permitted adjacent uses by reason of refuse matter, noise, light, vibration, or lack of proper maintenance of grounds or buildings.

(b) Outdoor storage of materials, products, equipment or vehicles, shall be screened by a solid wall not less than eight (8) feet in height that extend from the building closest to the street in a parallel manner to the street. Materials, products or equipment stored outdoors shall not be piled higher than the height of the fence or wall, nor encroach into required parking and landscape areas.

(c) A solid wall or fence not less than eight (8) feet in height is required along any rear or side lot line abutting property which is either used, zoned, or designated on the General Plan for residential purposes.

(d) Public utility electric distribution and transmission substations shall be enclosed within a solid wall or fence not less than eight (8) feet in height except as restricted by sections 36-45, 36-46, and 36-47 of the SAMC.

(e) All major compounding, processing, packaging or assembly of articles of merchandise, treatment of products and vehicle maintenance and repair, shall be conducted within a completely enclosed building. In addition, service bays for ancillary vehicle maintenance and repair shall be completely screened from view from the public street.

(g) Loading areas shall not be visible from arterial streets or from streets adjacent to front yards. Loading areas facing other streets shall be screened with decorative walls of a material compatible with the building design and by landscaping abutting such walls. Loading areas not facing a street shall be setback at least thirty-five (35) feet from the property line.

(h) Railroad tracks are not allowed on any street side of a building. If railroad tracks and loading docks are located other than at the rear of a building area, the tracks and the loading dock shall be completely screened from view from any street.

**J. Permit Requirements.** Table 4-1 provides for land uses that are:

1. Permitted subject to compliance with all applicable provisions of this Code, and Development Review in compliance with Chapter 4 of this Specific Plan. These uses are shown as " P " uses in Table 4-3-1;

2. Allowed subject to the approval of a Land Use Certificate, and shown as " LUC " in Table 4-3-1;

3. Allowed subject to the approval of a Conditional Use Permit, and shown as " CUP " in Table 4-3-1;

4. Not allowed in particular zones, and shown as " - " in Table 4-3-1.

4.1.040 - Organization and Use of Code

The following diagram illustrates the the contents of the code, the type of information in each component and the required action(s) by an applicant. This is a summary and subject to the actual processing and review by the City of Santa Ana.

| | Required Action by Applicant | Go to Page | Use this Code Component |
|---|---|---|---|
| 1 | Provide the required information and processing fee(s) for the City to review and process your application. | 4:3 | **Application Procedures and Requirements**<br>Consult City's application submittal requirements for types of drawings, information and quantities to be prepared and submitted with the application along with any required processing fee. |
| 2 | Find your parcel's zoning category. | 4:5 | **Regulating Plan and Zones**<br>• Rail Station<br>• Government Center<br>• Institutional<br>• Downtown<br>• Urban Center<br>• Corridor<br>• Urban Neighborhood 2<br>• Urban Neighborhood 1<br>• Residential / Industry |
| 3 | Find what uses are allowed on your parcel and what type(s) of permit(s) are required. | 4:9 | **Land Use Standards**<br>P Permitted - Zoning Clearance Required<br>LUC Land Use Certificate Required<br>CUP Conditional Use Permit Required<br>S Permit Requirement set by specific regulations*<br>- Use Not Alllowed<br>*Regulations for Specific Uses (i.e Adult Businesses, Telecommunications Facilties, Day Care, Recycling Facilities, Specialized Manufacturing, etc.) |
| 4 | If your site is 2 acres or larger, apply the standards to design new blocks using the allowed street types.<br>If not, go to step 5. | 4:55 | **Subdivision Standards**<br>• Blocks and Streets (Streets -- see page 4:61)<br>• Open Space |
| 5 | Apply the standards to identify the allowed building footprint, encroachments and height. | 4:11 | **Urban Standards**<br>• Building Placement<br>• Parking Placement<br>• Building Height - Profile<br>i - Building Types Allowed<br>ii - Frontage Types Allowed |
| 6 | Select from the allowed building types for your parcel and apply the standards to your parcel for each selected type. | 4:17 | **Building Type Standards**<br>• Tower-on-Podium<br>• Liner<br>• Hybrid Court<br>• Commercial Block<br>• Stacked Dwellings<br>• Courtyard Housing<br>• Live/Work<br>• Industrial Shed<br>• Rowhouse<br>• Duplex/Triplex/Quadplex<br>• Single Family Dwelling<br>• Carriage House |
| 7 | Select from the allowed frontage types for your parcel and apply the standards to your proposed design. | 4:31 | **Frontage Type Standards**<br>• Arcade<br>• Gallery<br>• Shopfront<br>• Forecourt<br>• Stoop<br>• Frontyard/Porch |
| 8 | Select from the allowed styles for your building(s) and apply the standards. | 4:37 | **Architecural Style Standards**<br>• Main Street Commercial<br>• Mission Revival<br>• Art Deco<br>• Western Victorian<br>• Craftsman<br>• California Contemporary |

SANTA ANA RENAISSANCE SPECIFIC PLAN 4:2
City of Santa Ana, California
DRAFT 27 April, 2007

**Fig. 4.12** Organization and use of the code

# Downtown Master Plan and Form-Based Code



## Benicia, California

THE CITY OF BENICIA is located along the Carquinez Strait in the San Francisco Bay area and has a population of approximately 28,000 people.[2] The last General Plan update process created a general Mixed-Use land-use category and applied it to the city's main street and to the surrounding neighborhood. The definition of Mixed-Use was left very vague within the General Plan; therefore, the city hired the consultants to refine the definition of Mixed-Use within the downtown neighborhoods through a publicly driven Master Plan process. The code team was selected, through an open Request for Proposal (RFP) process, to replace the zoning within this area with a Form-Based Code that would implement the vision plan and make the zoning consistent with the General Plan.

### Client's Background in Form-Based Coding

Jim Erickson, the city manager, had previously asked a group of FBC consultants to give a short presentation to the city council and planning commissioners in a joint workshop. Benicia then hired Charlie Knox, a community development director who had previously been a planning consultant with extensive experience implementing Form-Based Codes. Knox proceeded to put together an RFP process that selected the FBC consultant for the Downtown Master Plan and the Arsenal Specific Plan.

## Code Components

The primary goal of this process was to implement the vision plan and to create the Form-Based Zones, the Regulating Plan, and the Building Form Standards to replace the existing zoning. The Architectural Standards existed within the Downtown Historic Resource Plan that had been completed prior to the FBC process. The streets were all existing, and a previous set of recommended changes had been designed, including converting parallel parking to head-in angled parking to take advantage of overly wide curb-to-curb dimensions on the side streets. The FBC team reviewed these Street Standards and decided that they were in line with the Master Plan objective, but recommended that it was not completely necessary to alter the existing streets because they functioned fairly well already. Because of limitations in budget and the simplicity of the vision plan, which was preservation-oriented in nature, and the presence of few undeveloped lots, the FBC decided that Building Types Standards and Landscape Standards were not necessary.

### Organizing Principle

The transect was selected as the organizing principle for the FBC because it was an effective tool in educating the community about the ap-

| | Benicia Downtown Master Plan and FBC |
|---|---|
| Status: | Adopted on April 3, 2007 |
| Scale: | Part of a City/Town |
| Implementation Method: | Mandatory and Integrated |
| Site Context: | Redevelopment/Infill<br>Greyfield |
| Site Size: | |
| Administration: | City/County Staff |
| Organizing Principle: | Transect |
| Code Consultants(s): | Opticos Design, Inc.; Crawford, Multari & Clark Associates |
| Agency: | City of Benicia, California Community Development Department |

propriate levels of urbanism within its borders and how transect-based regulations could reinforce these patterns.

## Code Process

A documentation process at the macro scale and the micro scale initiated the process. At the macro scale, the team documented the existing neighborhoods, districts, and corridors and created a diagram of these elements to understand the role of the downtown within this framework and the role of streets that passed through or next to the planning area. The micro-scale details, such as lot sizes, setbacks, and heights, were gathered on a matrix that later evolved into the Building Form Standards. As the documentation progressed, the team took notes on a plan concentrating on how the physical form and the uses transitioned from the main street to the primarily residential fabric along the streets perpendicular to the main street.

After the documentation was complete, the FBC team ran a five-day public charrette process to engage local community members and stakeholders to help them establish their vision for the downtown. The charrette took place in a vacant shop along the main street in order to attract local business owners and to be onsite during the design process. In this project, most of the fabric was developed, and a large number of historic buildings were still intact. Therefore, one of the primary roles of this Master Plan and FBC was to preserve the historic character of the downtown and require that any new buildings be built in a manner that would reinforce the unique character of the downtown. During the charrette, a draft of the Form-Based Zones was created, with definitions. This draft, along with a template draft for the Building Form Standards pages, was shown to residents at the midpoint and final presentations to prepare them for the FBC that would come after the charrette.

Approximately six to eight weeks after the charrette, the Form-Based Code was completely drafted, went through a quick review process, and was approved by the city council within four months of the charrette.

### Public Participation

The team initiated the public process with a day-long one-on-one interview process for approximately 60 stakeholders and local decision makers. That same evening, they gave a short presentation on FBCs and the analysis completed to date and then had a breakout session with participants to find out what they did and did not like about their downtown. This was done with red and green dots, which were then compiled onto one base map to inform the team where there were issues that needed to be addressed and areas or elements of the downtown that needed to be enhanced or protected.

This was all leading up to an intense five-day charrette process through which the team created the Master Plan. The charrette was held according to the National Charrette Institute's (NCI) dynamic charrette process with three feedback loops, counting the first feedback loop that occurred at the precharrette workshop. There were three formal public presentations: one during the first evening, the next on the third evening, and the third on the final evening. Several breakout meetings were held with various stakeholders and decision makers during the process, and the doors were open to the public for most of the time.

## Advanced Application of FBCs

### A Simple Application as a Model for a Small-Town Downtown

Since the planning area was fairly small and easy to document and analyze, the FBC team could be very specific about the intent and application of the Form-Based Zones. In this way,

**Fig. 4.13** (previous page) Photos of Benicia, California

this code presents a really simple and efficient model that could be applied to the thousands of small towns across the country that are trying to make their downtowns and surrounding neighborhoods more vibrant while protecting the historic character.

### Adapting the Transect through the Creation of Subzones

A T5 Town Center zone was created to reinforce the vertical mixed-use character of First Street, Benicia's main street. This zone applied only to those lots facing directly on to the main street in order to focus the little energy that already existed. It encouraged the concentration of commercial and retail uses on this street. Many of the side streets were composed of historic, single-family residences that made for wonderful streetscapes. Therefore, the T3 Neighborhood General Form-Based Zone was created to reinforce the existing residential character while permitting mixed use to be defined by allowing workshops, artist studios, home offices, and ancillary units at the rear of the lots on the alleys.

As with most small-town downtowns, the trickiest areas to code were the areas of transition between the two- or three-story shopfront character and uses along the main street and the one- or two-story residential buildings and uses within the first few lots. During the charrette process, the team concentrated on understanding the existing conditions in these transitional areas to provide an appropriate transition in use and physical form. Because of the varying existing conditions, several additional Form-Based Zones were created. In some areas, the single-family homes had been converted to commercial and retail uses, thus already compromising the residential character of the street. In these areas, a Neighborhood General Open or T3-O zone was created to regulate a residential physical form, but allowing the uses to be open so that, as the market demands, they could be used for residential or commercial. With the performance standards-based land uses within this zone, any residential use would be compatible next to this use. This zone was also applied to lots that were still residential but due to

1886

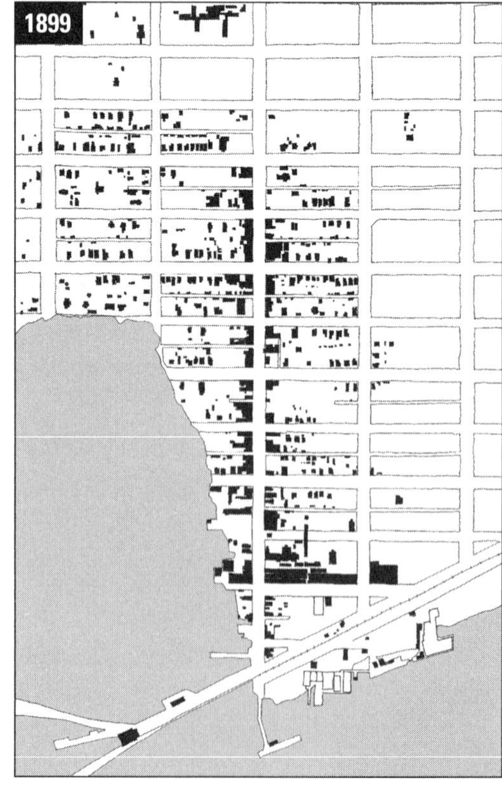

past adjacent development, had been compromised in some way, such as having a large parking lot or poorly designed apartment building next door. There were also instances in these transitional areas where the shopfront building type had turned the corners and several of the side-street lots had these shopfront types. In these instances, we created a Town Center-Open or T5-O zone that regulated a shopfront form that was a maximum of two stories, but allowed the uses to be flexible to accommodate a live/work or loft-type residence or small commercial uses.

### Form-Based Coding as a Tool for Preservation

This code also illustrated how FBCs can work in coordination with existing Historic Resource Plans to be a highly effective tool for preserving historic neighborhoods.

### Reinforcing the Unique Local Character

*Regulations to Support the Artist Community*

Benicia has a very strong artist community. Thus, it was important when defining the mixed-use nature of the entire downtown to consider how artist studios and galleries could be accommodated off of the alleys in a way that would support this way of life. In addition, the allowance of live/work, shopfront building types in the Town Center-Open zone was done with an artist's lifestyle in mind.

*Reintroducing Galleries to Main Street*

The downtown historically had wooden galleries over the sidewalks that, over time, had been torn down or had burned down. The Master Plan reintroduced the galleries along the main street, and the Form-Based Code allowed them to encourage reinstating this unique character in future building modifications or new construction.

## Implementation

### Code Administration

The Form-Based Code was adopted on April 3, 2007, and is currently being administered by the city staff.

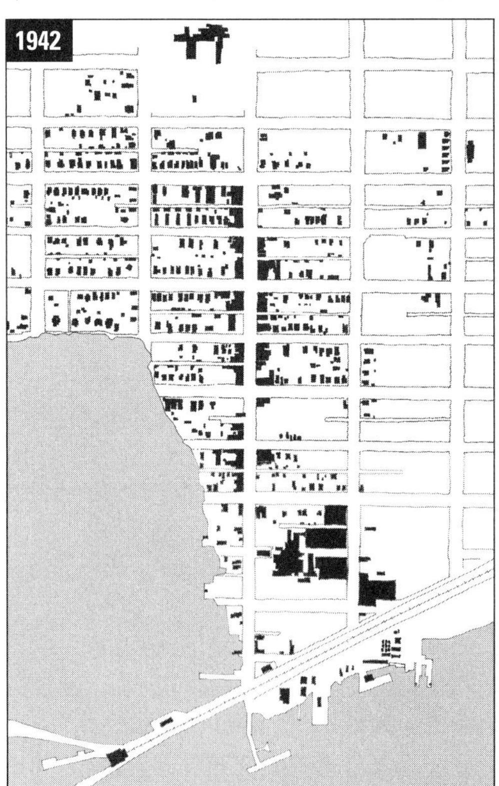


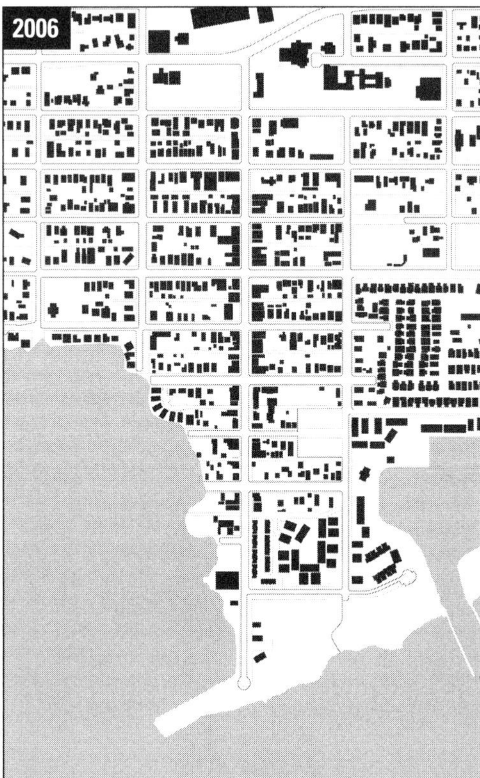


**Fig. 4.14** Historical analysis of downtown Benicia

### Lessons Learned

The Architectural Standards that existed within the Historic Resource Plan were merely adequate and will not ensure high-quality design consistent with the historic buildings. Therefore, if this process were done over again, the team would push to get the scope and budget expanded to include the creation of an architectural pattern book based on the local historic styles. Having a pattern book as a tool for review would help this community get higher-quality architectural design and reinforce the high-quality urbanism regulated by the FBC.

## Zone Descriptions

**Town Core (TC):** The primary intent of this zone is to enhance the vibrant, pedestrian-oriented character of First Street. The physical form and uses are regulated to reflect the urban character of the historic shopfront buildings. Mixed use within this zone primarily refers to vertical mixed use where retail or commercial uses are on the ground floor and residential or commercial uses are above.

**Town Core-Open (TC-O):** The primary intent of this zone is to regulate the physical form of shopfront buildings along the side streets between First and Second Street in order to provide an appropriate transition from First Street into the residential neighborhoods. The physical form of a shopfront building is regulated while allowing flexibility in use. Mixed use within this zone is defined by the flexibility and compatibility in use, allowing retail, commercial, or residential live/work uses in a shopfront form.

**Neighborhood Center (NC):** The primary intent of this zone is to reinforce and enhance the pedestrian-oriented character of locally serving retail and commercial uses along the existing commercial centers on East and West Second Streets. The physical form varies to reflect the urban character of the historic shopfront buildings, the residential character of adjacent residential buildings, or the civic character of existing buildings, such as old churches. Mixed use within this zone refers to vertical and horizontal mixed use where retail and commercial uses are permitted on the ground floor at the street edge and residential and commercial uses are permitted above or behind in ancillary buildings. All of this is at a scale and form that is appropriate to its neighborhood context adjacent to residential uses and forms.

**Neighborhood General (NG):** The primary intent of this zone is to protect the integrity and quality of the downtown residential neighborhoods. Appropriately scaled ancillary buildings are allowed to accommodate residential, home-office, or workshop uses.

**Neighborhood General-Open (NG-O):** The primary intent of this zone is to ensure a residential physical form to relate to adjacent residential buildings along the side streets between First Street and Second Street in order to provide an appropriate transition from First Street into the residential neighborhoods. The physical form of a residential building is regulated while allowing flexibility in use. This zone is applied to buildings with an existing residential form that has been compromised by on-site or adjacent development, making pure residential use inappropriate. Commercial and residential uses are allowed in this area in a residential form in the main buildings, as well as in the ancillary buildings.

# Neighborhood General (NG) Standards

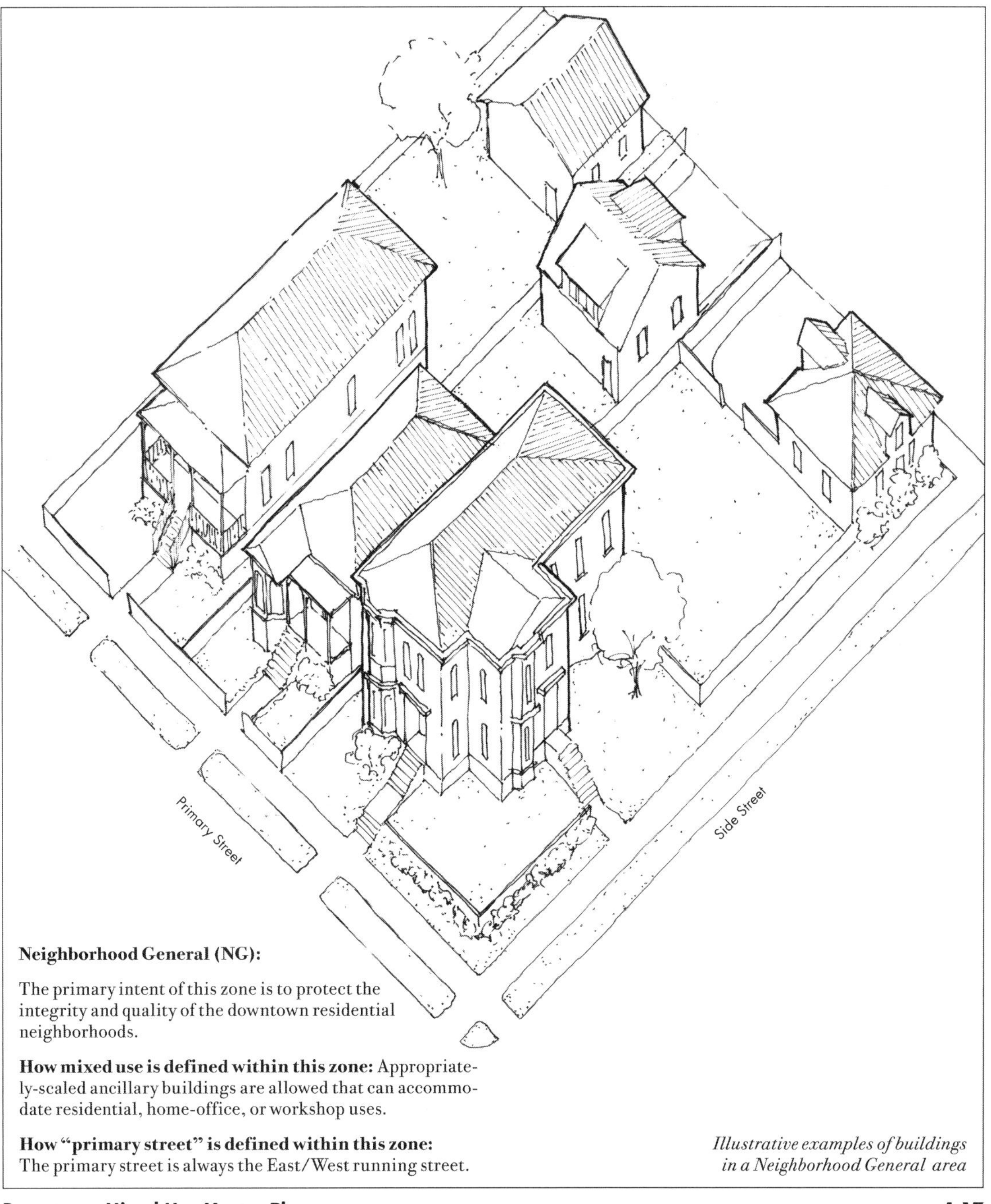


**Neighborhood General (NG):**

The primary intent of this zone is to protect the integrity and quality of the downtown residential neighborhoods.

**How mixed use is defined within this zone:** Appropriately-scaled ancillary buildings are allowed that can accommodate residential, home-office, or workshop uses.

**How "primary street" is defined within this zone:** The primary street is always the East/West running street.

*Illustrative examples of buildings in a Neighborhood General area*



**Fig. 4.15** Neighborhood General Building Form Standards, page 1

Chapter 4: Form-Based Code — Draft: 12.22.06

# Neighborhood General (NG) Standards

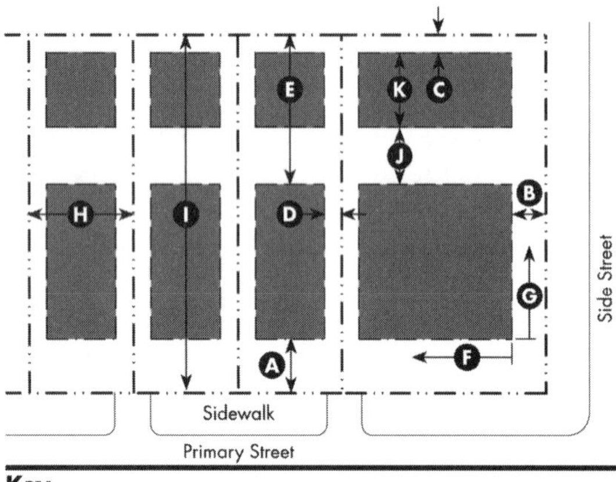




**Key**

-··- Property Line — --- Setback Line

-·- Build-to Line (BTL) — ■ Building Area

## Building Placement

| Build-to Line (Distance from Property Line) | | |
|---|---|---|
| Front | 20′ * | A |
| Side Street | 10′ | B |
| Rear, Ancillary Building | 5′ | C |

*May be reduced to meet furthest back adjacent BTL if adjacent BTL is less than 20′ from property line.

| Setback (Distance from Property Line) | | |
|---|---|---|
| Side | 4′ one side, 8′ other | D |
| Rear, Main Building | 40′ | E |

The windows along any portion of a building that project beyond the rear façade of adjacent homes must be privacy windows if the façade is 10′ or less from the side property line.

Any decks on the rear of homes greater than 2′ above grade must have a privacy screen toward neighboring lots.

| Building Form | | |
|---|---|---|
| Primary Street Façade built to BTL | 50% min. | F |
| Side Street Façade built to BTL | 30% min. | G |
| Lot Width | 50′ max. | H |
| Lot Depth | 150′ max. | I |
| Distance between buildings | 10′ min. | J |
| Depth of ancillary building | 28′ max. | K |
| Footprint of ancillary building | 700 sf max. | |

## Use

| | | |
|---|---|---|
| Ground Floor | Residential, or Services | L |
| Upper Floor(s) | Residential, or Services | M |

*See Table 4.4 for specific uses.

## Height

| | | |
|---|---|---|
| Building Max. | 2.5 stories and 30′ max.* | N |
| Ancillary Building Max. | 1.5 stories and 15′ max.* | |
| Finish Ground Floor Level | 18″ min. above sidewalk** | O |
| First Floor Ceiling Height | 10′ min. clear | P |
| Upper Floor Ceiling Height | 8′ min. clear | Q |

*All heights measured to eaves or base of parapet.

**6″ on downslope lots.

**Notes**

Mansard roof forms are not allowed.

4-22

Downtown Mixed Use Master Plan
Opticos Design, Inc.

**Fig. 4.16** Neighborhood General Building Form Standards, page 2

# Neighborhood General (NG) Standards

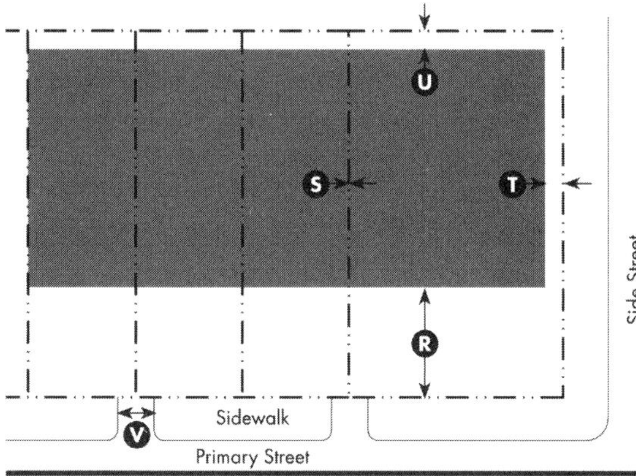


**Key**

- ·-·- Property Line
- ■ Parking Area

**Key**

- ·-·- Property Line
- - - Setback Line
- — — Build-to Line (BTL)
- ■ Encroachment Area

| Parking | | |
|---|---|---|
| **Location (Distance from Property Line)** | | |
| Front Setback | 20′ | R |
| Side Setback | 0′ | S |
| Side Street Setback | 5′ | T |
| Rear Setback | 5′ | U |
| **Required Spaces** | | |
| Residential Uses | | |
| Studio unit | ½ space | |
| 1-2 bedroom unit | 1 space | |
| 3+ bedroom unit | 1 space plus additional ½ space for every bedroom over two | |
| Other uses | | |
| Uses < 3,000 sf | No off-street parking required | |
| On lots without alley access, a one-unit ancillary structure up to 400 sf may be built without requiring additional parking. | | |
| **Notes** | | |
| Parking Drive Width | 11′ max. | V |
| No more than a single space of parking is allowed in front of the front façade plane. | | |
| 50% of the on-street parking spaces adjacent to lot can count toward parking requirements. | | |

| Encroachments | | |
|---|---|---|
| **Location** | | |
| Front | 10′ max. | W |
| Side Street | 8′ max. | X |
| **Notes** | | |
| Porches, Balconies, and Bay Windows may encroach into the setback on the street sides, as shown in the shaded areas. | | |

| Allowed Frontage Types *(see page 4-30)* | |
|---|---|
| Stoop | |
| Depth | 4′ min., 6′ max. |
| Forecourt | |
| Depth | 20′ min., not to exceed width |
| Width | 20′ min., 50% of lot width max. |
| Porch | |
| Depth | 8′ min. |
| Height | 2 stories max. |
| Common Lawn | |
| Porch Depth | 8′ min. |



**Fig. 4.17** Neighborhood General Building Form Standards, page 3

# Neighborhood General (NG) Standards

**Table 4.4: Neighborhood General (NG) Zone Allowed Land Uses and Permit Requirements**

| Land Use Type[1] | Permit Required | Specific Use Regulations |
|---|---|---|
| **Recreation, Education & Public Assembly** | | |
| Park, playground | MUP | |
| School, public or private | MUP | |
| **Residential** | | |
| Dwelling: Single family | P | |
| Home occupation | | |
| < 300 sf, 2 or fewer employees | P | |
| > 300 sf, 3 or fewer employees | P[3] | |
| > 300 sf, 3 or more employees | NA | |
| Dwelling: Multi-family-Duplex | P | |
| Ancillary Building | P | |

| Land Use Type[1] | Permit Required | Specific Use Regulations |
|---|---|---|
| **Retail** | | |
| General retail, except with any of the following features: | | |
| Alcoholic beverage sales | NA | |
| Floor area over 8000 sf | NA | |
| On-site production of items sold | P[3] | |
| Operating between 9 pm and 7 am | NA | |
| **Services: Business, Financial, Professional** | | |
| Office: Professional, administrative | P[3] | |
| **Services: General** | | |
| Bed & Breakfast | | |
| 4 guest rooms or less | P | |
| Greater than 4 guest rooms | MUP | |
| Day care center: Child or adult | MUP | |
| Day care center: Large family | UP | |
| Day care center: Small family | P | |
| **Transportation, Communications, Infrastructure** | | |
| Wireless telecommunications facility | MUP | |

| Key | |
|---|---|
| P | Permitted Use |
| MUP | Minor Use Permit Required - staff review only |
| UP | Use Permit Required |
| NA | Not an allowed use |

**End Notes**

[1] A definition of each listed use type is in the Glossary.

[2] Allowed only on upper floors or behind ground floor use.

[3] Allowed only in ancillary buildings



**Fig. 4.18** Neighborhood General Building Form Standards, page 4

T4R

# Miami 21 SmartCode

## Miami, Florida

**Fig. 4.19** (previous page) Illustrations of various transect zones in the Miami 21 FBC

THE CITY OF MIAMI, Florida, has an estimated population of 390,000.[3] The city decided to replace its existing zoning code with a SmartCode. Because of the size and complexity of Miami, it was first thought that the city would start by rezoning the corridors only. By the time the quarter-mile radius was added to the Plan from these corridors, almost the entire city was included. It was then that the city decided to split Miami into quadrants that would be coded individually. The first quadrant selected was the East Quadrant, which is bounded by the city limits at 82nd Street on the north, Interstate I-95 on the west, 15th Street and the Miami River on the south, and the Biscayne Bay on the east. This was more feasible, especially since it was decided that a Form-Based Code would be required, not optional as had originally been discussed.

#### Client's Background in Form-Based Coding

Prior to the initiation of Miami 21, Duany Plater-Zyberk & Company (DPZ) and various other firms had completed neighborhood plans that had proposed FBCs as an implementation tool that ultimately led to the discussion of the application of FBCs to the entire city. In addition, a booming economy reinforced inconsistencies in the existing code and highlighted the conflict between new towers and existing single-family neighborhoods. Manny Diaz, the mayor, was instrumental in pushing the Miami 21 process and a Form-Based Code as a means of making Miami a more sustainable city and protecting the character of neighborhoods while allowing growth and evolution. The mayor was strongly influenced by his participation in the Mayor's Institute on City Design.

## Code Components

Before the start of the Miami 21 code, there was no clear plan in place to guide development driven by the city's policies. The city's Comprehensive Plan established densities as the primary basis for build-out with little regulation to create predictable outcome from the zoning code. The Comprehensive Plan also opened the door for unlimited density in downtown to reinforce the downtown as the central node of the city. The challenge for the Miami 21 code was to work within these established densities and to strike a balance between the parts of the city that were dense or regulated to become dense, and those that existed as single-family neighborhoods, which also needed to be reinforced. In addition, the Miami 21 code was working to establish a nodal pattern of growth along es-

| | Miami 21 SmartCode |
|---|---|
| Status: | Submitted (June 2007) |
| Scale: | Part of a City/Town (Quadrant) |
| Implementation Method: | Mandatory and Integrated |
| Site Context: | Redevelopment/Infill<br>Greyfield |
| Site Size: | |
| Administration: | City/County staff |
| Organizing Principle: | Transect (SmartCode) |
| Code Consultants(s): | Duany Plater-Zyberk & Company |
| Agency: | City of Miami |

tablished corridors. All of this change and increased intensity was to be regulated to ensure an appropriate transition in height and density.

The Miami 21 code established Building Form Standards, Public Space Standards, Frontage Types, and general Landscape and Architectural Standards. This FBC chose not to regulate building types directly because the goal was to regulate the private realm simply to the point that it would produce a good public realm.

### Organizing Principle

Miami 21 is a SmartCode, which uses the transect as the organizing principle. The transect was customized to address the variety and complexity of physical size and use needed in Miami.

## Code Process

1. Complete analysis of uses; city narrowed list of uses to delete redundancies
2. Thorough analysis of existing code
3. Neighborhood, district, corridor analysis
4. Synoptic survey of different existing T-Zones
5. Determination of how existing zones translated into the T-Zones
6. Full analysis of development capacities in the current code versus proposed code
7. Studies of how corridors would evolve appropriately in size and transition into single-family neighborhoods
8. Building Form Standards draft

### Public Participation

An extended dialogue approach to outreach was used for the Miami 21 FBC, and possibly entailed one of the most extensive public outreach processes ever used in the country. The launch meeting was held in April 2005. Approximately three months after the launch, the code team presented general concepts to the public. This status presentation was quickly followed by open houses in each of the five sub-areas of the selected quadrant. Taking this information from the public meetings, the team worked to create the initial draft, which was presented to the public in May 2006. Also in May, public workshops were held for each of the individual sub-areas within the Plan. In July 2006, a general Miami 21 open house was held. In November, a progress presentation was given. The last open house was held in March 2007. On April 4, 2007, there was a Planning Advisory Board workshop, and on April 18, the Planning Advisory Board took action and approved the draft code and then sent it on to the city commission for review. As of May 30, 2007, dates for the city commission hearings have yet to be set. In addition to the formal meetings mentioned above, throughout the process the city staff and the consultants continually met with concerned property owners, their attorneys and architects, and other stakeholders to address issues related to the code.

During the evolution of the code and its components, the code team tested various graphic ways of presenting the intended size and character of each of the T-Zones. First they tried before-and-after images, next they tried video walk-throughs, and finally they decided upon the watercolor perspectives shown here. These have proven to be the most successful representation of the T-Zones for public understanding.

## Advanced Application of FBCs

As the first application to a major city, this code made really major advancements to the SmartCode and to the practice of Form-Based Coding in general. These advancements included the creation of several different types of subsets of the transect zones, the concept of allowing additional entitled square footage through a public benefit program, the reduction of uses from

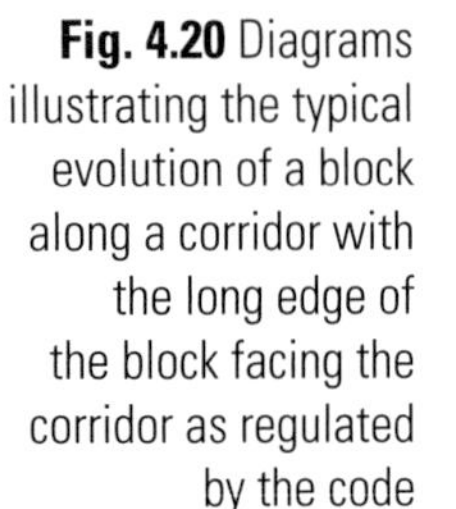

**Fig. 4.20** Diagrams illustrating the typical evolution of a block along a corridor with the long edge of the block facing the corridor as regulated by the code

360 to 46, the creation of different sections that are necessary for a city-wide code that were not previously in the SmartCode, the overall scale of the application of a Form-Based Code to a major American city, and a few other innovative elements mentioned below.

### Sub T-Zones

Each of the T-zones is broken down into subsets: Restricted (R), Limited (L), and Open (O). This differentiates areas that are generally zoned for a similar intensity of development but regulated for different uses, parking requirements, and/or frontages based on their exact location.

T3 replaces the R1 zones and is the only zone that requires detached housing types. The T3-R zone allows only a principal building with a maximum of 9 dwelling units (du)/acre, while T3-L and T3-O both allow up to 18 du/acre. T3-L allows one detached outbuilding with a minimum of 10 feet between structures, and T3-O allows an attached two-family residence, a duplex, or a detached outbuilding.

All the T4 zones have the same allowed density at 36 du/acre and the same regulations for general physical form. T4-R allows only residential uses and residential-appropriate frontages, T4-L allows residential or live/work, and T4-O allows residential, live/work, or commercial uses. Both T4-L and T4-O allow shopfront and awning frontages, but they are still regulated to maintain the 10-foot minimum setback that is standard in all T4 zones.

All the T5 zones have the same allowed density at 65 du/acre and the same regulations for general physical form. T5-R allows only residential uses and residential-appropriate frontages. T5-L allows residential or live/work. T5-O allows residential, live/work, or commercial uses. Both T5-L and T5-O allow shopfront and awning frontages, but they are still regulated to maintain the 10-foot minimum setback that is standard in all T5 zones.

There are two different ways in which the T6 zones divide into subzones. Similar to the above-described T-Zones, the T6 divides into R, L, and O subzones, but in addition, the Miami 21 FBC also breaks T6 zones into subzones based on differences in the allowed physical form, primarily height. T6-R allows only primarily residential and compatible uses. T6-L allows live/work, or commercial uses on up to four floors. T6-O allows all of the above or commercial uses on all floors. Since all these subzones regulate the same physical form and simply allow different uses, there is only one set of Building Form Standards for all of these. The differences are highlighted in Tables 3 and 4 of the code. Building Form Standards have been created for each of the T6-8, T6-12, T6-24, T6-36, T6-48 subzones. The numbers at the end of the zone name apply to the allowed number of floors.

### Public Benefit

This aspect of the code deals with the fact that the growing infrastructure needs of the city of Miami are greater than the city's capacity to provide them. The Public Benefits Program allows bonus building capacity in T6 zones in exchange for the developer's contribution either to a specific program within the project or outside the project, or simply through a financial contribution based on the additional square footages' value. The program includes workforce housing, waterfront access to parks, public space, historic preservation, development of brownfield sites, and Leadership in Energy and Environmental Design (LEED) rating of a building. An economic consultant carefully calculated the established values for this system. The program does not apply to T6 designated lots that are adjacent to T3 zones to ensure an appropriate transition between T6 and T3 zones.

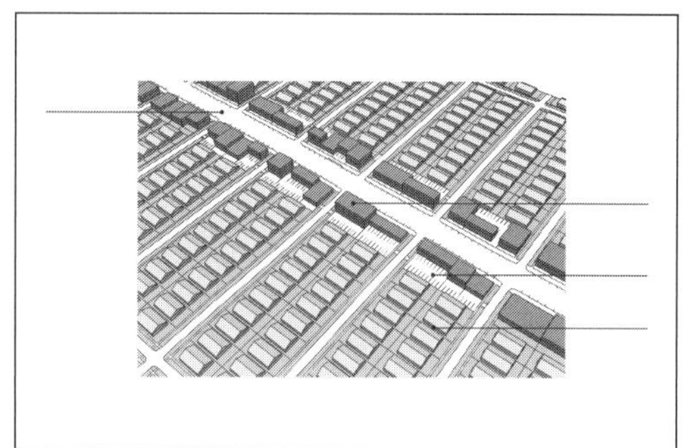

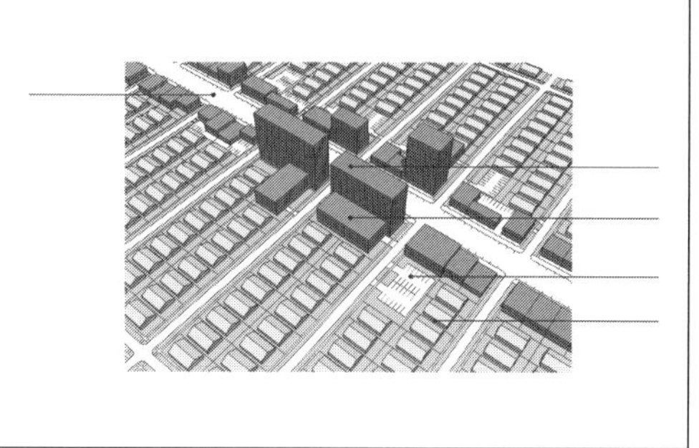

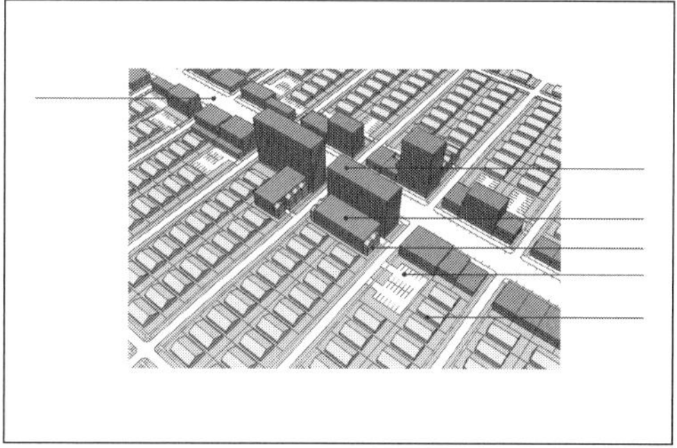

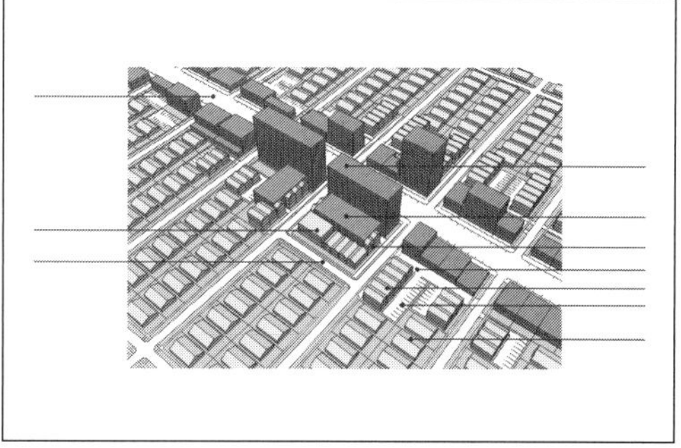

**Fig. 4.21** Diagrams illustrating the typical evolution of a block along a corridor with the short edge of the block facing the corridor as regulated by the code



Following is a summary of benefits extracted from the draft of the Miami 21 code.

*General*

- T6-8: eight-story maximum; bonus to 12 stories, FLR 5; bonus to 125 percent
- T6-12: twelve-story maximum; bonus to 20 stories, FLR 8, bonus to 130 percent

- T6-24: twenty-four story maximum; bonus to 48 stories, FLR 6, bonus to 130 percent
- T6-36: thirty-six-story maximum; bonus to 60 stories, FLR 12 or 22, bonus to 140 percent
- T6-48: forty-eight-story maximum; FLR 30; bonus to unlimited

*Green Building*

Additional square feet shall be allowed for buildings certified by the U.S. Green Building Council as follows:

- Silver: for buildings under 50,000 square feet, 2.0 percent of the floor lot ratio (FLR)
- Gold: 6.0 percent of the FLR
- Platinum: 14.0 percent of the FLR

This concept is further explained in *Section 3.12 Public Benefits Program* of the Miami 21 code.

### Structure of the Document

The structure of the Miami 21 code is a vast improvement over the general SmartCode in relation to a citywide application and is a good reference for other cities and FBC practitioners creating citywide Form-Based Codes. The following is the general structure:

Article 1: Definitions
Article 2: General Provisions
Article 3: General to All Zones
Article 4: Standards Tables
Article 5: Specific to Zones
Article 6: Supplemental Regulations
Article 7: Procedures and Nonconformities
Article 8: Thoroughfares

Overall, the scale of the application and size of the city to which it is being applied make the Miami 21 code an exemplar application of FBCs.

### Reinforcing the Unique Local Character

The following elements were included within the FBC to ensure that local conditions were appropriately addressed.

*Abutting T-Zone Transitions*

One of the primary objectives of the Miami 21 code was to provide appropriate relationships between the primarily single-family and the more intense adjacent zones. Therefore, a quick and appropriate transition into adjacent single-family neighborhoods was regulated, in the Building Form Standards, with the addition of different stepping and height requirements based on which T-Zone the lot or project abuts.

*Floor Plate Maximums*

Without proper regulations, new infill buildings were being built in Miami that had extremely large floor plates, which made it nearly impossible for them to fit into their context or provide a transition between zones. Therefore, within the T6 zones the Building Form Standards contain maximum floor plate sizes of 15,000 square feet for residential and lodging uses, and 30,000 square feet for office and commercial uses.

*Regulation by Net Lot Area and Gross Floor Area versus Gross Lot Area and Net Floor Area*

The existing Miami code calculated its FAR by using Gross Lot Area (GLA) and Net Floor Area (NFA). This made results incredibly unpredictable because buildings along wider thoroughfares, the waterfront, and parks and other public spaces automatically had more developable square footage than was allowed because the measurement of the gross lot size was taken from the centerline of the thoroughfare and a designated distance into the water or public space. In addition, the NFA regulation did not count parking, circulation, and other service-related square footage, thus allowing more overall square footage to fit within the regulated FAR.

The code team first considered removing FAR regulations and finding another way to regulate the same conditions. However, because of both the comfort the city and staff had with using FAR and the desire to create variety in building size and to provide assurance for developers and their attorneys, the FAR regulation was kept. The name was changed to Floor Lot Ratio (FLR), and it is calculated using Net Lot Area (NLA) and Gross Floor Area (GFA). This ensures more predictability of the ultimate developable envelope of the building because it is based on the actual size of the lot and aggregate square footage.

*Trees Required in Front Yards*

In T3 zones, a minimum of one tree is required in the front yard to provide reduction in solar heat gain and respite for pedestrians from the sun in the hot Miami climate.

*Parking Requirements Reduced near Transit-Oriented Development*

To create incentive for development near transit, parking requirements for such projects can be reduced. For all T-Zones, the parking requirement can be reduced by 30 percent for lots within 1/2-mile radius of Transit-Oriented Development (TOD) through a waiver.

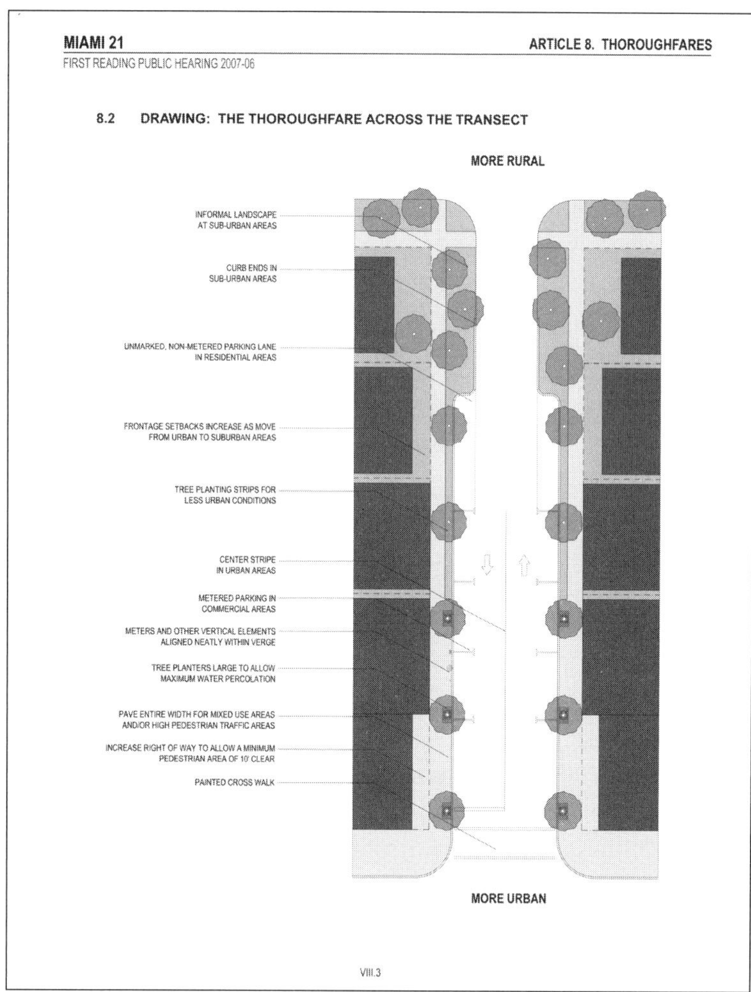


**Fig. 4.22** The thoroughfare across the transect

## Implementation

### Code Administration

The city planning staff will administer the code and have been integrally involved in its creation. In the last month of the revisions, the consultant and the city staff met twice a week to discuss the code modifications so the planning staff knows it well.

That being said, all agencies have not been as equally integrated into the process and are not as informed of the intent. An overview course on the SmartCode would have been beneficial for all the different agencies involved in the final code refinements and approvals.

The code was approved by the Planning Advisory Board and is scheduled to go to the City Commission in early 2008.

## MIAMI 21

DRAFT IN PROGRESS 03.16.07

### TABLE 3 BUILDING FUNCTION: USES

| | T3 SUB-URBAN | | | T4 URBAN GENERAL | | | T5 URBAN CENTER | | | T6 URBAN CORE | | | C CIVIC | | D DISTRICTS | |
|---|---|---|---|---|---|---|---|---|---|---|---|---|---|---|---|---|
| | R | L | O | R | L | O | R | L | O | R | L | O | CI | CS | D1 | D2 |
| DENSITY (UNITS PER ACRE) | 9 | 18 | 18 | 36 | 36 | 36 | 65 | 65 | 65 | 150** | 150** | 150** | AZ*** | N/A | 9 | N/A |
| **RESIDENTIAL** | | | | | | | | | | | | | | | | |
| SINGLE FAMILY RESIDENCE | R | R | R | R | R | R | R | R | R | R | R | R | | | | |
| COMMUNITY RESIDENCE | W | W | W | W | W | W | W | W | W | W | W | W | | | | |
| ANCILLARY UNIT | | R | | R | R | R | | | | | | | | | | |
| TWO FAMILY RESIDENCE | | | R | R | R | R | R | R | R | R | R | R | | | | |
| MULTI FAMILY HOUSING | | | | R | R | R | R | R | R | R | R | R | | | | |
| DORMITORY | | | | | E | E | | R | R | | R | R | | | | |
| HOME OFFICE | R | R | R | R | R | R | R | R | R | R | R | R | | | | |
| LIVE - WORK | | | | | R | R | | R | R | | R | R | | | R | |
| WORK - LIVE | | | | | | | | | | | | | | | R | |
| **LODGING** | | | | | | | | | | | | | | | | |
| BED & BREAKFAST | | | | W | R | R | E | R | R | E | R | R | | | | |
| INN | | | | | | R | | R | R | E | R | R | | | | |
| HOTEL | | | | | | | | R | R | | R | R | | | | |
| **OFFICE** | | | | | | | | | | | | | | | | |
| OFFICE | | | | | R | R | | R | R | | R | R | R | | R | R |
| **COMMERCIAL** | | | | | | | | | | | | | | | | |
| AUTO RELATED | | | | | | | | | W | | W | W | | | R | R |
| ENTERTAINMENT ESTABLISHMENT | | | | | | R | | W | R | | R | R | | | R | R |
| ENTERTAINMENT ESTABL - ADULT | | | | | | | | | | | | | | | | R |
| FOOD SERVICE ESTABLISHMENT | | | | | R | R | | R | R | W | R | R | E | E | R | R |
| ALCOHOL SERVICE ESTABLISHMENT | | | | | R | R | | R | R | | R | R | | | R | R |
| GENERAL COMMERCIAL | | | | | R | R | | R | R | W | R | R | E | E | R | R |
| MARINE RELATED | | | | | | | | W | W | | W | W | | | R | R |
| OPEN AIR RETAIL | | | | | | | | W | W | | W | W | W | W | R | R |
| PLACE OF ASSEMBLY | | | | | | | | R | R | E | R | R | W | W | R | R |
| RECREATIONAL ESTABLISHMENT | | | | | | | | R | R | | R | R | E | E | R | R |
| **CIVIC** | | | | | | | | | | | | | | | | |
| COMMUNITY FACILITY | | | | | W | W | | W | W | | W | W | W | | R | R |
| RECREATIONAL FACILITY | W | W | W | W | R | R | W | R | R | W | R | R | R | R | R | R |
| RELIGIOUS FACILITY | | E | E | | R | R | | R | R | E | R | R | R | | R | R |
| **CIVIL SUPPORT** | | | | | | | | | | | | | | | | |
| COMMUNITY SUPPORT FACILITY | | | E | | W | W | | W | W | | W | W | R | | R | R |
| INFRASTRUCTURE & UTILITIES | W | W | W | W | W | W | W | W | W | W | W | W | W | W | W | R |
| MAJOR FACILITY | | | | | | | | E | E | | E | E | E | | E | E |
| MARINA | | | | E | W | W | E | W | W | E | W | W | R | R | R | R |
| PUBLIC PARKING | | | | | W | W | E | W | W | E | W | W | R | | R | R |
| TRANSIT FACILITIES | | | | | W | W | E | W | W | E | W | W | R | | R | R |
| RESCUE MISSION | | | | | | | | | | | | | E | | E | W |
| **EDUCATIONAL** | | | | | | | | | | | | | | | | |
| CHILDCARE | | | | E | W | W | E | W | W | W | W | W | R | | E | |
| COLLEGE / UNIVERSITY | | | | | | | | W | W | | W | W | R | | E | |
| ELEMENTARY SCHOOL | E | E | E | E | E | E | | W | W | | W | W | R | | E | |
| LEARNING CENTER | | | | | E | E | | R | R | | R | R | R | E | E | |
| MIDDLE / HIGH SCHOOL | E | E | E | E | E | E | | W | W | | W | W | R | | E | |
| PRE-SCHOOL | E | E | E | E | E | E | | R | R | | R | R | R | | E | |
| SPECIAL TRAINING / VOCATIONAL | | | | | | E | | W | W | | W | W | R | | R | R |
| RESEARCH FACILITY | | | | | | | | | | | E | E | R | | W | R |
| **INDUSTRIAL** | | | | | | | | | | | | | | | | |
| AUTO RELATED | | | | | | | | | W | | | W | | | R* | R |
| MANUFACTURING & PROCESSING | | | | | | | | | | | | | | | W* | R |
| MARINE RELATED | | | | | | | | | | | | | | | R* | R |
| PRODUCTS & SERVICES | | | | | | | | | | | | | | | R* | R |
| STORAGE/ DISTRIBUTION FACILITY | | | | | | | | | | | | | | | R* | R |

R Allowed By Right
W Allowed By Warrant: Administrative Process - CRC (Coordinated Review Committee)
E Allowed By Exception: Public Hearing - granted by PZAB (Planning, Zoning & Appeals Board)

Some uses may require Compliance Reviews, Supplemental Regulations and/or State Regulations.
* Refer to Article 6, Section 6.
** Additional densities in some T6 zones are illustrated in Diagram 9.
*** AZ: Density of Abutting Zone

4

**Fig. 4.23** Building Function (Land-Use) Table

## EAST QUADRANT — CODE

DRAFT IN PROGRESS

ADMINISTRATIVE PROCEDURES - COMPARATIVE TABLE

| ZONING ORDINANCE 11000 | MIAMI 21 |
|---|---|
| **CERTIFICATE OF USE / BUILDING PERMIT**<br>**Issued by Zoning / Building staff** | **CERTIFICATE OF USE / BUILDING PERMIT**<br>**Issued by Zoning / Building staff** |
| **CLASS I SPECIAL PERMIT**<br>**Issued by Zoning Administrator**<br>1. Appeal to Zoning Board<br>2. Appeal to City Commission<br>3. Appeal to Circuit Court | **COMPLIANCE REVIEW**<br>**Issued by Zoning Administrator**<br>1. Appeal to Circuit Court |
| **CLASS II SPECIAL PERMIT**<br>May be referred to Urban Development Review Board<br>**Issued by Planning Director**<br>1. Appeal to Zoning Board<br>2. Appeal to City Commission<br>3. Appeal to Circuit Court | **WARRANT**<br>May be referred to Coordinated Review Committee<br>**Issued by Planning Director**<br>1. Appeal to Circuit Court |
| **SPECIAL EXCEPTION**<br>Review & recommendation by Zoning Department<br>Review & recommendation by Planning Department<br>Public hearing by Zoning Board<br>**Issued by Zoning Board**<br>1. Appeal to City Commission<br>2. Appeal to Circuit Court | **EXCEPTION**<br>Review & recommendation by Planning Department<br>Public hearing by Planning, Zoning & Appeals Board (**PZA**)<br>**Issued by PZA Board**<br>1. Appeal to Circuit Court |
| **MAJOR USE SPECIAL PERMIT**<br>Review & recommendation by Zoning Department<br>Review and recommendation by Large Scale Development Committee<br>Review and recommendation by Urban Development Review Board<br>Review & recommendation by Planning Department<br>Public hearing by Zoning Board<br>Public hearing by Planning Advisory Board<br>Public hearing by City Commission<br>**Issued by City Commission**<br>1. Appeal to Circuit Court | |
| **VARIANCE**<br>Review & recommendation by Zoning Department<br>Review & recommendation by Planning Department<br>Public hearing by Zoning Board<br>**Issued by Zoning Board**<br>1. Appeal to City Commission<br>2. Appeal to Circuit Court | **VARIANCE**<br>Review & recommendation by Planning Department<br>Public hearing by Planning, Zoning & Appeals Board (**PZA**)<br>**Issued by PZA Board**<br>1. Appeal to Circuit Court |
| **ZONING INTERPRETATION**<br>**Issued by Zoning Administrator**<br>1. Appeal to Zoning Board<br>2. Appeal to City Commission<br>3. Appeal to Circuit Court | **INTERPRETATION**<br>**Issued by Zoning Administrator**<br>1. Appeal to **PZA** Board<br>2. Appeal to Circuit Court |
| **DETERMINATION OF USE OR CHARACTERISTITCS OF USE NOT SPECIFIED**<br>**Issued by Planning Director**<br>1. Appeal to Zoning Board<br>2. Appeal to City Commission<br>3. Appeal to Circuit Court | **DETERMINATION**<br>**Issued by Planning Director**<br>1. Appeal to **PZA** Board<br>2. Appeal to Circuit Court |

B.3.4

Revision Date: 07.31.06

DUANY PLATER-ZYBERK & COMPANY

**Fig. 4.24** Administrative procedures: old versus new

MIAMI 21 — ARTICLE 5. SPECIFIC TO ZONES

PUBLIC HEARING-FIRST READING 2007-06 — 5.7 URBAN CORE TRANSECT ZONES (T6-48)

BUILDING DISPOSITION

LOT OCCUPATION

| | |
|---|---|
| a. Lot Area | 5,000 s.f. min. |
| b. Lot Width | 100 ft. min. |
| c. Lot Coverage | |
| -1-8 stories | 80%max. |
| - Above 8th story | 18,000 sq. ft. max. floorplate for Residential & Lodging<br>30,000 sq. ft. max. floorplate for Office & Commercial |
| d. Floor Lot Ratio (FLR) | 30 |
| e. Frontage at front setback | 70%min. |
| f. Open Space Requirements | 10%lot area min. |
| g. Density | 150 du/acre max. * |

BUILDING SETBACK

| | |
|---|---|
| a. Principal Front | 10 ft. min. |
| b. Secondary Front | 10 ft. min. |
| c. Side | 0 ft. min.; 30 ft. min. above 8th story |
| d. Rear | 0 ft. min.; 30 ft. min. above 8th story |
| e. Abutting T5 | 0 ft. min. 1st through 5th story<br>10 ft. min. 6th through 8th story<br>30 ft. min. above 8th story |

BUILDING CONFIGURATION

FRONTAGE

| | |
|---|---|
| a. Common Lawn | prohibited |
| b. Porch & Fence | prohibited |
| c. Terrace or L.C. | prohibited |
| d. Forecourt | permitted |
| e. Stoop | permitted |
| f. Shopfront & Awning | permitted |
| g. Gallery | permitted by Special Area Plan |
| h. Arcade | permitted by Special Area Plan |

BUILDING HEIGHT

| | |
|---|---|
| a. Min. Height | 2 stories |
| b. Max. Height | 48 stories |
| c. Max. Benefit Height | unlimited stories abutting all zones except T3 |

* Or as modified in Diagram 9

BUILDING PLACEMENT

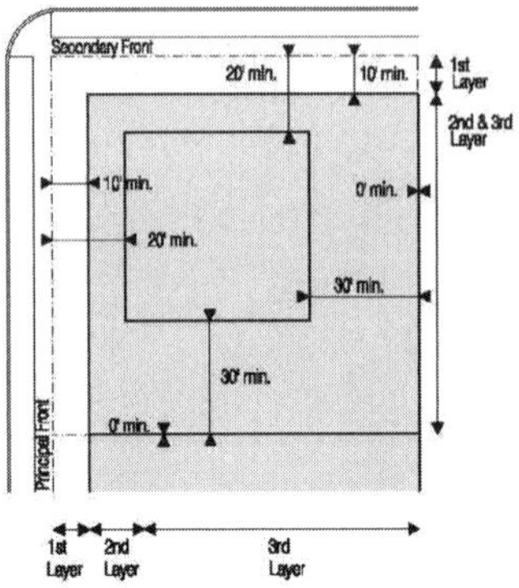

PARKING PLACEMENT

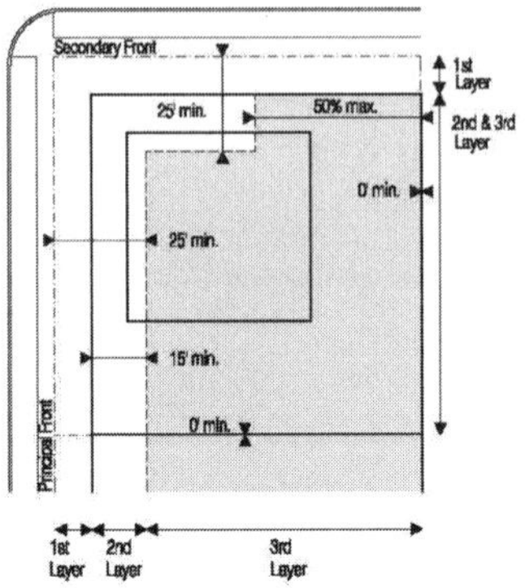

BUILDING HEIGHT

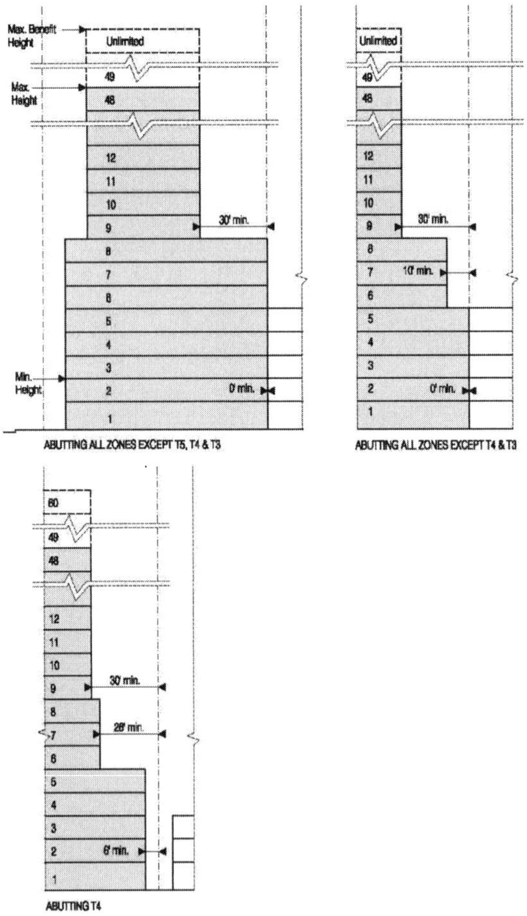

V.33

**Fig. 4.25** T6-48 Building Form Standards. Note how it regulates according to the adjacent zone on the bottom graphic.

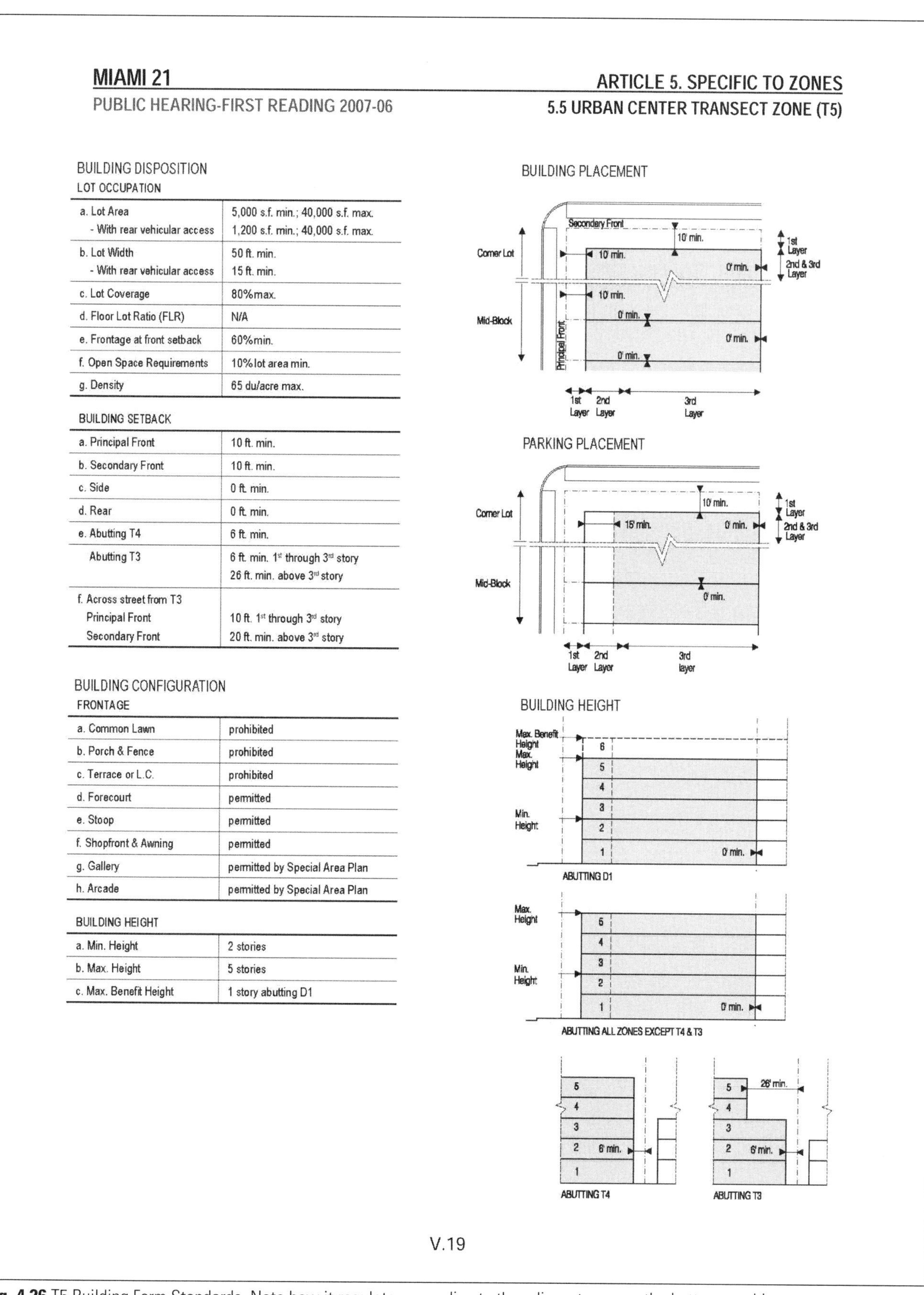

MIAMI 21 ARTICLE 5. SPECIFIC TO ZONES

PUBLIC HEARING-FIRST READING 2007-06 5.5 URBAN CENTER TRANSECT ZONE (T5)

BUILDING DISPOSITION

| LOT OCCUPATION | |
|---|---|
| a. Lot Area | 5,000 s.f. min.; 40,000 s.f. max. |
| - With rear vehicular access | 1,200 s.f. min.; 40,000 s.f. max. |
| b. Lot Width | 50 ft. min. |
| - With rear vehicular access | 15 ft. min. |
| c. Lot Coverage | 80%max. |
| d. Floor Lot Ratio (FLR) | N/A |
| e. Frontage at front setback | 60%min. |
| f. Open Space Requirements | 10%lot area min. |
| g. Density | 65 du/acre max. |

| BUILDING SETBACK | |
|---|---|
| a. Principal Front | 10 ft. min. |
| b. Secondary Front | 10 ft. min. |
| c. Side | 0 ft. min. |
| d. Rear | 0 ft. min. |
| e. Abutting T4 | 6 ft. min. |
| Abutting T3 | 6 ft. min. 1st through 3rd story<br>26 ft. min. above 3rd story |
| f. Across street from T3<br>Principal Front<br>Secondary Front | <br>10 ft. 1st through 3rd story<br>20 ft. min. above 3rd story |

BUILDING CONFIGURATION

| FRONTAGE | |
|---|---|
| a. Common Lawn | prohibited |
| b. Porch & Fence | prohibited |
| c. Terrace or L.C. | prohibited |
| d. Forecourt | permitted |
| e. Stoop | permitted |
| f. Shopfront & Awning | permitted |
| g. Gallery | permitted by Special Area Plan |
| h. Arcade | permitted by Special Area Plan |

| BUILDING HEIGHT | |
|---|---|
| a. Min. Height | 2 stories |
| b. Max. Height | 5 stories |
| c. Max. Benefit Height | 1 story abutting D1 |



V.19

**Fig. 4.26** T5 Building Form Standards. Note how it regulates according to the adjacent zone on the bottom graphic.

MIAMI 21
PUBLIC HEARING-FIRST READING 2007-06

ARTICLE 5. SPECIFIC TO ZONES
5.3 SUB-URBAN TRANSECT ZONE (T3)

BUILDING DISPOSITION

LOT OCCUPATION

| | |
|---|---|
| a. Lot Area | 5,000 s.f. min. |
| b. Lot Width | 50 ft. min. |
| c. Lot Coverage | 50% max. |
| d. Floor Lot Ratio (FLR) | N/A |
| e. Frontage at front setback | N/A |
| f. Green Space Requirements | 25% lot area min. |
| g. Density | T3 R=9 du/acre max.;<br>T3 L=9 du/acre max.;<br>T3 O=18 du/acre max. |

BUILDING SETBACK

| | |
|---|---|
| a. Principal Front | 20 ft. min. |
| b. Secondary Front | 10 ft. min. |
| c. Side | 5 ft. min. |
| d. Rear | 20 ft. min. |

OUTBUILDING SETBACK (T3 L & T3 O ONLY)

| | |
|---|---|
| a. Principal Front | 20 ft. min. |
| b. Secondary Front | 10 ft. min. |
| c. Side | 5 ft. min., 20% lot width total min. |
| d. Rear | 5 ft. min. |

BUILDING CONFIGURATION

FRONTAGE

| | |
|---|---|
| a. Common Lawn | permitted |
| b. Porch & Fence | permitted |
| c. Terrace or L.C. | prohibited |
| d. Forecourt | prohibited |
| e. Stoop | prohibited |
| f. Shopfront & Awning | prohibited |
| g. Gallery | prohibited |
| h. Arcade | prohibited |

BUILDING HEIGHT

| | |
|---|---|
| a. Principal Building | 2 stories and 25 ft. to eave max. |
| b. Outbuilding | 2 stories and 25 ft. to eave max. |

BUILDING PLACEMENT

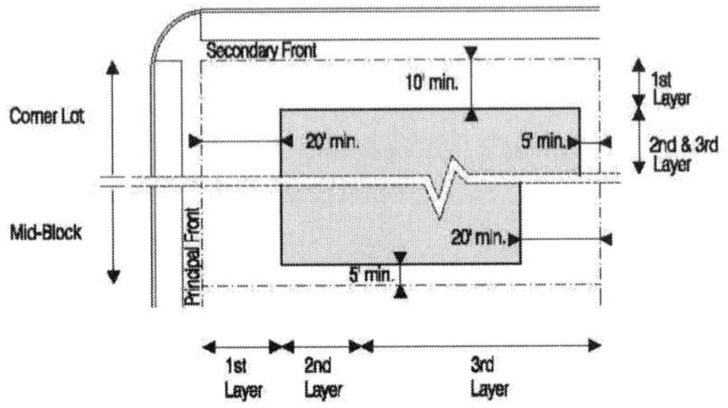

OUTBUILDING PLACEMENT

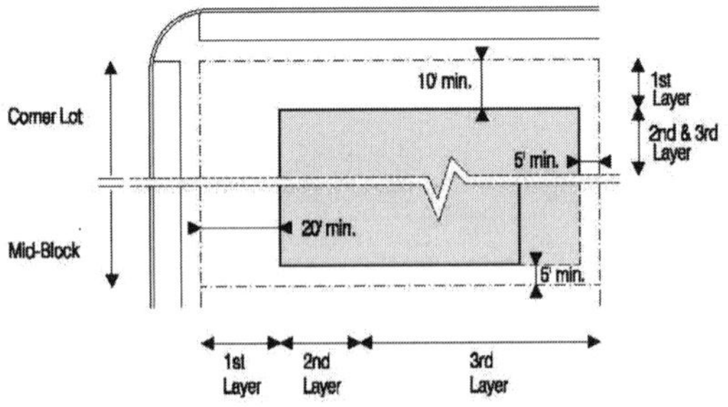

PARKING PLACEMENT

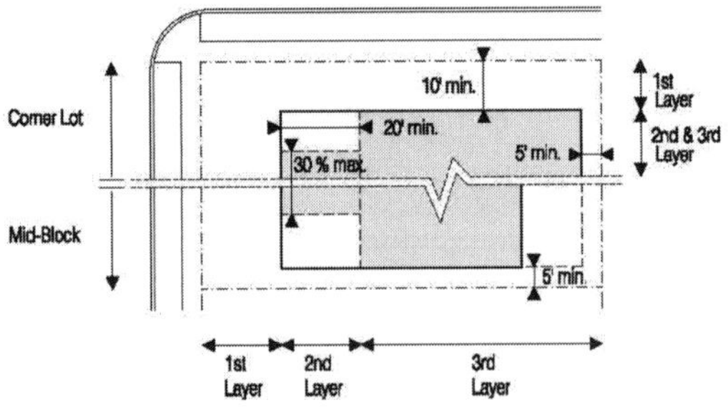

BUILDING HEIGHT

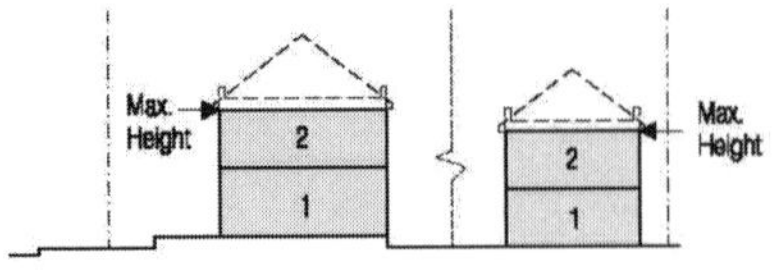

V.7

**Fig. 4.27** T3 Building Form Standards

# Development Code Update and Form-Based Code 

## Grass Valley, California

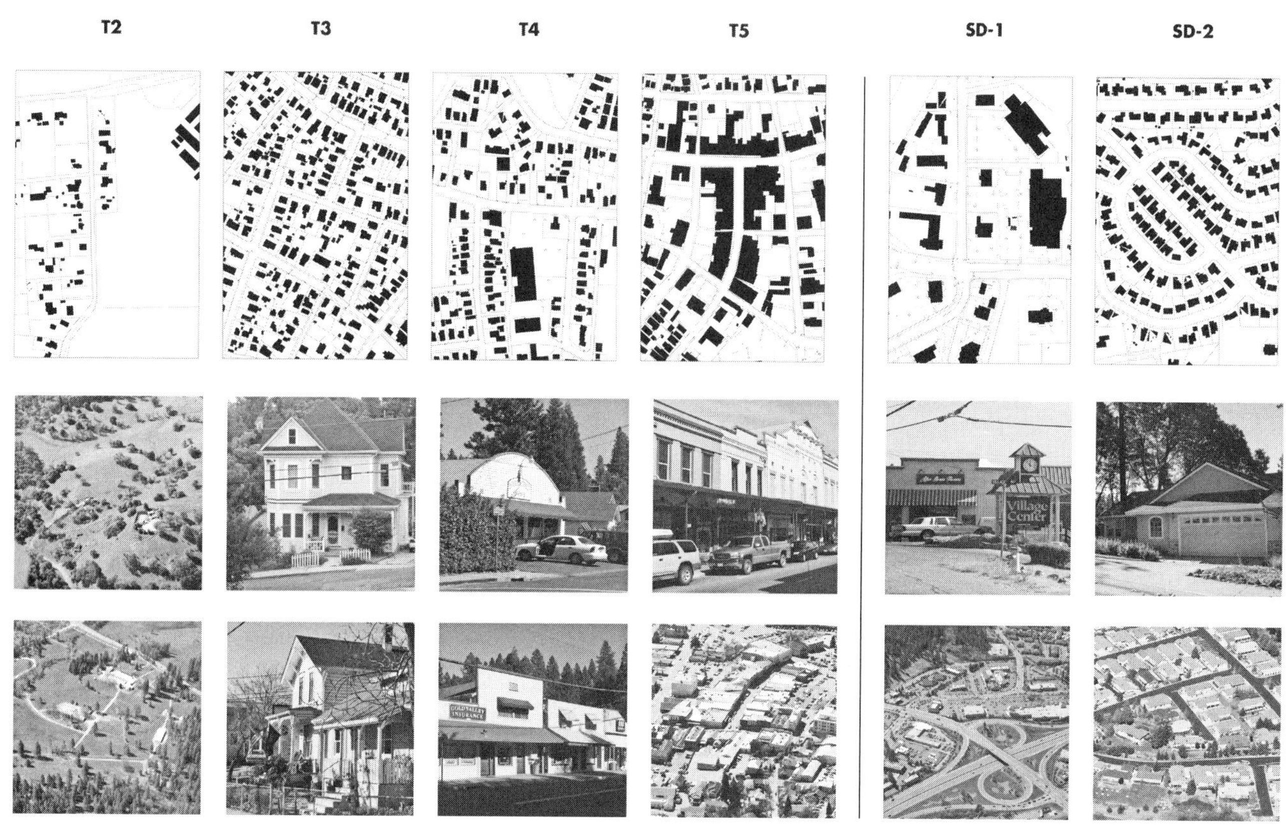

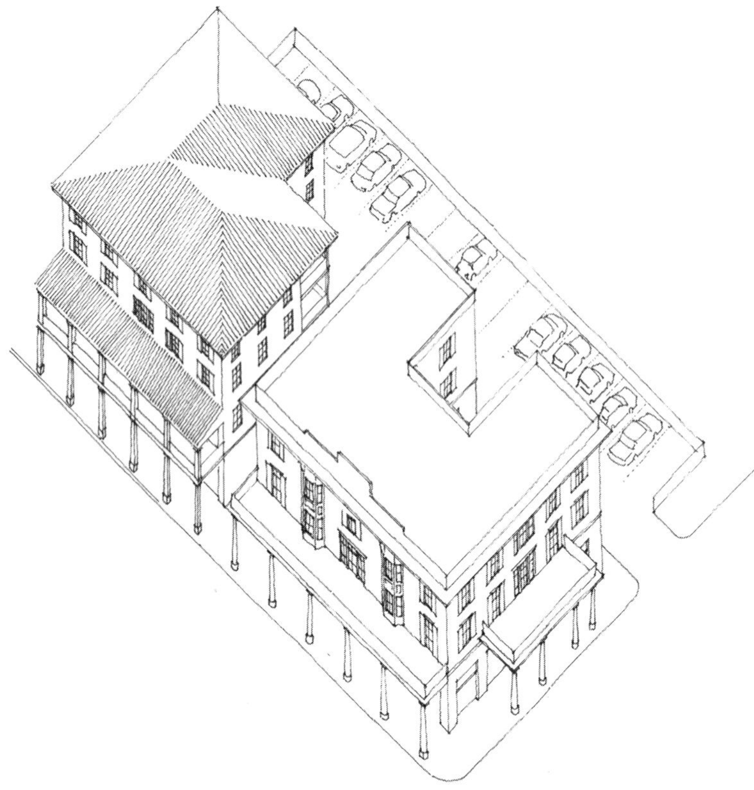

**Fig. 4.28** (previous page) Grass Valley existing conditions transect diagram

**Fig. 4.29** (above) Town Core (TC). The primary intent of this zone is to strengthen the mixed-use, pedestrian-oriented nature of the existing historic downtown. The secondary intent is to establish secondary mixed-use, pedestrian-oriented centers within large, regional districts that are likely to redevelop in the mid- and long-term.

THE CITY OF GRASS VALLEY is located in northern California along the Highway 49 corridor in Nevada County and has a current population of approximately 12,000.[4] The current Zoning Ordinance was originally adopted in 1965 but has been amended many times over the years. Therefore, it was in need of a comprehensive update. The existing development standards encouraged a built environment that is more suburban in context, rather than the type of compact, diverse style of development that had historically occurred in the community and that is further envisioned in the goals and objectives of the city's 2020 General Plan. To meet these goals, the team of Crawford Multari & Clark and Opticos Design, Inc. was selected as part of an open RFP process.

### Client's Background in Form-Based Coding

Community development director Joe Heckel had attended several regional workshops on FBCs. He was particularly impressed with a zoning update by the city of Sonoma, California, which was an early application of Form-Based Coding, and the way it used the design characteristics of the older neighborhoods to set standards for new projects. He decided that a similar FBC that emphasized form over function would be a good tool to help Grass Valley implement its General Plan policy of preserving the unique character of the community.

## Code Components

Although the Comprehensive Plan, or General Plan, had already been completed when the

| | Grass Valley Development Code and FBC Update |
|---|---|
| Status: | Adopted on March 6, 2007 |
| Scale: | Part of a City/Town |
| Implementation Method: | Mandatory and Integrated |
| Site Context: | Greenfield<br>Redevelopment/Infill<br>Greyfield |
| Site Size: | |
| Administration: | City/County staff |
| Organizing Principle: | Transect |
| Code Consultants(s): | Crawford, Multari & Clark Associates; Opticos Design, Inc. |
| Agency: | City of Grass Valley Community Development Department |

FBC team was hired, it had not been created with the foresight of laying the framework for an FBC. In addition, the city had already initiated a Streets Master Plan process and had completed a Downtown Master Plan and a Corridor Plan for the South Auburn Corridor, which was one of the corridors most likely to accommodate new growth in the near term. All the content from these studies and documents had to be reviewed and incorporated into the Development Code Update. In addition, architectural design guidelines were in place for the historic downtown.

### Organizing Principle

The transect was selected as the organizing principle because of its effectiveness in educating the community about the appropriate levels of urbanism within its borders and about the ways that transect-based regulations can reinforce these patterns.

## Code Process

Since a thorough documentation of the place was not completed during the General Plan process, a documentation and analysis phase was utilized to initiate the FBC process in order to gather the information necessary for the FBC. This documentation began at the macro scale and then transitioned to the micro scale. At the macro scale, the team documented the existing neighborhoods, districts, and corridors and created a diagram of these elements. Then the team used the General Plan objectives and planning studies completed by the city to add new neighborhoods, districts, and corridors and designate which elements should be regulated to evolve or be transformed. As part of this macro-scale documentation, the areas that represented typical desired conditions for each of the T-Zones or Form-Based Zones were selected. The characteristics of each of these sampling areas were documented to establish the base content for the Building Form Standards and the Subdivision Ordinance.

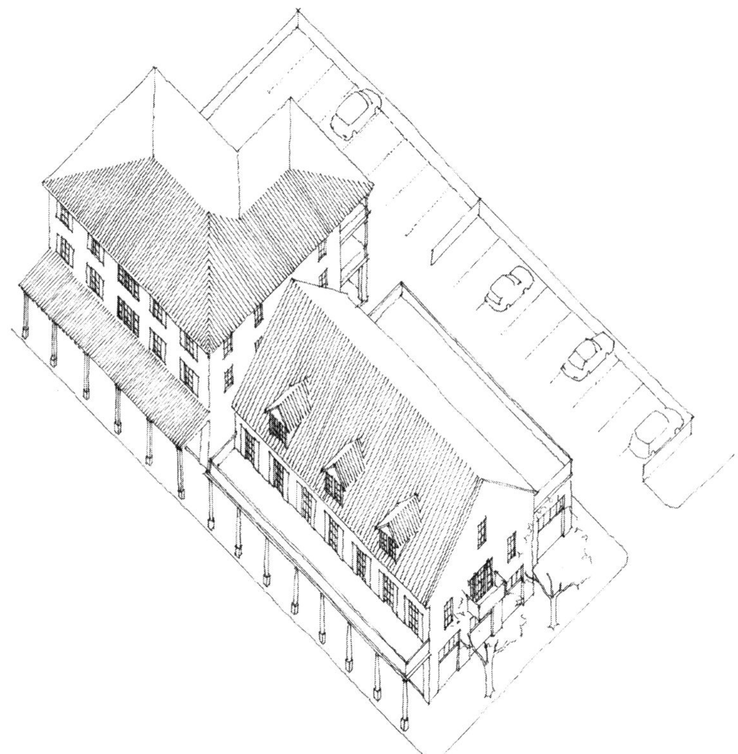

**Fig. 4.30**
Neighborhood Center (NC). The primary intent of this zone is to strengthen the existing neighborhood structure of Grass Valley by promoting and enhancing the vitality of existing neighborhood-serving commercial centers and, thus, promoting pedestrian-oriented neighborhoods. The secondary intent is to create additional mixed-use centers and nodes, for instance along corridors, that will provide focal points for mixed-use infill development.

After the documentation was complete, the FBC team worked with the city to select the areas where the Form-Based Zones would be applied.

Once the areas of application were selected, the FBC team created the document template and outline to be approved by the city. Once these templates were approved, the team worked with staff and the committee to create a draft of the Development Code, including the FBC standards.

### Public Participation

Since one of the primary objectives of the Development Code Update was to implement the goals and objectives of the General Plan, much of the necessary public outreach had been done during that prior process. An advisory com-

**Fig. 4.31** Neighborhood Center-Flex (NC-Flex). The primary intent of this zone is to work in combination with the NC zone to promote the vitality of corridors and centers within different neighborhoods. This zone intends to promote flexibility of use, allowing the market to determine ground-floor character while establishing the built form in order to ensure neighborhood compatibility.

mittee—consisting of two city council members, one planning commission member, and four other community representatives, including one from the local builder's association and a representative of the downtown association—ensured that the Code Update reinforced the Comprehensive Plan vision. Over the three and a half years of the process, the FBC team met a dozen times with the committee. This enabled the committee, as well as the staff, to be educated on how the FBC would work in coordination with the rest of the Development Code and enabled them to ask very specific questions and get answers back from the team. There were then two stakeholder meetings with the property owners and general public at the last two sessions. This process with the committee worked out quite well because it enabled the members of this group to take ownership of the document. When it came time for the document to be heard by the planning commission and the city council, the committee members representing each of these bodies could defend the FBC and answer questions about it.

## Advanced Application of FBCs

### Integrating Form-Based Zones into a Conventional Development Code Framework

In an ideal scenario, Form-Based Zones would have been applied to the entire city, but budget limitations dictated that select areas would be regulated by the Form-Based Zones and the others by conventional zones. The areas selected for the application for Form-Based Zones included the historic downtown, two historic neighborhoods adjacent to the downtown, and a strip commercial corridor in need of improvements. These areas would then become the case studies for later application to similar areas in the city. One of the neighborhoods primarily needed the Form-Based Code to preserve and enhance the existing character, the second needed the FBC to regulate the appropriate evolution of the neighborhood from a primarily single-family into a medium-density neighborhood, and the corridor needed the FBC to show how this single-use, auto-oriented corridor could evolve into a mixed-use, walkable neighborhood.

It is important to note that the framework was put in place so that if the FBC is successful, the Form-Based Zones can be applied to the remaining parts of the city. The Form-Based Zones, as defined, would be applicable to many other areas in the community, although a few new zones may need to be created to address any specific issues that arise as vision plans are created for these additional areas.

#### Adapting the Transect Zones

The Neighborhood General zone was adapted for its specific application to Grass Valley. This zone was broken down into three subzones of NG-1, NG-2, and NG-3, each representing primarily residential areas with different levels of allowed intensity of development. Ranging from lowest (NG-1) to highest intensity (NG-3), the numbers went up as the intensity increased similar to the overall transect. The NG-1 was ultimately dropped because it represented existing suburban subdivisions, which were not necessary to include in the FBC because the city had no desire to change these areas. The NG-3 regulates a creative approach to medium-density housing by regulating small-scale, well-designed infill that allows the historically single-family neighborhoods to evolve into medium-density neighborhoods without compromising the overall character.

A Neighborhood Center zone (T4) was created to reinforce the existing mixed-use neighborhood centers.

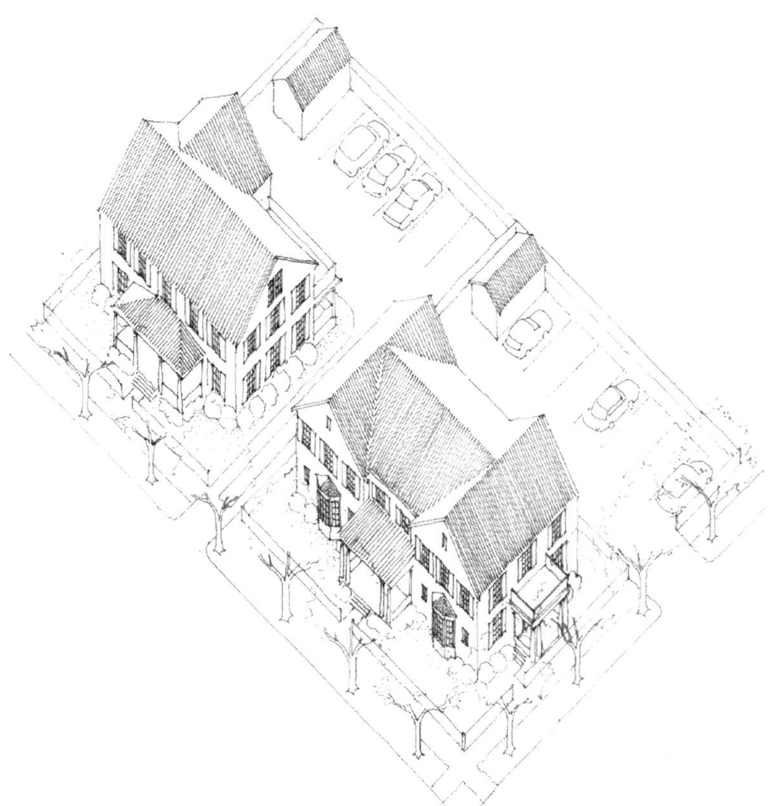

**Fig. 4.32**
Neighborhood General-3 (NG-3). The intent of this zone is to reinforce the character of the existing neighborhood fabric while encouraging additional housing to be provided. This zone will require well-designed density in the form of larger buildings that maintain a compatible size, shape, and scale with existing neighborhood architecture. Good examples of the scale and character of this housing should be large historic homes within the city that have been divided into multiple apartments.

#### Reinforcing the Unique Local Character

*Modifying Build-to Lines for Sites with Topographic Constraints*

Within the code, it was necessary to modify front build-to lines (BTLs) to respond to up-slope and down-slope conditions within the community. In addition, within the FBC, galleries are allowed to encroach over public ROWs in mixed-use areas due to historic precedent for this in the downtown.

*Encouraging Appropriate Infill at Neighborhood Centers*

The parking requirements within the code were very aggressive and, therefore, will go a long way in encouraging the creation of appropriate infill development. With the goal of reinforcing the existing framework of mixed-use, commercial, neighborhood centers, the team was able to incorporate no-parking requirements within Neighborhood Centers for uses under 3,000 square feet.

*Removing Single-Use Commercial District That Was Eroding a Neighborhood*

In addition, the process and Form-Based Code removed the single-use Professional Office zone that had been in place that was compromising the quality of the Empire Hill neighborhood. This zone was converted to NC-Flex to allow for well-designed residential and commercial infill that would support the viability of the Neighborhood Centers.

## Implementation

#### Code Administration

This code was adopted on April 10, 2007. The city is administering the Form-Based Code. Tom Last, the planning director, managed the project from start to finish and was extremely familiar with the FBC by the time it was adopted, which will enable him to work with the staff to administer the FBC. No projects have been submitted under the new Form-Based Code.

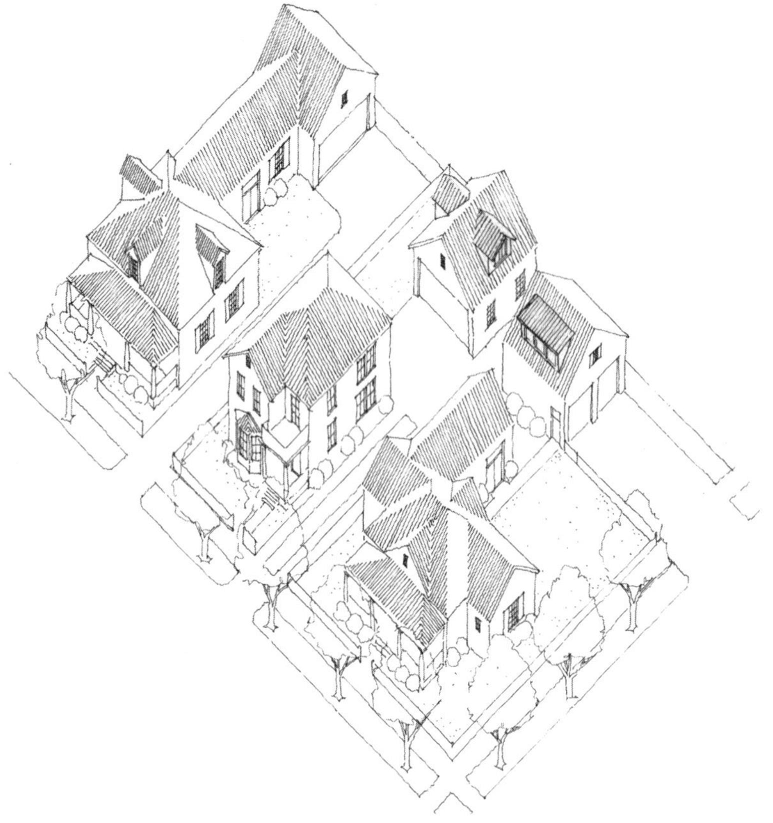

**Fig. 4.33** Neighborhood General-2 (NG-2). The primary intent of this zone is to strengthen the character of existing historic neighborhoods within Grass Valley.

### Lessons Learned

In the process, the one thing that hindered the application of the FBC was the existing General Plan Land-Use designations that had been created during the previous General Plan process. The city of Grass Valley wanted to avoid doing a General Plan update, so the Form-Based Zones had to be consistent with the General Plan Land-Use Map. In some instances, there was not enough flexibility in these uses to allow the form or uses that the team wanted to regulate in order to reinforce the neighborhoods, districts, and corridors within the community. In retrospect, these two processes should have been done in parallel to maximize the benefit and impact of the FBC.

With the components, four things would be approached differently if the code were done over today: (1) the interface with the Streets Master Plan would have been better coordinated; (2) the building types would have been more heavily integrated and regulated; (3) the application of Form-Based Zones would have been more comprehensive; and (4) and the transect zone names would have been more conventional.

The interface with the Streets Master Plan process should have been better coordinated. The very beginning of the Form-Based Coding process saw discussions of the importance of coordinating good street design with good development standards with the objective of creating great places, but the Streets Master Plan ultimately went off on its own tangent and the new street standards created were not pedestrian-oriented in nature.

## Another Form-Based Code for Grass Valley

As of this writing, the city of Grass Valley has a second Form-Based Code that has been submitted for approval. The FBC is within the Loma Rica Ranch Specific Plan, which is a developer-driven, 450-acre Traditional Neighborhood Development on the edge of Grass Valley. The city had specifically designated the several large, potential growth sites as Special Development Areas within their General Plan, requiring each of them to create a detailed Specific Plan to ensure that the growth meets the city's General Plan objectives.

To keep the administration of the Loma Rica Specific Plan FBC as simple as possible for city staff, knowing that the developer was already using the transect as an organizing principle for the FBC, the city requested that the developer use the same formatting and similar, if not the same, transect zones or Form-Based Zones for its Regulating Plan as the city had used for the FBC within its Development Code. The power of the transect as a regulating tool is demonstrated by the fact that it can be used as the organizing principle for a citywide FBC, to regulate within developed neighborhoods, to preserve the historic character, and to regulate growth in greenfield conditions that are in character with the historic patterns of Grass Valley.

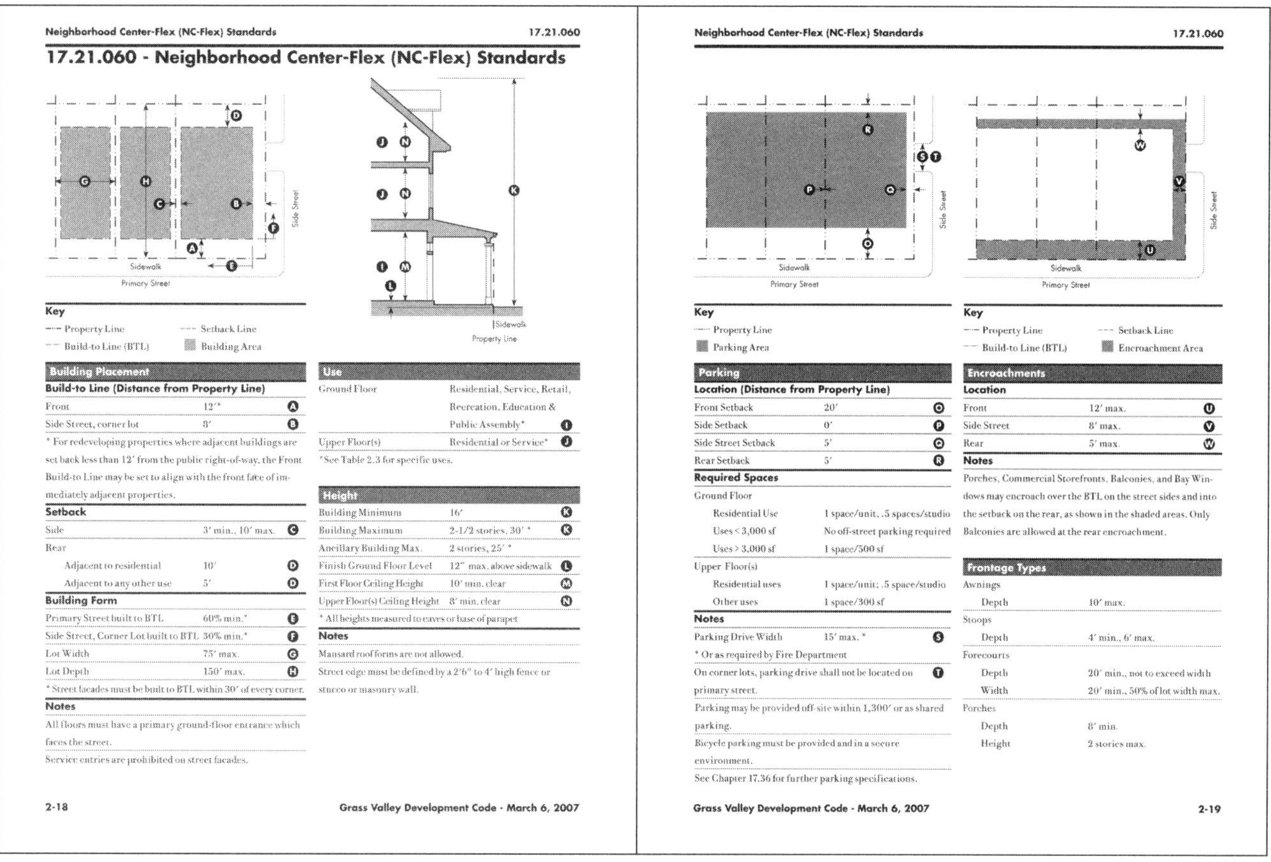

Neighborhood Center-Flex (NC-Flex) Standards 17.21.060

## 17.21.060 - Neighborhood Center-Flex (NC-Flex) Standards

Sidewalk

Primary Street

Side Street

Property Line

**Key**

Property Line — Setback Line — Build-to Line (BTL) — Building Area

**Building Placement**

| Build-to Line (Distance from Property Line) | | |
|---|---|---|
| Front | 12′* | A |
| Side Street, corner lot | 8′ | B |

* For redeveloping properties where adjacent buildings are set back less than 12′ from the public right-of-way, the Front Build-to Line may be set to align with the front face of immediately adjacent properties.

| Setback | | |
|---|---|---|
| Side | 3′ min., 10′ max. | C |
| Rear | | |
| Adjacent to residential | 10′ | D |
| Adjacent to any other use | 5′ | D |

| Building Form | | |
|---|---|---|
| Primary Street built to BTL | 60% min.* | E |
| Side Street, Corner Lot built to BTL | 30% min.* | F |
| Lot Width | 75′ max. | G |
| Lot Depth | 150′ max. | H |

* Street facades must be built to BTL within 30′ of every corner.

**Notes**

All floors must have a primary ground-floor entrance which faces the street.

Service entries are prohibited on street facades.

**Use**

| | | |
|---|---|---|
| Ground Floor | Residential, Service, Retail, Recreation, Education & Public Assembly* | I |
| Upper Floor(s) | Residential or Service* | J |

*See Table 2.3 for specific uses.

**Height**

| | | |
|---|---|---|
| Building Minimum | 16′ | K |
| Building Maximum | 2-1/2 stories, 30′ * | K |
| Ancillary Building Max. | 2 stories, 25′ * | |
| Finish Ground Floor Level | 12″ max. above sidewalk | L |
| First Floor Ceiling Height | 10′ min. clear | M |
| Upper Floor(s) Ceiling Height | 8′ min. clear | N |

* All heights measured to eaves or base of parapet

**Notes**

Mansard roof forms are not allowed.

Street edge must be defined by a 2′6″ to 4′ high fence or stucco or masonry wall.

2-18 Grass Valley Development Code - March 6, 2007

Neighborhood Center-Flex (NC-Flex) Standards 17.21.060

Sidewalk

Primary Street

Side Street

**Key**

Property Line — Parking Area

**Parking**

| Location (Distance from Property Line) | | |
|---|---|---|
| Front Setback | 20′ | O |
| Side Setback | 0′ | P |
| Side Street Setback | 5′ | Q |
| Rear Setback | 5′ | R |

| Required Spaces | |
|---|---|
| Ground Floor | |
| Residential Use | 1 space/unit, .5 spaces/studio |
| Uses < 3,000 sf | No off-street parking required |
| Uses > 3,000 sf | 1 space/500 sf |
| Upper Floor(s) | |
| Residential uses | 1 space/unit; .5 space/studio |
| Other uses | 1 space/300 sf |

**Notes**

Parking Drive Width 15′ max. * S

* Or as required by Fire Department

On corner lots, parking drive shall not be located on primary street. T

Parking may be provided off-site within 1,300′ or as shared parking.

Bicycle parking must be provided and in a secure environment.

See Chapter 17.36 for further parking specifications.

Grass Valley Development Code - March 6, 2007 2-19

Sidewalk

Primary Street

Side Street

**Key**

Property Line — Setback Line — Build-to Line (BTL) — Encroachment Area

**Encroachments**

| Location | | |
|---|---|---|
| Front | 12′ max. | U |
| Side Street | 8′ max. | V |
| Rear | 5′ max. | W |

**Notes**

Porches, Commercial Storefronts, Balconies, and Bay Windows may encroach over the BTL on the street sides and into the setback on the rear, as shown in the shaded areas. Only Balconies are allowed at the rear encroachment.

**Frontage Types**

| | |
|---|---|
| Awnings | |
| Depth | 10′ max. |
| Stoops | |
| Depth | 4′ min., 6′ max. |
| Forecourts | |
| Depth | 20′ min., not to exceed width |
| Width | 20′ min., 50% of lot width max. |
| Porches | |
| Depth | 8′ min. |
| Height | 2 stories max. |

**Fig. 4.34** NC-Flex Building Form Standards

Because of budget constraints, the team decided to work with city staff after the documentation phase to select the areas in which the budget would allow it to apply Form-Based Zones. The team ended up appropriately selecting the historic downtown, several of the adjacent historic neighborhoods, and one underutilized corridor for the application of the Form-Based Zones. In the end, having an FBC and conventional system in place doubled the work of creating the FBC and made the system less clean. Therefore, the team would apply the Form-Based Zones to all historic areas at a minimum to ensure clarity in the system.

**Table 2.3: Neighborhood Center-Flex (NC-Flex) Zone Allowed Land Uses and Permit Requirements**

| Land Use Type[1] | Permit Required | Specific Use Regulations |
|---|---|---|
| **Recreation, Education & Public Assembly** | | |
| Health/fitness facility | MUP | |
| Library, museum | P | |
| Meeting facility, public or private | UP | |
| Park, playground | P | |
| School, public or private | UP | |
| Studio: Art, dance, martial arts, music, etc. | P | |
| **Residential** | | |
| Dwelling: Multi-family - Duplex, triplex, fourplex | P | 17.44.160 |
| Dwelling: Multi-family - Rowhouse | P | 17.44.140 |
| Dwelling: Single family | P | 17.44.210 |
| Home occupation | P | 17.44.100 |
| Live/work unit | P | 17.44.130 |
| Mixed-use project residential component | P | 17.44.140 |
| Residential accessory use or structure | P | 17.44.020 |
| Residential care, 6 or fewer clients, in a home | P | |
| Residential care, 7 or more clients | UP | |
| Second unit or carriage house | P | 17.44.190 |
| **Retail** | | |
| Bar, tavern, night club | UP | |
| General retail, except with any of the following features: | P | |
| Alcoholic beverage sales | MUP | |
| Floor area over 10,000 sf | UP | |
| On-site production of items sold | MUP | |
| Operating between 9pm and 7am | UP | |
| Neighborhood market | MUP | |
| Restaurant, café, coffee shop | MUP | |
| **Services: Business, Financial, Professional** | | |
| ATM | P | |
| Business support service | P | |
| Medical services: Clinic, urgent care | P | |
| Medical services: Doctor office | P | |
| Medical services: Extended care | UP | |
| Office: Business, service | P | |
| Office: Professional, administrative | P | |
| **Services: General** | | |
| Day care center: Child or adult | MUP | 17.44.060<br>17.44.110 |
| Day care center: Large family | P | 17.44.060 |
| Day care: Small family | P | |
| Lodging: Bed & breakfast inn (B&B) | MUP | |
| Lodging: Hotel | MUP | |
| Personal Services | P | |
| Public Safety facility | UP | |
| **Transportation, Communications, Infrastructure** | | |
| Parking facility, public or commercial | UP | |
| Wireless telecommunications facility | UP | 17.46 |

| Key | |
|---|---|
| P | Permitted Use |
| MUP | Minor Use Permit Required |
| UP | Use Permit Required |
| NA | Use Not Allowed |

**End Notes**

[1] A definition of each listed use type is in Article 10 (Glossary).

**Fig. 4.35** Comparison of building types and land uses allowed in NC-Flex (above), NG-3 (top right), and NG-2 (bottom right)

## Table 2.4: Neighborhood General 3 (NG-3) Zone Allowed Land Uses and Permit Requirements

| Land Use Type[1] | Permit Required | Specific Use Regulations |
|---|---|---|
| **Recreation, Education & Public Assembly** | | |
| Library, museum | P | |
| Park, playground | P | |
| Meeting facility, public or private | UP | |
| **Residential** | | |
| Dwelling: Multi-family - Duplex, triplex, fourplex | P | 17.44.160 |
| Dwelling: Multi-family - Rowhouse | P | 17.44.160 |
| Dwelling: Single family | P | 17.44.210 |
| Home occupation | P | 17.44.100 |
| Residential accessory use or structure | P | 17.44.020 |
| Residential care, 6 or fewer clients, in a home | P | |
| Second unit or carriage house | P | 17.44.190 |

| Land Use Type[1] | Permit Required | Specific Use Regulations |
|---|---|---|
| **Retail** | | |
| | NA | |
| **Services: Business, Financial, Professional** | | |
| Medical services: Extended care | UP | |
| **Services: General** | | |
| Day care center: Large family | MUP | 17.44.060 |
| Day care center: Small family | P | |
| Lodging: Bed & breakfast inn (B&B) | MUP | |
| Public safety facility | UP | |
| **Transportation, Communications, Infrastructure** | | |
| | NA | |

## Table 2.5: Neighborhood General 2 (NG-2) Zone Allowed Land Uses and Permit Requirements

| Land Use Type[1] | Permit Required | Specific Use Regulations |
|---|---|---|
| **Recreation, Education & Public Assembly** | | |
| Library, museum | P | |
| Park, playground | P | |
| Meeting facility, public or private | UP | |
| **Residential** | | |
| Dwelling: Multi-family - Duplex | P | 17.44.160 |
| Dwelling: Single family | P | 17.44.210 |
| Home occupation | P | 17.44.100 |
| Residential accessory use or structure | P | 17.44.020 |
| Residential care, 6 or fewer clients, in a home | P | |
| Residential care, 7 or more clients | UP | |
| Second unit or carriage house | P | 17.44.190 |

| Land Use Type[1] | Permit Required | Specific Use Regulations |
|---|---|---|
| **Retail** | | |
| Neighborhood market | UP | |
| **Services: Business, Financial, Professional** | | |
| Medical services: Extended care | UP | |
| **Services: General** | | |
| Day care center: Large family | MUP | 17.44.060 |
| Day care center: Small family | P | |
| Lodging: Bed & breakfast inn (B&B) | MUP | |
| Public safety facility | UP | |
| **Transportation, Communications, Infrastructure** | | |
| | NA | |

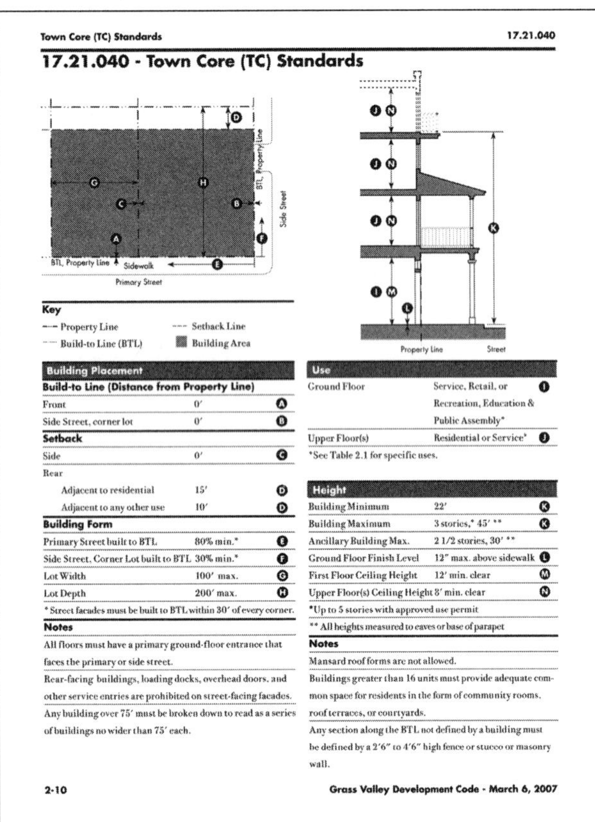

Town Core (TC) Standards 17.21.040

## 17.21.040 - Town Core (TC) Standards

Key
- Property Line
- Build-to Line (BTL)
- Setback Line
- Building Area

| Building Placement | | |
|---|---|---|
| **Build-to Line (Distance from Property Line)** | | |
| Front | 0′ | A |
| Side Street, corner lot | 0′ | B |
| **Setback** | | |
| Side | 0′ | C |
| Rear | | |
| Adjacent to residential | 15′ | D |
| Adjacent to any other use | 10′ | D |
| **Building Form** | | |
| Primary Street built to BTL | 80% min.* | E |
| Side Street, Corner Lot built to BTL | 30% min.* | F |
| Lot Width | 100′ max. | G |
| Lot Depth | 200′ max. | H |

* Street facades must be built to BTL within 30′ of every corner.

**Notes**

All floors must have a primary ground-floor entrance that faces the primary or side street.

Rear-facing buildings, loading docks, overhead doors, and other service entries are prohibited on street-facing facades.

Any building over 75′ must be broken down to read as a series of buildings no wider than 75′ each.

| Use | | |
|---|---|---|
| Ground Floor | Service, Retail, or Recreation, Education & Public Assembly* | I |
| Upper Floor(s) | Residential or Service* | J |

*See Table 2.1 for specific uses.

| Height | | |
|---|---|---|
| Building Minimum | 22′ | K |
| Building Maximum | 3 stories,* 45′ ** | K |
| Ancillary Building Max. | 2 1/2 stories, 30′ ** | |
| Ground Floor Finish Level | 12″ max. above sidewalk | L |
| First Floor Ceiling Height | 12′ min. clear | M |
| Upper Floor(s) Ceiling Height | 8′ min. clear | N |

*Up to 5 stories with approved use permit

** All heights measured to eaves or base of parapet

**Notes**

Mansard roof forms are not allowed.

Buildings greater than 16 units must provide adequate common space for residents in the form of community rooms, roof terraces, or courtyards.

Any section along the BTL not defined by a building must be defined by a 2′6″ to 4′6″ high fence or stucco or masonry wall.

2-10 Grass Valley Development Code - March 6, 2007

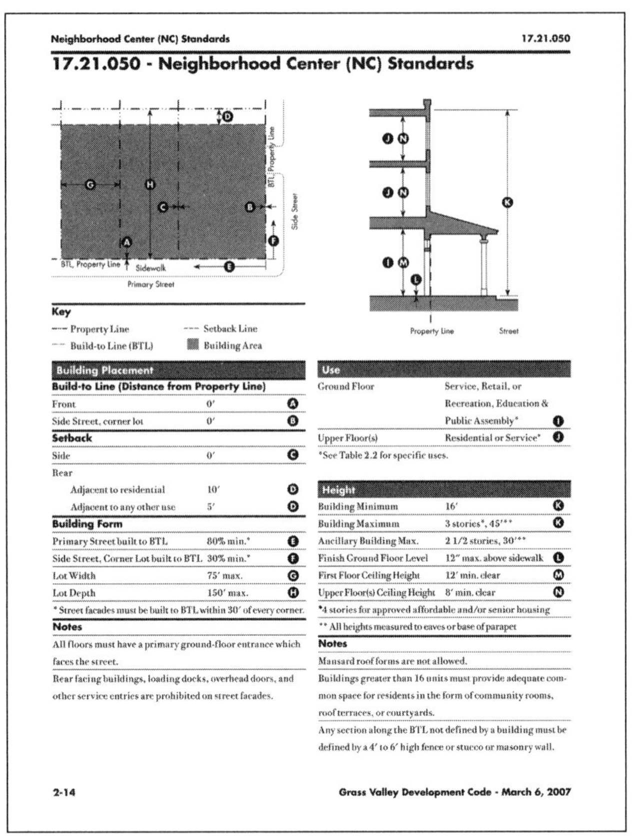

Neighborhood Center (NC) Standards 17.21.050

## 17.21.050 - Neighborhood Center (NC) Standards

Key
- Property Line
- Build-to Line (BTL)
- Setback Line
- Building Area

| Building Placement | | |
|---|---|---|
| **Build-to Line (Distance from Property Line)** | | |
| Front | 0′ | A |
| Side Street, corner lot | 0′ | B |
| **Setback** | | |
| Side | 0′ | C |
| Rear | | |
| Adjacent to residential | 10′ | D |
| Adjacent to any other use | 5′ | D |
| **Building Form** | | |
| Primary Street built to BTL | 80% min.* | E |
| Side Street, Corner Lot built to BTL | 30% min.* | F |
| Lot Width | 75′ max. | G |
| Lot Depth | 150′ max. | H |

* Street facades must be built to BTL within 30′ of every corner.

**Notes**

All floors must have a primary ground-floor entrance which faces the street.

Rear facing buildings, loading docks, overhead doors, and other service entries are prohibited on street facades.

| Use | | |
|---|---|---|
| Ground Floor | Service, Retail, or Recreation, Education & Public Assembly* | I |
| Upper Floor(s) | Residential or Service* | J |

*See Table 2.2 for specific uses.

| Height | | |
|---|---|---|
| Building Minimum | 16′ | K |
| Building Maximum | 3 stories*, 45′** | K |
| Ancillary Building Max. | 2 1/2 stories, 30′** | |
| Finish Ground Floor Level | 12″ max. above sidewalk | L |
| First Floor Ceiling Height | 12′ min. clear | M |
| Upper Floor(s) Ceiling Height | 8′ min. clear | N |

*4 stories for approved affordable and/or senior housing

** All heights measured to eaves or base of parapet

**Notes**

Mansard roof forms are not allowed.

Buildings greater than 16 units must provide adequate common space for residents in the form of community rooms, roof terraces, or courtyards.

Any section along the BTL not defined by a building must be defined by a 4′ to 6′ high fence or stucco or masonry wall.

2-14 Grass Valley Development Code - March 6, 2007

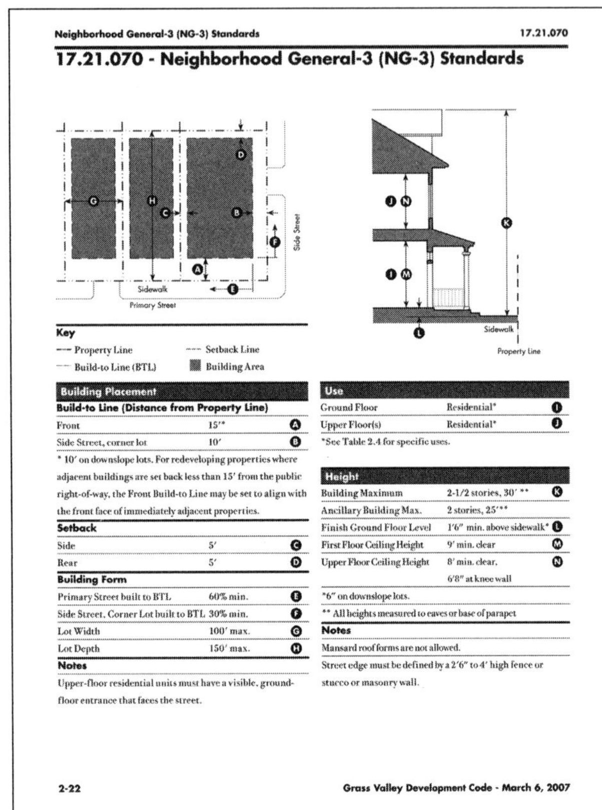

Neighborhood General-3 (NG-3) Standards 17.21.070

## 17.21.070 - Neighborhood General-3 (NG-3) Standards

Key
- Property Line
- Build-to Line (BTL)
- Setback Line
- Building Area

| Building Placement | | |
|---|---|---|
| **Build-to Line (Distance from Property Line)** | | |
| Front | 15′* | A |
| Side Street, corner lot | 10′ | B |

* 10′ on downslope lots. For redeveloping properties where adjacent buildings are set back less than 15′ from the public right-of-way, the Front Build-to Line may be set to align with the front face of immediately adjacent properties.

| **Setback** | | |
|---|---|---|
| Side | 5′ | C |
| Rear | 5′ | D |
| **Building Form** | | |
| Primary Street built to BTL | 60% min. | E |
| Side Street, Corner Lot built to BTL | 30% min. | F |
| Lot Width | 100′ max. | G |
| Lot Depth | 150′ max. | H |

**Notes**

Upper-floor residential units must have a visible, ground-floor entrance that faces the street.

| Use | | |
|---|---|---|
| Ground Floor | Residential* | I |
| Upper Floor(s) | Residential* | J |

*See Table 2.4 for specific uses.

| Height | | |
|---|---|---|
| Building Maximum | 2-1/2 stories, 30′ ** | K |
| Ancillary Building Max. | 2 stories, 25′** | |
| Finish Ground Floor Level | 1′6″ min. above sidewalk* | L |
| First Floor Ceiling Height | 9′ min. clear | M |
| Upper Floor Ceiling Height | 8′ min. clear, 6′8″ at knee wall | N |

*6″ on downslope lots.

** All heights measured to eaves or base of parapet

**Notes**

Mansard roof forms are not allowed.

Street edge must be defined by a 2′6″ to 4′ high fence or stucco or masonry wall.

2-22 Grass Valley Development Code - March 6, 2007

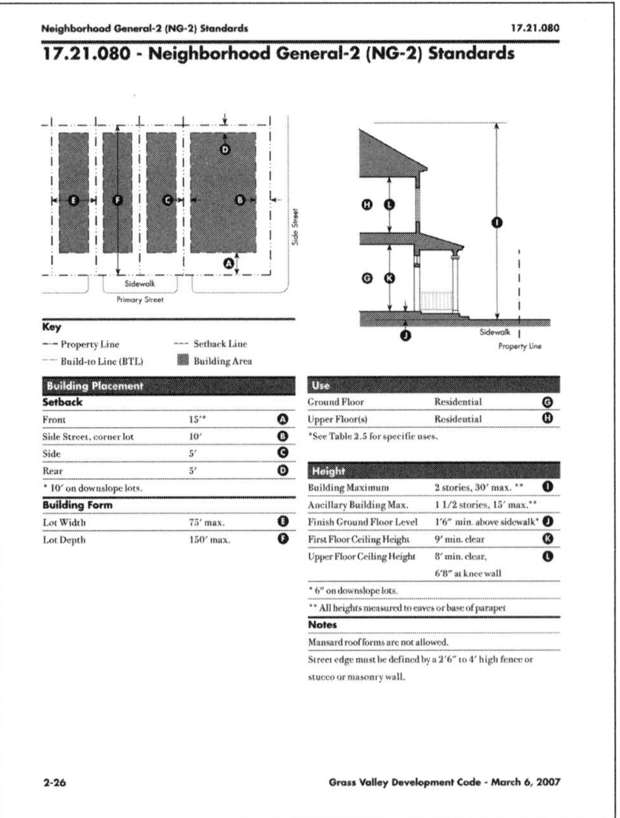

Neighborhood General-2 (NG-2) Standards 17.21.080

## 17.21.080 - Neighborhood General-2 (NG-2) Standards

Key
- Property Line
- Build-to Line (BTL)
- Setback Line
- Building Area

| Building Placement | | |
|---|---|---|
| **Setback** | | |
| Front | 15′* | A |
| Side Street, corner lot | 10′ | B |
| Side | 5′ | C |
| Rear | 5′ | D |

* 10′ on downslope lots.

| **Building Form** | | |
|---|---|---|
| Lot Width | 75′ max. | E |
| Lot Depth | 150′ max. | F |

| Use | | |
|---|---|---|
| Ground Floor | Residential | G |
| Upper Floor(s) | Residential | H |

*See Table 2.5 for specific uses.

| Height | | |
|---|---|---|
| Building Maximum | 2 stories, 30′ max. ** | I |
| Ancillary Building Max. | 1 1/2 stories, 15′ max.** | |
| Finish Ground Floor Level | 1′6″ min. above sidewalk* | J |
| First Floor Ceiling Height | 9′ min. clear | K |
| Upper Floor Ceiling Height | 8′ min. clear, 6′8″ at knee wall | L |

* 6″ on downslope lots.

** All heights measured to eaves or base of parapet

**Notes**

Mansard roof forms are not allowed.

Street edge must be defined by a 2′6″ to 4′ high fence or stucco or masonry wall.

2-26 Grass Valley Development Code - March 6, 2007

**Fig. 4.36** Building placement, use, and height standards for TC (top left), NC (top right), NG-3 (bottom left), and NG-2 (bottom right)

# TOD SmartCode 

## Leander, Texas

*Written by Scott Polikov, Principal, Gateway Planning Group*

LEANDER, TEXAS, STANDS at a crossroad of opportunity. Its location at the northwestern edge of the Central Texas growth corridor has made Leander one of the fastest-growing cities in the state. In 2003, it had a population of 13,846.[5] Leander will see much of its growth from the construction of the 183A Tollway by the Central Texas Regional Mobility Authority (CTRMA) and the regional urban commuter rail system by the Capital Metropolitan Transportation Authority (Capital Metro), linking Leander with downtown Austin. Gateway Planning Group was hired to facilitate a plan and Form-Based Code for the 2,000-acre area at the core of the growth onslaught. Known as the Leander Transit-Oriented Development (TOD), the plan area includes not only downtown Leander, but also adjacent greenfield primed for cosmopolitan development instead of conventional sprawl.

In presenting the Inaugural Driehaus Form-Based Code award, the jury for the Form-Based Codes Institute remarked:

*The code for Leander represents the initiative of a municipality planning ahead for development expected to result from projected transportation improvements. The current population of 17,000 is anticipated to exceed 200,000 as Leander is linked to Austin by tollway and regional commuter rail. This code is mandatory. It is an effective customization of the SmartCode template, addressing complicated issues of Texas planning law, as well as architectural standards intended to characterize the growing community.*

### Client's Background in Form-Based Coding

In the fall 2003, Leander Mayor John Cowman and the leadership of Central Texas traveled to the Washington, D.C., region to evaluate the New Urbanism and transit-oriented development. There, Andrés Duany hosted them for a tour of the Kentlands and Chairman Paul Ferguson of the Arlington County Board for a tour of the Orange Line Metro Corridor.

State Representative Mike Krusee (chairman of the House Transportation Committee and member of the National Board of Directors of the Congress for the New Urbanism), Capital Metro Transit Board Chairman Lee Walker, and Scott Polikov of Gateway Planning Group spearheaded the trip. After the trip, Mayor Cowman wanted to be the first in the region with a real TOD and hired Gateway Planning

| | Leander TOD SmartCode |
|---|---|
| Status: | Adopted on September 22, 2005 |
| Scale: | Part of a City/Town |
| Implementation Method: | Mandatory and Freestanding |
| Site Context: | Greenfield and Redevelopment/Infill |
| Site Size: | 2,000 acres |
| Administration: | Projects are reviewed by the city's Urban Design Officer [UDO] and Consolidated Review Committee that includes UDO and landowner representative, as called for in the implementation of a SmartCode |
| Organizing Principle: | Transect (SmartCode) |
| Code Consultants(s): | Gateway Planning Group, Inc. (Lead); PlaceMakers, Inc. |
| Agency: | City of Leander; Capital Metropolitan Transportation Authority |

Group to create the local context, formalize regional partnerships, craft a plan, and undertake the code reforms necessary to do just that. Capital Metro's initial commuter rail line from downtown Austin is scheduled to open in 2008 and will terminate in the Leander TOD. Cowman wanted a TOD waiting on opening day.

Walker, the former CFO of Dell Computers, became convinced that urbanism, local government growth policy, and regulatory reform were critical to rail's success. This set the stage to create a plan that capitalized on the recently won election authorizing a commuter rail line for the Austin area. Krusee knew that he could stake out a claim as a conservative Republican for transit by harnessing the "less expensive per mile" commuter rail through urban villages throughout the region. Polikov knew that if he put Krusee, Walker, and local political leaders all together on a trip, they would transcend their parochial politics and seek to implement partnerships for regional rail and urban village development. Polikov also knew that this trip would position his firm to facilitate implementation of early work to jump start momentum in the Austin region.

The delegation also included the local head of the Texas Department of Transportation, several other mayors, city managers, leaders from the real estate community, environmentalists, and community activists (both pro- and anti-rail).

Krusee and Polikov had served many years earlier on the governing board of the region's Metropolitan Planning Organization. Then representing Capital Metro, Polikov was pro–light rail for Austin. Representing the fast-growing suburbs of Round Rock, Krusee was pro-highway and anti–light rail. Polikov wanted rail no matter what, and Krusee considered the early light rail proposals "too much for too little." Over the next decade, Krusee and Polikov forged an alliance as Krusee embraced urbanism and Polikov embraced regionalism. They realized that regional rail transit and urbanism could be combined to create a sustainable growth pattern for all of Central Texas.

At the same time, the Envision Central Texas planning effort (facilitated by Fregonese/Calthorpe) had developed a regional growth vision and more alliances across Central Texas. Krusee and Polikov convinced Lee Walker of Capital Metro to host the trip with Gateway Planning Group to the D.C. area. Seeing it work through the eyes of Andrés Duany and Paul Ferguson, the Central Texas delegation became convinced that planning, Form-Based Code reforms, and leveraging transportation facilities can harness growth into sustainable, pedestrian-friendly, mixed-use neighborhoods.

**Fig. 4.37** (previous page) Perspective from the visioning process

**Fig. 4.38** (above) Illustrative Plan. Note that even for a project of this size that the street, block, and open space framework is clearly defined in the plan.

Once back home and fired up, Mayor Cowman and his political nemesis on the city council, David Siebold, reflected on the opportunities and decided they wanted a TOD adjacent to Leander's modest downtown, called Old Town. At the urging of the mayor, Polikov and Pix Howell, his Gateway Planning Group colleague, (who subsequently became the SmartCode Urban Design Officer for the City) began to meet with landowners near Old Town. Approximately 2,000 acres of greenfield sits adjacent to Old Town and will be anchored by Capital Metro's rail station connecting the commuter rail line set to open in 2008 with downtown Austin. The landowners of those 2,000 acres became intrigued with the potential for an urban village development pattern rather than low-density, single-family housing and some strip commercial along the major roadways.

TXP, Inc., a member of the consultant team, undertook a compelling fiscal impact analysis, concluding that the initiative at build-out would increase tax base value by almost an additional $1 billion within the 2,000 acres, as compared to conventional development. Consensus emerged to proceed with a detailed planning and code effort funded jointly by the major landowners, the city, and Capital Metro. A true public-private partnership had been formed.

## Code Components

All the code components were created in the process, including all zoning and subdivision standards, architectural guidelines, a localized plant palette, storm water drainage standards, street cross-sections, and a specially streamlined entitlement process. All these elements, among others, were incorporated into the SmartCode template. Gateway Planning Group modified approximately 30 percent of the SmartCode template to create the final unified development code.

### Organizing Principle

The transect was used as the guiding principle of the charrette master plan. The variety of conditions within the 2,000 acres of the planning area lent themselves to the transect: the existing downtown of Leander, an existing highway corridor with a parallel rail transit line set to open in 2008, a new tollway corridor also opening 2008, approximately 1,500 acres of greenfield across the highway/rail transit corridor from the existing downtown, a lake on the southern end of the planning area, and bluffs on the northern end.

A transect plan was formalized from the charrette plan and became the Regulating Plan for the code.

## Code Process

During the seven-day charrette for the 2,000-acre planning area, the Gateway Planning Group team tracked design elements and policies that needed to be implemented into the SmartCode. After the charrette, a draft of the adapted SmartCode was circulated to the seven major landowners, the city, and the city attorney. Over about four months, an iterative editing process facilitated the details of the unified development code.

Much of that process involved meetings with the landowner representatives to educate them that the code was facilitating a market-based dynamic for development, as opposed to micromanaging uses by the conventional zoning process of Leander. The existing regulatory environment of Leander had frustrated landowners, but they were skeptical about the SmartCode.

After months of meetings, the consultant team eventually convinced the landowners that prescription of the urban design elements of a project juxtaposed with wider latitude in uses would provide them with more flexibility. This flexibility would provide an opportunity for more density, wider markets in terms of residential demand, and a resulting higher quality of nonresidential uses that would evolve via market forces, not through planning and zoning commission votes. Thus, they finally embraced the details implemented in the Leander SmartCode to facilitate that shift in development philosophy.

#### Public Participation

The city of Leander hosted a public presentation to kick off the design charrette and a closing presentation. The process of implementation was discussed at those presentations, including the utilization of the SmartCode. After the landowner process was completed and a final draft of the SmartCode was secured, the Gateway team presented the SmartCode to the planning commission and city council at respective work sessions. Feedback resulted in minor edits.

Thereafter, a multi-item package was presented to the city council for adoption. First, the remaining land in the planning area not yet annexed was annexed by agreement of the landowners. Second, the Leander TOD Regulating Plan, which is the transect plan for the 2,000-acre planning area, was presented to the city council as an amendment to the city's Comprehensive Plan. Third, the SmartCode as the new unified land development code was presented to replace the existing land development code for the 2,000-acre planning area. All three were adopted in sequence after public hearing.

## Advanced Application of FBCs

The code requires a minimum mix of housing types for each project to ensure that people can "move up without moving out" of the neighborhoods. The implementing details are summarized here:

**Fig. 4.39** Perspectives from the visioning process

#### Residential Housing Mix (Subsection 3.4.4)

- T3 = three types, T4 and T5 = four types, T6 = no minimum (at least 5 percent of each type if more than one type required)

#### Residential Mix Phasing

- T3: The second of three types shall be started by second phase of construction (building permit), or more than 20 acres constructed, whichever occurs first. (3.4.5)
- T4/T5: The second of four types shall be started by second phase of construction (building permit), or more than 20 acres constructed, whichever occurs first. (3.4.6.)
- T4/T5: The third of four types shall be started by third phase of construction, or more than 40 acres constructed, whichever occurs first. (3.4.6)

The code included specific street cross-sections that were tailored for each specific major arterial

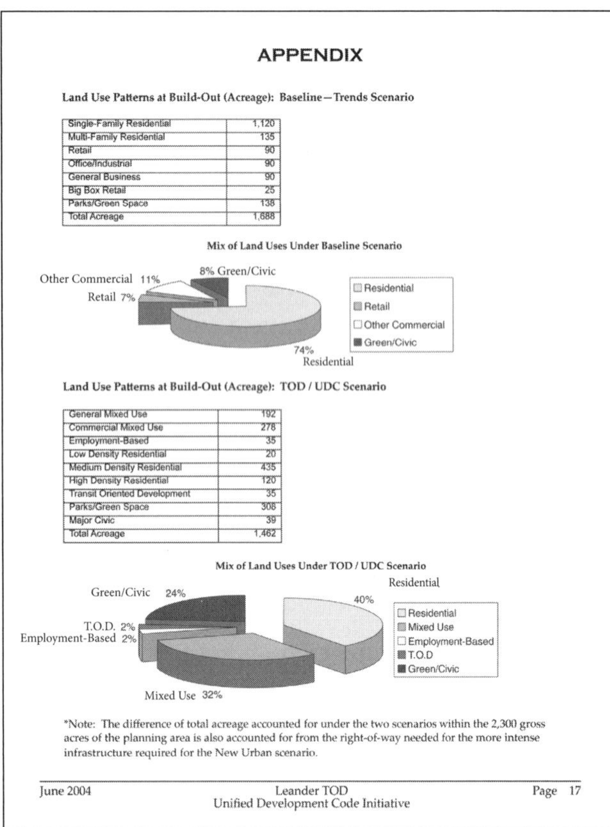

APPENDIX

Land Use Patterns at Build-Out (Acreage): Baseline—Trends Scenario

| | |
|---|---|
| Single-Family Residential | 1,120 |
| Multi-Family Residential | 135 |
| Retail | 90 |
| Office/Industrial | 90 |
| General Business | 90 |
| Big Box Retail | 25 |
| Parks/Green Space | 138 |
| Total Acreage | 1,688 |

Mix of Land Uses Under Baseline Scenario



Land Use Patterns at Build-Out (Acreage): TOD / UDC Scenario

| | |
|---|---|
| General Mixed Use | 192 |
| Commercial Mixed Use | 278 |
| Employment-Based | 35 |
| Low Density Residential | 20 |
| Medium Density Residential | 435 |
| High Density Residential | 120 |
| Transit Oriented Development | 35 |
| Parks/Green Space | 308 |
| Major Civic | 39 |
| Total Acreage | 1,462 |

Mix of Land Uses Under TOD / UDC Scenario



*Note: The difference of total acreage accounted for under the two scenarios within the 2,300 gross acres of the planning area is also accounted for from the right-of-way needed for the more intense infrastructure required for the New Urban scenario.

June 2004 — Leander TOD, Unified Development Code Initiative — Page 17

APPENDIX

Assumptions Used to Calculate Total Project Value: Baseline Scenario

| | Value/Unit | Unit/Acre | Total Value |
|---|---|---|---|
| Single-Family Residential | $160,000 | 3.5 | $627,200,000 |
| Multi-Family Residential | $50,000 | 16.0 | $108,000,000 |
| | Value/Sq. Ft. | F.A.R | Total Value |
| Retail | $125 | 0.15 | $73,507,500 |
| Office/Industrial | $130 | 0.20 | $101,930,400 |
| General Business | $100 | 0.15 | $58,806,000 |
| Big Box Retail | $150 | 0.15 | $24,502,500 |
| Parks/Green Space | N.A. | N.A. | N.A. |
| TOTALS | | | $993,946,400 |

Assumptions Used to Calculate Total Project Value: TOD / UDC Scenario

| | Value/Unit or Sq. Ft. | Unit/Acre or F.A.R. | Total Value |
|---|---|---|---|
| Mixed Use | | | |
| Non-residential | $130 | 0.15 | $163,088,640 |
| Residential | $125,000 | 6.00 | $144,000,000 |
| Commercial Mixed Use | | | |
| Non-residential | $155 | 0.15 | $281,550,060 |
| Residential | $125,000 | 16.00 | $139,000,000 |
| Employment Centers | $125 | 0.15 | $28,586,250 |
| Low Density Residential * | $175,000 | 3.50 | $12,250,000 |
| Medium Density Residential * | $175,000 | 8.00 | $609,000,000 |
| High Density Residential * | $55,000 | 16.00 | $105,600,000 |
| Transit Oriented Development | | | |
| Non-residential | $155 | 1.00 | $236,313,000 |
| Residential | $150,000 | 16.00 | $84,000,000 |
| Parks/Green Space | N.A. | N.A. | N.A. |
| TOTALS | | | $1,803,387,950 |

* Note: Numerous studies indicate that the premium for a residential unit in New Urban mixed-use project could be as much as 25%. In the interest of making a conservative estimate, the values for residential units under the Baseline scenario were increased only 10% for comparable units in the New Urban scenario.

June 2004 — Leander TOD, Unified Development Code Initiative — Page 18

**Fig. 4.40** (above left) Pie charts comparing the baseline-trends buildout scenario and the TOD/Unified Development Code buildout scenario

**Fig. 4.41** (above right) Value comparison based on the buildout scenarios

and the eventual redesign of the U.S. 183 state highway that will no longer serve as a regional arterial once the parallel tollway comes on line (Table 10C cross-sections in the code).

## Implementation

### Code Administration

The code calls for an Urban Design Officer (UDO) and a consolidated review committee (CRC). The initial UDO is Pix Howell, whom the city hired from Gateway Planning Group because of his intimate knowledge of the initiative and existing relationship with the major landowners and developers in the Leander TOD.

The UDO works for the city manager and serves not only as the city's staff for the Leander TOD and the SmartCode, but also as the coordinator of policies to implement the long-term financing of the project through support of the Tax Increment Financing (TIF) Board; this board governs the implementation of the TIF created to assist with the financing of major infrastructure for the Leander TOD as the tax base grows within it for recapture into the district. The CRC is composed of the UDO, additional city staff representatives, and landowner representatives.

### Lessons Learned

The charrette itself should be programmed to better inform the major landowners of the role of the SmartCode instead of waiting postcharrette to facilitate their education about the FBC as the implementing tool. The economics of Form-Based Codes proved to be the critical educational tool in implementing a successful plan for urbanism.

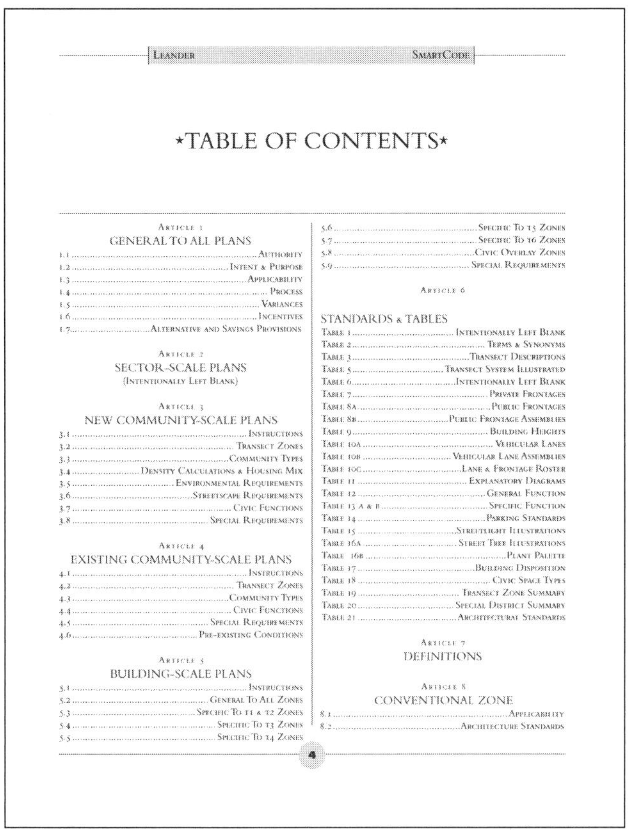

Leander SmartCode

★TABLE OF CONTENTS★



4

**Fig. 4.42** Table of contents

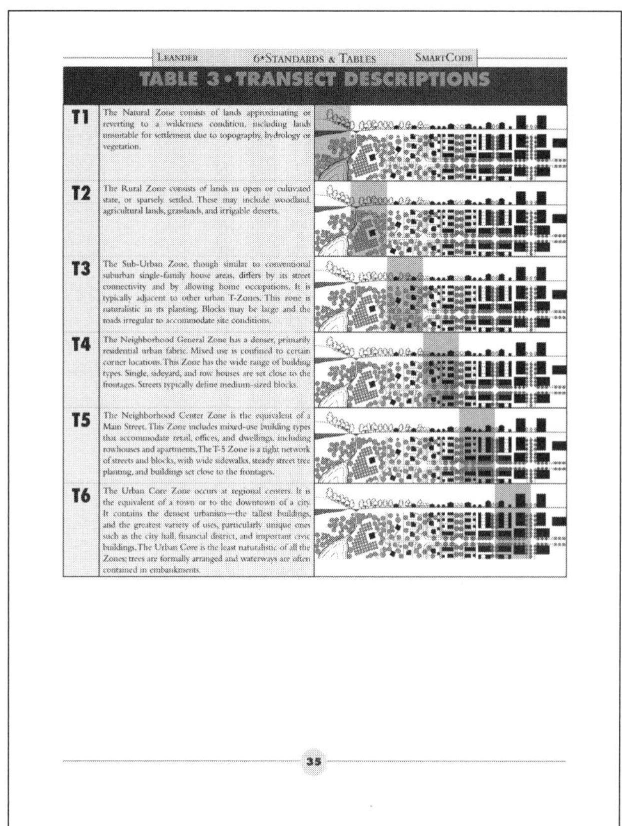

Leander 6•Standards & Tables SmartCode

TABLE 3 • TRANSECT DESCRIPTIONS

| | |
|---|---|
| T1 | The Natural Zone consists of lands approximating or reverting to a wilderness condition, including lands unsuitable for settlement due to topography, hydrology or vegetation. |
| T2 | The Rural Zone consists of lands in open or cultivated state, or sparsely settled. These may include woodland, agricultural lands, grasslands, and irrigable deserts. |
| T3 | The Sub-Urban Zone, though similar to conventional suburban single-family house areas, differs by its street connectivity and by allowing home occupations. It is typically adjacent to other urban T-Zones. This zone is naturalistic in its planting. Blocks may be large and the roads irregular to accommodate site conditions. |
| T4 | The Neighborhood General Zone has a denser, primarily residential urban fabric. Mixed use is confined to certain corner locations. This Zone has the wide range of building types. Single, sideyard, and row houses are set close to the frontages. Streets typically define medium-sized blocks. |
| T5 | The Neighborhood Center Zone is the equivalent of a Main Street. This Zone includes mixed-use building types that accommodate retail, offices, and dwellings, including rowhouses and apartments. The T-5 Zone is a tight network of streets and blocks, with wide sidewalks, steady street tree planting, and buildings set close to the frontages. |
| T6 | The Urban Core Zone occurs at regional centers. It is the equivalent of a town or to the downtown of a city. It contains the densest urbanism—the tallest buildings, and the greatest variety of uses, particularly unique ones such as the city hall, financial district, and important civic buildings. The Urban Core is the least naturalistic of all the Zones; trees are formally arranged and waterways are often contained in embankments. |

35

**Fig. 4.43** Transect descriptions

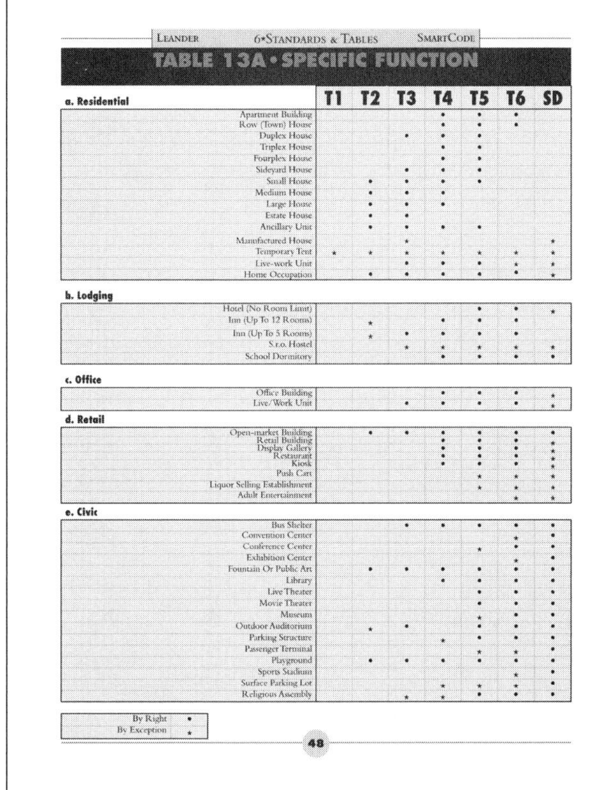

Leander 6•Standards & Tables SmartCode

TABLE 13A • SPECIFIC FUNCTION

| a. Residential | T1 | T2 | T3 | T4 | T5 | T6 | SD |
|---|---|---|---|---|---|---|---|
| Apartment Building | | | | • | • | • | |
| Row (Town) House | | | | • | • | • | |
| Duplex House | | | • | • | • | | |
| Triplex House | | | | • | • | | |
| Fourplex House | | | | • | • | | |
| Sideyard House | | | • | • | • | | |
| Small House | | • | • | • | • | | |
| Medium House | | • | • | • | | | |
| Large House | | • | • | • | | | |
| Estate House | | • | • | | | | |
| Ancillary Unit | | • | • | • | • | | |
| Manufactured House | | | ★ | | | | ★ |
| Temporary Tent | ★ | ★ | ★ | ★ | ★ | ★ | ★ |
| Live-work Unit | | | • | • | • | ★ | ★ |
| Home Occupation | | • | • | • | • | • | ★ |
| **b. Lodging** | | | | | | | |
| Hotel (No Room Limit) | | | | | • | • | ★ |
| Inn (Up To 12 Rooms) | | ★ | | • | • | • | |
| Inn (Up To 5 Rooms) | | ★ | • | • | • | • | |
| S.r.o. Hostel | | | ★ | ★ | ★ | ★ | ★ |
| School Dormitory | | | | • | • | • | • |
| **c. Office** | | | | | | | |
| Office Building | | | | • | • | • | ★ |
| Live/Work Unit | | | • | • | • | • | ★ |
| **d. Retail** | | | | | | | |
| Open-market Building | | • | • | • | • | • | • |
| Retail Building | | | | • | • | • | ★ |
| Display Gallery | | | | • | • | • | ★ |
| Restaurant | | | | • | • | • | ★ |
| Kiosk | | | | • | • | • | ★ |
| Push Cart | | | | | ★ | ★ | ★ |
| Liquor Selling Establishment | | | | | ★ | ★ | ★ |
| Adult Entertainment | | | | | | ★ | ★ |
| **e. Civic** | | | | | | | |
| Bus Shelter | | | • | • | • | • | • |
| Convention Center | | | | | | ★ | • |
| Conference Center | | | | | ★ | • | • |
| Exhibition Center | | | | | | ★ | • |
| Fountain Or Public Art | | • | • | • | • | • | • |
| Library | | | | • | • | • | • |
| Live Theater | | | | | • | • | • |
| Movie Theater | | | | | • | • | • |
| Museum | | | | | ★ | • | • |
| Outdoor Auditorium | | ★ | • | | • | • | • |
| Parking Structure | | | | ★ | • | • | • |
| Passenger Terminal | | | | | ★ | ★ | • |
| Playground | | • | • | • | • | • | • |
| Sports Stadium | | | | | | ★ | • |
| Surface Parking Lot | | | | ★ | ★ | ★ | • |
| Religious Assembly | | | ★ | ★ | • | • | • |

| | |
|---|---|
| By Right | • |
| By Exception | ★ |

48

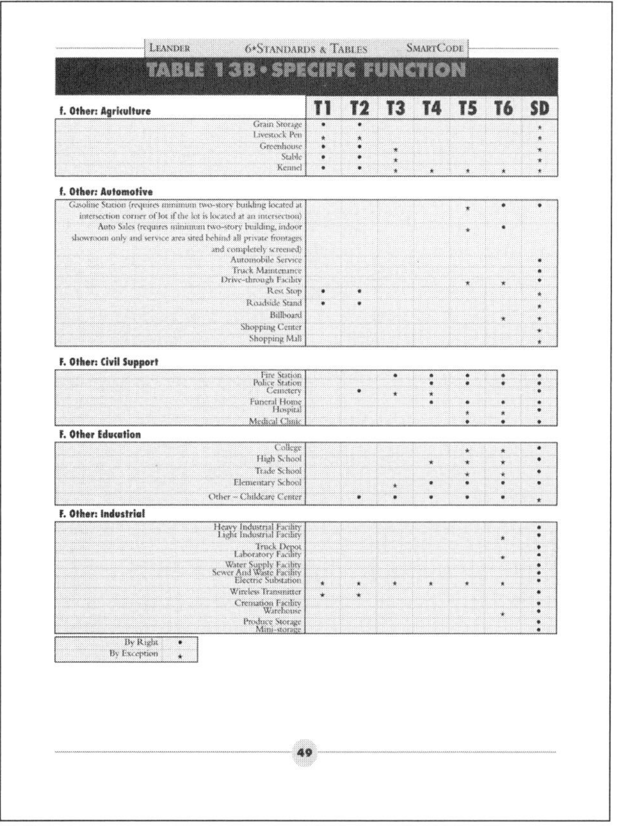

Leander 6•Standards & Tables SmartCode

TABLE 13B • SPECIFIC FUNCTION

| f. Other: Agriculture | T1 | T2 | T3 | T4 | T5 | T6 | SD |
|---|---|---|---|---|---|---|---|
| Grain Storage | • | • | | | | | ★ |
| Livestock Pen | ★ | ★ | | | | | ★ |
| Greenhouse | • | • | ★ | | | | ★ |
| Stable | • | • | ★ | | | | ★ |
| Kennel | • | • | ★ | ★ | ★ | ★ | ★ |
| **f. Other: Automotive** | | | | | | | |
| Gasoline Station (requires minimum two-story building located at intersection corner of lot if the lot is located at an intersection) | | | | | ★ | • | • |
| Auto Sales (requires minimum two-story building, indoor showroom only and service area sited behind all private frontages and completely screened) | | | | | ★ | • | |
| Automobile Service | | | | | | | • |
| Truck Maintenance | | | | | | | • |
| Drive-through Facility | | | | | ★ | ★ | • |
| Rest Stop | • | • | | | | | ★ |
| Roadside Stand | • | • | | | | | ★ |
| Billboard | | | | | | ★ | ★ |
| Shopping Center | | | | | | | ★ |
| Shopping Mall | | | | | | | ★ |
| **F. Other: Civil Support** | | | | | | | |
| Fire Station | | | • | • | • | • | • |
| Police Station | | | | • | • | • | • |
| Cemetery | | • | ★ | ★ | | | • |
| Funeral Home | | | | • | • | • | • |
| Hospital | | | | | ★ | ★ | • |
| Medical Clinic | | | | | • | • | • |
| **F. Other Education** | | | | | | | |
| College | | | | | ★ | ★ | • |
| High School | | | | ★ | ★ | ★ | • |
| Trade School | | | | | ★ | ★ | • |
| Elementary School | | | ★ | • | • | • | • |
| Other – Childcare Center | | • | • | • | • | • | ★ |
| **F. Other: Industrial** | | | | | | | |
| Heavy Industrial Facility | | | | | | | • |
| Light Industrial Facility | | | | | | ★ | • |
| Truck Depot | | | | | | | • |
| Laboratory Facility | | | | | | ★ | • |
| Water Supply Facility | | | | | | | • |
| Sewer And Waste Facility | | | | | | | • |
| Electric Substation | ★ | ★ | ★ | ★ | ★ | ★ | • |
| Wireless Transmitter | ★ | ★ | | | | | • |
| Cremation Facility | | | | | | | • |
| Warehouse | | | | | | ★ | • |
| Produce Storage | | | | | | | • |
| Mini-storage | | | | | | | • |

| | |
|---|---|
| By Right | • |
| By Exception | ★ |

49

**Fig. 4.44** (left and right) Land-use table

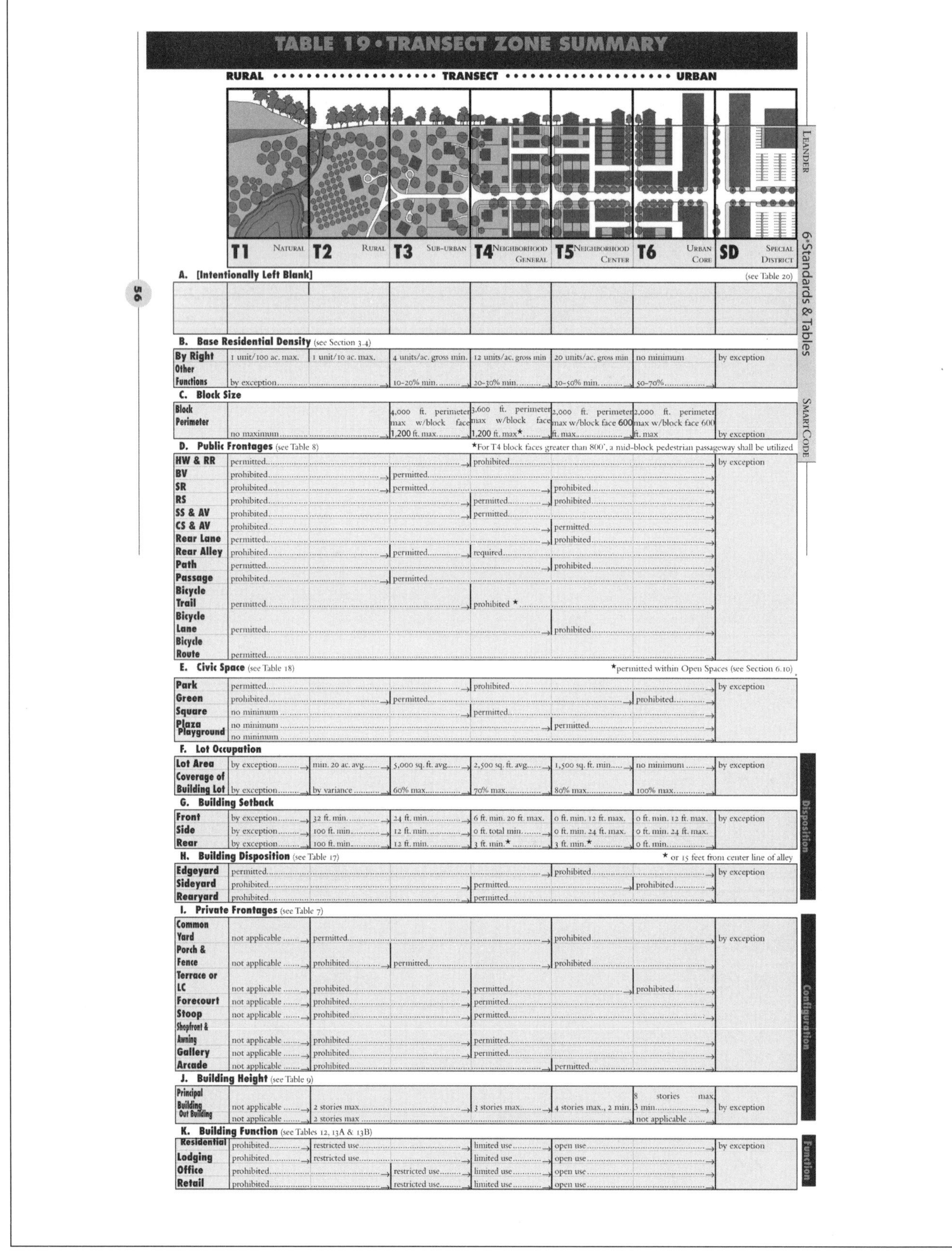

## TABLE 19 • TRANSECT ZONE SUMMARY

RURAL •••••••••••••••••••• TRANSECT •••••••••••••••••••• URBAN

| | T1 Natural | T2 Rural | T3 Sub-Urban | T4 Neighborhood General | T5 Neighborhood Center | T6 Urban Core | SD Special District |
|---|---|---|---|---|---|---|---|
| **A. [Intentionally Left Blank]** (see Table 20) | | | | | | | |
| **B. Base Residential Density** (see Section 3.4) | | | | | | | |
| By Right | 1 unit/100 ac. max. | 1 unit/10 ac. max. | 4 units/ac. gross min. | 12 units/ac. gross min | 20 units/ac. gross min | no minimum | by exception |
| Other Functions | by exception | | 10-20% min. | 20-30% min. | 30-50% min. | 50-70% | |
| **C. Block Size** | | | | | | | |
| Block Perimeter | no maximum | | 4,000 ft. perimeter max w/block face 1,200 ft. max. | 3,600 ft. perimeter max w/block face 1,200 ft. max*. | 2,000 ft. perimeter max w/block face 600 ft. max | 2,000 ft. perimeter max w/block face 600 ft. max | by exception |
| **D. Public Frontages** (see Table 8) | | | | | | | |
| HW & RR | permitted | | | prohibited | | | by exception |
| BV | prohibited | | permitted | | | | |
| SR | prohibited | | permitted | | prohibited | | |
| RS | prohibited | | | permitted | prohibited | | |
| SS & AV | prohibited | | | permitted | | | |
| CS & AV | prohibited | | | | permitted | | |
| Rear Lane | permitted | | | | prohibited | | |
| Rear Alley | prohibited | | permitted | required | | | |
| Path | permitted | | | | prohibited | | |
| Passage | prohibited | | permitted | | | | |
| Bicycle Trail | permitted | | | prohibited * | | | |
| Bicycle Lane | permitted | | | | prohibited | | |
| Bicycle Route | permitted | | | | | | |
| **E. Civic Space** (see Table 18) | | | | | | | |
| Park | permitted | | | prohibited | | | by exception |
| Green | prohibited | | permitted | | | prohibited | |
| Square | no minimum | | | permitted | | | |
| Plaza | no minimum | | | | permitted | | |
| Playground | no minimum | | | | | | |
| **F. Lot Occupation** | | | | | | | |
| Lot Area | by exception | min. 20 ac. avg. | 5,000 sq. ft. avg. | 2,500 sq. ft. avg. | 1,500 sq. ft. min. | no minimum | by exception |
| Coverage of Building Lot | by exception | by variance | 60% max. | 70% max. | 80% max. | 100% max. | |
| **G. Building Setback** | | | | | | | |
| Front | by exception | 32 ft. min. | 24 ft. min. | 6 ft. min. 20 ft. max. | 0 ft. min. 12 ft. max. | 0 ft. min. 12 ft. max. | by exception |
| Side | by exception | 100 ft. min. | 12 ft. min. | 0 ft. total min. | 0 ft. min. 24 ft. max. | 0 ft. min. 24 ft. max. | |
| Rear | by exception | 100 ft. min. | 12 ft. min. | 3 ft. min.* | 3 ft. min.* | 0 ft. min. | |
| **H. Building Disposition** (see Table 17) | | | | | | | |
| Edgeyard | permitted | | | | prohibited | | by exception |
| Sideyard | prohibited | | | permitted | | prohibited | |
| Rearyard | prohibited | | | permitted | | | |
| **I. Private Frontages** (see Table 7) | | | | | | | |
| Common Yard | not applicable | permitted | | | prohibited | | by exception |
| Porch & Fence | not applicable | prohibited | permitted | | prohibited | | |
| Terrace or LC | not applicable | prohibited | | permitted | | prohibited | |
| Forecourt | not applicable | prohibited | | permitted | | | |
| Stoop | not applicable | prohibited | | permitted | | | |
| Shopfront & Awning | not applicable | prohibited | | permitted | | | |
| Gallery | not applicable | prohibited | | permitted | | | |
| Arcade | not applicable | prohibited | | | permitted | | |
| **J. Building Height** (see Table 9) | | | | | | | |
| Principal Building | not applicable | 2 stories max. | | 3 stories max. | 4 stories max., 2 min. | 8 stories max, 3 min. | by exception |
| Out Building | not applicable | 2 stories max | | | | not applicable | |
| **K. Building Function** (see Tables 12, 13A & 13B) | | | | | | | |
| Residential | prohibited | restricted use | | limited use | open use | | by exception |
| Lodging | prohibited | restricted use | | limited use | open use | | |
| Office | prohibited | | restricted use | limited use | open use | | |
| Retail | prohibited | | restricted use | limited use | open use | | |

*For T4 block faces greater than 800', a mid-block pedestrian passageway shall be utilized

*permitted within Open Spaces (see Section 6.10)

* or 15 feet from center line of alley



**Fig. 4.45** Transect zone summary for the Building Form Standards

have been incorporated into the Transect Map and this Code and the associated plans have been adopted. Projects shall be processed consistent with this Code, State law and the City Charter.

1.4.3 An Urban Design Officer appointed by the City Manager with the advice of the Consolidated Review Committee ("CRC") and majority of the landowners, in terms of acreage within the area depicted by the Transect Map, shall be assigned to advise on the use of this Code and to aid in the design of the communities and buildings based on this Code. To aid in his or her mission, the Urban Design Officer may establish an urban design center if the Consolidated Review Committee and/or the City/landowners provide sufficient resources. The City Manager shall designate a temporary Urban Design Officer from his or her staff until a Consolidated Review Committee is established and an Urban Design Officer is appointed by the City Manager.

1.4.4 The City Manager and the City's Planning Department, in coordination with the landowners, shall develop a process to facilitate a Consolidated Review Committee comprised of the Urban Design Officer, City Representatives and Owner Representatives. The UDO shall coordinate with the CRC and have staff administrative jurisdiction over any processes authorized under this Code. The CRC shall expedite its reviews and advance the permitting process by undertaking any action consistent with this code, State law, and the City Charter to facilitate the permitting process under this Code.

1.4.5 All development within the area covered by the TOD Transect Map will be included within and approved as part of a Planned Unit Development ("PUD"). An approved PUD plan utilized for planned unit development zoning shall meet the requirements for a Preliminary Plan (not a final plat) for subdivision and be consistent with the Transect Map and the provisions of this Code. Zoning notices and procedures shall comply with state law. The Planning Commission shall give notice, hold a public hearing and have an opportunity to make a recommendation to the City Council on each PUD submitted for approval. The City Council shall give notice, hold a public hearing and act legislatively to approve or disapprove each PUD submitted for approval within the area. The PUD Plans (Preliminary Plan) shall be presented to and approved by the Planning Commission and the City Council, and a Final Plat shall be certified for recording when the Urban Design Officer certifies that all required infrastructure and construction has been installed, and inspected and accepted by the City as constructed and installed in compliance with the applicable rules, regulations, standards and ordinances of the City. An approved Site Plan and recorded Final Plat shall be required before the issuance of a building permit.

1.4.6 An applicant may appeal a decision of the UDO or CRC to the City Council. The City Manager or his or her designee shall provide a written recommendation to the City Council as the appeal is processed.

1.4.7 Should a violation of an approved plan occur during construction, the City Manager or the Urban Design Officer has the right to require the owner or developer to stop, remove, and/or mitigate the violation, or to require the owner or developer to secure an Exception to cover the violation.



**Fig. 4.46** The review process (Urban Design Officer)

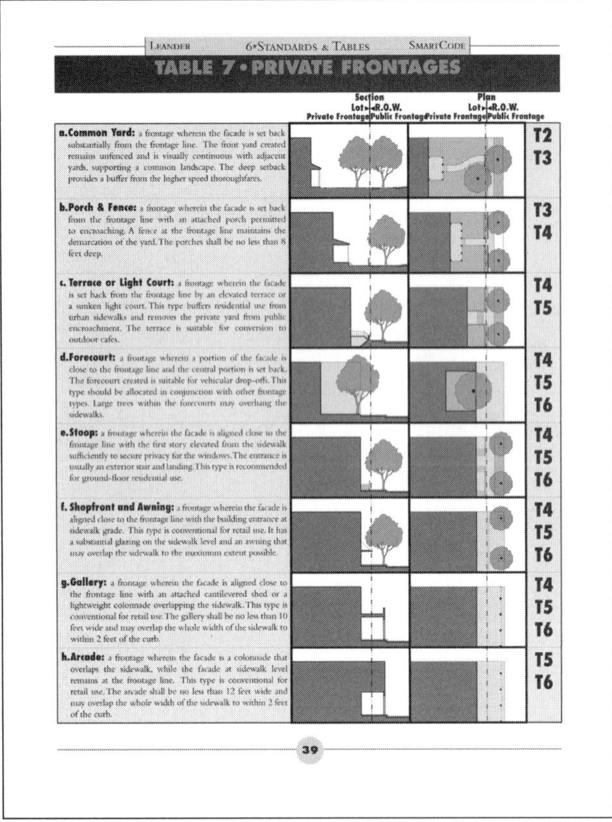

LEANDER 6•STANDARDS & TABLES SMARTCODE

## TABLE 7 • PRIVATE FRONTAGES

Section: Lot ▸◂ R.O.W. — Private Frontage | Public Frontage
Plan: Lot ▸◂ R.O.W. — Private Frontage | Public Frontage

| Frontage | Transect |
|---|---|
| **a. Common Yard:** a frontage wherein the facade is set back substantially from the frontage line. The front yard created remains unfenced and is visually continuous with adjacent yards, supporting a common landscape. The deep setback provides a buffer from the higher speed thoroughfares. | T2 T3 |
| **b. Porch & Fence:** a frontage wherein the facade is set back from the frontage line with an attached porch permitted to encroaching. A fence at the frontage line maintains the demarcation of the yard. The porches shall be no less than 8 feet deep. | T3 T4 |
| **c. Terrace or Light Court:** a frontage wherein the facade is set back from the frontage line by an elevated terrace or a sunken light court. This type buffers residential use from urban sidewalks and removes the private yard from public encroachment. The terrace is suitable for conversion to outdoor cafes. | T4 T5 |
| **d. Forecourt:** a frontage wherein a portion of the facade is close to the frontage line and the central portion is set back. The forecourt created is suitable for vehicular drop-offs. This type should be allocated in conjunction with other frontage types. Large trees within the forecourts may overhang the sidewalks. | T4 T5 T6 |
| **e. Stoop:** a frontage wherein the facade is aligned close to the frontage line with the first story elevated from the sidewalk sufficiently to secure privacy for the windows. The entrance is usually an exterior stair and landing. This type is recommended for ground-floor residential use. | T4 T5 T6 |
| **f. Shopfront and Awning:** a frontage wherein the facade is aligned close to the frontage line with the building entrance at sidewalk grade. This type is conventional for retail use. It has a substantial glazing on the sidewalk level and an awning that may overlap the sidewalk to the maximum extent possible. | T4 T5 T6 |
| **g. Gallery:** a frontage wherein the facade is aligned close to the frontage line with an attached cantilevered shed or a lightweight colonnade overlapping the sidewalk. This type is conventional for retail use. The gallery shall be no less than 10 feet wide and may overlap the whole width of the sidewalk to within 2 feet of the curb. | T4 T5 T6 |
| **h. Arcade:** a frontage wherein the facade is a colonnade that overlaps the sidewalk, while the facade at sidewalk level remains at the frontage line. This type is conventional for retail use. The arcade shall be no less than 12 feet wide and may overlap the whole width of the sidewalk to within 2 feet of the curb. | T5 T6 |

39

**Fig. 4.47** Private frontages

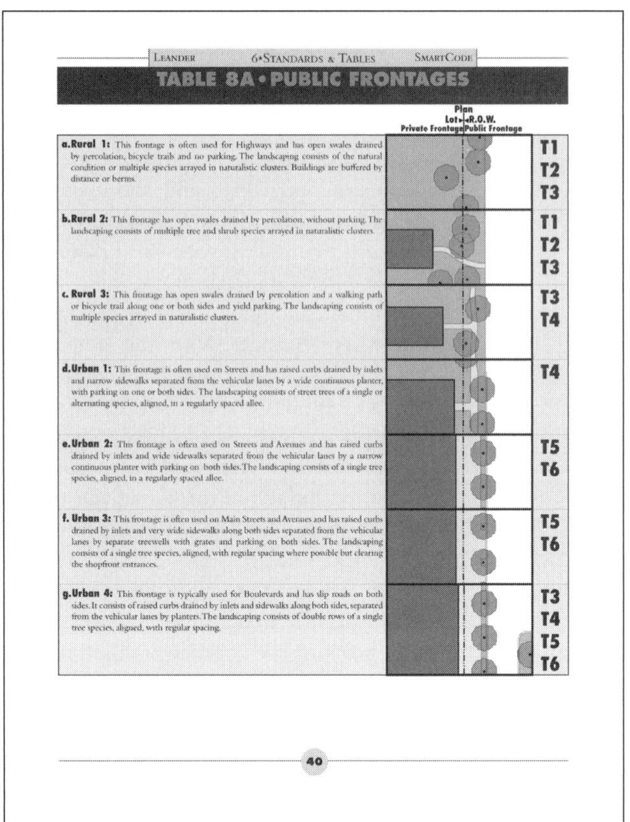

LEANDER 6•STANDARDS & TABLES SMARTCODE

## TABLE 8A • PUBLIC FRONTAGES

Plan: Lot ▸◂ R.O.W. — Private Frontage | Public Frontage

| Frontage | Transect |
|---|---|
| **a. Rural 1:** This frontage is often used for Highways and has open swales drained by percolation, bicycle trails and no parking. The landscaping consists of the natural condition or multiple species arrayed in naturalistic clusters. Buildings are buffered by distance or berms. | T1 T2 T3 |
| **b. Rural 2:** This frontage has open swales drained by percolation, without parking. The landscaping consists of multiple tree and shrub species arrayed in naturalistic clusters. | T1 T2 T3 |
| **c. Rural 3:** This frontage has open swales drained by percolation and a walking path or bicycle trail along one or both sides and yield parking. The landscaping consists of multiple species arrayed in naturalistic clusters. | T3 T4 |
| **d. Urban 1:** This frontage is often used on Streets and has raised curbs drained by inlets and narrow sidewalks separated from the vehicular lanes by a wide continuous planter, with parking on one or both sides. The landscaping consists of street trees of a single or alternating species, aligned, in a regularly spaced allee. | T4 |
| **e. Urban 2:** This frontage is often used on Streets and Avenues and has raised curbs drained by inlets and wide sidewalks separated from the vehicular lanes by a narrow continuous planter with parking on both sides. The landscaping consists of a single tree species, aligned, in a regularly spaced allee. | T5 T6 |
| **f. Urban 3:** This frontage is often used on Main Streets and Avenues and has raised curbs drained by inlets and very wide sidewalks along both sides separated from the vehicular lanes by separate treewells with grates and parking on both sides. The landscaping consists of a single tree species, aligned, with regular spacing where possible but clearing the shopfront entrances. | T5 T6 |
| **g. Urban 4:** This frontage is typically used for Boulevards and has slip roads on both sides. It consists of raised curbs drained by inlets and sidewalks along both sides, separated from the vehicular lanes by planters. The landscaping consists of double rows of a single tree species, aligned, with regular spacing. | T3 T4 T5 T6 |

40

**Fig. 4.48** Public frontages

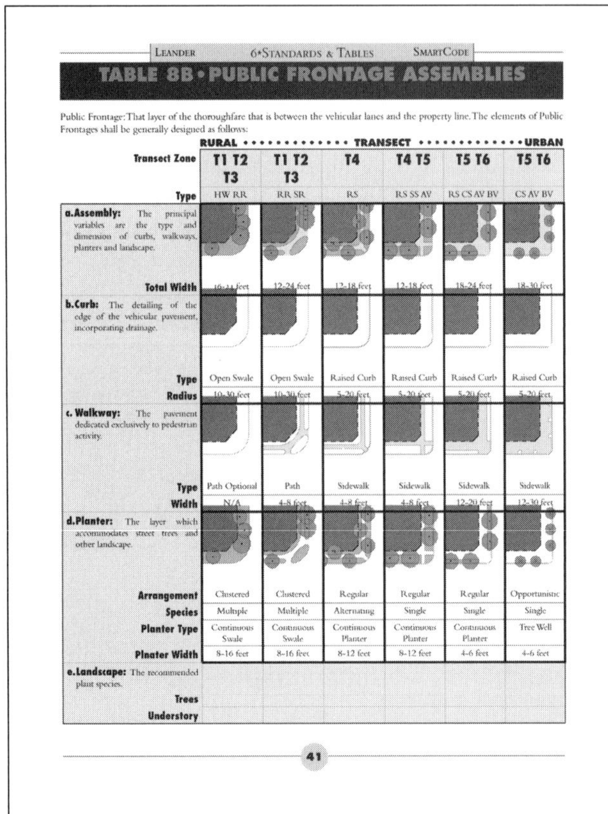

LEANDER 6•STANDARDS & TABLES SMARTCODE

## TABLE 8B • PUBLIC FRONTAGE ASSEMBLIES

Public Frontage: That layer of the thoroughfare that is between the vehicular lanes and the property line. The elements of Public Frontages shall be generally designed as follows:

RURAL • • • • • • • • • • • • • TRANSECT • • • • • • • • • • • • • URBAN

| | | | | | | |
|---|---|---|---|---|---|---|
| **Transect Zone** | T1 T2 T3 | T1 T2 T3 | T4 | T4 T5 | T5 T6 | T5 T6 |
| **Type** | HW RR | RR SR | RS | RS SS AV | RS CS AV BV | CS AV BV |
| **a. Assembly:** The principal variables are the type and dimension of curbs, walkways, planters and landscape. | | | | | | |
| **Total Width** | 16-24 feet | 12-24 feet | 12-18 feet | 12-18 feet | 18-24 feet | 18-30 feet |
| **b. Curb:** The detailing of the edge of the vehicular pavement, incorporating drainage. | | | | | | |
| **Type** | Open Swale | Open Swale | Raised Curb | Raised Curb | Raised Curb | Raised Curb |
| **Radius** | 10-30 feet | 10-30 feet | 5-20 feet | 5-20 feet | 5-20 feet | 5-20 feet |
| **c. Walkway:** The pavement dedicated exclusively to pedestrian activity. | | | | | | |
| **Type** | Path Optional | Path | Sidewalk | Sidewalk | Sidewalk | Sidewalk |
| **Width** | N/A | 4-8 feet | 4-8 feet | 4-8 feet | 12-20 feet | 12-30 feet |
| **d. Planter:** The layer which accommodates street trees and other landscape. | | | | | | |
| **Arrangement** | Clustered | Clustered | Regular | Regular | Regular | Opportunistic |
| **Species** | Multiple | Multiple | Alternating | Single | Single | Single |
| **Planter Type** | Continuous Swale | Continuous Swale | Continuous Planter | Continuous Planter | Continuous Planter | Tree Well |
| **Plnater Width** | 8-16 feet | 8-16 feet | 8-12 feet | 8-12 feet | 4-6 feet | 4-6 feet |
| **e. Landscape:** The recommended plant species. | | | | | | |
| **Trees** | | | | | | |
| **Understory** | | | | | | |

41

**Fig. 4.49** Public frontage assemblies

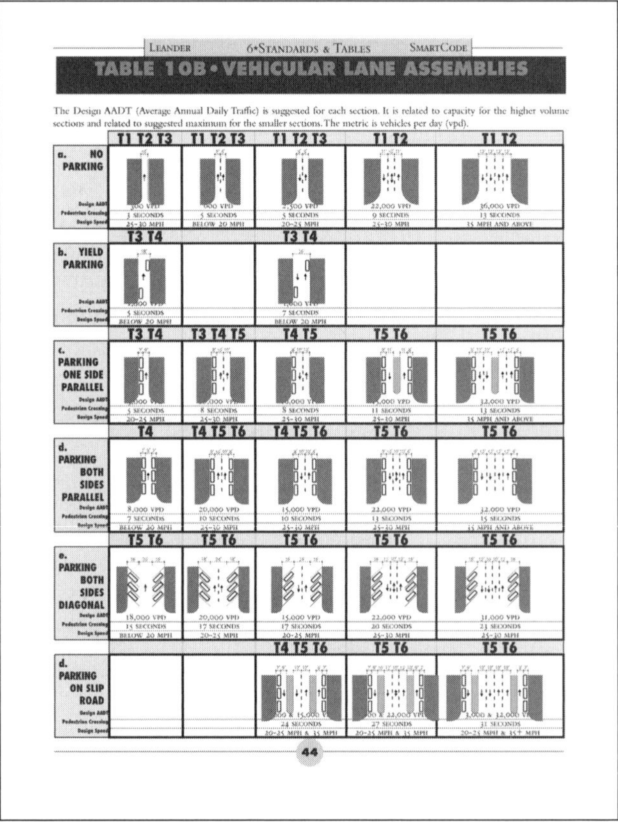

LEANDER 6•STANDARDS & TABLES SMARTCODE

## TABLE 10B • VEHICULAR LANE ASSEMBLIES

The Design AADT (Average Annual Daily Traffic) is suggested for each section. It is related to capacity for the higher volume sections and related to suggested maximum for the smaller sections. The metric is vehicles per day (vpd).

| | | | | | |
|---|---|---|---|---|---|
| **a. NO PARKING** | T1 T2 T3 | T1 T2 T3 | T1 T2 T3 | T1 T2 | T1 T2 |
| Design AADT | [illegible]00 VPD | [illegible]00 VPD | [illegible],500 VPD | 22,000 VPD | 36,000 VPD |
| Pedestrian Crossing | 3 SECONDS | 5 SECONDS | 5 SECONDS | 9 SECONDS | 13 SECONDS |
| Design Speed | 25-30 MPH | BELOW 20 MPH | 20-25 MPH | 25-30 MPH | 35 MPH AND ABOVE |
| **b. YIELD PARKING** | T3 T4 | | T3 T4 | | |
| Design AADT | [illegible],000 VPD | | [illegible],000 VPD | | |
| Pedestrian Crossing | 5 SECONDS | | 7 SECONDS | | |
| Design Speed | BELOW 20 MPH | | BELOW 20 MPH | | |
| **c. PARKING ONE SIDE PARALLEL** | T3 T4 | T3 T4 T5 | T4 T5 | T5 T6 | T5 T6 |
| Design AADT | [illegible],000 VPD | [illegible],000 VPD | [illegible],000 VPD | [illegible],000 VPD | 32,000 VPD |
| Pedestrian Crossing | 5 SECONDS | 8 SECONDS | 8 SECONDS | 11 SECONDS | 13 SECONDS |
| Design Speed | 20-25 MPH | 25-30 MPH | 25-30 MPH | 25-30 MPH | 35 MPH AND ABOVE |
| **d. PARKING BOTH SIDES PARALLEL** | T4 | T4 T5 T6 | T4 T5 T6 | T5 T6 | T5 T6 |
| Design AADT | 8,000 VPD | 20,000 VPD | 15,000 VPD | 22,000 VPD | 32,000 VPD |
| Pedestrian Crossing | 7 SECONDS | 10 SECONDS | 10 SECONDS | 13 SECONDS | 15 SECONDS |
| Design Speed | BELOW 20 MPH | 25-30 MPH | 25-30 MPH | 25-30 MPH | 35 MPH AND ABOVE |
| **e. PARKING BOTH SIDES DIAGONAL** | T5 T6 | T5 T6 | T5 T6 | T5 T6 | T5 T6 |
| Design AADT | 18,000 VPD | 20,000 VPD | 15,000 VPD | 22,000 VPD | 31,000 VPD |
| Pedestrian Crossing | 13 SECONDS | 17 SECONDS | 17 SECONDS | 20 SECONDS | 23 SECONDS |
| Design Speed | BELOW 20 MPH | 20-25 MPH | 20-25 MPH | 25-30 MPH | 25-30 MPH |
| **d. PARKING ON SLIP ROAD** | | | T4 T5 T6 | T5 T6 | T5 T6 |
| Design AADT | | | [illegible]00 & 15,000 VPD | [illegible]00 & 22,000 VPD | [illegible],000 & 32,000 VPD |
| Pedestrian Crossing | | | 24 SECONDS | 27 SECONDS | 31 SECONDS |
| Design Speed | | | 20-25 MPH & 35 MPH | 20-25 MPH & 35 MPH | 20-25 MPH & 35+ MPH |

44

**Fig. 4.50** Vehicular lane assemblies (Thoroughfare Standards)

# Heart of Peoria Land Development Code



## Peoria, Illinois

*Written by Geoffrey Ferrell, Principal, Ferrell Madden Associates*

PEORIA IS A CITY of approximately 113,000 people that is located along the Illinois River in Peoria County.[6] The team was initially hired to lead a public participation charrette and complete a detailed master plan and Form-Based Code for four redevelopment "vision areas" with minor revisions to the zoning ordinance to add balance to the core of the city. The project was ultimately expanded to be a comprehensive rewrite and translation of the zoning ordinance, for the core area, into a unified development code—the Heart of Peoria Land Development Code. The code had four integrated "pure" Form-Based Zones, called "Form Districts," derived from the detailed urban design and master planning effort.

#### Client's Background in Form-Based Coding

In 2002, the Peoria business community sponsored a DPZ charrette, creating a great deal of excitement and expectation about an urban renaissance in Peoria. In 2003, the Peoria city council "endorsed" the resulting Heart of Peoria Vision Plan, which included a recommendation for more detailed planning (and recoding) work for designated redevelopment areas.

Four years later, the enthusiasm had not translated to concrete change, and the city recognized the contradiction between its regulations and its vision. The city council established the Heart of Peoria Commission to make recommendations to invigorate the redevelopment vision.

## Code Components

A unified Land Development Code was created based on the existing zoning and subdivision regulations. Drawing on the lessons learned in the four vision areas, modifications were made to the existing code throughout the Heart of Peoria.

#### Organizing Principle

Frontages form the organizing principle for this code. This approach was used to emphasize first and foremost the importance of the way the building defines and engages the public realm.

## Code Process

Following a series of commission-sponsored workshops on Form-Based Codes in fall 2005, as well as extensive efforts by the commission and city planning staff on codifying the Heart of Peoria plan, Ferrell Madden Associates of Washington, D.C., and Code Studio of Austin, Texas, were selected to lead the urban design

| | Heart of Peoria Land Development Code |
|---|---|
| Status: | Adopted on April 30, 2007 |
| Scale: | Part of a City/Town &<br>Site-Specific (Four specific redevelopment "form districts") |
| Implementation Method: | Mandatory and Integrated |
| Site Context: | Redevelopment/Infill<br>Greyfield |
| Site Size : | 8,000 acres |
| Administration: | City/County staff |
| Organizing Principle: | Frontages |
| Code Consultants(s): | Ferrell Madden Associates; Code Studio, Inc. |
| Agency: | City of Peoria (Led by Planning and Growth Management Department) |

and Form-Based Coding effort. An interdisciplinary team from across the United States was assembled to plan for the redevelopment of the historic core of the city.

In May 2006, Peoria residents and businesspeople participated in an intensive week-long urban design charrette: the Studio Heart of Peoria (HOP). Building on the foundation laid in the Heart of Peoria Vision Plan, the Studio HOP team engaged the public and looked in greater detail at the physical urban design, traffic and transportation considerations, and underlying economic and market conditions.

#### Public Participation

Peoria residents and businesspeople took part in an intensive weeklong urban design charrette: the Studio HOP, a public-participation charrette.

The Studio HOP master planning process—particularly the level of consensus reached—illustrates the importance of citizen involvement in envisioning the future of their neighborhood and ensuring the viability and implementation of the Plan. Approximately 500 people—representing citizens, businesses, property owners, commissions, city staff, elected officials, and others—participated in the charrette-week activities, with many individuals attending multiple activities. With only minor differences in the fine-grained details, the consultant team heard consistent themes from participants throughout the week. That consensus laid the foundation for the district master plans and the Land Development Code that followed.

The consultant team was simultaneously responsible for refining details of the code in four specific "vision areas" and for code amendments to balance the area (about 8,000 acres). The end results were detailed urban designs and Form-Based Codes for each of the four vision

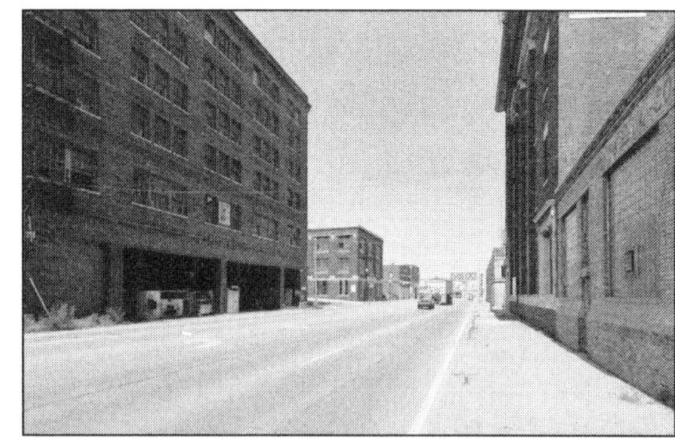

**Fig. 4.51** (previous page) Warehouse District illustrative plan

**Fig. 4.52** (left) Warehouse District photo simulation of proposed changes (Credit: Urban Advantage)

areas (Form Districts), which influenced the approach for the entire Heart of Peoria code.

Following the drafting of the new code by the consultants, the city staff moved the code through the public hearing process (planning and zoning commissions and city council) for review, approval, and adoption in the winter, spring, and summer of 2007.

## Advanced Application of FBCs

The following items are considered advanced application of Form-Based Coding.

#### Concision

The code was approach with simplicity and directness in mind and with extensive use of ap-

**Fig. 4.53** Sheridan Triangle photo simulation of proposed changes (Credit: Urban Advantage)

propriate graphics to make the code easy to understand and use.

### Integration of Form-Based Zones (Form Districts) into a Conventional Code Update

This is an approach to Form-Based Coding that many cities across the country can learn from. The Form-Based Zones (Form Districts) were integrated into a more conventional development code update. The specific areas selected for the application of the Form-Based Zones were carefully considered. The Regulating Plans show the precision that is necessary to establish the boundaries for the Form-Based Zones within the framework of the entire code.

As the vision plans evolved, the boundaries had to be very specifically considered for each of the individual areas. The Prospect Road Form District boundary focuses only on the lots facing the Prospect Road corridor; the Sheridan Triangle Form District boundary was extended along the various side streets to ensure that the goals of the vision plan could be met; the West Main Form District boundary included a block into the side streets to enable an appropriate transition from Main Street into the neighborhoods; and the Warehouse District boundaries established an entire section of town that has the potential to evolve into a mixed-use neighborhood.

### Potential Future Expansion of the FBC

An option for expansion of FBC areas, called the "Planned Form District," was included in the code. The concept was to allow future charrette work, or expansion of existing FBC areas through a defined formal process, similar to the one completed for these subareas.

### Reinforcing the Unique Local Character

This vision plan and code works to reinforce the unique aspects of the urban form of Peoria that once made the place vibrant.

*Revitalizing Pedestrian-Oriented Commercial Centers and Corridors*

One of the primary reasons for selecting the Sheridan Triangle, Prospect Road, and West Main study areas was to reinvigorate the neighborhood commercial centers and main streets that once served as the focal points for the community. The vision plan and codes were created to remove regulatory obstacles that were in place to prohibit the revitalization of these areas, so that they can once again serve as vibrant social centers within the community.

*Utilizing a Unique Aspect of the Community*

The warehouse district was selected because it represents a unique group of historic structures that played a vital role in the history of Peoria. The intent in this area was to create a code that would encourage the adaptive reuse of these beautiful historic warehouse buildings and new buildings in character with them to create a mixed-use neighborhood that was unique to Peoria.

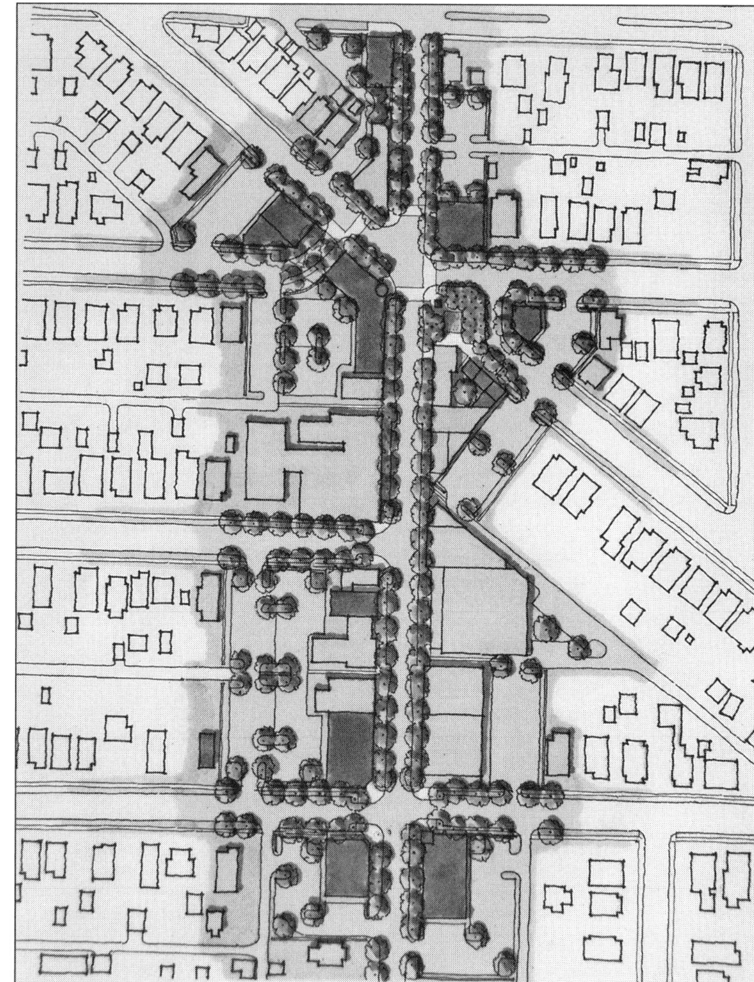

**Fig. 4.54** Sheridan Triangle Illustrative Plan

## Implementation

### Code Administration

Planning staff was involved throughout the process and clearly "own" the new code.

### Lessons Learned

The project was underfunded, to a level that the consultant team could not participate in the Public Hearing Process. Some simple issues, therefore, were magnified, and some simple fixes missed. (Despite this absence, the Form-Based Zones [Form Districts] passed without significant modification.)

## A. Warehouse District - General

HEIGHT

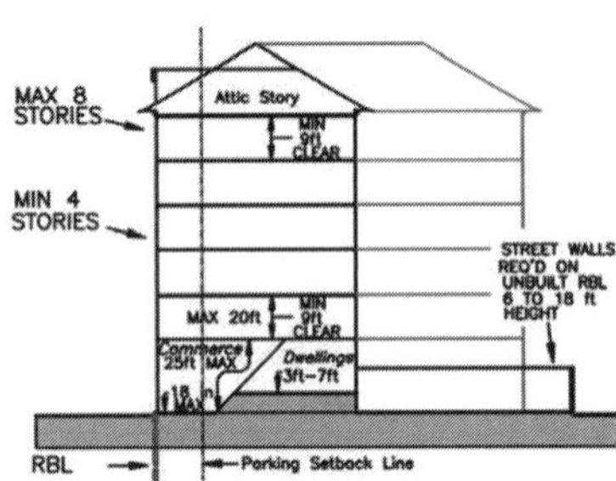


SITING

1. **Building Height**
   a. The height of the principal building is measured in stories.
   b. Each principal building shall be at least 2 stories in height, but no greater than 8 stories in height, except as otherwise provided on the regulating plan.
   c. An attic story shall not count against the maximum story height.
2. **Parking Structure Height**
   Where a parking structure is within 40 feet of any principal building (built after 2006) that portion of the structure shall not exceed the buildings eave or parapet height.
3. **Ground Story Height: Commerce/Industry Uses**
   a. The ground story finished floor elevation shall be equal to, or greater than the exterior sidewalk elevation in front of the building, to a maximum finished floor elevation of 18 inches above the sidewalk.
   b. The ground story shall have at least 12 feet of clear interior height (floor to ceiling) contiguous to the required building line frontage for a depth of at least 25 feet.
   c. The maximum story height for the ground story is 25 feet.
4. **Ground Story Height: Residential Units**
   a. The finished floor elevation shall be no less than 3 feet and no more than 7 feet above the exterior sidewalk elevation at the required building line.
   b. The first story shall have an interior clear height (floor to ceiling) of at least 9 feet and a maximum floor to floor story height of 22 feet.
5. **Upper Story Height**
   a. The maximum floor-to-floor story height for stories other than the ground story is 20 feet.
   b. At least 80% of each upper story shall have an interior clear height (floor to ceiling) of at least 9 feet.
6. **Mezzanines**
   Mezzanines having a floor area greater than 1/3 of the floor area of the story in which the mezzanine is situated shall be counted as full stories.
7. **Street Wall Height**
   a. A street wall not less than 6 feet in height or greater than 18 feet in height shall be required along any required building line frontage that is not otherwise occupied by the principal building on the lot.
   b. The height of the street wall shall be measured from the adjacent public sidewalk or, when not adjacent to a sidewalk, from the ground elevation once construction is complete.
8. **Street Facade**
   a. On each lot the building façade shall be built to the required building line for at least 80% of the required building line (RBL) length.
   b. The building façade shall be built to the required building line within 30 feet of a block corner.
   c. These portions of the building façade (the required minimum build to) may include jogs of not more than 18 inches in depth except as otherwise provided to allow bay windows, shopfronts, and balconies.
9. **Buildable Area**
   a. Buildings may occupy the portion of the lot specified by these building envelope standards.
   b. A contiguous open area equal to at least 5% of the total buildable area shall be preserved on every lot. Such contiguous open area may be located anywhere behind the parking setback, either at grade or at the second or third story.
   c. No part of any building, except overhanging eaves, awnings, or balconies shall occupy the remaining lot area.
10. **Side Lot Setbacks**
    There are no required side lot setbacks.
11. **Garage and Parking**
    a. Garage entries or driveways shall be located at least 75 feet away from any block corner or another garage entry on the same block, unless otherwise designated on the regulating plan.
    b. Garage Entries shall have a clear height of no greater than 16 feet nor a clear width exceeding 24 feet.
    c. Vehicle parking areas on private property shall be located behind the parking setback line, except where parking is provided below grade.
    d. These requirements are not applicable to on-street parking.
12. **Alleys**
    There is no required setback from alleys. On lots having no alley access, there shall be a minimum setback of 25 feet from the rear lot line.
13. **Corner Lots**
    Corner lots shall satisfy the code requirements for the full required building line length – unless otherwise specified in this code.
14. **Unbuilt Required Building Line and Common Lot Line Treatment**
    a. A street wall shall be required along any required building line frontage that is not otherwise occupied by a building. The street wall shall be located no more 8 inches behind the required building line.
    b. Privacy fences may be constructed along that portion of a common lot line not otherwise occupied by a building.



**Fig. 4.55** (left and right) Warehouse District Building Form Standards

## B. Warehouse District - General

### ELEMENTS

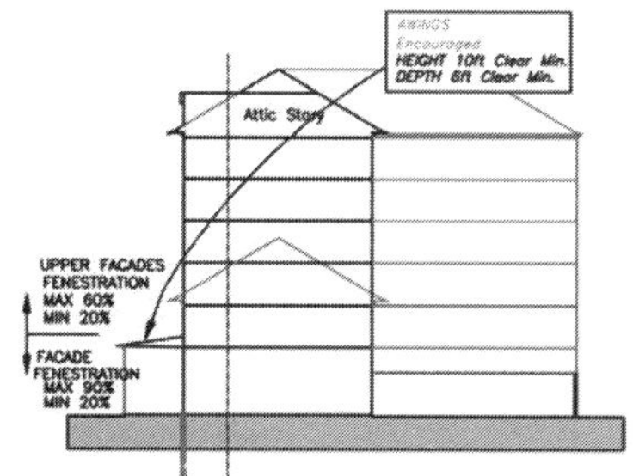


1. **Windows and Doors**
   a. Blank lengths of wall exceeding 20 linear feet are prohibited on all required building lines.
   b. Windows and Doors on the ground story facades shall comprise at least 20%, but not more than 90%, of the facade area (measured as a percentage of the facade between floor levels).
   c. Windows and Doors on the upper story facades shall comprise at least 20%, but no more than 60%, of the facade area per story (measured as a percentage of the facade between floor levels).
   d. No window may face or direct views toward a common lot line within 30 feet unless: that view is contained within the lot (e.g. by a privacy fence/garden wall) or, the sill is at least 6 feet above the finished floor level. All common lot lines within the warehouse form district are subject to the construction of building walls (with no setback) by the adjacent lot owner.
2. **Building Projections**
   a. Balconies and stoops shall not project closer than 5 feet to a common lot line.
   b. No part of any building, except overhanging eaves, awnings, balconies, bay windows, stoops, and shopfronts as specified by the code, shall encroach beyond the required building line.
   c. Awnings shall project a minimum of 6 feet and a maximum of within 1 foot of back of curb (where there are no street trees) or 1 foot into the tree lawn (where there are street trees.)
   d. Awnings that project over the sidewalk portion of a street-space shall maintain a clear height of at least 10 feet except as otherwise provided for signs, street lighting and similar appurtenances.
   e. Awnings may have supporting posts at their outer edge provided that they:
   f. Have a minimum of 8 feet clear width between the facade and the support posts or columns of the awning.
   g. Provide for a continuous public access easement at least 6 feet wide running adjacent and parallel to the awning columns/posts
3. **Doors/Entries**
   a. Functioning entry door(s) shall be provided along ground story facades at intervals not greater than 75 linear feet
   b. Each ground story residential unit shall have direct access to the street-space.
4. **Street Walls**
   A vehicle entry gate no wider than 18 feet or a pedestrian entry gate no wider than 6 feet shall be permitted within any required street wall.

### USE

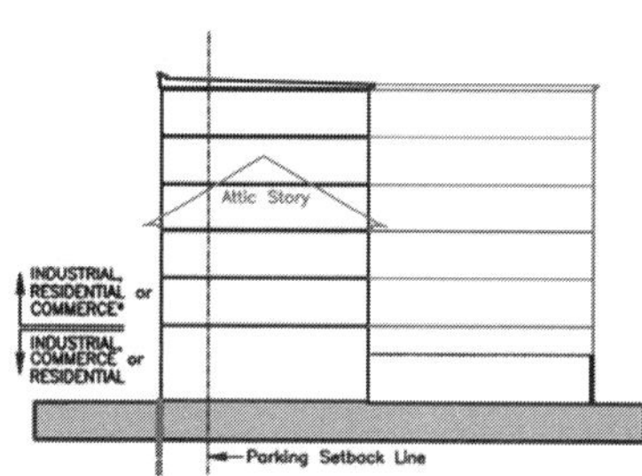


5. **Ground Story**
   The ground story shall house commerce, industrial or residential uses. See Height specifications above for specific requirements unique to each use.
6. **Upper Stories**
   a. The upper stories shall house commerce, industrial or residential uses. No restaurant or retail sales uses shall be allowed in upper stories unless they are second story extensions equal to or less than the area of the ground story use.
   b. Additional habitable space is permitted within the roof where the roof is configured as an attic story.
7. **Permitted Uses**
   a. Residential uses shall be considered to encompass all of the Residential use categories, as defined in Article 5.6.
   b. Commerce uses shall be considered to encompass all of the Commercial use categories, and all of the Civic use categories except passenger terminals and social service institutions, as defined in Article 5.6.
   c. Industrial uses shall be considered to encompass all of the Industrial use categories except the heavy industrial and waste-related services, as defined in Article 5.6.

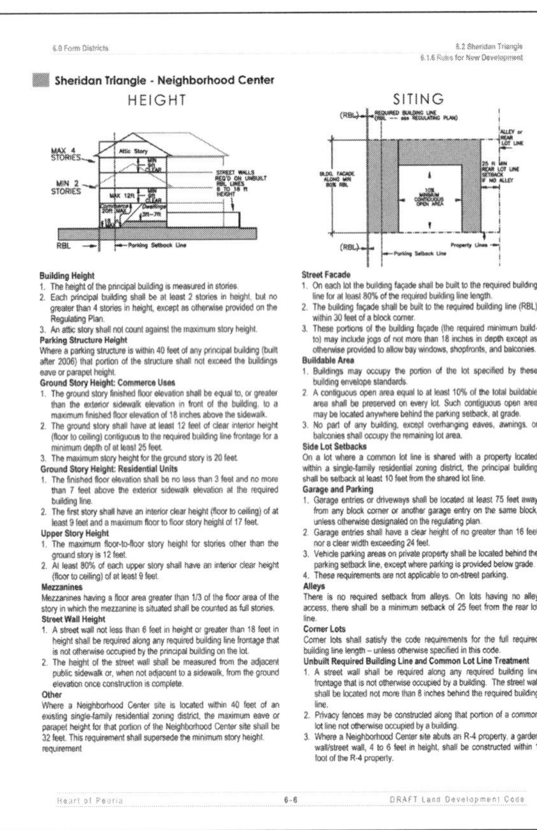

6.0 Form Districts

6.2 Sheridan Triangle
6.1.6 Rules for New Development

**Sheridan Triangle - Neighborhood Center**

HEIGHT

SITING

**Building Height**
1. The height of the principal building is measured in stories.
2. Each principal building shall be at least 2 stories in height, but no greater than 4 stories in height, except as otherwise provided on the Regulating Plan.
3. An attic story shall not count against the maximum story height.

**Parking Structure Height**
Where a parking structure is within 40 feet of any principal building (built after 2006) that portion of the structure shall not exceed the buildings eave or parapet height.

**Ground Story Height: Commerce Uses**
1. The ground story finished floor elevation shall be equal to, or greater than the exterior sidewalk elevation in front of the building, to a maximum finished floor elevation of 18 inches above the sidewalk.
2. The ground story shall have at least 12 feet of clear interior height (floor to ceiling) contiguous to the required building line frontage for a minimum depth of at least 25 feet.
3. The maximum story height for the ground story is 20 feet.

**Ground Story Height: Residential Units**
1. The finished floor elevation shall be no less than 3 feet and no more than 7 feet above the exterior sidewalk elevation at the required building line.
2. The first story shall have an interior clear height (floor to ceiling) of at least 9 feet and a maximum floor to floor story height of 17 feet.

**Upper Story Height**
1. The maximum floor-to-floor story height for stories other than the ground story is 12 feet.
2. At least 80% of each upper story shall have an interior clear height (floor to ceiling) of at least 9 feet.

**Mezzanines**
Mezzanines having a floor area greater than 1/3 of the floor area of the story in which the mezzanine is situated shall be counted as full stories.

**Street Wall Height**
1. A street wall not less than 6 feet in height or greater than 18 feet in height shall be required along any required building line frontage that is not otherwise occupied by the principal building on the lot.
2. The height of the street wall shall be measured from the adjacent public sidewalk or, when not adjacent to a sidewalk, from the ground elevation once construction is complete.

**Other**
Where a Neighborhood Center site is located within 40 feet of an existing single-family residential zoning district, the maximum eave or parapet height for that portion of the Neighborhood Center site shall be 32 feet. This requirement shall supersede the minimum story height. requirement

**Street Facade**
1. On each lot the building façade shall be built to the required building line for at least 80% of the required building line length.
2. The building façade shall be built to the required building line (RBL) within 30 feet of a block corner.
3. These portions of the building façade (the required minimum build-to) may include jogs of not more than 18 inches in depth except as otherwise provided to allow bay windows, shopfronts, and balconies.

**Buildable Area**
1. Buildings may occupy the portion of the lot specified by these building envelope standards.
2. A contiguous open area equal to at least 10% of the total buildable area shall be preserved on every lot. Such contiguous open area may be located anywhere behind the parking setback, at grade.
3. No part of any building, except overhanging eaves, awnings, or balconies shall occupy the remaining lot area.

**Side Lot Setbacks**
On a lot where a common lot line is shared with a property located within a single-family residential zoning district, the principal building shall be setback at least 10 feet from the shared lot line.

**Garage and Parking**
1. Garage entries or driveways shall be located at least 75 feet away from any block corner or another garage entry on the same block, unless otherwise designated on the regulating plan.
2. Garage entries shall have a clear height of no greater than 16 feet nor a clear width exceeding 24 feet.
3. Vehicle parking areas on private property shall be located behind the parking setback line, except where parking is provided below grade.
4. These requirements are not applicable to on-street parking.

**Alleys**
There is no required setback from alleys. On lots having no alley access, there shall be a minimum setback of 25 feet from the rear lot line.

**Corner Lots**
Corner lots shall satisfy the code requirements for the full required building line length – unless otherwise specified in this code.

**Unbuilt Required Building Line and Common Lot Line Treatment**
1. A street wall shall be required along any required building line frontage that is not otherwise occupied by a building. The street wall shall be located not more than 8 inches behind the required building line.
2. Privacy fences may be constructed along that portion of a common lot line not otherwise occupied by a building.
3. Where a Neighborhood Center site abuts an R-4 property, a garden wall/street wall, 4 to 6 feet in height, shall be constructed within 1 foot of the R-4 property.

Heart of Peoria 6-6 DRAFT Land Development Code

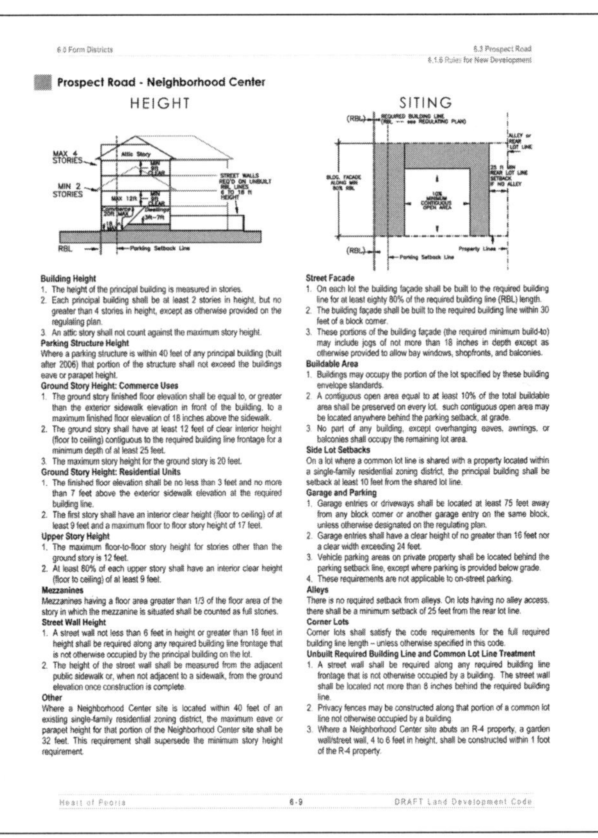

6.0 Form Districts

6.3 Prospect Road
6.1.6 Rules for New Development

**Prospect Road - Neighborhood Center**

HEIGHT

SITING

**Building Height**
1. The height of the principal building is measured in stories.
2. Each principal building shall be at least 2 stories in height, but no greater than 4 stories in height, except as otherwise provided on the regulating plan.
3. An attic story shall not count against the maximum story height.

**Parking Structure Height**
Where a parking structure is within 40 feet of any principal building (built after 2006) that portion of the structure shall not exceed the buildings eave or parapet height.

**Ground Story Height: Commerce Uses**
1. The ground story finished floor elevation shall be equal to, or greater than the exterior sidewalk elevation in front of the building, to a maximum finished floor elevation of 18 inches above the sidewalk.
2. The ground story shall have at least 12 feet of clear interior height (floor to ceiling) contiguous to the required building line frontage for a minimum depth of at least 25 feet.
3. The maximum story height for the ground story is 20 feet.

**Ground Story Height: Residential Units**
1. The finished floor elevation shall be no less than 3 feet and no more than 7 feet above the exterior sidewalk elevation at the required building line.
2. The first story shall have an interior clear height (floor to ceiling) of at least 9 feet and a maximum floor to floor story height of 17 feet.

**Upper Story Height**
1. The maximum floor-to-floor story height for stories other than the ground story is 12 feet.
2. At least 80% of each upper story shall have an interior clear height (floor to ceiling) of at least 9 feet.

**Mezzanines**
Mezzanines having a floor area greater than 1/3 of the floor area of the story in which the mezzanine is situated shall be counted as full stories.

**Street Wall Height**
1. A street wall not less than 6 feet in height or greater than 18 feet in height shall be required along any required building line frontage that is not otherwise occupied by the principal building on the lot.
2. The height of the street wall shall be measured from the adjacent public sidewalk or, when not adjacent to a sidewalk, from the ground elevation once construction is complete.

**Other**
Where a Neighborhood Center site is located within 40 feet of an existing single-family residential zoning district, the maximum eave or parapet height for that portion of the Neighborhood Center site shall be 32 feet. This requirement shall supersede the minimum story height requirement.

**Street Facade**
1. On each lot the building façade shall be built to the required building line for at least eighty 80% of the required building line (RBL) length.
2. The building façade shall be built to the required building line within 30 feet of a block corner.
3. These portions of the building façade (the required minimum build-to) may include jogs of not more than 18 inches in depth except as otherwise provided to allow bay windows, shopfronts, and balconies.

**Buildable Area**
1. Buildings may occupy the portion of the lot specified by these building envelope standards.
2. A contiguous open area equal to at least 10% of the total buildable area shall be preserved on every lot. such contiguous open area may be located anywhere behind the parking setback, at grade.
3. No part of any building, except overhanging eaves, awnings, or balconies shall occupy the remaining lot area.

**Side Lot Setbacks**
On a lot where a common lot line is shared with a property located within a single-family residential zoning district, the principal building shall be setback at least 10 feet from the shared lot line.

**Garage and Parking**
1. Garage entries or driveways shall be located at least 75 feet away from any block corner or another garage entry on the same block, unless otherwise designated on the regulating plan.
2. Garage entries shall have a clear height of no greater than 16 feet nor a clear width exceeding 24 feet.
3. Vehicle parking areas on private property shall be located behind the parking setback line, except where parking is provided below grade.
4. These requirements are not applicable to on-street parking.

**Alleys**
There is no required setback from alleys. On lots having no alley access, there shall be a minimum setback of 25 feet from the rear lot line.

**Corner Lots**
Corner lots shall satisfy the code requirements for the full required building line length – unless otherwise specified in this code.

**Unbuilt Required Building Line and Common Lot Line Treatment**
1. A street wall shall be required along any required building line frontage that is not otherwise occupied by a building. The street wall shall be located not more than 8 inches behind the required building line.
2. Privacy fences may be constructed along that portion of a common lot line not otherwise occupied by a building.
3. Where a Neighborhood Center site abuts an R-4 property, a garden wall/street wall, 4 to 6 feet in height, shall be constructed within 1 foot of the R-4 property.

Heart of Peoria 6-9 DRAFT Land Development Code

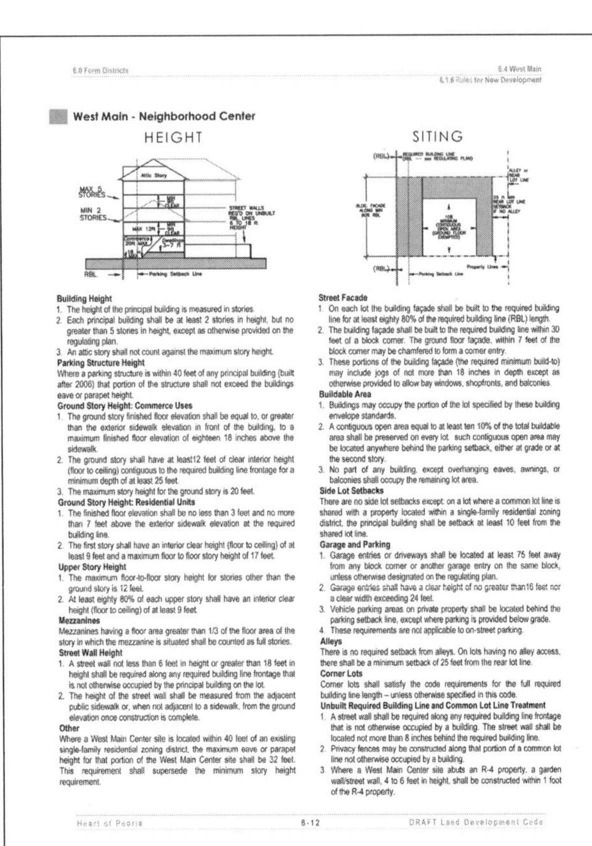

6.0 Form Districts

6.4 West Main
6.1.6 Rules for New Development

**West Main - Neighborhood Center**

HEIGHT

SITING

**Building Height**
1. The height of the principal building is measured in stories.
2. Each principal building shall be at least 2 stories in height, but no greater than 5 stories in height, except as otherwise provided on the regulating plan.
3. An attic story shall not count against the maximum story height.

**Parking Structure Height**
Where a parking structure is within 40 feet of any principal building (built after 2006) that portion of the structure shall not exceed the buildings eave or parapet height.

**Ground Story Height: Commerce Uses**
1. The ground story finished floor elevation shall be equal to, or greater than the exterior sidewalk elevation in front of the building, to a maximum finished floor elevation of eighteen 18 inches above the sidewalk.
2. The ground story shall have at least12 feet of clear interior height (floor to ceiling) contiguous to the required building line frontage for a minimum depth of at least 25 feet.
3. The maximum story height for the ground story is 20 feet.

**Ground Story Height: Residential Units**
1. The finished floor elevation shall be no less than 3 feet and no more than 7 feet above the exterior sidewalk elevation at the required building line.
2. The first story shall have an interior clear height (floor to ceiling) of at least 9 feet and a maximum floor to floor story height of 17 feet.

**Upper Story Height**
1. The maximum floor-to-floor story height for stories other than the ground story is 12 feet.
2. At least eighty 80% of each upper story shall have an interior clear height (floor to ceiling) of at least 9 feet.

**Mezzanines**
Mezzanines having a floor area greater than 1/3 of the floor area of the story in which the mezzanine is situated shall be counted as full stories.

**Street Wall Height**
1. A street wall not less than 6 feet in height or greater than 18 feet in height shall be required along any required building line frontage that is not otherwise occupied by the principal building on the lot.
2. The height of the street wall shall be measured from the adjacent public sidewalk or, when not adjacent to a sidewalk, from the ground elevation once construction is complete.

**Other**
Where a West Main Center site is located within 40 feet of an existing single-family residential zoning district, the maximum eave or parapet height for that portion of the West Main Center site shall be 32 feet. This requirement shall supersede the minimum story height requirement.

**Street Facade**
1. On each lot the building façade shall be built to the required building line for at least eighty 80% of the required building line (RBL) length.
2. The building façade shall be built to the required building line within 30 feet of a block corner. The ground floor façade, within 7 feet of the block corner may be chamfered to form a corner entry.
3. These portions of the building façade (the required minimum build-to) may include jogs of not more than 18 inches in depth except as otherwise provided to allow bay windows, shopfronts, and balconies.

**Buildable Area**
1. Buildings may occupy the portion of the lot specified by these building envelope standards.
2. A contiguous open area equal to at least ten 10% of the total buildable area shall be preserved on every lot. such contiguous open area may be located anywhere behind the parking setback, either at grade or at the second story.
3. No part of any building, except overhanging eaves, awnings, or balconies shall occupy the remaining lot area.

**Side Lot Setbacks**
There are no side lot setbacks except: on a lot where a common lot line is shared with a property located within a single-family residential zoning district, the principal building shall be setback at least 10 feet from the shared lot line.

**Garage and Parking**
1. Garage entries or driveways shall be located at least 75 feet away from any block corner or another garage entry on the same block, unless otherwise designated on the regulating plan.
2. Garage entries shall have a clear height of no greater than16 feet nor a clear width exceeding 24 feet.
3. Vehicle parking areas on private property shall be located behind the parking setback line, except where parking is provided below grade.
4. These requirements are not applicable to on-street parking.

**Alleys**
There is no required setback from alleys. On lots having no alley access, there shall be a minimum setback of 25 feet from the rear lot line.

**Corner Lots**
Corner lots shall satisfy the code requirements for the full required building line length – unless otherwise specified in this code.

**Unbuilt Required Building Line and Common Lot Line Treatment**
1. A street wall shall be required along any required building line frontage that is not otherwise occupied by a building. The street wall shall be located not more than 8 inches behind the required building line.
2. Privacy fences may be constructed along that portion of a common lot line not otherwise occupied by a building.
3. Where a West Main Center site abuts an R-4 property, a garden wall/street wall, 4 to 6 feet in height, shall be constructed within 1 foot of the R-4 property.

Heart of Peoria 6-12 DRAFT Land Development Code

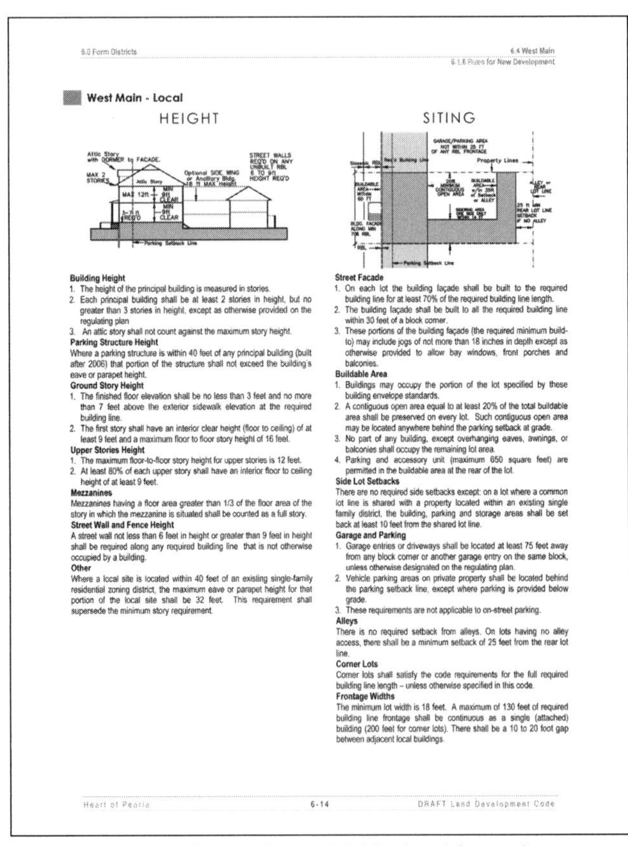

6.0 Form Districts

6.4 West Main
6.1.6 Rules for New Development

**West Main - Local**

HEIGHT

SITING

**Building Height**
1. The height of the principal building is measured in stories.
2. Each principal building shall be at least 2 stories in height, but no greater than 3 stories in height, except as otherwise provided on the regulating plan
3. An attic story shall not count against the maximum story height.

**Parking Structure Height**
Where a parking structure is within 40 feet of any principal building (built after 2006) that portion of the structure shall not exceed the building's eave or parapet height.

**Ground Story Height**
1. The finished floor elevation shall be no less than 3 feet and no more than 7 feet above the exterior sidewalk elevation at the required building line.
2. The first story shall have an interior clear height (floor to ceiling) of at least 9 feet and a maximum floor to floor story height of 16 feet.

**Upper Stories Height**
1. The maximum floor-to-floor story height for upper stories is 12 feet.
2. At least 80% of each upper story shall have an interior floor to ceiling height of at least 9 feet.

**Mezzanines**
Mezzanines having a floor area greater than 1/3 of the floor area of the story in which the mezzanine is situated shall be counted as a full story.

**Street Wall and Fence Height**
A street wall not less than 6 feet in height or greater than 9 feet in height shall be required along any required building line that is not otherwise occupied by a building.

**Other**
Where a local site is located within 40 feet of an existing single-family residential zoning district, the maximum eave or parapet height for that portion of the local site shall be 32 feet. This requirement shall supersede the minimum story requirement.

**Street Facade**
1. On each lot the building façade shall be built to the required building line for at least 70% of the required building line length.
2. The building façade shall be built to all the required building line within 30 feet of a block corner.
3. These portions of the building façade (the required minimum build-to) may include jogs of not more than 18 inches in depth except as otherwise provided to allow bay windows, front porches and balconies.

**Buildable Area**
1. Buildings may occupy the portion of the lot specified by these building envelope standards.
2. A contiguous open area equal to at least 20% of the total buildable area shall be preserved on every lot. Such contiguous open area may be located anywhere behind the parking setback at grade.
3. No part of any building, except overhanging eaves, awnings, or balconies shall occupy the remaining lot area.
4. Parking and accessory unit (maximum 650 square feet) are permitted in the buildable area at the rear of the lot.

**Side Lot Setbacks**
There are no required side setbacks except: on a lot where a common lot line is shared with a property located within an existing single family district, the building, parking and storage areas shall be set back at least 10 feet from the shared lot line.

**Garage and Parking**
1. Garage entries or driveways shall be located at least 75 feet away from any block corner or another garage entry on the same block, unless otherwise designated on the regulating plan.
2. Vehicle parking areas on private property shall be located behind the parking setback line, except where parking is provided below grade.
3. These requirements are not applicable to on-street parking.

**Alleys**
There is no required setback from alleys. On lots having no alley access, there shall be a minimum setback of 25 feet from the rear lot line.

**Corner Lots**
Corner lots shall satisfy the code requirements for the full required building line length – unless otherwise specified in this code.

**Frontage Widths**
The minimum lot width is 18 feet. A maximum of 130 feet of required building line frontage shall be continuous as a single (attached) building (200 feet for corner lots). There shall be a 10 to 20 foot gap between adjacent local buildings.

Heart of Peoria 6-14 DRAFT Land Development Code

**Fig. 4.56** Building Form Standards for Sheridan Triangle (top left), Prospect Road (top right), West Main Neighborhood Center (bottom left), and West Main Local (bottom right)

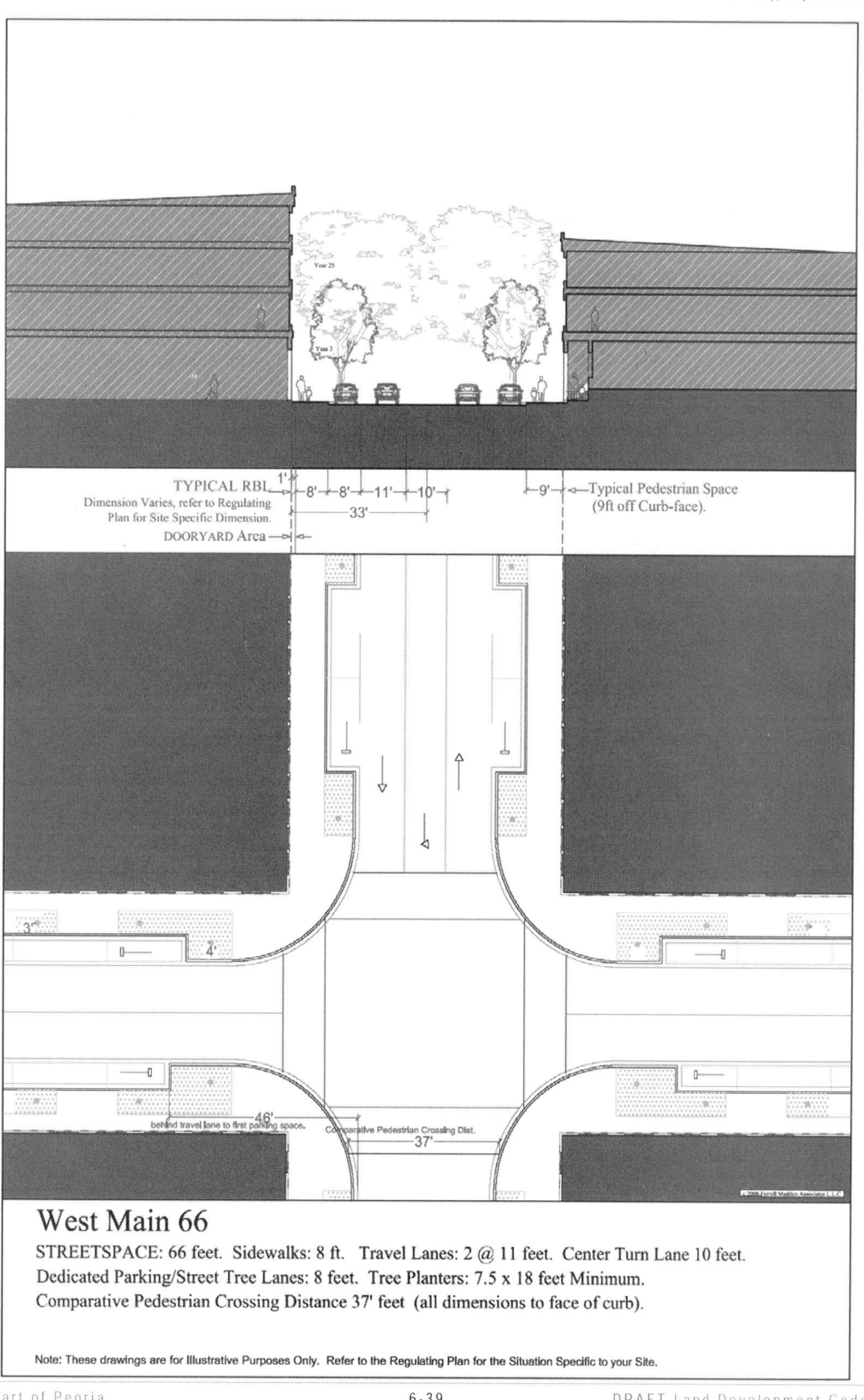
TYPICAL RBL
1'
8'
8'
11'
10'
33'
Dimension Varies, refer to Regulating Plan for Site Specific Dimension.
DOORYARD Area
9'
Typical Pedestrian Space (9ft off Curb-face).
3'
4'
46'
behind travel lane to first parking space.
Comparative Pedestrian Crossing Dist.
37'
West Main 66
STREETSPACE: 66 feet. Sidewalks: 8 ft. Travel Lanes: 2 @ 11 feet. Center Turn Lane 10 feet.
Dedicated Parking/Street Tree Lanes: 8 feet. Tree Planters: 7.5 x 18 feet Minimum.
Comparative Pedestrian Crossing Distance 37' feet (all dimensions to face of curb).
Note: These drawings are for Illustrative Purposes Only. Refer to the Regulating Plan for the Situation Specific to your Site.

**Fig. 4.57** Thoroughfare Standards for West Main 66

## 2.0 Administration

### 2.1 REVIEW BODIES

#### 2.1.1 Summary of Review Authority

The following table summarizes the required review and approval authority provided under this development code.

| Procedure | 2.1.2<br>Zoning Administrator | 2.1.3<br>Site Plan Review Board | 2.1.4<br>Planning Commission | 2.1.5<br>Zoning Commission | 2.1.6<br>Zoning Board of Appeals | 2.1.7<br>City Council | Reference |
|---|---|---|---|---|---|---|---|
| Zoning Compliance Certificates | D | R | | | | | 2.2 |
| Certificate of Occupancy | D | | | | | | 2.3 |
| Administrative Deviation | D | | | | | | 2.4 |
| Uses Permitted with Administrative Approval | D | | | | | | 2.5 |
| Minor Variations without Site Plan Review | D | | | | | | 2.6 |
| Minor Variations with Site Plan Review | D | R | | | | | 2.6 |
| Major Variations without Site Plan Review | R | | | | <D> | | 2.6 |
| Major Variations with Site Plan Review | R | R | | | <D> | | 2.6 |
| Appeals | | | | | <D> | | 2.7 |
| Amendments | R | R | | <R> | | <D> | 2.8 |
| Special Use | R | R | | <R> | | <D> | 2.9 |
| Official Development Plan | R | R | | <R> | | <D> | 2.10 |
| Critical Traffic Management Areas | R | R | | | | <D> | 2.11 |
| Traffic Impact Analysis | R | R | | | | R | 2.12 |
| Subdivision Plat (with waiver) | R | | <R> | | | <D> | 2.13 |
| Subdivision Plat (without waiver) | D | | | | | | 2.13 |
| Tract Survey | D | | | | | | 2.13 |
| Multifamily Plan | | | <R> | | | <D> | 2.13 |
| Certificate of Appropriateness (oNC only) | R | R | | <D> | | | 7.1 |
| Annexations | R | | <R> | | | | ?? |

**KEY:** R = Review or Recommendation D = Final Decision <> = Public Hearing

Heart of Peoria 2-1 City Council Review Draft Land Development Code

**Fig. 4.58** Administration of the code

# Form-Based Code for Mixed-Use Infill 

## Sarasota County, Florida

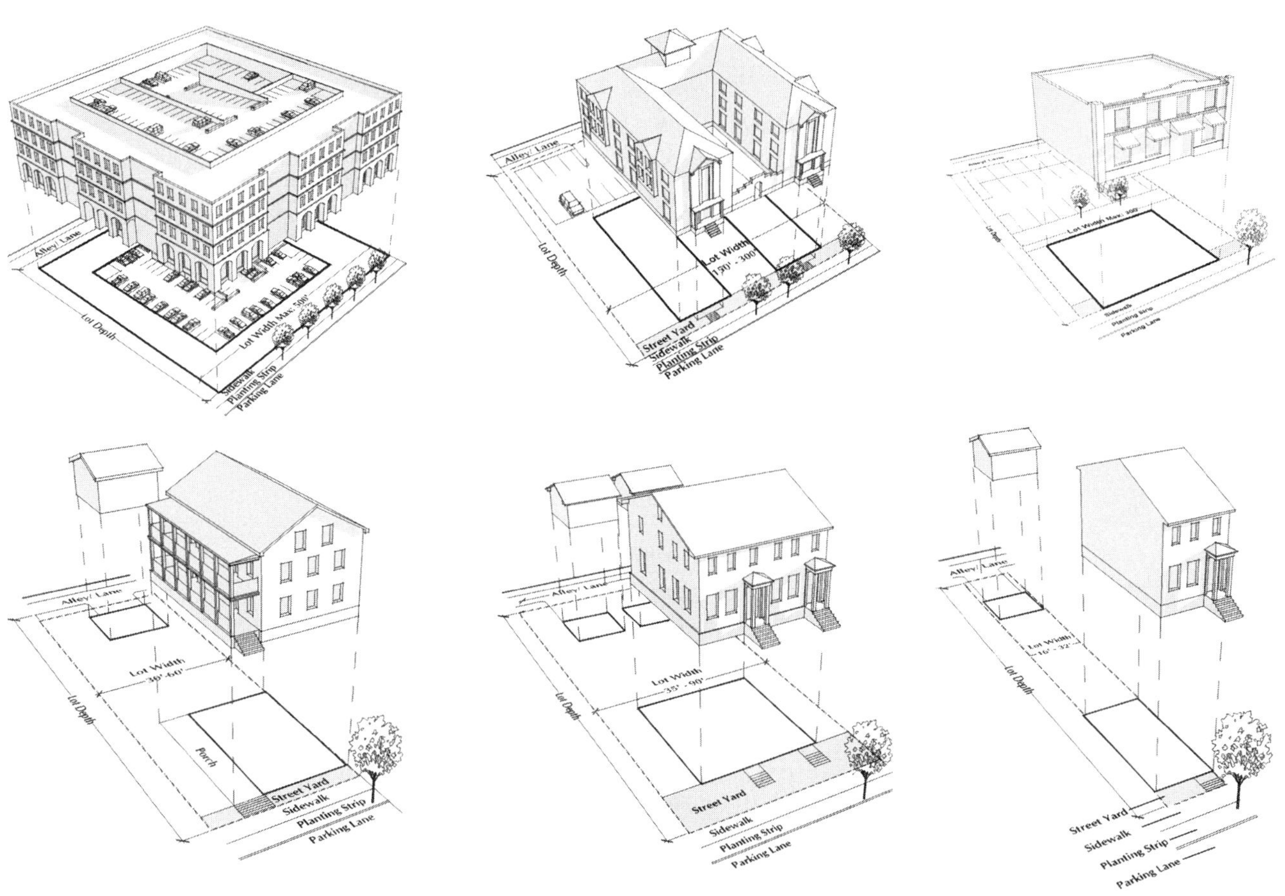

*Written by*
*William M. Spikowski,*
*Principal,*
*Spikowski Planning*
*Associates*

Sarasota County is located on the western coast of Florida south of Tampa. The 2005 population estimate for the county was 366,256.[7] The initial task for this process was to evaluate the county's existing and proposed regulations, including the ordinances implementing the "Sarasota 2050" regional plan for unincorporated Sarasota County, to determine whether they would achieve the county's goals for promoting higher densities in mixed-use developments in a largely suburban community.

The task was later expanded to include formulating a new FBC to replace alternative regulations that had been under consideration. The new code includes a mandatory charrette requirement to allow early input from other stakeholders.

#### Client's Background in Form-Based Coding

County officials had previously adopted a floating-zone infill code that contained many Form-Based techniques. No developers had chosen to use that code despite a robust economy; the reasons most commonly cited were insufficient flexibility in applying generally sound but quite rigid principles to difficult infill sites. County officials were determined to make their plan work and were willing to try something different: providing a more flexible coding option for developers who agreed to use charrettes to plan their development proposals.

#### Selection Process

County consultants Peter Katz and Bill Spikowski developed the concept for this code. Sarasota County retained six major planning and urban design firms to provide continuing consulting services on this and related projects through an open Request for Qualifications (RFQ) process. Dover, Kohl & Partners and Spikowski Planning Associates were then retained to prepare the code, to be assisted by Hall Planning and Engineering.

### Code Components

The foundations for the code were already in the Sarasota County Comprehensive Plan, which encourages higher densities in mixed-use developments and calls for reuse and development of vacant or underutilized commercial parcels as mixed-use neighborhoods.

| | Sarasota County Form-Based Code for Mixed-Use Infill |
|---|---|
| Status: | Adopted on August 28, 2007 |
| Scale: | Neighborhood (Designated growth nodes from Comprehensive Plan) |
| Implementation Method: | Floating Zone/TND |
| Site Context: | Redevelopment/Infill and Greyfield |
| Site Size: | Potentially applicable to about 12,275 acres in unincorporated Sarasota County |
| Administration: | Will be administered by county staff; rezoning approval for each infill site is required by the Board of County Commissioners. |
| Organizing Principle: | Transect |
| Code Consultants(s): | Dover, Kohl & Partners; Spikowski Planning Associates; Hall Planning and Engineering |
| Agency: | Sarasota County Board of County Commissioners |

### Organizing Principle

The code is based on two organizing principles, which must be shown on a proposed Regulating Plan for each infill sitet that requires approval through a planned development rezoning process. Each Regulating Plan must show transect zones and lot (building) types. Each Regulating Plan must also identify proposed street types that are consistent with the proposed allocation of transect zones.

## Code Process

The process described here created a new floating-zone code that was more flexible than the existing code. The new code can be used only by developers who undertake a full charrette-based planning process for their site, allowing early input from other stakeholders, including nearby property owners and county staff.

The code was drafted by the consulting team, working closely with county staff from nearly every department. Sarasota County hired a peer review team of leading national firms to extensively critique the code midway through its preparation. Adoption took place through the normal public hearing process.

### Public Participation

Two public processes underlie this code. First, the "Sarasota 2050" visioning process, completed in 2002, created a 50-year incentive-based plan that shapes future growth by preserving the county's natural, cultural, and physical resources and making all neighborhoods, both old and new, more livable. This plan grants density bonuses to landowners who build compact, mixed-use, walkable developments in appropriate areas. Second, through the standard Comprehensive Plan amendment process, Sarasota County in 2004 committed to allow higher densities in mixed-use centers within the urban service area.

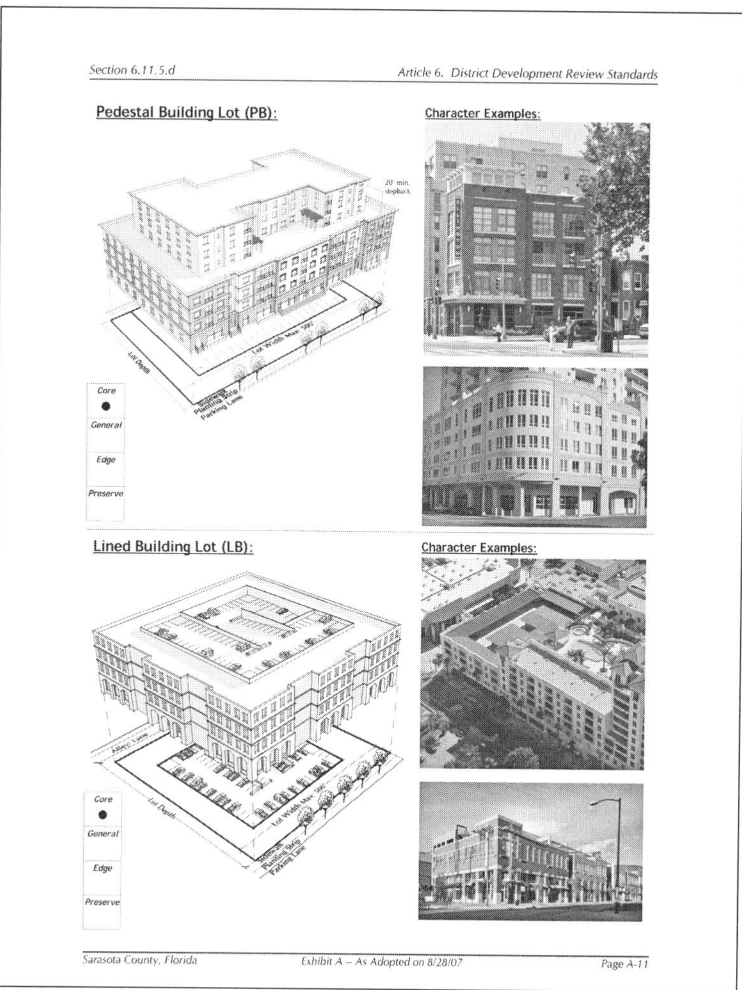


The adoption of this code followed the normal process for legislation: public workshops, planning commission public hearings, and county commission adoption hearings.

**Fig. 4.59** (previous page) A variety of building types

**Fig. 4.60** (above) Pedestal Building Lot and Lined Building Lot Standards

## Advanced Application of FBCs

The following are advanced aspects of Form-Based Coding inherent in this code.

### Application to Selected Growth Areas

Many communities wish to promote mixed-use infill development on a network of walkable streets. Every infill site has its own constraints. This code identifies the core components of urbanism and then allows them to be customized to individual sites by the private sector. In this new process, the developer's designer creates the Regulating Plan after each site

Street F:

Core
General
●
Edge
●
Preserve

Sidewalk | Planting Strip | Yield Condition With On Street Parking | Planting Strip | Sidewalk

6' | 6' | 7' | 9' | 9' | 6' | 6'

Typical Right-of-Way: 49'

Drive:

Core
General
●
Edge
●
Preserve

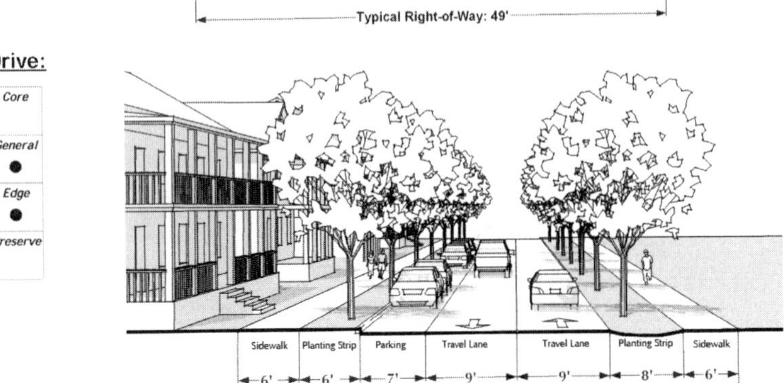


**Fig. 4.61** (above) "Street F" and "Drive" Thoroughfare standards
**Fig. 4.62** (below) Building Form Standards summary table

is planned through the charrette process. A prototypical Regulating Plan is shown in the code.

## County-Approved Design Firms

Developers must choose from a list of county-approved design firms to create the vision plan and Regulating Plans for their sites.

## Charrette Requirement

Only developers who agree to undertake a full charrette-based planning process for their site can use this code. The charrette process must follow the planning approaches outlined in *The Charrette Handbook* by Bill Lennertz and Aarin Lutzenhiser.

## Three Dimensional Code Graphics

In place of the plan and cross-section diagrams typically found in Form-Based Codes, this code

**TABLE 1**
**LOT SIZE AND DIMENSIONAL REQUIREMENTS**

| Lot Type | Lot Area (min / max in sf) | Lot Width (min / max) | Frontage Percentage (min / max) | Lot Coverage by all bldgs (max) | Yards: Street (min / max) Core | Yards: Street General | Yards: Street Edge | Yards: Side (min) | Yards: Rear[1, 2] (min) | Yards: Waterfront[3] (min) | Height[4] (min/max in stories; max in feet) Core | Height General | Height Edge | Accessory Dwelling Unit[5] (max bldg footprint in sf) |
|---|---|---|---|---|---|---|---|---|---|---|---|---|---|---|
| Pedestal Building Lot | no min / no max | no min / 500 | 90% / 100% | 100% | 0 / 10 | not permitted | not permitted | 0 | 0 | 20 / 30 | 2 / 7[6] 85' | not permitted | not permitted | not permitted |
| Lined Building Lot | no min / no max | no min / 500 | 90% / 100% | 100% | 0 / 10 | not permitted | not permitted | 0 | 0 | 20 / 30 | 2 / 5; 65' | not permitted | not permitted | not permitted |
| Mixed-Use Building Lot | no min / no max | no min / 300 | 90% / 100% | 100% | 0 / 10 | 0 / 10 | not permitted | 0 | 3 | 20 / 30 | 2 / 5; 65' | 2 / 3; 45' | not permitted | not permitted |
| Apartment Building Lot | 10,000 / no max | 100 / 200 | 80% / 100% | 100% | 0 / 10 | 5 / 10 | not permitted | 0 | 10 | 20 / 30 | 2 / 4; 55' | 2 / 3; 45' | not permitted | not permitted |
| Courtyard Building Lot[7] | 20,000 / no max | 150 / 300 | 50% / 90% | 70% | 0 / 10 | 5 / 10 | not permitted | 5 | 10 | 20 / 30 | 2 / 3½; 55' | 2 / 2½; 45' | not permitted | not permitted |
| Live-Work Building Lot | 1,800 / 7,200 | 16 / 60 | 60% / 100% | 80% | 0 / 6 | 5 / 10 | not permitted | 0 | 20 | 20 / 30 | 2 / 3; 45' | 2 / 2½; 45' | not permitted | 625 |
| Rowhouse Lot | 1,800 / 3,840 | 16 / 32 | 90% / 100% | 80% | 0 / 6 | 5 / 10 | not permitted | 0 | 20 | 20 / 30 | 2 / 3; 45' | 2 / 2½; 45' | not permitted | 625 |
| Apartment House Lot | 4,800 / 18,000 | 48 / 120 | 70% / 90% | 80% | not permitted | 10 / 25 | not permitted | 5 | 15 | 20 / 30 | not permitted | 1 / 3; 45' | not permitted | not permitted |
| Duplex Lot | 5,000 / 10,800 | 35 / 90 | 60% / 90% | 80% | not permitted | 10 / 20 | 15 / no max | 5 | 15 | 20 / 30 | not permitted | 1 / 3; 45' | 1 / 2½; 45' | not permitted |
| Cottage House Lot | 2,400 / 4,800 | 24 / 40 | 70% / 90% | 60% | not permitted | 5 / 20 | 10 / no max | 3 | 15 | 20 / 30 | not permitted | 1 / 2; 35' | 1 / 2; 35' | not permitted |
| Sideyard House Lot | 3,000 / 7,200 | 30 / 60 | 60% / 90% | 50% | not permitted | 5 / 10 | 10 / 15 | 0/ 10[8] | 15 | 20 / 30 | not permitted | 1 / 3; 45' | 1 / 2½; 45' | 800 |
| House Lot | 4,000 / 8,400 | 40 / 70 | 60% / 80% | 50% | not permitted | 10 / 20 | 15 / no max | 5 | 15 | 20 / 30 | not permitted | 1 / 3; 45' | 1 / 2½; 45' | 800 |
| Civic Building Lot | no min / no max | no min / no max | no min / no max | no max | no min / no max | no min / no max | no min / no max | 0 | 0 | 20 / 30 | 1 / 4; 55' | 1 / 4; 55' | 1 / 4; 55' | 1250 |
| Civic Space Lot | no min / no max | no min / no max | n/a | n/a | n/a | n/a | n/a | n/a | n/a | n/a | n/a | n/a | n/a | not permitted |

Core General Edge Preserve

[1] *Minimum rear yards apply to lots with alleys or lanes and to lots with neither alleys nor lanes; rear yards do not apply to through lots or to double-frontage lots.*

[2] *Minimum rear yards in this column apply to principal buildings. When alleys or lanes are provided, garages and accessory dwelling units must be built with one wall placed 3' from the property line which is adjacent to the alley or lane.*

[3] *Intracoastal waterway and bays – 30'; all other waterfront yards – 20'*

[4] *Buildings must comply with both maximum heights, as measured in stories and in feet. Building heights above 7 stories and 85 feet may not be approved as design variations, and building heights may not exceed any limitations in adopted Town Center or Village Center plans. Mezzanines that exceed the percentage of floor area for a mezzanine defined in the Florida Building Code are counted as a story for the purpose of measuring height. Habitable space within a roofline that is entirely non-habitable is not counted as a story with a 12:12 pitch or less counts as ½ story. For heights measured in feet, see Section 6.2.4 for details and exceptions.*

[5] *See requirements for accessory dwelling units in Sections 5.3.2.a and 6.11.5.e. The maximum sizes in this column supersede those in Section 5.3.2.a.*

[6] *One step-back of at least 20' must occur between the second through the fifth floor levels. Step-back is defined as at least 70% of a pedestal building's primary facade being built at least 20' further from all streets than the story below.*

[7] *On Courtyard Building Lots, the longer dimension of the central garden or courtyard must be at least 30' long if oriented east-west or 40' if oriented north-south. If the longer dimension is less than 35', architectural projections such as porches and balconies may only extend into the courtyard from one side. Elevator access is allowed only up to the courtyard level. Maximum lot coverage is measured immediately above the courtyard level.*

[8] *One side yard must be 10' min; the opposite side yard may be 0' if the adjacent lot is a Sideyard House Lot or if the adjacent lot provides a maintenance easement, otherwise the opposite side yard must 3' min.*

illustrates street types and building types with simple diagrams drawn in perspective, as well as with photographs, so the layperson can easily understand the intended character.

### Reinforcing the Unique Local Character

The following are unique aspects of the FBC included to ensure appropriate character of development.

*A Variety of Street Types Provided Within the FBC*

The code provides 14 acceptable street types and 12 acceptable lot (building) types. Urban designers are allowed considerable latitude in proposing additional street or lot types; every variation on the code's standard street and lot types must be able to be easily compared to the illustrations of the standard types.

*Block Standards*

The code contains strict standards on maximum block sizes. The creation of an appropriately scaled street network is one of the most critical aspects of a code for any site that does not have a walkable street network.

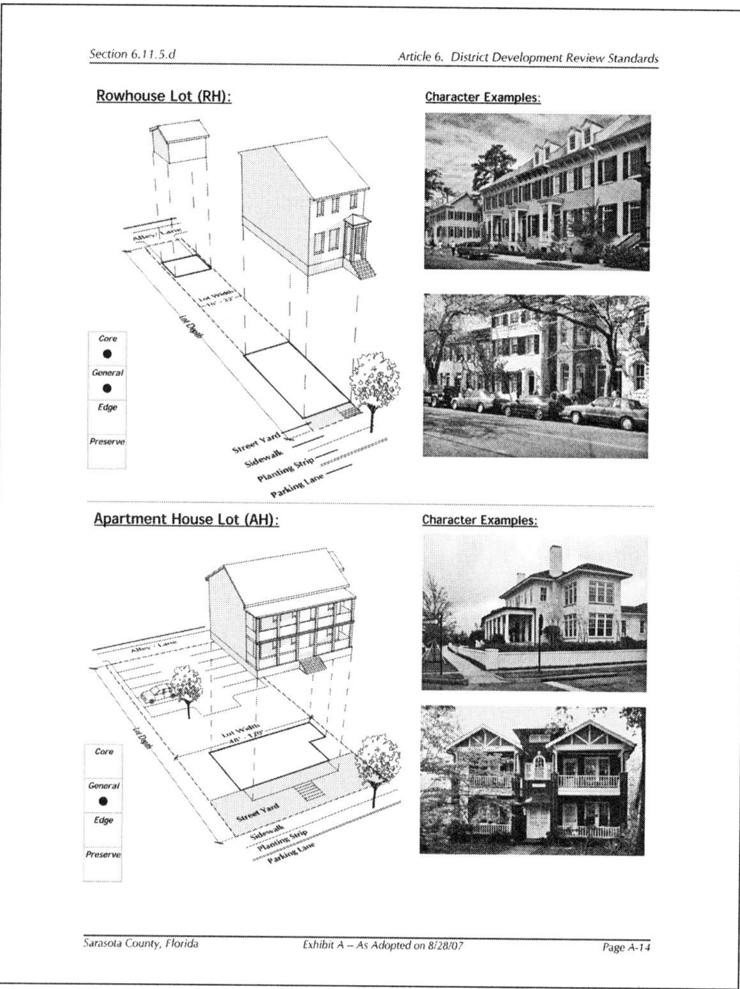


**Fig. 4.63** Rowhouse Lot and Apartment House Lot Standards

*Compatibility with Existing Adjacent Development*

Careful attention must be paid to the perimeter conditions around infill sites. Existing development is typically suburban in character; activist local residents have a history of objecting to infill development at higher intensities. The code will involve adjoining residents in the planning process to identify acceptable transitions from suburban to urban conditions.

*New Storm Water Requirements*

The code explicitly overrides the county's existing storm water management requirements that call for retention basins on every site. Fragmented basins are a deterrent to walkability and a burden on the use of individual lots.

## Implementation

### Code Administration

County staff will administer the code. Rezoning approval is required by the Board of County Commissioners; all later approvals will be made by county staff.

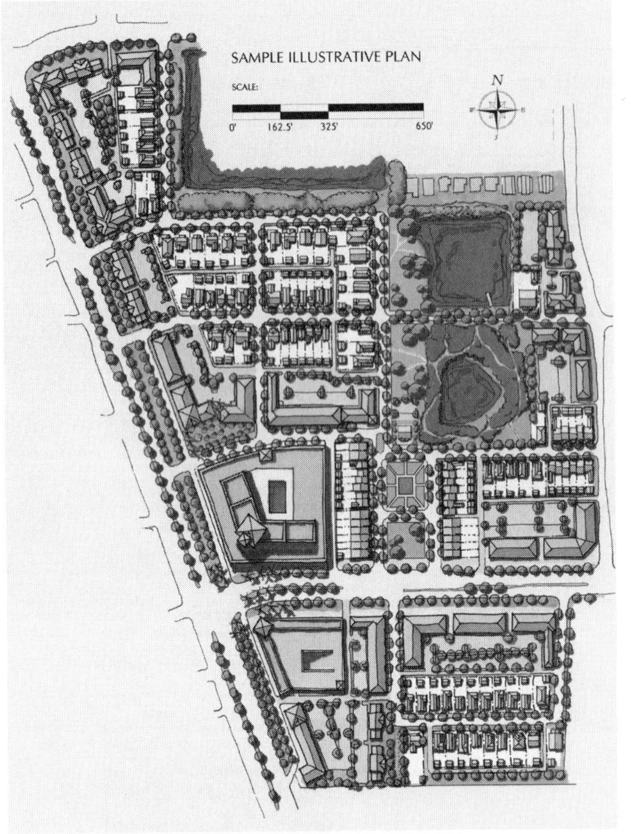


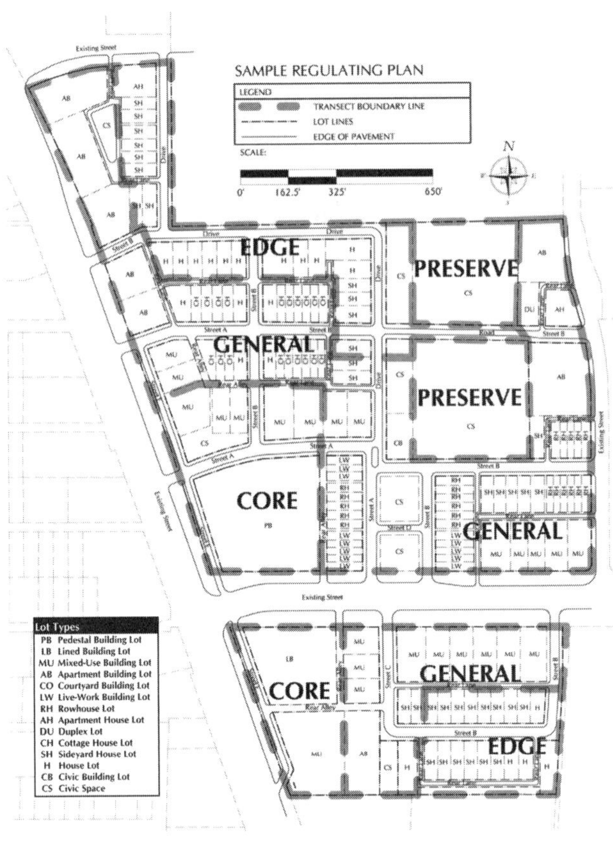


**Fig. 4.64** (above left) Prototypical Illustrative Plan

**Fig. 4.65** (above right) Prototypical Regulating Plan

**Fig. 4.66** (right) Summary of standards that apply to each transect zone

**i. "Core" transect zone**

PURPOSE: The Core transect zone is the most intensely occupied zone, with mostly attached buildings that create a continuous street facade within walking distance of surrounding primarily residential areas.

ALLOWABLE LOT TYPES in the Core transect zone: See Section 6.11.5.c.

- Pedestal Building Lot
- Lined Building Lot
- Mixed-Use Building Lot
- Apartment Building Lot
- Courtyard Building Lot
- Live-Work Building Lot
- Rowhouse Lot
- Civic Building Lot
- Civic Space (see Section 6.11.5.l)

BUILDING FORM AND PLACEMENT ON LOTS in the Core transect zone: See Section 6.11.5.d.

DEVELOPMENT STANDARDS in the Core transect zone: See Section 6.11.5.e.

PERMITTED USES in the Core transect zone: See Section 6.11.5.f.

ALLOWABLE STREET TYPES in the Core transect zone: See Section 6.11.5.g.

- Boulevard
- Avenue
- Street A
- Street C
- Street D
- Street E
- Rear alley

STREETSCAPE STANDARDS in the Core transect zone: See Section 6.11.5.j.

OFF-STREET PARKING in the Core transect zone: See Section 6.11.5.k.

CORE transect zone highlighted on sample regulating plan: See Section 6.11.5.n.

**ii. "General" transect zone**

PURPOSE: The General transect zone has a mixture of uses and a wide variety of lot types. Buildings may be attached or detached and are typically separated from the street with small street yards.

ALLOWABLE LOT TYPES in the General transect zone: See Section 6.11.5.c.

- Mixed-Use Building Lot
- Apartment Building Lot
- Courtyard Building Lot
- Live-Work Building Lot
- Apartment House Lot
- Rowhouse Lot
- Duplex Lot
- Cottage House Lot
- Sideyard House Lot
- House Lot
- Civic Building Lot
- Civic Space (see Section 6.11.5.l)

BUILDING FORM AND PLACEMENT ON LOTS in the General transect zone: See Section 6.11.5.d.

DEVELOPMENT STANDARDS in the General transect zone: See Section 6.11.5.e.

PERMITTED USES in the General transect zone: See Section 6.11.5.f.

ALLOWABLE STREET TYPES in the General transect zone: See Section 6.11.5.g.

- Boulevard
- Avenue
- Street A
- Street B
- Street C
- Street D
- Street E
- Street F
- Drive
- Rear Alley
- Rear Lane

STREETSCAPE STANDARDS in the General transect zone: See Section 6.11.5.j.

OFF-STREET PARKING in the General transect zone: See Section 6.11.5.k.

GENERAL transect zone highlighted on sample regulating plan: See Section 6.11.5.n.

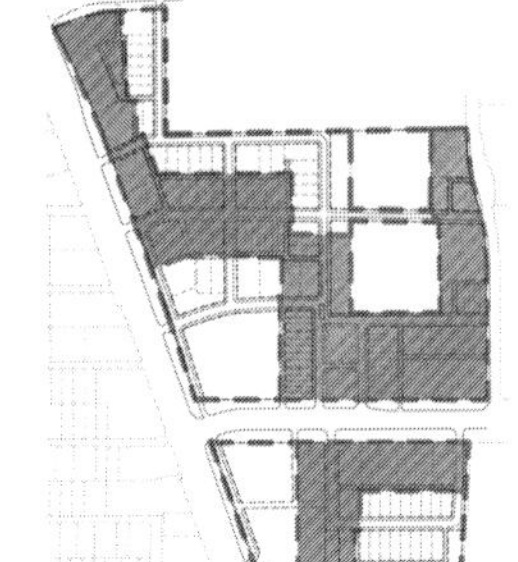

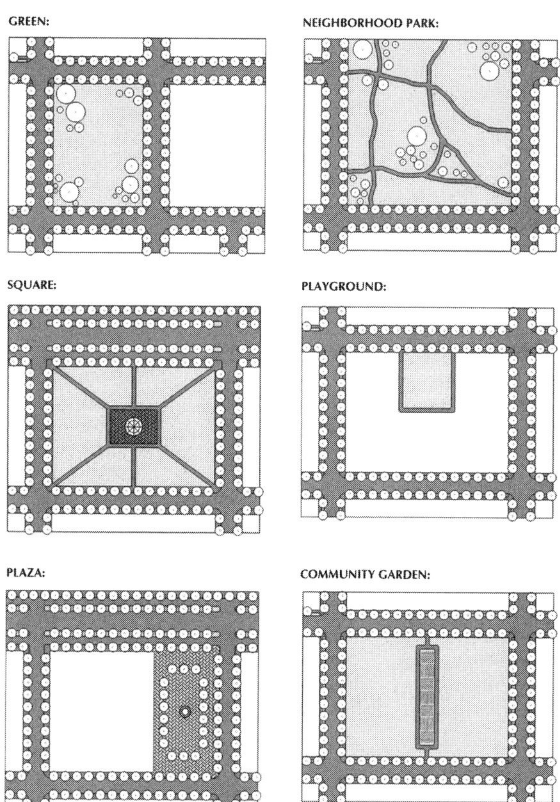


3. **CIVIC SPACES IN CORE, GENERAL, AND EDGE TRANSECT ZONES:** Each PMI district must contain at least one Civic Space Lot in Core or General transect zones. Civic spaces may be one of the following types, which are allowable in various transect zones as indicated by the letter "X" in the table below:
   i. **GREEN:** A green is an open space consisting of lawn and informally arranged trees and shrubs, typically furnished with paths, benches, and open shelters. Greens are spatially defined by abutting streets.
   ii. **SQUARE:** A square is a formal open space available for recreational and civic uses and spatially defined by abutting streets and building frontages. Landscaping in a square consists of lawn, trees, and shrubs planted in formal patterns and it is typically furnished with paths, benches, and open shelters.
   iii. **PLAZA:** A plaza is a formal open space available for civic and commercial uses and spatially defined by building frontages. Landscaping in a plaza consists primarily of pavement; trees and shrubs are optional.
   iv. **NEIGHBORHOOD PARK**: A neighborhood park is a natural landscape consisting of open and wooded areas, typically furnished with paths, benches, and open shelters. Neighborhood parks are often irregularly shaped but may be linear in order to parallel creeks, canals, or other corridors.
   v. **PLAYGROUND:** A playground is a fenced open space, typically interspersed within residential areas, that is designed and equipped for the recreation of children. Playgrounds may be freestanding or located within parks, greens, or school sites.
   vi. **COMMUNITY GARDEN:** A community garden is a grouping of garden plots available to nearby residents for small-scale cultivation.

| Civic Space Types | *Must Front On At Least:* | *Typical Lot Size* | Transect Zones: *Core* | *General* | *Edge* | *Preserve* |
|---|---|---|---|---|---|---|
| **Green** | 2 streets | 0.5 to 5 acres | | X | X | |
| **Square** | 3 streets | 0.5 to 2 acres | X | X | | |
| **Plaza** | 1 street | 0.1 to 2 acres | X | X | | |
| **Neighborhood Park** | 1 street | 0.5 to no max. | | X | X | |
| **Playground** | 0 streets | 0.1 to 1 acre | X | X | X | X |
| **Community Garden** | 0 streets | 0.1 to 1 acre | | X | X | X |

   vii. **COMBINED SIZE:** The combined size of all Civic Space Lots located in the Core, General, and Edge transect zones must be at least 5% of the total acreage of those zones, except where a comparable amount of civic space within 1/4-mile walking distance already exists or is committed. This 5% minimum is in addition to planting strips within street rights-of-way, open space provided on lots with private buildings, and open space in the Preserve transect zone.
   viii. **SQUARES AND PLAZAS:** Squares and plazas must be located so that building walls that will face the square or plaza will have at least 25% of their primary facade, including at least 40% of the ground story's primary facade, in transparent windows.
   ix. **RESTRICTION ON USES:** Civic Spaces Lots in Core, General, and Edge transect zones may not be used for any other purpose unless comparable civic spaces are approved through the rezoning process. These lots will not be restricted as open space in perpetuity as provided in Section 6.11.1.a.3 or elsewhere in this Code.
   x. **DESIGN:** Civic Space Lots must be designed, landscaped, and furnished to be consistent with the character of the transect zone in which they are located. Street frontage requirements are provided in the table above. One arrangement of each type of civic space is illustrated in the diagrams below:

**Fig. 4.67** (left and right) Civic Space Standards

**TABLE 2**

**USE TABLE**

| Lot Type | *Single-family detached* | *Two-family house* | *Upper story or attached residential* | *Family Day Care Home* | *Adult Day Care Home (up to 6)* | *Community Residential Home (see Section 5.3.2.b)* | *Guest house or accessory dwelling unit (see 5.3.2.a & d)* | *Live-work unit (see Section5.3.2.f)* | *Bed and Breakfast* | *Transient accommodations* | *Public & Civic Use Categories (limited to 5.2.4.a, b, c, d, h, & i)* | *Minor utilities (see Section 5.2.4.j)* | ENTIRE ZONING DISTRICTS: | Commercial Neighborhood (CN) | Office, Professional and Institutional (OPI) | Commercial General (CG) |
|---|---|---|---|---|---|---|---|---|---|---|---|---|---|---|---|---|
| **Pedestal Building Lot** | | | P | P | P | L | | P | P | P | P | P | | S | S | S |
| **Lined Building Lot** | | | P | P | P | L | | P | P | P | P | P | | S | S | S |
| **Mixed-Use Building Lot *** | | | P* | P* | P* | L | | P | P | P | P | P | | S | S | S |
| **Apartment Building Lot** | | | P | P | P | L | | | P | | | P | | | | |
| **Courtyard Building Lot** | | | P | P | P | L | | | P | | | P | | | | |
| **Live-Work Building Lot** | | | P | P | P | L | L | P | P | | P | P | | S | S | S |
| **Rowhouse Lot** | | | P | P | P | L | L | | P | | | P | | | | |
| **Apartment House Lot** | | | P | P | P | L | | | P | | | P | | | | |
| **Duplex Lot** | | P | | P | | L | | | P | | | P | | | | |
| **Cottage House Lot** | P | | | P | P | L | | | | | | P | | | | |
| **Sideyard House Lot** | P | | | P | P | L | L | | | | | P | | | | |
| **House Lot** | P | | | P | P | L | L | | | | | P | | | | |
| **Civic Building Lot** | | | | | | | L | | | | P | P | | | | |
| **Civic Space Lot** | | | | | | | | | | | P** | | | | | |

NOTES: *P = Permitted use (see Section 5.1.1.a.1)* | *L = Permitted with limitations (see Sec. 5.1.1.a.2)* | BLANK = *Use not permitted* | S = *Same permitted and limited uses as allowable for any parcel in the zoning district listed at the top of the column (see Section 6.11.5.f)*

* Residential uses in Mixed-Use Building Lots may not be placed in the ground (first) story.

** Civic Space Lots are not building sites; see Section 6.11.5.l for allowable uses on Civic Space Lots

Core
General
Edge
Preserve

**Fig. 4.68** Land-use table using terminology from the existing code

n. **Procedures**

1. **PREAPPLICATION REQUIREMENTS FOR THE PMI DISTRICT:** The use of the PMI District is optional. In order to qualify to apply for the PMI District, an applicant must control a qualifying site (see Section 6.11.5.a) and must commit to a charrette-based planning process.
   i. The purpose of this planning process is to analyze the prospective PMI site and surrounding land and to generate and evaluate alternate site plans for the property that meet the requirements of the Sarasota County Comprehensive Plan and that may qualify for rezoning to the PMI District.
   ii. An essential part of this planning process is an opportunity for public involvement in identifying issues and evaluating development alternatives for the site.
   iii. This planning process will produce a proposed regulating plan for the site that can meet the requirements of the PMI District.

2. **PLANNING PROCESS:** A three-phase dynamic planning process will be followed (see *Charrette Handbook: The Essential Guide for Accelerated, Collaborative Community Planning*, National Charrette Institute, 2006). The most visible public portion of this process will be a planning charrette, a multi-day collaborative design and planning workshop that will address the complex issues facing infill development. The three phases of the dynamic planning process are described below:
   i. The first phase of this process involves research, education, and charrette preparation. Community stakeholders and other affected parties are identified whose involvement is needed to produce a plan likely to be supported by the community. Community outreach begins in this phase, including distribution of information to the public and stakeholders about the site and the upcoming charrette. Base data and information are gathered for the site. Professional disciplines necessary to produce a feasible plan are identified and any necessary preliminary studies, such as market analysis or traffic study, are begun.
   ii. The second phase is the formal multi-day planning charrette which involves the public and multiple professional disciplines in a highly focused examination of the complex design issues inherent in mixed-use infill development on the site. All interested persons will be invited to participate in the charrette including the public, the sponsor, the professional design team, and county officials. The charrette typically includes several different avenues for input by participants, including public meetings and workshops, educational events, stakeholder meetings, and technical design meetings. The length of the charrette allow a series of short feedback loops where alternate site plans can be produced and evaluated by participants in a short period of time. Designs are tested for feasibility by the professional design team, which may include testing for market, physical, and permitting feasibility. The charrette process typically leads from multiple alternative concepts, through testing and input from participants, to a shared vision and preferred plan for sustainable development of the site.
   iii. The third phase is the post-charrette refinement of the preferred outcome and initial implementation steps. Refinement may include additional testing for market, financial, physical, and permitting feasibility. This phase concludes with the preparation of final drawings that document and illustrates the refined version of the preferred outcome.

3. **INITIATION OF PLANNING PROCESS AND COST RECOVERY:** A potential applicant may initiate this planning process as follows:
   i. A letter must be filed with Sarasota County that identifies the parcels proposed to be included in a PMI District and demonstrates that these parcels meet the minimum standards in Section 6.11.5.a. The letter must also assure Sarasota County that the landowner or developer controls or will control the property as required for planned development rezoning, and must identify generally the type of development or redevelopment that is anticipated.
   ii. After verifying eligibility of the essential parcels, county staff will review the site and surrounding area and determine the suitability of this planning process for these parcels. County staff may reject a request without prejudice and suggest changes that could make the parcels eligible, such as including adjoining parcels to create a more developable infill tract. If the request is acceptable, county staff will advise the applicant in writing and arrange a meeting to discuss the scope of the charrette process and the precise study area, which may include nearby properties.
      (a) The applicant will be advised of the list of consulting firms with extensive experience using charrettes to plan mixed-use infill development that Sarasota County has approved to conduct charrettes that can lead to an application for the PMI District.
      (b) The applicant must choose one of the firms on this list and must submit a proposed scope of services for written verification by county staff to ensure that the planning process will meet all the requirements of Section 6.11.5.
   iii. Participation in this process does not obligate a landowner or developer to petition for rezoning to the PMI District after completion of the process, nor does it obligate the Sarasota County to approve such a petition.
   iv. Sarasota County reserves the right to expand the study area beyond the essential and nearby properties to include additional land and/or related planning issues. Such additional planning may be performed by the same consulting firm or another group of professionals and may take place during the same or concurrent charrettes; however, additional costs will be the responsibility of Sarasota County.

4. **DENSITY AND INCENTIVES:** When the PMI District is used to qualify land for higher densities or other incentives allowable under the Comprehensive Plan, this planning process must be tailored to meet all requirements of the Critical Area Plan process and other requirements of the relevant policies of the Comprehensive Plan.

5. **REZONING PROCESS:**
   i. **Application Procedures:** Petitions for rezoning to the PMI District must meet the same requirements and follow the same procedures as other planned development districts, except as follows:
      (a) The required planning charrette may serve as the mandatory neighborhood workshop.
      (b) A proposed regulating plan that meets the requirements below must be drawn to the same scale and provided as a separate page in addition to the regular development concept plan.
   ii. **Regulating Plan:** A petitioner for the PMI District must submit a proposed regulating plan that complies with the following standards:
      (a) The plan must show the entire land area (including water bodies) being proposed for the PMI District and must also show the immediately adjoining roads, canals, and other rights-of-way or easements.
      (b) The plan must show the assignment of a transect zone to all land (including proposed streets) within the proposed PMI District. All land must be assigned one of the four transect zones described in Section 6.11.5.b; no land may be assigned two or more transect zones. Transect zone boundaries should follow proposed lot lines.
      (c) The plan must show the location of all streets within the proposed PMI District and must indicate the specific type of each street. Streets types must be allowed within the transect zones through which they pass (see Section 6.11.5.i) and must provide right-of-way in accordance with the standards in Section 6.11.5.i and j.
      (d) The plan must show proposed lot lines and lot types for all land to be subdivided into lots. Lot types must comply with the transect zones where the lots are to be located (see Section 6.11.5.c) and be able to meet the development standards for each lot type (see Section 6.11.5.e).
      (e) The level of detail and graphic format of the plan should be similar to the sample regulating plan shown in this section and should be produced at the same scale and sheet size as similar documents required for all other planned development districts.The plan must also be provided in a digital format acceptable to county staff.
   iii. **Illustrative Plan:** A petitioner for the PMI District must also submit a non-binding illustrative plan drawn to the same scale as the proposed regulating plan. The purpose is to illustrate the likely built results of the regulating plan by showing buildings on each lot and preliminary designs for streets and civic spaces in compliance with these regulations and the proposed regulating plan.
   iv. **Design Variations:** A petitioner for rezoning to the PMI District must clearly identify any design variations that are being requested from the specific standards in Section 6.11.5; county staff will present a recommendation to the Board of County Commissioners on each of the following requests:
      (a) Additional lot types (Section 6.11.5.c), which must be accompanied by proposed dimensional requirements (Section 6.11.5.e) and assignment of land uses (Section 6.11.5.f).
      (b) Modified dimensional requirements for lot types (Section 6.11.5.e).
      (c) Extension of stoops into the right-of-way (Section 6.11.5.e).
      (d) Additional street types (Section 6.11.5.g), which must be accompanied by proposed cross-sections and streetscape standards.
      (e) Modified cross-sections and streetscape standards for street types (Section 6.11.5.g).
      (f) Modified block standards (Section 6.11.5.h).
      (g) Alternative parking plans (Section 6.11.5.k).
   v. **Rezoning Approvals:** The approval process for the PMI District will follow the standard procedures for all other planned development districts, except as follows.
      (a) **STAFF REPORT:** County staff must submit a formal report containing a summary of the planning process, an analysis of the compliance of the petition with the design principles in Section 6.11.5.a, the Comprehensive Plan, and the technical regulations for the PMI District, and a recommendation on the entire petition and each requested design variation.
      (b) **RESPONSE TO REQUESTS FOR DESIGN VARIATIONS:** Prior to approving the PMI District, the Board of County Commissioners must explicitly respond to each request for a design variation from the specific standards in Section 6.11.5. Except to the extent that such requests are formally accepted or accepted with modifications, the written standards of the PMI District will apply.
      (c) **EFFECT OF REGULATING PLAN:** If the PMI District is approved, the proposed regulating plan, subject to modification by the Board of County Commissioners during public hearings, becomes a binding part of the rezoning approval and will regulate all development and future uses of land within the PMI District.
      (d) **EXPEDITED PROCESSING:** To effectuate Sarasota County's commitment to sustainable development practices, processing of complete PMI petitions, and where applicable, related Critical Area Plans, will be expedited to reach a final public hearing within six months in accordance with Resolution

**Fig. 4.69** Procedures for using the code

**g. Allowable Street Types by Transect Zone**

1. **STREET TYPES BY TRANSECT ZONE:** Specific street types are allowed within the corresponding transect zones as identified by the letter "X" in the following table. These streets must comply with the street cross-sections in Section 6.11.5.i as adjusted in accordance with the streetscape standards in Section 6.11.5.j.

| Street Type (movement type) | | Transect Zones | | | |
|---|---|---|---|---|---|
| | | Core | General | Edge | Preserve |
| **Boulevard** | (speed / slow) | X | X | | |
| **Avenue** | (slow) | X | X | | |
| **Street A** | (free) | X | X | | |
| **Street B** | (slow) | | X | X | |
| **Street C** | (slow) | X | X | | |
| **Street D** | (free) | X | X | X | |
| **Street E** | (slow) | X | X | | |
| **Street F** | (slow) | | X | X | |
| **Drive** | (slow) | | X | X | |
| **Road** | (free) | | | X | |
| **Rear Alley** | (slow) | X | X | | |
| **Rear Lane** | (yield) | | X | X | |

2. **ADDITIONAL STREET TYPES:** An applicant may propose additional street types or modified cross-sections and streetscape standards through the PMI application process. The County Engineer will review each additional street type or proposed modification and provide written comments. The Board of County Commissioners will decide to accept, modify, or reject such additions or modifications during the PMI approval process based on its determination as to the consistency of the additions or modifications with the planning, design, and compatibility principles set forth in the Comprehensive Plan and the PMI District.

**h. Design of Streets, Alleys, and Blocks**

1. **STREETS:** Each PMI District must provide a highly interconnected network of streets and must accommodate existing or anticipated public transit in accordance with transit standards adopted by Sarasota County.
   - i. Individual street types are classified in Section 6.11.5.g by movement type. Movement type describes the expected driver experience, as follows:
     - (a) **Speed:** Drivers can expect travel similar to conventional street design, but with continued emphasis on pedestrian safety and comfort. Design speed is 30-35 mph.
     - (b) **Free:** Drivers can expect to travel generally without delay at the design speed; street design supports safe pedestrian movement at the higher design speed. This movement type is appropriate for thoroughfares designed to traverse longer distances or connect to higher intensity locations. Design speed is 25-30 mph.
     - (c) **Slow:** Drivers can proceed carefully with an occasional stop to allow a pedestrian to cross or another car to park. The character of the street should make drivers uncomfortable exceeding design speed due to presence of parked cars, enclosure, tight turn radii, and other design elements. Design speed is 20-25 mph.
     - (d) **Yield:** Drivers must proceed slowly and with extreme care and must yield in order to pass a parked car or approaching vehicle (the functional equivalent of traffic calming). Design speed is 20 mph or less.
   - ii. The interconnected network of streets must extend into adjoining areas except where the general infill goal of integration with surrounding uses is deemed inappropriate for a particular infill site by the Board of County Commissioners during the PMI approval process. Street stubs must be provided to adjoining undeveloped areas to accommodate future street connectivity.
   - iii. Streets do not have to form a rectangular grid; they may be curved or bent but must connect to other streets. Intersections with designated arterials and collectors must have centerline offsets of at least 150 feet; this requirement does not apply to intersections that are limited to alleys, lanes, or local streets.
   - iv. The proposed street network should respect topography and designated environmental resources and be modified accordingly to avoid damages to such resources.
   - v. Sidewalks and rows of street trees must be provided on both sides of all streets; street trees may be omitted where arcades or colonnades meet the standards in Section 6.11.5.e or where a street adjoins a natural area being preserved. To allow healthy tree growth, when street trees will be planted in tree wells or in planting strips narrower than 10 feet, the developer must support the surrounding sidewalk and parking lane with structural soil or provide an equivalent soil volume using a method acceptable to the county's urban forester. See also Sections 6.11.5.i and j regarding street trees.
   - vi. Dead-end streets are not permitted except where physical conditions such as highways, sensitive natural resources, or unusual topography provide no practical connection alternatives. Each dead end must be detailed as a close (a small green area surrounded by a common driveway serving adjoining lots) and should provide pedestrian connectivity to the maximum extent practicable.
   - vii. All streets must be publicly dedicated. Private streets and closed or gated streets are prohibited.

CLOSE DETAILING EXAMPLE

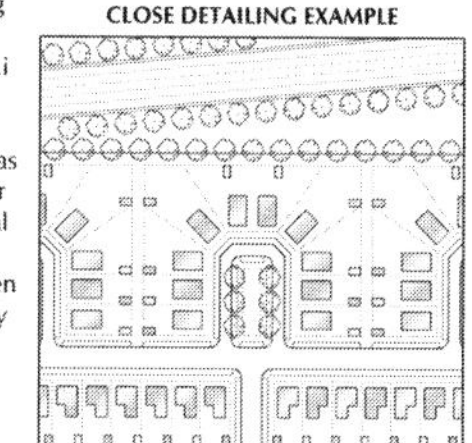

2. **ALLEYS AND LANES:** A continuous network of rear and side alleys or lanes must serve as the primary means of vehicular ingress to individual lots in the Core and General transect zones. Rear lanes are required in the Edge transect zone for all lots narrower than 60 feet (see special requirements in Section 6.11.5.e where vehicular ingress is from the street).
   - i. Alley or lane entrances should generally align so as to provide ease of ingress for service vehicles, but internal deflections or variations in the alley/lane network are encouraged to prevent excessive or monotonous views of the rear of structures resulting from long stretches of alleys or lanes.
   - ii. All alleys and lanes must be publicly dedicated.

3. **BLOCKS:** Except as otherwise provided, block perimeters may not exceed 1600 linear feet as measured along the inner edges of each street right-of-way. Blocks may also be broken by a Civic Space Lot provided that lot is at least 50 feet wide and will provide perpetual pedestrian access between the blocks and to any lots that front the Civic Space Lot. Smaller blocks are encouraged to promote walkability.
   - i. Block perimeters may exceed this limit, up to a maximum of 2000 linear feet, only if one or more of the following conditions apply:
     - (a) The block is assigned to the Core transect zone;
     - (b) The block has at least one block face on an arterial street; or
     - (c) The block contains valuable natural features or significant historic resources that should not be crossed by a street.
   - ii. Any single block face wider than 500 feet must include a publicly dedicated sidewalk, passage, or trail at least 8 feet in width that connects to another street.
   - iii. An applicant may propose minor modifications to these block size standards through the PMI application process. The Board of County Commissioners will decide to accept, modify, or reject such modifications during the PMI approval process based on its determination as to the consistency of the modifications with the planning and design principles set forth in the Comprehensive Plan and the PMI District.

**i. Street Cross-Sections**

1. The function of all PMI street types is to promote walkability and pedestrian comfort, with vehicle mobility as a secondary function.
   - i. These street types are provided for use in the PMI District with compatible lot types and transect zones.
   - ii. In the PMI District, these standards supersede any conflicting standards in this Code or in Chapter 74 or other land development or engineering regulations of Sarasota County.

2. Street types in all PMI districts must be assigned on the regulating plan in accordance with the standards in Section 6.11.5.
   - i. The specific design of each street must follow the cross-sections illustrated below for each street type, as adjusted for the transect zone it passes through in accordance with Sections 6.11.5.j.
   - ii. The lane widths shown include the width of horizontal extensions of curbs such as gutter pans.

**Fig. 4.70** Street and block standards

**m. Stormwater Management**

In mixed-use infill development, some best management practices for stormwater management differ from suburban practices. Compact development creates fewer pollutants by reducing expansive lawns and parking lots. However, because less land is available for stormwater treatment, excess stormwater may be infiltrated or detained in subsurface basins and oils and greases can be removed with skimmers. This subsection allows the use of a variety of best management practices to meet stormwater management standards. The use of these practices and their functional equivalents are presumed to comply with the stormwater management standards contained in the Land Development Regulations; if this subsection conflicts with any other provision of the Land Development Regulations, the provisions of this subsection will prevail.

1. Innovative and urban stormwater management designs and techniques may be considered for addressing stormwater treatment requirements, including but not limited to porous pavement, treatment inlet boxes with skimmers or traps, subsurface basins for infiltration or detention, prefabricated multi-chamber water quality devices, green roofs, stormwater treatment mitigation, etc. All stormwater management designs and techniques must be certified by a Florida professional engineer or other appropriate professional registered under Chapters 471 or 481 *F.S.* who is competent in the fields of hydrology, drainage, and flood control. The submittal must include a proposed maintenance schedule for each technique, identifying the timing of inspections and the maintenance activities that will be taken such as removing debris from inlet boxes, replacing filters, pumping out accumulated sediment, mechanical sweeping, etc.
2. Up to six inches of flooding in the deepest portion of parking areas may be allowed and included as one means of meeting stormwater attenuation or floodplain compensation volume requirements.
3. To minimize the amount of site fill and the associated impacts of such fill on existing native vegetation and trees, historical wet season water table levels may be controlled at lower elevations subject to the physical limitations of the receiving drainage system and compliance with the criteria for such set forth by the Southwest Florida Water Management District.
4. Stormwater attenuation requirements may be waived for sites located between the city limits of the City of Sarasota and the City of Venice and within one mile of the east coast of bays or the intracoastal waterway provided that post-development conditions will not cause an adverse increase in flood stages off site. This consideration is granted provided the site provides stormwater treatment for 150 percent of the site and adequate downstream capacity exists for the proposed discharge rate when considered within the context of the total watershed discharge and its timing, subject to the requirements of the Florida Department of Transportation, if applicable.



**Fig. 4.71** Storm water management standards

# Towns, Villages, and Countryside



## St. Lucie County, Florida

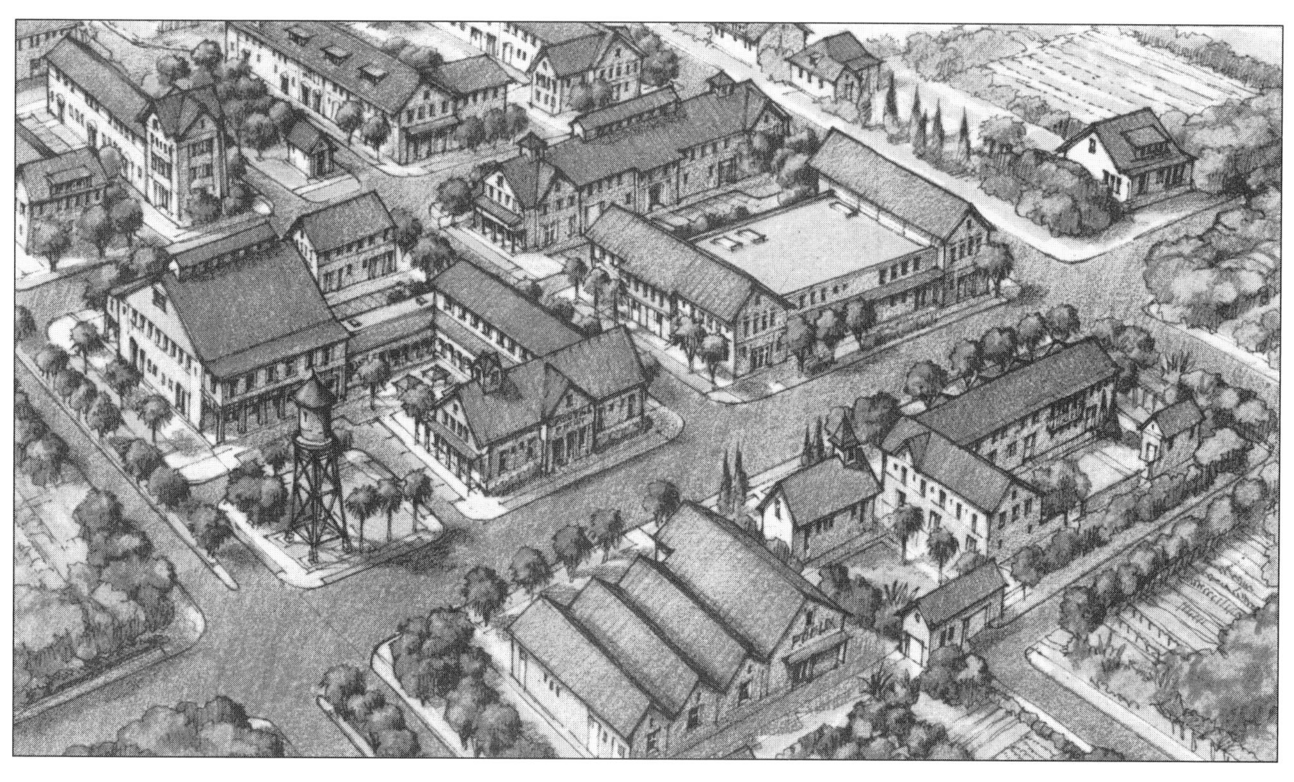

*Written by William M. Spikowski, Principal, Spikowski Planning Associates*

THIS FORM-BASED CODE implements a regional plan for 28 square miles just beyond the urban fringe of the city of Fort Pierce in unincorporated St. Lucie County, Florida, with an estimated 2005 population of 241,000.[8] This plan is known as the "Towns, Villages, and Countryside" (TVC) plan, prepared in 2004 by the Treasure Coast Regional Planning Council (TCRPC).

The TVC Plan combines agricultural preservation with limited urban development. Existing development rights can be exercised only by concentrating them in new villages, each to be surrounded by continued agricultural activity.

TCRPC is a public agency that created the initial vision under a consulting contract with St. Lucie County. TCRPC was rehired by the county to implement that vision. Implementation included amendments to the county's Comprehensive Plan and creation of land development regulations.

### Client's Background in Form-Based Coding

TCRPC advised county officials that a Form-Based Code was the only technique that could deliver the promised level of urbanism within towns and villages.

## Code Components

Two major components were created and adopted simultaneously: (1) amendments to the St. Lucie County Comprehensive Plan, and (2) amendments to the land development regulations. The latter amendments were adopted in two ordinances, one with the Form-Based Code and another with procedures for the transfer of development rights needed to guarantee preservation of the countryside.

During this same period, detailed planning was conducted for the backbone water management system, the major road network, and the overall public financing strategy.

St. Lucie County had adopted a unified land development code in 1990, effectively combining all land development regulations, including zoning, subdivision regulations, and the sign code. The new Form-Based Code was drafted to seamlessly fit into that unified code.

| | St. Lucie County Towns, Villages, and Countryside |
|---|---|
| Status: | Adopted on May 30, 2006 |
| Scale: | Region |
| Implementation Method: | Floating Zone/Traditional Neighborhood Development (TND) |
| Site Context: | Greenfield |
| Site Size: | 18,000 acres in north St. Lucie County, northeast of the city of Fort Pierce |
| Administration: | Will be administered by county staff; rezoning approval for each town and village is required by the Board of County Commissioners. During a transition period, the county is contracting with the Treasure Coast Regional Planning Council to administer the code and to train county staff. |
| Organizing Principle: | Transect<br>Building Types |
| Code Consultants(s): | Dover, Kohl & Partners; Spikowski Planning Associates |
| Agency Name: | St. Lucie County Board of County Commissioners |

The code provides a new zoning district suitable for an entire town or village and also provides two other potential zoning districts, one for minor subdivisions grandfathered under previous codes and the other for retail or workplace developments that are not part of a town or village (for instance, adjoining the existing urban service area or an I-95 interchange).

### Organizing Principle

This code is based on two organizing principles, the transect and lot (building) types. The Regulating Plan must designate both of these, as well as the proposed street types for each town or village that requires approval through a planned development rezoning process.

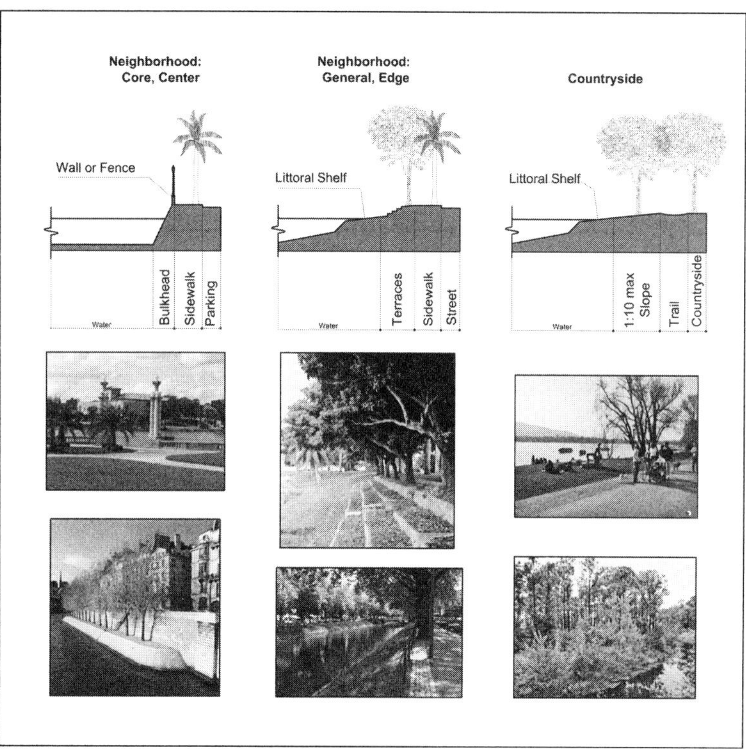


**Fig. 4.72** (previous page) Illustration of a village center prototype

**Fig. 4.73** (above) Illustration of flow way regulations

## Code Process

The vision plan was based on an intensive charrette process that began in February 2004. The plan amendments and new code were drafted by the consultants, with continual review by county staff. Several county-appointed committees also reviewed the various drafts and formulated recommendations. Adoption of the ordinance establishing the code took place through the normal public hearing process.

### Public Participation

The public process used an extended planning charrette, which was completed prior to initiation of code drafting. Because of the support created for the Master Plan, no public process will be required for the preparation of Regulating Plans for individual towns and villages.

## Advanced Application of FBCs

### Scale of Application

Most FBCs implement an urban design plan for a relatively small area, ranging from an individual development site, to an entire neighborhood or downtown, to the creation of an entirely new town. This code covers a much larger area, about 28 square miles, and will guide the creation of several new towns or villages.

### Preservation of Agricultural Lands through a Transfer of Development Rights (TDR) Program

This code also implements a plan to preserve 60 to 75 percent of the rural landscape by transferring existing development rights into pre-existing urban areas or into the new towns or villages. To do so, it created a new pattern for "floating zone" Form-Based Codes that provide clear guidance as to the kind of urbanism that the code requires for each new town or village, while also providing clear standards for acceptable use of the surrounding countryside. Floating-zone codes are usually optional, but this code is mandatory for any property owner who wishes to develop a new town or village.

### A Form-Based Code Without a Regulating Plan

In contrast to codes for smaller areas where a specific Regulating Plan is created for the original code, prospective developers of each new town or village will draft individual Regulating

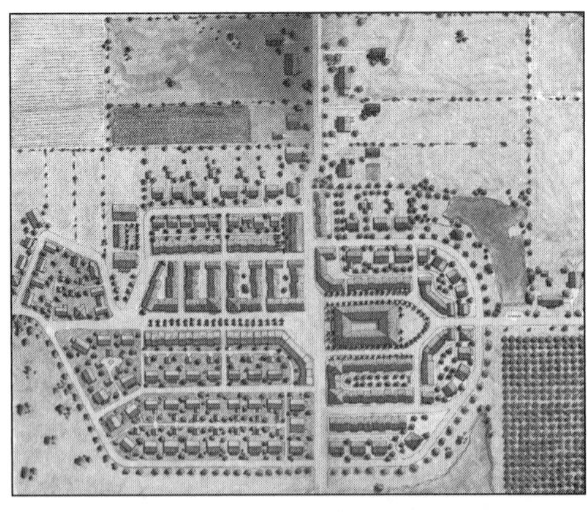

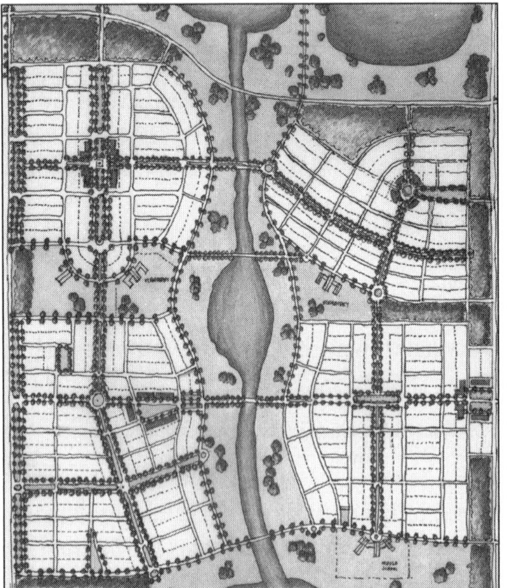

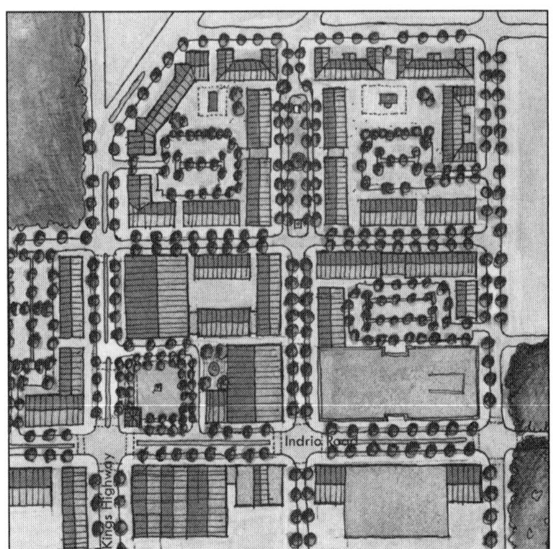


**Fig. 4.74** Prototype plans for a Hamlet (top), Neighborhood (middle), and Village Center (bottom)

Plans. After each proposed town or village is more specifically planned according to the requirements of the code, it is submitted for county approval through the rezoning process. Each Regulating Plan must meet the requirements in the ordinance for the Planned Town or Village (PTV) zoning district. Each Regulating Plan also must allocate the entire land parcel into urban and rural transect zones and must show the entire street network and proposed building types for all lots.

### Reinforcing the Unique Local Character

*A Variety of Street Types Provided Within the FBC*

This new pattern provides 11 acceptable street types and 11 acceptable lot (building) types. Urban designers are allowed considerable latitude in that they can propose additional street or lot types for a new town or village, with the check that every variation on the code's standard street and lot types can be easily compared to the illustrations of the standard types.

*Block Standards*

This code contains strict standards on maximum block sizes. The creation of an appropriately scaled street network is one of the most critical aspects of a greenfield code.

*Preserving the Rural Character of the County*

The rural areas that will be governed by this code were given considerable attention. Through the transfer of development rights of 60 to 75 percent of the land into the designated town and village locations, agricultural uses can continue without the pressure of urban land values, which so often displace farmland from metropolitan areas. These transfers will be memorialized by conservation easements, which explicitly allow continued farming at every scale (from the current citrus groves to niche agricultural uses that would supply produce to local residents).

*Addressing Regional Storm Water Issues*

The creation of a riverine surface water man agement system, required by the code, will al low appropriate handling of storm water on regional scale. The land surface is quite flat; th original sheet-flow drainage was altered with network of straight and deep agricultural drain age canals. The new riverine system will repai environmental damage caused by the existin canals by slowing drainage into coastal waters and raising groundwater levels, while creating a navigable recreational asset at the same time. This regional system also provides benefits to urbanism by avoiding fragmented retention basins in towns or villages, which are a deterrent to walkability and a burden on the use of individual lots.

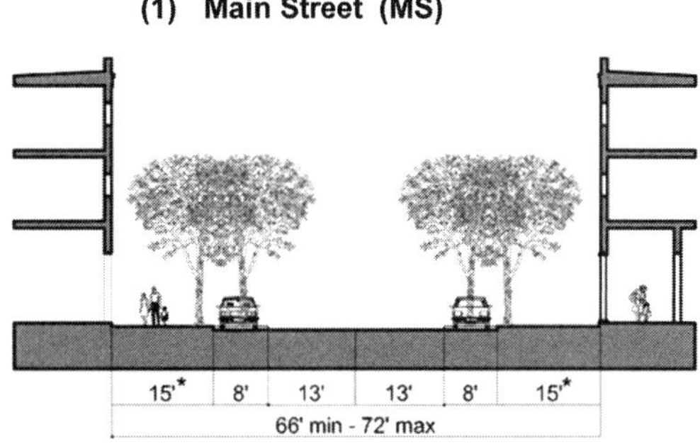


| | Transect Zones | | | | | |
|---|---|---|---|---|---|---|
| | Country-side | | Neighborhoods | | | |
| Street Types | Rural | Fringe | Edge | General | Center | Core |
| Main Street | | | | | X | X |
| Boulevard | X | X | X | X | X | X |
| Avenue | | | | X | X | X |
| East/West Street | | | X | X | X | |
| North/South Street | | | X | X | X | |
| Edge Drive | | | X | | | |
| Parkway | X | X | X | | | |
| Rural Road | X | X | | | | |
| Alley | | | | X | X | X |
| Lane | X | X | X | X | X | |
| Trail | X | X | X | X | X | X |

**Fig. 4.75** Thoroughfare Standards with a table allocating thoroughfare types by zone

## Implementation

### Code Administration

County staff will administer the code. The Board of County Commissioners requires rezoning approval for each town and village; county staff will make all later approvals.

During a transition period, the county is contracting with the Treasure Coast Regional Planning Council to administer the code and to train county staff.

Although this code was adopted by St. Lucie County in May 2006, the effective date had to be delayed until a legal challenge to the underlying Comprehensive Plan amendments is resolved. This is set for early 2008.

### Lessons Learned

*Written by Ramon Trias, Trias & Associates, Fort Pierce, Florida*

The adoption process proved longer and more complex than anticipated at the time of the initial charrette. At times, the existing procedures for adoption of comprehensive plan amendments and codes appeared to work against the shared vision developed during the charrette.

Although any ambitious reform of land development regulations requires substantial professional resources and time, the TVC proved to be an exceptional challenge to regulators. Thus, the process of review and approval of projects became expensive and slow. Several developers at first attempted to design projects consistent with the new requirements, but St. Lucie County was not able to process them right away. As the economy slowed, some of those developers chose to pursue the conventional development option instead due to delays on final adoption.

An important lesson, therefore, is that the state laws and county ordinances need to be revised to ensure that they assist in implementing the citizens' vision. Moreover, public agencies need to have adequate staffing and professional expertise to effectively manage the process of project review.

3.01.03.EE.1

**Section 3.01.03 "Zoning Districts" of the Land Development Code is amended to create new 3.01.03.EE, 3.01.03.FF, and 3.01.03.GG as follows** (these sections are being added to this code):

### 3.01.03 ZONING DISTRICTS

**EE. PTV (PLANNED TOWN OR VILLAGE)**

**1. PURPOSE**

The Planned Town or Village (PTV) district provides a specialized zoning district to expedite county approval of a Town or Village on land designated TVC on the Future Land Use Map of the St. Lucie County Comprehensive Plan.

**2. STANDARDS AND REQUIREMENTS**

Standards and requirements for Planned Town or Villages shall be as follows:

**a. DESIGN CONCEPTS FOR TOWNS AND VILLAGES**

Towns and Villages use the principles of traditional neighborhood design to create a sustainable growth pattern characterized by a mix of uses, building types, and income levels on a pedestrian-friendly block and street network. Each Town and Village also preserves a significant amount of Countryside that includes viable agriculture, public open space, and environmental preservation and restoration. Design concepts for Towns and Villages are described further in the TVC Element of the St. Lucie County Comprehensive Plan, which contains specific settlement principles which must be followed in the design of new neighborhoods.

**b. OVERALL REQUIREMENTS FOR TOWNS AND VILLAGES**

(1) Each Town consists of two or more neighborhoods and adjoining Countryside and must meet the following requirements:

| **SIZE:** | |
|---|---|
| Minimum parcel size for a Town outside USB: | 625 acres |
| Minimum parcel size for a Town inside USB: | 225 acres |
| Maximum parcel size: | n/a |
| **OPEN SPACE & COUNTRYSIDE:** | |
| Open Space & Countryside required outside USB: | 60% (50% Countryside min.) |
| Open Space & Countryside required inside USB: | 40% (40% Countryside min.) |
| **DENSITY REQUIRED IN NET DEVELOPABLE AREA:** | |
| Minimum average density required if inside USB: | 6 DU/acre |
| Minimum average density required if outside USB: | 5 DU/acre |

3.01.03.EE.2.c

(2) Each Village consists of one neighborhood and adjoining Countryside and must meet the following requirements:

| **SIZE:** | |
|---|---|
| Minimum parcel size for a Village outside USB: | 500 acres |
| Minimum parcel size for a Village inside USB: | 110 acres |
| Maximum parcel size: | 624 acres |
| **OPEN SPACE & COUNTRYSIDE:** | |
| Open Space & Countryside required outside USB: | 75% (65% Countryside min.) |
| Open Space & Countryside required inside USB: | 40% (40% Countryside min.) |
| **DENSITY REQUIRED IN NET DEVELOPABLE AREA:** | |
| Minimum average density required: | 5 DU/acre |

(3) Regional roadways are thoroughfares provided as links of the Future Street Network (Figure 3-15 of the TVC Element). The right-of-way of a regional roadway located within a neighborhood of a Town or Village is counted as part of the Net Developable Area and is included in the minimum average density requirement. The right-of-way of a regional roadway located outside of a neighborhood of a Town or Village is considered part of the Net Developable Area, but is not included in the calculation of the minimum average density requirement. Regional roadways are not counted toward the required amount of Open Space or Countryside.

FIGURE 3-8 – REGIONAL ROADWAYS

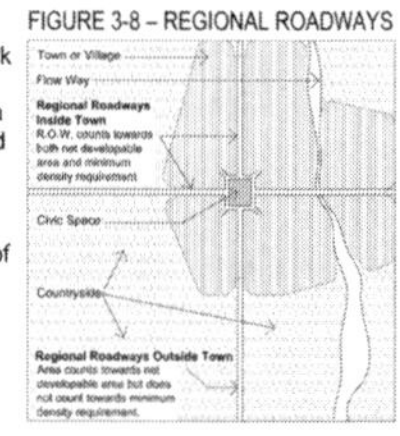


(4) For details on computing the minimum Open Space and Countryside percentages, see Section 3.01.03.EE.2.o. Civic Building Lots, including those used for public schools, that are located within the net developable area of a Town or Village are not included in the calculation of the required minimum average density.

**c. TRANSECT ZONES GENERALLY**

(1) **Transect zones.**

All land within each PTV must be allocated to one of the six transect zones described below. Each transect zone controls allowable street types and lot types, which then control the placement and intensity of buildings and other uses of land. Each neighborhood may be comprised of the following Neighborhood transect zones:

i. Core
ii. Center
iii. General
iv. Edge

The Countryside surrounding neighborhoods must be allocated to the following Countryside transect zones:

v. Fringe
vi. Rural

The general standards for each transect zone are described in Section 3.01.03.EE.2.d.

3.01.03.EE.2.d

(2) **Transect assignment concepts.**

Each PTV application must include a regulating plan that clearly identifies the proposed allocation of transect zones within the entire Town or Village and adjoining Countryside on the same parcel (see Section 3.01.03.EE.3). The allocation of transect zones is intended to ensure variety and mixture of use and lot types in neighborhoods and to delineate the Countryside that will be permanently protected after development of the Town or Village. The following general guidelines shall be followed when proposing transect zones:

i. Generally, a neighborhood has more intensity (Core or Center) in the center and less intensity (General or Edge) at the extremes.
ii. When the neighborhood is adjacent to a busy street or highway, or adjacent to an established urban area, the transect zones with greater intensity (Core or Center) may adjoin that highway or urban area.
iii. Similar uses should face across streets; changes in transect zones should generally occur along rear or side lot lines rather than along streets.
iv. The character of the neighborhood is determined by the transect zones of which it is comprised; neighborhoods vary in character internally. Some neighborhoods may be more intense and have a higher percentage of Core and Center while others may have a higher percentage of General and Edge. However, each neighborhood must meet the percentage requirements set forth below.
v. When a new neighborhood will adjoin an existing development, existing agriculture, or an existing or approved neighborhood, the new neighborhood should establish similar transect conditions (such as Core aligning with Core or Center, and Rural aligning with Rural) to ensure compatibility. Transect juxtapositions may be approved by St. Lucie County where natural conditions warrant them or where alignment of similar transect conditions would be inappropriate.

(3) **Transect assignment percentages.**

Each proposed regulating plan must allocate transect zones within the following percentage ranges. An applicant may propose minor variations on these percentages during the PTV rezoning process based upon site-specific constraints and compliance with the intent of the TVC Element and this Code. The Board of County Commissioners shall decide whether to accept, modify, or reject such variations during the approval process.

i. CORE: for Villages, no minimum; for Towns, 1% of each neighborhood minimum; 10% maximum in any neighborhood.
ii. CENTER: 5% of each neighborhood minimum; 30% maximum.
iii. GENERAL: 30% of each neighborhood minimum; 60% maximum.
iv. EDGE: 10% of each neighborhood minimum; 45% maximum.
v. FRINGE: no minimum; maximum 30% of Countryside
vi. RURAL: see Section 3.01.03.EE.2.b

**d. STANDARDS FOR EACH TRANSECT ZONE**

The general standards for each transect zone are described below.

**Fig. 4.76** (top left, top right, and bottom left) Description of the new Planned Town or Village (PTV) zoning district

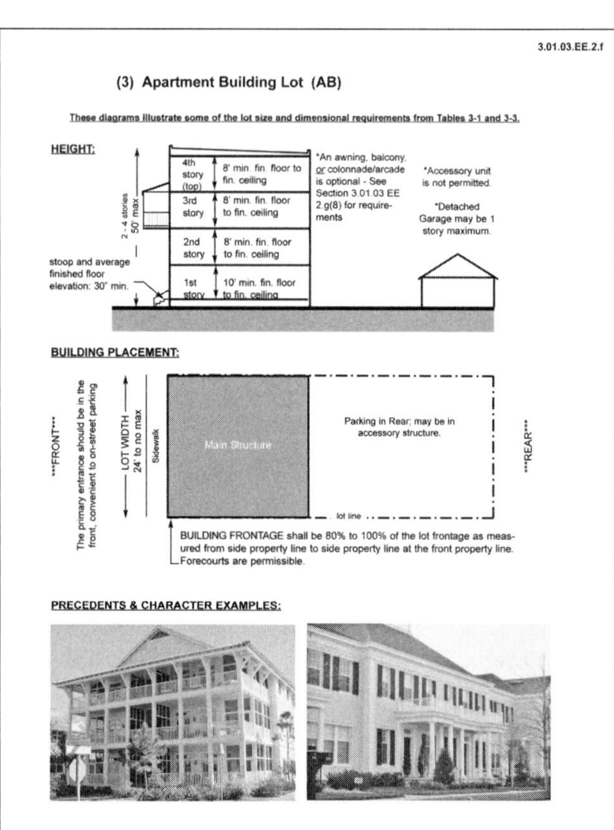
3.01.03.EE.2.f

**(3) Apartment Building Lot (AB)**

**These diagrams illustrate some of the lot size and dimensional requirements from Tables 3-1 and 3-3.**



**Fig. 4.77** Apartment Building Form Standards

**TABLE 3-1**
LOT SIZE AND DIMENSIONAL REQUIREMENTS

| Lot Type | Lot Size (min / max in sf) | Lot Width (min / max) | Building Frontage (min / max) | Lot Coverage by Bldgs. (max) | Yard | | | Height[3] (min/max in stories; max in feet) | First Story Elevation (min) | Accessory Dwelling[4] (max bldg footprint in sf) |
|---|---|---|---|---|---|---|---|---|---|---|
| | | | | | Front[1] (min / max) | Rear[2] (min) | Side (min) | | | |
| Mixed-Use Building Lot | 2,400 / no max | 24 / no max | 80% / 100% | 80% | 0 / 5 | 15 | 0 | 2 / 4; 56' | n/a | not permitted |
| Retail Building Lot | 2,400 / 7,200 | 24 / 60 | 80% / 100% | 80% | 0 / 5 | 15 | 0 | 1 / 4; 50' | n/a | not permitted |
| Apartment Building Lot | 2,400 / no max | 24 / no max | 80% / 100% | 80% | 0 / 10 | 15 | 0 | 2 / 4; 50' | 30"[6] | not permitted |
| Live/Work Building Lot | 1,800 / 7,200 | 16 / 60 | 80% / 100% | 80% | 0 / 10 | 15 | 0 | 2 / 3; 45' | n/a | 625 |
| Apartment House Lot | 4,800 / 18,000 | 48 / 120 | 70% / 90% | 80% | 5 / 10 | 15 | 0 | 1 / 4; 50' | 30"[6] | not permitted |
| Rowhouse Lot | 1,800 / 3,840 | 16 / 32 | 90% / 100% | 80% | 0 / 10 | 15 | 0 | 2 / 3; 35' | 30" | 625 |
| Cottage House Lot | 2,400 / 4,800 | 24 / 40 | 70% / 90% | 60% | 5 / 25 | 10 | 2 | 1 / 2; 35' | 30" | 800 |
| Sideyard House Lot | 3,000 / 6,000 | 30 / 60 | 60% / 90% | 50% | 5 / 10 | 10 | 0/ 10[5] | 1 / 3; 35' | 30" | 800 |
| House Lot | 4,000 / 8,400 | 40 / 70 | 60% / 80% | 50% | 20 / 30 | 10 | 5 | 1 / 3; 35' | 30" | 800 |
| Estate Lot | 7,200 / no max | 60 / no max | n/a | 30% | 20 / 50 | 20 | 10 | 1 / 3; 35' | 30" | 1000 |
| Civic Building Lot | 5,000 / no max | 50 / no max | n/a | 80% | n/a | 15 | 0 | 1 / 4; 50' | n/a | 1250 |
| Countryside Tract | 43,560 / no max | 200 / no max | n/a | 15% | 50 / n/a | 50 | 50 | 1 / 2; 35' | n/a | not permitted |

[1] *Corner lots must meet front yard requirements on both streets.*

[2] *Minimum rear yards in this column apply to principal buildings. Buildings for all accessory uses (including garages and accessory dwellings) must maintain a 5-foot minimum rear yard, except when the rear yard adjoins an alley (see Section 3.01.03.EE.2); no separation is required from an alley. Fences are regulated by Section 8.00.04.*

[3] *See definition of "story" for further details on height measurements. The building spacing formula in Section 7.04.03 does not apply in PTV districts.*

[4] *See additional requirements in Section 3.01.03.EE.2.g(3).*

[5] *See Section 3.01.03.EE.2.f(8) for further details.*

[6] *Non-elevator apartments three stories in height or less may be built at grade and shall provide a minimum front yard of 5 feet.*

**Fig. 4.78** Regulations table

**TABLE 3-2**
PERMITTED LAND USES

| Lot Type | Single-family detached dwellings | Two-family dwellings | Multiple-family dwellings (3 or more units) | Community Residential Homes | Family Day Care Homes | Family Residential Homes [beyond 1000'] | Family Residential Homes [within 1,000'] | Bed and Breakfast Residences | Residential Accessory Uses (subject to the requirements of Section 8.00.00) | Civic Uses (see Section 4.04.06) | Countryside Uses (see Section 3.01.03.EE.2.o) | Commercial, Neighborhood (CN) | Commercial, Office (CO) | Commercial, General (CG) | Industrial Light (IL) | Institutional (I) | Religious Facilities (RF) |
|---|---|---|---|---|---|---|---|---|---|---|---|---|---|---|---|---|---|
| Mixed-Use Building Lot * | - | P* | P* | P* | P* | P* | P* | P* | P* | P | - | S | S | - | - | S | S |
| Retail Building Lot | - | - | P | P | P | P | P | P | P | P | - | S | S | - | - | S | S |
| Apartment Building Lot | - | - | P | P | P | P | P | P | P | - | - | - | - | - | - | - | - |
| Live/Work Building Lot | - | P | P | P | P | P | P | P | P | P | - | S | S | - | - | S | S |
| Apartment House Lot | - | - | P | P | P | P | c | c | P | - | - | - | - | - | - | - | - |
| Rowhouse Lot | - | P | P | P | P | P | c | c | P | - | - | - | - | - | - | - | - |
| Cottage House Lot | P | - | - | - | P | P | c | - | P | - | - | - | - | - | - | - | - |
| Sideyard House Lot | P | - | - | - | P | P | c | - | P | - | - | - | - | - | - | - | - |
| House Lot | P | - | - | - | P | P | c | - | P | - | - | - | - | - | - | - | - |
| Estate Lot ** | P | - | - | c | P | P | c | c | P | - | - | - | - | - | - | - | - |
| Civic Building Lot | - | - | - | P | P | P | P | - | P | P | - | - | - | - | - | S | S |
| Countryside Tract | - | - | - | - | - | - | - | - | - | P | P | - | - | - | - | - | - |

NOTES: P = permitted use; c = conditional use; - = uses are not permitted; S = same uses as allowable for any parcel in listed zoning district (in addition to all uses specifically indicated in other columns)

* Residential uses in Mixed-Use Building Lots may not be placed in the first story.

** Estate Lots in Fringe transect zones are limited to a maximum of 5% of the land area for Open Space and Countryside components; the allowance for these lots must be acquired by TDR Credits transferred from an off-site eligible sending site (see Section 4.04.05).

**Fig. 4.79** Land-use table using terminology from the existing code

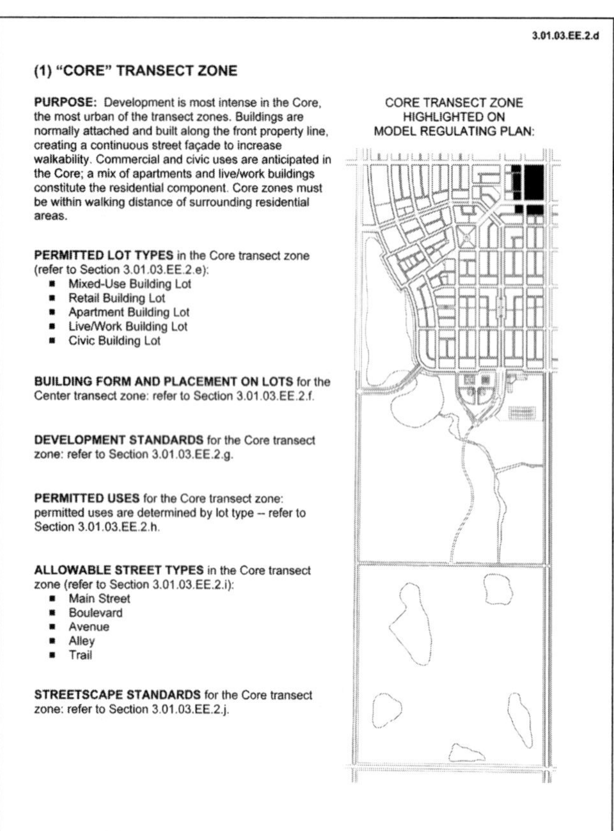

3.01.03.EE.2.d

**(1) "CORE" TRANSECT ZONE**

**PURPOSE:** Development is most intense in the Core, the most urban of the transect zones. Buildings are normally attached and built along the front property line, creating a continuous street façade to increase walkability. Commercial and civic uses are anticipated in the Core; a mix of apartments and live/work buildings constitute the residential component. Core zones must be within walking distance of surrounding residential areas.

CORE TRANSECT ZONE HIGHLIGHTED ON MODEL REGULATING PLAN:

**PERMITTED LOT TYPES** in the Core transect zone (refer to Section 3.01.03.EE.2.e):

- Mixed-Use Building Lot
- Retail Building Lot
- Apartment Building Lot
- Live/Work Building Lot
- Civic Building Lot

**BUILDING FORM AND PLACEMENT ON LOTS** for the Center transect zone: refer to Section 3.01.03.EE.2.f.

**DEVELOPMENT STANDARDS** for the Core transect zone: refer to Section 3.01.03.EE.2.g.

**PERMITTED USES** for the Core transect zone: permitted uses are determined by lot type -- refer to Section 3.01.03.EE.2.h.

**ALLOWABLE STREET TYPES** in the Core transect zone (refer to Section 3.01.03.EE.2.i):

- Main Street
- Boulevard
- Avenue
- Alley
- Trail

**STREETSCAPE STANDARDS** for the Core transect zone: refer to Section 3.01.03.EE.2.j.

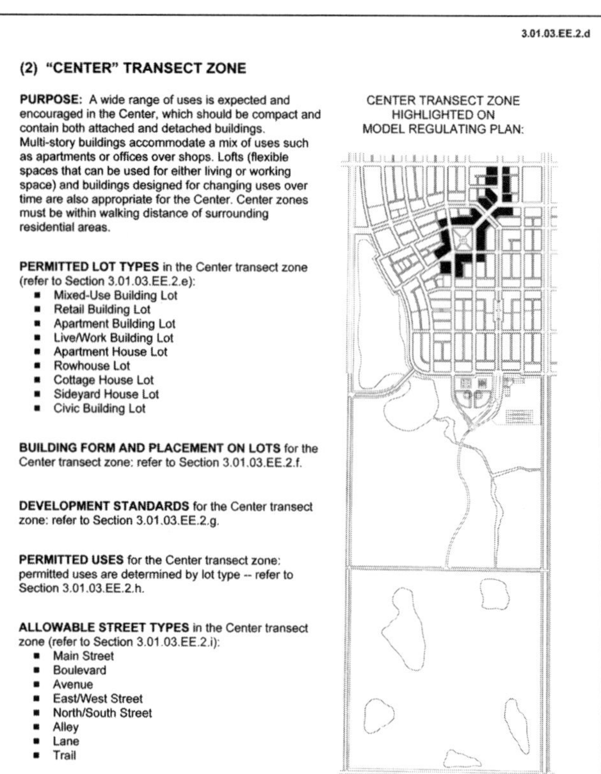

3.01.03.EE.2.d

**(2) "CENTER" TRANSECT ZONE**

**PURPOSE:** A wide range of uses is expected and encouraged in the Center, which should be compact and contain both attached and detached buildings. Multi-story buildings accommodate a mix of uses such as apartments or offices over shops. Lofts (flexible spaces that can be used for either living or working space) and buildings designed for changing uses over time are also appropriate for the Center. Center zones must be within walking distance of surrounding residential areas.

CENTER TRANSECT ZONE HIGHLIGHTED ON MODEL REGULATING PLAN:

**PERMITTED LOT TYPES** in the Center transect zone (refer to Section 3.01.03.EE.2.e):

- Mixed-Use Building Lot
- Retail Building Lot
- Apartment Building Lot
- Live/Work Building Lot
- Apartment House Lot
- Rowhouse Lot
- Cottage House Lot
- Sideyard House Lot
- Civic Building Lot

**BUILDING FORM AND PLACEMENT ON LOTS** for the Center transect zone: refer to Section 3.01.03.EE.2.f.

**DEVELOPMENT STANDARDS** for the Center transect zone: refer to Section 3.01.03.EE.2.g.

**PERMITTED USES** for the Center transect zone: permitted uses are determined by lot type -- refer to Section 3.01.03.EE.2.h.

**ALLOWABLE STREET TYPES** in the Center transect zone (refer to Section 3.01.03.EE.2.i):

- Main Street
- Boulevard
- Avenue
- East/West Street
- North/South Street
- Alley
- Lane
- Trail

**STREETSCAPE STANDARDS** for the Center transect zone: refer to Section 3.01.03.EE.2.j.

**Fig. 4.80** Summaries of Core (left) and Center (right) transect zone standards

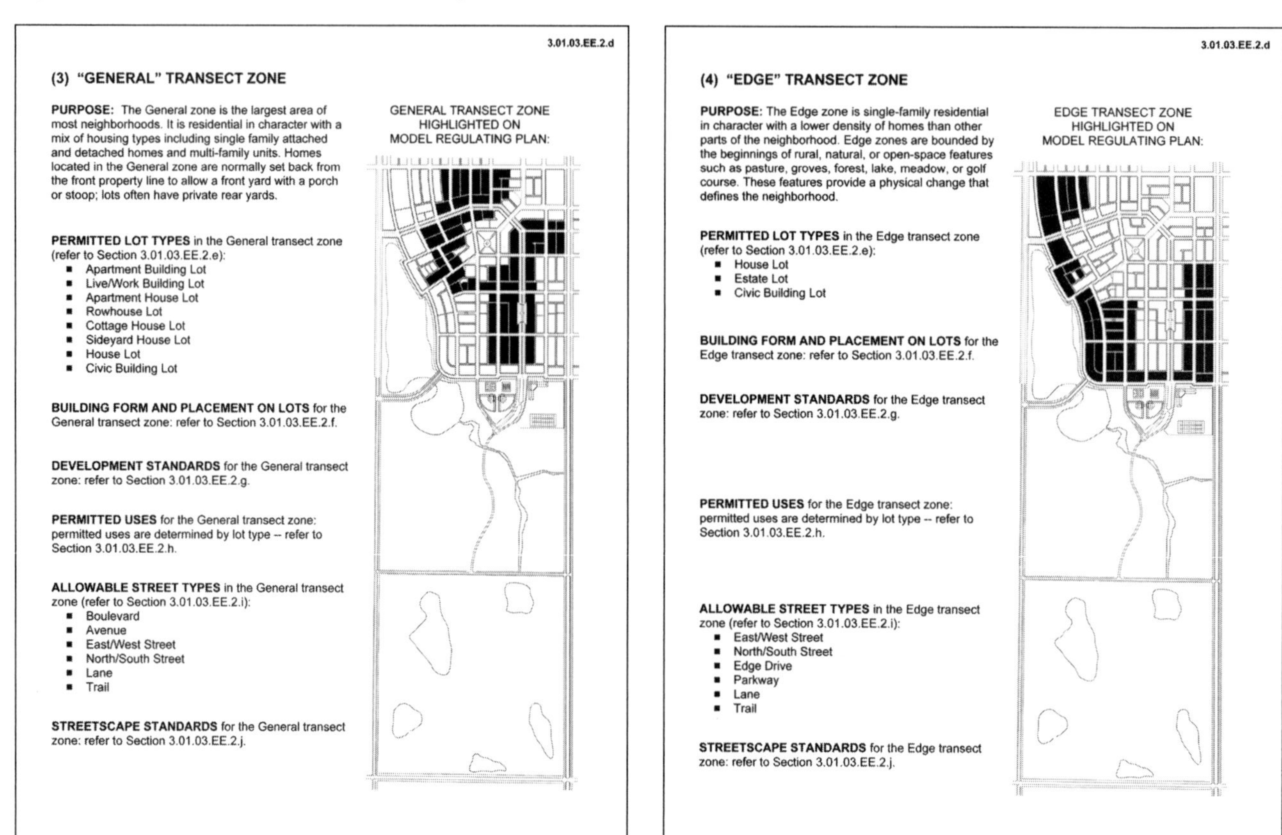

3.01.03.EE.2.d

**(3) "GENERAL" TRANSECT ZONE**

**PURPOSE:** The General zone is the largest area of most neighborhoods. It is residential in character with a mix of housing types including single family attached and detached homes and multi-family units. Homes located in the General zone are normally set back from the front property line to allow a front yard with a porch or stoop; lots often have private rear yards.

GENERAL TRANSECT ZONE HIGHLIGHTED ON MODEL REGULATING PLAN:

**PERMITTED LOT TYPES** in the General transect zone (refer to Section 3.01.03.EE.2.e):

- Apartment Building Lot
- Live/Work Building Lot
- Apartment House Lot
- Rowhouse Lot
- Cottage House Lot
- Sideyard House Lot
- House Lot
- Civic Building Lot

**BUILDING FORM AND PLACEMENT ON LOTS** for the General transect zone: refer to Section 3.01.03.EE.2.f.

**DEVELOPMENT STANDARDS** for the General transect zone: refer to Section 3.01.03.EE.2.g.

**PERMITTED USES** for the General transect zone: permitted uses are determined by lot type -- refer to Section 3.01.03.EE.2.h.

**ALLOWABLE STREET TYPES** in the General transect zone (refer to Section 3.01.03.EE.2.i):

- Boulevard
- Avenue
- East/West Street
- North/South Street
- Lane
- Trail

**STREETSCAPE STANDARDS** for the General transect zone: refer to Section 3.01.03.EE.2.j.

3.01.03.EE.2.d

**(4) "EDGE" TRANSECT ZONE**

**PURPOSE:** The Edge zone is single-family residential in character with a lower density of homes than other parts of the neighborhood. Edge zones are bounded by the beginnings of rural, natural, or open-space features such as pasture, groves, forest, lake, meadow, or golf course. These features provide a physical change that defines the neighborhood.

EDGE TRANSECT ZONE HIGHLIGHTED ON MODEL REGULATING PLAN:

**PERMITTED LOT TYPES** in the Edge transect zone (refer to Section 3.01.03.EE.2.e):

- House Lot
- Estate Lot
- Civic Building Lot

**BUILDING FORM AND PLACEMENT ON LOTS** for the Edge transect zone: refer to Section 3.01.03.EE.2.f.

**DEVELOPMENT STANDARDS** for the Edge transect zone: refer to Section 3.01.03.EE.2.g.

**PERMITTED USES** for the Edge transect zone: permitted uses are determined by lot type -- refer to Section 3.01.03.EE.2.h.

**ALLOWABLE STREET TYPES** in the Edge transect zone (refer to Section 3.01.03.EE.2.i):

- East/West Street
- North/South Street
- Edge Drive
- Parkway
- Lane
- Trail

**STREETSCAPE STANDARDS** for the Edge transect zone: refer to Section 3.01.03.EE.2.j.

**Fig. 4.81** Summaries of General (left) and Edge (right) transect zone standards

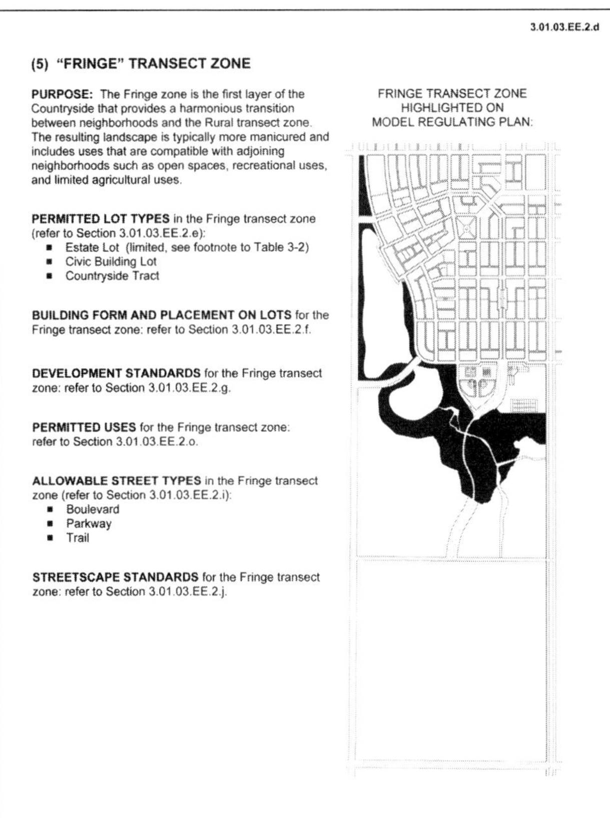

3.01.03.EE.2.d

(5) "FRINGE" TRANSECT ZONE

**PURPOSE:** The Fringe zone is the first layer of the Countryside that provides a harmonious transition between neighborhoods and the Rural transect zone. The resulting landscape is typically more manicured and includes uses that are compatible with adjoining neighborhoods such as open spaces, recreational uses, and limited agricultural uses.

**PERMITTED LOT TYPES** in the Fringe transect zone (refer to Section 3.01.03.EE.2.e):
- Estate Lot (limited, see footnote to Table 3-2)
- Civic Building Lot
- Countryside Tract

**BUILDING FORM AND PLACEMENT ON LOTS** for the Fringe transect zone: refer to Section 3.01.03.EE.2.f.

**DEVELOPMENT STANDARDS** for the Fringe transect zone: refer to Section 3.01.03.EE.2.g.

**PERMITTED USES** for the Fringe transect zone: refer to Section 3.01.03.EE.2.o.

**ALLOWABLE STREET TYPES** in the Fringe transect zone (refer to Section 3.01.03.EE.2.i):
- Boulevard
- Parkway
- Trail

**STREETSCAPE STANDARDS** for the Fringe transect zone: refer to Section 3.01.03.EE.2.j.

FRINGE TRANSECT ZONE HIGHLIGHTED ON MODEL REGULATING PLAN:

3.01.03.EE.2.d

(6) "RURAL" TRANSECT ZONE

**PURPOSE:** The Rural zone is the second layer of the Countryside that does not adjoin neighborhoods. Land uses in the Rural zone encompass the full range of permitted agricultural, recreational, and open space uses.

**PERMITTED LOT TYPES** in the Rural transect zone (refer to Section 3.01.03.EE.2.e):
- Countryside Tract

**BUILDING FORM AND PLACEMENT ON LOTS** for the Rural transect zone: refer to Section 3.01.03.EE.2.f.

**DEVELOPMENT STANDARDS** for the Rural transect zone: refer to Section 3.01.03.EE.2.g.

**PERMITTED USES** for the Rural transect zone: refer to Section 3.01.03.EE.2.o.

**ALLOWABLE STREET TYPES** in the Rural transect zone (refer to Section 3.01.03.EE.2.i):
- Boulevard
- Parkway
- Trail

**STREETSCAPE STANDARDS** for the Rural transect zone: refer to Section 3.01.03.EE.2.j.

RURAL TRANSECT ZONE HIGHLIGHTED ON MODEL REGULATING PLAN:

**Fig. 4.82** Summaries of Fringe (left) and Rural (right) transect zone standards

3.01.03.EE.2.k

k. **STREET NETWORK DESIGN**

(1) New development must accommodate the Future Street Network Plan (see Section 4.04.04.B).

(2) Each neighborhood must provide an interconnected network of streets, alleys or lanes, and other public passageways.

i. Neighborhood streets must be designed to encourage pedestrian and bicycle travel by providing short routes to connect residential uses with nearby commercial services, schools, parks, and other neighborhood facilities within the same or adjoining Towns or Villages. Sidewalks and rows of street trees must be provided on both sides of all neighborhood streets.

ii. Neighborhood streets should be organized according to a hierarchy based on function, size, and design speed. Rights-of-way are expected to differ in dimension and must meet the appropriate standards for the transect zones in which they are located (see Section 3.01.03.EE.2.i). There must be a minimum of two street types within each neighborhood.

iii. Neighborhood streets do not have to form an orthogonal grid and are not required to intersect at ninety-degree angles. These streets may be curved or bent but must connect to other streets. Jogs or centerline offsets shall be at least 100 feet for local streets; this requirement does not apply to alleys.

iv. Neighborhoods must accommodate one or more public transit nodes for future service to points beyond the neighborhood.

v. All streets must be publicly dedicated. Private streets and closed or gated streets are prohibited, notwithstanding the provisions of Sections 7.05.03.E and 7.10.15.

vi. The use of raised intersections, lateral shifts, and traffic circles are encouraged as alternatives to more conventional traffic calming measures such as speed bumps.

vii. A continuous network of rear and side alleys and/or lanes is desirable to serve as the primary means of vehicular ingress to individual lots. Such networks are mandatory in Core and Center transect zones and for Mixed-use, Retail, Live/Work, Apartment, and Rowhouse, and Cottage Lots regardless of transect zones. Alley and rear lane entrances should align so as to provide ease of ingress for service vehicles. Internal deflections or variations in the alley/rear lane network are encouraged to prevent excessive or monotonous views of the rear of structures resulting from long stretches of alleys and rear lanes.

viii. Cul-de-sacs are not permitted except where physical conditions such as freeways provide no practical alternatives for connection for through traffic. Canals may or may not be physical barriers; appropriate crossings will be considered at the time of PTV approval. Each cul-de-sac must be detailed as a close, with landscaping in the center (see Figure 3-9).

ix. Street stubs must be provided to adjacent undeveloped land to ensure an integrated street network is achieved over time, except where the adjacent land is being designated as Countryside through the PTV approval. Stub-out streets to connect to future development will not be considered cul-de-sacs if they are less than 300 feet long.

FIGURE 3-9
EXAMPLE OF CLOSE DETAILING

3.01.03.EE.2.l

x. Full access intersections along Indrio Road must be separated by at least 660 feet. Full access intersections along other roads on the regional street network must be separated by at least 330 feet (see Section 4.04.04.B).

(3) The average perimeter of all blocks within a neighborhood may not exceed 1,500 feet. The maximum perimeter of any block may not exceed 2,400 feet. The portion of any block between intersecting streets may not exceed 500 feet without a publicly dedicated pedestrian sidewalk or trail providing access to another street. Smaller block sizes are encouraged to promote walkability. An applicant may propose minor modifications to these block size standards during the PTV rezoning process; the Board of County Commissioners shall decide whether to accept, modify, or reject such modifications during the approval process.

(4) The Edge Drive street type is intended to demarcate the Edge transect zone from the Countryside. Edge Drives are primarily "single-loaded," having private lots on one side while providing visual and often physical access to the Countryside on the other. A double-loaded Edge Drive is limited to 30% of the linear edge; where Edge Drives are double-loaded, a physical line of demarcation (e.g. a split rail fence) must be provided separating private lots from public trails and the Countryside. An applicant may propose to exceed the 30% limitation during the PTV rezoning process where there is no significant view of the Countryside that would be lost or where it is deemed to be in the balanced public/private interest while remaining consistent with the TVC Element. The Board of County Commissioners shall decide whether to accept, modify, or reject a proposed increase in double-loaded Edge Drive during the approval process.

(5) In addition to its network of streets, each PTV shall also include a network of trails or greenways connecting urban, recreational, academic, and rural locations. Trails shall be provided along the Flow Way System and along remaining canals to provide connections and access to the Countryside. Trails in the Fringe transect zone should be located in the center of the Fringe zone or adjacent to the Rural zone to provide separation from private lots in the Edge zone. Existing hedgerows, environmentally significant or sensitive lands, tree clusters, flow ways, knolls, and viewsheds from scenic roads or parkways shall be considered for connecting linkages between Towns and Villages. Greenway lands shall be interconnected wherever possible to provide a continuous network of such lands within and adjoining each PTV and remaining separated from streets wherever possible.

(6) The street design requirements of Section 7.05 apply except where they conflict with standards for the TVC Overlay Zone or this zoning district. Further exceptions to the requirements of Section 7.05 may be authorized by the Board of County Commissioners through approval of a regulating plan during the PTV rezoning process.

l. **STREET CROSS-SECTIONS**

Street types in all PTV districts must be assigned in accordance with Section 3.01.03.EE.2.i. The specific design of each street must follow the cross-sections illustrated below for each street type, as adjusted for the transect zone they pass through in accordance with Section 3.01.03.EE.2.j. The lane widths shown include the width of gutter pans. In the event of direct conflicts, these standards shall supersede other standards in this Code or in public works manuals.

**Fig. 4.83** (left and right) Street network standards

3.01.03.EE.2.p

p. **REGIONAL FLOW WAY SYSTEM**

(1) **Purpose and intent.**

i. A regional Flow Way System will improve water quality through a comprehensive interconnected stormwater management system that also serves as a linear park. The Flow Way System is intended to provide for a high level of retention and treatment of stormwater, reduction in water lost to tide through storage and re-use of retained water, supplemental water supply for irrigation, habitat for fish and wildlife, wildlife corridors, opportunities for habitat mitigation, and the recreational and aesthetic values provided by natural riverine systems.

ii. The regional Flow Way System will be created incrementally and become a continuous water management system that enhances the conveyance functions of the existing drainage canals and incorporates the stormwater detention, conveyance, and discharge systems for new development so as to reduce total runoff volume and improve water quality prior to discharge into the Indian River Lagoon.

iii. Where not inconsistent with SFWMD permitting criteria, natural habitat restoration is preferred to open water systems for treating stormwater and may be eligible for higher multipliers offered for restoration and preservation.

(2) **Location and connectivity.**

i. The Flow Way System shall be integrated within each development site as well as with adjacent flow way systems and existing human and native habitats in order to create a fully integrated regional system.

ii. The Flow Way System shall be located within the Fringe or Rural transect zones where it can provide sufficient water storage to serve the neighborhoods while maximizing the viability of the adjacent land for agricultural uses and native habitat restoration. The system may pass through or between neighborhood transect zones provided the following criteria are met:
1) The location and width of that portion of the system does not negatively impact the desired walkable, compact structure required for each Town or Village;
2) An adequate number of crossings is provided in order to maintain the required connectivity of the street network and the navigability of the waterway; and
3) That portion of the system is detailed to reflect the appropriate urban or rural character of the neighborhood transect zones (see Figure 3-13).

(3) **Accessibility and edges.**

i. In order to reinforce the desired linear park quality intended for the Flow Way System, the water's edge must be easily and safely accessible. A pedestrian and bicycle trail system shall be provided and maintained along at least one side of the system. In neighborhoods, the trail may take the form of paved sidewalks that runs adjacent to the system. In the Countryside, trails of a suitable material for walking, cycling, or equestrian uses should be provided within the upland buffer adjacent to the system.

3.01.03.EE.2.p

ii. The edge of the Flow Way System should be varied and should reflect the character of the adjacent transect zone. The following edge conditions may be used (as illustrated in Figure 3-13) or other designs may be submitted for approval consistent with the following intent:
1) **Neighborhood: Core, Center.** Near the center of Towns and Villages, the system may be bulkheaded with adjacent sidewalks, railings, and formal landscaping. Bulkheaded sections should provide periodic access via stairs and landings to the waters' edge.
2) **Neighborhood: General, Edge.** The area from the waters' edge landward should be fairly level to gently sloping for a minimum of 15 feet, with any required elevation changes to an adjacent sidewalk accommodated by terraces or landscaped slopes. Landscaping may be either formal or informal, with care given to species selection on sloped areas for long-term maintenance.
3) **Countryside.** In order to create a natural relationship between land and water within the Countryside, the slope of the land from the water's edge landward shall be no steeper than 1 foot of vertical change in elevation for every 10 feet of horizontal distance for the first 20 feet landward from the waters' edge. A wide walking path can meander along the edge of the water within native habitat. This edge condition may also be appropriate along a park.

FIGURE 3-13

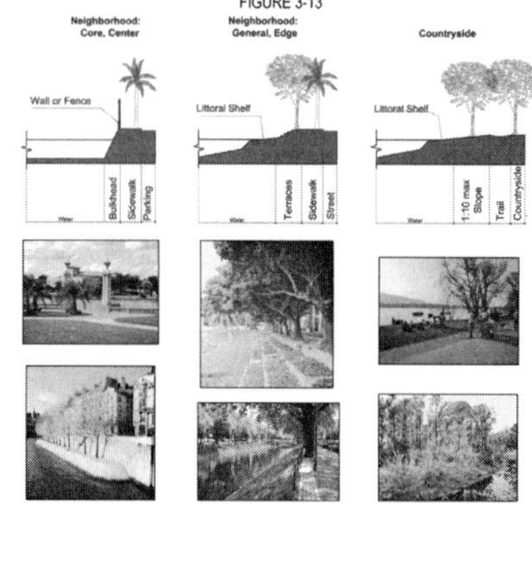


**Fig. 4.84** (left and right) Flow way regulations

3.01.03.EE.2.o

(3) **Location of Open Space and Countryside components in the transect.**

Open Space and Countryside components shall be located and arranged within the transect as described in this subsection. Figure 3-12 illustrates this description by applying vertical hatching to typical locations of Open Space and Countryside components.

FIGURE 3-12

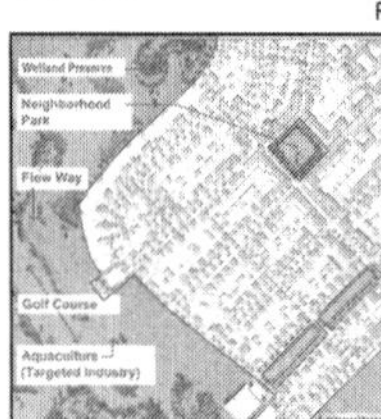


COUNTRYSIDE COMPONENTS

OPEN SPACE COMPONENTS

i. Within the PTV zoning district, the Flow Way System is to be designated as a Rural or Fringe transect zone. Where the Flow Way System runs through a neighborhood, its edges should reflect the character of adjacent transect zones as described in Section 3.01.03.EE.2.p.

ii. The continuation of viable agricultural uses in the Countryside and on neighboring properties is a primary design goal for the Countryside. Such uses constitute unique and irreplaceable resources and are major contributors to the economy. The assignment of transect zones must accomplish this goal in a manner consistent with Florida's Right to Farm Act. Once transect zones are assigned, the following limitations apply to agricultural uses and facilities within the PTV:
1) Agricultural uses and facilities in the Fringe transect zone are limited to passive agriculture that is compatible with nearby residential uses such as, but not limited to, horse and cattle pasture and native range.
2) Active agricultural uses must be located only in the Rural transect zone; such uses include crops that require extensive cultivation or spray applications of pesticide and fertilizer and concentrated livestock facilities.
3) Agricultural or utility uses or facilities that may generate noise or odor must be located only in the Rural transect zone.

iii. Other Countryside components shall also be located in the Fringe and Rural transect zones, except for community recreation areas which may be located in any transect zone.

iv. Open Space components may be located within any of the four neighborhood transect zones, except that Estate Lots may be located in the Fringe transect zone when limited in accordance with the footnote to Table 3-2.

**Fig. 4.85** Open space and countryside location regulations

4.04.03

**4.04.03 OVERVIEW OF TVC APPROVAL PROCESSES**

Development approvals for land designated TVC differ in several aspects from approvals in the remainder of unincorporated St. Lucie County. These processes can be summarized as follows:

A. Owners of 500 or more acres of land located **outside the USB** and owners of 110 acres or more of land located **inside the USB** may seek approval of a new Town or Village by applying to rezone the land to the PTV (Planned Town or Village) zoning district. See Section 3.01.03.EE.

B. Owners of less than 500 acres of land **outside the USB** may take any of the following actions:

1. Maintain the land in its natural state or with agricultural uses consistent with its agricultural zoning district and utilize the Transfer of Development Rights (TDR) program to move at least 90% of the unused transferable development value from the land to an eligible receiving site. See Section 4.04.05.

2. Subdivide the land into individual home sites using the transferable development value assigned to that land by applying to rezone the land to the PCS (Planned Country Subdivision) zoning district. See Section 3.01.03.FF. Upon approval, the TDR program may not be used to transfer density to or from the land.

3. Utilize the Transfer of Development Rights (TDR) program to move or permanently set aside at least 90% of the transferable development value from the land and subdivide the land into individual home sites using the remaining development rights. See Section 4.04.04.D.3.

4. When consistent with the retail standards under Objective 3.1.8 of the TVC Element or the workplace standards under Objective 3.1.10 of the TVC Element, apply to rezone the land to the PRW (Planned Retail/Workplace) zoning district. See Section 3.01.06.GG.

C. Owners of less than 110 acres of land **inside the USB** may take any of the following actions:

1. Develop or use the land for residential purposes in accordance with the TVC Overlay Zone requirements in Sections 4.04.01–4.04.06 of this Code.

2. Residential development is limited to the maximum residential densities on the Transferable Development Value Map (Figure 3-3 of the TVC Element), except that:
   a. Density may be increased as a county incentive for providing affordable housing, workforce housing, or mixed-use development.
   b. For development built in the form of a Town or Village, density may be increased through acquisition of TDR credits from eligible sending sites. See Sections 3.01.03.EE and 4.04.05.

D. Owners of land of any size **inside the USB** may seek rezoning of the land to the PRW (Planned Retail/Workplace) zoning district (Section 3.01.06.GG) to place retail or workplace land uses outside a Town or Village if those uses are fully consistent with the goals, objectives, and policies of the TVC Element. These proposals must meet the retail standards under Objective 3.1.8 and/or the workplace standards under Objective 3.1.10, in addition to the TVC Overlay Zone requirements in Section 4.04 of this Code.

E. Owners of land of any size may initiate, continue, or expand agricultural uses (including forestry and equestrian uses) in accordance with the requirements of the agricultural zoning district that applies to the land. This option is available both **inside and outside the USB**. See Section 3.01.03 for lists of permitted and conditional agricultural uses in each agricultural zoning district.

**Fig. 4.86** Approval process

# Ventura, California



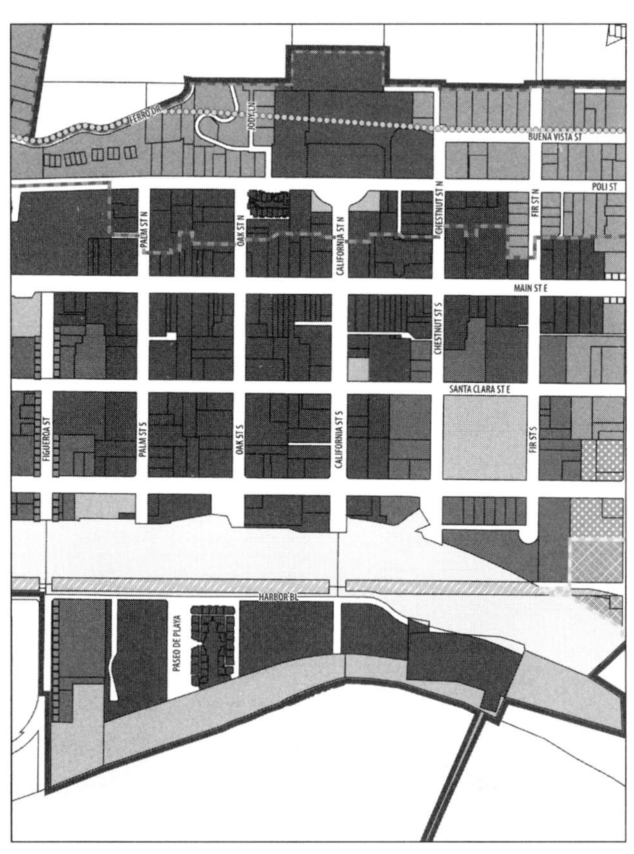

## The City's Approach to FBCs

The city of San Buenaventura (usually referred to as Ventura) is located in southern California along the Pacific Coast. It is the county seat of Ventura County, California and has a population of 106,744.[9] Ventura adopted a General Plan in September 2005 that was created in association with Crawford, Multari, Clark & Associates and took an aggressive stance by adopting the Ahwahnee Principles, the Charter of the New Urbanism, and the transect as tools for making policy and development decisions. This framework within the General Plan was created to allow the entire city to be systematically planned and regulated by FBCs. After the adoption of their General Plan in 2005, staff originally anticipated developing a "citywide" FBC, but later decided to focus on those areas facing the most urgent market demand. As a result, the Downtown Specific Plan, with a comprehensive FBC, has been adopted, and three other city-driven FBCs are in various stages covering other priority areas. In addition, private interests and developers have also begun to integrate FBCs into their Specific Plan applications.

The organizational framework for the General Plan was established as part of the "Ventura Vision" process. Its ten organizing elements are:

1. Our Natural Community
2. Our Prosperous Community
3. Our Well-Planned and Designed Community
4. Our Accessible Community
5. Our Sustainable Community
6. Our Active Community
7. Our Healthy and Safe Community
8. Our Educated Community
9. Our Creative Community
10. Our Involved Community

These principles were embellished with goals, policies, and actions to achieve these through a Smart Growth vision. The "Our Well-Planned and Designed Community" chapter integrated what typically occurs within the California state-mandated Land Use and Housing Elements, and further included optional elements, such as Community Design, to establish a framework for the application of transect-based Form-Based Codes for the entire city.

The following steps were taken within this chapter of the General Plan to establish an appropriate framework for future Form-Based Codes: (1) established a Neighborhoods, Districts, and Corridors Plan to provide a framework for prioritizing potential areas for infill and redevelopment; (2) established Planning Communities to emphasize specific existing conditions and potential improvements for each; (3) created Planning Designations that embody transect

**ARTICLE II. URBAN STANDARDS**

**2.30.070 T6.1 URBAN CORE**

**A. Building Placement**

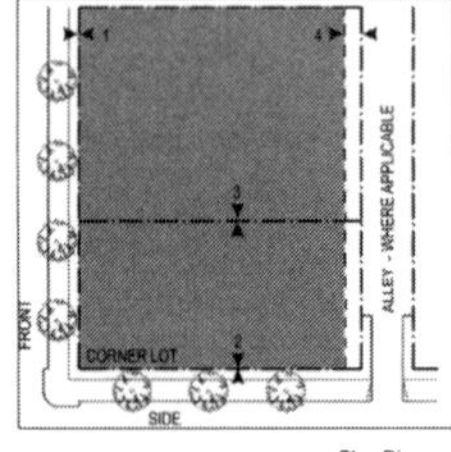


*Plan Diagram*

**1. SETBACKS**

a. Primary Buildings shall be placed within the shaded area as shown in the diagram above (unless specified otherwise by a permitted Building Type).
   1. Street Build-to Line: 0' to 5' min.
   2. Side Street Build-to Line: 0' to 5' min.
   3. Side Yard Setback: 0' min.
   4. Rear Yard Setback: 5' min.

**2. ARCHITECTURAL ENCROACHMENTS**

a. Balconies, bay windows, chimneys, cantilevered rooms, and eaves may encroach into required setbacks as identified below and as may be further limited by the California Building Code (CBC).
   1. Balconies: 6' max. into Street Build-to Line, Side Street Build-to Line and Rear Setback.
   2. Bay windows, chimneys, cantilevered rooms, and eaves: 3' max. into all Setback areas identified in Diagram A. Building Placement, above.

**B. Building Profile and Frontage**

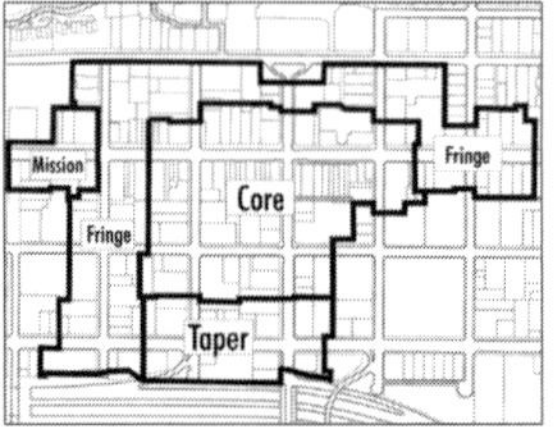


*Maximum Height Diagram*

**1. HEIGHT**

a. Maximum:
   1. **Core Area:** 4 stories for Primary Building (20% of building footprint may be 5 story).
   2. **Fringe Area:** 3 stories for Primary Building (25% of building footprint may be 4 story).
   3. **Taper Area:** 3 stories for Primary Building (25% of building footprint may be 4 story) + 25' setback for fourth story from Oak and California Streets. Taper area height limits apply to all T6.1 properties South of Hwy 101 (not shown in Maximum Height Diagram).
   4. **Mission Area:** 3 stories for Primary Building (15% of building footprint may be 4 story).

b. Floor to Floor: 18' max. ground floor; 12' max. second floor and above

**2. FRONTAGE TYPES**

a. Shopfront
b. Forecourt
c. Stoop
d. Porch (along Poli Street only)
e. Lightcourt
f. Dooryard (along Poli Street only)

City of San Buenaventura DOWNTOWN SPECIFIC PLAN
III-24

zones to establish program thresholds and general character parameters; and (4) produced a General Plan Diagram to show the application of these Planning Designations and the Plan's goals to the entire community.

The Planning Designations included a parenthetical reference to the transect zones they encompass that will provide guidance in interpreting them while drafting detailed plans and codes. While Planning Designations on the General Plan diagram are still tied to use and density, the application of the transect zones to each of these designated planning areas also establishes general parameters for the physical form within these areas. In addition, delineations of Neighborhood Centers, Districts, and Corridors allow flexibility in use by encouraging a mix of uses within these boundaries. It is also intended that the transect zones will be more specifically applied to a Regulating Plan as each of the designated planning areas has a vision plan and Form-Based Code created.

*The transect is a tool that can be used by the community to understand and describe the full range of unique environmental and built characteristics within each of Ventura's neighborhoods. Using the six parenthetical transect zones to better understand the broad Planning Designations of the General Plan Diagram, a finer-grained (site specific) set of development standards can be created to ensure that new development is in keeping with local preferences for building.* —Ventura General Plan, pp. 3-14

## The First Code: The Downtown Ventura Specific Plan

The first of the FBCs adopted by the city of Ventura was for its downtown in the Downtown Specific Plan (DTSP). The downtown was selected as the first area to plan and code to meet the city's General Plan policy of "infill first."

One of the goals that the city set for the Downtown Form-Based Code was to begin to establish a kit of parts and framework that would enable it to multiply the code and apply these parts to other areas of the community. The city began preparation of the Downtown Form-Based Code with three goals in mind: (1) clarity of rules, (2) certainty of process, and (3) high-quality design. A Specific Plan was selected as an appropriate tool for implementation to achieve the goal of having all regulations in a central, easy-to-find location. In California, the Specific Plan is the perfect tool for doing this because it enables the plan to establish Building Form Standards, a Regulating Plan, Building Type Standards, Thoroughfare and other Public Space Standards, and Architectural Standards that would override existing regulations when the Specific Plan was adopted. The Downtown

**Fig. 4.87** (previous page) The Regulating Plans for Ventura's Downtown Specific Plan (left) and the Main and Thompson FBC (right)

**Fig. 4.88** (below left and right) T6.1 Urban Core Building Form Standards from the Downtown Specific Plan (DTSP)

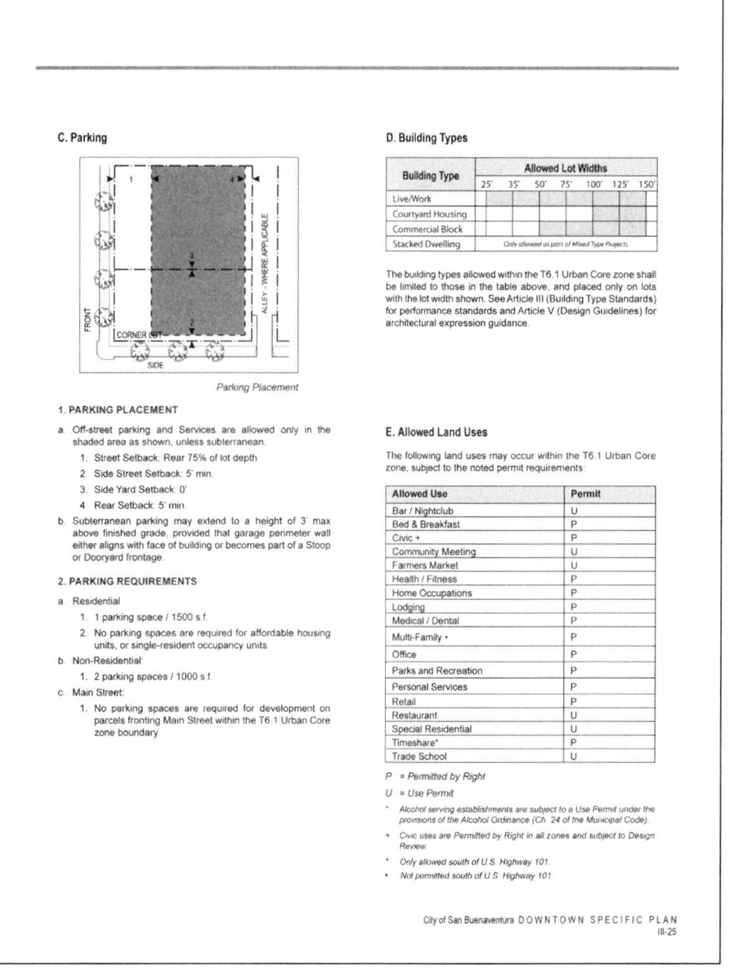

**C. Parking**



*Parking Placement*

**1. PARKING PLACEMENT**

a. Off-street parking and Services are allowed only in the shaded area as shown, unless subterranean.
   1. Street Setback: Rear 75% of lot depth
   2. Side Street Setback: 5' min.
   3. Side Yard Setback: 0'
   4. Rear Setback: 5' min.

b. Subterranean parking may extend to a height of 3' max above finished grade, provided that garage perimeter wall either aligns with face of building or becomes part of a Stoop or Dooryard frontage.

**2. PARKING REQUIREMENTS**

a. Residential
   1. 1 parking space / 1500 s.f.
   2. No parking spaces are required for affordable housing units, or single-resident occupancy units

b. Non-Residential:
   1. 2 parking spaces / 1000 s.f.

c. Main Street:
   1. No parking spaces are required for development on parcels fronting Main Street within the T6.1 Urban Core zone boundary.

**D. Building Types**

| Building Type | Allowed Lot Widths | | | | | | |
|---|---|---|---|---|---|---|---|
| | 25' | 35' | 50' | 75' | 100' | 125' | 150' |
| Live/Work | | | | | | | |
| Courtyard Housing | | | | | | | |
| Commercial Block | | | | | | | |
| Stacked Dwelling | *Only allowed as part of Mixed Type Projects* | | | | | | |

The building types allowed within the T6.1 Urban Core zone shall be limited to those in the table above, and placed only on lots with the lot width shown. See Article III (Building Type Standards) for performance standards and Article V (Design Guidelines) for architectural expression guidance.

**E. Allowed Land Uses**

The following land uses may occur within the T6.1 Urban Core zone, subject to the noted permit requirements:

| Allowed Use | Permit |
|---|---|
| Bar / Nightclub | U |
| Bed & Breakfast | P |
| Civic + | P |
| Community Meeting | U |
| Farmers Market | U |
| Health / Fitness | P |
| Home Occupations | P |
| Lodging | P |
| Medical / Dental | P |
| Multi-Family • | P |
| Office | P |
| Parks and Recreation | P |
| Personal Services | P |
| Retail | P |
| Restaurant | U |
| Special Residential | U |
| Timeshare* | P |
| Trade School | U |

*P = Permitted by Right*

*U = Use Permit*

* *Alcohol serving establishments are subject to a Use Permit under the provisions of the Alcohol Ordinance (Ch. 24 of the Municipal Code).*

\+ *Civic uses are Permitted by Right in all zones and subject to Design Review.*

* *Only allowed south of U.S. Highway 101.*

• *Not permitted south of U.S. Highway 101.*

City of San Buenaventura DOWNTOWN SPECIFIC PLAN
III-25

Form-Based Code was road-tested between September 2004 and March 2007 in the format of "Downtown Compatibility Guidelines," which were used to evaluate submitted projects. Substantial changes to the code resulted from this trial period.

The following are several of the innovations within the DTSP:

*Extensive Building-Type Regulations*

This Form-Based Code was one of the first to integrate a complete set of standards for each of a group of designated building types in addition to the regulations for building form in the Building Form Standards. For each building type, the code regulates access, parking and services, open space, frontage, and building size and massing.

**ARTICLE III. BUILDING TYPES**

**3.10.130 COMMERCIAL BLOCK**

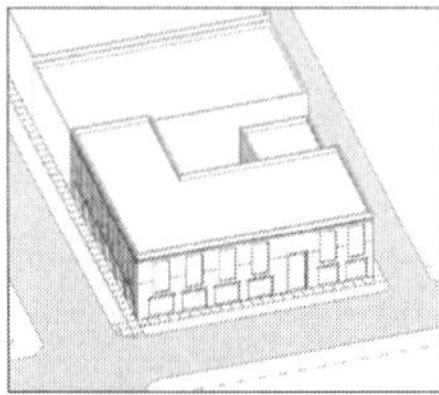

*Commercial Block Example Diagram*

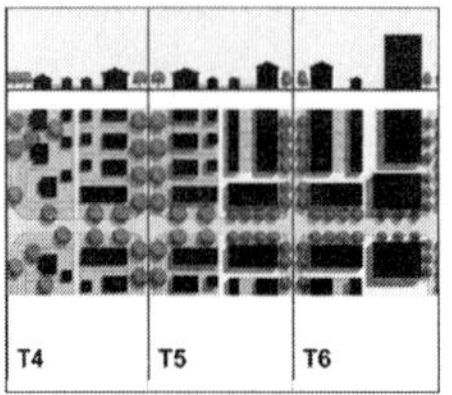


*Allowed in Transects: T4 through T6*

**A. DESCRIPTION**

A building designed for occupancy by retail, service, and/or office uses on the ground floor, with upper floors also configured for those uses or for dwelling units. A Commercial Block may be located upon a qualifying lot in the T4.4 Thompson Corridor, T5.1 Neighborhood Center and T6.1 Urban Core zones.

**B. ACCESS**

1. The main entrance to each ground floor area shall be directly from and face the street. [E]
2. Entrance to the residential and/or non-residential portions of the building above the ground floor shall be through a street level lobby or through a podium lobby accessible from the street. [E]
3. Elevator access shall be provided between the subterranean garage and each level of the building where dwelling and/or commerce access occurs. [W]
4. Interior circulation to each dwelling shall be through a corridor which may be single or double-loaded. [E]
5. Where an alley is present, parking shall be accessed through the alley. [E]
6. Where an alley is not present, parking shall be accessed by a driveway of 14' min. width. [E]
7. On a corner lot without access to an alley, parking shall be accessed by a driveway of 14' min. width. [E]
8. Dwellings can be accessed via a single-loaded, exterior corridor, provided the corridor is designed per the following requirements:
    a. The open corridor length does not exceed 40 feet. [W]
    b. The open corridor is designed in the form of a Monterey balcony, loggia, terrace, or a wall with window openings. [DR]

**C. PARKING & SERVICES**

1. Required parking may be at-grade or as subterranean. If provided at-grade, parking spaces may be within a garage, carport, or uncovered. [W]
2. Dwellings may have indirect access to their parking stalls. [DR]
3. Where an alley is present, services, above ground equipment and trash container areas shall be located on the alley. [W]
4. Where an alley is not present, above ground equipment and trash container areas should be located at least 10 feet behind the façade of the building and be screened from view from the street with landscaping or a fence. [DR]
5. Parking entrances to subterranean garages and/or driveways should be located as close as possible to the side or rear of each lot. [DR]

**D. OPEN SPACE**

1. Front yards are defined by the street build-to line or front yard setback and frontage type requirements of the applicable zone. [DR]
2. The primary shared open space is the rear yard, which shall be designed as a courtyard. Courtyards may be located on the ground or on a podium. Side yards may also be provided for outdoor patios connected to ground floor commercial uses. [E]
3. Minimum courtyard dimensions shall be 40 feet when the long axis of the courtyard is oriented East/West, and 30 feet when the courtyard is oriented North/South. [W]
4. The minimum courtyard area shall be twenty percent (20%) of the lot area. [W]
5. Courtyards shall not be of a proportion of less than 1:1 between their width and height. [W]

City of San Buenaventura DOWNTOWN SPECIFIC PLAN
III-54

The list of types regulated in this code are:

- Carriage House
- Front Yard House
- Side Yard House
- Duplex, Triplex, and Quadplex
- Villa
- Mansion
- Bungalow Court
- Row House
- Live/Work
- Side Court Housing
- Courtyard Housing
- Commercial Block
- Stacked Dwellings

*Height Overlay for T6 (in Building Form Standards)*

This regulation overlay was created to transition from the tallest buildings at the middle of the town center to those at the fringe of the core and adjacent to the historic mission. The heights are regulated by the overlay as follows:

- Core: Four stories maximum, 20 percent at five stories
- Fringe: Three stories maximum, 25 percent at four stories
- Taper: Three stories maximum, 25 percent at four stories (25-foot setback of fourth story in certain areas)
- Mission: Three stories maximum, 15 percent at four stories

*Hillside Overlay*

This overlay was created to ensure that new buildings tier with sloping topography and, in doing so, remain in scale with the existing and intended future building condition. It does this by regulating the maximum height above grade along the street and a maximum height above average natural grade for the rest of the site as it goes downhill.

*Secondary Regulating Plans for Overlay Regulations*

Several secondary Regulating Plans were created for the mixed-use portion of downtown. The first plan was to show locations where ground-floor commercial uses are required, and the second was to show appropriate locations for bar and nightclub locations. This second regulation was important to address police department staff deficiencies by concentrating new bar and nightclub establishments. In addition, two additional use type overlays were created to retain specific existing land uses (e.g., Patagonia in the Eastside neighborhood) and to allow for limited commercial uses in those designated for residential.

*Mixed-Type Regulations*

This was one of the first Form-Based Codes for infill conditions that specifically addressed regulations for blended densities on large infill lots and how these lots should be subdivided.

## Expanding the Application of FBCs to the City

The other two Form-Based Codes that are in process in Ventura are the Main Street and Thompson Boulevard Form-Based Code and the Victoria Avenue Corridor Plan and Code. The Saticoy and Wells Community Plan is also currently in draft format and will ultimately lead to the implementation of an FBC for the 1,000-acre planning area.

The Main Street and Thompson Boulevard FBC is a SmartCode calibrated by David Sargent and Robert Alminana of HDR | Town Planning and Paul Crawford to the local conditions of an aging corridor. The goal was to update the zoning to make it consistent with the General Plan goals and policies for this rapidly changing area. One of the unique aspects of this code is that it integrates Building-Type Regulations that were created for the Downtown Ventura Specific Plan to give it an additional depth of regulation to the standard SmartCode and to make it consistent with the Downtown FBC.

## Code Administration

In order to ensure that the city staff could easily administer all the various FBCs, a consistent common framework was needed. Ideally, this would have been done before starting the city-wide coding process, but the reality is that this has happened by default through the creation of the first several FBCs. The transect is the organizing principle, and subsets of the T-Zones are created as needed for each of the different neighborhood areas that are planned and coded. For example, T4 will ultimately need T4.1, T4.2, and the like to accommodate differences by planning area. That being said, an important goal of the city is to minimize the number of these subdistricts so that the code does not become unmanageable. Thus, many of the minor differences within the T-Zones are dealt with

**Fig. 4.89** (below left and right) Commercial Block Building Type Standards from the DTSP

*Illustrative Photo*

6. In 40-foot wide courtyards, the frontages and architectural projections allowed within the applicable zone are permitted on two sides of the courtyard; they are permitted on one side of a 30-foot wide courtyard. [W]
7. Private patios may be provided in side and rear yards. [DR]

E. LANDSCAPE

1. No private landscaping is required in front of the building. [DR]
2. Trees may be placed in side yards to create a particular sense of place. [DR]
3. At least one large tree should be provided in the rear yard, planted directly in the ground; except for podium courtyards. [DR]
4. Courtyards located over garages should be designed to avoid the sensation of forced podium hardscape through the use of ample landscaping. [DR]

F. FRONTAGE

1. Living areas (e.g., living room, family room, dining room, etc.), rather than sleeping and service rooms, should be oriented toward the fronting street and courtyard. [DR]
2. No arcade or gallery may encroach into the required minimum width of a courtyard. [W]

*Illustrative Photo*

G. BUILDING SIZE & MASSING

1. Buildings may contain any of three dwelling types: flats, townhouses, and lofts. [W]
2. Dwellings may be as repetitive or unique, as determined by individual designs [DR]
3. Buildings may be composed of one dominant volume, and may be flanked by secondary ones. [DR]
4. The intent of these regulations is to provide for buildings with varying heights. Suggested height ratios are as follows:
   a. 1.0 story: 100% 1 story [W]
   b. 2.0 stories: 85% 2 stories, 15% 3 stories [W]
   c. 3.0 stories: 85% 3 stories, 15% 4 stories [W]
   d. 4.0 stories: 75% 4 stories, 25% 5 stories [W]

   These height ratios are maximums that may exceed that allowed by the applicable zone (e.g., Commercial Block 4.0 may exceed the 4.0 75% 4-story, 25% 5-story limitation of the T6.1 Urban Core zone).
5. The visibility of elevators and of exterior corridors at the third, fourth and/or fifth stories should be minimized by incorporation into the mass of the building. [DR]

Deviations from a standard of guideline require the following Variance (pg. III-120):
[DR] = Design Review [W] = Warrant [E] = Exception

City of San Buenaventura DOWNTOWN SPECIFIC PLAN
III-55

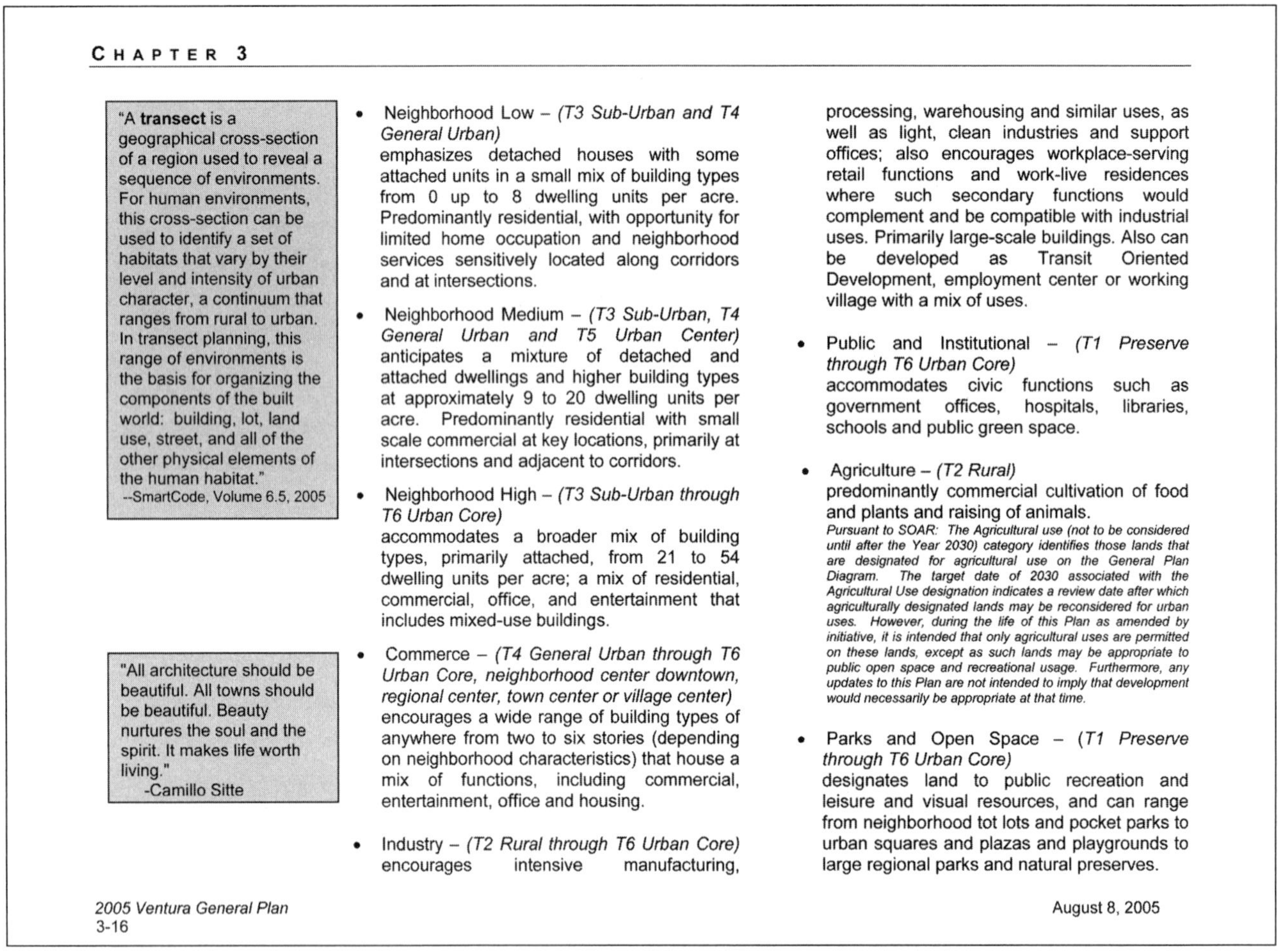

CHAPTER 3

> "A **transect** is a geographical cross-section of a region used to reveal a sequence of environments. For human environments, this cross-section can be used to identify a set of habitats that vary by their level and intensity of urban character, a continuum that ranges from rural to urban. In transect planning, this range of environments is the basis for organizing the components of the built world: building, lot, land use, street, and all of the other physical elements of the human habitat."
> --SmartCode, Volume 6.5, 2005

- Neighborhood Low – *(T3 Sub-Urban and T4 General Urban)*
  emphasizes detached houses with some attached units in a small mix of building types from 0 up to 8 dwelling units per acre. Predominantly residential, with opportunity for limited home occupation and neighborhood services sensitively located along corridors and at intersections.
- Neighborhood Medium – *(T3 Sub-Urban, T4 General Urban and T5 Urban Center)*
  anticipates a mixture of detached and attached dwellings and higher building types at approximately 9 to 20 dwelling units per acre. Predominantly residential with small scale commercial at key locations, primarily at intersections and adjacent to corridors.
- Neighborhood High – *(T3 Sub-Urban through T6 Urban Core)*
  accommodates a broader mix of building types, primarily attached, from 21 to 54 dwelling units per acre; a mix of residential, commercial, office, and entertainment that includes mixed-use buildings.
- Commerce – *(T4 General Urban through T6 Urban Core, neighborhood center downtown, regional center, town center or village center)*
  encourages a wide range of building types of anywhere from two to six stories (depending on neighborhood characteristics) that house a mix of functions, including commercial, entertainment, office and housing.
- Industry – *(T2 Rural through T6 Urban Core)*
  encourages intensive manufacturing, processing, warehousing and similar uses, as well as light, clean industries and support offices; also encourages workplace-serving retail functions and work-live residences where such secondary functions would complement and be compatible with industrial uses. Primarily large-scale buildings. Also can be developed as Transit Oriented Development, employment center or working village with a mix of uses.
- Public and Institutional – *(T1 Preserve through T6 Urban Core)*
  accommodates civic functions such as government offices, hospitals, libraries, schools and public green space.
- Agriculture – *(T2 Rural)*
  predominantly commercial cultivation of food and plants and raising of animals.
  *Pursuant to SOAR: The Agricultural use (not to be considered until after the Year 2030) category identifies those lands that are designated for agricultural use on the General Plan Diagram. The target date of 2030 associated with the Agricultural Use designation indicates a review date after which agriculturally designated lands may be reconsidered for urban uses. However, during the life of this Plan as amended by initiative, it is intended that only agricultural uses are permitted on these lands, except as such lands may be appropriate to public open space and recreational usage. Furthermore, any updates to this Plan are not intended to imply that development would necessarily be appropriate at that time.*
- Parks and Open Space – *(T1 Preserve through T6 Urban Core)*
  designates land to public recreation and leisure and visual resources, and can range from neighborhood tot lots and pocket parks to urban squares and plazas and playgrounds to large regional parks and natural preserves.

> "All architecture should be beautiful. All towns should be beautiful. Beauty nurtures the soul and the spirit. It makes life worth living."
> -Camillo Sitte

*2005 Ventura General Plan*
3-16

August 8, 2005

**Fig. 4.90** Pages from the General Plan pertaining to the transect

using overlays to regulate minor differences, such as height, setbacks, and frontages.

The city is pursuing several strategies to ensure that its staff has the ability to administer its FBCs. The city has started recruiting and hiring people who have an active interest and knowledge of New Urbanism, Smart Growth, and Form-Based Coding. It also plans to provide in-house training and to send staff to conferences and workshops to keep up to date with the latest evolution of these practices. The Planning Commission and city council also have begun to take tours to see projects that have components that are applicable to what they are trying to do in Ventura. Typical in Ventura is a very extensive series of public workshops every year on a variety of planning-related topics, of which one or more are likely to be dedicated to issues related to Form-Based Coding.

## Future Goals for the Application of FBCs

The intention is to continue to concentrate on areas in which change is expected as delineated in the city's General Plan, or areas that have a high potential for change, especially in terms of meeting its General Plan goals. The city realizes that it has just begun a very long process of reinforcing the unique qualities of its community, and is in it for the long haul because it knows that FBCs are an important tool in enabling the city to meet its goals.

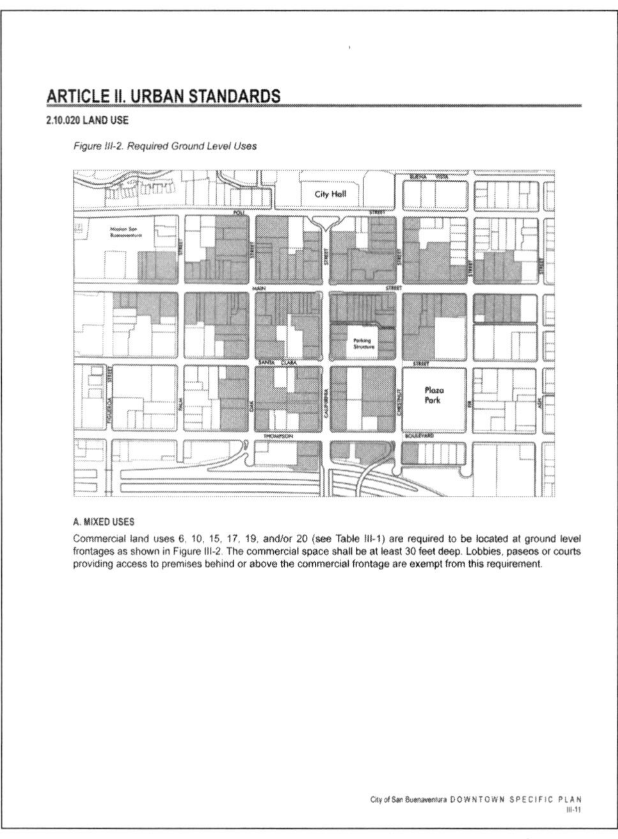

## ARTICLE II. URBAN STANDARDS

2.10.020 LAND USE

*Figure III-2. Required Ground Level Uses*



A. MIXED USES

Commercial land uses 6, 10, 15, 17, 19, and/or 20 (see Table III-1) are required to be located at ground level frontages as shown in Figure III-2. The commercial space shall be at least 30 feet deep. Lobbies, paseos or courts providing access to premises behind or above the commercial frontage are exempt from this requirement.

City of San Buenaventura DOWNTOWN SPECIFIC PLAN III-11

**Fig. 4.91** Required ground-level uses overlay from the DTSP

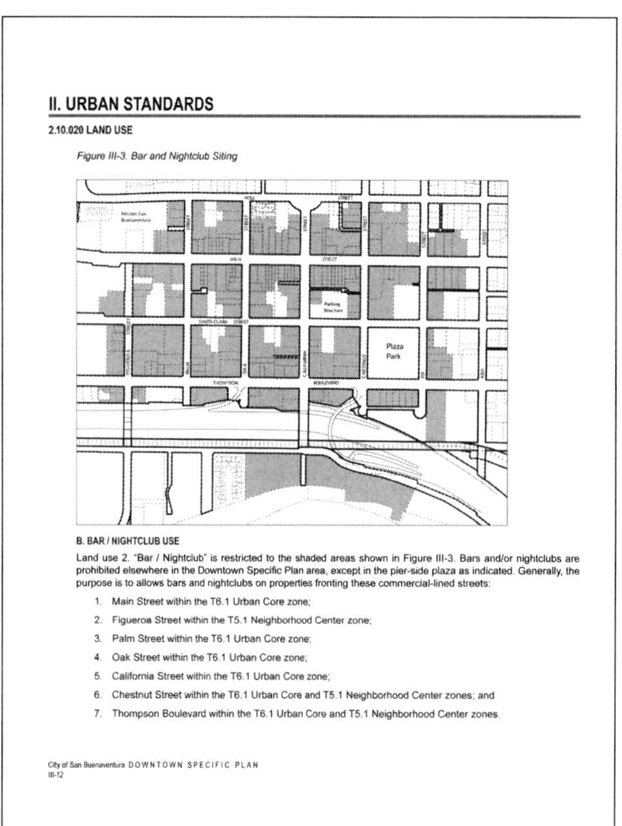

## II. URBAN STANDARDS

2.10.020 LAND USE

*Figure III-3. Bar and Nightclub Siting*



B. BAR / NIGHTCLUB USE

Land use 2, "Bar / Nightclub" is restricted to the shaded areas shown in Figure III-3. Bars and/or nightclubs are prohibited elsewhere in the Downtown Specific Plan area, except in the pier-side plaza as indicated. Generally, the purpose is to allows bars and nightclubs on properties fronting these commercial-lined streets:

1. Main Street within the T6.1 Urban Core zone;
2. Figueroa Street within the T5.1 Neighborhood Center zone;
3. Palm Street within the T6.1 Urban Core zone;
4. Oak Street within the T6.1 Urban Core zone;
5. California Street within the T6.1 Urban Core zone;
6. Chestnut Street within the T6.1 Urban Core and T5.1 Neighborhood Center zones; and
7. Thompson Boulevard within the T6.1 Urban Core and T5.1 Neighborhood Center zones.

City of San Buenaventura DOWNTOWN SPECIFIC PLAN III-12

**Fig. 4.92** Bar and nightclub overlay from the DTSP

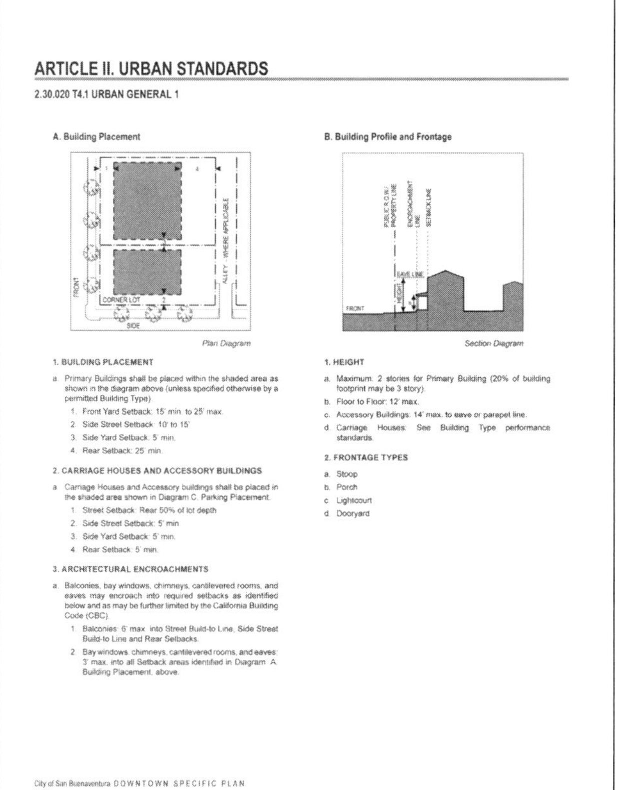

## ARTICLE II. URBAN STANDARDS

2.30.020 T4.1 URBAN GENERAL 1

A. Building Placement



*Plan Diagram*

B. Building Profile and Frontage



*Section Diagram*

1. BUILDING PLACEMENT

a. Primary Buildings shall be placed within the shaded area as shown in the diagram above (unless specified otherwise by a permitted Building Type).
   1. Front Yard Setback: 15' min. to 25' max.
   2. Side Street Setback: 10' to 15'
   3. Side Yard Setback: 5' min.
   4. Rear Setback: 25' min.

2. CARRIAGE HOUSES AND ACCESSORY BUILDINGS

a. Carriage Houses and Accessory buildings shall be placed in the shaded area shown in Diagram C. Parking Placement.
   1. Street Setback: Rear 50% of lot depth
   2. Side Street Setback: 5' min
   3. Side Yard Setback: 5' min.
   4. Rear Setback: 5' min.

3. ARCHITECTURAL ENCROACHMENTS

a. Balconies, bay windows, chimneys, cantilevered rooms, and eaves may encroach into required setbacks as identified below and as may be further limited by the California Building Code (CBC).
   1. Balconies: 6' max. into Street Build-to Line, Side Street Build-to Line and Rear Setbacks.
   2. Bay windows, chimneys, cantilevered rooms, and eaves: 3' max. into all Setback areas identified in Diagram A. Building Placement, above.

1. HEIGHT

a. Maximum: 2 stories for Primary Building (20% of building footprint may be 3 story).
b. Floor to Floor: 12' max.
c. Accessory Buildings: 14' max. to eave or parapet line.
d. Carriage Houses: See Building Type performance standards.

2. FRONTAGE TYPES

a. Stoop
b. Porch
c. Lightcourt
d. Dooryard

City of San Buenaventura DOWNTOWN SPECIFIC PLAN III-14

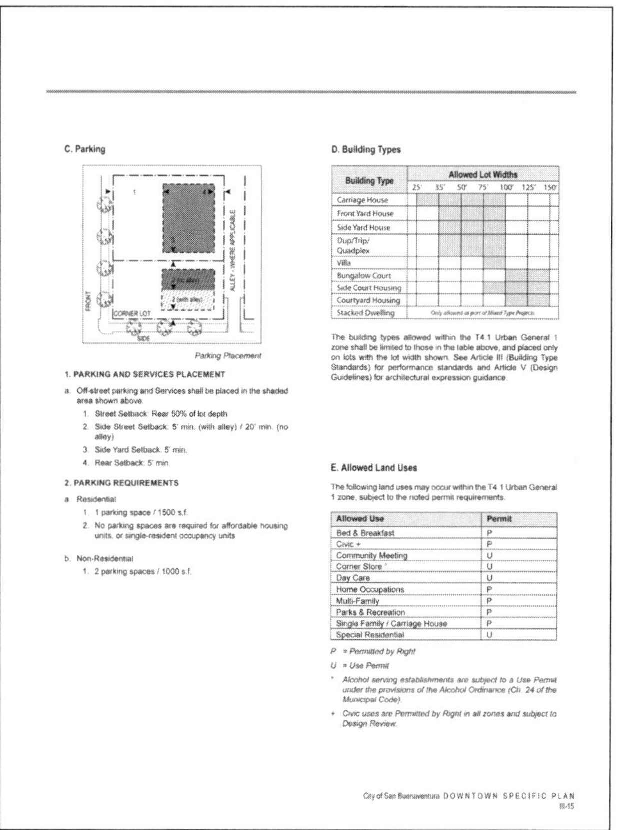

C. Parking



*Parking Placement*

1. PARKING AND SERVICES PLACEMENT

a. Off-street parking and Services shall be placed in the shaded area shown above.
   1. Street Setback: Rear 50% of lot depth
   2. Side Street Setback: 5' min. (with alley) / 20' min. (no alley)
   3. Side Yard Setback: 5' min.
   4. Rear Setback: 5' min.

2. PARKING REQUIREMENTS

a. Residential
   1. 1 parking space / 1500 s.f.
   2. No parking spaces are required for affordable housing units, or single-resident occupancy units

b. Non-Residential
   1. 2 parking spaces / 1000 s.f.

D. Building Types

| Building Type | Allowed Lot Widths | | | | | | |
|---|---|---|---|---|---|---|---|
| | 25' | 35' | 50' | 75' | 100' | 125' | 150' |
| Carriage House | | | | | | | |
| Front Yard House | | | | | | | |
| Side Yard House | | | | | | | |
| Dup/Trip/ Quadplex | | | | | | | |
| Villa | | | | | | | |
| Bungalow Court | | | | | | | |
| Side Court Housing | | | | | | | |
| Courtyard Housing | | | | | | | |
| Stacked Dwelling | Only allowed as part of Mixed Type Projects | | | | | | |

The building types allowed within the T4.1 Urban General 1 zone shall be limited to those in the table above, and placed only on lots with the lot width shown. See Article III (Building Type Standards) for performance standards and Article V (Design Guidelines) for architectural expression guidance.

E. Allowed Land Uses

The following land uses may occur within the T4.1 Urban General 1 zone, subject to the noted permit requirements.

| Allowed Use | Permit |
|---|---|
| Bed & Breakfast | P |
| Civic + | P |
| Community Meeting | U |
| Corner Store * | U |
| Day Care | U |
| Home Occupations | P |
| Multi-Family | P |
| Parks & Recreation | P |
| Single Family / Carriage House | P |
| Special Residential | U |

*P = Permitted by Right*

*U = Use Permit*

* *Alcohol serving establishments are subject to a Use Permit under the provisions of the Alcohol Ordinance (Ch. 24 of the Municipal Code).*

\+ *Civic uses are Permitted by Right in all zones and subject to Design Review.*

City of San Buenaventura DOWNTOWN SPECIFIC PLAN III-15

**Fig. 4.93** (left and right) T4.1 Urban General 1 Building Form Standards from the DTSP

**E. Stoop**

Stoops are elevated entry porches/stairs placed close to the frontage line with the ground story elevated from the sidewalk, securing privacy for the windows and front rooms. This type is suitable for ground-floor residential uses with short setbacks. This type may be interspersed with the shopfront frontage type. A porch or shed roof may also cover the stoop.

1. Configuration. A great variety of stoop designs are possible, but the following guidelines apply:
   a. 2 feet min. deep (clear)
   b. 3 feet min. wide (clear)
   c. Stoops may be at grade or raised to transition into the building. In no case may the ground story be elevated more than 3 feet above the adjacent sidewalk.
   d. Stoops must correspond directly to the building entry(s).
2. Elements
   e. Fences or walls defining the stoop or front setback may not exceed 30" from the highest adjacent finished grade.

*Illustrative Photo: Stoop*

*Axonometric Diagram: Stoop* — *Plan Diagram: Stoop* — *Section Diagram: Stoop*

**F. Porch**

Front yard porches are a common frontage primarily associated with single family houses, but used with other building types depending on the context in all cases, where the facade is set back from the right of way with a front yard. An encroaching porch may also be appended to the facade. A fence or wall at the property line may be used to define the private space of the yard. The front yard may also be raised from the sidewalk, creating a small retaining wall at the property line with entry steps to the yard.

1. Configuration. A great variety of porch designs are possible, but the following guidelines apply:
   a. 6 feet min. deep (clear);
   b. 12 feet min. wide (clear) for centered entry; 10 feet for asymmetrical entry and;
   c. 10 feet tall (clear).
   d. Porches may be at grade or raised to transition into the building. In no case may porches be raised more than 3 feet from the adjacent grade.
2. Elements
   e. Fences or walls defining and/or retaining the front yard may not exceed 4 feet in height from the adjacent sidewalk.

*Illustrative Photo: Frontyard/Porch*

*Axonometric Diagram: Frontyard/Porch* — *Plan Diagram: Frontyard/Porch* — *Section Diagram: Frontyard/Porch*

**Fig. 4.94** Frontages Type Standards from the DTSP

**2.50.020 HILLSIDE OVERLAY**

**A. Building Profile and Frontage**

*Primary Building Height Diagram*

1. HEIGHT

a. Primary Building height, as measured to the eave, shall not project above the following:
   1. T4.1 Urban General 1: 24' max. above any property line abutting a street (A) and the average natural grade (B).
   2. T6.1 Urban Core: 24' max. above Poli Street (A) and 36' max. above average natural grade (B).

b. Survey.
   1. Unless waived by the Director because plans adequately demonstrate no private or public views would be significantly obstructed, applications for new development shall include a survey accomplished by an architect, surveyor, or civil engineer licensed or registered to practice in the State of California to define the average natural grade.

2. FRONTAGE TYPES

Per underlying zone

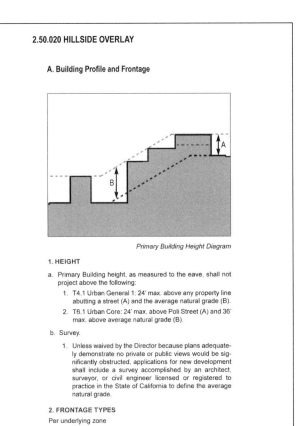

**Fig. 4.95** Hillside overlay from the DTSP

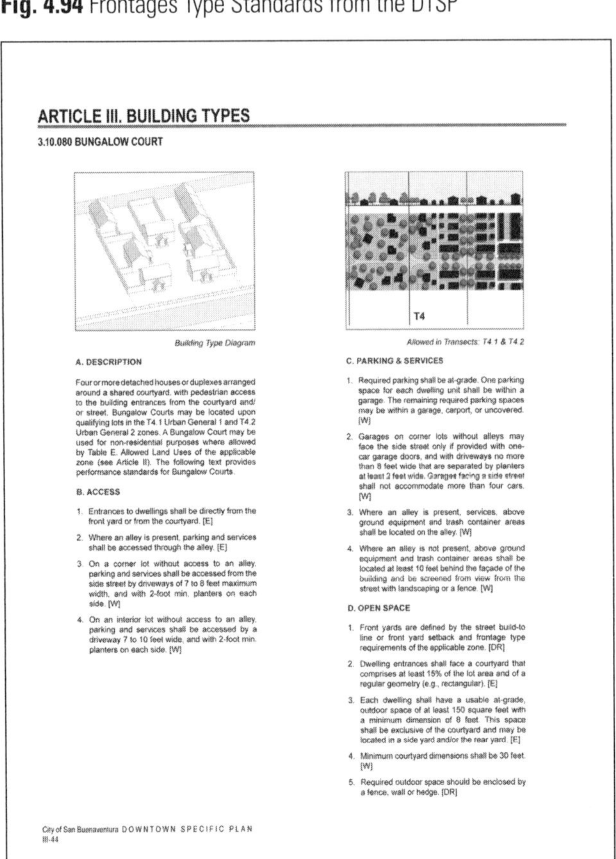

ARTICLE III. BUILDING TYPES

3.10.080 BUNGALOW COURT

*Building Type Diagram*

A. DESCRIPTION

Four or more detached houses or duplexes arranged around a shared courtyard, with pedestrian access to the building entrances from the courtyard and/or street. Bungalow Courts may be located upon qualifying lots in the T4.1 Urban General 1 and T4.2 Urban General 2 zones. A Bungalow Court may be used for non-residential purposes where allowed by Table E. Allowed Land Uses of the applicable zone (see Article II). The following text provides performance standards for Bungalow Courts.

B. ACCESS

1. Entrances to dwellings shall be directly from the front yard or from the courtyard. [E]
2. Where an alley is present, parking and services shall be accessed through the alley. [E]
3. On a corner lot without access to an alley, parking and services shall be accessed from the side street by driveways of 7 to 8 feet maximum width, and with 2-foot min. planters on each side. [W]
4. On an interior lot without access to an alley, parking and services shall be accessed by a driveway 7 to 10 feet wide, and with 2-foot min. planters on each side. [W]

T4

*Allowed in Transects: T4.1 & T4.2*

C. PARKING & SERVICES

1. Required parking shall be at-grade. One parking space for each dwelling unit shall be within a garage. The remaining required parking spaces may be within a garage, carport, or uncovered. [W]
2. Garages on corner lots without alleys may face the side street only if provided with one-car garage doors, and with driveways no more than 8 feet wide that are separated by planters at least 2 feet wide. Garages facing a side street shall not accommodate more than four cars. [W]
3. Where an alley is present, services, above ground equipment and trash container areas shall be located on the alley. [W]
4. Where an alley is not present, above ground equipment and trash container areas shall be located at least 10 feet behind the façade of the building and be screened from view from the street with landscaping or a fence. [W]

D. OPEN SPACE

1. Front yards are defined by the street build-to line or front yard setback and frontage type requirements of the applicable zone. [DR]
2. Dwelling entrances shall face a courtyard that comprises at least 15% of the lot area and of a regular geometry (e.g., rectangular). [E]
3. Each dwelling shall have a usable at-grade, outdoor space of at least 150 square feet with a minimum dimension of 8 feet. This space shall be exclusive of the courtyard and may be located in a side yard and/or the rear yard. [E]
4. Minimum courtyard dimensions shall be 30 feet. [W]
5. Required outdoor space should be enclosed by a fence, wall or hedge. [DR]

City of San Buenaventura DOWNTOWN SPECIFIC PLAN
III-44

*Illustrative Photo*

E. LANDSCAPE

1. Landscape should not be used to separate a front yard from front yards on adjacent parcels. Front yard trees should be of porch scale (no more that 1.5 times the height of the porch at maturity) except at the margins of the lot, where they may be of house scale (no more that 1.5 times the height of the house at maturity). [DR]
2. Trees may be placed in side yards to protect the privacy of neighbors. [DR]
3. At least one large tree should be provided in each rear yard for shade and privacy. [DR]

F. FRONTAGE

1. Buildings should be designed so that living areas (e.g., living room, family room, dining room, etc.), rather than sleeping and service rooms, are oriented toward street build-to lines and the courtyard. [DR]

*Illustrative Photo*

G. BUILDING SIZE AND MASSING

1. Buildings should be composed of one and/or two story volumes and massed as houses. [DR]
2. Building elevations abutting side yards should be designed to provide at least one horizontal plane break of at least three feet, and one vertical break. Architectural elements such as bay windows, projecting rooms or covered balconies may be provided in lieu of one plane break. [DR]
3. Buildings on corner lots should be designed with two facades of equal architectural expression. [DR]
4. Dwellings within a duplex may be flats and/or townhouses. [DR]
5. Attic space may be occupied and not count as a story when applying the height limits of the applicable zone. [DR]

Deviations from a standard of guideline require the following Variance (pg. III-120):
[DR] = Design Review [W] = Warrant [E] = Exception

City of San Buenaventura DOWNTOWN SPECIFIC PLAN
III-45

**Fig. 4.96** (left and right) Bungalow Court Building Type Standards from the DTSP

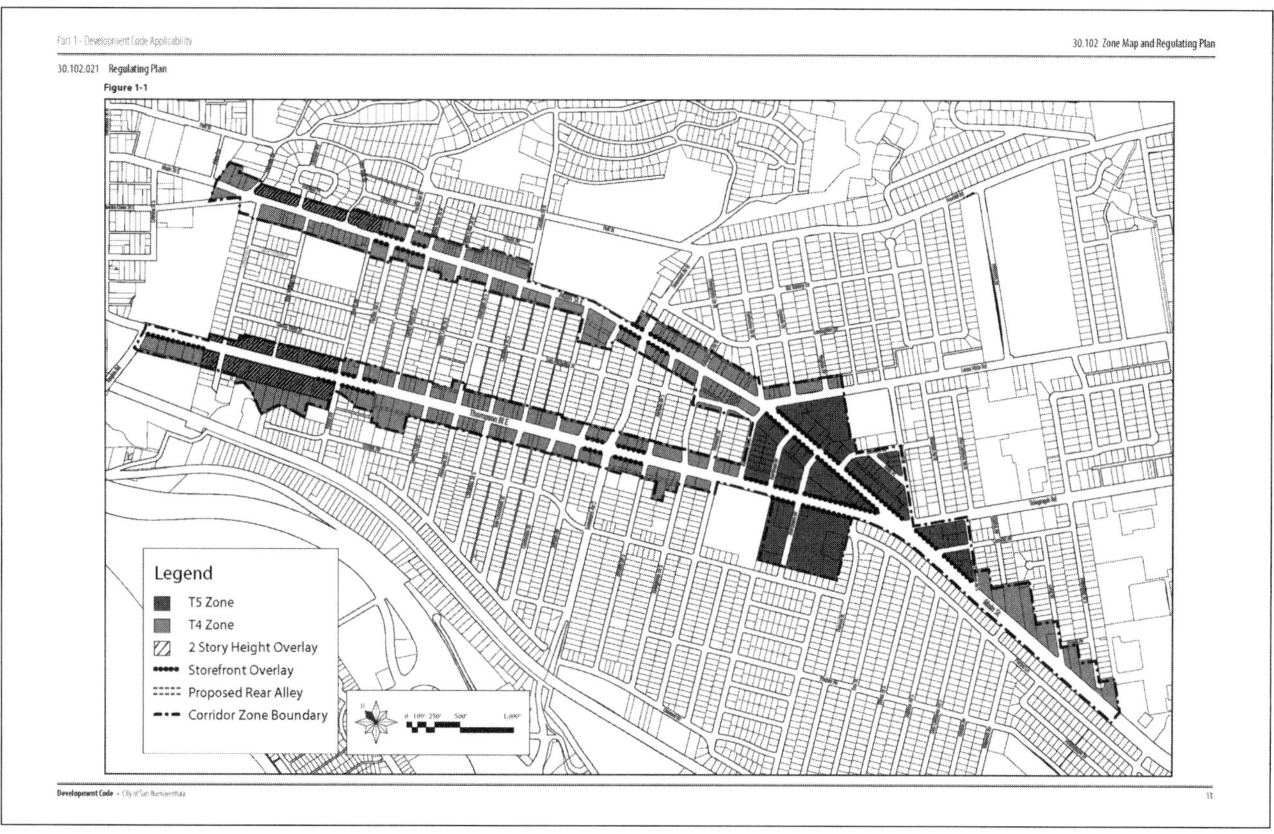


**Fig. 4.97** The Regulating Plan from the Main and Thompson FBC

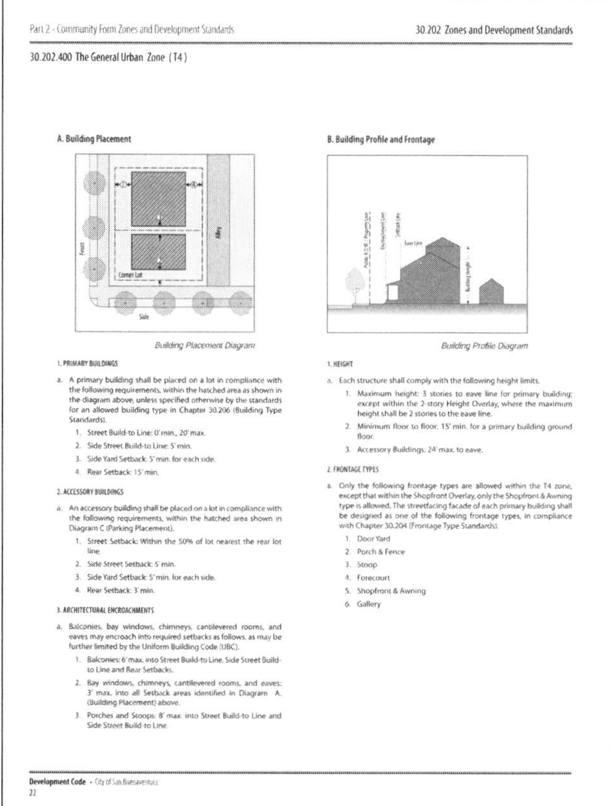

Part 2 - Community Form Zones and Development Standards

30.202 Zones and Development Standards

30.202.400 The General Urban Zone (T4)

A. Building Placement

*Building Placement Diagram*

1. PRIMARY BUILDINGS

a. A primary building shall be placed on a lot in compliance with the following requirements, within the hatched area as shown in the diagram above, unless specified otherwise by the standards for an allowed building type in Chapter 30.206 (Building Type Standards).
   1. Street Build-to Line: 0' min., 20' max.
   2. Side Street Build-to Line: 5' min.
   3. Side Yard Setback: 5' min. for each side.
   4. Rear Setback: 15' min.

2. ACCESSORY BUILDINGS

a. An accessory building shall be placed on a lot in compliance with the following requirements, within the hatched area shown in Diagram C (Parking Placement).
   1. Street Setback: Within the 50% of lot nearest the rear lot line.
   2. Side Street Setback: 5' min.
   3. Side Yard Setback: 5' min. for each side.
   4. Rear Setback: 3' min.

3. ARCHITECTURAL ENCROACHMENTS

a. Balconies, bay windows, chimneys, cantilevered rooms, and eaves may encroach into required setbacks as follows, as may be further limited by the Uniform Building Code (UBC).
   1. Balconies: 6' max. into Street Build-to Line, Side Street Build-to Line and Rear Setbacks.
   2. Bay windows, chimneys, cantilevered rooms, and eaves: 3' max. into all Setback areas identified in Diagram A. (Building Placement) above.
   3. Porches and Stoops: 8' max. into Street Build-to Line and Side Street Build-to Line.

B. Building Profile and Frontage

*Building Profile Diagram*

1. HEIGHT

a. Each structure shall comply with the following height limits.
   1. Maximum height: 3 stories to eave line for primary building; except within the 2-story Height Overlay, where the maximum height shall be 2 stories to the eave line.
   2. Minimum floor to floor: 15' min. for a primary building ground floor.
   3. Accessory Buildings: 24' max. to eave.

2. FRONTAGE TYPES

a. Only the following frontage types are allowed within the T4 zone, except that within the Shopfront Overlay, only the Shopfront & Awning type is allowed. The streetfacing facade of each primary building shall be designed as one of the following frontage types, in compliance with Chapter 30.204 (Frontage Type Standards).
   1. Door Yard
   2. Porch & Fence
   3. Stoop
   4. Forecourt
   5. Shopfront & Awning
   6. Gallery

Development Code • City of San Buenaventura
22

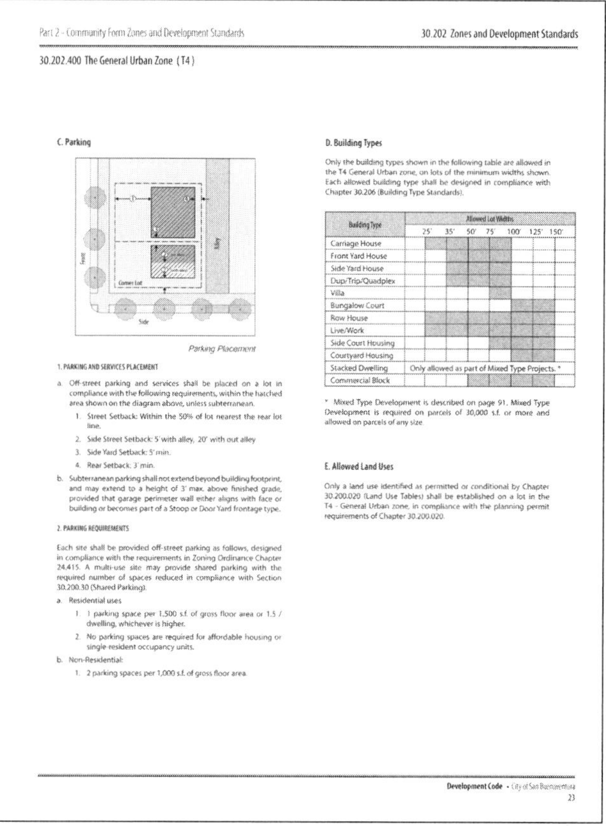

Part 2 - Community Form Zones and Development Standards

30.202 Zones and Development Standards

30.202.400 The General Urban Zone (T4)

C. Parking

*Parking Placement*

1. PARKING AND SERVICES PLACEMENT

a. Off-street parking and services shall be placed on a lot in compliance with the following requirements, within the hatched area shown on the diagram above, unless subterranean.
   1. Street Setback: Within the 50% of lot nearest the rear lot line.
   2. Side Street Setback: 5' with alley, 20' with out alley
   3. Side Yard Setback: 5' min.
   4. Rear Setback: 3' min.

b. Subterranean parking shall not extend beyond building footprint, and may extend to a height of 3' max. above finished grade, provided that garage perimeter wall either aligns with face or building or becomes part of a Stoop or Door Yard frontage type.

2. PARKING REQUIREMENTS

Each site shall be provided off-street parking as follows, designed in compliance with the requirements in Zoning Ordinance Chapter 24.415. A multi-use site may provide shared parking with the required number of spaces reduced in compliance with Section 30.200.30 (Shared Parking).

a. Residential uses
   1. 1 parking space per 1,500 s.f. of gross floor area or 1.5 / dwelling, whichever is higher.
   2. No parking spaces are required for affordable housing or single-resident occupancy units.

b. Non-Residential:
   1. 2 parking spaces per 1,000 s.f. of gross floor area.

D. Building Types

Only the building types shown in the following table are allowed in the T4 General Urban zone, on lots of the minimum widths shown. Each allowed building type shall be designed in compliance with Chapter 30.206 (Building Type Standards).

| Building Type | Allowed Lot Widths | | | | | | | |
|---|---|---|---|---|---|---|---|---|
| | | 25' | 35' | 50' | 75' | 100' | 125' | 150' |
| Carriage House | | | | | | | | |
| Front Yard House | | | | | | | | |
| Side Yard House | | | | | | | | |
| Dup/Trip/Quadplex | | | | | | | | |
| Villa | | | | | | | | |
| Bungalow Court | | | | | | | | |
| Row House | | | | | | | | |
| Live/Work | | | | | | | | |
| Side Court Housing | | | | | | | | |
| Courtyard Housing | | | | | | | | |
| Stacked Dwelling | Only allowed as part of Mixed Type Projects. * | | | | | | | |
| Commercial Block | | | | | | | | |

* Mixed Type Development is described on page 91. Mixed Type Development is required on parcels of 30,000 s.f. or more and allowed on parcels of any size.

E. Allowed Land Uses

Only a land use identified as permitted or conditional by Chapter 30.200.020 (Land Use Tables) shall be established on a lot in the T4 - General Urban zone, in compliance with the planning permit requirements of Chapter 30.200.020.

Development Code • City of San Buenaventura
23

**Fig. 4.98** (left and right) T4 General Urban Building Form Standards from the Main and Thompson FBC

## 30.208.030 Main Street A - Existing

### Existing Condition:

From approximately Lincoln Drive to N. Catalina St., Main Street is defined by one and two-story buildings which are primarily of a residential character. Many of these buildings were constructed in the early 1920's and reflect a distinct and historically significant architectural period. This segment of Main Street represents the edge of the surrounding neighborhoods and has therefore been identified as a T4 Zone. The northern streetscape is defined by stoops and dooryards towards the west and shopfronts toward the east. The southern streetscape is defined almost entirely by shopfronts. It is an urban thoroughfare with two travel lanes, a turning lane, a bike lane and parallel parking each side. The pedestrian experience is fairly austere as no landscape elements exist, only archaic serpent -head street lights and power poles.

| | Existing Main Street A |
|---|---|
| Thoroughfare Type | Street |
| Transect Zone Assignment | T4 |
| Right-of-Way Width | 80' |
| Pavement Width | 64' |
| Movement | Free Movement |
| Design Speed | 35 MPH |
| Pedestrian Crossing Time | 8 - 11 seconds |
| Traffic Lanes | 3 lanes |
| Parking Lanes | Both sides @ 9' |
| Curb Radius | 10' |
| Public Frontage Type | -- |
| Walkway Type | Sidewalk, 8' min. |
| Planter Type | None |
| Curb Type | Curb |
| Landscape Type | None |
| Transportation Provision | None |

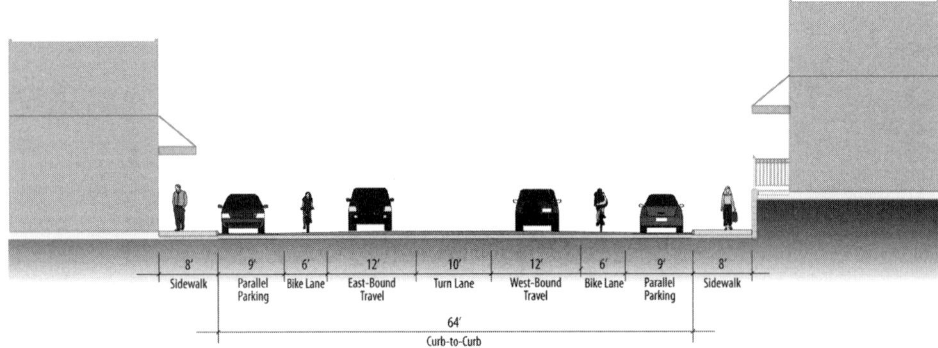




**Fig. 4.99** Existing (left) and proposed (right) Main Street sections from the Main and Thompson FBC

## 30.208.031 Main Street A - Proposed

### Proposed Approach:

The proposed alterations are focused on maintaining the existing street's residential character and increasing the quality of the pedestrian experience. Main Street is almost exclusively a commercial street with a few mixed-use buildings. Future development on Main Street should maintain the established streetscape and land use pattern. Buildings should not exceed 2 stories in height and, where appropriate, be provided with awnings that strengthen a sense of enclosure for shoppers and strollers. The pedestrian experience should be enhanced with sidewalks that have street trees in wells and pedestrian-scale lighting. The existing on-street parallel parking helps to support the businesses along both sides of Main Street.

Recommended Adjustments:

- Decrease the bike lane to 5', each side.
- Decrease the parking lane to 8', each side.
- Increase the sidewalk to 7', each side.
- Add 5' tree wells @ 30' o.c., each side.
- Relocate power poles underground.
- Replace serpent-head street lights with single-head column street lights.

| | Proposed Main Street A |
|---|---|
| Thoroughfare Type | Street |
| Transect Zone Assignment | T4 |
| Right-of-Way Width | 80' |
| Pavement Width | 56' |
| Movement | Free Movement |
| Design Speed | 35 MPH |
| Pedestrian Crossing Time | 8 - 11 seconds |
| Traffic Lanes | 3 lanes |
| Parking Lanes | Both sides @ 8' |
| Curb Radius | 10' |
| Public Frontage Type | -- |
| Walkway Type | Sidewalk, 12' min. |
| Planter Type | Tree wells, 5' |
| Curb Type | Curb |
| Landscape Type | Trees at 30' o.c. Avg. |
| Transportation Provision | None |

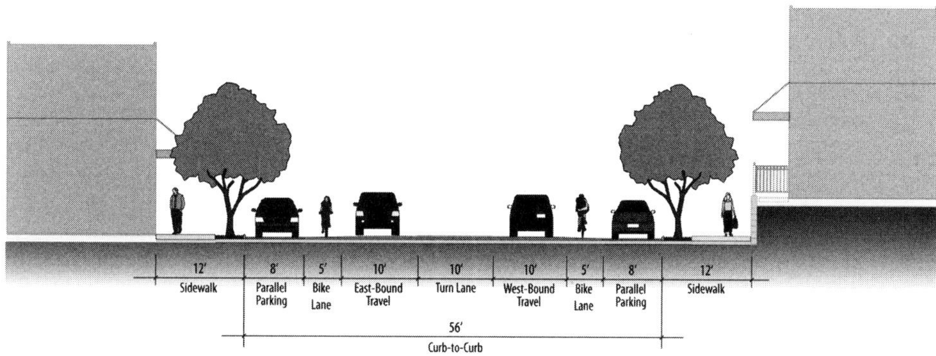

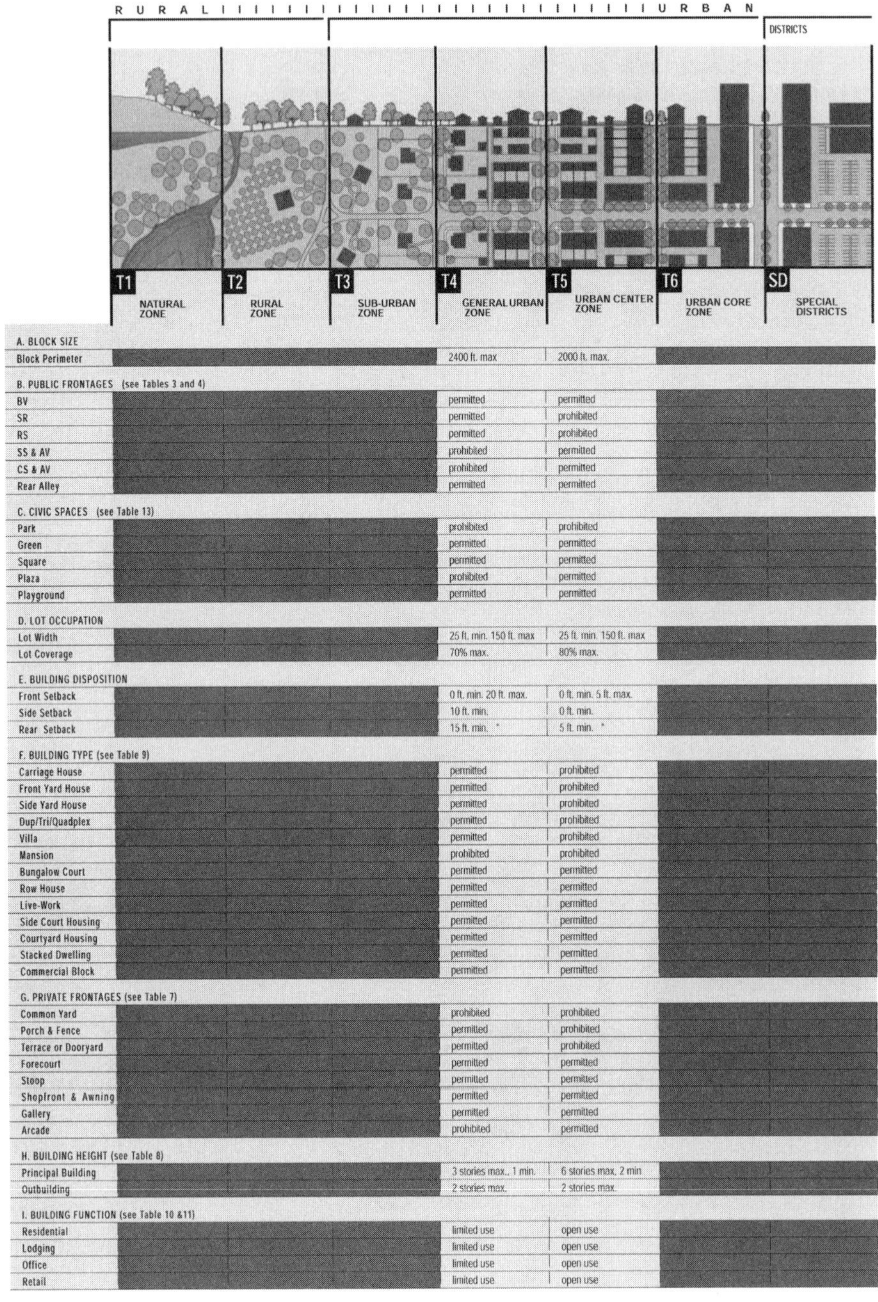



30.1000 Transect Zones Summary Table

**TABLE H: Transect Zones Summary.**



| | T1 NATURAL ZONE | T2 RURAL ZONE | T3 SUB-URBAN ZONE | T4 GENERAL URBAN ZONE | T5 URBAN CENTER ZONE | T6 URBAN CORE ZONE | SD SPECIAL DISTRICTS |
|---|---|---|---|---|---|---|---|
| **A. BLOCK SIZE** | | | | | | | |
| Block Perimeter | | | | 2400 ft. max | 2000 ft. max. | | |
| **B. PUBLIC FRONTAGES (see Tables 3 and 4)** | | | | | | | |
| BV | | | | permitted | permitted | | |
| SR | | | | permitted | prohibited | | |
| RS | | | | permitted | prohibited | | |
| SS & AV | | | | prohibited | permitted | | |
| CS & AV | | | | prohibited | permitted | | |
| Rear Alley | | | | permitted | permitted | | |
| **C. CIVIC SPACES (see Table 13)** | | | | | | | |
| Park | | | | prohibited | prohibited | | |
| Green | | | | permitted | permitted | | |
| Square | | | | permitted | permitted | | |
| Plaza | | | | prohibited | permitted | | |
| Playground | | | | permitted | permitted | | |
| **D. LOT OCCUPATION** | | | | | | | |
| Lot Width | | | | 25 ft. min. 150 ft. max | 25 ft. min. 150 ft. max | | |
| Lot Coverage | | | | 70% max. | 80% max. | | |
| **E. BUILDING DISPOSITION** | | | | | | | |
| Front Setback | | | | 0 ft. min. 20 ft. max. | 0 ft. min. 5 ft. max. | | |
| Side Setback | | | | 10 ft. min. | 0 ft. min. | | |
| Rear Setback | | | | 15 ft. min. * | 5 ft. min. * | | |
| **F. BUILDING TYPE (see Table 9)** | | | | | | | |
| Carriage House | | | | permitted | prohibited | | |
| Front Yard House | | | | permitted | prohibited | | |
| Side Yard House | | | | permitted | prohibited | | |
| Dup/Tri/Quadplex | | | | permitted | prohibited | | |
| Villa | | | | permitted | prohibited | | |
| Mansion | | | | prohibited | prohibited | | |
| Bungalow Court | | | | permitted | permitted | | |
| Row House | | | | permitted | permitted | | |
| Live-Work | | | | permitted | permitted | | |
| Side Court Housing | | | | permitted | permitted | | |
| Courtyard Housing | | | | permitted | permitted | | |
| Stacked Dwelling | | | | permitted | permitted | | |
| Commercial Block | | | | permitted | permitted | | |
| **G. PRIVATE FRONTAGES (see Table 7)** | | | | | | | |
| Common Yard | | | | prohibited | prohibited | | |
| Porch & Fence | | | | permitted | prohibited | | |
| Terrace or Dooryard | | | | permitted | prohibited | | |
| Forecourt | | | | permitted | permitted | | |
| Stoop | | | | permitted | permitted | | |
| Shopfront & Awning | | | | permitted | permitted | | |
| Gallery | | | | permitted | permitted | | |
| Arcade | | | | prohibited | permitted | | |
| **H. BUILDING HEIGHT (see Table 8)** | | | | | | | |
| Principal Building | | | | 3 stories max., 1 min. | 6 stories max. 2 min | | |
| Outbuilding | | | | 2 stories max. | 2 stories max. | | |
| **I. BUILDING FUNCTION (see Table 10 &11)** | | | | | | | |
| Residential | | | | limited use | open use | | |
| Lodging | | | | limited use | open use | | |
| Office | | | | limited use | open use | | |
| Retail | | | | limited use | open use | | |



Fig. 4.100 Transect zone summary table from the Main and Thompson FBC

# Montgomery, Alabama



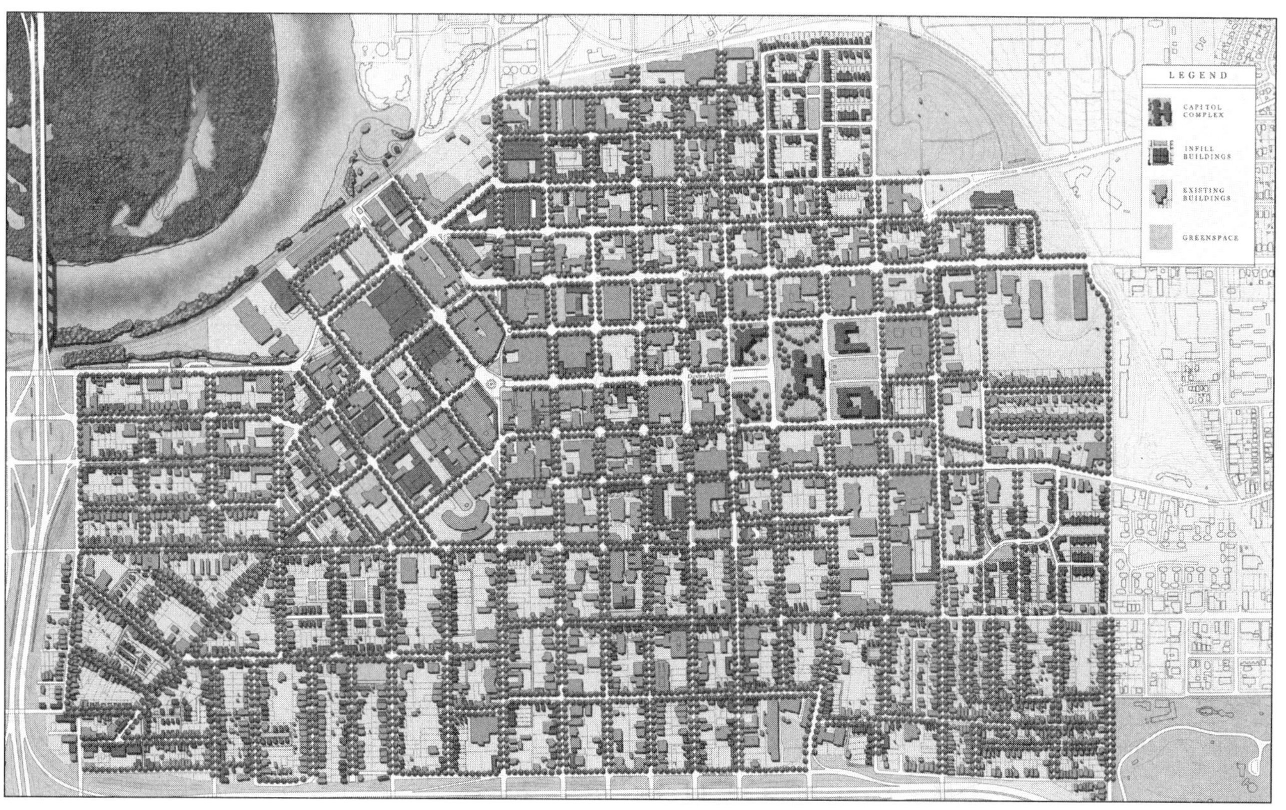

## The City's Approach to FBCs

MONTGOMERY IS LOCATED in central Alabama and has a population of approximately 200,000 in the city and a metropolitan area population of almost 470,000 people.[10] According to Chad Emerson, the author of *The SmartCode Solution to Sprawl*, Montgomery had some of the best urban form in the United States that fell victim to Euclidean zoning practices. If you look closely at photos of historic downtown Montgomery and images of what currently exists, you would easily agree. However, first through the adoption of an optional SmartCode to allow and encourage New Urbanist development on greenfield sites, and subsequently through the adoption of a mandatory SmartCode for downtown Montgomery, the city is now on its way to reestablishing this high-quality urban environment and establishing more sustainable development patterns.

## The First Code: An Optional Citywide SmartCode

Several years before the first SmartCode was adopted, Ken Groves, the planning director, began efforts to educate the community members and elected and appointed officials about Smart Growth. While the general public became interested, the city council and Planning Commission were anything but enthusiastic. A great opportunity dropped into the planning department's lap when a prominent local builder, who was historically anti-zoning, approached the city about doing a Traditional Neighborhood Development (TND) on a greenfield site within the city. His approvals would depend on the adoption of the SmartCode. These changes in the political environment ultimately led to the support of the mayor for the SmartCode, and after a dinner with Andrés Duany, many other key decision makers seemed to be on board. Because of the general reluctance toward regulatory change, the city took the approach of an unmapped and optional SmartCode that would, at the very least, promote and permit vertical mixed-use projects within the entire city and allow TNDs.

This proved successful when, in fall 2005, the Planning Commission unanimously approved the SmartCode floating zone, and the city council did the same in front of a packed council chambers in January 2006. Since the adoption, there have been at least four developers using the SmartCode to implement New Urbanist projects on greenfield sites in the city.

This initial, parallel SmartCode was calibrated by Chad Emerson and was adopted as an overlay zone. There were only minor modifications

**Fig. 4.101** (previous page) The Illustrative Plan for downtown Montgomery

**Fig. 4.102** (below) Transect diagram from the Montgomery SmartCode

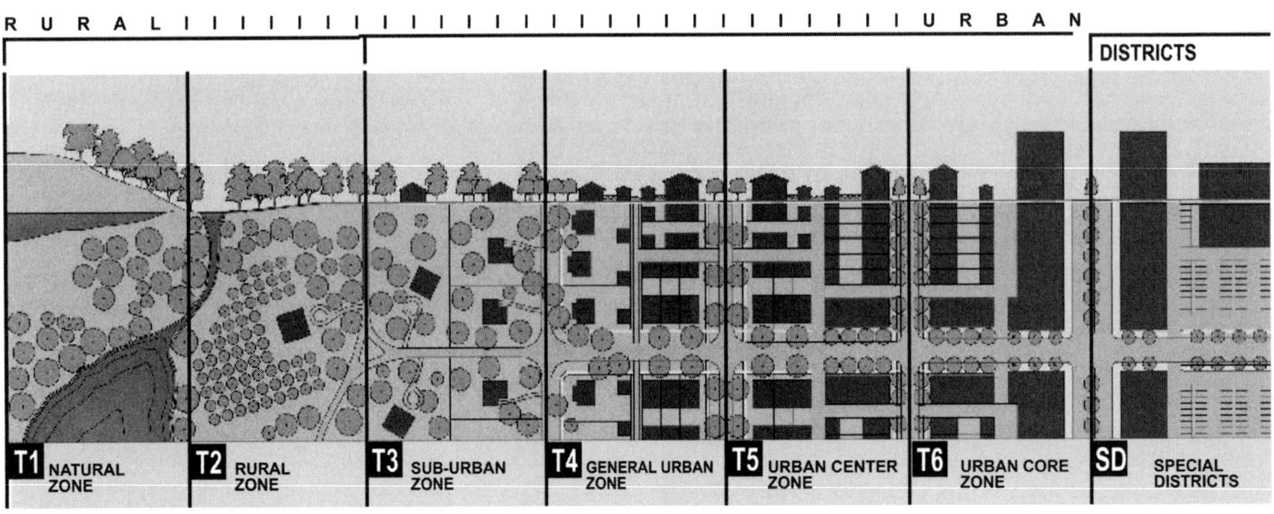

**Fig. 4.103** (above) Image of a revitalized Bell Street

to the SmartCode template as adopted. The first TND submitted under the SmartCode was a project called Hampstead, a 415-acre project planned by DPZ and submitted in July 2006. Subsequently, several other greenfield projects, including Chanticleer, whose SmartCode regulations were done by 180° Design Studio in Kansas City, have been submitted and approved.

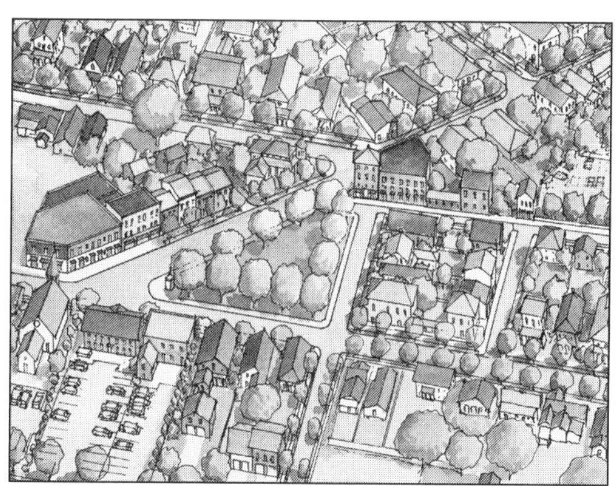

**Fig. 4.104** (left) Rendering of a new neighborhood center

## Expanding the Application of FBCs to the City

These efforts to get the optional SmartCode adopted and supported politically, and then working toward a mandatory mapped version of the SmartCode, are proving to be a good approach. In April 2006, Montgomery announced that it had hired Dover, Kohl & Partners to develop a downtown Master Plan and a mandatory SmartCode to implement it. The master planning process and downtown SmartCode were so successful that the SmartCode, with adjustments to support the Master Plan for downtown, became mandatory in the downtown when it was unanimously adopted by the city council on May 1, 2007. To illustrate the impact of the SmartCode over an extremely short time,

**Fig. 4.105** Photographic illustration of a redesigned public plaza

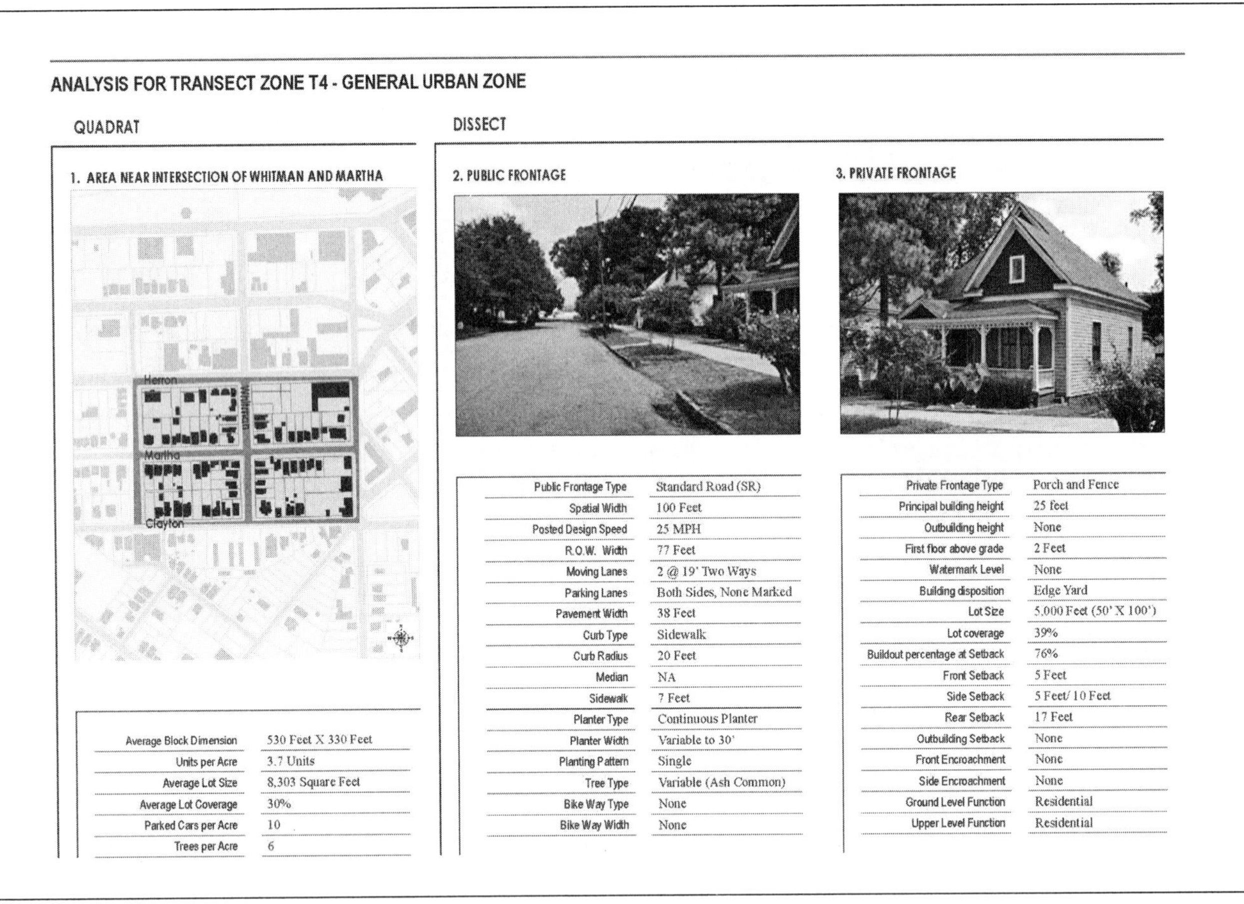

ANALYSIS FOR TRANSECT ZONE T4 - GENERAL URBAN ZONE

QUADRAT

1. AREA NEAR INTERSECTION OF WHITMAN AND MARTHA



| | |
|---|---|
| Average Block Dimension | 530 Feet X 330 Feet |
| Units per Acre | 3.7 Units |
| Average Lot Size | 8,303 Square Feet |
| Average Lot Coverage | 30% |
| Parked Cars per Acre | 10 |
| Trees per Acre | 6 |

DISSECT

2. PUBLIC FRONTAGE

| | |
|---|---|
| Public Frontage Type | Standard Road (SR) |
| Spatial Width | 100 Feet |
| Posted Design Speed | 25 MPH |
| R.O.W. Width | 77 Feet |
| Moving Lanes | 2 @ 19' Two Ways |
| Parking Lanes | Both Sides, None Marked |
| Pavement Width | 38 Feet |
| Curb Type | Sidewalk |
| Curb Radius | 20 Feet |
| Median | NA |
| Sidewalk | 7 Feet |
| Planter Type | Continuous Planter |
| Planter Width | Variable to 30' |
| Planting Pattern | Single |
| Tree Type | Variable (Ash Common) |
| Bike Way Type | None |
| Bike Way Width | None |

3. PRIVATE FRONTAGE

| | |
|---|---|
| Private Frontage Type | Porch and Fence |
| Principal building height | 25 feet |
| Outbuilding height | None |
| First floor above grade | 2 Feet |
| Watermark Level | None |
| Building disposition | Edge Yard |
| Lot Size | 5,000 Feet (50' X 100') |
| Lot coverage | 39% |
| Buildout percentage at Setback | 76% |
| Front Setback | 5 Feet |
| Side Setback | 5 Feet/ 10 Feet |
| Rear Setback | 17 Feet |
| Outbuilding Setback | None |
| Front Encroachment | None |
| Side Encroachment | None |
| Ground Level Function | Residential |
| Upper Level Function | Residential |

**Fig. 4.106** (left and right) Results from the synoptic survey of downtown assisted in the local calibration of the transect zones for the Downtown Montgomery Plan SmartCode

in May 2007, Groves stated, "Since the adoption of the SmartCode, every major development submitted to the city has used the SmartCode in lieu of conventional zoning."

The mandatory downtown SmartCode uses the original optional SmartCode framework and simply makes amendments as necessary to implement the detailed Master Plan completed by Dover, Kohl & Partners. The primary amendments to the code were as follows:

1. A T4 Open Subzone was added to regulate an appropriate transition between the T4 and T5 zones, allowing a great flexibility in use and a transition of physical form.
2. The required size of civic spaces was reduced to encourage the creation of more civic spaces in the downtown.
3. The minimum acreage of a TND was reduced from 80 acres to 40 acres, thus making it more applicable to sites within the downtown.
4. Section 3.1.7, dealing with transect succession, was eliminated.
5. The synoptic surveys were added to the appendix to provide a rationale for coding decisions.
6. Minor adjustments were made in the land-use table.

The supporting graphics for this master plan and SmartCode make an extremely compelling argument for the SmartCode. Look at Figure C.14 in the color section of this book, which represents the likely build-out according to the existing zoning and proposed SmartCode, to see the dramatic difference that having a master

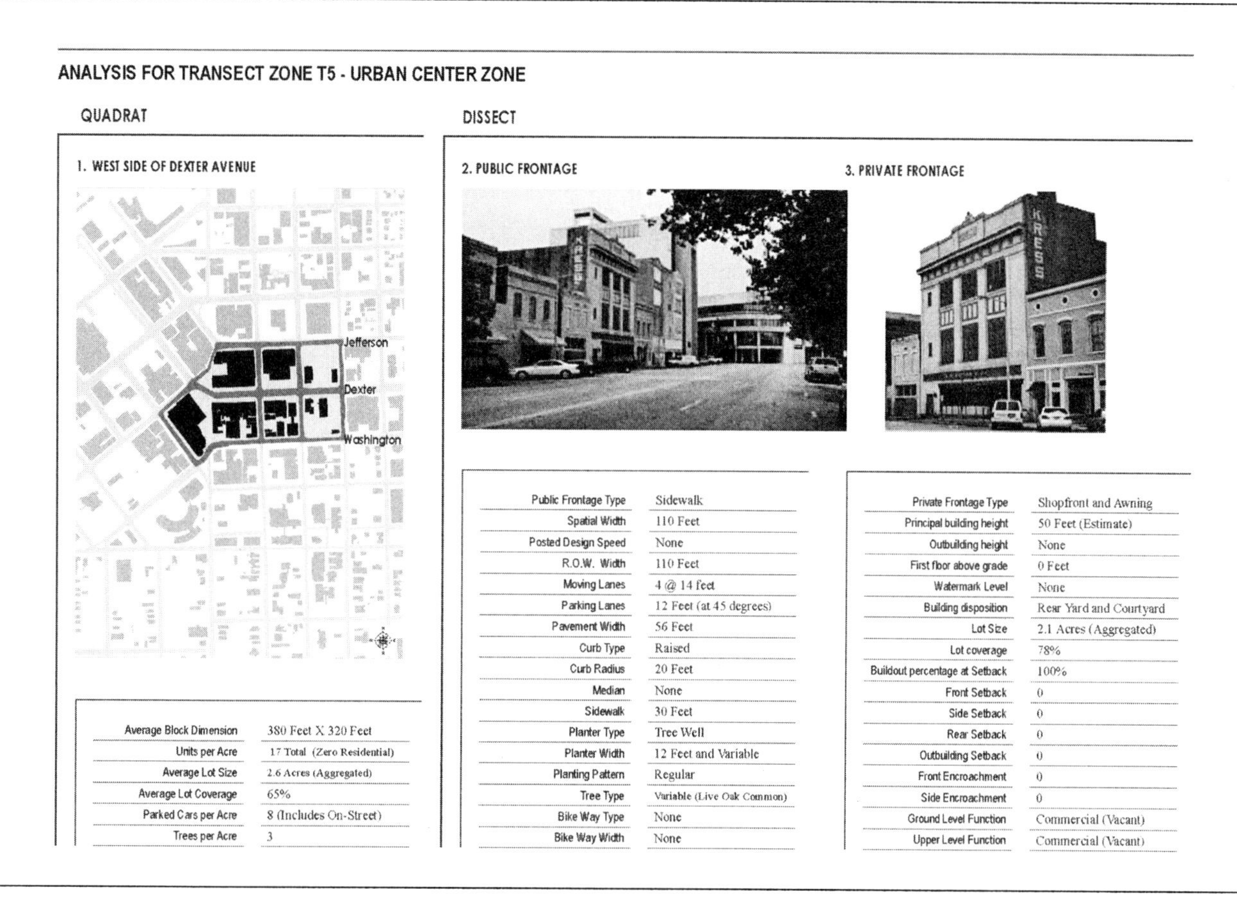


| | |
|---|---|
| Average Block Dimension | 380 Feet X 320 Feet |
| Units per Acre | 17 Total (Zero Residential) |
| Average Lot Size | 2.6 Acres (Aggregated) |
| Average Lot Coverage | 65% |
| Parked Cars per Acre | 8 (Includes On-Street) |
| Trees per Acre | 3 |

| | |
|---|---|
| Public Frontage Type | Sidewalk |
| Spatial Width | 110 Feet |
| Posted Design Speed | None |
| R.O.W. Width | 110 Feet |
| Moving Lanes | 4 @ 14 feet |
| Parking Lanes | 12 Feet (at 45 degrees) |
| Pavement Width | 56 Feet |
| Curb Type | Raised |
| Curb Radius | 20 Feet |
| Median | None |
| Sidewalk | 30 Feet |
| Planter Type | Tree Well |
| Planter Width | 12 Feet and Variable |
| Planting Pattern | Regular |
| Tree Type | Variable (Live Oak Common) |
| Bike Way Type | None |
| Bike Way Width | None |

| | |
|---|---|
| Private Frontage Type | Shopfront and Awning |
| Principal building height | 50 Feet (Estimate) |
| Outbuilding height | None |
| First floor above grade | 0 Feet |
| Watermark Level | None |
| Building disposition | Rear Yard and Courtyard |
| Lot Size | 2.1 Acres (Aggregated) |
| Lot coverage | 78% |
| Buildout percentage at Setback | 100% |
| Front Setback | 0 |
| Side Setback | 0 |
| Rear Setback | 0 |
| Outbuilding Setback | 0 |
| Front Encroachment | 0 |
| Side Encroachment | 0 |
| Ground Level Function | Commercial (Vacant) |
| Upper Level Function | Commercial (Vacant) |

plan and Form-Based Code in place will likely have on the downtown in the long term.

## Code Administration

The city staff will administer the SmartCode. The city staff was integrally involved in the charrette process to ensure that staffers understood the rationale behind what was being regulated in the code. It is also likely that the staff will continue to attend SmartCode workshops as needed for continued education about the SmartCode as a regulatory tool.

## Future Goals for the Application of FBCs

The city of Montgomery does have plans for further application of the SmartCode. The local AIA chapter has sponsored planning charrettes for three older neighborhoods (1930s to 1940s era) that still have a functional social or commercial center with traditional residential areas surrounding them. The geographic area studied in each of these efforts was limited to the commercial center itself in which plans were prepared anticipating application of our SmartCode. The city will be expanding the areas studied in each case to see if the minimum acreage required for an infill TND (40 acres) can be planned for application of the SmartCode. Synoptic analysis of the area surrounding the three centers is scheduled to be conducted to see whether application of the SmartCode makes sense.

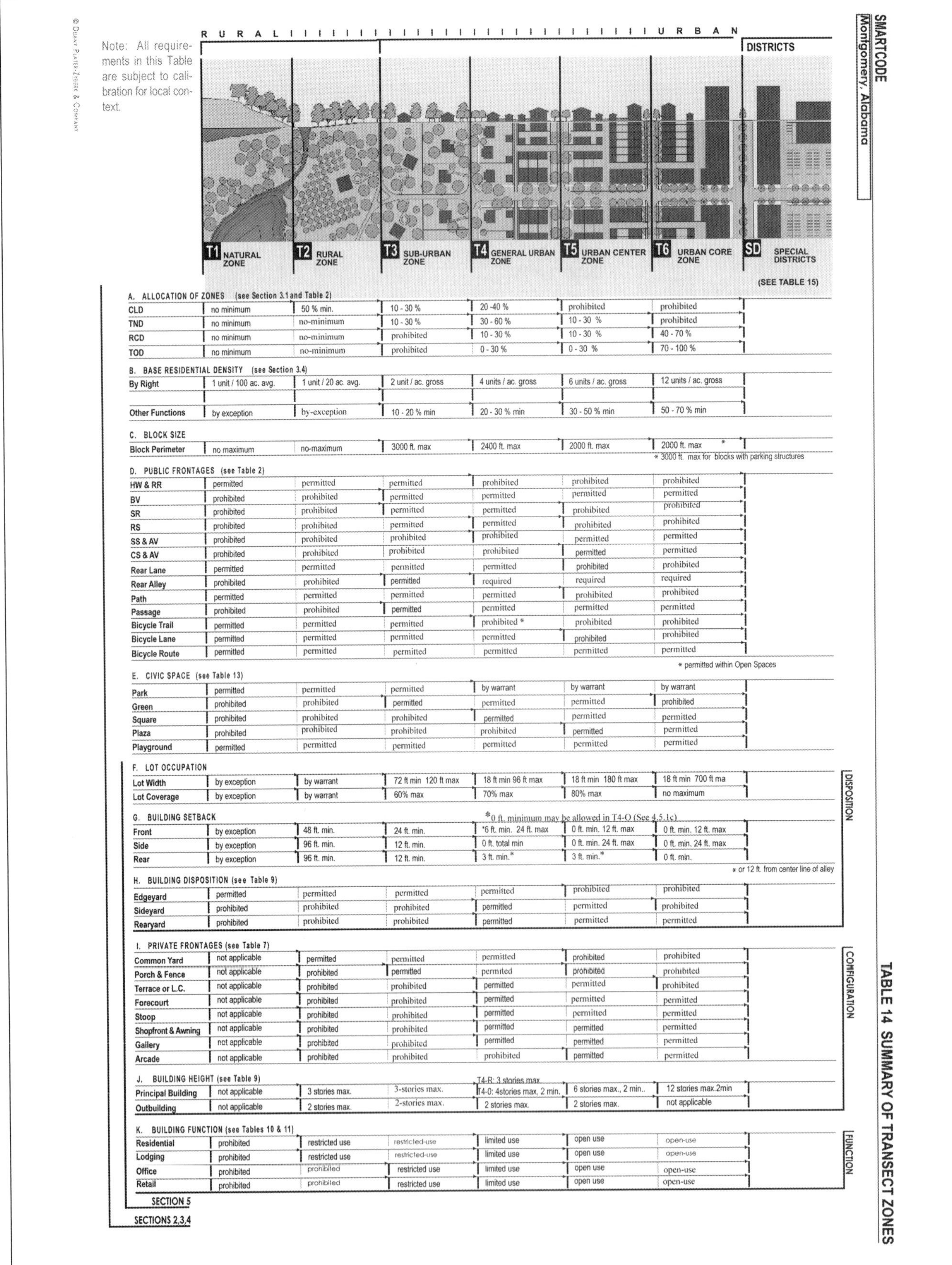

SMARTCODE
Montgomery, Alabama

TABLE 14 SUMMARY OF TRANSECT ZONES

© Duany Plater-Zyberk & Company

Note: All requirements in this Table are subject to calibration for local context.

R U R A L I I I I I I I I I I I I I I I I I I I I I I I I I U R B A N — DISTRICTS

| | T1 NATURAL ZONE | T2 RURAL ZONE | T3 SUB-URBAN ZONE | T4 GENERAL URBAN ZONE | T5 URBAN CENTER ZONE | T6 URBAN CORE ZONE | SD SPECIAL DISTRICTS (SEE TABLE 15) |
|---|---|---|---|---|---|---|---|
| **A. ALLOCATION OF ZONES (see Section 3.1 and Table 2)** | | | | | | | |
| CLD | no minimum | 50 % min. | 10 - 30 % | 20 -40 % | prohibited | prohibited | |
| TND | no minimum | no-minimum | 10 - 30 % | 30 - 60 % | 10 - 30 % | prohibited | |
| RCD | no minimum | no-minimum | prohibited | 10 - 30 % | 10 - 30 % | 40 - 70 % | |
| TOD | no minimum | no-minimum | prohibited | 0 - 30 % | 0 - 30 % | 70 - 100 % | |
| **B. BASE RESIDENTIAL DENSITY (see Section 3.4)** | | | | | | | |
| By Right | 1 unit / 100 ac. avg. | 1 unit / 20 ac. avg. | 2 unit / ac. gross | 4 units / ac. gross | 6 units / ac. gross | 12 units / ac. gross | |
| Other Functions | by exception | by-exception | 10 - 20 % min | 20 - 30 % min | 30 - 50 % min | 50 - 70 % min | |
| **C. BLOCK SIZE** | | | | | | | |
| Block Perimeter | no maximum | no-maximum | 3000 ft. max | 2400 ft. max | 2000 ft. max | 2000 ft. max * | |
| **D. PUBLIC FRONTAGES (see Table 2)** | | | | | | | |
| HW & RR | permitted | permitted | permitted | prohibited | prohibited | prohibited | |
| BV | prohibited | prohibited | permitted | permitted | permitted | permitted | |
| SR | prohibited | prohibited | permitted | permitted | prohibited | prohibited | |
| RS | prohibited | prohibited | permitted | permitted | prohibited | prohibited | |
| SS & AV | prohibited | prohibited | prohibited | prohibited | permitted | permitted | |
| CS & AV | prohibited | prohibited | prohibited | prohibited | permitted | permitted | |
| Rear Lane | permitted | permitted | permitted | permitted | prohibited | prohibited | |
| Rear Alley | prohibited | prohibited | permitted | required | required | required | |
| Path | permitted | permitted | permitted | permitted | prohibited | prohibited | |
| Passage | prohibited | prohibited | permitted | permitted | permitted | permitted | |
| Bicycle Trail | permitted | permitted | permitted | prohibited * | prohibited | prohibited | |
| Bicycle Lane | permitted | permitted | permitted | permitted | prohibited | prohibited | |
| Bicycle Route | permitted | permitted | permitted | permitted | permitted | permitted | |
| **E. CIVIC SPACE (see Table 13)** | | | | | | | |
| Park | permitted | permitted | permitted | by warrant | by warrant | by warrant | |
| Green | prohibited | prohibited | permitted | permitted | permitted | prohibited | |
| Square | prohibited | prohibited | prohibited | permitted | permitted | permitted | |
| Plaza | prohibited | prohibited | prohibited | prohibited | permitted | permitted | |
| Playground | permitted | permitted | permitted | permitted | permitted | permitted | |
| **F. LOT OCCUPATION** | | | | | | | |
| Lot Width | by exception | by warrant | 72 ft min 120 ft max | 18 ft min 96 ft max | 18 ft min 180 ft max | 18 ft min 700 ft ma | |
| Lot Coverage | by exception | by warrant | 60% max | 70% max | 80% max | no maximum | |
| **G. BUILDING SETBACK** | | | | | | | |
| Front | by exception | 48 ft. min. | 24 ft. min. | *6 ft. min. 24 ft. max | 0 ft. min. 12 ft. max | 0 ft. min. 12 ft. max | |
| Side | by exception | 96 ft. min. | 12 ft. min. | 0 ft. total min | 0 ft. min. 24 ft. max | 0 ft. min. 24 ft. max | |
| Rear | by exception | 96 ft. min. | 12 ft. min. | 3 ft. min.* | 3 ft. min.* | 0 ft. min. | |
| **H. BUILDING DISPOSITION (see Table 9)** | | | | | | | |
| Edgeyard | permitted | permitted | permitted | permitted | prohibited | prohibited | |
| Sideyard | prohibited | prohibited | prohibited | permitted | permitted | prohibited | |
| Rearyard | prohibited | prohibited | prohibited | permitted | permitted | permitted | |
| **I. PRIVATE FRONTAGES (see Table 7)** | | | | | | | |
| Common Yard | not applicable | permitted | permitted | permitted | prohibited | prohibited | |
| Porch & Fence | not applicable | prohibited | permitted | permited | prohibited | prohibited | |
| Terrace or L.C. | not applicable | prohibited | prohibited | permitted | permitted | prohibited | |
| Forecourt | not applicable | prohibited | prohibited | permitted | permitted | permitted | |
| Stoop | not applicable | prohibited | prohibited | permitted | permitted | permitted | |
| Shopfront & Awning | not applicable | prohibited | prohibited | permitted | permitted | permitted | |
| Gallery | not applicable | prohibited | prohibited | permitted | permitted | permitted | |
| Arcade | not applicable | prohibited | prohibited | prohibited | permitted | permitted | |
| **J. BUILDING HEIGHT (see Table 9)** | | | | | | | |
| Principal Building | not applicable | 3 stories max. | 3-stories max. | T4-R: 3 stories max. T4-0: 4stories max, 2 min. | 6 stories max., 2 min.. | 12 stories max.2min | |
| Outbuilding | not applicable | 2 stories max. | 2-stories max. | 2 stories max. | 2 stories max. | not applicable | |
| **K. BUILDING FUNCTION (see Tables 10 & 11)** | | | | | | | |
| Residential | prohibited | restricted use | restricted-use | limited use | open use | open-use | |
| Lodging | prohibited | restricted use | restricted-use | limited use | open use | open-use | |
| Office | prohibited | prohibited | restricted use | limited use | open use | open-use | |
| Retail | prohibited | prohibited | restricted use | limited use | open use | open-use | |

* 3000 ft. max for blocks with parking structures (C)

* permitted within Open Spaces (D)

*0 ft. minimum may be allowed in T4-O (See 4.5.1c) (G)

* or 12 ft. from center line of alley (G)

DISPOSITION (F–H) · CONFIGURATION (I–J) · FUNCTION (K)

SECTION 5 (F–K) · SECTIONS 2,3,4 (A–E)

**Fig. 4.107** Zone regulation summary table from the optional SmartCode

**SMARTCODE** — Montgomery, Alabama — **TABLE 10 BUILDING FUNCTION-SPECIFIC**

■ By Right
□ By Exception

| a. RESIDENTIAL | T1 | T2 | T3 | T4 | T5 | T6 | SD |
|---|---|---|---|---|---|---|---|
| Apartment building | | | | ■ | ■ | ■ | |
| Rearyard house | | | | ■ | ■ | ■ | |
| Duplex house | | | | ■ | ■ | | |
| Sideyard house | | | ■ | ■ | ■ | | |
| Edgeyard House | | ■ | ■ | ■ | | | |
| Outbuilding | | ■ | ■ | ■ | ■ | | |
| Manufactured house | | | □ | | | | □ |
| Temporary tent | □ | □ | □ | □ | □ | □ | □ |
| Live-work | | | ■ | ■ | ■ | ■ | □ |
| **b. LODGING** | | | | | | | |
| Hotel (no room limit) | | | | | ■ | ■ | □ |
| Inn (up to 12 rooms) | | □ | | ■ | ■ | ■ | |
| Inn (up to 5 rooms) | | □ | ■ | ■ | ■ | ■ | |
| S.R.O. hostel | | | □ | □ | □ | □ | □ |
| School dormitory | | | | ■ | ■ | ■ | ■ |
| **c. OFFICE** | | | | | | | |
| Office building | | | | ■ | ■ | ■ | □ |
| Live-work | | | ■ | ■ | ■ | ■ | □ |
| **d. RETAIL** | | | | | | | |
| Open-market building | | ■ | ■ | ■ | ■ | ■ | ■ |
| Retail building | | | | ■ | ■ | ■ | □ |
| Restaurant | | | | ■ | ■ | ■ | □ |
| Kiosk | | | | ■ | ■ | ■ | □ |
| Push cart | | | | ■ | ■ | ■ | □ |
| Adult entertainment | | | | | | □ | □ |
| **e. CIVIC** | | | | | | | |
| Bus shelter | | | ■ | ■ | ■ | ■ | ■ |
| Convention center | | | | | ■ | □ | ■ |
| Conference center | | | | | □ | ■ | ■ |
| Fountain or Public art | | ■ | ■ | ■ | ■ | ■ | ■ |
| Library | | | | ■ | ■ | ■ | ■ |
| Movie Theater | | | | | ■ | ■ | ■ |
| Museum | | | | | □ | ■ | ■ |
| Outdoor auditorium | | □ | ■ | | ■ | ■ | ■ |
| Parking structure | | | | | ■ | ■ | ■ |
| Passenger terminal | | | | | □ | □ | ■ |
| Playground | | ■ | ■ | ■ | ■ | ■ | ■ |
| Sports stadium | | | | | ■ | □ | ■ |
| Surface parking lot | | | | □ | □ | □ | ■ |
| Religious assembly | | | | ■ | ■ | ■ | ■ |



**SMARTCODE** — Montgomery, Alabama — **TABLE 10 BUILDING FUNCTION-SPECIFIC (CONTINUED)**

| f. OTHER: AGRICULTURE | T1 | T2 | T3 | T4 | T5 | T6 | SD |
|---|---|---|---|---|---|---|---|
| Grain storage | ■ | ■ | | | | | □ |
| Livestock pen | □ | □ | | | | | □ |
| Greenhouse | ■ | ■ | □ | | | | □ |
| Stable | ■ | ■ | □ | | | | □ |
| Kennel | ■ | ■ | □ | □ | □ | □ | □ |
| **f. OTHER: AUTOMOTIVE** | | | | | | | |
| Gasoline station | | □ | | | □ | □ | ■ |
| Automobile service | | | | | | | ■ |
| Truck maintenance | | | | | | | ■ |
| Drive-through facility | | | | | □ | □ | ■ |
| Rest stop | ■ | ■ | | | | | □ |
| Roadside stand | ■ | ■ | | | | | □ |
| Billboard | | | | | | □ | □ |
| Shopping center | | | | | | | □ |
| Shopping mall | | | | | | | □ |
| **f. OTHER: CIVIL SUPPORT** | | | | | | | |
| Fire station | | | ■ | ■ | ■ | ■ | ■ |
| Police station | | | | ■ | ■ | ■ | ■ |
| Cemetery | | ■ | □ | □ | | | ■ |
| Funeral home | | | | ■ | ■ | ■ | ■ |
| Hospital | | | | | □ | □ | ■ |
| Medical clinic | | | | □ | ■ | ■ | ■ |
| **f. OTHER: EDUCATION** | | | | | | | |
| College | | | | | □ | □ | ■ |
| High school | | | | □ | □ | □ | ■ |
| Trade school | | | | | □ | □ | ■ |
| Elementary school | | | □ | ■ | ■ | ■ | ■ |
| Childcare center | | ■ | ■ | ■ | ■ | ■ | □ |
| **f. OTHER: INDUSTRIAL** | | | | | | | |
| Heavy industrial facility | | | | | | | ■ |
| Light industrial facility | | | | | | □ | ■ |
| Truck depot | | | | | | | ■ |
| Laboratory facility | | | | | | □ | ■ |
| Water supply facility | | | | | | | ■ |
| Sewer and waste facility | | | | | | | ■ |
| Electric substation | □ | □ | □ | □ | □ | □ | ■ |
| Cremation Facility | | | | | | | ■ |
| Large Storage | | | | | | □ | ■ |
| Mini-storage | | | | | | | ■ |



**Fig. 4.108** (left and right) Land-use table from the optional SmartCode

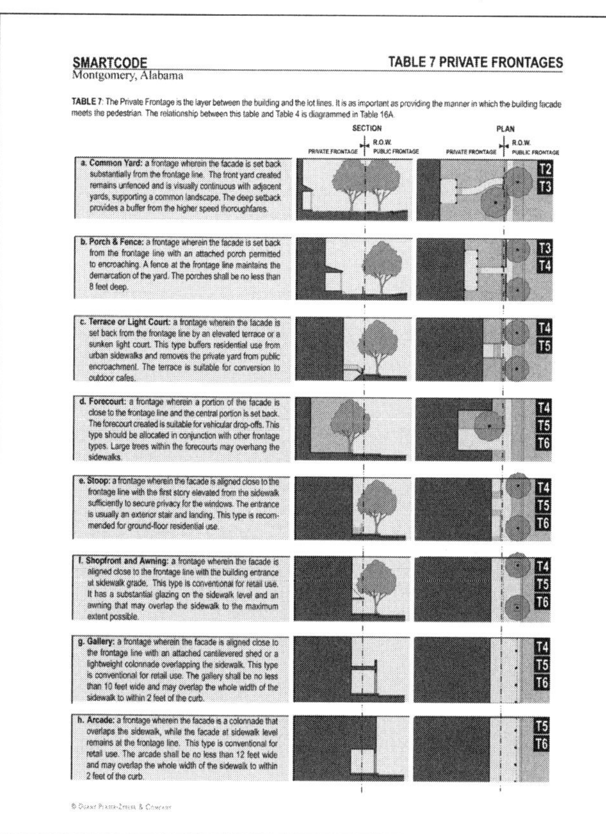

**SMARTCODE** — Montgomery, Alabama — **TABLE 7 PRIVATE FRONTAGES**

TABLE 7: The Private Frontage is the layer between the building and the lot lines. It is as important as providing the manner in which the building facade meets the pedestrian. The relationship between this table and Table 4 is diagrammed in Table 16A.

| | SECTION (PRIVATE FRONTAGE / R.O.W. PUBLIC FRONTAGE) | PLAN (PRIVATE FRONTAGE / R.O.W. PUBLIC FRONTAGE) |
|---|---|---|
| **a. Common Yard:** a frontage wherein the facade is set back substantially from the frontage line. The front yard created remains unfenced and is visually continuous with adjacent yards, supporting a common landscape. The deep setback provides a buffer from the higher speed thoroughfares. | | T2 T3 |
| **b. Porch & Fence:** a frontage wherein the facade is set back from the frontage line with an attached porch permitted to encroaching. A fence at the frontage line maintains the demarcation of the yard. The porches shall be no less than 8 feet deep. | | T3 T4 |
| **c. Terrace or Light Court:** a frontage wherein the facade is set back from the frontage line by an elevated terrace or a sunken light court. This type buffers residential use from urban sidewalks and removes the private yard from public encroachment. The terrace is suitable for conversion to outdoor cafes. | | T4 T5 |
| **d. Forecourt:** a frontage wherein a portion of the facade is close to the frontage line and the central portion is set back. The forecourt created is suitable for vehicular drop-offs. This type should be allocated in conjunction with other frontage types. Large trees within the forecourts may overhang the sidewalks. | | T4 T5 T6 |
| **e. Stoop:** a frontage wherein the facade is aligned close to the frontage line with the first story elevated from the sidewalk sufficiently to secure privacy for the windows. The entrance is usually an exterior stair and landing. This type is recommended for ground-floor residential use. | | T4 T5 T6 |
| **f. Shopfront and Awning:** a frontage wherein the facade is aligned close to the frontage line with the building entrance at sidewalk grade. This type is conventional for retail use. It has a substantial glazing on the sidewalk level and an awning that may overlap the sidewalk to the maximum extent possible. | | T4 T5 T6 |
| **g. Gallery:** a frontage wherein the facade is aligned close to the frontage line with an attached cantilevered shed or a lightweight colonnade overlapping the sidewalk. This type is conventional for retail use. The gallery shall be no less than 10 feet wide and may overlap the whole width of the sidewalk to within 2 feet of the curb. | | T4 T5 T6 |
| **h. Arcade:** a frontage wherein the facade is a colonnade that overlaps the sidewalk, while the facade at sidewalk level remains at the frontage line. This type is conventional for retail use. The arcade shall be no less than 12 feet wide and may overlap the whole width of the sidewalk to within 2 feet of the curb. | | T5 T6 |



**Fig. 4.109** Frontage Standards from the optional SmartCode

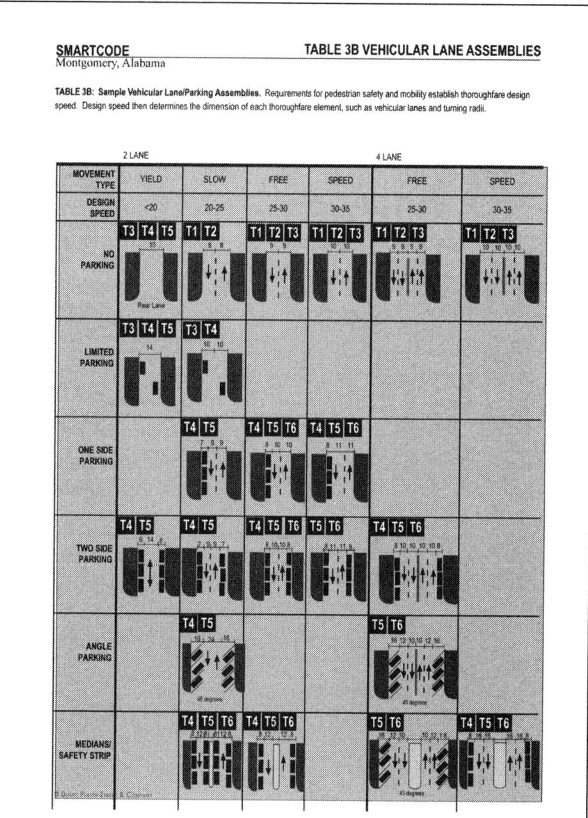

**SMARTCODE** — Montgomery, Alabama — **TABLE 3B VEHICULAR LANE ASSEMBLIES**

**TABLE 3B: Sample Vehicular Lane/Parking Assemblies.** Requirements for pedestrian safety and mobility establish thoroughfare design speed. Design speed then determines the dimension of each thoroughfare element, such as vehicular lanes and turning radii.

| | 2 LANE | | | | 4 LANE | |
|---|---|---|---|---|---|---|
| MOVEMENT TYPE | YIELD | SLOW | FREE | SPEED | FREE | SPEED |
| DESIGN SPEED | <20 | 20-25 | 25-30 | 30-35 | 25-30 | 30-35 |
| NO PARKING | T3 T4 T5 (10; Rear Lane) | T1 T2 (8 8) | T1 T2 T3 (9 9) | T1 T2 T3 (10 10) | T1 T2 T3 (9 9 9 9) | T1 T2 T3 (10 10 10 10) |
| LIMITED PARKING | T3 T4 T5 (14) | T3 T4 (10 10) | | | | |
| ONE SIDE PARKING | | T4 T5 (7 9 9) | T4 T5 T6 (8 10 10) | T4 T5 T6 (8 11 11) | | |
| TWO SIDE PARKING | T4 T5 (8 14 8) | T4 T5 (7 9 9 7) | T4 T5 T6 (8 10 10 8) | T5 T6 (8 11 11 8) | T4 T5 T6 (8 10 10 10 10 8) | |
| ANGLE PARKING | | T4 T5 (18 24 18; 45 degrees) | | | T5 T6 (18 12 10 10 12 18; 45 degrees) | |
| MEDIANS/ SAFETY STRIP | | T4 T5 T6 | T4 T5 T6 (8 12 12 8) | | T5 T6 (18 12 10 10 12 18; 45 degrees) | T4 T5 T6 (8 16 16 16 16 8) |



**Fig. 4.110** Vehicular lane assemblies from the optional SmartCode

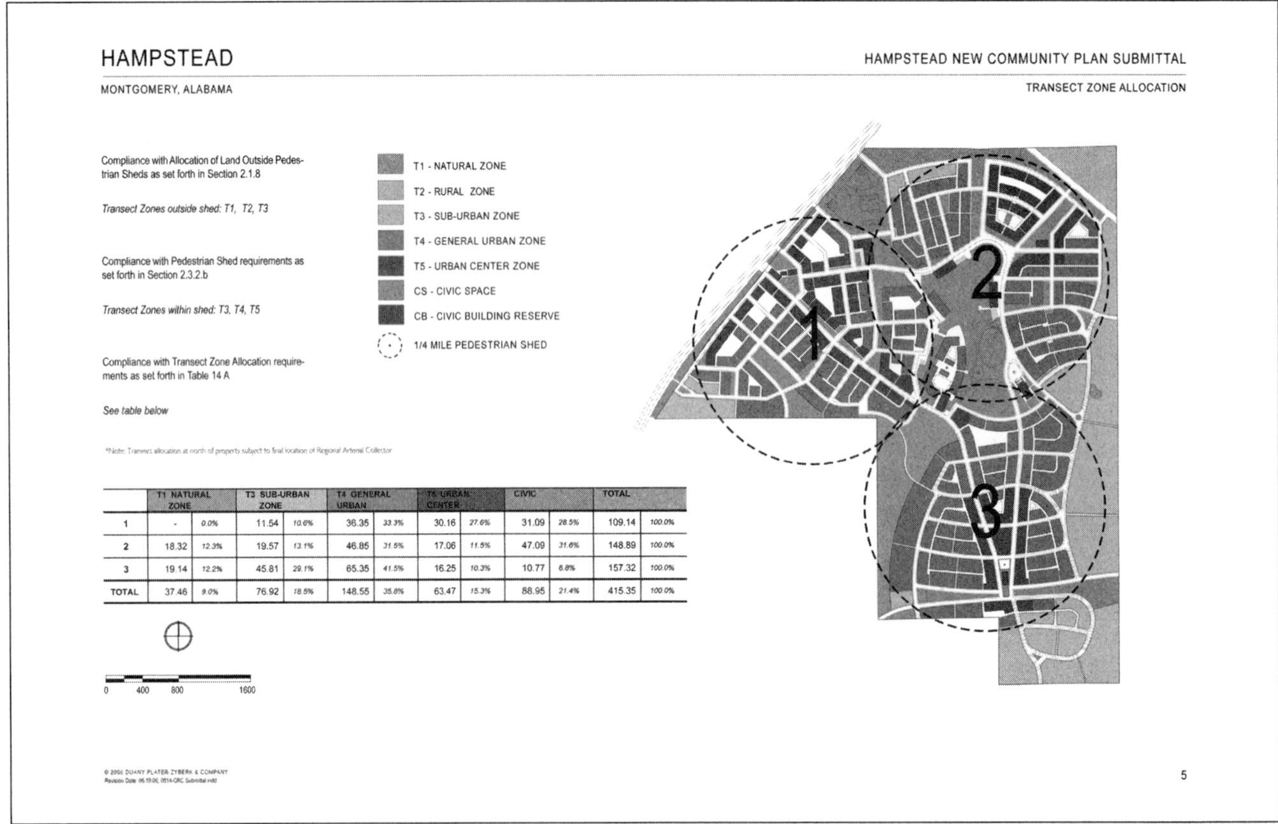


| | T1 NATURAL ZONE | | T3 SUB-URBAN ZONE | | T4 GENERAL URBAN | | T5 URBAN CENTER | | CIVIC | | TOTAL | |
|---|---|---|---|---|---|---|---|---|---|---|---|---|
| 1 | - | 0.0% | 11.54 | 10.6% | 36.35 | 33.3% | 30.16 | 27.6% | 31.09 | 28.5% | 109.14 | 100.0% |
| 2 | 18.32 | 12.3% | 19.57 | 13.1% | 46.85 | 31.5% | 17.06 | 11.5% | 47.09 | 31.6% | 148.89 | 100.0% |
| 3 | 19.14 | 12.2% | 45.81 | 29.1% | 65.35 | 41.5% | 16.25 | 10.3% | 10.77 | 6.8% | 157.32 | 100.0% |
| TOTAL | 37.46 | 9.0% | 76.92 | 18.5% | 148.55 | 35.8% | 63.47 | 15.3% | 88.95 | 21.4% | 415.35 | 100.0% |

**Fig. 4.111** Transect zone allocations from the Hampstead project application

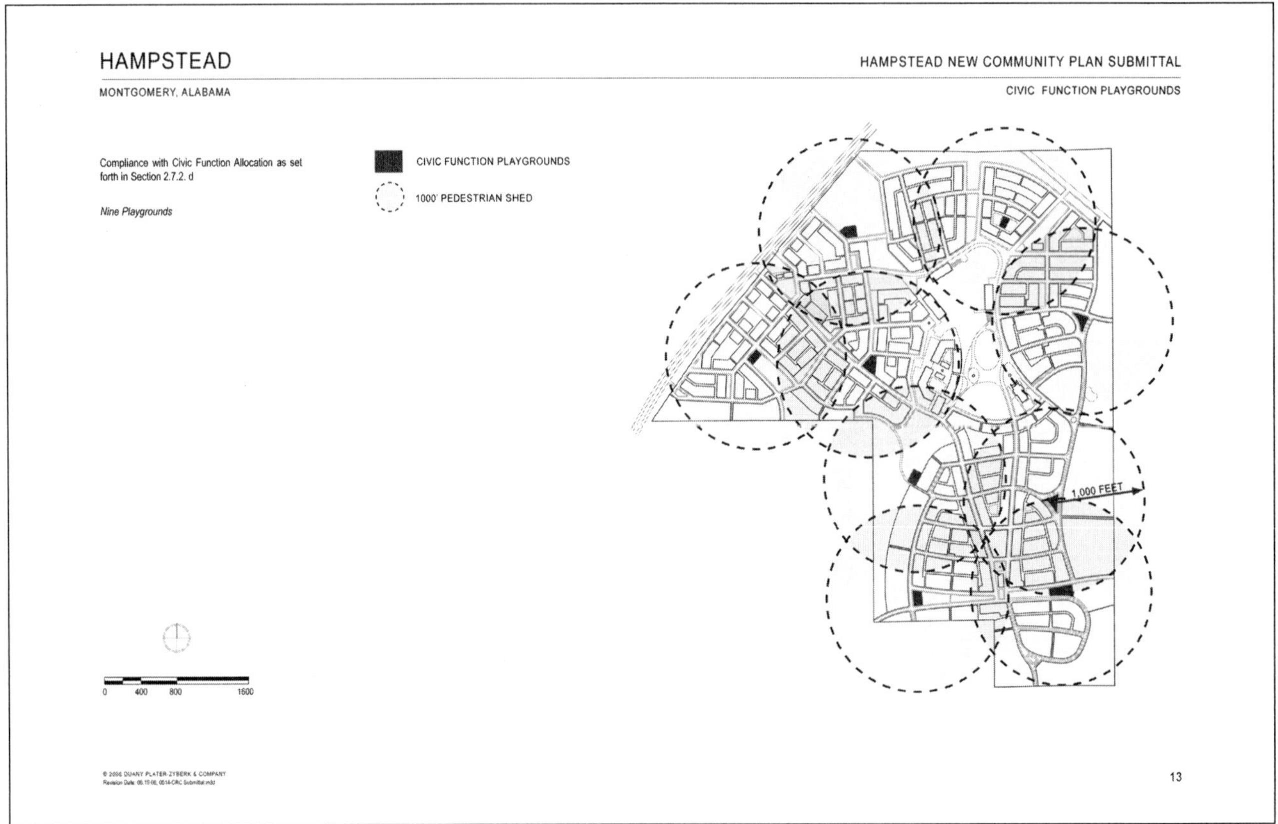


**Fig. 4.112** Civic space allocations from the Hampstead project application

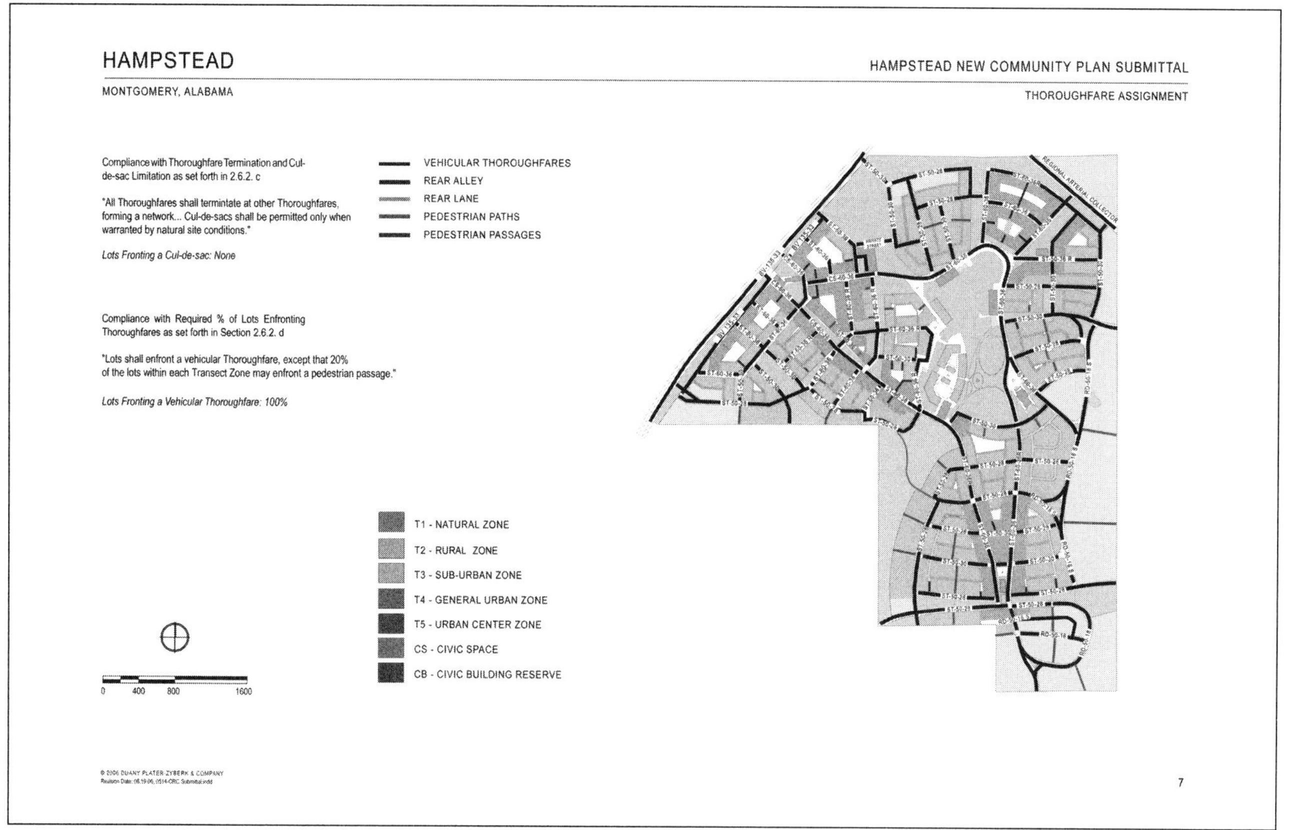


**Fig. 4.113** Thoroughfare allocations from the Hampstead project application

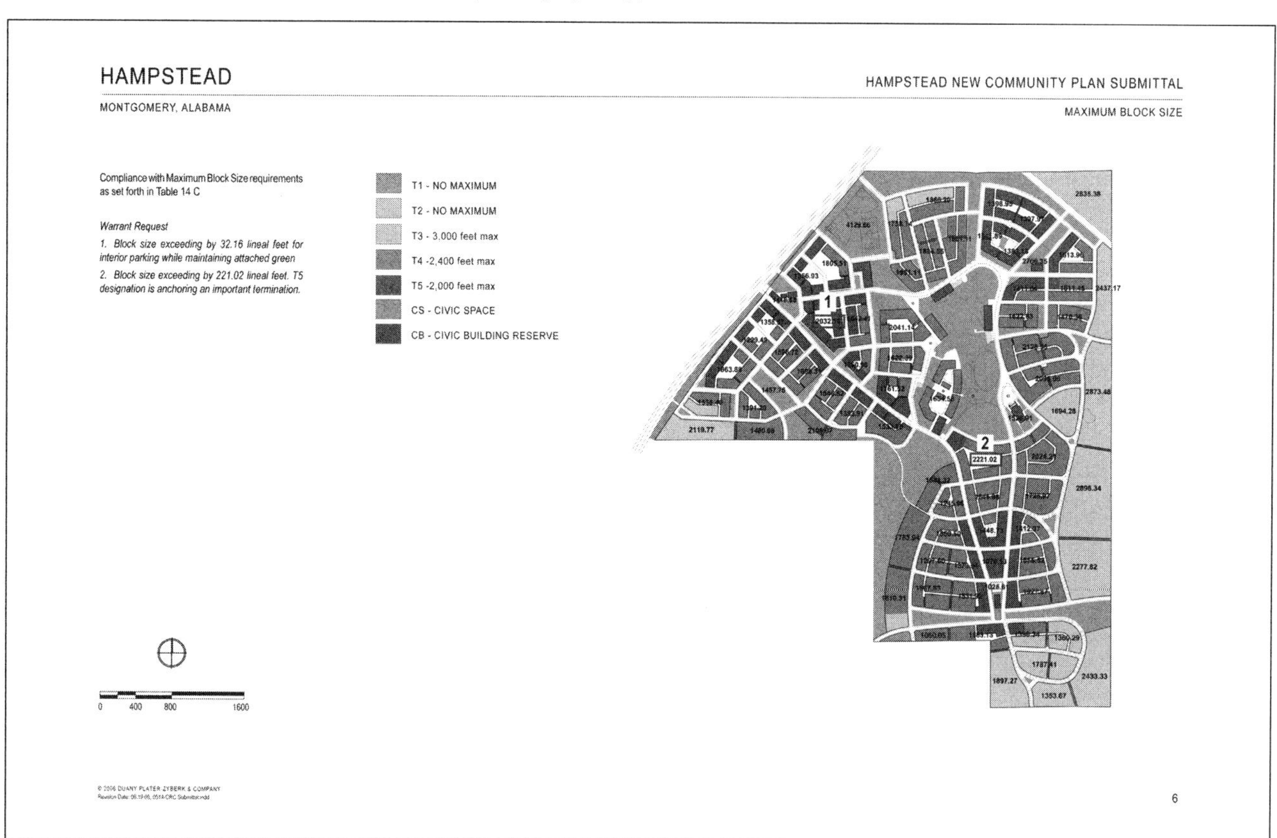


**Fig. 4.114** Block Standards from the Hampstead project application

The following graphics from the SmartCode contain new Thoroughfare Assemblies which should be added to the Montgomery SmartCode Table 3C. In addition new versions of tables 3A and 3B have been provided to replace the earlier versions. These new Thoroughfare Assemblies and tables were developed to customize the standard SmartCode for the unique conditions of Montgomery.

**SMARTCODE** **TABLE 3C THOROUGHFARE ASSEMBLIES (continued)**

*Montgomery, Alabama*

**TABLE 3C: Thoroughfare Assemblies.** These thoroughfares are assembled from the elements that appear in Tables 3A and 3B and incorporate the Public Frontages of Table 4. The key gives the thoroughfare type followed by the right-of-way width, followed by the pavement width, and in some instances followed by specialized transportation capability.

**KEY** **ST-57-20-BL**

Thoroughfare Type
Right of Way Width
Pavement Width
Transportation

**THOROUGHFARE TYPES**

| | |
|---|---|
| Boulevard: | BV |
| Avenue: | AV |
| Commercial Street: | CS |
| Street: | ST |
| Road: | RD |
| Rear Alley: | RA |
| Rear Lane: | RL |
| Bicycle Trail: | BT |
| Bicycle Lane: | BL |
| Bicycle Route: | BR |
| Path: | PT |
| Transit Route: | TR |

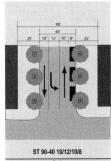

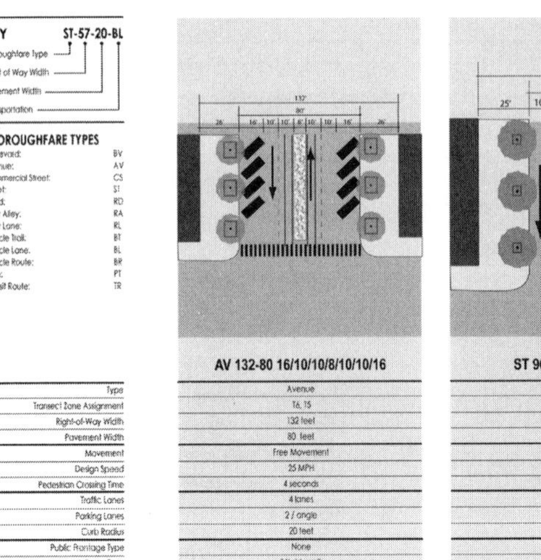


| | AV 132-80 16/10/10/8/10/10/16 | ST 90-40 10/12/10/8 |
|---|---|---|
| Type | Avenue | Street |
| Transect Zone Assignment | T6, T5 | T6,T5 |
| Right-of-Way Width | 132 feet | 90 feet |
| Pavement Width | 80 feet | 40 feet |
| Movement | Free Movement | Free Movement |
| Design Speed | 25 MPH | 25 MPH |
| Pedestrian Crossing Time | 4 seconds | 10 seconds |
| Traffic Lanes | 4 lanes | 3 lanes |
| Parking Lanes | 2 / angle | 1 / parallel |
| Curb Radius | 20 feet | 20 feet |
| Public Frontage Type | None | |
| Walkway Type | 26' sidewalk | 25' sidewalk |
| Planter Type | tree wells; 50' o.c. | tree wells; 50 o.c. |
| Curb Type | vertical curb | vertical curb |
| Landscape Type | | |
| Transportation Provision | TR, BR | BR |

Page A.12
January 2007
DOWNTOWN MONTGOMERY PLAN

SMARTCODE AMENDMENTS

This following amendments are recommended for the Montgomery SmartCode. Text with strikethroughs indicate existing text to be removed and italic text with underlines indicate new text to be added. The amendments accomplish the following:

1. Create a T4 Open (T4-O) sub-zone as a transition step in building form and use between T5 (high-intensity downtown commercial areas) and T4-Restricted, (T4-R), (low-rise residential neighborhoods).

2. Change the provision of childcare facilities from a required item of Traditional Neighborhood Developments (TNDs) Pedestrian Sheds to an encouraged item.

3. Decrease the size requirements of civic space in order to encourage the creation of civic space.

4. Change the minimum acreage of TNDs and Infill Plans from 80 acres to 40 acres.

5. Add to the number of allowable uses in the Downtown.

6. Adopt a Downtown Transect Map to guide infill development.

7. Eliminate Transect Succession portion Section 3.1.7.

8. Calibrate the allowed roadway types in the Montgomery SmartCode to the existing urban condition of the downtown for use with Infill Plans.

9. Add Synoptic Surveys to the SmartCode Appendix in order to provide the rationale for local calibrations to the original SmartCode V8.0 Template.

**Complete Amendments**

1. Create a T4-O (T4-Open) sub-zone which provides a transition in the city's physical form from the predominately two-story, small structure residential uses set back from the road in T4-R (T4-Restricted) and the taller, larger commercial and office buildings with a zero setback in T5. The T4-O sub-zone will have a minimum requirement of two stories and maximum of four in order to create the proper proportion between building height and the width of the streets. T4-O may have a zero setback if provided for in a community plan. The sub-zone also allows neighborhood sized commercial within walking distance of city neighborhoods.

The T4-O sub-zone designation for us in the downtown was allotted on the basis of blocks and neighborhoods with the exception of the corridor which follows Goldthwaite Street, Clayton Street, and Scott Street and the corridor which follows Mobile Street and Mildred Street. All parcels along these corridors that were within 165 feet from the centerline of the road were designated T4-O. Generally, 150 feet of lot depth is required in order to construct a three story building with street-level commercial and three rows of parking at the rear of the lot. Fifteen feet was added to the 150 feet to account for the 30 foot average street width. The only exemptions were lots which were 500 feet in depth which were designated T4-O starting from the front lot line to 150 feet deep into the lot.

a) Section 4.5: *"4.5 Specific to General Urban Zones (T4) (Includes T4-R and T4-O)"*

b) Section 4.5.1c: *"A zero setback line shall be allowed in T4-O if a build-to line requires a zero setback pursuant to an approved New Community Plan or Infill Plan provided a 5 foot clear path is available for pedestrians in the public frontage (sidewalk)."*

c) Section 4.5.5d: "Buildings shall have sloped roofs. Buildings with flat roofs shall be allowed in T4-O which are in accordance with Section 4.2.5h.

d) Table 4A(e), (SS)(AV) For Standard Streets or Avenues: Add "T4-O" to the column which lists "T5" and "T6" to make this street type allowable in T4-O

e) Table 4B: Add "T4-O" to the column heading which lists "T5" and "T6" and reads "RS-CS-AV-BV".

f) Table 8: Table 8 does not reflect Table 14J. All of the graphics need to be either updated or removed. If updated then a graphic must be created that would should show T4-O and T4-R and their maximum and minimum heights.

g) Table 11: Add to the heading column of Table 11 (which lists "T3", "T4", "T5", and "T6") a "T4-O" to the column which lists "T5" and T6". Change the Column which lists "~~T4~~" to "T4-R".

h) Table 12. Add to the heading column of Table 11 (which lists "T3", "T4", "T5", and "T6") a "T4-O" to the column which lists "T5" and T6". Change the Column which lists "~~T4~~" to "T4-R".

i) Table 14, 14J Principal Building: "~~4 stories max, 2 min~~". "T4-R: 3 stories max.", and "T4-O: 4 stories max., 2 stories min."

j) Table 14, 14G Building Setback, Front, Column Referring to T-4:

"*0 ft. minimum may be allowed in T4-O (See 4.5.1c)"

A zero setback provision should be added to allow the construction of places with a more urban character, typically commercial storefronts, in areas where a build-to line has been designated in an approved New Community Plan or Infill Plan.

Page A.9
APPENDIX A
January 2007

**Fig. 4.115** New thoroughfare assemblies (top) and general amendments (bottom) added by the Downtown Montgomery Plan to the original, optional SmartCode to calibrate it to downtown conditions

# Appendix

# Abbreviated Timeline of Form-Based Coding



1981 Duany Plater-Zyberk & Company (DPZ) creates the first contemporary Form-Based Code (FBC) for Seaside, Florida.

1989 A TND code is created for Key West, Florida, by Buff Chace, Douglas Storrs, Dan Cary, Jean Francois LeJeune, and Andrés Duany.

1991 Miami/Dade County, Florida, adopts a Traditional Neighborhood Development (TND) ordinance created by DPZ (led by Geoffrey Ferrell), Sam Poole, and Gary Greenan that later becomes a model for dozens of other communities.

1991 Andrés Duany and Elizabeth Plater-Zyberk and DPZ's early Form-Based Coding efforts are published in *Towns and Town Making Principles.* Vincent Scully's foreword highlights their coding capabilities and the power of this alternative to conventional coding. Bill Lennertz introduces the components of the codes.

1991 Riviera Beach, Florida adopts a Master Plan and Form-Based Code created by Mark Schimmenti in association with Dover Correa Kohl Cockshut Valle and Geoffrey Ferrell, which wins the Progressive Architecture Awards Urban Design Citation (with special mention of the code).

1993 South Miami, Florida, adopts the Hometown District Ordinance by Dover, Kohl & Partners.

1994 Peter Katz writes *The New Urbanism: Toward an Architecture of Community,* which highlights the latest in Form-Based Coding practice by New Urbanist practitioners.

1995 Correa Valle Valle produces the Traditional Village Ordinance code for Monroe County, Florida.

1995 West Palm Beach, Florida, adopts a new downtown plan and mandatory urban code prepared by Jonathan Barnett, Elizabeth Plater-Zyberk, and Andrés Duany.

1995 The city of Belmont adopts the first TND Code in North Carolina.

1996 At CNU IV in Charleston, South Carolina, participants ratify the Charter of the New Urbanism, which specifically promotes the use of graphical codes (an early name for Form-Based Codes).

1996 The Traditional Town Overlay District Code by Dover, Kohl & Partners is adopted for Port Royal, South Carolina.

1996 Cornelius, North Carolina, adopts the first mandatory TND Code under Craig Lewis, planner.

1998 Sonoma, California, adopts a Development Code by Paul Crawford and Moule & Polyzoides that integrates a framework of neighborhoods, districts, and corridors into the hybrid code.

1998 Winter Springs, Florida, adopts the Winter Springs Town Center District Code by Dover, Kohl & Partners.

1999 DPZ creates a plan for the entire county of Onondaga County, New York, using the transect as the basis.

2000 DPZ develops the first draft of the SmartCode.

2001 Chicago-based consultant Carol Wyant coins the term *Form-Based Code*.

2001 Peter Katz, Geoffrey Ferrell, Carol Wyant, and Steve Price advise Mayor Daley's Committee to Rewrite the City of Chicago's Zoning Ordinance about Form-Based Coding.

2001 Hercules, California, adopts the Central Hercules Plan and Form-Based Code by Dover, Kohl & Partners. It is the first FBC enacted into law in California.

2001 Contra Costa County, California, approves the Pleasant Hill Transit Village Master Plan by Lennertz and Coyle and FBC by Geoffrey Ferrell. Opticos Design is hired as the Town Architect.

2001 Iowa City, Iowa, adopts an FBC written by Geoffrey Ferrell with Jim Tischler as a new chapter in the city's zoning code. It is established to implement the Peninsula Neighborhood and promote other New Urbanist projects.

2002 The Congress for the New Urbanism (CNU) "Codes Council" convenes in Santa Fe, New Mexico.

2003 SmartCode version 1 is released.

2003 The Brookings Institute Center on Urban and Metropolitan Policy and the American Planning Association (APA) sponsor a day-long conference on zoning reform in Chicago, instigated and partially organized by Peter Katz and Carol Wyant. The central theme was whether conventional zoning ordinances that regulate use, height, and bulk should be replaced by Form-Based Codes.

2003 Paul Crawford and Moule & Polyzoides organize and sponsor the conference "The California Codes Challenge: Implementing Smart Growth and New Urbanism Through General Plans and Zoning Codes" in Pasadena, California.

2003 The California APA Conference in Santa Barbara includes sessions called "Smart Growth and New Urbanism in Practice: Form-Based Codes," with Paul Crawford, Lois Fisher, Daniel Parolek, and Stefanos Polyzoides, and "Smart Growth and New Urbanism in Practice: The Statewide Planning Framework," with Paul Crawford, Andrés Duany, and Tal Finney, the director of the California Governor's Office of Planning and Research.

2003 PlaceMakers, in conjunction with Andrés Duany, conducts its first SmartCode Workshop at the Kentlands in Gaithersburg, Maryland.

2003 Steve Tracy of the Local Government Commission authors *Smart Growth Zoning Codes: A Resource Guide.*

2003 Arlington County, Virginia, adopts the Columbia Pike Special Revitalization District FBC by Ferrell Madden Associates, based on the Dover Kohl & Partners charrette and Master Plan.

2003 Petaluma, California, becomes the first U.S. municipality to adopt the SmartCode through the Petaluma Central District Specific Plan. Fisher & Hall, Paul Crawford, and David Sargent calibrated the code.

2003–4 Cotati, California, adopts a citywide land use code and FBC by Paul Crawford.

2003–5 Azusa, California, adopts a Development Code and FBC by Paul Crawford and Moule & Polyzoides.

2004 CNU and APA publish *Codifying New Urbanism: How to Reform Municipal Land Development Regulation,* by Ellen Greenberg, Joel Russell, Jonathan Barnett, Paul Crawford, Rick Bernhardt, and Gianni Longo.

2004 Judy Corbett with Jeff Speck at National Endowment for the Arts organizes the Mayor's Institute on City Design (Sacramento region) with a segment on FBCs in Napa, California.

2004 APA National Conference in Washington, D.C., includes a panel called "Form-Based Zoning Codes: Principles and Practice," with Paul Crawford, Bill Dennis, and Geoffrey Ferrell.

2004 Governor Arnold Schwarzenegger of California signs Assembly Bill 1268, sponsored by Assembly Member Wiggins with text written by Paul Crawford, making California the first state to specifically enable FBCs.

2004 The Form-Based Codes Institute (FBCI) is founded by Peter Katz, Carol Wyant, and 15 FBC practitioners with funding from the Richard H. Driehaus Charitable Lead Trust.

2004 APA publishes *Form-Based Zoning* by Paul Crawford, Bill Dennis and Geoffrey Ferrell as an American Institute of Certified Planners training CD.

2004 The Michigan Society of Planning hosts Geoffrey Ferrell as keynote speaker to present FBCs and convene a two-session workshop on the topic.

2004 Sarasota, Florida, adopts a downtown SmartCode.

2004–5 The Local Government Commission sponsors workshops "Developing Smart Growth Zoning Codes" in Chino, Oakland, Pasadena, Sacramento, and San Diego, California.

2005 Andrés Duany and DPZ organize the Mississippi Renewal Forum with an unprecedented gathering of more than 200 community leaders and national, multidisciplinary professionals to create a vision to rebuild Mississippi after Hurricane Katrina. The SmartCode is proposed as a tool to implement the vision plans.

2005 The SmartCode is provided without a licensing fee.

2005–6 The FBCI teaches its first course in Alexandria, Virginia, and establishes a 3-level curriculum of courses to be taught across the country.

2007 The FBCI presents the first Driehaus Form-Based Codes Awards funded by the Richard H. Driehaus Charitable Lead Trust at CNU XV in Philadelphia. Awards are given to Farmers Branch, Texas; Gulfport, Mississippi; Leander, Texas; and St. Lucie County, Florida.

2007 Miami 21, the first Form-Based Code and SmartCode for a major city, is submitted to the City Commission.

# Common Mistakes

Even in the relatively short time that Form-Based Codes (FBCs) have been prepared, adopted, and administered, a number of common mistakes have been observed in their design and application. These mistakes often can invalidate the quality of an FBC and its intent very quickly. Even one of these mistakes can threaten the predictability of the form and character of new development, and reduce public confidence in the code, as well as its effectiveness. The following are the most common mistakes.

## Confusing, Overly Detailed, or Insufficiently Detailed Land-Use Tables

As mentioned earlier, a land-use table should not attempt to list every possible use. This is nearly impossible to do and only causes confusion for code users and administrators. An important part of the FBC process is to distill the use tables down to one page or just over one page for each zone, but at the same time ensure appropriate compatibility of adjacent uses. It is helpful to use a performance-criteria approach to land uses, such as the hours that a business can operate, the size of a business, and whether the business has a drive-through. Discuss land-use tables early and often during FBC preparation to ensure that land-use decisions are part of the education process and that they are well thought out.

## Using Density to Regulate Development

Density as a primary tool for regulating built form does not produce predictable results and, thus, should be avoided in an FBC. For example, a yield of 20 units per acre can be reached by building a two-story eight-plex on a lot 166 feet wide by 105 feet deep, but it can also be achieved by building two small, one-story bungalows on a 40-foot-wide by 110-foot-deep lot. Therefore, density should be used only if required to help establish a cap in capacity of a city or site, such as to calculate a maximum yield for an environmental impact report.

It is often a challenge during the FBC process to educate local elected officials and planning staff about the benefits of regulating physical form first and not by density. This education is most successfully achieved by taking walking tours through neighborhoods and housing types that are above what the community thinks is acceptable density-wide, but are well designed and would be appropriate within the particular community. An example is the typical courtyard apartment housing type found in southern California, more particularly in and near Santa Barbara. Most citizens, elected or appointed officials, and professionals like this building type after seeing it in person and would not mind having it in their communities. When they are told that it typically yields a density of 40 units/acre, they are quite shocked and begin to understand the importance of the physical form over density numbers.

## Not Calibrating Parking to the Transect

Restrictive parking requirements have been one of the biggest obstacles for high-quality infill and greenfield development. It is a mistake if parking requirements are not calibrated by transect zone in an FBC. In short, suburban parking standards are being required for more urban areas. This typically prohibits, or at the very least often discourages, the desired type of development. For example, retail and commercial uses at mixed-use neighborhood centers located within walkable neighborhoods should not have the same high off-street parking requirement as the same uses in a suburban strip-mall context. Using land within a neighborhood center for off-street parking is detrimental to walkable neighborhoods for a variety of reasons, including increasing walking distance to retail and creating holes in the street/building edge. If there is a fear that a large use will locate at a neighborhood center that would require more parking, it is possible to use performance-criteria-based regulations, such as the maximum size of a store, to ensure that only smaller shops are allowed in these locations. (See the sidebar "Parking" in Chapter 2.)

## Not Calibrating Open Space Requirements to the Transect

Similar to the parking regulations described above, we often see suburban open-space requirements being required in urban areas. These requirements should decrease as you move from rural to urban transect zones. Along with parking, this requirement is often a big obstacle for good infill and redevelopment projects. For example, if a code in a downtown requires a certain square footage of shared open space for each project, this will often prohibit projects on smaller lots, thus encouraging lot aggregation and larger buildings that may not be as in character with the community as the smaller buildings would be.

## Building Placement

Most of the issues we see with building placement also have to deal with the standards not being calibrated by transect zone, but instead being coded to a suburban standard. These regulations typically make it difficult, if not impossible, to develop or redevelop sites in existing areas.

Another issue we have seen is Building Placement Standards that are not specific enough or predictable enough from either a community's or a developer's standpoint. There should be some wiggle room within these regulations, but not so much that the built result is not predictable or that the intent is not clear. A community should know what results to expect from a development, and at the same time a developer should know that if a submitted project adheres to all the regulated criteria, then the project will get approval. In addition, the developer will know that the value of the project is ensured because the adjacent property will develop in the same manner.

## Using Lot Coverage Percentage

Typically, lot coverage percentage regulations are not used in FBCs, and we recommend against using them. If they need to be used for political or other similar reasons, they must be based on a thorough documentation of an area and must be calibrated by transect zone. The maximum percentage of coverage is typically established based on suburban development patterns that are inappropriately applied to historic neighborhoods and town centers, and applied to subdivision standards in a way that limits a good mix of housing types within a project. Including noncalibrated percentages in your FBC can automatically prevent the revitalization of existing neighborhoods, as well as the creation of new neighborhoods with a character similar to those of the old ones.

## Using Floor-Area Ratio

Floor-area ratio (FAR) has absolutely no role in FBCs and should not be used. If FAR is used as a primary tool for regulation and entitlement, a developer will simply max out the FAR, thus creating very "boxy" buildings with little variation in massing. Other regulation parameters provide more predictable results and should be used in its place. An appropriate combination of height, maximum building depth, distance between buildings, and size and massing requirements within Building Type Standards should be used instead.

## Not Addressing Frontages

This is a much less critical mistake than the others, but worthy of inclusion. Documentation of typical frontages and their application to the FBC regulating system should be considered an integral component because they regulate an appropriate interface between the public and private realms within a community. Hire a consultant who knows what frontages are.

## Not Using Administrative Review

The intent of going through the FBC process, including the visioning process, is to establish community and political support for a specific vision that the FBC then regulates for predictable results. Therefore, once the vision is established and the FBC is written, projects that meet FBC requirements should be approved administratively. This provides the incentive for developers to meet the requirements of the FBC, which means that there must be full confidence in the FBC.

Removing the discretionary review process is often difficult when special interest groups have historically exercised significant participation in a project review. The solution is to engage these groups in the FBC process early and often to ensure that the team has their full support for the vision plan and full confidence in the FBC.

# References 

## Form-Based Codes and Related Planning Documents

The following is a list of the code and planning documents referred to directly in this book. Links to these documents will be listed as they are available at www.opticosdesign.com/fbcbook.html. References and links to additional Form-Based Codes (FBCs) can be found on the Form-Based Codes Institute Web site at www.formbasedcodes.org.


180° Design Studio. "Blue Springs Downtown Development Code." City of Blue Springs, Missouri, April 2, 2007.

180° Design Studio. "Chanticleer Design Manual." Montgomery, Alabama, 2007.

"2005 Ventura General Plan." City of Ventura, California, August 8, 2005.

Dover, Kohl & Partners. "Downtown Montgomery Plan." City of Montgomery, Alabama, January 11, 2007.

Dover, Kohl & Partners and Spikowski Planning Associates. "Proposed Form-Based Code for Mixed-Use Infill." Sarasota County, Florida, April 5, 2007.

"Downtown Specific Plan." City of Ventura, California, draft, December 2006.

Duany, Andrés, William Wright, and Sandy Sorlien. *SmartCode & Manual, v. 8.0.* New Urban Publications.

Duany Plater-Zyberk & Company. "Hampstead." Montgomery, Alabama, 2006.

Duany Plater-Zyberk & Company. "Miami 21 Draft." City of Miami, Florida, March 16, 2007.

Ferrell Madden Associates and Code Studio. "Heart of Peoria, Land Development Code." City of Peoria, Illinois, public review draft, October 10, 2006.

Ferrell Madden Associates and Urban Advisors. "Heart of Peoria, Implementation Charrette Report & Master Plan." City of Peoria, Illinois, public review draft, May 2006.

HDR | Town Planning. "Midtown Corridor Development Code: Main Street and

Thompson Boulevard," City of Ventura, California. January 9, 2007.

Moule & Polyzoides. "Santa Ana Renaissance Specific Plan." City of Santa Ana, California, draft, October 8, 2007.

Moule & Polyzoides. "Uptown Whittier Specific Plan." City of Whittier, California, June 2006.

Moule & Polyzoides and Crawford, Multari & Clark Associates. "Placentia-Westgate Specific Plan." City of Placentia, California, draft, October 12, 2006.

Moule & Polyzoides, et al. "Downtown Newhall Specific Plan." City of Santa Clarita, California, draft, September 13, 2005.

Moule & Polyzoides, et al. "Visalia Southeast Area Specific Plan." City of Visalia, California, 100 percent administrative draft, April 27, 2007.

Opticos Design, Inc. "Benicia Downtown Mixed Used Master Plan." City of Benicia, California, 2007.

Opticos Design, Inc. and Crawford, Multari & Clark Associates. "City of Grass Valley Municipal Code, Title 17: Development Code." City of Grass Valley, California, April 10, 2007.

Spikowski Planning Associates. "St. Lucie County Land Development Code: Towns, Villages and Countryside." St. Lucie County, Florida, May 30, 2006.

Transect Codeware Company. "Leander SmartCode." City of Leander, Texas, September 22, 2005.

Treasure Coast Regional Planning Council. "North St. Lucie County Charrette: A Citizens' Master Plan." St. Lucie County, Florida, February 2004.

## Books

Burden, Dan. *Street Design Guidelines for Healthy Neighborhoods.* Local Government Commission's Center for Livable Communities, January 1999.

Crawford, Paul, Bill Dennis, and Geoffrey Ferrell. *Form-Based Zoning.* American Institute of Certified Planners, Chicago, 2004.

Duany, Andrés, and Elizabeth Plater-Zyberk. *Towns and Town-Making Principles.* 2nd ed. New York: Rizzoli, 1992.

Emerson, Chad. *The SmartCode Solution to Sprawl.* Environmental Law Institute, 2007.

Ewing, Reid, Keith Bartholomew, Steve Winkelman, Jerry Walters, and Don Chen. *Growing Cooler: The Evidence on Urban Development and Climate Change.* Urban Land Institute, 2007.

Frumkin, Howard, Lawrence Frank, and Richard Jackson. *Urban Sprawl and Public Health.* Island Press, 2004.

Greenberg, Ellen, Joel Russell, Jonathan Barnett, Paul Crawford, Rick Bernhardt, and Gianni Longo. *Codifying New Urbanism: How to Reform Municipal Land Development Regulations.* Chicago: American Planning Association, Congress for the New Urbanism, 2004.

Institute of Transportation Engineers. *Context Sensitive Solutions in Designing Major Urban Thoroughfares for Walkable Communities.* Institute of Transportation Engineers, 2006.

Katz, Peter. *The New Urbanism: Toward an Architecture of Community.* New York: McGraw-Hill Professional, 1993.

Lennertz, Bill, and Aarin Lutzenhiser. *The Charrette Handbook.* Chicago: American Planning Association, 2006.

Polyzoides, Stefanos, Roger Sherwood, James Tice, and Julius Shulman. *Courtyard Housing in Los Angeles.* Princeton Architectural Press, 1992.

Slater, David C. *Management of Local Planning.* Municipal Management Series. Washington, D.C.: International City Management Association, 1984.

Toll, Seymour I. *Zoned American.* New York: Grossman Publishers, 1969.

Tracy, Steve. *Smart Growth Zoning Codes: A Resource Guide.* Local Government Commission, 2003.

Weaver, Clifford L., and Richard F. Babcock. *City Zoning: The Once and Future Frontier.* Chicago: American Planning Association, 1979.

Zucker, Paul C. *The ABZs of Planning Management.* San Diego: West Coast Publishers, 1997.

## Articles

Burdette, Jason Todd. "Form-Based Codes: A Cure for the Cancer Called Euclidean Zoning?" *Digital Library and Archives.* Virginia Tech, April 2004.

Crawford, Paul, Daniel Parolek, Karen Parolek, and Stefanos Polyzoides. "Downtowns and Form-Based Codes: The Other Side of the Story." *CalPlanner,* May–June 2007.

Davis, Dave, ed. "Form-Based Codes: Implementing Smart Growth." Local Government Commission, June 2006.

Dover, Victor. "Alternative Methods of Land Development Regulation." Town of Fort Myers Beach, Florida, September 2, 1996.

Duany Plater-Zyberk & Company. "Introduction to Existing Code." *Miami 21.* City of Miami, July 31, 2006.

Duany Plater-Zyberk & Company. "Introduction to Transect Theory." *Miami 21.* City of Miami, July 31, 2006.

Duany Plater-Zyberk & Company. "PAB Presentation." *Miami 21.* City of Miami, July 31, 2006.

Ferrell Madden Associates. "FAQ's: Form-Based Codes." City of Farmers Branch, Texas, 2006.

Katz, Peter. "Form First." *Planning Magazine,* November 2004.

Klipp, Luke H. "The Real Cost of San Francisco's Off-Street Residential Parking Requirements." *Livable City.* University of California at Berkeley, May 27, 2004.

Leinberger, Christopher B. "Turning Around Downtown: Twelve Steps to Revitalization." The Brookings Institute, March 2005.

Madden, Mary E., and Bill Spikowski. "Place Making with Form-Based Codes." *Urban Land,* September 2006.

Miller, Jason. "Smart Codes Smart Places." *Realtor.org.* National Association of Realtors, Summer 2004.

National Association of Realtors. "Successful Growth Begins with Five Principles." *Realtor.org.*

Peirce, Neal. "A Cure for Cluttered Roadways?" *Washington Post Writers Group*, 2003.

Rangwala, Kaizer. "Retooling Planners." *Places,* 17.1.

Rouse, Dave, and Nancy Zobl. "Practice: Form-Based Zoning." *Zoning Practice,* May 2004.

Sitkowski, Robert, and Brian Ohm. "Form-Based Land Development Regulations." *Urban Lawyer,* Winter 2006.

Sperber, Bob, ed. "Function Follows Form." *Professional Builder,* September 1, 2005.

Sullivan, J. "Future Tense: Trend 12." *Builder*, December 2005.

## Web Sites

Charrette Institute
www.charretteinstitute.org

Charter of the New Urbanism
www.cnu.org/charter

City of Grass Valley, California
www.cityofgrassvalley.com

City of Miami, Florida
www.miamigov.com

City of Montgomery, Alabama
www.montgomeryal.gov

City of Peoria, Illinois
www.ci.peoria.il.us

Congress for the New Urbanism
www.cnu.org

Fannie Mae Location Efficient Mortgage (LEM) Calculator
www.locationefficiency.com

Form-Based Codes Institute
www.formbasedcodes.org

Local Government Commission
www.lgc.org

New Urban Timeline
www.nutimeline.net

Smart Growth Network
www.smartgrowth.org

St. Lucie County, Florida
www.stlucieco.gov

Wikipedia
www.wikipedia.org

# End Notes 

## Chapter 1

[1] For more information on the effects of sprawl on our health, see *Urban Sprawl and Public Health* by Howard Frumkin, Lawrence Frank, and Richard Jackson, Island Press, 2004. For more information on the effects of land development and climate change, see *Growing Cooler: The Evidence on Urban Development and Climate Change* by Reid Ewing, Keith Bartholomew, Steve Winkelman, Jerry Walters, and Don Chen, Urban Land Institute, 2007.

[2] Peter Katz, *Eight Advantages to Form-Based Codes*, http://www.formbasedcodes.org/advantages.html.

[3] Form-Based Codes Institute, *Definition of a Form-Based Code*, www.formbasedcodes.org/definition.html, June 27, 2006.

[4] As an example, see the story of the Pleasant Hill BART station in *The Charrette Handbook* by Bill Lennertz and Aarin Lutzenhiser, p. 151.

[5] Reid et al., *Growing Cooler.*

[6] *Codifying New Urbanism: How to Reform Municipal Land Development Regulations.* Chicago: American Planning Association, Congress for the New Urbanism, 2004.

[7] *Future Tense: Trend 12* by J. Sullivan, *Builder*, December 2005.

[8] http://www.realtor.org/smart_growth.nsf/Pages/formbasedcodes?OpenDocument.

[9] Christopher B. Leinberger, *Turning Around Downtown: Twelve Steps to Revitalization,* The Brookings Institute, March 2005.

[10] These include an 8-page fact sheet produced by the Local Government Commission called "Form-Based Codes: Implementing Smart Growth," Chad Emerson's "The SmartCode Solution to Sprawl," and the SmartCode, as well as several short magazine articles, and a few Web sites, including that of the Form-Based Code Institute (http://www.formbasedcodes.org).

[11] Reid et al., *Growing Cooler.*

## Chapter 2

[1] Form-Based Codes Institute, *Definition of a Form-Based Code*, www.formbasedcodes.org/definition.html, June 27, 2006.
[2] Ibid.
[3] Based on: Form-Based Codes Institute, *Definition of a Form-Based Code*, www.formbasedcodes.org/definition.html, June 27, 2006.
[4] Institute of Transportation Engineers. *Context Sensitive Solutions in Designing Major Urban Thoroughfares for Walkable Communities.* Institute of Transportation Engineers, 2006.
[5] Dan Burden, *Street Design Guidelines for Healthy Neighborhoods.* Local Government Commission's Center for Livable Communities, January 1999.
[6] Based on the thoroughfare types in the *SmartCode v.8* (Duany, Wright, and Sorlien) and *Street Design Guidelines for Healthy Neighborhoods* (Burden).
[7] Burden, *Street Design Guidelines for Healthy Neighborhoods,* p. 25.
[8] Based on civic space types in the *SmartCode v.8* (Duany, Wright, and Sorlien) and various Form-Based Codes by Moule & Polyzoides.
[9] Based on regulations in the *SmartCode v.8* (Duany, Wright, and Sorlien).
[10] Ibid.
[11] Klipp, Luke H. "The Real Cost of San Francisco's Off-Street Residential Parking Requirements." *Livable City.* University of California at Berkeley, May 27, 2004.
[12] Fannie Mae Location Efficient Mortgage (LEM) calculator. Available at http://www.locationefficiency.com.
[13] This process is based on one developed by Moule & Polyzoides.

## Chapter 3

[1] Katz, *The New Urbanism,* p. xvii.
[2] Ibid., p. xix.
[3] Ibid., p. xx.
[4] Duany, Wright, and Sorlien, *SmartCode v.8,* p. A5.

## Chapter 4

[1] www.wikipedia.com.
[2] Ibid.
[3] Ibid.
[4] Ibid.
[5] Ibid.
[6] Ibid.
[7] Ibid.
[8] Ibid.
[9] Ibid.
[10] Ibid.

# Index 

## C

## T